AEROSPACE
PHYSIOLOGY

AEROMEDICAL AND HUMAN PERFORMANCE
FACTORS FOR PILOTS

AEROSPACE PHYSIOLOGY

AEROMEDICAL AND HUMAN PERFORMANCE FACTORS FOR PILOTS

Steven C. Martin

gatekeeper press
Columbus, Ohio"

Aerospace Physiology: Aeromedical and Human Performance Factors for Pilots

Published by Gatekeeper Press
2167 Stringtown Rd, Suite 109
Columbus, OH 43123-2989
www.GatekeeperPress.com

The editorial work for this book is entirely the product of the author. Gatekeeper Press did not participate in and is not responsible for any aspect of this element.

Library of Congress Control Number: 2021943400

ISBN (paperback): 9781662917653
eISBN: 9781662917660

PREFACE

Aviation human factors issues have been around since the dawn of aviation, and the first attempts at human factors and flight physiology training were not far behind. This type of training was born in the military, and the military has continuously invested in Aerospace Physiology training for more than 80 years, with decades of research beyond those 80 years.

This author's experience attempting to locate research or studying material on this subject matter has been met with frustration, as the material is either too simplistic, too complicated, or located in too many different sources. Much of the material includes misinformation, incomplete information, or information irrelevant to the vast majority of aviators or applicable only to military pilots. Unfortunately, not enough *relevant* information has filtered down to the civilian aviation training communities. For many civilian aviators, aerospace physiology subject matter remains almost as much of a mystery today as it was to Orville and Wilbur Wright. Mr. Martin's desire to change this information void, as well as elevate the standard of training for professional aviators, was ultimately the driving force behind authoring this text.

This book is designed to be an easily understandable, enjoyable, and memorable narrative of all aerospace physiology subject matter considered relevant in today's world of flight. The book is NOT intended to produce Aeromedical Examiners out of every student; however, aviators need to have a solid understanding of this information to minimize many of the human performance-related issues and fatalities in aviation. The information in this book is modeled after the US Air Force's Physiological Training Program for pilots, as well as European Union Aviation Safety Agency's (EASA) human performance standards.

Aerospace physiology is a fascinating subject, as the majority of Mr. Martin's students have indicated over the years. This being said, many frightening issues can occur in aviation as with virtually any other form of transportation. It is not this author's intention to scare anyone wishing to fly out of flying, but rather make prospective pilots aware of human performance issues which truly exist in aviation but may be rarely spoken about. The more an aviator knows, the better prepared they will be!

ACKNOWLEDGEMENTS

As one may or may not imagine, attempting to recognize everyone assisting in the contribution of my personal knowledge or motivation for the discipline of aerospace physiology over decades is a difficult task. With a list of literally hundreds of colleagues and thousands of students who have contributed to my specific experience and understanding of this subject matter, there is no possible way to acknowledge all involved.

Starting with those closest to me, my ever-patient, self-sacrificing, and love-of-my-life wife Kimberley must receive top acknowledgement. Kim's faith in my professional direction is nothing short of a blessing, and I am continually thankful she allows me the freedom and space necessary to pursue the passion I have for aerospace physiology. Followed by my wife are my daughters Jessica and Amanda, who have always believed in me, if not necessarily listened to me! I am equally and eternally proud of both of their professional accomplishments, and love and value them immensely.

My father Ray (deceased), a private pilot, instilled a love and curiosity for aviation in me from an early age, giving me my first flight in an airplane at age four. Both my father and mother Doris encouraged me and ensured I followed a path necessary for success. My sister Carrie and brother Paul have always had my back, and have provided essential advice to me numerous times throughout the years.

On the professional end of the spectrum, out of the many people I have worked with over the years, several stand out. Staff Sergeant Everett Onifer provided me with pivotal guidance during two distinct points in my career, and I would probably not be where I am without him, so thank you! The following have also provided leadership, mentorship, motivation, and crucial knowledge: Colonel John Greene (deceased), Dr. Kent Gillingham (deceased), Major Mike Boehme, Captain Eric Young, Senior Master Sergeant Frank Stegemeier, Dr. Warren Jensen, Chief Master Sergeant Joe Shalk, John D. Odegard (deceased), and Professor Tom Zeidlik (who prodded me into writing this book).

Perhaps the most important people involved in providing the motivation to pursue aerospace physiology with the intensity I have are all of those aviators who have been injured or died over the years, and in particular those who were injured or died from the topics covered in this text. This book is truly for all of you.

CONTENTS

1. INTRODUCTION TO AEROSPACE PHYSIOLOGY

Almost every day somewhere in the world someone (or many people) will die as a result of aviation-related accidents. These accidents range from one person flying their own airplane, helicopter medical transport flights, single or dual pilot cargo flights, corporate jets, crop-dusters, any number of military aviation operations, to a commercial airline with hundreds of souls on board. Each and every fatal aviation accident is tragic, and the reality is a large percentage of aviation accidents may have been prevented had the pilot been given the proper tools to recognize and react properly to those hazardous situations.

Human Factors, as defined by the Federal Aviation Administration (FAA), is a "multidisciplinary effort to generate and compile information about human capabilities and limitations and apply that information to equipment, systems, facilities, procedures, jobs, environments, training, staffing, and personnel management for safe, comfortable, and effective human performance (Role of Human Factors in the FAA, 2014)."

Federal Aviation Administration (FAA) experts estimate the percentage of aviation incidents and accidents caused by human influence is approximately 60 – 80%. Those outside the aviation industry may assume pilots were to blame for all those incidents and accidents, but nothing could be further from the truth. Many other humans are involved in the aviation operations chain: aerospace and aviation engineers, software engineers and programmers, air traffic control, maintenance personnel, flight line workers, dispatchers, managers, and many others. Pilots, unfortunately, are the end-of-the-line recipients of whatever problems develop and are left trying to figure out how to correct complex issues in real time, usually while trying to fly the airplane. Some of those in-flight problems may be a result of pilot action (or inaction); however, in many cases the problem developed somewhere upstream before the pilots ever entered the flight deck. Regardless of the problem's origin, the pilot is the one person in the chain that holds the key to life or death in their hands. For that reason, the pilot should be operating at their utmost peak efficiency, both cognitively and physiologically, to give themselves and their passengers the greatest chance for survival "if something" happens.

Human cardiovascular, respiratory, musculoskeletal, intellectual, and orientation systems developed to function with peak efficiency at sea level, where people operate at relatively slow speeds, maintain a ground level visual perspective, have their body in constant contact with the ground, and breathe copious amounts oxygen under a certain amount of atmospheric pressure.

Flight conditions cause faster speeds, elevated visual perspectives, misleading orientation cues, reduced oxygen and atmospheric pressure, and many other abnormal environmental factors. As part of the overall Human Factors spectrum, *Aerospace Physiology* (also known as Flight Physiology, Aviation Physiology, and Aeromedical Factors) is the scientific discipline studying the effects of flight on human physiological and cognitive systems. The goal of aerospace physiology is to teach aviators to optimize their performance in abnormal environments. In essence, training aviators to survive the "worst days" of their aviation career; the day they experience smoke or fumes on the flight deck, experience hypoxia inflight, become spatially disoriented, or experience any of the other myriad of physiologically or psychologically incapacitating events. Students of aerospace physiology learn to continuously analyze the environments they are exposed to, recognize physical or physiological symptomology potentially leading to impairment or incapacitation, and successfully react to prevent impairment and incapacitation instinctively and possibly instantaneously.

Aviators must ask themselves what the difference is between a fatal accident and non-event. Is it one checklist item? 0.4 seconds of reaction time? One quick glance at an instrument at the right time? During a mid-air crisis pilots need to take all of their training, synthesize critical and complex information, and develop an action plan possibly within a split-second timeframe. Aerospace physiology training provides significant information necessary for aviators to make the correct decision at critical times.

Although some form of aerospace physiology is taught throughout various phases of pilot training, historically APT is an under-trained facet of the aviation training curriculum. Training and learning to a standard is not enough. Pilots must learn what is truly necessary. Many pilots associate this training with simply "high-altitude hypoxia" training or "hypoxia awareness" training. The reality is this training encompasses much more than simply hypoxia.

Effective aerospace physiology training occurs when one intersects the domains of "aviation" with "physiology." Aviators teaching the subject matter may miss critical nuances of physiology, and physiologists teaching the subject matter may miss crucial nuances of flight management. Aerospace physiologists merge the two domains with research and experience-based information, coupled with practical training, to provide the most effective aeromedical training available.

To effectively retain this information, military forces attend regularly scheduled APT refresher courses at intervals of three to five years. The same interval should apply to you, as much of the information presented in this book applies to all phases of an aviator's career span and varying experience levels. For you to apply this knowledge most effectively over your flying career, retain and review this book every three to five years to ensure the information remains fresh in your mind.

1.1 HISTORY OF AEROSPACE PHYSIOLOGY TRAINING (APT)

According to USAF aerospace physiologist Irena Farlik, the first aircraft flight took place at Kitty Hawk, NC by the Wright Brothers on December 17th, 1903; surprisingly taking five years before the first fatal airplane accident occurred. The military recognized the strategic importance of flight and the mobility it provided. Less than 10 years following the first flight, the U.S. military invested in some aircraft to start training. The mishap rate in the first year of flight training was atrocious. Of the 100 aviators killed, it was determined that 90 of those deceased were killed by some type of pilot error. This led to the recognition that human error was a major factor in aviation-related deaths, and concept of "human factors" training was born. This epiphany led to the development of aerospace medicine and aviation physiology training.

U.S. Military Aviation Safety Initiatives

In 1916, U.S. involvement in World War I led to the formation of an air service in the armed forces. The U.S. War Department issued a special order directing the establishment of the field of Aerospace Medicine for the research of human factors issues and the training of such to pilots. This eventually led the development of the Air Service Medical Research Laboratory in 1918 at Hazelhurst Field, Mineola, Long Island, where the term "Flight Surgeon" was adopted describing those physicians devoted to the health and well-being of aviators. This laboratory and flight surgeon training center became known as the School of Aviation Medicine (SAM) in 1922, and in 1926 the school was relocated to Brooks Field, San Antonio, TX. The school was relocated around Texas a couple more times before settling back at Brooks in 1957, becoming the USAF School of Aerospace Medicine (USAFSAM) in 1961. In 2005, USAFSAM moved from Brooks to Wright-Patterson AFB, OH.

Through the 1920's and 30's, military necessity for speed, altitude, distance, and duration was growing. By 1930, the B-17 Flying Fortress could cruise at altitudes of FL300 without bombs and travel at 230 mph. With this increase in altitude, questions began to emerge regarding the physiological hazards of flight at such altitudes for extended periods of time.

By 1935, the Physiological Research Unit at Wright Field in Dayton, OH, received a new low-pressure chamber and also had a human centrifuge installed for high-G research. Interestingly, this new lab sparked some competition from the scientists at USAFSAM. Research at Wright Field sparked the publishing of over 30 papers and "Principles and Practice of Aviation Medicine," which became the standard authority in aerospace medicine for decades.

Following the beginning of World War II in 1942, the U. S. Air Surgeon instituted a new "Altitude Training Program." This program was Air Force-wide and mandatory for aircrew members to complete. During program expansion, doctors and instructors were assembled into 45 units to instruct military aviators on oxygen equipment and the physiological hazards of flying. Other training topics included night vision training, G-forces, and thermal stress. Following the ending of the war, training tempo slowed, and the doctors and instructors reentered private practice and teaching in the civilian sector. The Aerospace Physiology program was reactivated in 1949 by the Surgeon for the 8th Air Forces. The Surgeon expanded the program into the Aerospace Physiology Training Branch where he initiated written tests, altitude chamber technical orders, modified altitude chambers to allow rapid decompression training, night vision trainers, and the first training charts and slides. He opened 13 Aerospace Physiology Training Units in 1950 (Farlik, 2015).

The program accelerated through the 1950s, and by 1956 there were 51 Physiological Training Units (PTUs). Oxygen consoles, pressure suits, and ejection seat trainers were added to the training. The 1960s brought even more advancement, and the program was reorganized under the Aerospace Medicine Division. High-altitude airdrop support (HAAMS) began in the early 1960s, which became prominent during the Vietnam Conflict. NASA also included crucial aerospace physiology training to astronauts from the earliest days of space flight, and continues this training to this day. By the 1980's, 22 USAF PTU existed world-wide supporting a wide variety of military training and support missions including physiology of flight, hypobaric chamber, oxygen equipment, ejection seat, emergency parachuting, survival and survival kits, spatial disorientation, vision and visual illusions, high-G centrifuge, full-pressure suit, hyperbaric chamber, and high-altitude airdrop/parachutist missions.

Civilian Aviation Safety Initiatives

The U.S. military was fully engaged in aviation safety training, but what about civilian aviators? The oldest (by far) organization established to investigate "aviation" safety and support & maintain high professional standards in aerospace disciplines was the Royal Aeronautical Society (RAeS), which became active in 1866. The RAeS today has an international network of 67 branches in virtually every corner of the world.

The International Civil Aviation Organization (ICAO) was established in 1944 at the Chicago Convention, funded and directed by 193 nations supporting cooperation in air transport.

In 1961, the recently-formed Federal Aviation Administration established the Civil Aeromedical Research Institute (CARI) in Oklahoma City, OK. In 1965, the scope of CARI's mission was enlarged and renamed the FAA's Civil Aeromedical Institute (CAMI) and initiated a Physiological Training Program for civilian pilots – a short course designed to give civil airmen basic aeromedical education on the concepts of APT.

The Civil Aviation Authority (CAA) was established in the United Kingdom in 1972, responsible for aviation safety standards. The European Union joined aviation safety in earnest as far back as 1996, legally establishing the European Union Aviation Safety Agency (EASA) in 2002. Others include the Air Transport Association (ATA), Experimental Aircraft Association (EAA), Flight Safety Foundation (FSF), International Air Transport Association (IATA), as well as many other organizations established in aviation's long history as well.

In 1989, the University of North Dakota's School of Aerospace Sciences started the nation's first non-government APT program as part of their Commercial Pilot degree program, including practical altitude chamber and spatial disorientation (SDO) training, which was ground-breaking at the time. UND's immersive three-credit hour APT program now incorporates not only altitude chamber and SDO/visual illusions training in a full-motion trainer, but cockpit smoke and enhanced vision lab training as well, and is still the premier collegiate Aerospace Physiology Training program in the country. A shortened version of this training is also offered to professional corporate and commercial aviators as well.

Civilian APT refresher training should be accomplished on a five- to ten-year recurrent basis. Memory fades, technology changes, new research comes available, and new trends emerge. The Air Force required APT training for aviators every three years for decades and enjoyed a relatively low human factors-related mishap rate. In a wave of military budget-cutting under President Obama, the USAF moved the training to a five-year cycle and closed some the APT units. Interestingly enough, the USAF human factors mishap rate increased not long after the increased training cycle.

1.2 HUMAN RESPONSE TO FLIGHT

Changes in atmospheric pressure, a reduction in the amount of oxygen we ingest, changing our visual perspective and typical orientation processes, increased radiation exposure, and a myriad of other environmental factors can have profound effects on the way we cognitively process information and physiologically function.

The reality of flying is a pilot may potentially be presented with physical, cognitive, or physiological pressures resulting in impairment or incapacitation of the pilot. For example, let us look at a young, relatively inexperienced visual flight rules (VFR) pilot who inadvertently flies into a cloud while working on an aircraft equipment issue. A possible response to this situation would be for the pilot to look up from their task-at-hand, erroneously believe the aircraft is turning or tumbling out-of-control, realize they are unable to orient themselves with the horizon, and panic. The resulting intellectual incapacitation causes the pilot to start instinctively over-controlling the airplane, truly losing control, and exiting the cloud in a vertical descent, ultimately impacting terrain.

While younger, less-experienced pilots may be somewhat more susceptible to many of these scenarios, more experienced pilots may never have been presented with many of the problems which may occur. Having never experienced these issues previously, their response could be just as catastrophic if the right issue happens at the wrong time. One way to view these potential problems is as "low-probability, high-consequence" events. Examples may include:

- Loss of runway visibility on short final due to weather
- Deviation from aircraft approach glide path due to automation failure
- Rapid loss of aircraft pressurization at high altitude
- Toxic fume intrusion onto the flight deck
- Debilitating sinus block on approach
- Failure to monitor instrumentation due to distracting personal problems

The list of potential problems regarding a pilot's inability to cognitively or physiologically cope is almost endless. Because situations such as these rarely present themselves, any pilot may be unprepared to respond appropriately simply because of lack of exposure or awareness.

The mission of APT is to enable pilots and aircrew members to effectively mitigate physical, physiological, or psychological incapacitation, with the ability to turn potential incidents and/or accidents into non-events. By knowing the proper responses and steps to mitigate the above-listed issues (and many, many others), the aviator can improve their safety margin by a very large degree.

If we examine historical causes of aviation incidents and accidents, one disturbing trend is the same things which were killing pilots decades ago are still killing pilots today, despite the advancement of technology. Technology has caused overall numbers of incidents and accidents to fall greatly over the years, but has also created new sets of problems.

The most recent Worldwide Commercial Jet Fleet Aviation Occurrence Category statistics compiled by the International Civil Aviation Organization (ICAO) reveal the occurrence killing most crewmembers and passengers in commercial aviation from 2007 through 2016 is loss-of-control inflight (LOC-I) accidents with 1,345 fatalities during the timeframe (Accident Statistics, 2020).

One may wonder why LOC-I conditions even exist in a day and age where automated aircraft control is the norm for passenger-carrying aircraft. The National Aeronautics and Space Agency (NASA) has performed studies on LOC-I accidents and found 46% occurred as result of the cockpit crew's "inappropriate response or interaction with aircraft equipment (Jacobson, 2013)." One may interpret this statement to mean the pilots failed to program the automated system correctly, failed to monitor the automated systems correctly, failed to respond to system failure correctly, failed to fly the airplane after system failure, or any number of other interpretations.

The simple fact remaining after analysis is flying still relies on human input, ability, cognition, and attention-to-detail. The phase of flight contributing to the highest overall number of incidents is the approach and landing phase, which involves human perception, judgement, calculation, rapid intellectual scene-building, and ability.

The common denominator is "human." Humans still need to remain engaged with the aircraft, correctly program and monitor the aircraft, and actually fly it in cases of non-automated flight conditions. Of course, engineers will argue technology can solve many of the life-threatening problems associated with flight, and perhaps those systems can so long as the systems work as advertised. The only problem with this theory is anyone with even a simple understanding of mechanized or electrical systems knows those systems can break, fail, be improperly programmed, or otherwise be rendered inoperable. So long as those systems have a less-than-100% success rate, humans still need to be on the flight deck ensuring the aircraft remains safe.

Aerospace physiology training is about enhancing human performance in adverse aviation environments. A complete and thorough understanding of the concepts of APT will undoubtedly make ANY pilot safer, regardless of their experience level. This book should be used as a career-long resource for professional aviators for the prevention of physiological issues in the flight environment.

Chapter 1 Core Competency Questions

1. According to FAA experts, what percentage of aviation accidents are caused by human influence?
2. When the U.S. military first invested time and resources into aviation training, what number of pilots died from "pilot error" out of the first 100 fatalities?
3. What civilian aviation safety organization was the first, and when were they established?
4. According to NASA's studies on loss of control inflight (LOC-I) accidents, what percentage occurred from the aircrew's "inappropriate response or interaction with aircraft equipment?

2. SCIENCE OF THE ATMOSPHERE

The atmosphere (think environment) humans typically survive and thrive in has a profound effect on the way human's function. As such, aviators need to have a basic understanding of the atmospheric function in general to better understand the overall influence it has on our human cognitive and physiological processes.

In this chapter we will discuss:

1. Definition of atmosphere
2. Atmospheric functions
3. Physical characteristics of the atmosphere
4. Climate change and aviation operations
5. Composition of the atmosphere
6. Physiological acclimatization
7. Physical divisions of the atmosphere
8. Physiological divisions of atmosphere
9. Physical gas laws
10. The partial pressure of oxygen

2.1 DEFINITION OF ATMOSPHERE

The Earth's *atmosphere* is a protective gaseous envelope surrounding the Earth consisting of gases, vapor, and solid particles held to the Earth by gravity.

Barometric pressure is measuring the weight, or pressure, of air molecules above the point the measurement is taken, which means barometric pressure decreases with altitude. As a result of air being compressible, the pressure decrease is not linear, as molecular density plays a role. This also means the closer one gets to the Earth's surface, the denser air molecules become.

One may think of the surface of the Earth as being the bottom of an "ocean" of air; the closer to the bottom one gets, the exponentially denser the barometric pressure. With this in mind, the greatest amount of barometric pressure change aviators will be exposed to is below 10,000 feet MSL.

2.2 ATMOSPHERIC FUNCTIONS

The basic *atmospheric functions* as far as humans are concerned are to provide life support, protect us from the harmful effects of radiation, thermal variations, and orbital material striking the Earth.

The life support function is provided through the proper amount of atmospheric pressure on our bodies for normal function, and to provide vital amounts of oxygen to allow us to operate normally. We will discuss those issues in depth later.

With regards to thermal protection, the atmosphere prevents extreme thermal loss. Think of the thermal extremes of the moon, for example. When the sun strikes the moon's surface, temperatures can reach a robust 260 degrees Fahrenheit, whereas when sun goes down, temperatures can dip to a chilly -280 degrees F. Because of the insulating capability the Earth's atmosphere provides, our temperature variations are not nearly as extreme.

Orbital material enters the Earth's atmosphere, where the friction of the atmosphere heats the material up to the point of incineration. This material may be space exploration junk left in orbit from previous experiments, space pebbles, meteors, or any other material floating around in space.

The radiation protection the Earth's atmosphere provides deserves somewhat more respect. Ultraviolet (UV) and/or galactic cosmic (ionizing) radiation could severely damage our human organs were it not for the protection afforded to us by ozone in the stratosphere and the mesosphere. Were it not for the atmosphere, acute and/or chronic symptoms of radiation overexposure would make survival of the species difficult.

Because radiation exposure increases with altitude, aviators do have an increased exposure to both UV and ionizing radiation; enough so that the Federal Aviation Administration classifies pilots as "Occupational Radiation Workers." Based on FAA research, findings reveal a typical flight from New York, NY to Tokyo, Japan yields almost as much ionized radiation as one chest X-ray, the flight equating to .0754 millisieverts (mSv) of radiation exposure. The average U.S. citizen receives approximately 2.96 mSv radiation exposure per year from natural causes, while the average pilot adds another 2.2 mSv per year on top of that number. The FAA limits pilots to 20 mSv per year, so few pilots would be able to get close to that figure as 20 mSv would equal close to 225 New York to Tokyo flights per year. Even so, it is estimated flying at FL350 increases ionized radiation exposure by approximately 70% over ground level. Ionized radiation is known to promote free-radical production in the body, which is atoms losing orbital electrons, thus becoming cancerous. Taking all factors into consideration, the increase in fatal cancer risk in pilots has been observed to be an average of .5% over the general population. In addition to increased ionized radiation, UV radiation can reach up to 3,500% of Sea Level values near the top of the Troposphere (approximately 35,000 feet).

How do we protect ourselves from radiation? One method is flying where the protective elements of the atmosphere are at their greatest. The atmosphere is not a perfect sphere; in reality, it is more of an oblong shape. The atmosphere is thinnest at the polar regions of the Earth and thickest at the Equator. This occurs mainly because the angle of the sun striking the Earth is at its lowest angle at the poles, and at its highest angle at the equator. More heat from the Earth's surface is radiated into the air, resulting in a higher troposphere in equatorial regions; thus, more atmospheric radioactive protection.

Another protection strategy is to protect our skin and eyes from UVA radiation. UVB and UVC ray are mitigated for the most part by the skin and windscreens of the aircraft, but UVA rays are still a concern. UVA rays can cause long-term cumulative damage to the eyes and skin, so wearing a high sun protection factor (SPF) sunscreen and UVA-protectant sunglasses is advised. The protective factor for sunscreen should be at least SPF 50, and sunglasses should provide 99% UV blockage below 400 nanometers.

Dr. Adrian Chorley of Aviation Vision Services conducted research from 2008-2015 studying the effects of ultraviolet radiation on a pilot's eyesight. The study showed even though UVA is the least energetic of UV radiation, it causes the most harm to a pilot's eyes and eyesight because a higher percentage of the radiation penetrates the flight deck and cabin of an aircraft. The study concluded there is good evidence long-term exposure to solar radiation, especially the ultraviolet and blue light components, is a risk factor for cataracts and, to a lesser extent, age-related degeneration of the retina."

2.3 PHYSICAL CHARACTERISTICS OF THE ATMOSPHERE

The Earth's atmosphere shows relatively predictable characteristics in that barometric pressure, temperature, and water vapor all decrease as we ascend to higher altitudes.

According to the International Civil Aviation Organization (ICAO), the standard temperature at mean sea level (MSL) is 59 degrees F, or 15 degrees C. Temperature decreases as we ascend to altitude at a rate of 3.5 degrees F or 2.0 degrees C per 1,000 feet altitude. This temperature lapse rate continues until approximately the top of the troposphere, where the temperature stabilizes in the vicinity of -67 degrees F or -55 degrees C.

Gaseous atmosphere is influenced by Earth's gravitational pull, and atmospheric (barometric) pressure is the combined gasses' force on the environment at any given point. Barometric pressure is expressed in measurements of Pounds per Square Inch (PSI), Inches of Mercury (in/Hg) or Millimeters of Mercury (mm/Hg) as referenced in the chart below:

Figure 2.1 Barometric Pressure Table

Altitude (feet)	Pressure (in/Hg)	Pressure (mm/Hg)	Pressure (psi)	Temperature (Celsius)	Temperature (Fahrenheit)
Sea Level	29.92	760	14.69	15	59
10,000	20.58	522.6	10.11	-4.8	23.3
18,000	14.95	379.4	7.34	-20.7	-5.3
20,000	13.76	349.1	6.75	-24.6	-12.3
25,000	10.51	281.8	5.45	-34.5	-30.1
30,000	8.9	225.6	4.36	-44.4	-48
34,000	7.4	187.4	3.62	-52.4	-62.3
35,332	6.8	175.9	3.41	-55	-67
40,000	5.56	140.7	2.72	-55	-67
43,000	4.43	119	2.3	-55	-67
50,000	3.44	87.3	1.69	-55	-67

Note that in terms of barometric pressure density, the half-way point is 18,000 feet. This means half of the Earth's atmospheric density is below 18,000 feet, and the other half extends to the boundary of space, which is a complete vacuum. As pressure decreases, air becomes less dense due to the kinetic nature of atoms and molecules, which are in constant state of motion. As pressure around the molecules is reduced, the molecules travel further apart; therefore, air becomes less dense and gas expands. ¾ atmospheric pressure would equate to approximately 8,000 feet, which is a common cabin altitude for commercial aircraft, and ¼ atmospheric pressure would equate to approximately 34,000 feet, which is a common ambient cruise altitude for commercial aircraft.

As barometric pressure decreases, so does its ability to affect and assist bodily function. As mentioned, barometric pressure decrease is not a linear progression; rather, an exponential progression. Since pressure density increases the nearer we get to the Earth's surface, the most likely place for human pressure-induced issues, such as ear blocks and sinus blocks, is below 10,000 feet.

The combination of barometric pressure and oxygen determines our human ability to perform. Another important question to answer is where, exactly, does reduced barometric pressure begin to seriously affect humans? The answer is some physiological and higher-level cognitive functions are already being affected as low as 5,000 feet for a sea level-equilibrated individual. One may note physical performance begins to degrade rapidly as altitude increases, as anyone who has skied, tried running, climbed mountains, or engaged in any physical activity at altitudes above 4,000 MSL.

At altitudes below 10,000 feet, humans can perform somewhat normally, even given the great amount of barometric pressure change between sea level and 10,000 feet which can be as much as 237 mm/Hg. As mentioned, barometric pressure decreases exponentially, so the same 10,000 feet altitude increase between 30,000 feet and 40,000 feet yields a decrease of 84.9 mm/Hg. Although the pressure change is less, the impact on human performance is greatly magnified at those altitudes.

Barometric pressure, temperature and water vapor variations interact and contribute to weather formation and climate. In the troposphere, air rises as it is heated by the sun, then falls towards the surface of the Earth as it cools. It will then intermix with evaporated water from the oceans, seas, lakes and rivers of the world to form clouds and precipitation. Uneven heating of the Earth's surface due to sunlight, combined with the Earth's rotation, cause rising, falling and horizontal air movements (also known as "wind"). These processes combined result in the development of snow and rain, and heat or freezing temperatures, and is called "weather." Long-term trends with regards to weather patterns affecting the entirety of Earth is called "climate," which is typically tracked in 30-year blocks of time. Variations in climate behavior over longer periods (100-year blocks or so) is referred to as "climate change."

2.4 CLIMATE CHANGE AND AVIATION OPERATIONS

NASA scientists attribute the increasing global warming trend seen since the mid-20th century to the human contribution of the "greenhouse effect", or warming which occurs when the atmosphere traps heat radiating from Earth toward space.

Certain gases in the atmosphere block radiated heat from escaping. Gases that remain semi-permanently in the atmosphere and do not respond physically or chemically to variations in temperature are described as "forcing" climate change. Gases, like water vapor, which respond physically or chemically to changes in temperature are seen as "feedbacks."

According to NASA, gases that contribute to greenhouse effect include:

- Water vapor. The most abundant greenhouse gas. Crucially, it acts as a feedback to the climate. Water vapor increases as atmosphere warms, but also contributes to the possibility of clouds and precipitation. This effect makes these some of the most important feedback mechanisms to the greenhouse effect.

- Carbon dioxide (CO_2). A relatively small but very important component of the atmosphere, carbon dioxide is released through natural processes such as respiration, volcanic eruptions and through human activities such as deforestation, land use changes, and burning fossil fuels. Humans have increased atmospheric CO_2 concentration by more than a third since the Industrial Revolution began. This is the most prolific, long-lived "forcing" of climate change.

- Methane. A hydrocarbon gas produced both through natural sources and human activities, including the decomposition of wastes in landfills, agriculture, and especially rice cultivation, as well as digestive processes and manure management associated with domestic livestock. On a molecule-for-molecule basis, methane is a much more active greenhouse gas than carbon dioxide, but also much less abundant in the atmosphere.

- Nitrous oxide. A powerful greenhouse gas produced by soil cultivation practices, especially through the use of commercial and organic fertilizers, fossil fuel combustion, nitric acid production, and biomass burning.

- Chlorofluorocarbons (CFCs). Synthetic compounds designed entirely for industrial purposes and used in a number of applications, CFCs are now highly regulated regarding production and release into the atmosphere by international agreements for their ability to contribute to destruction of the ozone layer. They are also greenhouse gases.

Much research has gone into the development and effects of climate change in recent history, and climate change is destined to have a profound impact on aviation operations as we know it at the present time. The United States Environmental Protection Agency (US EPA) predicts a global climate shift that contains a decrease in extreme cold weather, and an increase in extreme hot weather. Based on NASA and EPA research findings, the following are some of the effects of climate change to consider for aviators:

- Ozone depletion in the stratosphere increases wind speeds in that region of the atmosphere, and can create shifts in the Intertropical Convergence Zone (ITCZ) located five degrees North and South of the Equator. These ITCZ shifts can cause global wind and rain belt fluctuation, causing more extreme weather in areas of the world that historically have not experienced such potentially hazardous conditions.
- Scientists predict a 50% increase in lightning strikes in the coming century. While most aircraft are arguably equipped to disburse lightning strikes somewhat effectively, having a highly electrical-dependent aircraft receive a 1,000,000,000-joule energy surge has the potential to create problems with aircraft electrical systems.
- Storm size and intensity is predicted to increase due to the increase in global temperatures. Flying into unpredictable weather that has the potential to blossom catastrophically and reach higher altitudes than the aircraft can fly, or increase the chances of icing conditions creating serious controllability issues. Research has shown the majority of business jet LOC-I accidents occur below 1,000 feet above ground level (AGL), and increasing the chances for turbulence, icing or flight control binding could possibly create an increase in those issues occurring.
- Warmer global temperatures may also impact typical arrival and departure patterns for airports in historically warmer regions, such as the American Southwest. Warm temperatures will affect atmospheric pressure density, making landing and/or taking off from the aircraft more difficult at certain times of the day, which could in turn demand a change in runway lengths, or even change the amount of weight a particular aircraft model could safety transport.
- A predicted increase in carbon dioxide (CO_2) in the atmosphere has the potential to dramatically increase turbulence. Turbulence has the capacity to injure passengers and flight cabin crew members who are moving around the aircraft at the time of turbulence entry.

Figure 2.2 Two Hurricanes and the ITCZ

With the above-mentioned information in mind, what does this mean to you? Unpredictable weather can potentially cause aviators to find themselves immersed in a psychologically challenging situation in a matter of seconds or even split-seconds.

2.5 COMPOSITION OF THE ATMOSPHERE

The main atmospheric gases we as humans are concerned with are oxygen, nitrogen, and carbon dioxide. Oxygen is our primary life-support gas; it is essential for human and animal life and supports body metabolism (the catabolic breakdown of glucose for the production of heat energy). Nitrogen is inert to humans but still physiologically significant as we ascend to higher altitudes. Carbon dioxide is simply the by-product of human metabolic processes. The remaining atmospheric gases are considered noble gases, which have no bodily function. The table below lists the various atmospheric gases and the total percentage of that gas in the atmosphere.

Figure 2.3 Percentages of Gases in the Atmosphere

GAS	PERCENTAGE
Nitrogen (N2)	78.09%:
Oxygen (O2)	20.95%
Carbon Dioxide (CO2)	00.04%
Argon (A)	trace

Neon (Ne)	trace
Helium (He)	trace
Krypton (Kr)	trace
Xenon (Xe)	trace
Hydrogen (H2)	trace

The percentages of these gases remain consistent to the outer edge of the atmosphere (which is anywhere from 50 to 1,000 miles, depending on which scientist is asked), but as already mentioned, the overall pressure decreases. In the lower reaches of the atmosphere, water vapor, dust and pollution make up the rest of atmospheric composition.

2.6 PHYSIOLOGICAL ACCLIMATIZATION

Humans have the unique ability to adapt to their environment fairly effectively, with full physiological and cognitive function, up to an altitude of 10,000 feet. Based on research conducted by Dr. Zubieta-Calleja of the University of Copenhagen, full physiological adaption takes about 18.4 days per mile (5,280 feet) of altitude up to 10,000 feet.

Long-term physiological changes that occur to compensate for environmental pressure changes include:

- Increases in red blood cell (RBC) mass. Oxygen transport in the body is the responsibility of RBC's binding to and carrying oxygen, so the body compensates by increasing the capacity of the transportation system.
- Increase in cellular mitochondria. Cellular mitochondria are responsible for oxygen metabolizing processes of the body, so the body increases production capacity.
- Increases in cardiovascular system capillaries. Capillaries are responsible for the exchange of oxygen between the blood stream and body tissue, so the body increases its ability to diffuse oxygen into tissue.
- Increases in arterial blood pressure. The body's arteries are responsible for transportation of oxygen-rich RBC's, so the body wants to increase its ability to transport decreasing amounts of oxygen around the system.

Individuals that do not fully physiologically acclimatize can expect the following symptomology:

- Hyperventilation: involuntary faster and/or deeper breathing rate.
- Shortness of breath, or air starvation, during exertion.
- Changing breathing patterns during periods of sleep.
- Awakening frequently at night.
- Increased urination.

What about people that live their lives at altitudes above 10,000 feet, or extreme mountain climbers who spend months at altitudes in excess of 10,000 feet? Indigenous mountain dwellers such as the famous Sherpa of the Himalayan Mountains of Asia have actually undergone an evolutionary physiological adaption over centuries to enable them to function normally at extreme altitudes. Their physiology has permanently adapted to be hyper-efficient with lower barometric pressures and lower oxygen-levels. Mountain climbers, or more appropriately sea-level adapted people, undergo the changes listed above over a period of time, but would never achieve peak physical or cognitive performance.

Knowing what we do so far about the lack of human efficiency at altitude, why do aviation operations risk flight at high altitudes? The answers are:

- Less air resistance equals more efficient fuel consumption, potentially saving an airline operator thousands of dollars per flight.
- Better routing as a result of the ability to fly over mountainous or hostile terrain.
- Potential for more favorable winds (again, better fuel efficiency) if a flight lines up correctly with the Jetstream.
- The opportunity to fly above hostile weather systems, ensuring a smoother, more comfortable and predictable customer experience.

Humidity

Water as a substance is unique, as it may exist as a liquid, solid, or gas. Water, or moisture, increases in the atmosphere primarily through evaporation from rivers, lakes, oceans, plants and the majority is typically contained below 10,000.

Absolute humidity is a measure of the actual amount of water vapor in the air, regardless of air temperature. Obviously, the higher the content of water vapor, the higher the absolute humidity.

Relative humidity is typically expressed as percent, and measures water vapor relative the air temperature. Typically, warm air may possess more water vapor than cold air so if both types of air possess the same absolute humidity, cold air would have higher relative humidity and warm air would have lower relative humidity. What humans feel outside in an unprotected environment is the actual amount of moisture, or relative humidity, in the air.

As mentioned, altitude and temperature play a role regarding moisture in air. The higher and colder the ambient altitude, the lower the relative humidity, and this dry air is being used to pressurize most commercial or corporate aircraft. As this ambient air is modified and warmed for use in the fuselage it gets even drier resulting in a very dry cabin environment. Most commercial aircraft operate with a very low internal relative humidity of 20% or less, especially on long flights. Aircraft are not equipped with humidifiers as the volume of water required to be stored on board would create significant operational weight penalties.

These low relative humidity levels may cause discomfort to passengers and crew such as sore eyes and less visual effectiveness, dry skin, and drying out of mucosal membrane. Dry mucosal membrane in nasal passages may crack and therefore become more susceptible to rhinovirus cold viruses penetration.

One may *mitigate the effects of low humidity* by:

- **Inhaling steam from hot coffee or tea**
- **Using moisturizing creams**
- **Staying hydrated with bottled water**
- **Using saline solution for dry eyes**
- **Wearing a protective face mask.**

2.7 PHYSICAL DIVISIONS OF THE ATMOSPHERE

As we know, atmospheric pressure decreases and temperature variances exist throughout the entire spectrum of the envelope of air surrounding the Earth. In the lowest division of the atmosphere, the Troposphere, this occurs as result of differential heating of air from the sun's rays striking the Earth (radiant energy) at various angles, depending on where those rays strike. The sun's rays will be at a very low angle at the poles, resulting in less heating and as such, less "lift", so the Tropospheric layer at the poles can be relatively thin. The sun's rays strike the Earth at a higher angle at the equator, resulting in more heating (higher "lift") and a much thicker Tropospheric layer.

Each physical division of the atmosphere has specific characteristics associated with it, in that temperature, chemical composition and physical properties differentiates that division from the others. The list below describes these divisions:

Troposphere: Sea level – approximately 23,000 feet (poles) to 50,000 feet (equator). Variable temperature, water vapor, turbulence, storms, weather, temperature lapse rate. This is the common cruise altitude for most piston- and turbo-prop-powered aircraft.

Tropopause: While not officially a division of the atmosphere, the tropopause is a region of temperature stability that forms the boundary separating the Troposphere and Stratosphere.

It should be noted at this point that a large amount of ozone gas exists in the atmosphere exceeding tropospheric levels. Ozone is an important component of the atmosphere that filters out ultraviolet radiation. Heavier concentrations of ozone typically exist in the winter and spring seasons, and while flying northern routes.

Unfiltered, ozone gas ingestion in humans can cause a variety of symptoms, including headaches, fatigue, shortness of breath, chest pains, nausea, coughing, pulmonary distress, and exacerbation of asthma.

On aircraft capable of flying at those altitudes, catalytic ozone converters should be effective at filtering out 90-98% of ozone entering the occupied cabin. Issues that can arise is filter efficiency can degrade with age like any other mechanical device, and smoke events can lessen filter effectiveness.

Stratosphere: Approximately 36,000 feet - 165,000 feet. Relatively constant temperature of -55 degrees C or -67 degrees F at the lower levels, little water vapor, jet streams, little turbulence. Temperatures in the stratosphere may actually increase with altitude because of increasing amounts of ozone. This is a common cruise altitude for most commercial and corporate turbine-powered aircraft.

Mesosphere: Approximately 165,000 feet – 287,000 feet. The coldest regions of our atmosphere exist in this layer and reach -90 degrees C. Provides protection from UV rays, and gets its name from the ionized gas within this layer (UV rays strip electrons from gaseous molecules and creates ions). This layer also allows for effective radio communication.

Thermosphere: 287,000 feet – 1,650,000 feet (approximately 300 miles). The fourth layer of the Earth's atmosphere is the region the International Space Station or space shuttles orbiting the Earth spend their time. The thermosphere is extremely sensitive to the sun's activity, and can heat up to 1,500 degrees C as a result of solar influence.

Exosphere: 300,000 feet +. Gradually becomes the vacuum of space, and has so little pressure and density gaseous molecules rarely collide.

<u>Space</u>: Complete vacuum, average temperature between celestial bodies averages -270 degrees C or -458 degrees F.

Figure 2.4 Physical Divisions of the Atmosphere

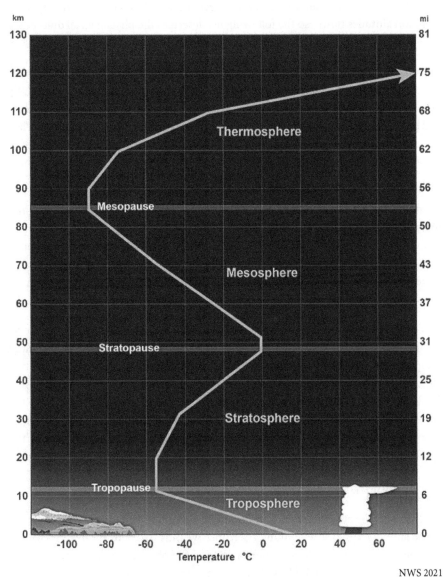

NWS 2021

2.8 PHYSIOLOGICAL DIVISIONS OF ATMOSPHERE

In the scientific discipline of Aerospace Physiology, we classify the atmosphere in phases of how human function will be affected, and our life-support needs for peak performance. Modern aircraft quickly exceed human limitations with respect to common altitudes flown, so the following list describes the physiological divisions of the atmosphere:

Zone of Normal Adaptation. This zone extends from sea level to 10,000 feet. Humans can adapt and function relatively normally at these altitudes. Generally speaking, the human body has adapted to operate at peak efficiency in the lower regions of this zone and can experience minor physiological and cognitive problems resulting from a lack of oxygen in the upper reaches. Problems with the equalization of gas trapped in certain body cavities may occur as humans descend through this part of atmosphere.

Zone of Physiologic Deficiency. This zone extends from 10,000 feet to 50,000 feet. Most humans are unable to adapt and function with peak efficiency in this region of the atmosphere, so conventional aviation life-support equipment is necessary to support peak, or even normal, physiological and cognitive function. Life-support equipment efficiency needs to vary with increasing altitudes and conditions, as increasing amounts of oxygen and pressure ingestion are necessary to allow humans to continue to operate normally.

Space Equivalent Zone. This zone starts at 50,000 feet and extends until the outer edge of the atmosphere. Exposure to these altitudes would most certainly cause incapacitation, followed very shortly by death, in extremely short periods of time (seconds as opposed to minutes.) Survival at these altitudes would require the use of full-body pressure suits (space suits), sealed pressurization systems, etc. FL630 is known as Armstrong's Line; the point in the atmosphere where liquid boils simply by exposure to the environment. Barometric pressure is so low and gas expansion so high that human blood would virtually boil at a temperature of 65 degrees F.

2.9 PHYSICAL GAS LAWS

As discussed, the atmosphere is complex mixture of gases, and these gases are subject to the laws of physics like anything else. Since we must strive to survive in whatever environment we fly in, a basic understanding of the physical gas laws and how they interplay with the human body and aviation equipment you will use is necessary.

We will discuss the actions of gases when gases are subjected to pressure, subjected to thermal variation, and when gases are dissolved in a solution. We also explain the actions of gases when they diffuse, and their component structure.

Boyle's Law. A volume of gas is inversely proportional to its subjected pressure, temperature remaining constant.

What Boyle is so eloquently saying is when a volume of gas exists, the environmental pressure surrounding it determines its size. Think of a balloon blown up half-way to its fullest volume; if one could reduce the atmospheric pressure around the balloon, its size would increase. If one could increase the atmospheric pressure on the balloon, its size would decrease.

The same phenomena occur in the human body when we ascend or descend in the atmosphere. There are areas of "trapped gas" inside the body whereas the gas expands as we ascend in altitude and contracts as descend in altitude. This may cause excruciating problems if that gas cannot be equalized as we ascend and descend, so Boyle's Law explains how trapped gas issues occur in the body as we fly.

Charles' Law. The pressure of a gas is directly proportional to its temperature.

What Charles' Law explains is the propensity of gas volume to increase as it is heated, or contract as it is cooled. The significance of this in aviation has nothing to do with human physiology; rather, it mainly has to do with aircraft oxygen bottles.

Oxygen bottles must be filled to a certain pressure prior to flight, and the filling process takes place in a hanger or on the ramp where the temperature is 80 degrees F, for the purposes of this discussion. We know when we ascend to altitude, the temperature cools, so when we check the pressure of those oxygen bottles at altitude the pressure reading will be less than when we checked the pressure on the ground. Charles' Law simply explains the fluctuation of oxygen bottle pressure at altitude vs. what they read on the ground.

Henry's Law. The amount of gas dissolved in a solution is proportional to the partial pressure of that gas over the solution.

Henry's Law is explaining what happens when opening a bottle or can of carbonated beverage. In a carbonated drink, the partial pressure of carbon dioxide over the liquid compresses carbon dioxide gas into the liquid itself. When we open the bottle or can, the liquid in the container fizzes as the partial pressure of carbon dioxide over the liquid is reduced, allowing carbon dioxide in the liquid to escape.

The physiological significance of Henry's Law is because 78% of atmosphere consists of nitrogen, the resulting consequence is we have a lot of nitrogen molecules in body tissue and bodily fluids. When we ascend to altitude, especially under certain conditions (to be discussed later), those nitrogen (N_2) molecules can supersaturate in the tissues and fluid and form bubbles. Depending on where those bubbles form and collect in the body, significant and profound issues to human function can arise. This bubble formation is known as Evolved Gas Disorders, or Decompression Sickness.

Graham's Law (The Law of Gaseous Diffusion). Gases will diffuse from an area of high concentration to an area of low concentration.

Graham's Law simply states the movement of smells and gases occur as a direct result of pressure differentials. If there is an area with a pressure of "100", for example, and an adjacent area of pressure of "75", the gas from the area of high pressure will naturally move to the area of low pressure until both areas' pressure is equal. The same thing happens with high- and low-pressure weather systems, creating wind on the surface of the Earth.

The physiological significance of Graham's Law is explaining how we can get oxygen from our environment into our lungs, blood stream and body tissues. The process simply depends on pressure gradients and varying concentrations to keep those gasses moving in the correct direction. Ultimately, Graham's Law explains the respiration process of the human body.

Dalton's Law. The total pressure of a mixture of gas is equal to the sum of the partial pressure of each gas in the mixture.

This isn't a hard concept to comprehend; there are a number of fractions which equal a whole number. Each gas in the Earth's atmosphere can be isolated, and that gas is referred to as a "partial pressure," so when you add up all the partial pressures of each gas in the atmosphere (O_2, N_2, CO_2, H_2, etc.) you have the total atmospheric pressure.

The physiological impact to us is when we ascend, the total atmospheric pressure decreases, which means the partial pressure of oxygen we have grown accustomed to receiving from our environment is steadily decreasing along with the decrease in overall pressure. If we continue to ascend, we will reach a point in the atmosphere where we start to fail, both cognitively and physiologically, so Dalton's Law explains how the phenomena of hypoxia occurs as we ascend.

2.10 THE PARTIAL PRESSURE OF OXYGEN

The environmental partial pressure of oxygen humans need is one of the main physiological issues of aviation, as oxygen is the "currency" by which we live and function. It is critical for aviators to have a thorough understanding of the relationship between the partial pressure of oxygen and human function.

To determine the partial pressure of oxygen in the atmosphere, we use a simple equation; PO2 = PB x %oxygen (the atmospheric partial pressure of oxygen equals the total atmospheric pressure multiplied by the percentage of oxygen in the atmosphere).

Let us figure out the partial pressure of oxygen at Sea Level: 760 mm/Hg (total SL atmospheric pressure) x .21 (percentage of oxygen in the air) = <u>159 mm/Hg</u> (the partial pressure of oxygen).

159 mm/Hg is the amount of atmospheric oxygen humans need to be at our physiological and cognitive peak efficiency.

Let us see what the partial pressure of oxygen would be at 18,000 feet (FL180): 380 mm/Hg x .21 = <u>80 mm/Hg</u>.

FL180 being the half-way point in terms of atmospheric pressure, it stands to reason the PO2 would be 50 percent that of sea level. Now that we know this, what can aviators do to maintain peak efficiency? The answer: use properly-calibrated oxygen equipment.

If we add an oxygen system that is properly calibrated, the system should be delivering adequarte partial pressure of oxygen at FL180 to keep us relatively close to sea level equivalency, as this is where we function at our peak. In order to achieve that goal, we need to figure out what the proper amount of oxygen would be. If we multiply 380 mm/Hg by .42, we end up with 159.6 mm/Hg as a PO2, so the oxygen system should be delivering somewhere between 40% - 42% PO2 to keep us fully functional.

This is the key to a properly functioning and calibrated oxygen system; either the aviator or the system itself has to continuously be aware and/or monitor the barometric pressure at any given altitude and provide the proper partial pressure of oxygen to keep the aviator safely flying the aircraft. This information will be covered in much greater detail later in this book.

Conclusion

Now we have a better understanding of the atmosphere and how we, as humans, fit into it. The atmosphere is a wonderful place that keeps humans alive through oxygen, pressure, maintaining a habitable temperature, and protecting us from UV & galactic cosmic radiation and meteorites. As aviators, we are offered the chance to fly at the higher altitudes, and see and experience things humans were not really expected to see and experience. The atmosphere provides us with career and income opportunities, beautiful horizons, and can be our best friend if respected accordingly.

The atmosphere may also be a formidable adversary, if disrespected and misused. We should not forget our human physiological and cognitive systems developed as surface-dwellers; any time we fly we are in a hostile environment, at a disadvantage, and must constantly protect ourselves from the many potentially disastrous issues that face us in the air.

Chapter 2 Core Competency Questions

1. How much does temperature decrease per 1,000 feet as we ascend into the atmosphere?
2. Where does temperature stabilize in the atmosphere?
3. Where is atmospheric pressure the densest?
4. How long does a human take to fully physiologically acclimatize to a given altitude?
5. To what altitude can humans fully physiologically acclimatize?
6. What is percentage of oxygen and nitrogen in the atmosphere?
7. What altitudes apply to the Zone of Physiologic Efficiency?
8. What altitudes apply to the Physiological Deficient Zone?
9. Where does the Space Equivalent Zone begin?
10. What is the partial pressure of atmospheric oxygen at SL?
11. What physiological issue does Boyle's Law apply to?
12. What physiological issue does Henry's Law apply to?
13. What physiological issue does Charles' Law apply to?
14. What physiological issue does Graham's Law apply to?
15. What physiological issue does Dalton's Law apply to?

3. RESPIRATION AND CIRCULATION

People are dimly aware of how their body works; however, for aviators it is crucial to have a thorough understanding of physiological processes to better understand the abnormal impacts the flying environment can have on the body and mind. Two human systems most directly affected by flight are the respiratory and circulatory systems, and this chapter will provide a better understanding of these sophisticated systems.

The most obvious benefit of these systems is to enable humans to extract oxygen from the atmosphere, move oxygen to our lungs, and then transport oxygen around the body and deposit it at the body tissue that needs it. Oxygen is the catalyst to create energy at the cellular level to enable us to think, calculate, move in a meaningful way, respond to external stimuli, and so forth. Therefore, oxygen's timely delivery to the cells of the body is what makes us the intelligent species we are. Unfortunately, disruption of oxygen delivery makes us somewhat less intelligent in many cases.

In this chapter we will discuss:

1. Respiration
2. Cardiovascular system
3. Oxygen Processing in the human body
4. Ventilation
5. Diffusion
6. Oxygen Transport (Circulation)
7. Utilization
8. Homeostasis

3.1 RESPIRATION

Respiration is basically defined as an exchange of gases between a living organism and its environment. The most important point to remember is the fact every cell in the organism is involved in this process, and for aviators, the brain cells have the most importance. We will discuss how the brain is oxygenated normally, and in future chapters how the brain is prevented from normal oxygenation as a result of various factors and forces imposed on us through the flight environment.

Human Physiology

Although fascinating to the point of appearing like magic, some people find the operation of the body to be somewhat confusing. We can paint a simpler picture of bodily function if we look at human physiology in terms of a functioning mechanical object, like an automobile or an aircraft:

- Fuel = Oxygen: Like any other "engine", the body needs oxygen to function like an engine needs fuel to function. When the engine runs out of fuel, the engine stops functioning. The same happens to the body; if it runs out of oxygen; the body (and brain) stops working.
- Fuel tank = Lungs: The fuel tank holds its supply of fuel, and the body's "fuel tank" are the lungs. The lungs maintains its supply of oxygen at-the-ready so the body tissues maintain a continuous supply of "fuel" for energy creation.
- Fuel pump = Heart: The engine's fuel pump sends the energy-rich fuel to its fuel-management system and cylinders for combustion. The heart pumps oxygen-rich blood through the cardiovascular system for delivery to body tissues for metabolization (combustion).
- Fuel lines = Arteries: The fuel being pumped around the engine travels in the fuel lines, and the oxygen-rich blood moves through the body's arteries.
- Cylinders = Mitochondria: The fuel that reaches the cylinders is combusted to create energy. Once blood reaches the cellular mitochondria, the mitochondria metabolizes the oxygen to create energy.
- Exhaust gases = Carbon Dioxide: Once the combustion process is complete, the by-product of that process is the exhaust gas, or waste gas. Once the mitochondria has metabolized oxygen, the byproduct of that process is carbon dioxide (CO_2).
- Exhaust System = Veins. The engine needs to vent off its exhaust gases, so it routes those gases through the exhaust system. The body's "exhaust system" are the veins, which transport excess carbon dioxide to the lungs so we can exhale the excess CO_2 out of our body.
- Gyroscopic System = Vestibular System: An aircraft transmits aircraft spatial orientation information though gyroscopic instrumentation, whereas the body's spatial orientation system rests with the vestibular system, located in the inner ear of the cranium.
- Navigation System = Visual System: An aircraft needs to provide navigation information to its pilot so the pilot does not get lost; whereas the body's visual system (eyes) provide navigational guidance through visual input.

The body was developed to operate in an environment that provides a generous supply of oxygen, with the appropriate atmospheric pressure to ensure proper oxygen distribution around the body, moving about three to four miles per hour, and in a more-or-less two-dimensional world with our bodies touching the Earth in some way. When those operational parameters are altered, i.e. flying at a higher altitude with less oxygen and atmospheric pressure, adding a third dimension, changing visual perspectives, and moving faster than we should be, our bodily functions and senses may have difficulty keeping up. Given the right circumstances, our functions and senses can shut down altogether, or provide such confusing information to our brain we simply do not figure out what is going on in the moment, and become momentarily inactive and indecisive; the point when incidents and accidents start to occur.

The most essential thing for an aviator to remember in flight is the environment they are currently operating in is a foreign environment. Aviators need to respect the connection they have directly with the atmosphere, and be mindful of the fact that when the environment changes, their bodily functions change along with it. If one were to experience a rapid decompression, for instance, people transition extremely rapidly from a high-atmospheric pressure environment to a low-pressure environment in seconds, and the corresponding physiological changes will be devastating to normal function. If aviators experience toxic fumes in the cockpit, the very air they breathe is changing chemically, significantly affecting normal physiology. When aviators descend in their aircraft, they are moving from a low-pressure environment to a high-pressure environment and the trapped gas volumes inside their bodies need to equalize, or intense and excruciating pain could result.

3.2 CARDIOVASCULAR SYSTEM

The cardiovascular system is responsible for transportation of blood and nutrients throughout the body. The cardiovascular system is comprised of the heart and blood vessels, creating an incredibly efficient delivery system for oxygen, nutrients, hormones, and cellular waste to the entirety of the human body. The heart is merely the size of a closed fist, but is a very powerful pump to energize the system for the movement of the blood cells throughout the body.

Figure 3.1 The Human Heart

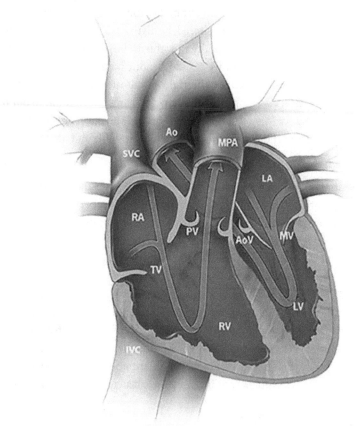

CDC 2021

The human heart pumps blood throughout the body. Blood transports and provides oxygen and nutrients to body tissues and removes carbon dioxide and waste products. As blood travels throughout the body, oxygen is delivered to tissues and the blood becomes *oxygen poor*.

1. Oxygen-poor blood returns from the body to the heart through the *superior vena cava* (SVC) and *inferior vena cava* (IVC), the two main veins that bring blood back to the heart.
2. The oxygen-poor blood enters the right atrium (RA), or the right upper chamber of the heart.
3. From there, the blood flows through the *tricuspid valve* (TV) into the right ventricle (RV), or the right lower chamber of the heart.

4. The right ventricle (RV) pumps oxygen-poor blood through the *pulmonary valve* (PV) into the main pulmonary artery (MPA).
5. From there, the blood flows through the right and left pulmonary arteries into the lungs, called *pulmonary circulation*.
6. In the lungs, oxygen is diffused into the blood and carbon dioxide is diffused out of the blood during the process of breathing. After the blood gets oxygen in the lungs, it is called *oxygen-rich* blood.
7. Oxygen-rich blood flows from the lungs back into the left atrium (LA), or the left upper chamber of the heart, through four pulmonary veins.
8. Oxygen-rich blood then flows through the *mitral valve* (MV) into the left ventricle (LV), or the left lower chamber.
9. The left ventricle (LV) pumps the oxygen-rich blood through the *aortic valve* (AoV) into the *aorta* (Ao), the main artery that takes oxygen-rich blood out to the rest of the body, called *systemic circulation* (How the Heart Works, 2017).

The number of times one's heart pumps blood through the cardiovascular system is called *pulse rate*. One's pulse rate may be determined by a variety of factors such as air temperature (heat increases pulse rate), emotions, body mass index (higher BMI usually raises pulse rate), and medication use. *Stroke volume* (SV) is the amount of blood one's left ventricle pumps with each beat.

Cardiac output is stroke volume x heart (pulse) rate. One's heart needs to supply vital organs and the brain with adequate oxygen and nutrient levels, and the average cardiac output for adults is five to six liters of blood per minute, with average heart rates between 60 and 100 beats-per-minute.

Measurement of one's blood pressure is gauged using *systolic* (the first number) and *diastolic* (the second number) blood pressures. Systolic blood pressure indicates the pressure one's blood exerts on arterial walls when one's heart beats. Diastolic blood pressure indicates the pressure one's blood exerts on arterial walls when one's heart is resting between beats. According to the CDC, normal adult blood pressure is measured at 120/80 mmHg. It is common for blood pressure to elevate slightly with age, as arteries lose elasticity.

Hypertension and Hypotension

Hypertension is a condition causing blood pressure to be higher than normal, whereas *hypotension* is blood pressure lower than normal. Either condition may have negative consequences regarding a pilot's medical certificate.

Hypertension may cause some individuals to experience headaches, shortness of breath, nosebleeds, especially if hypertension reaches severe stages. Severe hypertension may also cause damage to heart, brain, kidneys, and eyes. Hypertension may develop as a result of unhealthy lifestyles, such as not getting enough exercise, obesity, or having diabetes. Untreated hypertension may damage arteries making them less elastic, in turn decreasing the flow of blood and oxygen to the heart causing *heart disease*. This can lead to *angina* (chest pain), *heart attack* (blood supply to the heart is blocked and damage occurs), or *heart failure* (the heart cannot pump blood and oxygen to organs of the body). Angina may be a sign of the development of *coronary artery disease (CAD),* which is plaque buildup causing the interior walls of arteries to narrow over time, which can partially or totally block the blood flow caused by being overweight, physical inactive, a tobacco smoker, or eating unhealthy foods.

High blood pressure may cause arteries supplying blood and oxygen to one's brain to burst or be blocked, causing a *stroke*. Brain cells die during a stroke as a result of a lack of oxygen. Strokes may cause serious disabilities with speech, movement, and other basic functions. A stroke may also be severe enough to kill.

High blood pressure and CAD may be mitigated by exercising 30 minutes per day for five days per week, not smoking, maintaining a healthy diet low in sodium and alcohol, maintaining a healthy weight, and managing stress. In more severe cases, medications may be prescribed or surgery may be performed to help restore blood flow to the heart.

Hypotension is blood pressure lower than 90/60 mmHg. Factors causing low blood pressure in individuals include medications, bleeding, aging processes, as well as conditions including dehydration, pregnancy, heart problems, and diabetes. Typically, older adults maintain higher risks for symptoms of low blood pressure including trips or falls, fainting, or dizziness upon standing or following a meal. Older adults are more at risk of developing low blood pressure as a side effect of high blood pressure medications.

Low blood pressure may go unnoticed by some individuals. Others may experience light-headedness, confusion, fatigue, physical weakness, blurry vision, headaches, neck/back pain, nausea, or heart palpitations. Sitting down may offer immediate relief of these symptoms. Should blood pressure drop too low, vital bodily organs may not get sufficient oxygen and nutrients. Should this happen, low blood pressure may lead to shock, requiring immediate medical attention. Signs of shock include cold and sweaty skin, rapid breathing, a blue skin tone, or a rapid but weak pulse. If signs of shock are noticed in yourself or someone else, immediately call for professional medical assistance.

Physicians will perform a blood pressure test for low blood pressure diagnoses. Additional tests may include blood, urine, or imaging tests, and possibly a tilt-table test if fainting occurs often. Treatment for low blood pressure may not be necessary depending on signs and symptoms, or treatment may include drinking more fluids, taking medicines to raise one's blood pressure, or adjusting medicines causing low blood pressure. Recommended lifestyle changes include adjusting what and how one eats as well as how one sits and stands up. Other recommendations could include compression stockings for those required to stand for long periods.

3.3 OXYGEN PROCESSING IN THE HUMAN BODY

As mentioned, respiration is the exchange of gases between a living organism and its environment. The obvious benefits of this mechanism is absorption of oxygen into the body, and removal of carbon dioxide from the body. There are four recognized steps regarding oxygen movement and use in the human body:

1. Ventilation: The process of bringing air to the lung from the external environment, and expelling excess gases out of the body.
2. Respiration: Gas exchange in the air sacs (alveoli) of the lung.
3. Transportation: Oxygen is transported (circulated) through arteries of the body, and excess carbon dioxide is removed through the veins.
4. Utilization: Oxygen is metabolized by the cells of the body to create energy.

We will look at each one of these steps in detail to gain a basic understanding of these normalized processes, which provides us a clearer picture of what could potentially happen to us in an abnormal environment. Please note these discussions apply to physiologically normal and healthy humans. Pre-existing illnesses such as anemia, asthma, Chronic Obstructive Pulmonary Disease (COPD), and coronary arterial disease require much deeper discussion.

3.4 FIRST STEP: VENTILATION

Ventilation involves drawing oxygen into the lungs from the atmosphere around us. In order for the body to be able to use this oxygen effectively, it must be modified for the respiratory system to use it to its fullest advantage. Modifications to this oxygen include:

- *Filtering the oxygen.* Our nasal cavities possess perfect air foils to spin the air as it enters our sinuses, creating a centrifugal effect to separate particles (dirt, dust pollution) from the oxygen. Cilia (hair cells) and mucous provide the rest of the filtering tasks.
- *Warming the oxygen.* This oxygen needs to be at body temperature to maximize absorption, and to prevent damage from occurring to the delicate tissues that form the respiratory system.
- *Humidifying the oxygen.* Oxygen needs to be infused with water vapor to provide for and facilitate the transfer of oxygen from the lungs to the bloodstream and prevent damage to lung tissue.

The mechanical process of inhaling the oxygen into the body involves several muscle groups contracting all at the same time. The muscles of the chest (pectorals) and rib cage (intercostal) contract to expand the rib cage, and the diaphragm contracts and moves downward, therefore allowing the lungs to expand. As the lungs expand, air is sucked into the body through the nose and mouth, travels down the throat and trachea, and into the bronchial tubes and lungs. More on that later.

The process of breathing occurs at a normalized rate of 12 to 20 breaths per minute, and a volume of approximately eight liters per minute. The normal breathing rate will become more important in future discussions.

Under normal circumstances, inhaling air is considered the *active* phase of breathing as a result of the muscular contraction required. The exhalation phase of breathing is considered the *passive* phase, as muscles relax to allow the lungs to contract in size and push excess air and carbon dioxide out of the body.

When flying at high altitudes, a certain amount of excess pressure is required from an aviator's life support equipment to maintain normal oxygen transfer at the lung level. This excess pressure is called *pressure breathing,* and it is virtually a reversal of the normal breathing cycle. Pressure breathing can create problems for uninitiated aviators, as it is unlike anything they've likely experienced previously, which can create quite a panic if not controlled. Receiving training and practicing pressure breathing is highly recommended for aircraft equipped with pressure-demand oxygen regulators, which will be discussed in future chapters. Pressure breathing may also impair an aviator's ability to communicate, as normal verbal communication takes place during the passive phase of breathing. Attempting to talk against pressure being rammed into the body can be very frustrating; again, necessitating the need for training in dealing with pressure breathing effectively.

Mentioned previously was the rate of breathing was eight to twenty breaths-per-minute, as long as all is normal. The rate of breathing can be significantly affected by many factors, including:

- Fever
- Depressant drugs
- Anxiety
- Insufficient oxygen
- Stimulant drugs
- The proper amount of sleep
- Fatigue

Controls of Respiration

There are several natural controls of respiration in humans. Two are chemical-based, and one is cognitively based.

The *primary control of respiration* in humans is the amount of *carbon dioxide* in body tissues. This chemical is constantly monitored by peripheral chemoreceptors located in the carotid and aortic bodies. These chemoreceptors are sensitive to variations of carbon dioxide in the blood stream and relay this information to the pons of the brain, triggering the breathing mechanism if too much carbon dioxide is detected in the lungs. You can experiment on yourself by holding your breath for 20 – 30 seconds; before long, the build-up of carbon dioxide will cause you to <u>have</u> to take a breath of fresh air!

Figure 3.2 Human Brain

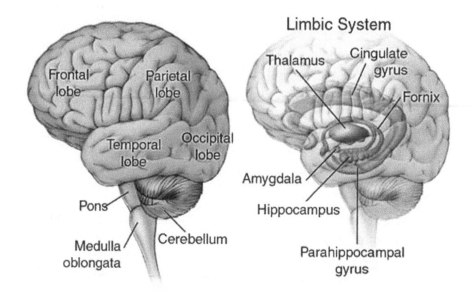

The *secondary control of respiration* is the aortic body monitoring *oxygen saturation* levels in the blood. When the body registers too little oxygen in the blood, the body automatically increases breathing rate as a compensatory measure to increase oxygen intake. Conversely, if too much oxygen is detected, the body will slow breathing rate in an attempt to maintain chemical equilibrium.

The *cognitive control of respiration* is to *voluntarily control* your rate and depth of breathing. Central chemoreceptors located on the ventrolateral surface of the medulla oblongata detect changes in the pH of spinal fluid. This mechanism is used mainly as a defense mechanism against over-breathing in the event the aviator is pressure breathing, or during periods of acute hyper-stress, leading to hyperventilation (breathing too rapidly) based on external stimulus.

Lung Structure

Oxygen travels down the throat to the trachea, into the bronchial tubes and ultimately the lungs. Once oxygen enters the lungs, it flows into the large bronchial tubes which branch a total of 16 times, growing progressively smaller at each branch. At the very end of the 16th branch, known as terminal bronchioles, are the *alveoli* (air sacs). These alveoli are extremely tiny, but are present in huge qualities. It is estimated that 300,000 alveoli exist in normal adult human lungs. Though each individual alveoli is tiny, if every alveoli was removed and placed on a flat surface, it would occupy a space the size of a large room. Each alveoli is encapsulated by a dense sheet of capillaries. These capillaries are so dense they actually resemble a sheet of blood around each alveoli. The alveolar wall is a very thin, permeable membrane that is just one cell (1/50,000th of an inch) thick. This allows oxygen, as well as other gases, to diffuse across the membrane into and out of the capillaries, and therefore blood.

Figure 3.3 Human Lung Structure

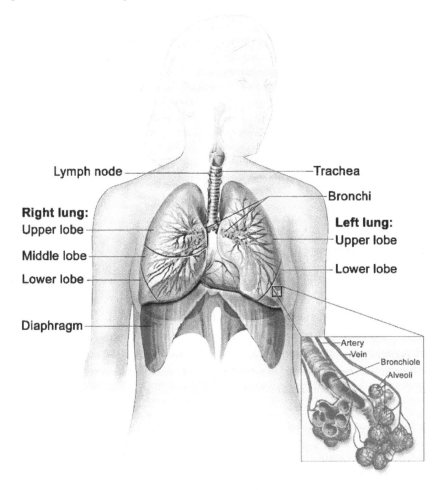

Figure 3.4 Alveolar Structure

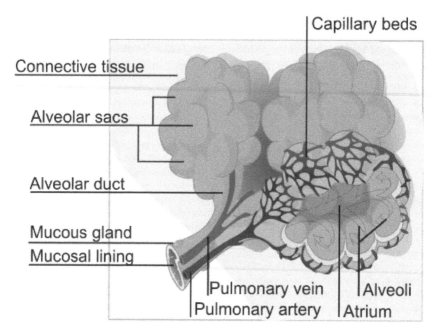

Capillary beds

Connective tissue

Alveolar sacs

Alveolar duct

Mucous gland
Mucosal lining

Pulmonary vein
Pulmonary artery

Alveoli
Atrium

Wpclipart 2021

3.5 SECOND STEP: DIFFUSION

The partial pressure of oxygen forces oxygen through alveolar membrane and into the bloodstream. The partial pressure of atmospheric oxygen is approximately 21% of the total atmospheric pressure. If at sea level, this would equate to 159 mm/Hg of pressure (21% of the total atmospheric pressure of 760mm/Hg). The alveolar environment not only includes the air we inhale, but also the carbon dioxide we produce and the water vapor our bodily tissues generate. As a result of these off-setting components, the amount of oxygen in the alveoli, known as *oxygen tension*, is reduced from that of the sea level partial pressure of oxygen in the atmosphere (PO2). The formula for such is as follows:

PAO2 (partial pressure of alveolar oxygen) = PO2 (159 mm/Hg) minus PH2O minus PCO2 = 100 to 104 mmHg. This represents oxygen tension in human lungs allowing us to operate at our physiological and psychological peak.

Due to the function of Graham's Law which states: "Gases will diffuse from an area of high concentration to an area of low concentration", this causes gases to move back and forth across a gas-permeable membrane (such as the alveoli). The high partial pressure of oxygen in the alveoli (104 mm/Hg) now diffuses oxygen molecules across the alveolar membrane and into the blood. This in turn raises the partial pressure of oxygen in venous blood (blood that has left the cells and therefore is low in oxygen) from 40 mm/Hg to 104 mm/Hg. At the same time this is occurring, the high pressure of carbon dioxide (approximately 47 mm/Hg) in the blood will cause excess carbon dioxide to diffuse into the alveoli where carbon dioxide pressure is a constant 40 mm/Hg.

As a direct result of Graham's Law, positive pressure gradient in the alveolus versus the bloodstream is necessary for oxygen to transfer from the lungs to the red blood cells (RBCs). Under normal circumstances, because of the robust pressure gradient at Sea Level, this diffusion is extremely effective and takes place in microseconds. Obviously at higher altitudes the pressure gradient naturally declines as a result of decreasing atmospheric pressure. In order for oxygen molecules to continue diffusing, a pressure gradient of at least two to three mm/Hg is required to force oxygen molecules through the one-cell thick permeable membrane of the alveolus. When pressure gradient is lost altogether, oxygen stops diffusing. Since optimum physiological and psychological performance is our goal when we fly, how then do we compensate for this decrease in pressure gradient? The answer is to increase the percentage of the oxygen in the air we breathe.

With that concept in mind, let us examine the oxygen percentage required to allow us full functionality as we ascend into the atmosphere. The aviation term for this additional oxygen requirement is *supplemental oxygen,* which is what life support equipment should supply to aviators if used correctly. The table below lists the oxygen percentage requirements providing us full physiological equivalency to sea level:

Figure 3.4 Human Oxygen Requirements

Altitude (m/ft)	Barometric Pressure	Lung Oxygen % Requirement
Sea Level	760	21%
1515/5,000	632	25%
3030/10,000	532	31%
4545/15,000	429	40%
6060/20,000	329	49%
7575/25,000	282	62%
9090/30,000	225	81%
10,300/34,000	187	100%

Even flying at relatively benign altitudes such as 5,000 requires an increased percentage of oxygen over sea level to maintain full physiological ability. Simply put, our bodies are already losing function, albeit hardly noticeable, at easily attainable altitudes in virtually any aircraft.

From the chart above, notice that humans need 100% oxygen (with a tight-fitting oxygen mask) at 34,000 feet to maintain full physiological function. At 34,000 feet (FL340), our atmospheric pressure gradient ceases, with the pressure in our lungs equal to the pressure in the atmosphere and no longer providing for the transfer of oxygen from lungs to blood. The next obvious question to ask is "what happens if we are exposed to altitudes higher than FL340?" The answer is to pressurize the air entering into the body.

According to Graham's Law, if a human were to continue ascent beyond FL340 without pressurizing the air to the lungs, the pressure gradient would actually reverse itself and humans would start exporting oxygen as opposed to importing oxygen. Breathing 100% oxygen without pressure will sustain an aviator up to an altitude of FL400: however, the physiological equivalency increases. The result is unpressurized 100% oxygen at FL400 equals 10,000 feet equivalency to the body. Remember, *sea level equivalency* is our goal.

Demand-style aircraft oxygen equipment are equipped with air-metering regulators to roughly follow the oxygen percentage values represented on the chart above. In fact, most oxygen regulators are designed to keep aviators supplied with *higher oxygen percentages* than the values on the chart to ensure pilots stay ahead of the power-curve, so to speak. Most Pressure-Demand oxygen regulators used in professional transport aircraft not only automatically adjust the oxygen percentage to the altitude (depending on the setting on the regulator), but have the additional benefit of automatically introducing the oxygen under pressure before pressure is necessary. Most pressure-demand-style oxygen regulators begin delivering pressure between FL280 and FL320, steadily increasing the pressure volume the higher an aircraft ascends. The mathematical formula to determine the partial alveolar pressure of oxygen is:

$$PAO2 = [(PB - PH2O) \times FIO2] - PCO2[FIO2 + 1 - FIO2/0.85)].$$

There is a limit as to what altitude pressuring breathing will effectively sustain an aviator at full physiological efficiency, and the limiting factor is *lung tissue*. Lung tissue is not designed for long-term or high-volume pressurized air, and can reach a point where it may be damaged. Based on the above formula, using pressurized oxygen the human limit is FL450. Beyond that altitude, either physiological efficiency is lost or increased pressure would cause lung damage. The next obvious question is "What about civilian corporate aircraft which fly higher than FL450?" Great question, so let us examine.

Let us look at a corporate aircraft flying at FL500, which experiences a rapid decompression with its cabin pressure reaching flight altitude pressure in under five seconds. The crew is wearing pressure-demand oxygen masks. Using the above-mentioned formula:

$PAO2 = [(87+40 - 47) \times 1.0] - 40[0.82]$, therefore $PAO2 = 80 - 32.8 = 47.2$ mm/Hg.

The pilot's alveolar oxygen tension is 47.2 mm/Hg, with a peak efficiency goal of 100 mm/Hg. According to the calculation, the pilot only has roughly 50% of the oxygen at lung level required to perform at a very high cognitive level. How would you expect this scenario to work out?

Let us examine that same scenario at FL500 where the pilots failed to get their oxygen masks on in time:

$PAO2 = [(87 - 47) \times 0.21] - 40[0.96]$, therefore $PAO2 = 8.4 - 39.6 = -31.2$ mm/Hg.

Since the pilots' alveolar oxygen tension is a **minus** 31.2 mm/Hg, they are now rapidly exporting oxygen from their lungs and body. In this scenario Boyle's Law is forcing residual oxygen out of the lungs during the ascent, so when the aircraft reaches FL500 there is virtually no oxygen in the lungs to take advantage of. A pilot in this situation could expect to maintain consciousness for a maximum of perhaps five seconds, as it takes approximately four and a half seconds for a red blood cell to travel from the lungs to the brain. This scenario results in an unconscious pilot.

3.6 THIRD STEP: OXYGEN TRANSPORT (CIRCULATION)

The circulatory system is tasked with transporting blood throughout the body. Blood transports food, oxygen, and water to body tissues and waste materials from tissues. Blood has the additional function of maintaining body heat.

The components of the body that comprise the circulatory system are the heart, arteries, veins, and capillaries.

The heart is a pumping organ capable of forcing blood through the vessels as tissue requirements dictate. The interior of the heart is divided into the right and left halves and each half has two chambers: the atrium and ventricle.

The *arteries* are blood vessels that carry oxygenated blood away from the heart. The elastic walls of the arteries are muscular and strong, permitting the arteries to vary its carrying capacity. Small arteries connect larger arteries to capillaries. The capillaries convey blood from the arteries to body tissue, and from tissue to veins. They are very small, thinly walled, and usually form a network in body tissues in which the exchange of gases take place.

The veins are blood vessels responsible to carry deoxygenated blood back to the heart. Veins have thinner walls and are less elastic than the corresponding-sized arteries. Blood enters the veins from the capillaries under low pressure. Therefore, some method is necessary to get blood back to the heart, especially from the lower regions of the body. The muscles around the veins produce a milking action of the veins forcing blood towards the heart. Valves located in veins prevent a back flow of blood.

Composition of Blood

Blood is made up of two parts, plasma and solids. Approximately 90% of plasma is water, in which many substances are dissolved or suspended. The solid part of blood is made up of white blood cells (WBC) and red blood cells (RBC).

WBCs are composed largely of a substance that act as anti-bodies to assist in fighting diseases and infections. The RBCs are formed in bone marrow and approximately 35 trillion total RBCs exist in the body.

Each RBC is largely made up of a substance called hemoglobin. Each RBC contains approximately 250 million hemoglobin molecules. Each hemoglobin molecule within the RBC can carry 4 molecules of oxygen, so each RBC can carry approximately 1 billion oxygen molecules. The secret of hemoglobin is it contains one atom of iron for every hemoglobin molecule. This gives the blood a chemical attraction for oxygen as well as its red color. The RBCs carry 95% of all oxygen, while the remainder is suspended in plasma. This can be readily seen for a person suffering from *anemia*, which is a lack of RBCs, does not have enough functioning RBCs and will begin to suffer the effect of lack of oxygen at a relatively low altitude. Normal arterial oxygen saturation is about 95 - 97 %. The ability of hemoglobin to take up or release oxygen is not a linear function of partial pressure; however, the relationship is well defined and is usually shown in the form of the oxygen dissociation curve.

One could reason, then, if a decline in hemoglobin were to occur, so would oxygen carrying-capacity of the RBC. For example, if an aviator were a habitual blood-donor, the reduction in RBC count would significantly reduce oxygen delivery to the cells, resulting in deoxygenation issues occurring at much lower altitudes than expected. Therefore, it is imperative an aviator wait an appropriate period of time after blood or plasma donations before flying. Recommendations are to wait 24 hours after plasma donation, and 72 hours following blood donations.

As mentioned, the oxygen dissociation curve is a factor in circulation. The further a RBC gets from the heart, the weaker the bond with oxygen becomes. Typically, this is not an issue in aviation as the brain is close enough to the lungs to ensure oxygenation to function (oxygen supply depending). The oxygen dissociation curve can, however, become a physiological issue at altitude. Once the atmospheric pressure drops to approximately 329 mm/Hg (FL200), the oxygen-hemoglobin bonding process begins to weaken. A strong bonding process is heavily dependent on pressure-gradient in the lungs, which we know is steadily decreasing as we ascend in atmosphere. Therefore, an aviator's *effective performance time* without oxygen decreases rapidly after humans pass the FL200 barrier.

3.7 FOURTH STEP: UTILIZATION

Cells in the body require a constant supply of oxygen for the burning of food material to produce energy. This process, called *metabolism*, converts glucose (blood sugar) and oxygen into energy, as well as carbon dioxide and water. Carbon dioxide produced from this reaction must be removed from the body. In review, the lungs receive oxygen from the atmosphere, which then diffuses into the blood. The blood, at the same time, releases carbon dioxide into the lungs to be exhaled. The oxygen is then transported by the blood to all cells that are low in oxygen. Once the oxygen is in the cell, and metabolism has taken place, carbon dioxide then leaves the cell for the blood. Once in the blood, the carbon dioxide is transported back to the lungs for exhalation.

Previously mentioned was the process to convert glucose to energy requires a constant supply of oxygen, so without oxygen cellular energy production ceases immediately. Once the supply of oxygen is disrupted, the brain's neurons, or brain cells, are some of the first in the body to be affected.

According to the National Institutes of Health, the brain comprises approximately 2% of human body weight, uses 20% of the oxygen provided to the body, and 25% of the total glucose used for energy supply. While the brain is one of the highest energy-demanding tissues of the body, per capita retinal energy demand is even higher with visual processing alone accounting for over 40% of the brain's energy consumption. Consequently, any reduction of oxygen to humans has an almost immediate effect on high cognitive and visual function. Since higher cognitive and visual functions require the most energy production (oxygen), higher reasoning skills, judgement, diagnostic abilities, and high vision function are the first processes in danger of failure, which is not optimum for an aviator in an emergency situation.

Cellular metabolic activity takes place in the mitochondria of the cell, which under normal circumstances converts biochemical energy into adenosine triphosphate (ATP). This metabolic activity may be improved and maximized by maintaining good diet and exercise practices. Some issues reducing or disrupting a human's cerebral metabolic efficiency include:

- Cyanide ingestion
- Lack of oxygen
- Previous concussions (traumatically injured brain tissue)
- Cancer
- Age

3.8 HOMEOSTASIS

According to NASA and the FAA, *homeostasis* may be defined as "the tendency of an organism or cell to regulate its internal functions so as to maintain health and functioning." Translating for aviation, homeostasis is "the condition compatible with optimum cellular and bodily function." Whatever interior or exterior environment we fly in, we must strive to maintain optimum human physiological and psychological function. We may have to modify the air we breathe, the altitude we are flying at, the air quality of the cabin, the ambient temperature we're operating in; the end goal is to maintain optimum function to ensure safe flight.

For peak human performance, we need to keep our cells (specifically neurons) in a normal operating environment with regards to the following:

- Oxygen
- Nutrition
- Rest
- Hydration

As long as we have adequate quantity and quality of those four components, we should operate as close to peak human function as possible. Think about the last time you attempted to take an important exam on three hours' sleep, or you engaged in hard physical labor after skipping breakfast; chances are the task did not go very well. The same concept applies to flying aircraft; the pilot needs to be at their obligatory peak to ensure safe passage for themselves and their passengers. Most flight departments or operations have *Safety Management System (SMS)* programs designed to give the aircrew members guidelines for optimum performance, and it is highly recommended to follow those guidelines.

Long-Term Health

Extensive research has repeated shown diet and exercise programs have major *medicinal* benefits for the user. Those benefits include controlling lifestyle-related chronic illnesses and leading causes of death and disability, such as heart disease, diabetes, obesity, depression and many others. Health issues requiring medication may possibly be mitigated simply by maintaining a healthy diet and exercise program.

Another major benefit of staying physically active and being fit is those individuals are *harder to kill*. This may seem like a grim topic-of-discussion, but the reality is aircraft can and have crashed, generating tremendous forces threatening to tear a human body apart. The more muscular strength and muscle-mass an individual maintains, the better protected against those forces they remain.

Discussions concerning physical exercise and proper diets for aviators could be never-ending and topics for another book or two. The last chapter of this book contains easy-to-understand and rational information concerning diet, exercise, and medical maintenance any serious aviator will find useful.

Conclusion

The concept of respiratory and circulatory systems of the human body is fairly simplistic, yet efficient. It gives the human body the capability to adjust and function in a variety of environments; however, the body has its limitations. If changes are too abrupt, then these systems can not adjust quickly enough and the body and mind will suffer the effects. Now we have a basic understanding of normal physiological function, and will now begin to discuss the body's limitations at altitude, perceptual challenges and other abnormal environmental considerations. Most importantly, we will learn to take appropriate measures to compensate for those limitations.

Chapter 3 Core Competency Questions

1. What is the basic definition of respiration?
2. Proper oxygenation of what cell(s) in the respiration process are most important for aviators?
3. The primary control for respiration in humans is regulated by what gas?
4. The secondary control for respiration in humans is regulated by what gas?
5. True or false: human respiration can be voluntarily controlled?

6. What are the tiny air sacs in the lungs where oxygen diffuses into the blood stream called?
7. What are the four phases of respiration?
8. What cell is responsible to transport oxygen in the cardiovascular system?
9. What do oxygen molecules bind to in the transport process?
10. What four elements need to be maintained in humans for homeostasis with your environment?

4. HYPOXIA IN AVIATION

Hypoxia is, or at least should be, a concern for every aviator that flies an aircraft. Hypoxia is a well-recognized word by aviators, and is covered in all pilot training programs to some degree; mainly as a conversation in a classroom or similar setting. The problem is while most aviators believe they know all they need to know about hypoxia, precious few could actually recognize or respect it for what it really is if it were happening to them in flight. Although altitude-induced hypoxia is all most aviators think they need to worry about, other forms of hypoxia exist pilots rarely consider that could potentially impair a pilot at altitudes far below what is expected or anticipated.

In this chapter, we'll discuss:

1. Definition of hypoxia
2. Types of hypoxia
3. Hypoxic hypoxia
4. Histotoxic hypoxia
5. Hypemic hypoxia
6. Stagnant hypoxia
7. Subjective symptoms of hypoxia
8. Objective signs of hypoxia
9. Characteristics of hypoxia
10. Factors influencing hypoxia effective performance time
11. Effective performance times
12. Treatment for hypoxia
13. Preventative measures for hypoxic hypoxia

4.1 DEFINITION OF HYPOXIA

According to the FAA, *hypoxia* is defined as: "An oxygen deficiency in blood, body tissue and cells sufficient to cause impairment of function."

With regards to aviation, the main focus of our discussions will have to do with cerebral deoxygenation, or how the brain is being deprived of adequate amounts of oxygen.

As mentioned in the definition, an *impairment* of function is the main issue. Impairment can mean different things based on different interpretations, but for our purposes we'll simply define impairment as: *A reduction or loss of function or ability.*

One of the main problems with identifying impairment in an operational aviation setting is the fact an aviator may feel completely normal, yet still be experiencing a reduction in intellectual abilities. The reduction in cognitive functionality may not necessarily mean a loss of "normal" abilities; it may mean when an unexpected emergency event presents itself an aviator's ability to respond quickly and decisively may be reduced to a dangerous level.

One of the issues we discuss throughout many topics we cover in aerospace physiology is the loss or reduction of *cognitive ability* or *cognition*. Again, depending on who is asked, it is certain the term *cognition* can mean different things to different people, so we will define cognition as "the mental action or process of acquiring knowledge and understanding through thought, experience, and the senses."

Now that we have a general definition of cognition, what does it truly mean? If we imagine having an inflight emergency and what cognitive brain processes need to occur to successfully mitigate the emergency, we could further define cognition in aviation as "assessing all of your training and knowledge up to this point in your flying career, and being able to diagnose and fix a complex inflight problem."

Now that we have workable definitions of hypoxia: impairment, and cognition; this brings us to the most lethal fact concerning the onset of hypoxia; it may slow or completely strip an aviator's ability to deal with a complex problem or emergency condition inflight. Hypoxia may be profound enough to prevent a pilot from successfully performing even normalized tasks, such as maintaining straight and level flight. Even worse, many pilots never even see it coming.

Perhaps the most effective way an aviator can be trained to recognize hypoxia is in a controlled environment training device such as a *hypobaric chamber*. A hypobaric chamber (aka altitude chamber) is a large, low-pressure solid-steel box that has the capability of bringing aviators to low-pressure environments by vacuuming the air out. Once at "altitude", the trainees can then experience exactly what hypoxia feels like in themselves, and what it looks like in other people. Other training options exist for hypoxia training, but none as effective as altitude chamber training. This type of training has been an integral part of military aviation training for many decades, and a few institutions exist in the civilian community that can provide the training, including the FAA in Oklahoma City, OK, and the University of North Dakota in Grand Forks, ND.

According to U.S. Air Force research, aviators who have never experienced hypoxia training in an altitude chamber were almost 25 times more likely to lose consciousness because of hypoxia than those that have experienced altitude chamber training. The main reason for this statistic is when many pilots begin to feel hypoxia symptoms developing, pilots may not respect the symptoms as dangerous as opposed to something more benign.

Dalton's Law

In the first chapter, we briefly talked about how Dalton's Law dictates when the overall atmospheric pressure drops, so does the partial pressure of oxygen. In review, Dalton's Law states: "the total pressure of a mixture of gas is equal to the sum of the partial pressure of each gas in the mixture." This explains why lower atmospheric pressures fail to provide sufficient oxygen for human to adequately function, which explains how and why altitude-induced hypoxia occurs.

4.2 THE TYPES OF HYPOXIA

The following are the four types of hypoxia recognized as potential threats to aviators:

- Hypoxic hypoxia: affects the flow of oxygen to the lungs.
- Histotoxic hypoxia: affects how the cells utilize (metabolize) oxygen.
- Hypemic hypoxia: affects the ability of Red Blood Cells to transport oxygen.
- Stagnant hypoxia: affects the normal circulation of blood around the body and arriving at the cells.

We will examine each type of hypoxia in detail.

4.3 HYPOXIC HYPOXIA

Hypoxic hypoxia is a condition that interrupts the flow of oxygen into the lungs. The most common causes of hypoxic hypoxia are:

- Altitude
- Drowning
- Pneumonia
- Chronic lung disease

Altitude-induced hypoxic hypoxia is the most obvious concern to aviators, so that is the causal factor we will concentrate on first.

Hypoxic hypoxia may be a factor flying at normal cabin altitudes above sea level. One may wonder why 10,000 feet or higher was not mentioned as the "magic" altitude where hypoxic hypoxia can occur, and the reason is even slight cerebral hypoxic hypoxia can still be a concern below those altitudes. Flying at night at altitudes above 5,000 feet can significantly impair night vision, as the retina of the eye experiences failure of complex visual elements with even a slight reduction of retinal oxygenation.

A typical question asked of pilots is "when does a lack of oxygen become a concern?" Unfortunately answers range from 12,500 feet, 15,000 feet, 18,000 feet or higher. The fact is physical, intellectual, and physiological performance is affected as low as 5,000 feet in normal, heathy humans. Night vision, in particular, is significantly affected at the 5,000 feet to 6,000 feet levels. Physical performance such as walking, running, etc. is affected at those same altitudes. As we will find out, even the highest cognitive functions may be affected at 5,000 feet to 6,000 feet. *Short-term memory loss* may be acutely affected at altitudes above FL200.

Hypoxic hypoxia may be brought on by improper use of oxygen equipment as well. Many accidents have occurred in which the aviator had their oxygen mask available or even on their face, and still succumbed to hypoxia. Failure to properly don (put on) or secure the oxygen mask with a proper seal can incapacitate an aviator as fast as having no oxygen mask available.

Another crucial issue to discuss with hypoxic hypoxia is slow versus rapid-onset hypoxia.

Slow-onset hypoxia can be an extremely insidious event; in other words, it can happen over a long enough period-of-time to make hypoxia almost imperceptible to humans. One may reason any abnormality should have perceptible symptoms, and they do. The problem is pilots tend to pass those symptoms off as something more normal and/or less threatening, such as not getting enough sleep, skipping breakfast, not enough coffee, etc. Consequently the developing condition is not given the respect it deserves, the aviator loses their cognitive abilities, and they end up in an accident report on an NTSB investigator's desk. Unfortunately, many times "fatigue" or "sleepiness" is among the first symptoms and all it takes is for an aviator to close their eyes, seemingly for a couple of seconds, and end up taking a very sound nap until the aircraft runs out of fuel and begins an uncontrolled, final descent.

Rapid-onset hypoxia is obviously at the opposite end of the spectrum. At the higher altitudes, debilitating hypoxia symptoms can manifest themselves at such a rapid rate an unsuspecting aviator's ability to effectively respond to the condition simply is not good enough. Under many circumstances the hypoxia event will be brought on by another catastrophic event such as a rapid decompression, which may bring on its own set of problems. Imagine flying at FL390 on autopilot, talking to your first officer about the next football game or your children's current report card, and BOOM! Cabin pressure is rapidly lost; flying debris is swirling around the flight deck, the temperature drops dramatically, condensation develops, and windblast is deafening. In a scenario similar to this, it may be completely normal to be somewhat distracted and disorientated for a period of 15 to 30 seconds while one attempts to assess the situation. During this limited time period, one may not recognize reflexes getting dangerously slow, simple instructions becoming hard-to-comprehend, and before 10 seconds has elapsed one is no longer able to perform *any* function beyond staring dumbly at the instrument panel trying to make sense of something.

In the above scenario, rapid-onset hypoxia may be so devastatingly quick an intellectual response may be inadequate. In cases such as these, an automatic or conditioned (muscle-memory) response may be the only adequate action to prevent pilot incapacitation. Automatic or conditioned responses to hyper-critical events may only be gained through copious and repetitive training sessions.

Supplemental Oxygen Requirements

The following chart shows the percentage of oxygen a human must sustain in order to maintain sea level physiological equivalency, based on USAF School of Aerospace Medicine research:

Figure 4.1 Human Supplemental Oxygen Requirements

Altitude (m)	Barometric Pressure (ft)	Lung Oxygen (mmHg)	Requirement %
Sea Level		760	21%
1515	5,000	632	25%
3030	10,000	532	31%
4545	15,000	429	40%
6060	20,000	329	49%
7575	25,000	282	62%
9090	30,000	225	81%
10,300	34,000	187	100%

As one can see, as low as 5,000' an aviator would require an increase in atmospheric oxygen percentage of 4% above normal to maintain physiological equilibration to sea level. At 10,000', an aviator would require 10% above normal PO2 to maintain normal function.

The following chart reveals what our arterial oxygen saturation would be at given altitudes:

Figure 4.2 Blood Oxygen Saturation by Altitude

Altitude (ft)	Arterial O2 Saturation w/o supplemental O2	Barometric Pressure (mmHg)
Sea Level	96%	760
5,000	95%	632
7,500	93%	575
10,000	89%	532
12,500	87%	474
14,000	83%	446
16,500	77%	403
20,000	65%	329
25,000	Sub-60%	282

Now we have a basis for how much our oxygen saturation levels drop with altitude (assuming no supplemental oxygen), let us look at what that means to our performance levels:

Figure 4.3 Human Oxygen Saturation versus Symptoms

Oxygen Saturation Range	Typical Symptomology
100% - 95%	No detectable cognitive impairment, night vision decreases at 95%
95% - 85%	High-level cognitive impairment w/normal intellectual function unaffected, coordination slows
85% - 75%	Mid-level cognitive impairment w/normal intellectual function affected, coordination sloppy
75% - 65%	Low-level cognitive impairment, normal intellectual functions affected, physical functions affected
60% & below	Little-to-no cognitive function, potential collapse

As we can see from the above chart, the first section of "impairment" falls between 95% and 85%, with "high-level cognitive impairment." (The altitudes 95% to 85% saturation levels fall between is approximately 5,000' to 12,500'.) One could also refer to this area as "the danger zone," as the highest cognitive functions are beginning to be impaired with few noticeable symptoms of hypoxia. Normal tasks at these oxygen saturation levels will not be overtly affected; hence, the reason few aviators expect flying at those altitudes to be a threat.

Consider the effects of battery depletion on a flashlight's beam. When the battery is fresh, the beam is very bright, but as the battery charge depletes, the beam gradually gets dimmer. The brain operates the same way; as oxygen supply to the brain begins to deplete, its higher functions begin to degrade. The question is what qualifies as higher brain function?

Lower brain function would control things such as breathing, muscular movement, walking, sitting upright, etc. Middle brain function could be considered normal tasks such as driving a car, flying an aircraft in straight and level flight, performing a routine job, and so forth. Higher brain functions include complex computations and analytics; think of those tasks as being able to diagnose and fix an inflight problem such as instrument failure, loss-of-control, loss-of-thrust, and the myriad of other issues which may arise out of nowhere. One's ability to diagnose and fix complex inflight problems are among the first functions to fail! This fact should be of major concern for most pilots.

The next zone, which runs from 85% to 75% oxygen saturation (12,000' to 18,000'), brings noticeable neurological symptoms of hypoxia. The symptoms may not be considered strong, but difficulties with calculations, recalling emergency procedures, and lack of concentration will be more pronounced.

Once an aviator falls below 75% oxygen saturation they essentially become "test-pilots." Hypoxia symptoms are highly individualized and subjective, but it is safe to assume the majority of aviators will be experiencing significant physical and neurological hypoxia symptoms by these levels.

Typically, unconsciousness tends to occur below 60% oxygen saturation levels, but some trainees have been observed to be conscious and functional as low as 45%. On the other end of the spectrum, trainees have been close to unconsciousness in the mid-80% range. As mentioned, everyone responds differently and experiences different symptoms with hypoxia, which makes it critical to able to experience it first-hand in the controlled-environment of a hypobaric chamber.

As we can see based on our discussions, higher cognitive function may be affected in relatively benign flight environments where pilots typically would never expect hypoxia to be an issue. Considering most pilots fly perfectly normal flights without having an in-flight emergency develop at lower altitudes, pilots may potentially fly their entire career without a problem. However, should an in-flight emergency develop from 5,000' to 10,000' it is entirely possible the pilot's response to the specific emergency could be catastrophically compromised if the emergency demands a split-second reaction-times from the pilot-in-command.

Low-Altitude Hypoxic Hypoxia

Research has proven even mild forms of hypoxic hypoxia may make information interpretation difficult, and make humans slow to respond to novel (non-standard or emergency) events.

Consider the complexity of cockpit systems for the average turbine or turboprop aircraft in today's flight environment. Many different control systems exist; communication systems, power management, flight director, primary information display (PFD), navigation controls, radar, and enhanced or synthetic vision systems to name a few. Each system has its own set of instructions and knowledge to operate, control switches or knobs may vary, displays may vary, programming between systems may be inconsistent, and the list goes on. In many cases, even manipulating these systems with a fully functioning and alert brain can be daunting! Slight amounts of intellectual impairment may cause mistakes to occur easier than one would imagine.

In August of 2005, the scientific journal *Aviation, Space, and Environmental Medicine's* Adrian Smith conducted a survey depicting hypoxia symptoms distributed to Australian Helicopter crewmembers, all of whom flew exclusively below 10,000'. The article's name was 'Hypoxia symptoms reported during helicopter operations below 10,000 feet; a retrospective survey', and below is a synopsis of results:

- 87% of non-pilot crewmembers and 60% of pilots reported feeling one or more symptoms regularly
- 60% of non-pilot crewmembers and 17% of pilots reported four or more symptoms regularly
- Most common symptoms recognized: difficulty with calculations, light-headed, delayed reaction time, and mental confusion

Remember, these are all aviators flying <u>exclusively below 10,000 feet</u>.

In the 1960's hypoxia research was conducted at the Royal Air Force (RAF) Institute of Aviation Medicine by a scientist named Dr. John Ernsting. Dr. Ernsting was concerned that airline pilots flying at routine cabin altitudes (5,000 feet to 8,000 feet) may be experiencing some degree of cognitive decline. He used the RAF Institute's altitude chamber to test two control groups of subjects: those breathing cockpit air at 5,000 feet and those breathing supplemental oxygen at 5,000 feet.

Concluding his research, Dr. Ernsting found those subjects breathing cockpit air had an impaired ability to perform novel (emergency) tasks. On average, the "cockpit air" group took two-to-three times as long to recognize, diagnose, and respond to unexpected tasks. How long does it take to respond to an emergency situation, such as an unexpected stall? Two seconds? Three seconds? Five seconds? Whatever the timeframe is, doubling or tripling the time to respond could very well be the difference between life and death.

If two airplanes are flying a collision course from a distance of one nautical mile (nm) with a closing speed of 240 knots (120 knots each) they would collide in 14 seconds. FAA research shows the average pilot takes 12 seconds to see the oncoming target, comprehend and analyze the situation, decide on a course of action, and implement the decision. Obviously, this leaves a margin-of-error of two seconds. Mild hypoxic hypoxia may not necessarily double the time it takes to make the same life-saving decision, but delaying it by even three seconds may be catastrophic.

We will examine hypoxia and many other emergency mitigation strategies later in this chapter, as well as throughout this entire textbook.

Let us take a moment to review a few random hypoxia incidents, each illustrating slightly different scenarios, taken from NTSB accident investigation files:

Incident Review - May 2014: A pilot and his wife, also a pilot, were flying a TBM 900 along the East Coast at FL280 on autopilot. While enroute, the pilot contacted ATC and requested a descent to FL180 due to an "indication that was not correct." ATC cleared the pilot to FL250, at which point the pilot responds "We need to get lower." ATC clears the pilot to FL200, which the pilot acknowledged but never initiated. ATC contacts military authorities, who in turn scramble some fighters to intercept the TBM 900 to evaluate the situation. The fighters intercept the aircraft, and find the pilot and passenger slumped over the controls and the windows frosted over. One of the fighter pilots get close enough to the cockpit to see the pilot's chest rising and falling, and it was determined the pilot was alive, but incapacitated. The aircraft continued automated flight until it ran out of fuel 14 miles off the coast of Jamaica and disappeared into the ocean.

Analysis: The NTSB determined the pilot noted warnings on the crew alerting system, but did not declare an emergency, don an oxygen mask (which were present on the aircraft), or initiate an emergency descent. Contact was lost 4.5 minutes after the first radio call to ATC. The aircraft fault codes indicate cabin pressure bled down to ambient atmospheric pressure in about 4 minutes, and the NTSB determined the accident was a result of pilot incapacitation due to hypoxia following a loss of pressurization.

Conclusion: The pilot noticed a loss of pressurization occurring, and should have immediately donned an oxygen mask, declared an emergency, and initiated a descent to a safe altitude (in that order). Failure to recognize hypoxia symptoms by both pilots resulted in loss-of-life.

Incident Review - May 2016: A Cessna Citation I/SP was in cruise flight at FL430 over Texarkana, AR, with one pilot and three passengers. The aircraft quickly lost pressurization. The pilot lost consciousness and the aircraft entered an uncontrolled descent. Around 7,000 feet the pilot regained consciousness and realized the aircraft was out-of-control. The pilot regained control, sustaining substantial damage to both wings due to excessive wing loading during the descent and recovery. The pilot was extremely shaken but managed to safely land the aircraft.

Analysis: The NTSB determined the primary pressurization duct into the cabin was separated from its connection to the water separator, causing the aircraft to lose pressurization. The NTSB also determined the pilot was in violation of Part 91 oxygen use regulations, which require the use of oxygen masks if one pilot is at the controls above FL350.

Conclusion: Some oxygen masks are uncomfortable to wear, and some Part 91 pilots tend to ignore the oxygen usage rule for this reason. The rules exist specifically for rapid loss-of-pressurization incidents, and the pilots' and passengers' lives are at risk by violating the rule.

Incident Review – January 2017: A pilot and friend were flying around Gurdon, AR, in a Columbia Aircraft 400-LC41 at 17,500 feet when the pilot contacted ATC and requested an ascent to FL250 to do an "equipment test." The aircraft remained at FL250 for three minutes before requesting a descent due to "a little bit of an equipment issue." Four minutes later the pilot declared an emergency and upon ATC contacting the pilot, the pilot's response was unintelligible. Two minutes after that radio contact, the aircraft impacted terrain at high speed with no further ATC contact.

Analysis: NTSB investigators determined the pilot-in-command (PIC) had just purchased a new oxygen mask and was going to check it out inflight and at altitude. The NTSB also learned the PIC had just recently completed "altitude chamber training" from an undisclosed location.

Conclusion: Having recently completed some sort of Aerospace Physiology Training the pilot should have been aware of their individual hypoxia symptoms. The PIC should also have been aware of the limitations and proper deployment and usage of oxygen equipment. Evidently neither lesson was retained.

Incident Review – January 2018: A medical physician was flying a Pilots-N-Paws volunteer dog rescue mission from Oklahoma City, OK -Georgetown, TX – Las Vegas, NV in a Cirrus SR22T. The pilot left OKC at 1419 local time flying at a cruise altitude of FL190 on autopilot and was scheduled to arrive in Georgetown at 1530 local time. ATC verbal contact was lost approximately 30 minutes prior to arrival, and USAF fighters were deployed to intercept the aircraft. The fighters were unable to gain the attention of the pilot, who was unresponsive at the controls. The aircraft continued on autopilot over the Gulf of Mexico and was last seen on radar at 1715 and 15,000 feet before it disappeared.

Analysis: Investigators were unable to determine the physical status of the pilot due to the aircraft has yet-to-be recovered. It is presumed the pilot suffered from a case of altitude-induced hypoxia, continued on course, and eventually ran out of fuel.

Conclusion: The pilot was a medical physician and should have recognized physiological and psychological impairment manifestations. Assuming the pilot suffered from hypoxic hypoxia, the insidious symptoms of hypoxia were not recognized in time. The aircraft was equipped with oxygen equipment capable of sustaining cognitive function at that altitude and was either not used properly or at all.

Incident Review – May 2019: A Citation 560 Encore flown as a single pilot flight was enroute at FL390 from St. Louis, MO to Fort Lauderdale, FL. Approximately one hour before reaching its destination, ATC communication was lost, and the aircraft overflew the destination. USAF fighters were dispatched to intercept the aircraft, but didn't reach the aircraft until shortly before it went down in the Atlantic Ocean 300 miles East of Fort Lauderdale.

Analysis: The aircraft has yet to be recovered. Investigators assume the aircraft experienced a decompression, the pilot got hypoxic and became incapacitated, and the aircraft ran out of fuel.

Conclusion: Once again, assuming the pilot suffered from hypoxic hypoxia, the insidious symptoms of hypoxia were not recognized in time. The aircraft was equipped with oxygen equipment capable of sustaining cognitive function at that altitude and was either not used properly or at all.

4.4 HISTOTOXIC HYPOXIA

Histotoxic hypoxia is the condition interfering with normal oxygen metabolic activity and/or neurotransmission in the cells, specifically the brain cells. The most common causes of histotoxic hypoxia are:

- Cyanide
- Alcohol
- Narcotics
- Phosgene gases
- Pyrolyzed oil or hydraulic fluid

Cyanide

Certain chemicals prohibit effective neurotransmission by inhibiting an enzyme in the human nervous system called cholinesterase, which is used to break down acetylcholine, a neurotransmitter carrying signals between nerves and muscles. To simplify, the brain may be receiving copious amounts of oxygen, but simply can not process the oxygen effectively to communicate with the body's nervous system.

Cyanide produces a profound drop in tissue O2 consumption since the reaction of the enzyme cytochrome oxidase with oxygen is blocked by cyanide. This stops oxidative phosphorylation and prevents cellular mitochondria from producing adenosine triphosphate (ATP), the energy component of cellular metabolism.

Alcohol and Altitude

You would surmise not much needs to be said against drinking alcohol or taking illegal drugs and flying. The fact is every year many professional pilots are stopped at the gate or even on the flight deck ready to fly with alcohol on their breath. Predictably, many accidents have occurred while the pilot is impaired by drugs or alcohol. Mixing alcohol-induced hypoxia with altitude-induced hypoxia is an extremely dangerous endeavor, as altitude may make the effects of alcohol much worse and vise-versa. If a prospective pilot needs to be convinced drinking alcohol and flying is not a good idea, maybe a change of occupation should be considered.

Let us examine one such incident:

Incident Review – August 2016: A charter first officer (FO) reported to a flight piloting a Bombardier Challenger 604 in Traverse City, MI, met the captain, and started his pre-flight checklist. The captain noticed the first officer was acting unusually erratic, and called company dispatch. Dispatch called the local police department, who responded to the scene. The FO was administered a field sobriety test and breathalyzer test which showed a blood-alcohol content of .30% – more than seven times the FAA's legal limit of .04% for operation of an aircraft. The FO was taken into custody.

Analysis: A corporate aircraft first officer showed up legally drunk to fly passengers, and was subsequently charged with a crime. On 10/13/17, the FO was sentenced to one year in prison.

Conclusion: The FO was presumably a functioning alcoholic, who likely had previously flown legally drunk. Even under normal operating conditions, the FO was an accident waiting to happen. Fortunately, the FO was removed from flight duties prior to a fatal accident.

Narcotics and Medications

Another area of concern is over-the-counter and prescription medication. Even the mildest medications may produce side-effects and these side-effects may be amplified at altitude. Typical adverse effects of medication combined with altitude are as follows:

- Visual deterioration
- Pronounced drowsiness
- Impaired bodily thermal regulation
- Reduced oxygen metabolization resulting in hypoxic hypoxia at lower altitudes
- Increased gastrointestinal distress
- Increased vestibular system excitation, resulting in increased sensitivity to spatial disorientation
- Increased hemorrhaging resulting from crash injuries

As a result of potential side-effects of medications and for the pilot's safety, it is necessary to get any medications one intends on taking or are prescribed to be approved by an Aeromedical Examiner to ensure you are aware of the effects while flying, or to be ordered not to fly while on that medication.

The NTSB conducted a study on toxicology findings for fatally injured accident pilots from 1990 through 2017. The chart below illustrates the findings:

Figure 4.5 NTSB Pilot Toxicology Study 1990 - 2017

Legend:
- At Least 1 Positive Drug Finding
- More Than 1 Positive Drug Finding
- More Than 2 Positive Drug Findings

NTSB 2021

What the study reveals is for pilots fatally injured in an aircraft accident in 2017, almost 50% registered at least one positive drug finding, almost 30% had more than one drug finding, and almost 15% had more than two drug findings in their system. 96% of the study pilots were general aviation (GA) pilots.

In the same study, the overall GA pilot population showed 16% tested positive for potentially impairing drugs. If only 16% of GA pilots tested positive for drugs but 40% of GA pilots had drugs in their system when they died, what correlation can be drawn from this data? The answer appears to be simple; mixing the side-effects of drugs, inflight emergencies, and the effects of altitude can be a lethal mixture.

In 2012, the FAA, NTSB, and the General Aviation Joint Steering Committee conducted a similar study on pilots fatally injured in loss-of-control accidents from 2001 to 2010, and the results were remarkably similar to the 2017 study. 42% of the fatally injured pilots were found positive for drugs or medications; however, in this study the most common impairing drug was found to be diphenhydramine.

Diphenhydramine is an antihistamine and common ingredient found in more than 50 over-the-counter and prescription drugs designed to control allergy or cold symptoms. The most common side effects of diphenhydramine include sleepiness and dizziness, but can include fatigue, blurred or double vision, headache, dry mouth, confusion, and feeling anxious. Once again, the side-effects of medications may be amplified if combined with slight hypoxic hypoxia, so ingesting diphenhydramine and flying would not be recommended.

As we all know, the real world can operate differently than the textbook world. Professional pilots often find themselves in situations in which they may feel a slight illness developing and may decide to self-medicate with OTC medicine in order to complete their flight segment. If such a situation occurs, the best course of action is to ensure the other pilot is aware of your less-than-peak condition, and adjust cockpit tasks accordingly.

Phosgene Gases

Phosgene gases may be formed as chlorinated hydrocarbon compounds are combusted or exposed to extremely high temperatures, such as fire onboard an aircraft causing certain materials to catch fire. The vapors of chlorinated solvents, such as solvents used in metal cleaning, paint stripping, and dry cleaning, may cause phosgene gases when exposed to high temperatures as well. Phosgene gases are heavier-than-air, so gases tend to sink to the floor as opposed to the top of the cabin.

Pyrolysis and Cabin Air Contamination

Organophosphate intrusion (as a result of pyrolysis of jet engine oil or hydraulic fluid) into aircraft cabins is a controversial subject without many "conclusive" scientific findings behind any claims of organophosphate ingestion. Some people have termed this and other cabin air contamination *"Aerotoxic syndrome."* Aerotoxic Syndrome is a generic phrase coined by two pilots, Chris Winder and Jean-Christophe Balouet, in 2000 to describe their claims of short- and long-term adverse health effects of breathing aircraft cabin air allegedly contaminated to toxic levels.

While some authorities consider this information only worthy of conspiracy theorists, enough empirical evidence exists as to warrant some discussion on this area of concern. According to research by Dr. Scholz of Hamburg University of Applied Science, "contaminations of cabin air happen on every flight with cabin air being supplied through bleed air, regardless of odors or no odors on board, as engine seals leak small amounts of engine oil by design." While many toxins exist that can contaminate aircraft cabins, for this singular discussion we will focus on organophosphates.

Modern jetliners have environmental control systems (ECS) that manage the flow of air entering and leaving the aircraft cabin. Outside air enters the engines and is then compressed in the forward section prior to the combustion section, theoretically ensuring no combustion byproducts enter the cabin. A portion of compressed bleed air is used to pressurize the cabin. The ECS then recirculates some of the cabin air through HEPA filters, while the remainder is directed to outflow valves, ensuring there is a constant supply of fresh, uncontaminated air coming into the aircraft cabin at all times.

Air contamination is certainly possible when contaminants enter the cabin through the air-supply system and through other means. Chemical substances used in the maintenance and treatment of aircraft, including aviation engine oil, hydraulic fluid, cleaning compounds and de-icing fluids, can contaminate the ECS.

Organophosphates are neurotoxins and can be found in insecticides, medications, oil, and chemical weapons. One compound contained in synthetic jet engine oil is tri-cresyl phosphate (TCP), and TCP is an organophosphate. As mentioned, some feel long-term, low-level exposure to organophosphates in aircraft cabins can be a health risk. TCP fumes tend to be lighter-than-air so the fumes congregate towards the top of aircraft cabins, putting those frequently walking around the cabin (i.e. flight attendants) at greater risk for exposure.

According to medical research, approximately 10% of human population is at an increased risk for organophosphate contamination, while the other 90% of the population may be able to de-metabolize these contaminants more efficiently.

Common symptoms of organophosphate contamination include:

- Impaired memory and concentration
- Confusion
- Irritability
- Headaches
- Nausea
- Muscular weakness
- Loss of appetite
- Speech difficulties
- Reaction time difficulties
- Increased disorientation

Let us examine some potential cases of organophosphate contamination:

Incident Review – October 2011: An A380-800 was on climb-out from Frankfurt, Germany when some cabin crew members noticed an odor similar to dirty socks; however, the cockpit had no abnormal smell. The captain contacted dispatch, who relayed one engine had been washed prior to departure. The captain deactivated the bleed air feed from that engine, and the smell apparently went away. On approach into their final destination of San Francisco, CA, USA, the smell reappeared and one flight attendant noticed concerning neurological and physical symptoms developing in herself. The aircraft landed, passengers disembarked, and the flight attendant went to see a local physician, who could not identify the illness. Eyewitnesses stated the flight attendant was bright and alert at the beginning of the flight, and severely impacted by the end of the flight.

The flight attendant (FA) continued to experience symptoms, was permanently, and eventually tested positive for TCP contamination.

Analysis: The flight attendant was apparently normal at the onset of the flight, and severely neurologically and physically impacted at the end. The FA maintains she has ongoing issues with headaches, permanent fatigue, lack of concentration, lack of energy, and burning eyes. The FA tested positive for TCP contamination, no longer qualifies for a flight physical and is permanently grounded.

Conclusion: The FA apparently encountered some type of toxin during the flight, and based on testing positive for TCP, the toxins were most likely organophosphates. The airline has repeatedly declined her attempts at receiving worker's compensation as a result of losing her flight status.

Incident Review – February 2019: An A319-100 airliner was enroute at FL330 NE of Las Vegas, NV, USA, when the cockpit crew decided to divert to Las Vegas after reporting smoke in the cockpit. The FAA reported that upon landing, three flight attendants were transported to a hospital with unknown injuries.

One of the affected flight attendants suffered a cerebral hemorrhage as well as additional nerve damage. Initial laboratory toxicology results suggest a critically low value of cholinesterase enzymes (neurotransmitters). FAA research has linked this issue to exposure to organophosphate fume contamination.

Analysis: Three flight attendants suffered exposure to toxic substances as a result of smoke on the aircraft, and one tested positive for possible organophosphate exposure.

Conclusion: Flight attendants continue to be at the greatest threat of exposure to harmful contamination from toxins that are lighter-than-air, as their heads are close to the top of the cabin. No smoke event on any aircraft should be taken lightly, and all crew members should be medically checked following any smoke or fume event. Timely use of oxygen equipment may have prevented injury to crewmembers.

4.5 HYPEMIC HYPOXIA

Hypemic Hypoxia is the condition interfering with the ability of the blood cells to transport oxygen. The most common causes of hypemic hypoxia include:

- Carbon monoxide poisoning
- Anemia
- Blood loss or blood donation

Carbon Monoxide (CO) is produced through incomplete combustion, and may be produced in aviation settings through the burning of many different materials. CO being the main culprit in Hypemic hypoxia regarding aviation, this gas will be our focus for this discussion.

What makes CO such a concern for humans is CO is more attractive than O2 to hemoglobin in the red blood cell (RBC) by a large factor – some 250 to one. This means any CO molecules in the lung are going to bind to the RBC's hemoglobin; once this process occurs, the affected RBC will no longer be efficient at transporting O2 until CO molecules de-metabolize. Once CO is bound to hemoglobin it is known as *carboxyhemoglobin*. A major problem with carbon monoxide is the gas is odorless, colorless and tasteless making it difficult to detect until psychological and physical symptoms manifest themselves. Once noticeable, it is possible the contamination may be severe enough to incapacitate the pilot.

Habitual cigarette smokers experience mild hypemic hypoxia; enough so to impair night vision even at ground level. Individuals smoking one pack of cigarettes per day may experience the equivalent physiological altitude of 6,000 feet to 8,000 feet at sea level.

The CO de-metabolization process can take a relatively long period of time. The half-life of carboxyhemoglobin is three to four hours at rest breathing fresh air. The de-metabolization of carboxyhemoglobin may be accelerated down to 30 to 90 minutes by breathing 100% oxygen with a tight-fitting oxygen mask; however, the de-metabolization process can best be accomplished by providing hyperbaric high-pressure dive chamber) therapy to the patient. Hyperbaric therapy can complete the de-metabolization process in as little as 15 to 23 minutes.

Smoke, fumes, or fire events may happen on airliners somewhat more often than one would imagine. FAA and European Aviation Safety Administration (EASA) estimates range from 900 to 3,000 global commercial airline events per year (although the FAA doesn't currently officially track those events.) Some EASA experts believe fumes events occur on every commercial airline flight. The Los Angeles Times reported over

400 passengers and flight attendants became ill from toxic fumes between 01/19 and 12/19, with NASA Aviation Safety Reporting System (ASRS) reports indicating 48 pilots in the same time period became too incapacitated from fumes to perform their duties successfully. Regardless of the number of smoke, fire, and fumes events occurring, it is certainly frequent enough to be a concern for any aviator.

Let us take a look at some incidents where CO poisoning was suspected:

Incident Review – May 2017: A 787-800 was on climb-out from Orlando, FL, USA when the pilots stopped the climb at 15,000 feet reporting two flight attendants became sick, reporting nausea and dizziness. The aircraft returned to the airport where 27 people in total were treated at the airport for fumes ingestion, and four were taken to an area hospital. A Hazardous Materials team checked the cabin air but found nothing abnormal.

Analysis: 27 people on board the aircraft exhibited symptoms of fumes ingestion and were provided oxygen at the airport by rescue personnel, with four people serious enough to be taken to a hospital for further observation and evaluation.

Conclusion: The assumption by authorities is carbon monoxide intrusion caused this event. The problem with that theory is Boeing 787's are the only airliner not using engine bleed air to pressurize the cabin to prevent CO events. The pressurization system is completely autonomous, which in theory means no engine exhaust byproducts could possibly enter the cabin; because of that design, the cause of these fumes is a mystery.

Incident Review – January 2018: An A380-200 was enroute at FL380 from Akron, OH to Fort Lauderdale, FL when one passenger complained about an abnormal smell. Flight attendants attending to the passenger confirmed the smell, which became stronger and stronger until the cabin air became nearly "not breathable." The pilots informed ATC about the condition, confirmed the odor in the cockpit, and the pilots donned their oxygen masks. Flight attendants were feeling increasingly nauseous and some indicated they nearly passed out because of the odor.

After descending below 10,000 feet the captain depressurized the aircraft and the cabin air improved. After landing, emergency services transported all passengers and crew to hospitals. First medical findings indicated seriously elevated levels of CO with all cabin crewmembers, with several flight attendants reaching near lethal levels of contamination.

Maintenance personnel could not detect any odor and were about to return the aircraft to service when the captain intervened insisting a serious fumes event had just occurred. Maintenance rechecked the aircraft, subsequently finding an engine wet seal had breached.

Analysis: The aircraft had a serious fumes incident in which some members of the cabin crew had levels of CO poisoning in near-fatal doses. At the captain's insistence, maintenance finally located and repaired the suspected issue.

Conclusion: A breached engine wet oil seal allowed CO to enter the cabin in high enough concentrations to almost kill crewmembers. Following proper maintenance protocols should never be taken lightly, and may have prevented this incident. Recognition of the condition and donning oxygen masks may have prevented injury to crewmembers.

Incident Review – February 2018: A 767-300 was enroute at FL360 near Greenland when one flight attendant exhibited symptoms of a heart attack and four flight attendants felt light headed, dizzy, headaches and showed symptoms of poisoning. The affected flight attendants reported they felt "there was low oxygen in the cabin" and "issues with air quality." The aircraft diverted, landed, and the alleged "heart attack" victim was transported to a hospital, where she tested positive for high levels of CO in blood samples. The aircraft was sent to a maintenance facility for servicing.

Analysis: Another in-flight fumes event occurs over the North Atlantic Ocean, causing suspected CO poisoning of cabin crewmembers.

Conclusion: One cannot predict if and when dangerous fumes events will occur. The aircraft must be inspected according to protocol, and crewmembers need to recognize the condition and have aircrew life-support gear readily available to combat the effects of fumes events.

Lithium-Ion Batteries and In-flight Fires

With modern society's fascination with electronic devices, the proliferation of lithium-ion batteries to power these devices is tantamount to an insect infestation. Li-Ion batteries are everywhere, powering millions of devices, and each battery is a potential time-bomb waiting to overheat and/or explode. Li-Ion batteries overheating creates a condition known as *thermal runaway*, and the resulting explosion/fire is a threat to every airline passenger and crewmember trapped on an airborne aircraft.

Many confirmed incidents involving Li-Ion batteries starting on fire in laptops, electronic cigarettes, cell phones, headsets, and even heated socks have occurred in passenger baggage, clothing, in-hand, under seats, and overhead compartments. Each and every incident is a potential disaster, as Li-Ion batteries are extremely difficult to extinguish due to the temperature at which they burn.

Inhalation of fumes caused by burning Li-Ion batteries includes Phosphorous Pentafluoride. Symptoms of ingestion include skin and eye irritation, followed by pulmonary edema (fluid in the lungs) in severe cases.

The first major incident bringing the dangers of bulk Li-Ion battery transport into focus is as follows:

Incident Review – September 2010: A cargo 747-400 was on departure out of Dubai. 22 minutes into the flight the crew reported smoke in the cockpit, donned their oxygen masks and initiated a climb to FL200. After the climb failed to extinguish the fire, the crew decided to return to Dubai. Enroute to Dubai, ATC suggested diverting to a closer alternate airfield, which was refused by the crew. The captain, unable to breathe through his oxygen mask, left the cockpit in search of a portable oxygen cylinder and never returned. The FO flew to the final approach phase-of-flight and went missed-approach as result of zero (smoke-induced) visibility in the cockpit. The aircraft crashed on go-around, resulting in the crew suffering fatal injuries.

Analysis: The aircraft cargo hold contained thousands of Li-Ion batteries, and the crew experienced an on-board fire caused by thermal runaway. The crew attempted a climb to starve the fire of oxygen (which was accepted practice at the time), which failed. The captain's oxygen mask supply line was damaged by the intense heat in the cargo hold, feeding smoke and contaminants into the mask. As the captain went in search of an alternate mask, he presumably was overcome by smoke and fumes (hypemic hypoxia), and possibly hypoxic hypoxia. The FO experienced smoke in the cockpit to the degree where he could not successfully aviate.

Conclusion: Unfortunately, accidents like this help shape future emergency training requirements. The lessons learned were "do not climb to extinguish the fire - instead attempt landing at the earliest possible time; have alternate oxygen sources readily available; develop systems to enable pilots to see in smoke-filled cockpits; do not transport large amounts of Li-Ion batteries in the same space."

As a direct result of the above-mentioned accident and others, the FAA studied the task of bulk Li-Ion transport by aircraft. Testing and research revealed:

- One overheating battery can quickly spread to other batteries.
- Fire suppression systems retard the initial flames, but extreme heat causes the battery to reignite after the suppression system is exhausted.
- If many batteries are burning in close proximity, explosive gases can build up and cause an intense explosive fire
- Even one battery can burn with such intensity it can be almost impossible to extinguish the battery with a single fire extinguisher.

Several commercial companies sell Li-Ion battery containment devices to assist containment of thermal runaway. These can easily be researched online.

In the absence of such a device, a GA pilot may designate a passenger to oversee mitigation of such incidents. The following checklist will minimize the emergency:

1. Remember to *Isolate, Extinguish and Cool.*
2. **Isolate: Direct (throw) the burning device to an area that does not start a secondary fire.**
3. **Extinguish: Use halon to extinguish the flames.**
4. **Cool: Use water to cool the device; either by immersion or dousing.**

In-flight fires of any kind can be a life-threatening condition, as active fires can escalate quickly. According to FAA research, the average active aircraft fire has the potential to cause fatalities as quickly as 15 minutes after initial combustion. If flying a pressurized aircraft, the FAA recommends the following checklist to deal with In-Flight Fires:

1. **Don oxygen mask with smoke goggles at the earliest possible time.**
2. **Initiate an immediate emergency descent whether you have ATC clearance or not.**
3. **DO NOT use typical smoke/fume elimination procedures (opening windows as this can feed the fire), or reset circuit breakers unless absolutely necessary.**
4. **Aggressively pursue fire suppression activities using any and all resources.**

5. Have fire-fighting committee communicate severity of the fire to the pilots.
6. Egress the aircraft as soon as possible.

The following incidents illustrate how quickly a fire emergency may escalate:

Incident Review – July 2011: A 747-400 cargo jet departed Incheon International Airport, South Korea at 2:47 AM. At 4:03 AM the crew reported an onboard fire and diverted to Jeju, South Korea. Radio contact was lost at 4:11 AM and is believed to have crashed 66 miles SW of Jeju Island. The cargo hold held 880 pounds of Li-Ion batteries.

Analysis: The flight crew noticed a fire developing onboard the aircraft, notified ATC, and attempted a rapid diversion. Investigators estimate the aircraft crashed 18 minutes after the fire was first detected.

Conclusion: The extreme rapidity of which fire incidents may escalate are evidenced here. Crew oxygen masks, immediate descent and landing (however accomplished) are critical concerns and have to be initiated without delay.

Incident Review – May 2016: An A320-200 was enroute with 76 souls onboard from Paris to Cairo at FL370 about 3 hours and 25 minutes into the flight when the aircraft inexplicably disappeared from radar over the Mediterranean Sea. No "Mayday" call was received by ATC from the aircraft, which exhibited a 90 degree turn to the left, 360 degree turn to the right, initiated a steep descent through 15,000 feet and impacted the Sea. The last communications from the aircraft was two transmissions from its emergency locator transmitter prior to submersion.

Analysis: Speculation centered on possible terrorist activity was initially the focus of the investigation; however, recovery of the aircraft flight data recorders (FDR) indicate intense heat and smoke in the aircraft at the time of the crash. Aircraft wreckage showed signs of soot and exposure to high temperatures as well. Analysis of the cockpit voice recorder (CVR) revealed the crew mentioning the existence of fire on board. As of 07/18, investigators feel the most likely cause of the accident was fire in the cockpit.

Conclusion: If indeed the cause of the accident was fire and smoke in the cockpit, aircrew oxygen masks and a proper smoke/fire mitigation strategy may have prevented this accident.

Carbon monoxide, organophosphates, and *phosphorous pentafluoride* have been identified as possible dangerous agents from fume intrusion. *Polychlorinated*

Biphenyls fumes caused by electrical fires is another chemical to be aware of, and symptoms include numbness, weakness, limb pain, partial loss of sensation and headaches.

In the end, protecting oneself by donning an oxygen mask delivering 100% oxygen at the first sign or smoke or fumes to protect oneself from debilitating fumes is the goal.

4.6 STAGNANT HYPOXIA

Stagnant hypoxia is the condition that interferes with normal circulation of blood arriving at cells throughout the body. The most common causes of stagnant hypoxia are as follows:

- G-forces
- Shock
- Fainting
- Heart failure or other compromised cardiac output
- Cold temperature
- Hyperventilation

G-forces will affect the flow blood through the body simply because at increased G-levels bodily fluid molecules weigh more. The heart is only designed to pump blood at 1G.

Shock may cause a condition called vasovagal syncope, which causes a dilation, or opening, of blood vessels preventing adequate blood flow to the brain. *Fainting* is the typical end-result of a vasovagal response.

Heart failure or compromised cardiac output will obviously prevent an adequate flow of blood, with the "fuel pump" not working correctly.

Cold temperatures force the body to protect its internal organs by redirecting the flow of blood to the intrathoracic region. The body constricts the flow of blood to the extremities, in turn increasing intrathoracic flow, warming the internal organs.

Hyperventilation creates a chemical imbalance in the blood between oxygen and carbon dioxide. The body's response is to constrict blood vessels (therefore blood flow) in an attempt to rebalance O_2 and CO_2.

Deep Vein Thrombosis (DVT)

One condition that may develop as a result of not moving for a long time, such as a crewmember or passenger may experience on an overseas flight, is *deep vein thrombosis (DVT)*. Remember that the flow of venous blood depends on muscular contraction, and if a person sits still for many hours on end, the lack of flow can create blood clots (typically in the legs). The potential result of blood clots detaching and flowing to the heart is *pulmonary embolism*, which may block blood flow in the pulmonary artery of the lung, thus preventing oxygen transfer. Symptoms include:

- Sudden shortness of breath
- Lightheadedness, dizziness or fainting
- Rapid pulse
- Coughing up blood
- Potential death

DVT can be prevented on long flights by simple movement. Do not sit in one position for extended periods of time; get up and move around, stretch, walk down the aisle, flex muscles – anything you can do to prevent blood stagnation should assist in preventing DVT.

Some cells have the ability to store an emergency supply of oxygen. Unfortunately for aviators, central nervous system cells (including brain cells) are not included in this group. Remember, 20% of oxygen flowing into the body feeds the brain, so any loss of blood flow to the body results in cerebral deoxygenation. Once neural blood flow is reduced, the higher brain functions such as judgement and cognition are the first to go.

4.7 SUBJECTIVE SYMPTOMS OF HYPOXIA

The *subjective symptoms of hypoxia* are those abnormal neurological and physical indications you feel within yourself. As one experiences a reduction of oxygen (therefore a loss of energy production) to the central nervous system the number of symptoms observed may be almost endless as virtually everyone is affected differently.

The most commonly observed symptoms are as follows:

- Air hunger
- Apprehension
- Headache
- Nausea
- Fatigue

- Hot and cold flashes
- Blurred vision
- Tunnel vision
- Euphoria
- Tingling sensations
- Numbness in extremities
- Loss of situational awareness

Air hunger makes a person feel that no matter how much air they inhale, it just is not enough. This can easily lead a person to hyperventilate.

Apprehension is the feeling that something just is not "right"; a feeling of doom, nervousness, nothing makes sense.

Headache is self-explanatory, as is *nausea*. These symptoms are actually considered good to have, as no one wants to stay off oxygen if they feel bad, which in turn propels them to do something to correct the situation.

Fatigue may be profound and come on very rapidly. People refuse to work on problems or tasks and prefer to just sit and do nothing.

Hot and cold flashes may be interchanging sensations of warmth and chill in the same part of the body, and occasionally in different parts (my hands feet cold, but my feet feel hot).

Blurred or tunnel vision is very common, as the eyes are highly oxygenated organs and sensitive to oxygen fluctuations. Peripheral vision may be decreased due to lack of retinal blood flow, as is visual acuity and color contrast and sensitivity.

Euphoria is the feeling of well-being, excitement, or happiness making a potentially dangerous symptom to experience. Happy, giggly people who feel great may be difficult to convince oxygen is necessary.

Tingling may feel like tiny pin-pricks on the skin, similar to a limb falling asleep, and *numbness* is a loss of sensation.

Loss of situational awareness (SA) refers to the narrowing of attention. Aviators losing SA may be fascinated with and focused on one singular task or problem. Once this occurs, the aviator loses concentration on all other information they may be required to successfully process to mitigate the emergency at hand.

Recognition of an individual's subjective symptoms of hypoxia in their earliest stages are crucial to avoid becoming incapacitated, and must be respected for what they are.

Slow onset of symptoms could be (and often are) mistaken for signs of other issues, such as missing breakfast, getting old, not enough coffee and so on. If an aviator feels any mental or physical abnormality, hypoxia must be suspected first and treated immediately and correctly. Passing the symptoms off as some other issue can and has caused many fatalities.

Once established, individual hypoxia symptoms typically remain consistent throughout an aviator's career. The intensity and order of occurrence of symptoms is highly individualized and unique to each person. Due to the dynamic nature of flight recognition of symptoms may need to occur in an emergency situation, such as a high-altitude rapid decompression, where time to think simply does not exist. The opportunity to experience those symptoms first-hand in an altitude chamber is invaluable for these reasons and should be an experience every professional aviator should strive for.

Also worth mentioning is not all of these symptoms will manifest themselves in every case. Some may experience only one symptom, and others may experience many. The symptoms apply to all forms of hypoxia and may change between different types of hypoxia as well. Recognition of something intellectually or physically abnormal and respecting the condition for what these symptoms truly represent, which is hypoxia, is the main point to remember.

4.8 OBJECTIVE SIGNS OF HYPOXIA

The *objective signs of hypoxia* are the mental and physical indicators one would notice in someone else. This is a critical skill for professional aviators as the person getting hypoxic may not recognize it, whereas an observant fellow crewmember may. The most commonly recognized objectives symptoms are:

- Mental confusion
- Loss of eye focus and coordinated eye movement
- Poor judgement
- Increase in rate and depth of breathing
- Loss of muscle coordination
- Cyanosis
- Euphoria
- Belligerence
- Unconsciousness

An important component in the recognition of objective signs is to be aware of your fellow crewmembers' signs of hypoxia. One cannot hesitate if they believe their fellow pilot is getting hypoxic, as timely correction is paramount. One must also be aware a hypoxic pilot may not or will not treat themselves; the observing pilot will need to correctly treat the affected pilot.

An important note: the subjective symptoms and objective signs of hypoxia apply to all types of hypoxia. Many pilots believe hypoxia is only an issue when flying at high altitudes; therefore, a pilot may start getting symptoms at 5,000 feet and feel hypoxia "can not be the problem" because they are too low an altitude. However, they may be experiencing hypemic or histotoxic hypoxia from carbon monoxide poisoning or some other contaminant or condition which may be equally as dangerous as hypoxic hypoxia.

4.9 CHARACTERISTICS OF HYPOXIA

The following list contains typical characteristics of hypoxia:

- Insidious onset
- Onset rate varies depending on certain factors
- Intellectual impairment will occur
- Reaction time will be delayed
- Painless

Earlier we discussed how hypoxia can impair a pilot before they truly understand the ramifications of the symptoms they are experiencing. This is called *insidious onset*; the hypoxic condition is so difficult to detect, especially in slow-onset settings, it may be hard to differentiate from a more benign condition. This is perhaps the <u>most dangerous characteristic</u> – failure to recognize.

How fast hypoxia manifests itself can vary depending on circumstances. Many different factors can influence onset rates and severity and will be discussed in the following section.

Intellectual impairment is another dangerous component of the hypoxic condition. For the untrained pilot there is difficulty in recognizing the extent of cognitive impairment. A simple rule to follow is <u>if you start doing or thinking something that does not make sense, descend or get on oxygen!</u> Many hypoxic incidents have occurred where the pilot does not care what their altitude is, how fast they're flying, giggling over ATC commands, fly straight into the side of a mountain, etc. Even to the pilot experiencing intellectual impairment those actions may not match their normal flight discipline, but still fail to "connect the dots" with what is truly happening. If hypoxia is suspected, great care must be exercised regarding following checklists or procedures as well, as intellectual impairment may cause one to skip critical steps. Checklists and procedures should be followed multiple times, if necessary, to ensure all steps are completed.

Reaction time to standard, and even more importantly non-standard, operations will be slower-than-normal. Extra awareness and "leading the event" should be employed if possible.

Hypoxia is a painless condition; in many cases, hypoxia may even be pleasant to experience. This allows those affected by it to misunderstand the seriousness of the condition.

4.10 FACTORS INFLUENCING HYPOXIA EFFECTIVE PERFORMANCE TIME

Effective performance time (a.k.a. Time of Useful Consciousness) is defined by the FAA as "the time from exposure to hypoxic conditions until an individual is no longer able to manage safe operations." If a pilot is hypoxic but still able to fly, they are within the effective performance time (EPT) limit. If the pilot can no longer fly safely, they are outside the EPT limit.

A number of factors influence how fast and severe a hypoxic incident may be, as listed below:

- Altitude
- Rate of ascent
- Individual tolerance
- Physical activity
- Environmental temperature
- Duration of exposure
- Psychological stress
- Physical fitness
- Fatigue
- Medications
- Nutrition
- Concussions

Altitude as a factor is self-explanatory; the greater altitude one is exposed to, the quicker hypoxia manifests itself.

Rate of ascent is a major factor regarding EPT. The faster one ascends, the more air (therefore oxygen) is expelled from the lungs in accordance with Boyle's Law. A rapid ascent, such as a rapid decompression, expels virtually all residual oxygen from the lungs, resulting in no oxygen flow from the lungs to the brain if altitude is above FL340.

Individual tolerances vary greatly depending on personal physiological efficiency, especially concerning altitudes below FL300. Some individuals are simply more tolerant of altered psychological states as well.

Being engaged in *physical activity* results in skeletal muscles requiring more energy, which uses greater amounts of oxygen. This increased bodily oxygen consumption results in less oxygen transferring to the brain.

Colder environmental temperatures result in the body's physical and physiological systems working harder to stay warm, thus requiring more oxygen.

Longer duration of exposure causes the body to use up oxygen reserves to maintain function, with residual oxygen levels eventually reaching the point where they can no longer sustain normal physiological functions.

Psychological stress increases the brain's oxygen metabolization activity, burning up more oxygen reserves in the body.

Varying degrees of *physical fitness* may play a role in either extending or contracting EPT.

FAA research has suggested aerobically-training individuals (runners, swimmers) potentially train their bodies to operate more efficiently with lower levels of oxygen than the general population, in turn extending their EPT. Anaerobically-training (weight lifters, football players) may train their bodies to use large amounts of oxygen quickly, in turn contracting their EPT.

Fatigue may retard bodily and brain functions, with deteriorated brain function processing oxygen less efficiently.

Medications affect many psychological and physiological processes, potentially resulting in less efficient metabolization of oxygen.

Nutrition seriously affects a body's physiological processes as the body requires optimal levels of nutrients for optimal metabolization and function. Based on observations, undernourished people may become incapacitated due to hypoxia two to three times quicker and at higher oxygen saturation levels than their well-nourished counterparts.

Research has been conducted on *concussions* and *traumatically-injured brain tissue,* and their ability to effectively process oxygen. Although the research is far from complete, initial findings suggest injured neurons may be less effective at metabolizing oxygen than uninjured neurons, particularly at higher altitudes than the individual is equilibrated to. This equates to previously concussed pilots possibly being more susceptible to debilitating degrees of hypoxia at altitudes legal to breathe cockpit air. If a pilot has suffered a previous concussion, increased sensitivity to the effects of hypoxia must be stressed, and great care must be taken to maintain safe flight operations.

4.11 EFFECTIVE PERFORMANCE TIMES

The following chart depicts the average observed EPT for various altitudes:

Figure 4.6 Effective Performance Times

FL180	20 to 30 minutes
FL220	8 to 10 minutes
FL250	3 to 5 minutes
FL300	1 to 2 minutes
FL350	30 to 60 seconds
FL400	15 to 20 seconds
FL430	9 to 12 seconds

FL500 and above 9 to 12 seconds

To understand that the times listed are averages and may not accurately reflect real-life flight conditions is important. The EPT's listed were researched in USAF and FAA altitude chambers with people on oxygen masks at the given altitudes, then removing oxygen to see how long they could last. Few situations exist in the real world aviation operations where those exact conditions would be replicated. The most likely scenarios include slow ascents to altitude or rapid decompressions, at which time the listed EPT times would be invalidated as the pilot may not even be conscious upon reaching the actual peak altitude.

Effective Performance Time following Rapid Decompression

Experiencing a rapid decompression to high altitudes can and will significantly reduce one's EPT dramatically. As a result of exhaling all residual oxygen out of the lungs, EPT may be reduced by 30% to 50% or greater. Current FAA regulations stipulate a pilot flying a pressurized aircraft at high altitudes must be able to don and correctly configure their quick-don oxygen mask in five seconds or less with one hand. The five-second rule is a direct result of research into high-altitude decompressions; a five-second time-to-altitude rapid decompression at or above FL380 means the pilot <u>may</u> have five seconds EPT before they're unconscious.

FAA and Dr. Ernsting's research at the RAF Civil Aeromedical Institute suggests that even with an oxygen mask <u>on the pilot's face,</u> five-second FL380 RD's may result in the pilot becoming unconscious. Fortunately if the oxygen mask is on the pilot's face, the pilot should recover fairly quickly with no ill effects.

Seeing as pilots can lose consciousness as result of rapid ascent to altitude, passengers will be subjected to the same stresses. The FAA has addressed the issue with the "FAA Interim Policy on High Altitude Decompression," which states passengers have a limited amount of time to be unconscious at given altitudes to avoid "medical damage." It is the responsibility of the pilots to ensure the following timeline is met to descent passengers from altitude:

Figure 4.7 FAA Time of Safe Unconsciousness

Cabin Pressure Altitude	Maximum Total Exposure Time (minutes)
Above FL450	0
Above FL400	1
Above FL250	3
Above 10,000 feet	6

Synergistic Effects

Of equal importance as EPT are the number of physiological variables present in any given incident. In most circumstances physiological issues will most like manifest themselves synergistically rather than as separate components. It is safe to assume one physiological issue may potentially induce or enhance many other physiological problems. Consider the following scenarios:

- Mild hypoxic hypoxia may exacerbate or induce spatial disorientation.
- Spatial disorientation may exacerbate visual illusions.
- Visual illusions may exacerbate cognitive indecisiveness.
- A pilot who smokes, is on medications, is flying at altitude, and is cold in the cockpit may be experiencing all four types of hypoxia at once.

Let us examine one such incident:

Incident Review – June 2013: A Bellanca 17-31ATC with three people onboard was on a VFR flight over mountainous terrain in Oregon, USA. Clouds and turbulence existed up to FL250. According to radar returns, the flight lasted one hour, with 28 minutes at 12,500 feet and 8 minutes at 14,000 feet. The last two minutes of radar returns depict a course reversal, erratic flight and an irregular, rapid descent into terrain.

Analysis: NTSB investigators discovered the aircraft was equipped with an oxygen tank, but carried no oxygen masks or oxygen hoses. Investigators theorize the accident was a suspected case of spatial disorientation, exacerbated by hypoxia, resulting in uncontrolled flight into terrain with three fatalities.

Conclusion: The pilot most likely flew into conditions they were not prepared for. The aircraft also contained an oxygen bottle that could not be used due to missing oxygen masks and hoses. The pilot was flying at altitudes that produce slow-onset hypoxia in potentially poor visibility conditions which resulted in spatial disorientation. A combination of poor planning, physiological issues, and flight errors led to fatalities for the pilot and passengers. Wearing oxygen and maintaining cognitive decisiveness may have prevented this accident from occurring.

4.12 TREATMENT FOR HYPOXIA

Now that the dangers of hypoxia are well understood, what exactly does one do about it? The following is the checklist for the treatment of any hypoxic incident:

1. **Don the oxygen mask with 100% oxygen & emergency pressure, or descend**
2. **Return rate and depth of breathing to normal**
3. **Check oxygen equipment connects (if applicable)**
4. **Descend below 10,000 feet if possible**

The most critical element of the checklist is for the pilot or crewmember to immediately protect themselves for the deprivation of cerebral deoxygenation. *Donning the oxygen mask* and selecting 100% oxygen with emergency pressure, or descending (depending on equipment availability), is of upmost importance. Nothing else matters until this step is accomplished. One must also understand the altitude is not important, as histotoxic or hypemic hypoxia may occur well below 10,000 feet.

Returning the rate and depth of breathing to normal is necessary as most people facing acute stress could possibly hyperventilate due to confusion and the startle factor. Additionally, taking a deep initial breath may complicate one's physiological ability to rapidly recover from hypoxia, so one must take care to breathe normally when donning the oxygen mask. The normal breathing rate is 12 – 20 breaths-per-minute, which translates to one breath every three to five seconds. Consciously monitoring breathing rate should be repeated for a few breath cycles to establish normality.

Checking oxygen equipment connections should be accomplished prior to flight, but in an emergency simple movement can cause some oxygen supply hoses to become disconnected.

Descent below 10,000 feet, if possible, will ensure all aircraft occupants are in atmosphere that readily sustains life. It's also possible a 10,000 foot altitude may not be attainable, due to the following circumstances:

- Terrain
- Weather
- Traffic
- Fuel restrictions
- Political instability

If flight is conducted over *terrain* exceeding 10,000 feet, then it's highly advisable to maintain terrain clearance.

Fuel restrictions come into play should an aircraft lose pressurization or encounter fumes in the cabin while hundreds of miles out-to-sea. Altitudes above 10,000 feet may need to be maintained to ensure fuel quantity is not exhausted prior to arriving over land. If this is the case pilots need to balance fuel vs. oxygen consumption, whereas if sufficient oxygen is available, oxygen may be a range-multiplier to allow travel to safer flight conditions.

Weather may be severe enough, such as tornadic activity/hail/turbulence/icing, to warrant staying above it.

Traffic may prevent an immediate descent; all efforts should be made for ATC to clear airspace below an incident aircraft prior to an emergency descent. If an immediate descent is warranted, turn on all exterior lights, turn away from your assigned route or track and descend while broadcasting position and intention to ATC and other aircraft on frequency 121.5, switch transponder to 7700, and monitor the Traffic Collision Avoidance System (TCAS) closely.

Political instability is a descent consideration to be taken seriously, as many parts of the world are militarily unstable. FAA advisories need to be monitored closely, as flight into the wrong airspace could generate a surface-to-air missile attack on civilian aircraft if below certain altitudes.

The key to remember if a diversion from altitude is necessary is the descent is the beginning of the emergency, not the end. One must always remember their oxygen mask could fail, smoke or windblast could cause visual impairment, or oxygen could be depleted prior to reaching a safe altitude or condition so pilots should plan for these contingencies.

An oxygen mask should never be removed from its container by the oxygen hose because if this hose separates from the mask or is rendered inoperative in any way, the pilot is placed in a compromising situation in a hostile environment. Pilots should always have a back-up oxygen mask within easy reach for this reason. The emergency is only truly over when the aircraft reaches the gate.

Reoxygenation Unconsciousness

One rare physiological response to oxygen entering a person's body under these circumstances is *vasovagal response* or *vasovagal syncope*. The rapid influx of oxygen into the brain may trigger a nervous system response that regulates heart rate and blood pressure to malfunction. Heart rate slows, blood vessels in one's legs dilate and blood pools in the legs, blood pressure in the brain drops, and one faints. If able, lying on one's side or putting one's head between their legs restores cerebral blood flow and recovery is initiated; however, the risk of re-fainting will remain for 15 to 30 minutes if rapid transition to the sitting or standing position occurs.

Another rare physiological response to reoxygenation is called *oxygen paradox*. Recovery from hypoxia typically occurs within seconds after re-establishing normal alveolar oxygen partial pressure; however, mild physical symptoms such as headache or fatigue may linger following the hypoxic episode. The persistence of symptoms seems to have a higher degree of correlation with the duration of the episode than with its severity. In some episodes following the administration of oxygen to correct the hypoxic insult the individual may develop a temporary increase in the severity of hypoxia symptoms. This condition known as Oxygen Paradox may cause the individual to lose consciousness or develop convulsions for periods up to 60 seconds.

Accompanying symptoms are mental confusion, visual deterioration, dizziness, and nausea.

Initially arterial blood pressure falls and the rate of blood flow decreases. The hypotension produced by the restoration of oxygen may be due to vasodilation occurring in the pulmonary vascular bed brought about by the direct action of oxygen on pulmonary vessels. *Hypocapnia* (lack of adequate carbon dioxide) is produced by hypoxia and a decrease in blood pressure, which follows reoxygenation, and act together to reduce cerebral blood flow. The reduced cerebral blood flow intensifies the symptoms of hypoxia for a short period until the cardiovascular effects have passed and carbon dioxide tension returns to normal. As the partial pressure of CO_2 returns to normal, the respiratory center is stimulated to resume normal ventilation the hypoxia symptoms resolve (DeHart, 1996).

4.13 PREVENTATIVE MEASURES FOR HYPOXIC HYPOXIA

Hypoxic hypoxia may be largely mitigated through the following measures:

- **Cabin pressurization**
- **Supplemental oxygen**
- **Preflight oxygen equipment**
- **Fly at lower altitudes**
- **Fly in accordance with Federal Aviation Regulations (FARs)**
- **Keep cabin altitude under 10,000'**

Cabin pressurization is obviously to keep your cabin altitude at a lower-than-flight altitude, optimizing occupant's comfort and safety. Cabin altitudes should always be maintained below 10,000 feet.

Supplemental oxygen will assist the aviator to maintain normal cognitive and physiological function if cabin altitudes exceed 10,000 feet. If the pilot feels the need to use oxygen below 10,000 feet, such as flying above 5,000 feet at night, they should absolutely feel justified in doing so.

Pre-flight inspecting oxygen equipment is a necessity to ensure proper operation if employed on a flight. We will cover this in much greater depth in a later chapter.

Flying at lower altitudes is always going to make the flight safer. Many pilots believe if their aircraft is rated to fly at higher altitudes, this is where they should be flying. High-altitude flight, especially for General Aviation, should only be used in cases where lower altitudes cannot be maintained.

Adherence to Federal Aviation Regulations will generally ensure a flight will be as safe as possible. A rule-of-flight to remember regarding regulations is: Rules are created because someone likely died.

Keep cabin altitude under 10,000 feet. If possible, one should attempt to keep cabin altitudes as close to sea level as possible to maintain optimum cognitive function.

Conclusion

A solid understanding of the phenomena of hypoxia should now be realized. You know what hypoxia is, the types and causal factors, subjective symptoms and objective signs of the various forms of hypoxia, and proper treatment and preventative measures for hypoxia episodes. The key is if any cognitive or physiological abnormality is noticed, corrective actions must be initiated immediately and correctly.

Next, we will discuss a closely-related condition known as *hyperventilation*.

Chapter 4 Core Competency Questions

1. What is the first human function lost to hypoxia?
2. What are the four types of hypoxia?
3. Which type of hypoxia relates to altitude?
4. Which type of hypoxia is caused by carbon monoxide poisoning?
5. True or false: hypoxia may affect higher cognitive function at altitudes as low as 5,000'.
6. Below what oxygen saturation level does collapse normally occur at?
7. Alcohol is an example of which type of hypoxia?
8. True or false: the effects of medications may exacerbate the effects of hypoxia at altitude.
9. What three steps should be taken during a lithium ion battery thermal runaway event?
10. Hyperventilation may cause what type of hypoxia?
11. What is the most dangerous characteristic of hypoxia?
12. True or false: a lack of nutrition may affect an individual's effective performance time.
13. What is the first step one should take in treating hypoxia of any type?
14. Is it always possible to descend to 10,000 feet in emergencies?
15. True or false: Effective Performance Times are guaranteed times a pilot can depend on to maintain consciousness at a given altitude.

5. HYPERVENTILATION (HYPOCAPNIA)

Hyperventilation produces a condition known as *hypocapnia*, and is arguably a component of virtually all aviation accidents to some degree. Anyone experiencing acute stress has the normal tendency to over-breath, which can lead to physiological responses ranging from mild symptomology to incapacitation. Understanding the body's response to hyperventilation and how to control it is an essential skill for aviators immersed in an emergency situation.

In this chapter we will discuss:

1. Hyperventilation and aviation accidents
2. Normal breathing rate in humans
3. Abnormal breathing rate
4. Causes of hyperventilation
5. Hypoventilation (Hypercapnia)
6. Subjective symptoms of hyperventilation
7. Objective signs of hyperventilation
8. Comparison of hyperventilation to hypoxia symptomology
9. Treatment for hyperventilation in yourself and others
10. Prevention of hyperventilation

5.1 HYPERVENTILATION AND AVIATION ACCIDENTS

It is a safe assumption most people have experienced hyperventilation to some degree at some point in their lives. Imagine the first time you asked a significant other out on a date, the first time you made a presentation in front of your class, the first time you got caught doing something wrong…that lightheadedness, faintness, and nausea you experienced was a result of hyperventilation. Did you notice you were breathing too fast? Most likely not, as few people do.

Hyperventilation resulting from an aviation incident or accident is a normal human response, as mentioned. While not necessarily causing accidents, many aviators may experience a severe startle effect if and when an abnormal condition develops in their aircraft, in turn causing an emotional response. Should hyperventilation go uncontrolled, the condition may absolutely impair an aviator's ability to continue responding to the task with any kind of cognitive clarity and most likely result in unconsciousness.

5.2 NORMAL BREATHING RATE IN HUMANS

Under normal circumstances the body does a wonderful job managing its functions. Our normal breathing rate is 12 to 20 breaths-per-minute. Human breathing rate is based on the constant monitoring of the chemical content of the blood stream, thus providing the correct physiological inputs to the brain.

The process of metabolism combines oxygen and glucose in the cells whereas the glucose releases heat and kinetic energy through catabolic reaction. This reaction converts oxygen and glucose to carbon dioxide and water as shown in the following formula:

$$6O_2 + C_6H_{12}O_6 \text{ to } 6H_2O + 6CO_2$$

Where $6O_2$ (6 oxygen molecules) combines with $C_6H_{12}O_6$ (glucose) resulting in the liberation of $6H_2O$ (6 molecules of water) and $6CO_2$ (6 carbon dioxide molecules). This reaction takes place in every cell of the human body and is the basis of metabolism.

About 7% of CO_2 released from the cell will dissolve in simple solution (plasma) and will be circulated to the lungs in this fashion for exhalation. Approximately 23% combines with RBC's and forms carbaminohemoglobin. Approximately 70% of carbon dioxide molecules will be carried as bicarbonate ions and adheres to the following reaction:

$$H_2O + CO_2 \text{ to } H_2CO_3 \text{ to } H^+ + HCO_3^-$$

Where H_2CO_3 is carbonic acid, a hydrogen ion (H^+) is taken from the carbonic acid and forms HCO_3^- (bicarbonate ion).

As mentioned, 70% of all CO_2 will be carried in the blood in this fashion. Once the venous blood arrives at the alveoli, the reaction will reverse, and CO_2 and water vapor will be expelled.

The body requires a sufficient amount of oxygen through the arterial network to maintain this process and excess carbon dioxide must be transported out of the body, which occurs through the venous network. When everything works correctly, the amount of oxygen humans ingest is balanced by the amount of carbon dioxide we dispose of. The *primary gas* controlling your breathing rate is the amount of CO_2 in the bloodstream, with the *secondary gas* affecting breathing rate is O_2.

The volume of CO_2 liberated during metabolism processes dictates the volume of bicarbonate, and perhaps more importantly, the amount of H+ (hydrogen) ions in the bloodstream. The H+ ion concentration in the blood is monitored by chemoreceptors in carotid and aortic bodies. Within these large arteries, chemoreceptors respond to increasing and decreasing H+ ion concentrations. During exercise there is increased production and liberation of CO_2. This causes a corresponding increase in H+ ion content of the blood. As the chemoreceptors sense this increase, a message to the brain is generated instructing it to increase the breathing rate. As breathing rate increases, two primary objectives are met; an increase in O_2 uptake to feed the exercising muscles and to decrease the amount of hydrogen ions, as well decrease CO_2 built up in the blood as a result increased O_2 consumption. This process works great during exercise, but if breathing is increased voluntarily (blowing up a balloon) or involuntarily (startle effect) without an increase in muscular activity, this process may bring about unconsciousness.

5.3 ABNORMAL BREATHING RATE

An *abnormal* rate and depth of breathing is called *hyperventilation*. Hyperventilation essentially creates a condition whereas carbon dioxide loss exceeds the body's production of the gas. Low carbon dioxide in the bloodstream causes a condition known as *hypocapnia*.

In acutely stressful events a person's breathing is controlled emotionally instead of chemically. Due to the natural release of adrenaline, the breathing rate will increase while physical activity remains normal. When the person begins rapidly breathing with no increased activity, the oxygen and hydrogen ion levels of the blood are normal. When rapid breathing continues, O_2 levels remain normal but the CO_2 levels and H+ ion levels rapidly drop. This shifts the pH balance of the blood to alkaline, known as *respiratory alkalosis*. The chemoreceptors sense the H+ ion drop and begin constricting blood flow in an attempt to chemically rebalance. Alkaline rich blood, if left in cells long enough, may begin to cause cellular damage. The brain, in defense mode, will start cerebral vasoconstriction, or restrict blood flow to the brain. O_2 transfer to the brain slows and the brain goes into a hypoxic state. Since blood flow is affected, hyperventilation effectively produces Stagnant Hypoxia. If breathing is not slowed down in a reasonable period of time, unconsciousness will occur. Once the person is unconsciousness, breathing rate slows and the H+ ion level will return to normal levels and decrease blood pH.

5.4 CAUSES OF HYPERVENTILATION

The following list depicts the most common causes of hyperventilation:

- Voluntary
- Emotional
- Pain
- Hypoxia
- Pressure Breathing

Voluntarily increasing one's breathing rate may seem strange enough, but consider what happens when blowing up a large balloon, an air mattress, or something similar. Most often, one ends up feeling lightheaded, dizzy, or faint as a result of the increased respiratory effort.

As mentioned, *emotional responses* are the most common cause of hyperventilation in aviators. Fear, anxiety, stress or tension can bring on adrenaline-induced hyperventilation mainly because the aviator is facing the unknown, or dealing with an unfamiliar event.

Pain may bring on adrenaline-induced hyperventilation as well, as humans have a tendency to solely focus on the unfamiliar sensation and are unsure of how to cope with it.

Hypoxic hypoxia causes a decrease in oxygen at the lung level, and the body's natural response is to breathe faster to compensate.

Pressure breathing is the act of oxygen-under-pressure being forced into an aviator's lungs via the oxygen system regulator. The act of pressure breathing is unnatural, and if not consciously monitored can easily lead to hyperventilation.

Let us examine a case of suspected hyperventilation in a real case:

Incident Review – February 2016: A cockpit crew flying a de Havilland Dash 8-400 was climbing through 17,000 feet towards FL190 when the crew heard a loud, metallic noise followed by a rush of air throughout the cabin. The first officer stopped the climb at 17,400 feet when both pilots noticed symptoms including lightheadedness, tightness of the chest, and tingling in the fingers. Suspecting hypoxia, the pilot-in-command ordered the crew don their oxygen masks and initiated an immediate descent to 10,000 feet.

Analysis: Subsequent inspection and investigation by authorities discovered the aircraft pressurization system outflow valve failed inflight causing the metallic noise, and a decompression, producing the rush of air. It was discovered the cabin altitude never exceeded 10,000 feet following the decompression.

Conclusion: While the crew responded appropriately to the event, the cause of their symptoms is believed to have been caused by hyperventilation. The cabin altitude never reached an altitude where symptoms of hypoxic hypoxia would have been immediately noticeable.

5.5 HYPOVENTILATION (HYPERCAPNIA)

Hypoventilation is exactly the opposite of *hyperventilation*; individuals breathing too slowly. This creates a condition of excessive carbon dioxide in the bloodstream, resulting in low oxygen levels, known as *hypercapnia*. A variety of medical conditions may cause hypercapnia, including COPD, unconsciousness, muscle and nerve damage, lung embolism, sleep apnea, brainstem stroke, hypothermia, obesity, and overdosing on drugs; however, the one cause aviators need be concerned with is *environmental*. Environmental causes may include ingestion of volcanic ash as a result of flight through a volcanic eruption, lack of air filtration, smoke and fumes ingestion, or ingestion of dry ice fumes (high concentration of CO_2).

The most common symptoms of hypoventilation are:

- Deeper breathing
- Twitching of muscles
- Increased blood pressure and pulse rate
- Headache
- Loss of judgement
- Unconsciousness (may occur in less than one minute when CO_2 concentrations rise by 10%)

The following incident is an example of how hypoventilation may occur:

Incident Review – January 2017: After taxing a single-pilot flight Cessna 208B cargo aircraft to Runway 30R at the Bakersfield, CA airport, the pilot-in-command experienced "strong sleepiness" and difficulty breathing. The PIC stopped the airplane in the run-up area and closed their eyes for a brief rest. ATC tried contacting the airplane after a few minutes with no response, and continued to try to contact the pilot for a total of 25 minutes. The local fire department was called, and when fire fighters reached the aircraft the PIC was found in the cockpit "with his head rolled back and mouth open." The fire fighter removed the PIC from the cockpit and revived him successfully.

Analysis: A FAA inspector responding to the incident found "numerous boxes labeled 'Dry Ice' positioned behind the pilot and stacked to the ceiling of the upper cargo pod." The final determination was the PIC succumbed to CO_2 fumes resulting from the proximity of dry ice to the cockpit.

Conclusion: The PIC has recognizable personal symptoms of contamination or a lack of oxygen. Had the dry ice boxes not been placed immediately behind the cockpit or the PIC recognized the abnormal condition occurring and opened a window or donned an oxygen mask, this incident would likely not happened.

5.6 SUBJECTIVE SYMPTOMS OF HYPERVENTILATION

Hyperventilation will produce definitive personal symptoms similar to those of hypoxic conditions. As with hypoxia, early recognition is the key to successful mitigation of symptomology. These symptoms are mainly the result of blood-alkalinity and constriction of cerebral blood flow. The following is a list of common symptoms:

- Tingling sensations
- Dizziness and/or lightheadedness
- Nausea
- Visual problems
- Muscular cramping or twitching
- Carpopedal spasms

Tingling sensations are a direct result of alkaline-rich blood reacting with the sensitive nerves of the extremities.

Dizziness and lightheadedness are typically a result of cerebral blood flow restriction, and very similar to what is experienced with hypoxia.

Nausea is usually associated with the perfusion of adrenaline into the body.

Visual problems are a result of cerebral blow flow restriction, thus preventing retinal blood perfusion. Typical visual issues include blurry or tunnel vision.

Muscular cramping or twitching is caused by alkaline rich blood entering the muscles, whereas the muscle reacts with spasms. Muscles of the face and large skeletal muscles are commonly affected.

Carpopedal spasms are a flapping and contraction of hands and feet, although forearms may be affected as well.

5.7 OBJECTIVE SIGNS OF HYPERVENTILATION

Understanding the symptomology fellow crewmembers may exhibit while hyperventilating is an important skill for any aviator, so one may assist them prior to their losing consciousness. Research has shown unconscious crewmembers do not successfully contribute to the flying mission!

These are the most common objective signs of hyperventilation:

- Muscle twitching
- Muscle tetany (spasm)
- Carpopedal spasms
- Cold, clammy skin
- Paleness
- Unconsciousness

Muscular twitching is caused by alkaline increases in the blood and the blood penetrates deep within the muscle, the muscle will progress from the twitch to *tetany* (an eventual muscle spasm). Once skeletal muscles spasm, the body stiffens up as if a straight board of wood.

Carpopedal spasms are a flapping and contraction of hands towards the wrist. Feet may be affected as well.

Cold, clammy skin and *paleness* are caused by vasoconstriction (constriction of blood vessels), the natural response of the body responding to elevated CO_2 levels.

As mentioned previously, unconsciousness occurs once cerebral vasoconstriction restricts blood flow adequately.

5.8 COMPARISON OF HYPERVENTILATION TO HYPOXIA SYMPTOMOLOGY

One may have noticed the subjective symptoms of hyperventilation mirror those of hypoxia, and there is a good reason for that. Hyperventilation causes cerebral vasoconstriction, which restricts the flow of blood (therefore oxygen) to the brain and the brain encounters stagnant hypoxic. Internal subjective symptoms make differentiating hypoxia from hyperventilation difficult for the person experiencing either condition. External objective signs are much easier to differentiate, as the demeanor and appearance of the person experiencing either condition is dramatically dissimilar.

5.9 TREATMENT FOR HYPERVENTILATION IN YOURSELF AND OTHERS

The fact of hypoxia and hyperventilation being so similar in subjective symptom presentation makes it extremely difficult to tell them apart in the middle of an inflight emergency. This necessitates treating both conditions exactly the same:

1. **Get on 100% oxygen with emergency pressure, or descend**
2. **Return rate and depth of breathing to normal**
3. **Check oxygen equipment connects (if applicable)**
4. **Descend below 10,000 feet if possible**

The only true mitigating factor for hyperventilation is controlling the rate and depth of breathing, but the rest of the checklist needs to be accomplished to ensure the secondary threat of hypoxia is prevented.

We know if other crewmembers or passengers were hypoxic, ensuring they are provided with oxygen is the only effective strategy to employ, but what is the strategy for those hyperventilating? How does one effectively get another to slow their breathing rate while trying to maintain control of an airplane?

Based on personal observations, prompting the affected person to talk or verbalize is the most effective, "hands-off" method of hyperventilation intervention as long as the condition is in its earlier stages. The individual needs to calm down and focus on something else, so reciting emergency procedures or reading a checklist may be appropriate.

If the individual is beyond the talking stage and starting to exhibit spasms and dilated pupils, the best intervention method may be to have the person lie on their side. This action will effectively restore blood flow to the brain, and the person should recover rather quickly. The main step to remember in this case is to allow the affected person to stay in the prone position for several minutes, even if they appear awake and alert. To allow them to sit up seconds after recovery invites a condition known as *vasovagal syncope*, which causes a rapid drop in cerebral blood pressure resulting in the person going unconscious a second time.

5.10 HYPERVENTILATION PREVENTION

The best method of mitigating hyperventilation is to prevent it from manifestation in the first place. We know acute stress (or startle effect) leading to panic and the resulting "breathing too fast" are the main causes for hyperventilation in aviation environments. Obviously, then, the best prevention strategy calls for an aviator to not panic and control your breathing. This sounds easy enough, but a pilot simply cannot push the "no panic" button on their dash when they experience engine failure on take-off and everything will turn out fine. How then does an aviator not panic in any given condition?

5.11 MAINTAINING CONTROL IN HYPER-STRESS ENVIRONMENTS

The topic of life-or-death events is a grim subject to contemplate. No one hopes they have to face such an event, but in aviation as well as everyday life situations may arise that requires us to respond with almost superhuman speed and skill for any chance of survival. We will now examine proven methods of dealing with those events successfully.

If we examine intellectual effect in the event of "startle effect," we find people tend to hyper-focus on what caused the event itself. For example, if a pilot experiences engine failure, they may focus on why they lost an engine. If loss of hydraulics occurs, the pilot may focus on why hydraulics were lost. This period of hyper-focus tends to last up to 30 seconds, during which time pilots may lose track of their responsibilities (airspeed/altitude/attitude), fail to monitor their instruments, and experience a loss of energy state awareness. Valuable seconds are lost in search of what caused the problem and situational awareness suffers, which in turn may prevent the pilot from actually rectifying the problem in time.

The split-second period-of-time a pilot has to make a decision which will either save their life or kill them is a fascinating place; why do some people make the right decision where other people fail in the same situation? What gives a pilot the "right stuff" to deal with extreme stress in the face of almost certain death?

When faced with extreme stress, human heart rates increase to between 115 to 145 beats-per-minute and neural impulse speed increases exponentially from 70 feet-per-second (fps) to approximately 300 fps. Motor and cognitive reaction times and visual processing efficiency are at their peak to prepare the individual to "fight or flight." Most people who experience a motor vehicle accident, for example, state at the time of accident "time seems to slow down." Time obviously is not slowing down, but rather neural impulse speed is dramatically increasing. In those situations some people panic and freeze, while others respond to the event. The obvious question is how do we harness this energy so we all do something meaningful in times of extreme stress?

U.S. Air Force flight operations are fraught with danger for a variety of reasons, so it stands to reason the Air Force would have developed a successful method to train aviators for extreme events. The methodology revolves around establishing neural pathways for conditioned responses to emergency events, and this is accomplished is through repetition. Every conceivable emergency event has a "bold-faced" checklist, and those checklist items are committed to memory through constant verbal recitation of the checklist. Instructors continuously drill student pilots on their bold-faced procedures for the wide variety of emergencies, and in doing so prepare the students to respond automatically if and when the time comes. This continuous series of verbal and intellectual drilling builds a *conditioned response* or *muscle memory*. A civilian pilot may accomplish the same training simply by drilling themselves repeatedly on any given emergency procedure until such point the procedure becomes rote memory.

U.S. military special operations soldiers have also developed techniques for dealing with extreme stress situational responses, which we'll discuss in the following paragraphs.

Along with muscle memory is the technique of *tactical breathing,* which is the main ingredient in controlling hyperventilation in the first place. Upon initial stress exposure, immediate conscious breath control at three to five breaths-per-minute helps establish and stabilize normal cerebral function.

Visualization and desensitization are powerful techniques to use in defense of traumatic events. The more one visualizes an event, a more effective neural pathway is built to deal with the event, similar in scope to muscle memory. The more mentally prepared an aviator becomes with visualization, the more desensitized to the event they become, thus preventing panic from occurring.

Some aviation professionals *talk themselves through the emergency.* By verbalizing each step of the process the brain stays focused on the proper response steps, thus helping ensure no single step is missed.

One more stress-response technique is *stay outwardly focused* and *NEVER give up* on the task-at-hand. One has to eliminate any negative mental distraction and feelings of doubt in the midst of an emergency. The only thing that matters is following the checklist completely and continuing this action until the event is resolved one way or the other. Aviators who give up and believe they are going to die most likely will.

Conclusion

Hyperventilation is not common, but can happen to anyone. To successfully navigate life-or-death events, one has to convince themselves that if they have to die, then they will die trying to save themselves. One has to focus on <u>what they have to work with</u>

and what they CAN do, and not what one doesn't have or can't do. Many instances have been recorded in which people thought they were going to die but worked the checklist, stuck with their emergency plan, and saved themselves in the end. Be one of those aviators!

Hyperventilation-inducing events can be dealt with effectively and efficiently with some preparation and forethought. Remember to treat the causes of hyperventilation, and not the symptoms. Put the work in before-hand so you aren't required to make it up as you go.

Chapter 5 Core Competency Questions

1. How many breaths-per-minute does the average human maintain?
2. What is the primary gas chemically controlling human breathing rate?
3. What is the secondary gas chemically controlling breathing rate?
4. True or false: the loss oxygen occurring from breathing too fast causes hyperventilation.
5. What form of hypoxia is produced by hyperventilation?
6. What typically causes hyperventilation in pilots?
7. Hypercapnia is caused by low amounts of what gas in the bloodstream?
8. True or false: the subjective symptoms of hyperventilation are similar to hypoxia.
9. True or false: pilots should treat hyperventilation exactly the same as hypoxia.
10. What type of pilot response is best used in extreme-stress events?

6. TRAPPED GAS IN HUMANS

As has been discussed in earlier chapters, gas expands with decreasing atmospheric pressures, and compresses with increasing atmospheric pressures. Gas expands and compresses in accordance with Boyle's Law, which states: "A volume of a gas is inversely proportional to the pressure to which it is subjected, temperature remaining constant." Aviators need to have a good understanding of the mechanisms of and treatment for trapped gas, as the painful symptoms associated with these disorders may seriously distract from a pilot's ability to control their aircraft.

In this chapter we will discuss:

1. Trapped gas definition
2. Common areas of human trapped gas
3. Trapped gas in the middle ear (Barotitis Media)
4. Trapped gas in sinuses (Barosinusitis)
5. Trapped gas in teeth (Barodontalgia)
6. Trapped gas in gastrointestinal tract (GI Barotrauma)
7. Trapped gas in lungs (Pulmonary Barotrauma)

6.1 TRAPPED GAS DEFINITION

According to the FAA, we may define human trapped gas in aviation as "any volume of gas in the human body unable to equalize with ambient atmospheric pressures."

The human body has various cavities that contain amounts of gas. Most of these cavities have an opening that will allow the gas to enter and escape. If the opening is reduced in size or closed, then the gas is trapped. Once trapped, it is still subject to gas expansion and compression in accordance with Boyles Law. The "formula" to remember is expansion or compression minus equalization equals pain (and often times excruciating pain.)

6.2 COMMON AREAS OF HUMAN TRAPPED GASES

Certain areas of the human body contain areas that contain an existing volume of gas. Equalization of these gases is rarely a problem at sea level; however, once humans are exposed to radical changes in atmospheric pressures these volumes of gas can create serious physical issues. The areas of concern are:

- Middle ears
- Sinus cavities
- Teeth
- Gastrointestinal (GI) Tract
- Lungs

6.3 TRAPPED GAS IN THE MIDDLE EAR (BAROTITIS MEDIA OR OTIC BAROTRAUMA)

One of the most common problems descending in an airplane is a pressure-equalization issue called *Barotitis Media*; also known as an *ear block*. Ear blocks occur in the presence of a pressure gradient (either increasing or decreasing) in the middle ear (located behind the tympanic membrane or eardrum) and an ineffective eustachian tube. When these two conditions present themselves, gas will attempt to either expand or contract in the middle ear (in accordance with Boyle's Law).

The eustachian tube connects the middle ear cavity to the throat and typically remains somewhat flaccid. Normally during ascent, as pressure decreases and the volume of gas in the middle ear expands, air is forced down through the eustachian tube, inflating it to equilibrate the pressures. On descent when ambient pressure increases, negative pressure or a relative vacuum occurs in the middle ear and the eustachian tube will often not open without conscious effort. Due to the fixed cavity space of the middle ear (see below), pressure in the middle ear will either be exerted out against the walls on ascent or pulling against the walls as a relative vacuum forms on descent. For this reason, ear blocks are most common on descent for aviators. This phenomenon is worsened with the presentation of inflammation or congestion in the tissues surrounding the eustachian tubes, which often accompanies allergies or upper respiratory infections (aka the common cold).

Figure 6.1 Middle Ear Anatomy

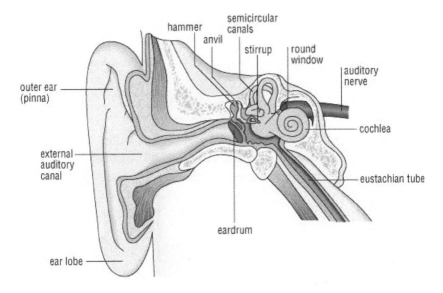

Wpclipart 2021

Symptoms of Ear Block

When the eustachian tube is compressed due to inflammation and swelling from an acute upper respiratory infection or allergies and cannot function effectively, pressures do not equilibrate, and as a result symptoms will be experienced by the aviator:

- Fullness or stuffiness
- Hearing impairment
- Increasing pain
- Rupture of eardrum

The feeling of *fullness* or *stuffiness* is generally the first recognizable symptom of an ear block, as well the most opportune time to remedy the condition. Fixing small problems is more effective then fixing big problems.

Hearing impairment may be noticed by the aviator. In some cases, pilots may assume this is a result of tight-fitting headsets as opposed to an ear block condition.

Pain will begin to develop if the descent continues. The pain may simply an irritant at first, eventually becoming excruciating pain severe enough to impair aircraft operation.

In extreme cases, the eardrum can potentially rupture and a small tear or hole will develop. Due to the possibly movement of fluids in the vestibular apparatus, spatial disorientation may immediately develop as a result of ruptured tympanic membrane. Should a rupture happen, the best course of action is to visit the Aeromedical Examiner and avoid flight for two to three weeks to allow the damaged tissue to heal adequately.

Ear Block Clearing Methods

In order to avoid ear blocks inflight, aviators need to consciously force the eustachian tube open, allowing the vacuum developing in the middle ear to equilibrate with the higher pressure of the changing external environment. This can be accomplished by learned (conscious) control of the muscles responsible for opening the tube, and several other maneuvers. The best methods to treat inflight ear blocks are:

- **Yawn**
- **Swallow**
- **Move or jut the jaw forward**
- **Valsalva**
- **Vasoconstrictor spray**

Yawning, swallowing and *moving the jaw* all flex the neck and jaw muscles, potentially allowing the eustachian tube to open more effectively. These techniques are individualized and may not be effective for all.

Surprisingly enough, many aviators are not familiar with the correct mechanism of a properly-performed *Valsalva* maneuver. Due to the anatomical architecture of the neck and jaw, effective positioning of the eustachian tube needs to be accomplished. Aviators should perform the maneuver as follows:

- **Keep the shoulders level and face straight ahead**
- **Slant the head sideways towards the shoulder opposite the fullness or pain**
- **Lower the jaw onto the chest**
- **Pinch off both nostrils and keep the mouth closed tight**
- **Blow in this position as if blowing your nose**

Vasoconstrictor sprays are a last-resort method used to clear ear blocks when all other methods have failed. Vasoconstrictors contain medications used to shrink nasal blood vessels, therefore the lining, of the nose considerably. After use, the nasal breathing passages will feel incredibly wide-open and should easily equalize. However, if misused for longer periods of time (three days or so), a rebound effect may occur in which after the medication wears off, the symptoms are worse than before. Vasoconstrictor sprays should always be carried in your flight bag for emergency use only. The sprays should never be used so a pilot *can* fly, but if already *in flight* and the ears severely block, vasoconstrictor sprays can literally be a life-saver.

Ear Block Inflight Treatment

If an ear block is experienced inflight, the following procedures should be followed:

1. **Level off and Valsalva**
2. **Climb 1,000 feet to 2,000 feet if unable to clear ears**
3. **Retry Valsalva**
4. **Use reduced rates of descent and land**

Leveling the aircraft will stop the pressure change from occurring. If pain is present, ascent to a lower atmospheric pressure will immediately alleviate the pain. These maneuvers make clearing the condition more effective. Perform a proper Valsalva, and if unsuccessful, resort to vasoconstrictor spray.

Most of the inventors of these maneuvers have solidified their place in medical history as demonstrated by the various names- the Valsalva maneuver, the Toynbee maneuver, the Frenzel maneuver, or the Politzer device. These various maneuvers and devices will be discussed later.

6.4 TRAPPED GAS IN SINUSES (BAROSINUSITIS)

The physiological mechanism of *barosinusitis,* also known as a *sinus block,* is very similar to barotitis media (ear block). As the name indicates, the main difference between the two conditions is the location of the pressure-induced blockage. Humans have four symmetrical pairs of air-filled paranasal sinuses: frontal, maxillary, ethmoidal and sphenoidal sinuses. These can be examined in the diagram below. Each sinus is lined with mucosa and has a small opening to the external environment to allow for and ensure air and pressure exchange.

Figure 6.2 Paranasal Sinuses

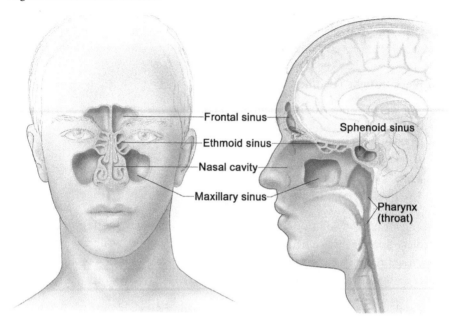

Frontal sinus

Ethmoid sinus

Nasal cavity

Maxillary sinus

Sphenoid sinus

Pharynx (throat)

cancer.gov 2021

Symptoms of Sinus Block

The blockage condition most commonly occurs when moving from a relatively low-pressure environment into one of higher-pressure, or what happens on descent from altitude. As with ear blocks, a negative pressure gradient in the sinuses may become difficult to equalize caused by mucosal congestion and possibly a hematoma (collection of blood), occasionally culminating in damaged tissue. The main symptom of sinus blockage is:

-    The sudden and possibly excruciating onset of pain

The blockage pain experienced by the aviator normally occurs with little-to-no warning. This pain may interfere with the pilot's ability to safely operate an aircraft, or possibly even make rational decisions.

Sinus blocks are mainly experienced due to an underlying cold/upper respiratory infection or allergic rhinitis. If the underlying condition is severe enough, sinus blocks may occur on ascent as well. In rare cases the victims of recurrent sinus blocks have some physical abnormality of the sinuses or openings to the sinuses, and surgery by an otolaryngologist (ear, nose and throat surgeon) may be necessary to correct the condition.

Treatment for Inflight Sinus Blocks

If sinus blocks occur inflight, following the following procedures:

1. **Level off and Valsalva**
2. **Reverse the direction of pressure change**
3. **Retry Valsalva**
4. **Vasoconstrictor spray should be used if Valsalva is ineffective**
5. **Descend at reduced rates and land**

Leveling the aircraft will stop the pressure change from occurring. If pain is present, ascent or descend depending on when the block occurs immediately to alleviate the pain. These maneuvers make clearing the condition more effective. Perform a proper Valsalva, and if unsuccessful, resort to vasoconstrictor spray.

6.5 TRAPPED GAS IN TEETH (BARODONTALGIA)

An inflight pressure-induced issue with air pockets in teeth is called *Barodontalgia*, also known as a *tooth block*. Boyle's Law is again at issue as trapped gas expands in a closed space in the tooth provoking pain and/or tissue destruction. Gas may be trapped in teeth during any number of dental procedures such as when placing a filling. In this closed space will reside ambient air, which obviously expands as we ascend. There are also types of bacteria which may produce gas during infectious processes such as tooth abscesses.

These small pockets of inter-tooth air may be inconsequential in most people, but for a pilot or the result can be incredible pain or even fracture of the tooth with pressure changes on ascent. While tooth blocks have been observed at very low altitudes, aviators at higher risk for rapid decompressions remain at risk for dental barodontalgia. As a result, a variety of dental procedures require a pilot to not fly for a specific duration of time.

Treatment of Inflight Tooth Blocks

If tooth pain is experienced inflight, follow the following procedures:

1. **Immediately descend**
2. **Identify the tooth**
3. **See your dentist**

As tooth blocks occur on ascent, immediate descent will alleviate any associated pain. The <u>exact tooth</u> needs to be identified. A pilot experiencing barodontalgia should revisit their dentist to have a second procedure with the goal of removing the offending space, or treating the underlying condition.

Referred Sinus Pain

Referred sinus pain occurs when a maxillary sinus block occurs, but feels like all of the teeth in the upper jaw are in pain. Often times this condition will be confused with tooth pain when, in fact, it is a sinus block exerting pressure on the upper row of teeth.

Should several or all of the teeth of the upper jaw hurt simultaneously, the condition must be treated as any other sinus block with ascent or descent to relieve the pain, Valsalva, and slower rate-of-descent.

6.6 TRAPPED GAS IN GASTROINTESTINAL TRACT (GI BAROTRAUMA)

Gas expansion in the gastrointestinal (GI) tract may cause inflight discomfort and pain known as *GI Barotrauma*, also known as simply *GI Gas*. The GI tract is a 30-foot long continuous gas-filled tube extending from the mouth and esophagus through the stomach, small intestine, large intestine and exiting out of the rectum and anus. This tube has two openings to allow gas to pass (either as a belch or flatus depending on the location of gas), but decreasing pressure on ascent will invoke symptoms as the volume of GI gas expands.

Figure 6.3 Human Gastrointestinal Tract

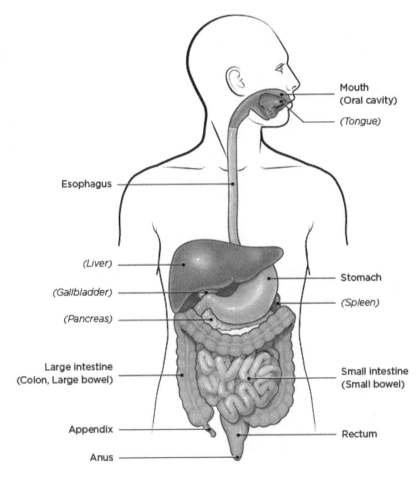

Mouth
(Oral cavity)

(Tongue)

Esophagus

(Liver)

(Gallbladder)

(Pancreas)

Large intestine
(Colon, Large bowel)

Appendix

Anus

Stomach

(Spleen)

Small intestine
(Small bowel)

Rectum

CDC 2021

The GI tract was not designed to accommodate expansion. As gas expands in the GI tract, pain receptors sensitive to stretch often will induce abdominal discomfort and/or pain. This expansion of gas at altitude can be so profound that descension of the diaphragm is prevented, disallowing the lungs from full inflation during inhalation, ultimately disrupting respiration.

Sources and Expansion Ratios of GI Gas Expansion

Most aviators are well-aware of the foods that "give them gas." Typically, the most notorious offenders are beans, broccoli, cauliflower, brussel sprouts, cabbage, and carbonated beverages. Natural digestive processes may produce excess gas, as well as swallowing air from pressure breathing.

Once the aviator begins ascent to higher altitudes, Boyle's Law takes over and begins the process of expanding trapped gas in the GI tract to increasing levels the higher one flies. The dry gas expansion ratios aviators may expect as they climb are as follows:

Figure 6.4 Altitude Gas Expansion Ratio in Humans

Altitude	Expansion Ratio Over Sea Level
FL180	2 to 1
FL250	3 to 1
FL300	5 to 1
FL350	7 to 1
FL430	9 to 1
FL500	17 to 1

To put these numbers into perspective, consider the fact the average human body contains approximately one liter of gas in its GI tract. At a cabin altitude of FL180, the volume increases to two liters; at FL250 volume increases to three liters. At each interval gas discomfort and bloating becomes more pervasive, eventually leading to the threshold of pain.

Now imagine experiencing a rapid decompression to FL430 in five seconds; GI tract expansion reaches nine liters in five seconds! The ability of the body to dispel that volume of gas quickly enough to avoid severe intestinal stretching is almost impossible, and it is safe to assume the aviator would experience extreme discomfort and/or pain until GI gas could equalize.

Treatment of Inflight GI Gas

The most obvious way of avoiding discomfort and/or pain as a result of GI tract gas expansion inflight is to get rid of it before it becomes a problem. The following are recognized methods of minimizing the effects of GI tract gas:

1. **Pass gas**
2. **Avoid gas-forming foods**
3. **Stomach massage**
4. **Loosen restrictive clothing**

Passing gas has been taught from an early age to be publicly unacceptable, and for that reason many people find this step difficult. Abdominal discomfort and pain may be avoided by early belching and passing of flatus. Leaning to the left assists in belching out upper abdominal gas.

Avoiding gas-forming foods is preventative medicine for high-altitude flights. Not exacerbating the problem in the first place helps avoid potential problems later.

Stomach massage is a method whereas the aviator can assist the body in breaking up larger gas bubbles in the GI tract into smaller gas bubbles to assist in their passing. An aviator takes their fist, presses it into the upper right corner of the abdominal cavity, and rolls their fist diagonally across the cavity to the lower left. This allows intestinal folds to fluctuate and relax, allowing for the passage of gas.

Loosen restrictive clothing is a simple but effective technique to avoid gas discomfort. Many aviation uniforms require the use of belts and slacks, and allowing for more expansion in those areas of the body reduces discomfort.

6.7 TRAPPED GAS IN LUNGS (PULMONARY BAROTRAUMA)

In addition to the conditions listed above, *pulmonary barotrauma* has implications that the aviation professional need be aware. Atmospheric air enters and exits the body through the trachea and in the lungs, air also expands with ascent. Normally air in the lung is passively expired on ascent, but in cases where ascent-to-altitude and the resulting lung gas expansion is rapid, it may become difficult to inhale as expanding lung air escapes through the trachea. Coupled with an oxygen system delivering pressure above certain altitudes, the very process of breathing may come to a complete halt until cabin altitude is equalized.

Figure 6.5 Human Lung Air Pathways

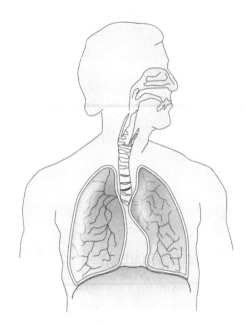

If lung gas expansion is too rapid lung tissue can potentially tear. This condition may ultimately result in:

- Pneumothorax (abnormal collection of air in the pleural space between the lung and chest wall),
- Pneumomediastinum (alveolar hyperinflation)
- Arterial gas embolism (blockage of blood supply to organs caused by bubbles in an artery).

In order for an ascent-to-altitude to be considered <u>too rapid</u> for lung tissue to adjust, the ascent rate would approach incredible speeds; specifically experiencing an *explosive decompression*. Explosive decompression criteria equal traversing a 10-psi pressure differential in .1 to .5 seconds, or the equivalent of flying at FL420 with the cabin pressurized to 4,000 feet, and losing total cabin pressure in a half-second or less.

Treatment of Inflight Pulmonary Barotrauma

Avoiding problems associated with lung gas expansion is as simple as allowing the air in the lungs to escape naturally. If a rapid ascent-to-altitude is experienced, open your mouth to allow the gas to discharge. Do not hold the breath or try to inhale against the forces of escaping gases; don your oxygen mask, allow the cabin altitude to equalize and continue on with your mission.

Conclusion

Gases are continuously present in the body and the consequences must be considered for every flight, pressurized aircraft or not. Allowing the gases to escape and equalize with the surrounding environment minimizes potential problems. However, if the gases become trapped and equalization is difficult, the result tends to be very painful.

The major problems with ears and sinuses will usually occur below 10,000 feet, teeth could be affected anywhere, and GI gas normally above FL180. These three steps provide guidance on preventing trapped gas issues from occurring inflight:

1. **Do not fly with an upper respiratory infection**
2. **Avoid gas-forming foods prior to flight**
3. **Maintain proper dental hygiene**

Chapter 6 Core Competency Questions

1. Which gas law applies to Trapped Gas issues in aviators?
2. What are the common areas of trapped gas in humans?
3. What two areas of trapped gas are most likely to occur on ascent?
4. What two areas of trapped gas are most likely to occur on descent?
5. What pathway connects the middle ear with throat?
6. True or false: ear blocks are always accompanied by pain.
7. What is the most effective method of clearing an ear or sinus block?
8. Should vasoconstrictor sprays be used to clear normal ear blocks?
9. What is the best way to clear GI gas?
10. What is the gas expansion ratio at FL250?
11. What is the best way to avoid ear and sinus blocks inflight?

7. EVOLVED GAS IN HUMANS

Most problems associated with flying at high altitude are caused by the drop in atmospheric pressure as one ascends. One notable problem an aviator may face is the threat of *evolved gas disorders,* also known as *decompression sickness.* Decompression sickness (DCS) in aviation is the evolution of nitrogen molecules in bodily fluids and tissues developing into nitrogen bubbles at altitude. The location of bubble formation greatly influences the severity of the problem.

In this chapter we will discuss:

1. Cause and mechanism of evolved gas formation
2. Altitude-induced decompression sickness
3. Types of decompression sickness
4. Bends (Arthopathy) symptoms
5. Skin (Cutaneous) symptoms
6. Central Nervous System (Neurologic) symptoms
7. The Chokes (cardiopulmonary) symptoms
8. Predisposing factors of DCS
9. Treatment for altitude-induced DCS
10. Prevention of altitude-induced DCS

7.1 CAUSE AND PATHOPHYSIOLOGY OF EVOLVED GAS FORMATION

Evolved gas disorders, or DCS, are not exclusive to aviation and are certainly not a recent discovery. The first cases of decompression sickness affected caisson workers in the early 1800s. Caissons were pressurized, watertight retaining structures workers used to build the foundations of bridge piers. The workers performed their tasks in this pressurized environment which could be dozens of feet below Sea Level. When depressurizing following their shift, many workers would report previously unknown painful symptoms in their joints, lungs, and skin, and cognitive difficulties. Some injuries resulted in permanent injury or even death in some cases.

In due time doctors were able to isolate the cause of these mysterious illnesses, which today we know was caused by nitrogen bubble formation in various parts of the body in accordance with Henry's Law. Henry's Law states: "the amount of gas dissolved in a solution is proportional to the partial pressure of that gas over the solution." One of the best practical analogies of this law is demonstrated by opening a soft drink. When the cap is removed from the bottle, gas is heard escaping and bubbles are seen forming in the liquid. This is carbon dioxide gas coming out of solution as a result of sudden exposure to lower barometric pressure.

The problem of DCS has been studied for nearly 200 years, yet there is still a lot to be discovered concerning this potentially life-threatening disorder. The pathophysiology of DCS stems from nitrogen molecules saturated in body tissue and fluids; decreasing environmental atmospheric pressure causes supersaturation of the molecules leading to bubble formation and lodging in various tissues, blood vessels, or fluids of the body. DCS symptoms result from the pressure and inflammation on these tissues, but first we need to more closely examine bubble formation.

Nitrogen Bubble Formation

While at sea level, humans breathe air composed of 78% nitrogen. Nitrogen is an inert gas, and will not be metabolized in the human body. The inhaled nitrogen is taken into the lungs at a pressure of 593 mmHg (78% of total atmospheric pressure [760mm Hg] at sea level). The nitrogen is distributed throughout bodily fluids and tissues via the circulatory system and stored at a pressure of about 593 mmHg. As long as humans remain at sea level, the nitrogen partial pressure inside and outside the body are at equilibrium. However, when atmospheric pressure is reduced such as flying unpressurized at altitude, the equilibrium is upset. This causes the nitrogen to de-metabolize and naturally leave the body. If pressure differential is not too radical and the rate of ascent is slow enough nitrogen will leave as a gas and simply exhaled. If the fluid and tissue nitrogen expand too quickly, the fluids and tissues become supersaturated with nitrogen and bubbles may form. While the knowledge of exactly how the bubbles initially form is currently unclear, research performed by Dr. Sander Wilderman at the Centre for Fluid Dynamics, University of Twente, The Netherlands, suggests potential mechanisms are *tribonucleation* or *heterogenerous nucleation*.

Tribonucleation creates small gas bubbles caused by two solid surfaces making and breaking contact while immersed in a liquid, such as the synovial fluid of a human joint (shown below). The small bubbles may act as nuclei promoting the growth of bubble as atmospheric pressure is reduced. *Heterogenerous nucleation* may create bubble formation as a result of a surface in contact with a liquid with microbubble formation in the liquid itself.

Figure 7.1 Human Joint and Synovial Fluid

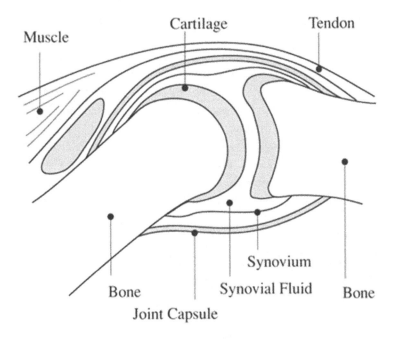

Wpclipart 2021

Once microbubbles form, they may grow resultant from a reduction in pressure or diffusion of gas into the gas surrounding the microbubble. Bubbles may manifest themselves in tissues or transported through the bloodstream.

DCS may occur during exposure to altitude or during ascent from depth (mining or diving). The first documented cases of DCS (Caisson's Disease) were reported in 1841 by a mining engineer who observed pain and muscle cramps occurring among coal miners exposed to pressurized mine shafts designed to keep water out. In 1869 the first medical description of a DCS case resulting from undersea diving while wearing a pressurized hard-hat was reported. Today, most physicians consider DCS a SCUBA diver's disease due to amount of atmospheric pressure change divers transcend, which equates to one atmosphere's worth of pressure (760 mmHg) every 33 feet of depth. While the onset of DCS is known in diving settings, many medical professionals fail to realize the potential of the condition in aviation settings.

7.2 ALTITUDE-INDUCED DECOMPRESSION SICKNESS

Altitude DCS became a commonly encountered problem associated with high-altitude balloon and aircraft flights in the 1930s, when altitude-setting flights could reach in excess of FL500. Today, technology allows civilian aircraft (commercial, corporate and private) to fly higher, faster and greater distances than ever before. Although modern aircraft are safer and more reliable, aircrew members and passengers are still subject to unique stresses of high-altitude flight and related problems. Over a century after the first altitude-induced DCS case was observed, scientific understanding of DCS has improved and related knowledge has accumulated; however, the problem is far from being definitively solved. Pressurization systems provide vital protection against DCS at altitude, but we continue to fly aircraft to higher altitudes where the risk of exposure is greater.

Assessing DCS Risk

Humans at increased risk for DCS can be calculated using the following mathematical formula:

$R = PN2/PB$

R is the *Risk Value*, which is determined by dividing an individual's tissue Nitrogen saturation level (*PN2*) by the total atmospheric pressure they are being exposed to (*PB*). If R equals or is greater than 1.5, then the individual is at increased risk for DCS. Let's examine what this looks like for a Sea Level-equilibrated aviator who will be flying unpressurized to FL180:

Tissue N2 @ Sea Level: 760 mmHg x .78 = 593 mmHg

FL180 atmospheric pressure = 396 mmHg

593/396 = 1.5 R value

This equation shows us a sea level-equilibrated human can expect potential DCS problems starting at FL180. Since not everyone lives exactly at sea level, we can also calculate to what unpressurized altitude an aviator can expect to fly to when equilibrated to a higher altitude by calculating PN2/R = PB:

Here is the equation for 4,000 feet equilibration: 656.3 mmHg (.78)/1.5 = 341.3 mmHg (approximately 21,700')

For 8,000 feet: 564.4 mmHg x .78/1.5 = 293.5 mmHg (approximately 25.400 feet)

From these results we can deduce equilibrating to a higher altitude provides increased R Value protection.

7.3 TYPES OF DECOMPRESSION SICKNESS

Mentioned previously was the fact DSC symptomology may present itself in a variety of bodily fluids and/or tissue. Some presentations of the disease are more dangerous than others; thus DCS presentation is broken down into two groups Type I (Simple) and Type II (Serious):

- Type 1 Decompression Sickness (musculoskeletal presentation)
  a. Bends (Arthopathy)
  b. Skin Symptoms (Cutaneous)
- Type 2 Decompression Sickness (neurological/circulatory presentation)
  c. Central Nervous System (Neurologic)
  d. Chokes (Cardiopulmonary)

Type 1 DCS is considered a milder form of the disease with rare fatalities, while Type 2 DCS can be very serious and potentially fatal. It is important to note Type 1 DCS can revert to Type 2 DCS rapidly, so any DCS symptomology should be considered a serious medical threat and treated accordingly.

7.4 BENDS (ARTHOPATHY) SYMPTOMS

The bends are perhaps the most common and recognized form of decompression sickness to the general population. The bends derives its name from the actions of the person suffering from the disease; if a person experienced pain in their elbow, for example, the person would "bend" the elbow repeatedly to try to disperse the developing pain.

The bends account for 60% - 70% of all altitude DCS cases and are by far the most common. The bends are formed by negative pressures generated in the large joints of the body, leading to N2 bubble formation in synovial fluid. The main joints affected in aviation settings include shoulders, elbows and wrists, while diver settings mainly affect hips, knees, and ankles. This is mainly due to which parts of the body are moving at the time of bubble formation are most affected.

Symptomology of the bends include a localized mild, deep pain gradually evolving to excruciating pain if ascent is continued. Aggressive movement of the joint may aggravate the condition. The pain will typically resolve on descent; however, pain can last for hours or even days after the flight.

7.5 SKIN (CUTANEOUS) SYMPTOMS

Skin symptoms are the result of N2 bubble formation under the cutaneous layer of skin. Skin DCS is usually mild; however, the onset of skin symptoms could potentially lead to more severe manifestations of DCS.

Skin DCS in aviation is relatively rare, comprising approximately 10% – 15% of all altitude DCS cases.

Symptomology of Skin DCS may be itching and tingling sensations, hot or cold sensations, and typically a red, blotchy rash. The condition may be advanced to mottled or marbled skin lesions, which at these presentation levels should be treated with hyperbaric treatment protocols as soon as possible.

7.6 CENTRAL NERVOUS SYSTEM (CNS - NEUROLOGIC) SYMPTOMS

CNS DCS is a particularly nasty presentation of the disease, as the resulting physical and neurologic manifestations can be quite severe. The cause of CNS DCS is N2 bubble formation in the brain neurons, spinal cord or peripheral nerves.

Fortunately, CNS DCS is another relatively rare condition in aviation settings, only comprising approximately 10% - 15% of all altitude DCS cases. The symptomology of CNS DCS may vary widely depending on the location of the disease, hence we will examine the brain, spinal cord and peripheral nerve symptoms separately:

Brain: Confusion or memory loss, headache, spots in visual field, tunnel vision, double vision, blurry vision, unexplained extreme fatigue or behavior changes, seizures, dizziness, vertigo, nausea, vomiting, unconsciousness

Spinal cord: Abnormal sensations such as numbness, burning, stinging and tingling around the lower chest and back, symptoms may spread from the feet up and may be accompanied by ascending weakness or paralysis, girdling abdominal or chest pain

Peripheral nerves: Urinary or rectal incontinence, abnormal sensations such as numbness, burning, stinging and tingling, muscle weakness or twitching

Headache and visual disturbances are the most common occurring symptoms of CNS DCS. Recognition of these symptoms should prompt immediate hyperbaric treatment.

Let us examine an incident involving CNS DCS in general aviation:

Incident Review – April 2016: The elderly pilot-in-command of a Cirrus SR-22T was flying with his wife from California to their destination of Pueblo, CO. The PIC and wife went on supplemental oxygen at 10,000 feet while wearing pulse oximeters to monitor oxygen saturation, and climbed to FL250 where they remained enroute for over two hours.

Upon approach to their destination, the pilot reportedly suffered from slurred speech, then could not talk at all. The PIC also suffered from abdominal pain, confusion, visual problems, extreme vertigo, nausea, fever, sweats, and even lost consciousness briefly during the approach, according to his wife. Once on the ground, the pilot's severe vertigo prevented him from walking away from the aircraft, instead resorting to crawling.

The PIC and his wife went to a local Emergency Room, where the attending physician diagnosed High Altitude Cerebral Edema and treated with steroids for several days with no resolution of symptoms. The physician contacted the Mayo Clinic Hyperbaric Medical Treatment Division, where the PIC's condition was re-diagnosed as Central Nervous System DCS. The PIC was recommended for hyperbaric therapy.

Analysis: The pilot-in-command suffered severe inflight neurological symptoms and was fortunately able to successfully land the aircraft. The PIC reported to a local hospital, was misdiagnosed by the attending physician, and finally correctly diagnosed by physicians from Mayo Clinic. While hyperbaric therapy was recommended for the patient, the outcome of the therapy is not known to the author at the time of this writing.

Conclusion: The PIC experienced what appeared to be CNS DCS, and attempted to do the right thing by reporting to a hospital. Unfortunately, misdiagnoses of DCS by physicians is all-too-common as they generally have little training identifying DCS as an altitude-induced disease. Searching out an Aeromedical Examiner who is trained in DCS identification and appropriate treatment protocols is critical.

7.7 THE CHOKES (CARDIOPULMONARY) SYMPTOMS

The chokes are a rare, but serious presentation of DCS involving the evolution of N2 bubbles in venous blood, eventually becoming lodged in the arterial side of the pulmonary capillaries of the lungs. This causes an obstruction in those capillaries and ultimately prevents normal oxygen transfer in the lungs. The condition can be rapidly fatal even with appropriate treatment.

Fortunately, the chokes are extremely infrequent in aviation and occur is less than 2% of all altitude DCS cases.

The symptomology of pulmonary DCS include chest pain on inhalation (located deep underneath the sternum), difficulty breathing (noted as a feeling of suffocation), a dry, hacking, non-productive continuous cough, and ultimately stagnant hypoxia and/or death.

7.8 PREDISPOSING FACTORS OF DCS

The following list contains common influencing factors predisposing aviators to DCS:

- Altitude
- Rate of ascent
- Duration of exposure
- Exercise at altitude
- Obesity
- Age
- Dehydration
- Recent SCUBA diving
- Repetitive exposures above FL180
- Individual susceptibility
- Ambient temperature
- Previous injury

Altitude is the most obvious predisposing factor to be considered, as exposure above FL180 for sea level-equilibrated aviators significantly increases risk. Although no specific altitude can be considered an absolute altitude exposure threshold, there is little evidence of altitude DCS occurring among healthy individuals below 18,000 feet who have not been SCUBA diving. Aviation-related exposures to altitudes between FL180 and FL250 reveal a low incidence rate of altitude DCS; the majority of altitude DCS cases occur among individuals exposed to altitudes of FL250 and above. A U.S. Air Force study of altitude DCS cases reported that only 13% occurred below FL250. The higher the exposure altitude, the greater the risk of developing altitude DCS. An important note to consider is although exposures to altitudes above FL180 show an incremental risk of altitude DCS, a direct relationship with the severity of the types of DCS is not seen.

Rate of ascent greatly influences the onset of altitude DCS, as slow ascents will allow the body to naturally off-gas N2 as N2 molecules expand in bodily fluids and tissues.

A rapid ascent, such as a rapid decompression, exposes the individual to a greater risk of DCS as bodily fluids and tissues simply cannot off-gas N2 fast enough.

Duration of exposure predisposes individuals to altitude DCS as the more time-at-altitude, the more chance N2 molecules have to expand into bubbles.

Exercise at altitude aggravates large-joint negative pressures, assisting N2 bubble formation.

Obesity typically assists altitude DCS as high body-fat content promotes poor blood supply, and N2 molecules are much more soluble and stored in greater volumes in fatty tissues. Although fat represents only 15% of a normal adult body, fat stores over half of the total amount of N2 (about 1 liter) normally dissolved in the body.

Age has been proven in some studies to promote altitude DCS, possibly as a result of a loss of muscle-mass and increased fat stores.

Dehydration will increase the likelihood of altitude DCS possibly because hydration may enhance inert gas removal or increase surface tension of blood cells.

Recent SCUBA diving produces much greater risks of N2 bubble formation as a result of the body recently experiencing major barometric pressure changes and enhanced N2 saturation, predisposing N2 molecules to evolve into bubbles. SCUBA diving requires breathing air under high pressure. Under such conditions, a significant increase in the amount of N2 dissolved in body tissue is experienced (body nitrogen saturation). The deeper the SCUBA diving, the greater the incidence rate of body N2 saturation. Additionally, SCUBA diving in high-elevation bodies of water (mountain lakes) at any given depth results in greater body N2 saturation when compared to SCUBA diving at Sea Level at the same depth. Following SCUBA diving, sufficient time must be allowed to eliminate excess N2 stored in body fluids or tissues, or altitude DCS may occur at altitude exposures as low as 5,000 feet or less.

Repetitive exposures above FL180 within a short period of time (i.e. a few hours) increases the incidence rate of altitude DCS as N2 tissue saturation hasn't had enough time to normalize.

Individual susceptibility may play a role in altitude DCS susceptibility for a variety of physiological factors. USAF high-altitude training observations have revealed some individuals experience DCS at certain altitudes for a limited period of time, returning to normal for no apparent reason.

Ambient temperature possibly plays a role in altitude DCS development, as scientific evidence suggests individuals exposed to very cold ambient temperatures may increase their risk levels.

7.9 TREATMENT FOR ALTITUDE-INDUCED DCS

If any crewmember or passenger exhibits signs of any form of DCS inflight, the condition needs to be treated as an immediate-response medical emergency. Depending on the presentation of the disease, the condition may rapidly escalate to a life-threatening condition, making quick diagnoses to therapy immensely important. The following inflight patient protocol should be followed:

1. **100% oxygen with tight-fitting oxygen mask**
2. **Re-pressurize (emergency descent)**
3. **Render supportive measures**
4. **Notify and land at the nearest airport**
5. **Contact AME to continue treatment**

100% oxygen with a tight-fitting mask is the essential first-step to ensure the patient starts extricating as much nitrogen out of their tissues as possible, as 100% oxygen will assist in displacing nitrogen. A tight-fitting mask, or crew-style mask, is necessary to ensure no ambient air is entering the patient's body. The flimsy, thin-rubber passenger oxygen masks simply do not provide a proper seal to ensure proper absorption of highly-oxygenated gas.

Re-pressurize, or start an immediate emergency descent, to begin the process of compressing nitrogen bubbles. It's important to note even if symptoms disappear on descent, ensure the patient stays on 100% oxygen and continue the descent.

Render supportive measures as the patient may unexpectedly lapse into a hypoxic state, or may suffer from shock. Ensure the patient keeps their oxygen mask on, remains calm, does not move unnecessarily, and is lying down. Most commercial and corporate flight crews have inflight medical care services available by radio or telephone contact, which may help manage the situation.

Notify and land at the nearest airport as the patient needs to get on the ground and seek medical evaluation with no delay.

Contact AME to continue treatment to ensure the patient receives the proper and necessary medical evaluation and treatment protocol, if needed. Ultimately, treatment in a hyperbaric (dive) chamber may the *only* treatment option capable of suppressing the condition and related symptoms.

A major consideration of altitude DCS treatment options revolves around the fact many aviation-related DCS incidents are misdiagnosed by non-AME physicians. The pilot-in-charge has to be the advocate for proper treatment of DCS patients, whether it's themselves or others, as an attending physician not specializing in aviation or hyperbaric medicine may not be familiar with the disease. Another point worth noting is delayed signs and symptoms of altitude DCS can occur after return to ground level whether they were present inflight or not.

A viable DCS treatment resource is the Diver's Alert Network (DAN), which can direct the pilot to properly manage the patient and direct the flight to the nearest hyperbaric therapy center. The DAN telephone number is 919-684-9111.

7.10 PREVENTION OF ALTITUDE-INDUCED DCS

Altitude DCS is a potential risk on every flight exceeding FL180, or after any SCUBA diving activities. The prevention options for altitude DCS are as listed:

- **Cabin pressurization**
- **Denitrogenation by pre-breathing 100% oxygen**
- **Ascend to altitude slowly**
- **Avoid unnecessary strenuous activity prior to flights above FL180 & 24 hours after the flight**
- **Limit altitude exposure to lower pressures**
- **No SCUBA diving prior to any flights**

Cabin pressurization was specifically designed to assist aviators in preventing DCS and hypoxia, but always be aware DCS is a potential risk in the event of a sudden loss of pressurization.

Denitrogenation is the pre-breathing of 100% oxygen prior to high-altitude flights, and is one of the most significant scientific breakthroughs regarding DCS protection in aviators. Pre-breathing is the main safety precaution used in high-altitude chamber training, and has proven to be a reliable DCS prevention method.

100% Oxygen pre-breathing promotes elimination of body tissue nitrogen. Extensive USAF School of Aerospace Medicine research has shown pre-breathing oxygen for 30 minutes prior to ascent reduces the risk of DCS for 10- to 30-minute exposures to altitudes from FL180 to FL430. Uninterrupted oxygen usage has to be continued without interruption inflight to maximize protection against altitude DCS. However, it's critical to understand breathing 100% oxygen only during flight (ascent, enroute, and descent) does not decrease the risk of DCS and must not be relied upon for adequate DCS protection. Additionally, while pre-breathing is effective it is usually not considered a logistically viable nor inexpensive option for most civilian aviation operations. At the present time, pre-breathing is only used by military, space missions, and high-altitude chamber operations.

Slow ascent simply allows the body to naturally off gas nitrogen as N2 molecules expand.

Unnecessary strenuous activity may aggravate negative pressure in the large joints involved in the movement, predisposing that joint for N2 bubble evolution.

Limiting exposure to altitudes above FL180 may prevent N2 bubble evolution from occurring, as the longer an aviator lingers at altitude the greater the chance for N2 bubble development. Should an aviator experience an inflight rapid decompression, they should not fly for at least 24 hours following the incident; also remain vigilant for a potential onset of delayed symptoms of altitude DCS. If delayed symptoms or signs of DCS are experienced, seek proper medical attention ASAP.

No SCUBA diving prior to any flights is of urgent importance to avoid altitude DCS at any altitude, as discussed previously. The following are DAN recommendations regarding SCUBA diving-to-flight times:

- After *single, no-decompression dives,* **12-hour minimum wait to fly**
- After *multiple no-decompression dives per day* or *multiple days of diving,* **18-hour minimum wait to fly**
- After *dives requiring decompression stops,* a **"substantially longer-than-18-hour" wait time to fly is suggested (the Professional Association of Diving Instructors say at least 24 hours is recommended)**

A significant note is waiting these specific times comes with *no guarantees* the individual will not experience DCS. The longer one waits to fly, the better chance they have of not getting altitude DCS.

Let us examine an incident where diving and flying without waiting resulted in the onset of altitude DCS:

Incident Review – May 2019: A man from Frisco, TX, flew to Bali to fulfill a desire to learn deep diving in the ocean. He made his final dive shortly before leaving on his return trip, the first leg of which was uneventful. On the second leg flying from South Korea to Texas, he noticed all of his joints started to hurt. Upon arrival to DFW, he was feeling dizzy while walking through the terminal and eventually collapsed on the terminal floor. The man was rushed to the hospital, ultimately being diagnosed with DCS. He was treated successfully with a five-hour hyperbaric therapy protocol.

Analysis: The man flew to Bali to learn to ocean dive, and during dive training was most likely warned of the dangers of SCUBA diving and immediately flying, which he chose to ignore.

Conclusion: This incident is a perfect example of why rules are made to be followed, not broken. Part of every SCUBA diver's training includes appropriate underwater decompression measures to follow, as well as diving-to-flight interval times. The only advocate who can ensure rules are followed to minimize DCS occurrence is the person themselves.

Conclusion

The opportunity for evolved gas problems is present on virtually every flight above FL180, pressurized or not, and any flight to any altitude following SCUBA diving. Familiarize yourself with the signs and symptoms of altitude DCS and monitor all aircraft crewmembers and passengers (including yourself) whenever cabin altitude exceeds FL180. Even if flying a pressurized aircraft, altitude DCS may occur resulting from inadvertent loss of pressurization.

If delayed symptoms or signs of altitude DCS are experienced, seek appropriate medical support immediately and do not fly again until medically cleared to do so. Remember breathing 100% oxygen during flight without oxygen pre-breathing does not prevent altitude DCS. Don't disregard symptoms or signs resolving during descent, as this may confirm the presence of altitude DCS.

Chapter 7 Core Competency Questions

1. Which law dictates the mechanism behind evolved gas disorders?
2. Which atmospheric gas evolves into bubbles to create evolved gas disorders?
3. What is the critical Risk Value above which evolved gas issues are prevalent?
4. For someone equilibrated to sea level, what altitude represents the threshold for evolved gas problems?
5. Which type of DCS (Type I or Type II) is most likely to occur in aviators?
6. Which type of DCS (Type I or Type II) is most likely to be life threatening?
7. Which presentation of DCS is most likely to occur in aviators?
8. Which presentation of DCS is the least likely to occur and also the most dangerous?

9.   Doing what prior to flight increases the probability of DCS exponentially?

10. What is the number one step in treatment of suspected DCS?

11. What aircraft system provides the best prevention measure against DCS?

12. What medical professional should be standing by to receive DCS patients?

13. What the four presentations of DCS?

8. OXYGEN EQUIPMENT AND OXYGEN SYSTEM INSPECTION

Oxygen equipment development has paralleled aircraft performance evolution. Without supplemental life-support systems humans become the limitation for aircraft performance, and from the earliest days of aviation aviators quickly learned human physiological performance needs to be enhanced to fly in more challenging environments. Therefore, the proper use of supplemental oxygen inflight is one of the most important components for humans to fly in hostile environments of higher altitude.

Unfortunately, in many cases aircrew oxygen equipment knowledge in pilots is either lacking or ignored for a variety of reasons. In observations of aviation operations, the majority of pilots do not demonstrate superior knowledge regarding routine inspections, handling, configuring, storing, or in some cases even when to effectively deploy an oxygen mask. A pilot's oxygen mask is the <u>one</u> piece of equipment on board the aircraft specifically designed to save their life in the event of a high-altitude decompression or smoke and fumes contingency, and therefore <u>must</u> be intimately familiar with all aspects of this crucial piece of equipment. An oxygen mask should be considered the pilot's "friend" as opposed to their adversary or something to fear.

In this chapter, we will discuss:

1. Dangerous assumptions regarding oxygen equipment
2. Purpose of oxygen equipment
3. Forms of aircraft oxygen storage
4. Aircraft oxygen systems
5. Aircraft oxygen system safety
6. Aircraft oxygen delivery systems
7. Aircraft oxygen breathing systems
8. Smoke hoods
9. FAA oxygen equipment use regulations
10. Preflight and inflight oxygen equipment inspection

8.1 DANGEROUS ASSUMPTIONS REGARDING OXYGEN EQUIPMENT

Pilots typically perform a thorough preflight inspection of their aircraft. They check the tires for wear, control surfaces for unobstructed movement, avionics and communications systems, engine function, brakes, yet few take the time to thoroughly check their oxygen equipment. Why would a conscientious pilot carefully check every mechanical device on the aircraft, yet fail to thoroughly inspect the *one system on the aircraft designed to save their life in an inflight emergency?* Having trained and conversed with thousands of aviators from virtually every type of aviation operation imaginable, the following *dangerous, yet common, assumptions* appear to permeate the aviation industry regarding oxygen systems:

- Oxygen never needs to be used below 10,000 feet.
- The oxygen system is in perfect working condition
- Adequate oxygen is available in emergency oxygen walk-around bottles
- The maintenance crew has checked the oxygen system
- The bleed and dump valves are adjusted per operating instructions
- The pilot before me likely checked the oxygen equipment

The major problem aviators face when assuming the above is they will not find out if those assumptions were correct or not until an inflight emergency occurs, and they truly need their oxygen equipment to work perfectly. Unfortunately, documented fatal accident sequences have proven over and over again those assumptions to be false.

In 2019, <u>Business and Commercial Aviation</u> author Patrick R. Veillette studied 100 records submitted to the NASA Aviation Safety Reporting System (ASRS) from 2016 and 2017 involving incidents in which oxygen masks were employed. The study revealed in 29 of those incidents the oxygen system failed to operate as expected, and in seven of those incidents the oxygen mask or oxygen hose *physically failed.* Had a proper oxygen equipment inspection been performed, those issues would have been caught and/or repaired prior to flight.

8.2 PURPOSE OF OXYGEN EQUIPMENT

Generally considered an *emergency system,* aircrew oxygen equipment was designed to allow aviators to ascent to altitudes humans were not developed to optimally perform. As we know by now, the increased percentage of inhaled oxygen allows our bodies to maintain normal function in the zone of physiological deficiency above 10,000 feet.

Supplemental oxygen systems can allow small, unpressurized aircraft operators to climb over weather, terrain or obstacles, or gain better fuel consumption rates at higher altitudes; in these circumstances aircraft oxygen systems can be considered as a "get me up" system. To this end, most general aviation oxygen equipment is more comfortable for extended use, but less robust and not designed for use at extreme altitudes above FL250.

For the pilots of larger, pressurized passenger-carrying aircraft, the oxygen system is designed to be used in the event of an inflight emergency in which supplemental oxygen is required to enable the pilots to maintain full physiological or psychological function. These systems are very robust, made to don quickly, and designed to seal tightly and deliver oxygen under pressure if necessary. As a result of their ability to fit tight to virtually any face, they are not designed for <u>comfort</u> as much as <u>function</u>. These masks are not only uncomfortably tight, but communication with ATC and crewmembers is usually impaired as well. This makes their use for extended periods unfavorable as these masks tend to be uncomfortable, which runs contrary to FAA regulatory continuous oxygen-use requirements specifying pilots remain on oxygen under certain conditions (to be covered later in this chapter).

8.3 FORMS OF AIRCRAFT OXYGEN STORAGE

Aircraft equipped with fixed-place or portable oxygen equipment generally fly either pressurized or unpressurized flights at altitudes in excess of 10,000 feet.

The methods in which oxygen is stored onboard aircraft takes one of three forms:

- Gaseous
- Liquid
- Chemical or solid-state
- On-board oxygen generating system (OBOGS)

Gaseous oxygen systems are considered either high or low-pressure, with high-pressure oxygen cylinders the most common civilian oxygen systems. Low-pressure oxygen cylinders are almost exclusively used by military aviation operations. The most common type of oxygen used on aircraft is *Aviator's Breathing Oxygen*, which is formulated to meet the following criteria:

- Grade A Type 1, 99.5% pure oxygen
- Must not contain more than .005 mg of water vapor at 68 degrees F
- Should be odorless, colorless, and tasteless
- Must be cryogenic oxygen (the purest form)

Aviator's Breathing Oxygen is known to be extremely dry (little water vapor), which can dry nasal and oral passages with extended use.

Liquid oxygen systems are, once again, almost exclusively military equipment.

Chemical or solid-state oxygen systems are a solid mixture of chemicals which create an oxygen-rich gas when blended together.

On-Board Oxygen Generating Systems are molecular sieves filtering out gases and contaminants other-than-oxygen, allowing the aviator to breathe an unlimited supply of oxygen. OBOGS are generally military systems, but some have been developed for civilian use as well.

8.4 AIRCRAFT OXYGEN SYSTEMS

Aircraft oxygen systems are based on the forms of oxygen: *gas, liquid, chemical, or OBOGS* and need to be constructed with appropriately matching components to ensure proper operation. Aircraft oxygen equipment systems can be simple or sophisticated, but they all have the same basic components consisting of a storage system with pressure gauge, pressure regulating valves, plumbing, delivery system, and breathing system.

For pressurized passenger-carrying aircraft, the oxygen equipment normally consists of gaseous containers secured within the aircraft and filled or serviced through an exterior fuselage port.

Fixed oxygen systems offer longer duration times; however, actual times depend upon the size and number of oxygen cylinders in the system, and volume of occupants using the system.

Light aircraft normally flying below 10,000 feet often use portable oxygen equipment in order to save weight and avoid bulk problems. Portable oxygen cylinders are normally limited in oxygen supply duration. Typical breathing time for four people at 18,000 feet is in the range of 1-1/2 hours using a 22-cubic foot container.

Let us examine the individual oxygen systems based of forms of oxygen storage.

Gaseous Oxygen Systems

Gaseous oxygen systems using high-pressure oxygen cylinders are typically color-coded bright green. These systems are considered full at 1,800 – 2,000 psi, and serviceable down to 200 psi.

An aviator should try to avoid breathing an oxygen cylinder down to completely empty, as contaminants may enter the cylinder and would require purging by qualified technicians.

Low-pressure oxygen cylinders typically used by the military are color-coded bright yellow. These systems are considered full at 400 – 450 psi, and are serviceable down to 100 psi. Do not confuse civilian yellow air cylinders with aviation oxygen cylinders as those generally contain nothing more than compressed air, which is not what an aviator needs to breathe at altitude.

Commercial aircraft typically use gaseous aviator's oxygen as their primary oxygen source as gaseous oxygen provides the purest form of oxygen.

Liquid Oxygen Systems

Liquid oxygen (LOX) converter systems are another "military-only" system, and has the advantage of being light-weight, compact, and very dangerous as the boiling point of liquid oxygen is minus 297 degrees F. Liquid oxygen maintains an expansion ratio of 860:1. The compact size makes these systems ideal for fighter and trainer aircraft, but LOX systems are also used in large tanker, transport and bomber aircraft as well. LOX converters can range in size from 5 to 35 liters, and operate at pressures from 60 to 300 psi.

Chemical or Solid-State Oxygen Systems

Chemical oxygen generators release oxygen via chemical reaction, and are primarily used for *passenger emergency oxygen* purposes in civilian aircraft. These devices are not used for crew oxygen purposes as they do not deliver 100% oxygen. Once ignited, a sodium-chlorate compound mixes with small amounts of barium peroxide and potassium perchlorate, which thermally decompose and release oxygen. Because the chemical reaction happens at extreme temperatures, the canister can reach temperatures of 500 degrees F. Once activated the device cannot be stopped until all chemicals have been depleted, and continuously deliver oxygen for 12 to 22 minutes.

Oxygen candles, also known as chlorate candles, contain a mix of sodium chlorate and iron powder. These devices work similarly to chemical oxygen generators.

On-Board Oxygen Generating Systems (OBOGS)

On-board oxygen generating systems were developed for military aircraft use in the 1980's as a source of limitless oxygen, with varying degrees of success. OBOGS has since been developed for very limited use in civilian aircraft as well, but as yet has not been embraced by the civilian aviation community on a wide-spread basis.

The OBOGS system works by purifying air drawn from the aircraft's engine compressor (bleed air) before it reaches combustion. The air is run through a series of molecular scrubbers, or *sieve beds*, removing nitrogen and other contaminants, and delivers at or above 93% oxygen. Current military OBOGS system operations require a back-up supply of gaseous 100% oxygen in case of OBOGS system failure.

8.5 AIRCRAFT OXYGEN SYSTEM SAFETY

Any time people work around aircraft oxygen systems, there are some safety items to keep in mind:

- Oxygen supports combustion
  - o Ensure aircraft is properly grounded during oxygen servicing – no smoking in area
- Grease and oil must be kept away from oxygen equipment
  - o This includes oil or petroleum based cosmetics and lip balms
- Handle oxygen cylinders and valves carefully
- Keep oxygen equipment clean
- Protect your oxygen mask from direct sunlight and dust
- Chemical cylinders can get extremely hot
  - o Chemical cylinders have caused burns
- Exercise extreme caution around liquid oxygen systems (LOX)
  - o LOX is highly dangerous and should be avoided

When servicing aircraft oxygen systems:

- Use only qualified personnel.
- Aircraft electrical switches need to be turned off.
- No ground powered equipment should be operating within 50 feet of aircraft.
- Ensure aircraft is not being serviced with fuel, oil, or anti-ice fluids at the same time.
- No combustibles should be evident in the servicing area.

On oxygen cylinders, ensure the *hydrostatic test date* is current. The cylinders should be tested to 1.67 times maximum cylinder pressure (2,000 psi tank is tested to 3,340 psi). This test date should be stamped on the side of the bottle.

8.6 AIRCRAFT OXYGEN DELIVERY SYSTEMS

Aircraft oxygen delivery systems, more commonly known as *oxygen regulators,* are designed to meter the flow of oxygen to the aviator depending on altitude and environmental circumstances. These systems are separated into three main categories:

- Continuous flow
- Diluter-demand
- Pressure-demand

Continuous-Flow Regulators

Continuous-flow oxygen regulators are mechanically simple devices which supply aviators with a *continuous* flow of 100% oxygen. The rate of flow is typically adjusted and measured in liters-per-minute. Normally flow-rate may be adjusted manually; however, some regulators utilize an altitude-sensing aneroid to adjust flow-rate automatically. The rate-of-flow is normally set to one liter per 10,000 foot altitude (i.e. 1.5 liters/15,000 feet, 2.0 liters/20,000 feet, etc.)

Continuous flow oxygen regulators will deliver oxygen to the aviator whether inhaling or exhaling, in turn making these regulators inefficient and of relatively short-duration. This also limits their effectiveness to a maximum ceiling of FL250, dependent on the breathing system used.

Continuous flow oxygen regulators are mainly used in unpressurized general aviation aircraft.

Diluter-Demand Oxygen Regulators

Diluter-demand oxygen regulators, as the name implies, provides the aviator oxygen only when <u>inhaled or demanded.</u> A lever usually enables the aviator to set the regulator to automatically provide a mixture of cabin air and oxygen, or purely 100% oxygen. The lever providing this function is referred to as the *auto-mix lever*, and allows the aviator to select either *Normal (mixed) or 100% Oxygen* settings. The diluter-demand oxygen regulator is designed to provide varying amounts of oxygen dependent on altitude, thereby making oxygen usage more efficient and less wasteful. As a result of this efficiency, diluter-demand regulators may be safely used to FL350. Federal Aviation Regulations (FARs) state diluter-demand oxygen regulators may be used to FL400; however, FL400 should be considered the emergency cabin altitude for these regulators, and not for standard operations.

The main selection difference between the two settings is *normal oxygen* is used in normal operational settings, where conserving oxygen is beneficial. The regulator will automatically adjust the percentage of inhaled oxygen to maintain near-Sea Level physiological equivalency for the aviator. *100% Oxygen* is selected to isolate the aviator from possible smoke, fumes, or high-altitude loss-of-pressurization situations where conservation of oxygen is not the goal, but preservation of life is.

The main caveat in allowing for oxygen to flow on-demand is the fit of the oxygen mask. The oxygen mask must be sealed to the face air-tight so as to generate the proper amount of negative pressure in the mask to cause the demand diaphragm to open, allowing a flow of oxygen to the mask. Failure to properly fit the mask will not allow the regulator to operate to specifications.

Pressure-Demand Oxygen Regulators

Pressure-demand oxygen regulators are designed to operate the same as diluter-demand regulators, with the additional benefit of adding *positive pressure*. A positive pressure application of oxygen to the oxygen mask enables the aviator's lungs to be pressurized with oxygen, which raises the partial pressure of oxygen at the alveolar level, therefore increasing oxygen transfer to the bloodstream at high altitudes. Pressure-breathing oxygen may cause its own physiological problems, such as hyperventilation, fatigue, communication difficulties and physical effects in lung tissue.

The pressurized flow of oxygen may be manually controlled or function automatically on some regulators at a given altitude through aneroid action. Most often, pressure-demand oxygen regulators automatically deliver 100% oxygen under pressure around FL300. Pressure may also be manually selected to decrease recovery time from hypoxia, and force smoke & fumes out of the mask.

As a result of positive pressure, the operational ceiling of pressure-demand oxygen regulators is raised to FL400 in civilian oxygen equipment, and FL450 in most military equipment. The absolute emergency ceiling with *any* pressure-demand oxygen equipment is limited to FL500, at which maximum pressure would provide the physiological equivalent of 10,000'. The main limiting factor is lung tissue simply cannot withstand more pressure without rupturing. Federal Aviation Regulations (FARs) state pressure-demand oxygen regulators are unrestricted in terms of altitude use; however, FL450 should be considered the_emergency cabin altitude for civilian pressure-demand regulators, and not for standard operations.

8.7 AIRCRAFT OXYGEN BREATHING SYSTEMS

Oxygen masks must match the capabilities of and be compatible with the aircraft oxygen delivery systems. It is crucial the oxygen mask connector perfectly mate with the oxygen regulator connector, or the integrity of the entire system will be compromised. Many aircraft accidents have occurred resulting from a private pilot trying to make an oxygen mask work with a different type of oxygen regulator, literally duct taping the pieces together. Full functionality of oxygen equipment can only be assured using Original Equipment Manufacturer (OEM) parts. Supplemental oxygen should be used any time the cabin altitude exceeds 10,000 feet, to improve night vision above 5,000 feet, or *any time* an aviator feels they would benefit from its use.

Continuous-Flow Breathing Systems

Continuous-flow breathing systems, or oxygen masks, may either *oro-nasal* or *nasal cannula*. *Oro-nasal oxygen masks* do not provide an air tight face seal, which permits the aviator to exhale around the face piece or through small ports or openings designed to allow for exhalation, as well as dilute the oxygen with ambient air. The face-piece sits on the face over the nose and under the lips, such as passenger-style oxygen masks on commercial aircraft. Most continuous-flow masks currently in operation use a rebreather bag. This plastic bag is attached to the mask and enables the aviator to repurpose part of their exhaled oxygen. The oxygen hose typically contains a flow indicator enabling the aviator to confirm oxygen is flowing through the hose. Oro-nasal masks provide maximum effectiveness up to FL250, and are not meant to isolate the aviator from smoke or fumes.

Airline drop-down units, also known as "Dixie Cup" oxygen masks, are phase-sequential continuous-flow mask, which looks similar to general aviation oro-nasal oxygen masks. However, both masks function differently, as the phase-sequential mask allows the user to go to higher altitudes. This mask uses a series of one-way ports which allow a mixture of 100% oxygen and cabin air into the mask. Exhalation is vented out of the mask, and as a result the bag does not inflate. This mask can be safely used at emergency altitudes up to FL400, but is not suitable to be worn for cockpit crew functions.

Nasal cannulas are typically plastic tubing, suspended on an aviator's head by wrapping over the ears with the tubing routed under the nose, where two small ports are inserted into each nostril. 100% oxygen will obviously be diluted by inhaling air through the mouth, which makes these breathing systems scientifically uncertain as to the quality and mixture of oxygen entering the body. Therefore, nasal cannulas provide maximum effectiveness up to FL180, and not meant to isolate the aviator from smoke or fumes.

Diluter-Demand Breathing Systems

Diluter-demand breathing systems are designed and intended to accommodate an air-tight seal to the face, without which the mask will not build the necessary negative pressure to allow the regulator to flow oxygen. Diluter-demand masks should also be sealed to retain all inhaled oxygen, keep out smoke and fumes, and not be diluted by ambient air intrusion. The diluter-demand mask fits over the nose and under the lower lip or chin, and provides more efficiency resulting in higher altitude capabilities than most continuous-flow masks. It is essential diluter-demand masks be properly fitted to the head by an adequate harness and the masks be fitted with tension adjustments for the aviator to maintain an air-tight seal to the face. The higher the aviator flies, the more crucial this seal becomes.

Diluter-demand masks provide maximum effectiveness up to FL350, and are effective isolating the aviator from smoke and fumes.

Pressure-Demand Breathing Systems

Pressure-demand breathing systems are designed and intended to accommodate an air-tight seal to the face, similar to the diluter-demand masks. The *Inhalation/exhalation valve* designed into the mask is designed to allow oxygen pressure build-up within the mask, thus supplying oxygen under pressure to the lungs. Most civilian pressure-demand masks fit over the nose and under the lower lip, while military masks fit over the nose and under the chin for more long-term comfort.

Virtually all pressure-demand oxygen masks currently used in commercial and corporate aviation are *quick-don* oxygen masks, which self-adjust to a tight fit for all face-types effectively eliminating the need to meticulously adjust and fit the mask. This self-adjustment is attained through a pressurized harness that expands around an aviator's head when activated, and contracts to a tight fit when released. As a result of their self-adjusting, tight-fitting nature, quick-don pressure-demand masks are extremely effective for emergency use, but usually extremely uncomfortable for regulatory and long-term wear. As a result of their efficiency, quick-don pressure-demand masks provide maximum effectiveness up to FL400 to FL450, depending on the model, and emergency use up to FL500.

Most quick-don oxygen masks have the oxygen regulator built in the face piece, eliminating the need for an additional component in the cockpit. While effective, most quick-don oxygen regulators are difficult-to-impossible to see when the mask is one the face, necessitating the ability to operate "by feel" as opposed to visually. Familiarity with one's oxygen equipment is paramount to ensure the mask is configured properly under any and all conditions. Any pilot should instantly be able to visually confirm whether the oxygen switch settings are correct or not.

Most commercial and corporate aviation operations maintain smoke goggles for use with the oxygen masks. Smoke goggles may either be integrated into the mask, clip onto the mask, or worn as separate component. Ensure smoke goggles fit and seal correctly to prevent visual impairment, and the goggles are not scratched to the point incoming light refracts off the lens prohibiting vision.

Practice Donning the Oxygen Mask and Smoke Goggles

Current FAA regulations stipulate a quick-don oxygen be donned, properly sealed and configured in five seconds or less with one hand. In order to accomplish this rather difficult task, it is essential aviators' practice with their specific oxygen equipment in their own aircraft. The ability to don the quick-don oxygen mask in a timely manner every time and under any conditions requires muscle-memory and pre-rehearsed choreography.

Most quick-don mask harnesses do not fit easily over headsets, eyeglasses or sunglasses, requiring the pilot to remove those items first. The pilot needs to ensure no cockpit obstructions prevent retrieval of the oxygen mask inflight, as well as ensure nothing is routinely placed on the oxygen mask container such as iPads, charts, lunchboxes, etc. It is entirely possible visual impairment from smoke, wind-blast or flying debris may present itself, which requires the pilot to be able to appropriately respond by feel.

Practicing attaching or donning smoke goggles is a critical skill as well, as most recurrent training curriculum doesn't require it. Ensuring smoke goggles work with your prescription or sun glasses is relevant information to acquire prior to a smoke incident at altitude. The donning process should also be practiced with eyes closed, as visibility in the cockpit could be compromised.

Included in this emergency training should be a contingency plan for oxygen equipment failure, as few aircrews consider that possibility, although such cases have occurred.

8.8 SMOKE HOODS

Smoke hoods are separate life-support components some personal and professional flight crews use as a supplement or back-up emergency system in the event of fire or smoke in the aircraft. Smoke hoods provide visibility and limited-time breathing ability in dense smoke environments, and should be considered for use in all aircraft.

Many professional aviators feel their oxygen masks and smoke goggles are enough to successfully navigate an inflight smoke event; however, not all crewmembers may have immediate access to their oxygen masks. The possibility also exists the cockpit and cabin crewmembers may have to evacuate through a smoke- and toxic fumes-filled cabin once on the ground, which most fixed oxygen masks cannot help with.

Smoke hoods are available in a wide variety of configurations, from simple charcoal-filter hoods to full pressurized oxygen-fed devices. All smoke hoods feature a rubber neck-seal, preventing smoke and fumes from entering the breathing space. All hoods feature some degree of heat-resistant head protection, with a heat-resistant visor. The most robust smoke hoods can withstand 1,800 degrees F up to five seconds.

For breathing protection, the simplest smoke hoods feature a charcoal filter providing smoke and fumes protection for a limited amount of time. More sophisticated smoke hoods known as *PBE's, or portable breathing equipment,* provide hood-injected oxygen via pressurized gaseous oxygen or chemical oxygen generators. Obviously smoke hoods with oxygen-fed capability are effective for only as long as oxygen supply lasts. Of particular note is if chemical oxygen generator smoke hoods are used, the aviator must be aware the oxygen generators may get hot enough to cause burns on their neck, as the following incident portrays:

Incident Review – October 2014: An Airbus A330-200 was being pushed back by ground crew from the park position when smoke developed in the cabin. The flight attendants donned their chemical oxygen PBE's. One flight attendant's PBE self-ignited upon activation and caught fire, causing injuries and at which time the flight attendant promptly removed the PBE and threw it to the floor.

Analysis: Smoke developed on pushback, and the flight attendants followed Standard Operating Procedures by donning and activating their PBE's. One PBE caught on fire while on a flight attendant's head.

Conclusion: All emergency should be regularly inspected, and that fact was not clear with this incident. The flight attendants responded as trained, but no equipment involving any type of pyrotechnics is completely safe.

8.9 FAA OXYGEN EQUIPMENT USE REGULATIONS

The Federal Aviation Administration maintains rules governing the use of oxygen equipment on aircraft flight of all types and altitudes. This information is contained in Title 14 of the Code of Federal Regulations.

The following is an excerpt pertaining to **FAR Part 91 General Operating and Flight Rules** requiring use of oxygen equipment:

"§91.211 Supplemental Oxygen

(a) General. No person may operate a civil aircraft of U.S. registry –

1) At cabin pressure altitudes above 12,500 feet mean seal level (MSL) up to and including 14,000 feet (MSL) unless the required minimum flight crew is provided with and uses supplemental oxygen for that part of the flight at those altitudes that is more than 30 minutes duration;

2) At cabin pressure altitudes above 14,000 feet (MSL) unless the required minimum flight crew is provided with and uses supplemental oxygen during the entire flight at those altitudes; and

3) At cabin pressure altitudes above 15,000 feet (MSL) unless each occupant of the aircraft is provided with supplemental oxygen.

    a. Pressurized cabin aircraft. (1) No person may operate a civil aircraft of U.S. registry with a pressurized cabin –

    b. At flight altitudes above flight level 250 unless at least a 10-minute supply of supplemental oxygen, in addition to any oxygen required to satisfy paragraph (a) of this section, is available for each occupant of the aircraft for use in the event that a descent is necessitated by loss of pressurization; and

    c. At flight altitudes above flight level 350 unless one pilot at the controls of the airplane is wearing and using an oxygen mask that is secured and sealed and that either supplies oxygen at all times or automatically supplies oxygen whenever the cabin pressure altitude of the airplane exceeds 14,000 feet (MSL), except that one pilot need not wear and use an oxygen mask while at or below flight level 410 if there are two pilots at the controls and each pilot has a quick-donning type of oxygen mask that can placed on the face with one hand from the ready position within 5 seconds, supplying oxygen and properly secured and sealed.

(2) Notwithstanding paragraph (b)(1)(ii) of this section, if for any reason at any time it is necessary for one pilot to leave the controls of the airplane when operating at flight altitudes above flight level 350, the remaining pilot at the controls shall put on and use an oxygen mask until the other pilot has returned to that crewmember's station."

The following is an excerpt pertaining to **FAR Part 135 Operating Requirements: Commuter and On Demand Operations and Rules Governing Persons On-Board Such Aircraft** requiring use of oxygen equipment:

"§ 135.89 – Pilot requirements: Use of oxygen.

(a) Unpressurized aircraft. Each pilot of an unpressurized aircraft shall use oxygen continuously when flying—

(1) At altitudes above 10,000 feet through 12,000 feet MSL for that part of the flight at those altitudes that is of more than 30 minutes duration; and

(2) Above 12,000 feet MSL.

(b) Pressurized aircraft.

(1) Whenever a pressurized aircraft is operated with the cabin pressure altitude more than 10,000 feet MSL, each pilot shall comply with paragraph (a) of this section.

(2) Whenever a pressurized aircraft is operated at altitudes above 25,000 feet through 35,000 feet MSL, unless each pilot has an approved quick-donning type oxygen mask—

(i)At least one pilot at the controls shall wear, secured and sealed, an oxygen mask that either supplies oxygen at all times or automatically supplies oxygen whenever the cabin pressure altitude exceeds 12,000 feet MSL; and

(ii) During that flight, each other pilot on flight deck duty shall have an oxygen mask, connected to an oxygen supply, located so as to allow immediate placing of the mask on the pilot's face sealed and secured for use.

(3) Whenever a pressurized aircraft is operated at altitudes above 35,000 feet MSL, at least one pilot at the controls shall wear, secured and sealed, an oxygen mask required by paragraph (b)(2)(i) of this section.

(4) If one pilot leaves a pilot duty station of an aircraft when operating at altitudes above 25,000 feet MSL, the remaining pilot at the controls shall put on and use an approved oxygen mask until the other pilot returns to the pilot duty station of the aircraft."

All pilots should adhere to the oxygen use rules set forth by the FAA. As uncomfortable as quick-don masks may be, wearing an oxygen mask at the right time could well be the difference between life and death.

8.10 PREFLIGHT AND INFLIGHT OXYGEN EQUIPMENT INSPECTION

It is incumbent on the captain of the flight to ensure the aircraft oxygen and other emergency equipment is inspected and prepared prior to flight. It is essential the equipment be ready to deploy at a moment's notice, with assurance knowing it will work as expected. This applies not only to the pilots' emergency equipment, but the equipment for the rest of the crew and passengers as well. While the captain is responsible to ensure emergency equipment is available and ready for use, they can and should designate the inspection tasks accordingly to the individual crewmembers.

The *SCREAM Check* is a preflight, inflight, or diagnostic check of an aviator's oxygen equipment. SCREAM stands for **S**upply, **C**onnections, **R**egulator, **E**mergency Equipment, **A**djustments to the mask, **M**ask condition. This check should be:

- Performed prior to every flight to ensure the aircraft oxygen system is prepared for emergencies
- Performed inflight if oxygen equipment is deployed for use
- Performed inflight if the oxygen system is not operating correctly to identify the specific problem

As with any routine inspection, starting and ending with the same checklist components each and every time an inspection is conducted ensures inspection familiarity and consistent compliance. Although all preflight checklists list some manner of oxygen inspection, following the *SCREAM* checklist listed below ensures the entire oxygen system is operational and deployment-ready.

S = Supply

Check the aircraft oxygen supply to ensure:

- A continuous supply of oxygen to the oxygen masks. This involves physically breathing through the mask and ensuring the oxygen pressure gauge "back-fills" to fill the void in the oxygen line caused by inhaling oxygen. If the pressure gauge does not back-fill, the main oxygen supply valve may be turned off. This check may also be accomplished by depressing the Emergency Pressure button for five seconds.

- The volume of oxygen pressure available in the oxygen cylinders is sufficient to provide sufficient oxygen to all crew and passengers for any and all foreseeable inflight contingencies which may occur. Each aircraft should carry an *Oxygen Consumption Data Chart* depicting how much oxygen is required for any assigned altitude depending on number of occupants, and the flight should not be allowed to progress until those volumes are met. Medical and/or therapeutic oxygen should be checked, if applicable.

- Oxygen masks have not been previously deployed, as referenced by the following incident:

Incident Review – May 2013: A Boeing 737 was enroute when it lost cabin pressure. The pilots donned their oxygen masks, and passenger oxygen masks were deployed in the cabin. The aircraft diverted and made an uneventful landing, and maintenance crews re-stowed the oxygen masks.

The FAA audited that incident, and determined the aircraft made a subsequent 123 flights before company maintenance checked the oxygen bottles, and the following two days after the incident were flown two of four portable oxygen units unserviceable.

Analysis: The aircraft had an inflight incident, deployed oxygen masks, and landed. According to FAA rules, any time oxygen masks are deployed inflight, the oxygen system **must** be checked prior to the next flight.

Conclusion: The aircraft flew 123 times prior to maintenance checking the oxygen bottles and portable oxygen bottles. This indicates 123 Captains failed to ensure the oxygen system and emergency equipment was serviceable prior to flight, and the airline was fined by the FAA.

Not only should oxygen supply be checked prior to take-off, but inflight as well. Oxygen cylinders and connections are not immune from leakage, and having an oxygen system leak down inflight compromises inflight safety, as the following incident shows:

Incident – November 2013: A Boeing 767-300 was enroute at FL340 on the Atlantic Ocean 450 nautical miles South East of New York when the crew declared an emergency. The crew realized the oxygen pressure gauge read "zero pressure", which prompted the crew to descent to 10,000 feet for the remainder of the flight.

Conclusion: One would assume oxygen pressure was not lost instantaneously, and presumably the crew may have had the opportunity to see the system leaking down prior to this point. Although the cause of the leak is unclear, in many cases an oxygen system leak is caused by a faulty oxygen mask and therefore mitigatable inflight. Had the crew been checking oxygen supply routinely inflight, this incident may have been negated.

C = Connections

Physically check the oxygen mask hose and aircraft oxygen supply hose coupling to ensure proper connection. Physically check the microphone intercom connection as well. Failure to ensure proper connections may result in loss of oxygen or communications inflight.

R = Regulator

The oxygen regulator should be given a functional check to ensure:

- All switches work-as-expected.
- The flow indicator works.
- Oxygen flows under pressure.
- No contaminants on the regulator face or ports.
- No missing screws.
- No illegible writing on tags.

The regulator should be placed in the "emergency flow" position with the mask tight to the face, and breath held. If the regulator is operating properly, the flow indicator should indicate "no flow". If a flow of oxygen is detected, the regulator may have an internal leak.

E = Emergency Equipment

All aircraft personal emergency equipment should be checked to ensure proper placement and operation. This check includes portable walk-around oxygen bottles, protective breathing equipment (PBE's), smoke hoods, and smoke goggles.

A = Adjustments to the Mask

If oxygen masks require personal adjustment to ensure proper fit, the mask needs be adjusted prior to flight. A number of inflight fatalities have occurred with an aviator donning an oxygen mask during a smoke or altitude event, only to realize too late the mask wasn't properly sealed. With regards to quick-don oxygen masks, this step may be skipped as quick-don mask are self-adjusting.

M = Mask Condition

The oxygen mask itself needs to be inspected to ensure no damage and proper operation. These checks should include:

- Breathing into the mask to ensure proper operation of the inhalation/exhalation valve.
- Ensuring oxygen masks are set to 100% oxygen.
- No holes or tears in the face piece or mask hose.
- No missing components.
- No debris or clear plastic shipping covers in the mask cup.
- Ensuring the microphone/intercom works, as crew and ATC communication is essential in emergencies.
- Ensuring the pressure harness is not twisted and ready for deployment.

The following incidents show the crucial nature of ensuring oxygen equipment is ready-for-deployment:

Incident – August 2016: A Boeing 787-800 was enroute from Chicago, IL to Tokyo, Japan at FL380 760 nm NW of Seattle, WA when the cockpit crew noticed indications of decreasing pressure of the crew oxygen system. The crew consulted with dispatch and maintenance, and eventually decided to divert to Seattle. Subsequent maintenance checks revealed the captain's oxygen mask was leaking, causing the oxygen system to bleed down.

Incident – September 2016: An Airbus A330-300 was enroute from Rome, Italy to Philadelphia, PA at FL360 over the Atlantic Ocean when the crew reported a problem with the crew oxygen system and requested a diversion to Ireland. A short time later the crew declared an emergency reporting a lack of crew oxygen supply, and descended to 10,000 feet. Subsequent maintenance checks isolated an oxygen leak at the captain's oxygen mask, and the mask assembly was replaced.

Incident – July 2017: A commercial aircraft was enroute above FL350 when the first officer needed to use the restroom. The FO was returning to the cockpit when they heard a "whooshing" sound. The FO regained access to the cockpit to find the captain struggling to hold the oxygen mask together, as the mask hose had blown off the face piece. Repeated attempts were made to reattach the mask hose to no avail. The pilots noticed oxygen was rapidly depleting out of the system, so a descent and diversion were initiated.

Incident – November 2017: In cruise flight above FL350, the First Officer needed to use the restroom and left the cockpit. The Captain pulled his oxygen mask out of the storage container, and the mask fell apart in his hands. The mask hose/intercom connection was broken and dangling off the front of the face piece, and could not be reconnected. The pilots elected to perform an emergency descent.

Conclusion: Each one of these incidents may have prevented with a thorough oxygen equipment preflight check, saving inconvenient diversions, irritable passengers, and thousands of dollars in additional costs. Never take for granted "someone else" checked your equipment for you.

Conclusion

Aircraft oxygen systems are engineered to protect aviators to the maximum certified flight altitude of the aircraft. The oxygen masks and personal emergency equipment may never be used during an actual inflight emergency; however, should the equipment ever be needed it is essential the equipment function perfectly to ensure a safe conclusion to the incident. A pilot should *never* trust maintenance or the pilot before him checked the equipment properly, and should take personal initiative to ensure a proper oxygen and emergency equipment inspection is completed prior to every flight. A pilot must also ensure they have an adequate back-up plan should their primary oxygen equipment fail during emergency operations.

Chapter 8 Core Competency Questions

1. True or false: A pilot may be comfortable knowing maintenance checked their oxygen mask prior to flight.
2. Physiologically, supplemental oxygen should be used above what altitude?
3. Which two forms of oxygen storage systems are found on civilian aircraft?
4. Which type of oxygen is typically found on commercial aircraft?
5. Is it safe to use petroleum-based products around 100% oxygen?
6. What are the three types of aircraft oxygen delivery systems?
7. What is the purpose of pressure-demand regulators?
8. True or false: a smoke hood should always be used before a pilot dons an oxygen mask.
9. For Part 92 flight operations, above what altitude should a pilot be using supplemental oxygen?
10. What is the SCREAM Check?

9. AIRCRAFT FIRES AND TOXIC FUMES

Our everyday environment is permeated with airborne toxins, even though the majority of the time we remain unaware of their presence. In present-day society toxins may originate from second-hand smoke and vaping, paint, cleaning products, and industrial waste as well as micro-organisms such as mold, mildew, bacteria, viruses and dust mites.

Toxic contamination on aircraft may originate from both combustion and non-combustion sources; however, some of the most prolific producing sources of toxic fumes tend to be combustion, or fires. Research by Pratt and Whitney in 1953/1954 confirmed some chemicals used in aircraft engines and other systems do no harm to the human body at normal ambient temperatures; however, as soon as they get heated these substances become highly toxic.

The atmosphere of a fire can be deadly, making an understanding of environmental concerns surrounding active aircraft fires and the fumes produced is of fundamental importance to aviators. Fire can cause aircraft occupants to be exposed to heat, smoke, depleted oxygen, carbon monoxide and other gases such as cyanide, hydrogen chloride, and acrolein to name a few. Fluids, chemicals, and synthetic materials may release highly toxic gases increasing the possibility of inhalation injury to all on board.

Inflight non-combustion smoke, fume or odor events may present themselves without obvious visual or olfactory cues. Although some of these events may not be of major concern, potential adverse health effects to passengers and crew demand prompt and decisive action, and may require targeted and timely action to protect aircraft occupants. Professional aviation operations should ensure their emergency checklists specifically address recognition, differentiation and mitigation of fire, smoke, fumes or odors in the aircraft.

In this chapter we will discuss:

1. Toxic fumes in aviation
2. Contaminants from external sources
3. Contaminants from internal sources
4. Contaminants from aircraft systems
5. Aircraft fires and thermo-toxic environments
6. Pyrolytic toxicology

9.1 TOXIC FUMES IN AVIATION

The limited environment of an aircraft cabin can be a likely place for toxins to reside. These toxins may be introduced to the cabin environment through people, chemicals used for aircraft operation and maintenance, equipment malfunction or failure, altitude, or air-quality of the air space being flown through by inadvertent or intentional actions. Concerns have been expressed by passengers and crews alike regarding chemical contaminant exposure and potential adverse health effects. Depending on levels of exposure and individual tolerance, these contaminants may or may not actually cause health issues among those exposed.

Potential sources of airborne contamination in aircraft cabins may include the following:

- Ozone (O_3)
- Carbon dioxide (passengers exhaling CO_2)
- Carbon monoxide (CO from jet exhaust fumes or ambient airport air)
- Off-gassing from interior material and cleaning agents
- Allergens, infectious, or inflammatory agents
- Cabin pressurization
- Forest fires
- Volcanic ash
- De-icing fluid
- Particulate matter (including dust which contains microbes)
- Dry ice used to keep food cold
- Pyrethroid pesticides

Ground and flight crews, as well as passengers themselves can be sources of contaminants such as pesticides, bioeffluents, viruses, bacteria, allergens, and fungal spores.

The contaminants encountered inflight may come from external sources, internal sources, or aircraft systems.

9.2 CONTAMINANTS FROM EXTERNAL SOURCES

Contaminants originating from outside sources are drawn in the cabin through ventilation air provided to the cabin by the Environmental Control System (ECS) from ambient air around the aircraft. During the normal course-of-flight, an aircraft will encounter the following types of air:

- Ground-level air at departure or arrival airports
- Urban air aloft of the cities being flown from and to
- Tropospheric air
- Upper tropospheric and lower stratospheric air

Ground-level air can include emissions from local airport sources or urban pollution. These sources of contaminants will be encountered for a relatively short period of time with respect to the entirety of the flight. At airports, combustion-generated pollutants are emitted from aircraft jet engines and diesel-powered service vehicles. A key factor for airport-generated emissions is the amount of time the aircraft is on the ground and factors extending ground-time, such as traffic, inclement weather, or equipment malfunctions. Flight attendants may be at increased risk as they board the aircraft prior to and deplane after the passengers.

Urban air aloft varies with altitude, as expected. Virtually all air pollution has ground-level or low-altitude sources. This pollution mixes through the lower troposphere via wind blowing over rough ground surfaces causing turbulent mixing, and being sent in a vertical motion by the Sun heating the Earth's surface. The "well-mixed" layer extends from a few hundred to a few thousand meters above ground level, with pollutants declining steeply above those altitudes. Predictably, exposure to the well-mixed layer of pollution is very brief during most flights, only lasting for minutes after departure and before arrival.

Tropospheric air contamination may originate from forest fire smoke, volcanic ash, dust and industrial chemicals. While ECS filters provide a large degree of protection from environmental contaminants, odors may penetrate the cabin, particularly during flight through smoke or volcanic ash. Many cases of airliners reporting smoke-in-the-cockpit were, in reality, caused by forest fire smoke, while volcanic ash may infuse the fuselage with a sulfuric smell.

Upper tropospheric and lower stratospheric air's primary ambient air pollutant at airliner cruise altitudes is ozone, or O_3. Oxygen molecules (O_2) at altitude undergo photodissociation provided by UV radiation from the sun. Oxygen atoms combine with O_2 molecules to produce O_3. Ozone is reactive and decomposes relatively rapidly in the stratosphere by photodissociation, reaction with oxygen atoms, or catalytic destruction (reactions with nitrogen oxides or chlorine oxides).

At typical airliner cruise altitudes (FL290 to FL390), the average ozone concentration is much higher at high latitudes (greater than 60°N) than at low latitudes (approximately 30°N). Additionally, the effects of latitude and altitude causes O_3 to vary seasonally and fluctuates over short periods of time because of air exchange between the lower stratosphere and the upper troposphere. In airliners, exposure to O3 has been associated with adverse health effects: headaches, fatigue, shortness of breath, chest pains, nausea, coughing, pulmonary distress, and exacerbation of asthma.

Outdoor air exchange rates tend to be more effective in aircraft than in homes or commercial buildings. Air exchange rates in commercial aircraft range from 10 to 27 exchanges-per-hour, whereas U.S. residences and office buildings range from 0.2 to 2 air exchanges-per-hour. The more effective air-exchange rates in commercial aircraft tends to limit the adverse effects of ozone contamination. However, potentially high ozone concentrations in aircraft cabins compared with ordinary buildings may offset the effect of faster air exchange.

Catalytic ozone converters are designed to filter out the majority of ozone entering the ECS system, decomposing 90% to 98% of the O3 entering into the system. The designed useful life for catalytic ozone converters is 10,000 to 20,000 flight hours, however, particularly concerning is the potential for fouling of the converters by air-quality incidents. Sizeable exposures of the bleed-air system to aerosolized engine oil, hydraulic fluid, or even jet engine exhaust could possibly contribute to performance degradation of the system.

9.3 CONTAMINANTS FROM INTERNAL SOURCES

Sources of contaminants inside aircraft cabins are typically connected with the passengers and crew with regards to viruses, bacteria, bioeffluents, allergens, and spores. Human-produced contaminants are shed from clothing and skin or expelled from oral, nasal, or rectal orifices. Structural components of the aircraft, luggage, personal articles, food, and sanitation fluids can also be sources of vapors or particles. Additionally, surface residue on aircraft interior components may be sources of cleaning compounds, pesticides, or accumulated debris.

Through metabolic activity and personal sanitary habits, passengers and crewmembers may emit odors that others perceive as unpleasant, such as body odor, belching or passing flatus. Passengers and crew are the primary sources of CO2 in the cabin as well. Passengers may apply odor-producing products including nail polish, nail-polish remover, cologne, and perfume.

Airplane dust may contain minerals, metals, textile, paper and insulation fibers, combustion soot, nonvolatile organics, and various materials of biological origin (e.g., hair, skin flakes, and dander). Dust can be a vehicle for absorbed organic compounds, such as polycyclic aromatic hydrocarbons. In addition, airplane dust can include residues from cleaning agents and pesticides.

The aircraft cabin environment may influence individual perceptions of cabin air quality, as when cooler, drier, and clean air becomes permeated with even slight odors, those odors are more perceptible than warm and humid environments.

9.4 CONTAMINANTS FROM AIRCRAFT SYSTEMS

Contaminants originating from aircraft systems are typically resultant from combustion or pyrolysis of chemicals which perfuse the cabin bleed air. The bleed air may come from two different sources, depending on the aircraft and flight segment. Bleed air may be supplied by the aircraft engines, or could be supplied by the auxiliary power unit (APU). The APU is a small turbine engine usually located in the tail cone of the aircraft, and will provide bleed air when the main engines are not operating, or main-engine power demands in certain flight segments dictate bleed air cannot be spared.

Physiological issues can arise when fumes, aerosols, or smoke produced from fluids used in the operation and maintenance of the aircraft entered the ECS through engine bleed air. These chemical mixtures may contain *ultrafine particles,* which are very small airborne liquids and solids suspended in the air with diameters less than 0.1 micrometers. These particles are typically formed in copious amounts through pyrolysis of oil, coolants, cleaning and deicing agents, hydraulic fluid, and combustion of fossil fuels.

Notable events of high ultrafine-particle counts could be experienced when engine or ground-equipment exhaust enters the aircraft fuselage. In addition to catastrophic engine oil-seal failures, which are accompanied by visible smoke in the cabin, slowly leaking oil that comes into contact with hot ECS or engine components would result in ultrafine-particle formation that might not be perceived in the cabin air.

These particles may be inhaled into the deepest recesses of the lungs and pass directly into the bloodstream, and may produce symptoms such as stinging eyes and throat, tightness in the chest, and coughs, as well as many other physical and neurological symptomology.

Toxic exposure resulting from fumes, aerosols or smoke may occur with little-to-no warning or emergency notification. There are no current requirements for airborne toxic warning capabilities or alarm systems. The specific scenario may prevent access to adequate oxygen equipment for inhalation protection, and aviators must be cognizant of altered human performance indications, unusual smells and cargo contamination.

9.5 AIRCRAFT FIRES AND THERMO-TOXIC ENVIRONMENTS

Aircraft fires and thermo-toxic environments are incredibly frightening and dangerous scenarios to consider, but professional aviators must develop adequate procedures to mitigate emergencies of such nature. Development of fire, smoke, and fumes emergency procedures is better accomplished <u>before</u> the emergency occurs rather than <u>during</u> the emergency. Some considerations in development of those procedures are as follows:

- Egress efforts may be difficult
- Thermal injury
- Loss-of-pressurization places crew and passengers at risk
- Venting the aircraft may increase the rate of combustion
- Current ventilation systems increase toxic exposure
- Fear, panic and secondary trauma
- Large fuel stores present significant risk

Egress efforts can be difficult in smoke-filled environments simply from a lack-of-visibility. Disorientation resulting from thick smoke is to be expected, and could cause errors in orderly evacuation. Not every occupant of the aircraft will be trained in maintaining a low profile to stay under the smoke/fumes in the upper portion of the cabin, potentially hindering escape efforts by others. Fire location may prevent the use of some exits, requiring occupants to re-direct to other exits, in turn causing delay and confusion.

Thermal injury due to intense heat exposure may severely complicate evacuation and survival efforts. Burn depth, extent-of-injury, and anatomic location of burn victims may potentially render those individuals immobile, requiring additional care from rescuers and distracting care from other survivors.

Loss-of-pressurization may amplify the emergency as a result of lack-of-oxygen, temperature and windblast effects, creating increasing levels of confusion and panic. Hypoxic hypoxia may also increase the mortality rate of toxic exposure, or lower an individual's exposure tolerance levels to certain toxic products, particularly carbon monoxide.

Venting the aircraft may sound like a good theory to clear the fuselage of smoke; however, in reality such action could potentially increase oxygen availability to the fire source, thus increasing the intensity.

Current ventilation systems may transport fumes from one section of aircraft interior to another, thereby increasing the likelihood of personal exposure and injury.

Fear, panic and secondary trauma are components of most aircraft fire or thermo-toxic emergency scenarios, and require a practiced, coordinated response by the crew to ensure successful mitigation of the event. Passenger fear-leading-to-panic can foil the most comprehensive of plans, and the disposition of passengers must be strictly, thoroughly and rapidly enforced by the crew to prevent further mishap. Secondary trauma may result from passenger injury during aircraft exit or injury from incoming emergency response vehicles.

Large fuel stores exponentially increase the potential for disaster, as fuel is obviously flammable, explosive and dispersible should the aircraft fuel tanks rupture upon ground contact. Spraying flammable liquid over a crash-site would most definitely complicate survival and rescue efforts.

All aircraft fires will be battled using water and/or foam, both of which come with their own considerations and side-effects. Water used to cool fires inevitably turns to steam which can super-heat, becoming invisible to the naked eye. Super-heated steam may damage lungs, eyes and skin extremely rapidly. If water is blasted onto molten metal, the resulting reaction can be explosive dramatically worsening the situation.

Carbon dioxide foam typically deprives fires of oxygen, thus dousing the flames; however, using CO_2 extinguishers on burning metal can cause the metal to burn hotter. Another consideration is when the blast of air from the extinguisher hits the burning metal, the air may send flaming metal dust flying in all directions, exacerbating the emergency.

While aircraft crashes can be traumatizing events, fatalities are rarely caused by the impact itself. 80% of all survivable aircraft crash fatalities are instead causing by inhalation of toxic gases rather than impact or thermal injuries. Toxic fume build-up in the cabin tends to happen rapidly following impact, making egress or evacuation of paramount importance. According to FAA research, commercial aircraft should be evacuated in 90 seconds or less following crash impact, as after 90 seconds toxic fume build-up will increase mortality of the event.

As a cause of mortality, aircraft fires have been somewhat mitigated through use of less-combustible materials in the cabin. Natural materials such as wood and cloth have rapid rates of combustion, while newer materials such as plastics and urethanes improve fire resistance. Unfortunately, the use of unnatural or composite materials increases the likelihood of toxic chemical permeation in the event of fire. As the composite materials heat up, combustible gases are released. These gases being lighter-than-air, the natural tendency of those gases is to collect towards the top of the cabin, creating a breathing zone in the lower third of the cabin. As these composite gases continue to heat up to approximately 1,200+ degrees F, the gases ignite in what is known as *flashover*. At that point, mortality rates climb exponentially.

9.6 PYROLYTIC TOXICOLOGY

Thermal degradation and toxic production of combustible products will be determined via the temperature those products are burned at, so different toxins are produced by varying temperatures. Smoldering fires will have a more pronounced insidious onset of poisoning than a more intense, rapidly burning fire. In aircraft cabins, this translates to fires in inaccessible areas may contaminate without any obvious signs of a fire.

Carbon monoxide is the most common chemical product of incomplete combustion, and as mentioned in the chapter on hypoxia, is odorless, colorless and tasteless making CO difficult to detect during certain pyrolytic events. Remember, CO has a greater affinity to hemoglobin in red blood cells (RBC's) by a factor of some 250 times that of oxygen. As a result of increased affinity, a high level of carbon monoxide (CO) exposure isn't necessarily a prerequisite for high CO blood levels.

Once CO binds to hemoglobin, it becomes *carboxyhemoglobin,* or *CO-Hb.* Specific CO-Hb levels in the blood produce the following symptomology:

- 12% - 20%: Headache and weakness
- 20% - 30%: Weakness, dizziness, nausea
- 30% - 40%: Muscular coordination problems
- 55% - 75%: Coma and death

For aviation settings, it must be remembered that altitude-induced (hypoxic) hypoxia may exacerbate CO symptoms dramatically.

Cyanide (HCN) is a dangerous gas produced from burning urethane, wool, and some flame-retardant materials. Death may occur at relatively small toxicity levels, such as less than 3.3 to 5 micrograms/kg. Cyanide is approximately 1,000 times more toxic than carbon monoxide, making ingestion a virtual certain case of mortality. The presence of CO-Hg in the human body creates a synergistic effect with HCN, which lowers lethal contamination levels to 20% CO-Hg and 2 mcg/Kg HCN. Cyanide is the most dangerous gas aviators may potentially be exposed to.

Carbon dioxide (CO), as we know, is a natural human respiration by-product, but may also be toxic above certain levels in enclosed spaces. CO2 is a common fire-retardant, and as such rapidly could produce a toxic environment for humans in the vicinity during fire-fighting activities. CO2 may also be shipped in gaseous or solid form, such as dry ice. Excessive CO2 will displace oxygen in enclosed environments, creating hypoxic hypoxia conditions. In extreme cases, CO2 could potentially replace enough O2 in the environment to cause death-by-asphyxia. CO2 is heavier-than-air, and as such will concentrate towards the floor of a contaminated area. Symptoms of excess CO2 exposure include:

- Shortness of breath and/or rapid breathing
- Rapid heartrate
- Headaches
- Dizziness
- Fatigue and/or loss of consciousness

Organophosphates are a potential neurotoxic by-product of pyrolysis of engine oil, as discussed in the Hypoxia chapter. Based on laboratory analysis, synthetic jet engine oil contains approximately 3% tricresyl phosphate (TCP) and the neurotoxic isomer tri-o-cresyl phosphate (TOCP) at 0.1%. When oil is exposed to a hot engine surface, the oil can release TCP or TOCP isomers which can be trapped in air at room temperature. These compounds can remain airborne, and are most likely associated with smoke particles. As previously mentioned, substantial quantities of CO may be generated as well, producing synergistic symptomology to those exposed to the smoke and fumes.

Many other irritant gases, such as aerosolized acids, may be present as well. Most aerosolized acids are water soluble, and their primary effect is on skin and respiratory tract tissue producing swelling, pain, and difficulty breathing.

The primary concern for flight crews, quite obviously, are the incapacitating or performance-impairing airborne contamination.

9.7 KEYS TO SURVIVAL IN TOXIC AIRCRAFT ENVIRONMENTS

For professional aircrew exposed to fire, smoke and fume conditions, a proper understanding of the unfolding situation is paramount in proper and effective mitigation. The given conditions can and will quickly overcome aviators and other aircraft occupants, rendering them incapacitated and therefore ineffective. The following are the main *keys to survival in toxic aircraft environments*:

- **Respect the emergency**
- **Protect your lungs**
- **Protect your vision**
- **Know your breathing zone**
- **Decrease risk of incapacitation**

Respecting the emergency is of utmost importance and *time* will be the aviator's most beneficial ally or nemesis. According to FAA research, commercial aircraft must be fully evacuated in 90 seconds or less to prevent a rapid increase in mortality, as previously discussed. A comprehensive escape plan is a necessity; however, familiarity and frequent practicing of the escape plan is what saves lives. Immediate implementation of the evacuation plan must be initiated without delay or hesitation. A smoke-filled environment will be confusing and chaotic, especially for passengers, so using known non-visual cues for escape-route orientation may be necessary. Knowing the location of emergency escape doors by feel (counting seats, etc.) will assist in the timely evacuation of passengers in opaque aircraft cabins, as well as choosing seats close to emergency escape doors if flying as a passenger.

Protecting your lungs requires complete isolation from environmental air, and is a critical first step to accomplish. The first and foremost action needs to be donning the oxygen mask with smoke goggles, and needs to be accomplished at the earliest opportunity. Serious damage to the aviator can occur in the first seconds of a smoke or fume event, and time cannot be lost trying to "sniff out" the source of the smoke or fumes.

The oxygen mask needs to be air-tight, and providing 100% oxygen with emergency pressure to eliminate the possibility of contaminants entering the mask. Passenger oxygen masks (so-called "dixie cup" masks) are not designed for isolation from smoke and fumes, and should not be utilized by the flight crew if any other option exists. If passengers are exposed to or exhibit smoke inhalation symptoms, wet towels placed over their face can potentially minimize toxin exposure.

The smoke goggles protect your vision whether they are permanently mounted or donned separately and need to have an air-tight seal on the face as well. Some oxygen masks automatically blow pressurized oxygen into the goggle once the goggle is attached to assist clearing smoke; other oxygen masks may need to be manually manipulated to blow oxygen into the goggle.

The key is to ensure all equipment fits tight, works properly, and is operating to protect your lungs and vision as efficiently as possible. Damaged oxygen masks, or ill-fitting and seriously-scratched goggles will do little to ensure efficient mitigation of the emergency.

As a viable back-up system, some aviation operations provide a separate smoke hood for use if the primary oxygen mask fails, or to assist in cockpit evacuation operations as the oxygen mask alone will not suffice for evacuation. Aviators should be familiar with the operation and limitations of smoke hoods, if available, as many different models and configurations exist.

Knowing your breathing zone is critical for safe evacuation of the flight crew and occupants. Generally, the lower third of the cabin is where one can expect the breathable air to collect. The upper two-thirds of the cabin may be a dangerous "toxic soup" causing serious temporary or possibly permanent damage to humans.

Decreasing the risk of incapacitation includes ensuring not only your emergency equipment is prepared, but your "personal equipment" as well. You may consider your clothing material, clothing options and any accessories "personal equipment."

Clothing material should be non-synthetic fibers, such as cotton, as synthetic material will cling to the skin if burning, creating more opportunity for serious injury.

Clothing options should include long-sleeve shirts, full-length pants, full shoes and socks. Wearing short-sleeve shirts, short pants, and wearing sandals provides minimal protection in a thermal-toxic environment, and may expose the user to gross injury attempting to evacuate through flames and hot, jagged metal or glass fragments.

Accessories to consider are anything to assist in protection and evacuation in the event of an emergency. Items include light gloves to protect your hands, a flame-resistant hat to protect hair, a wet cotton wash-cloth packed in a plastic bag for airway protection, or wrap-around glasses for eye protection.

Conclusion

Smoke, fire and fumes events in aircraft, whether on the ground or inflight, are extremely serious conditions due to their effect on human performance and well-being. Immediate initiation of an appropriate and well-rehearsed evacuation plan is essential to minimize the harmful effects of thermal-toxic environments on aircrews and passengers alike. Ensuring effective aircrew protection equipment is strategically placed in the aircraft and properly inspected is critical. Always remember "smooth is fast" when accomplishing emergency procedures; chaotic, hap-hazard instructions or crew performance creates a confusing and dangerously inefficient situation.

Chapter 9 Core Competency Questions

1. True or false: ground crews, flight crews, and passenger may be a source of toxic fumes.
2. What on the aircraft is designed to filter out ozone in the atmosphere?
3. What three mechanisms contribute to contaminants in aircraft?
4. According to the FAA, what is the time frame in which aircraft should be evacuated following an aircraft crash?
5. What is the most common chemical product of incomplete combustion?
6. Carbon monoxide has a greater affinity for hemoglobin over oxygen by how much?
7. What is the most dangerous gas aviators could potentially be exposed to?
8. What is a critical first step to for aviators to take in dealing with toxic fumes events? .

10. HUMAN ORIENTATION SYSTEMS

Human orientation systems assist us in maintaining awareness with the environment utilizing a variety of interactive sensory inputs including vision, touch, muscles, tendons, joints, pressure, hearing, and accelerative forces. These inputs provide feedback to the brain, which interprets this feedback as position, motion, direction, and speed data. Obviously, these sensory systems originated to provide us environmental orientation with a human's feet touching the ground while moving at a relatively slow pace. As humans began to fly it was not long before problems arose resulting from altered visual perceptions, increased speeds, and an orientation system built for a two-dimensional environment now operating in three-dimensional airspace.

Since powered flight's origins, some of the aviator's greatest problems have revolved around *visual* and *intellectual interpretation* of approach and landing phase-of-flight environmental cues, and maintaining orientation in reduced visibility flight conditions. Historically, visual illusions and spatial disorientation (SDO) have been the leading causes of the largest number of aircraft incidents and fatal accidents, respectively. Ironically, these two physiological issues were among the first to be identified as "human factors" problems causing the deaths of pilots over one hundred years ago, and still provide some of the biggest problems for aviators today.

In this chapter we will discuss:

1. Human orientation overview
2. Proprioception system
3. Vestibular systems
4. Visual systems
5. Physiology of vision
6. Visual blind spots
7. Empty field myopia
8. Relative motion and attention
9. Effective scanning
10. Common inflight visual illusions
11. Autokinesis
12. Vision and FAA standards
13. Introduction to enhanced visual systems

10.1 HUMAN ORIENTATION OVERVIEW

Human orientation organically developed around our environment being at sea level, with some part of our body touching the Earth in some way, moving fairly slowly such as walking or running, and being able to see our environment. Our orientation systems integrate and interpret information provided to our central nervous system (CNS) through:

- Proprioception (our body sense of orientation and motion)
- Vestibular (detect head motion and position relative to gravity)
- Visual (the ability to interpret visible light to build a representation of our surrounding environment, maintaining geospatial awareness)
- Auditory (the ability to use sound as a localization source using three dimensions: azimuth, height, and distance. Not generally considered significant in aviation as a primary orientation source)

Humans developed to thrive at ground-level as slow-moving creatures with some part of our body touching a solid surface; therefore, when our environmental operational parameters change our brain's ability to interpret orientation cues may rapidly disintegrate. When our environment speeds up while driving an automobile, for instance, events (car crashes) may occur so quickly it's beyond our ability to see and react. When we try to intellectually process too much information at once, such as texting on a phone while driving a car, we tend to drive off the road (or worse) because we cannot interpret that much information simultaneously. With flying, not only are we increasing our speed of movement and bombard our brains with information, we place ourselves in a three-dimensional environment, trick our body's pressure sensors, and change our visual perspective (or eliminate vision entirely) which may rapidly overwhelm our orientation systems to the degree pilots literally fall out of the sky because they do not know which way is "up."

Why is vision such a concern for flight? The answer is 90% of human orientation information comes from the eyes, and the challenge for aviators is to correctly interpret and reconcile the information our eyes provide us in visual perspective conditions we, as humans, were not built to operate in. Low visibility and/or precipitations are factors in more than 70% of approach and landing incidents and accidents, the reasons being our lack of depth perception abilities, loss of field-flow, misperceived angle interpretation, and inability for intellectual scene-building.

Obviously, the lower the visibility due to darkness, clouds/fog, and precipitations (or a combination thereof), the higher the chances for incidents and accidents to occur.

Loss of visual references may result in SDO, which is the leading cause of controlled or uncontrolled flight into terrain (CFIT/UFIT). Over 90% of aircraft accidents caused by spatial disorientation (SDO) involve fatalities, the reason being the extreme angle-of-attack normally achieved upon terrain contact resulting from inability to orient oneself to the surface of the Earth.

10.2 HUMAN NERVOUS SYSTEM

Orientation mechanisms must transmit and interpret information on one's position and movement activities, and this information is processed through the *human nervous system*. The human nervous system sends and receives electrochemical-based signals throughout the body to control bodily functions. The main parts of the nervous system consist of the *central nervous system, or CNS* (brain and spinal cord) and *peripheral nervous system, or PNS* (nerve fibers that attach to and lie outside the brain and spinal cord). The *autonomic nervous system, or ANS,* is a division of the PNS supplying smooth muscle and glands, influencing the function of internal organs such as heart rate, digestion, respiratory rate, pupillary response, urination, and sexual response. The ANS is the primary mechanism controlling the "*fight or flight response.*"

The human nervous system has two major components, motor (efferent) and sensory (afferent), responsible for carrying information from and to, respectively, the central nervous system. The human brain is the organ of thought, emotion, and processing of the various senses. The brain acts as the command center, communicating with and controlling a variety of other systems and functions. The nervous system also provides special senses such as sight, hearing, taste, feel, and smell. The eyes, ears, tongue, skin, and nose are utilized to gather information about the body's environment. Stimulus must be sensed in order to be acknowledged by the brain, and *sensory receptors* are specialized to detect energy and transmit information to sensory nerves.

Sensory threshold is the weakest stimulus organisms can detect. It is possible for sub-threshold stimulus to go undetected by the brain, therefore defeating the brain's ability to maintain proper orientation. Visual references may be so low-contrast the brain may not properly interpret the visual information correctly.

Sensory adaptation refers to a reduction in one's sensitivity to a stimulus after constant exposure to it, theoretically freeing up our attention and resources to attend to other stimuli. Imagine flying a particular approach and each time the approach is flown ground proximity warning sensors (GPWS) emit a warning, even though no danger of ground contact exists. Eventually, a pilot may learn to ignore GPWS warnings as insignificant, creating a hazardous lack of acknowledgement of GPWS for other approaches.

10.3 PROPRIOCEPTION SYSTEM

Proprioception is the perception of self-movement, connection to the environment, and position of the body and limbs independent of vision. Generally this perception is sensed at a subconscious level, gained by sensory nerve terminals in muscles, tendons, and joints, so pressure applied to nerves in the body translates into motion sensations and body stabilization activities.

Proprioceptive impulses originate with *proprioceptors*; mechanosensory neurons embedded in muscles, tendons, and joints of the human body. Distinct behaviors enable activation of multiple types of proprioceptors, thus encoding specific types of neural information such as limb loads and limits, limb movement and velocity, joint angle, pressure on muscles, and even voice modulation.

Imagine sitting in a cockpit seat, and the aircraft begins to accelerate. The forward movement of the fuselage pushes the aviator back into their seat, and pressure sensors in the back sends neural impulses to the brain indicating forward movement is occurring. The same process takes place during deceleration and pitch, roll, and yaw movements. As these learned sensations become habitual and normal to a pilot, these sensations may be thought of as the "seat-of-the-pants" sensation.

Proprioception works to near-perfection in our normal, two-dimensional environment on the ground; however, proprioception may easily be misled in the three-dimensional environment of flight through the absence of visual references.

10.4 VESTIBULAR SYSTEMS

The *vestibular system (or apparatus)* is the human sensory system designed to detect angular and linear acceleration, head position, and spatial orientation. The vestibular system allows us to keep our balance, stabilize our head, eyes, and body during movement, and maintain allow us to maintain posture.

The vestibular apparatus is relatively small; approximately the size of an adult's small finger nail. The vestibular apparatus is adapted to motion on Earth; therefore, the system's propensity to be misled in flight conditions is high. Two of the ways the apparatus may be tricked in flight is the system cannot detect steady states-of-motion, and it is also possible to turn an aircraft slower than the apparatus can detect. Both conditions will be examined in depth in this chapter.

The vestibular apparatus is located in the inner ear, and consists of auditory and non-auditory sensory systems.

Figure 10.1 Ear Anatomy

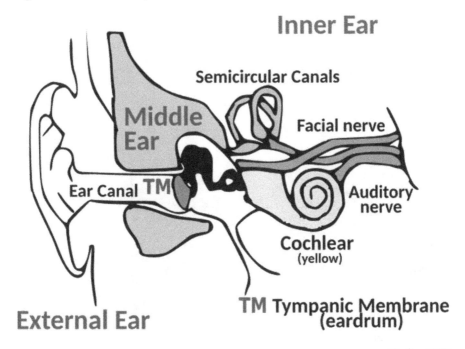

The vestibular apparatus is composed of two separate organs:

- Otolith organs
- Semicircular canals

The vestibular apparatus is both the *semicircular canals* (SCC) and *otolith organs,* which are comprised of the *utricle* and *saccule.* The SCC lie at approximately 90-degree angles to each other, and are designed to detect the speed and direction of angular acceleration in the pitch, roll, and yaw axes. The otolith organs are designed to detect the speed and direction of linear acceleration and head tilt. Both SCC and otoliths are filled with a thick fluid called *endolymph,* and located in the end of the enlarged areas of the canals called the *ampullae* extends very fine, sensitive hair cells named *cilia.*

Figure 10.2 Ampullae Hair Cells of the Vestibular Apparatus

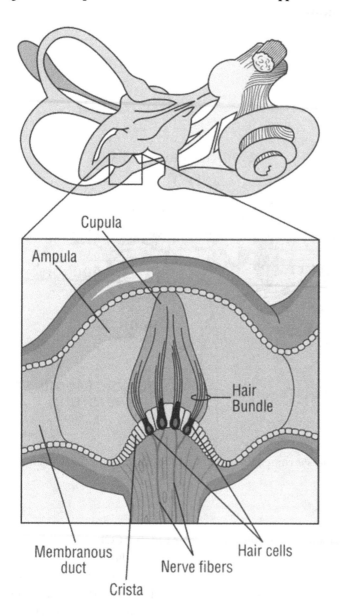

Cupula

Ampula

Hair Bundle

Membranous duct

Nerve fibers

Hair cells

Crista

Wpclipart 2021

The vestibular apparatus assists with maintaining orientation to our surroundings, assisting with balance and movement as well as coordinating eye movement, which is of particular importance during visual tracking tasks. These functions are accomplished by sensing movement of the body through hair cell stimulation in the SCC and otolith fluid.

The *vestibulo-ocular reflex* is a reflexive eye movement occurring when the head turns, producing an eye movement in the direction opposite the turn. This movement assists stabilizing images on the retina during head movements, allowing the eyes to accurately track and interpret the image. The SCC canals detect the head rotation, and drive the rotational vestibulo-ocular reflex automatically, which may cause problems if unexpected in flight. This will be discussed more in depth later in this chapter.

Vestibular System Functions

Angular, rotational, or linear acceleration of the body will move the fluid in a respective SCC or otolith canal. These movements occur along the yaw, pitch, or roll axis or linear forward, rearward, or sideways acceleration. This bodily movement causes the canal fluid to lag behind the movement of the body, which displaces the sensory hair cells in the ampulla. At this point an impulse is generated and sent to the brain to be interpreted as motion in a known axis-of-movement.

Acceleration in excess of three degrees-per-second causes the hair cells to displace and depending on which way the hair cells deflect, the brain will determine the plane of rotation or direction of acceleration/deceleration. This system works well in flight for short periods of time; however, if the turn continues at a constant rate for approximately 20 seconds the motion of the fluid catches up to the speed of the canal walls, and the hair cells are no longer deflected. Once the fluid and canal walls are at equilibrium, the aviator will no longer sense acceleration.

Undetected Motion and False Sensations

If a pilot were executing a constant rate right turn for over 20 seconds, the pilot would sense the initial angular acceleration accurately. Once the time of the turn extended beyond 20 seconds, the pilot would no longer feel angular acceleration and may assume the aircraft is flying straight and level if no visual confirmation of the turn could be made. Once the turn is truly returned to straight and level flight beyond the 20 seconds, the fluid in the SCC will be re-stimulated, deflecting the hair cells in the opposite direction. This would make the pilot feel as though a left turn were being initiated, lacking proper visual confirmation.

Should a pilot execute a gentle turn or slow roll of less than three degrees-per-second, the fluid in the SCC and otoliths may not receive adequate stimulation to provide any sensory input. The body, canal fluid and hair cells are all moving at the same speed and in the same direction, and movement not sensed is not easily acknowledged by the brain. This effect is known as *sub-threshold acceleration*. Once again, without adequate visual confirmation of the maneuver, the aircraft may be changing attitude or altitude undetected.

Typically if these sensations were experienced while able to visually confirm aircraft attitude, visual input will take precedence over vestibular inputs and aviators have no problem.

When visual input is lacking, serious orientation conflicts may occur that can cause the human orientation system to become tricked and/or overwhelmed to the degree an aviator can be rendered intellectually incapacitated. In certain situations a pilot will return to the original turn or action to feel as if they are flying straight and level, when in fact they are not. Upon the realization the aviator has no true idea which way is up or down, the resulting confusion can be an absolutely terrifying experience for the uninitiated pilot. Spatial disorientation can be extremely convincing to an aviator's brain, even to the point where pilots actually refuse to believe the aircraft instruments are correct.

 All spatial disorientation illusions have a name associated with them. The names are based on the root problem (turning, accelerating, and gravity) and the part of the body affected (eyes, body). The spatial disorientation (SDO) terminology is based on the following:

- Vestibulo: refers to the vestibular system, including both SCC and otolith organs.
- Oculo/ocular: refers to the eyes.
- Somato: refers to the body.
- Gyric: refers to a turning motion.
- Gravic: refers to linear acceleration or gravity.

For instance, *somatogravic illusion* refers to the body being affected by forward acceleration or deceleration. An *oculogyric illusion* refers to the eyes being affected by a turning motion. We will investigate all the SDO illusions in depth in the chapter dealing with spatial disorientation.

10.5 VISUAL SYSTEMS

Visual systems allow humans to locate themselves within an environment, or provide geospatial positioning information. An aviator's understanding of vision can assist aviators to realize the full potential of visual input and its contribution to orientation, and learn the "visual interpretation traps" causing incidents and accidents. The eye is highly reliable for orientation, responsible for 90% of orientation processing given an adequate number of reference points. Most people do not bother thinking about how visual truly works, which is unfortunate; visual processing in humans is a complex and fascinating process. Vision allows humans to see the beauty of colors & landscapes, shapes and textures, near and distant, in three dimensions, and many other features. In aviation, however, vision used correctly allows pilots to determine distance and depth, judge altitude and angles, spot small obstacles from great distances, see low-contrast threats, and build comprehensible scenes.

Despite the inclusion of various electronic systems such as radar, GPS, TCAS, ADS-B, and others, an aviator's effective use of vision remains of significant important to maintain safety-of-flight.

Main Visual Systems

Two main visual systems exist in human vision:

- Central (Focal) vision
- Peripheral (Ambient) vision

Central vision comprises a small window in the overall visual field; the central two degrees of human visual perception. Central vision is processed with a high degree of *consciousness* or attention. In simpler terms, an aviator has to be thinking about what they are looking at in order to understand what they're looking at. One may think of central vision as providing the "what" of things we look at, as this visual system is specialized for object recognition and identification. Central vision can be finely-focused by compressing the lens of the eye, and provides images in high detail.

Peripheral vision is all visual input outside the above-mentioned two degrees of visual perception. Peripheral vision is processed with little or no conscious thought, known as sub-conscious image processing. The images generated from the visual periphery are of coarse detail with little-to-no object recognition. These images provide very powerful environmental movement information, so peripheral vision is specialized for spatial location and orientation cues involving large stimulus patterns. These orientation cues (or lack thereof) may quickly convince the brain we are moving when in fact we are not, and vice-versa. This can quickly become unnerving to aviators, causing a severe loss of situational awareness.

Phases of Vision

In terms of visual processing, the amount of ambient light plays an important role in how much information our eyes generate to our brain. The three phases of vision are as follows:

- Photopic (day) vision
- Scotopic (night) vision
- Mesopic (intermediate) vision

Photopic vision occurs during periods of full luminance, commonly known as "day vision." The *cone photoreceptor cells* in the retina of the human eye are responsible for processing of photons (light energy) under well-lit conditions. Photopic vision provides for the best processing of our elements of vision, to be discussed in this chapter. Adaption to photopic vision takes place rapidly, usually within five minutes.

Scotopic vision occurs during periods of low illuminance, known as "night vision." The *rod photoreceptor cells* in the retina of the eye are responsible for processing of low-light level photons, as the cone cells are non-functional in low visible light. The basic visual elements are typically very poor during periods of scotopic vision. Rod cells are not immediately available for peak usage; adaption to peak scotopic vision occurs over a period of 30- to 45- minutes. This low-light level vision process requires a regeneration of the photo-pigment *rhodopsin* in the rod cells, making those cells highly sensitive to light. Exposure to high-intensity light will bleach the rhodopsin out in a matter of seconds, requiring restarting the regeneration process.

Mesopic vision occurs during periods of intermediate luminance, known as "intermediate vision." Both cone and rod cells are employed during mesopic visual phases, providing inaccurate visual and color cues. Typically, this phase of vision is dangerous for aviators as their impression is their vision is better than it truly is, in which important distance and contrast cues can be missed.

Elements of Vision

The following list are recognized elements of vision to considered for the various phases of vision, as these elements change with each phase:

- Visual acuity
- Accommodation
- Field of view
- Color sensitivity
- Contrast sensitivity
- Depth perception

Visual acuity refers to visual clarity, and is essential for spotting inflight threats such as a small, distant speck that evolves into an aircraft flying a collision course with you. The generally accepted normal visual acuity for adults using photopic vision is 20/20. This peak visual acuity is contained within the two-degree cone of central vision, and visual acuity rapidly degrades beyond central vision. As the phases of vision change, objects which may have been comprehensible in photopic peripheral vision may be incomprehensible in the mesopic and scotopic phases of peripheral vision. This lapse in comprehension may cause those objects to be missed and create unsafe conditions and/or incidents and accidents involving collisions to occur.

Accommodation refers to the process in which the eye adjusts optical power to maintain clear images or focus on objects in varying distances. Imagine flying the aircraft and focusing on a display on the instrument panel, then looking out the windscreen to scan for oncoming aircraft in the distance; this ability is accommodation. Accommodation is best accomplished in the photopic vision phase and predictably degrades transitioning through subsequent phases. One needs to realize their eyes may require several seconds to refocus when switching views between the instrument panel and distant objects.

Accommodation may strain a pilot's eyes unnecessarily and may be mitigated through a gradual focal transition from instruments to distant targets. One way to accomplish a gradual focal transition is to focus the eyes from the instruments, to the left-wing tip, and out into airspace. One may bring focal transition back in by focusing the eyes from airspace, to the right-wing tip, and back to the instruments.

Field of view (FOV) is our entire comprehensible binocular visual picture that can be seen at one time. This picture reaches approximately to 120 degrees horizontally and 120 degrees vertically, although these parameters are somewhat debatable depending on how one measures "vision." Independently, eyes produce a monocular (flat) image, and both eyes working synergistically creates a binocular (depth) image. The various phases of vision do not affect FOV, but the ability to distinguish objects in the far periphery degrades significantly through loss of light energy.

Color sensitivity is the ability of humans to perceive differences between visible light energy (photons) composed of differential wavelengths, resulting in color perception. Good color vision is necessary to enable aviators to spot inflight threats against a visually cluttered background, such as searching for an aircraft silhouetted against a cityscape. The characteristic colors humans distinguish from the visible electromagnetic wavelength spectrum, from long-to-short wavelength, are red, orange, yellow, green, blue, and violet. The color of light wavelengths we view objects in plays a major role in what color those objects are perceived; therefore, viewing red lines on a map with a red-tinted flashlight in the cockpit will change the color of the lines or make them disappear completely.

The *definition of light* is "visually perceived radiant energy." Visible light is a small segment of the entire electromagnetic wavelength spectrum. As visibly perceived radiant energy, light powers the mechanism of human sight, so the light allowing us to see those objects is known as *illuminance*. The visible light reflected off objects allowing humans to perceive the object in a particular color is known as *luminance*. Luminance levels indicate how much luminance power can be detected while viewing a particular item or surface from a particular angle. Therefore, illuminance and luminance will influence human visual color processing of objects under varying conditions. One may notice it is much easier to focus on red lights at night due to our perception of long wavelengths; whereas viewing blue lights at night makes it difficult to focus on those lights.

The ability to distinguish colors is of critical concern for aviators, as correct interpretation of aircraft displays, terrain recognition, lights of other aircraft, runway lighting systems and many others may literally be the difference between life and death. Aviators must take color blindness tests when applying for all levels of pilot medical certificates, unless allowed to possess a certificate with a waiver.

For sunglasses, the choice of tints for is almost infinite. Most commonly, sunglass tints are gray, gray-green, and brown, any of which are excellent choices for aviators. Gray (neutral density filter) is highly recommended because it distorts color least. However, some pilots report gray-green and brown tints enhance vividness and minimize scattered (blue and violet) light, thus enhancing contrast in hazy conditions. Yellow, amber, and orange (i.e., "Blue Blockers") tints eliminate short-wavelength light from reaching the wearer's eyes and reportedly sharpen vision, although no scientific studies support this claim. In addition, these tints are known to distort colors, making it difficult to distinguish the color of navigation lights, signals, or color-coded maps and instrument displays. For flying, sunglass lenses should screen out only 70 - 85% of visible light and not appreciably distort color. Tints blocking more than 85% of visible light are not recommended for flying due to the possibility of reduced visual acuity, resulting in difficulty seeing instruments and written material inside the cockpit (Federal Aviation Administration Medical Facts for Pilots, 2021).

Contrast Sensitivity is the ability to detect subtle environmental shade and pattern differences. Contrast sensitivity allows aviators to detect objects without clear outlines and discriminate those objects from their background. Imagine flying through hilly or mountainous terrain in foggy or low-light conditions; being able to distinguish terrain through the fog may rapidly turn into a life-or-death situation if unable to climb above the terrain. For aviators, an aerial perspective may make distinguishing power lines against background clutter difficult, or trying to detect the height of a particular tree against the background clutter of a forest can be misleading. Lower light illumination levels make contrast sensitivity an even greater threat. Our ability to perceive rising terrain may become near-impossible if flying towards a mountain range with the sun setting behind the mountains or snow-covered mountains blending in with a grey sky.

Depth Perception is the ability to judge distance and the spatial relationship, or three-dimensional judgement, of objects at differential distances in our visual field. Depth perception is essential for aviators to judge distance to the threshold, altitude, obstacle clearance, flare height, wing clearance during taxi, and many others. The depth cues the brain interprets come from two different sources; binocular and monocular.

Binocular cue sensory input is resultant from having two functioning eyes, thus allowing humans to see in dimension. Dimensional judgement works for human eyes to a distance of approximately 200 meters, which admittedly isn't far enough for most aviation operational concerns. Beyond 200 meters, we switch to *monocular cue sensory input* to assist in distance judgement. Monocular cues can include object size references, perspective, object contrast and texture, overlaying or occlusion of objects, object motion, and light and shade among other factors. Object size reference is very important in long-distance judgement. If one does not know the relative size of an object they are looking at (mountains or clouds), the ability to estimate distance is extremely difficult. These distance judgement activities are typically processed subconsciously.

Air clarity can play a major role in human depth perception. Clear air, such as one would find in the mountains or other rural areas, may make objects appear to be closer than they truly are. Haze or precipitations may make objects appear to be father away.

10.6 PHYSIOLOGY OF VISION

We will now examine the complex subject of human vision from a simple perspective.

Human vision is powered by two sources: light energy (photons) and metabolic energy (oxygen). Loss of either energy source leads to a degradation of visual effectiveness.

Human visual ability results from the brain's processing of information gained from photons focused on the retina. The *Iris* and *pupil* control the amount of light energy (photons) passing through the *vitreous body*, those photons eventually contacting the *photoreceptor* cells of the *retina*. The pupil will expand in low light conditions to allow

Figure 10.3 Human Eye

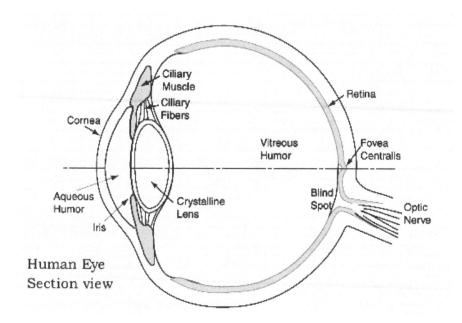

Human Eye
Section view

Photoreceptor cells in the retina are tasked with beginning the visual process, and these cells are made up of *cone* cells and *rod* cells.

Cone cells function best by absorption of high-intensity light, and number approximately six million per retina. Cone cells are densely packed in the *fovea centralis*, located in the center of the retina, thus allowing for the best visual acuity and color processing skills in the central two degrees of our visual field. Cone cell density quickly reduces towards the periphery of the retina.

Rod cells function best in low-intensity light, are extremely light-sensitive and number approximately 90 to 100 million per retina. Rod cells are usually concentrated towards the periphery of the retina, thus assisting with peripheral vision and have nearly sole responsibility for night vision. A complete absence of rod cells exists in the fovea centralis, resulting in a *blind spot* for night vision. The rod cell's sensitivity to light increases primarily due to the pigment *rhodopsin,* which increases the rod cell's light sensitivity to its maximum level over 30 to 45 minutes. This results in humans experiencing their best night vision after 30 to 45 minutes. Re-exposure to high light intensity will desensitize the rod cells, leading to a loss of maximum night vision in seconds.

Photons energize the photoreceptor cells, creating an *electrochemical neural impulse*. These neural impulses pass through photoreceptor neurons, and then are conducted across synapses to the bipolar neurons located in the intermediate zone of the nervous layer of the retina. Neural impulses then transmit to the ganglion neurons. The axons of the ganglion neurons extend posteriorly to a small section of the retina called the *optic disc*. The optic disk maintains openings through which the axons of the ganglion neurons exit as the *optic nerve*. The optic nerve transmits the impulses via optic nerve fibers to the *visual cortex* of the brain. Once the brain receives these neural impulses, the visual cortex decodes the information, generating a perceived image. This process is completed in milliseconds for millions of images per second. Each image we see over our lifetime is stored as a memory, as well as input from the senses of hearing, touch, taste and smell.

The adult human brain arguably contains some 100 billion individual neurons. Each neuron may contain up to 1,000 synaptic connections, each of which some scientists believe could be a sensory memory. This means the brain could potentially be sorting through 100 *trillion* electrochemical codes trying to determine if what is being currently experienced is new information, or information stored in a memory, all of which occurs in fractions of a second.

Since the optic disk contains no rod or cone photoreceptor cells, photons striking this area of the retina cannot be perceived; thus, the optic disk creates a second blind spot in human vision.

Having a basic understanding of electrochemical impulse processing of visual information in the brain, what does that have to do with aviation? When the brain decodes impulses, it has to categorize the image as to what it is and if we have seen that image before. If the image matches previous memory, we know rapidly what we are looking at and continue operations. If the image does not match previous memory, the brain has to figure out what it is looking at. Sometimes this process may take a little more time than usual, at which point we typically "stop and stare" until a conclusion is reached.

Imagine flying into an airport you have never flown an approach to previously and something about the approach looks abnormal, but you can't pinpoint what looks different. At this point, one of two things may happen; the brain goes into a holding pattern trying to build a scene that makes sense, or the brain subconsciously tries to align you on an approach path that appears normal but potentially causes you abnormal ground contact. Neither option is preferable as either critical time is being wasted or you may damage the aircraft (or worse). We will investigate ways to counteract this phenomenon later in this chapter.

10.7 VISUAL BLIND SPOTS

As discussed in the previous section, two anatomical blind spots exist in our field of view; one blind spot affecting photopic and scotopic vision, and the second affecting scotopic vision only.

Day Blind Spot

Because the optic nerve enters the retina, no photoreceptor cells occupy the retinal lining in this space. This space is called the *optic disk*. The location of the optic disk in the retina represents the *first* blind spot affecting photopic and scotopic vision. Locating the blind spot in the field of view is simple; it is located 15 degrees outside the vertical meridian as shown in the following diagram.

Figure 10.4 Optic Disk Visual Blind Spot

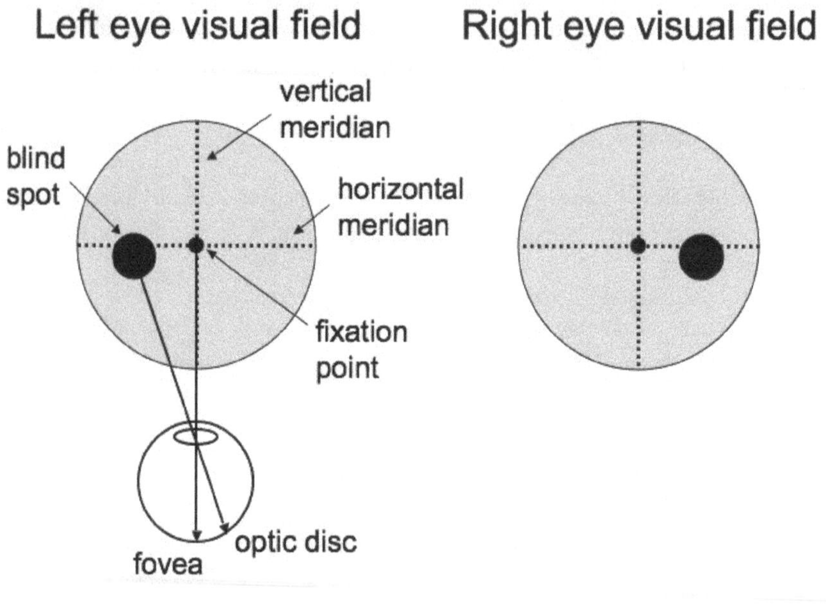

Typically, the blind spot is not noticeable as the brain fills in the missing visual scene and peripheral vision of one eye fills in for the opposite eye, provided one possesses binocular vision. The blind spot still exists, however, and a distant aircraft flying a collision course with your aircraft could potentially stay in the blind visual quadrant until such a time where reaction time would be limited.

One may perform a simple test to observe the blind spot in action:

Figure 10.5 Visual Blind Spot Test

Look at the picture of the cross and the circle on this page. Sit with your nose pointing in between the cross and the black circle. Following the listed directions:

1. Cover your **LEFT** eye and stare at the cross with your **RIGHT** eye.
2. SLOWLY move your head towards the page while still staring at the cross with your **RIGHT** eye.
3. Between 10-14 inches from the page the black circle will <u>disappear</u> and the area where the black circle appears will now be all white...this is the visual **BLIND SPOT**.

If you move closer to the page or farther away, the circle re-appears. At just the right distance, the circle will disappear.

One may now try the other eye, but this time cover the **RIGHT** eye and look at the **CIRCLE** with your **LEFT** eye, and as you move closer you will see that the **CROSS** now disappears.

Night Blind Spot

The lack of rod cell concentration in the fovea centralis creates the *second* blind spot, noticeable only at night. This blind spot is most commonly referred to as "the night-blind spot," for obvious reasons.

Because of the high concentration of cone cells in the fovea centralis, the central two-degree zone of our FOV provides our best visual acuity in normal light conditions; however, this also creates a void of rod cells for virtually no effective night vision.

The night-blind spot is central to both eyes, and the further an object gets from the eye, the larger the blind spot becomes. This may present a significant problem if flying directly at an object which remains in the night-blind spot, potentially resulting in a collision.

As a result of being unable to see objects at night by looking directly at them, the key in combating the night visual blind spot is look approximately 10 – 15 degrees to the side the object. This is called using an *off-center scan,* which will allow the aviator to engage rod cells in the immediate periphery surrounding central vision. This technique will not allow an aviator to see those objects with perfect visual clarity, but will allow visual contact with the object with the best visual acuity available given the conditions.

10.8 EMPTY FIELD MYOPIA

Empty field myopia is a condition in which the eyes, having nothing specific within the available visual field upon which to focus, will automatically focus at range of a few meters ahead. As a result of this condition, a daydreaming aviator simply "staring off into space" while flying is not visually focused in the medium- to far-distance where potential inflight collision risks exist. Detection of objects outside this few-meter distance will be delayed, leading to increased risk of midair collisions. If an object of interest does enter the field of view, visual determination of its size, range, or closure rate may be problematic.

Conscious effort must be made to calibrate the eyes to a specific distance. This can be easily accomplished in the cockpit by focusing on a distant object on the ground of a specific distance, such as a water tower five miles away. Once focused on that object, raise the eyes to the sky and now the eyes are effectively focused for five miles. The same technique can be employed to 10 miles, 15 miles or whatever range zone the aviator wishes to see into.

10.9 RELATIVE MOTION AND ATTENTION

Relative motion is the calculation of the motion of an object with regard or in relation to another object. In aviation, this term normally applies to the speed of another aircraft in relation to yours.

The reason an understanding of relative motion is important for pilots is an aircraft flying a parallel flightpath at the same speed as an aircraft will not attract attention. Typically, when an object is seen with peripheral vision, it needs to be moving across your visual field for the brain to acknowledge the object. If the parallel aircraft is moving at the speed as an aircraft, no movement in the visual field is detected and no attention may be given to that aircraft. As a result of this phenomena, more mid-air collisions occur with aircraft flying converging flight paths versus opposing flight paths. According to Dr. Craig Morris of the Bureau of Transportation Statistics, U.S. civil aviation averages approximately 15.6 midair collisions per year.

TCAS, ATC, and ADS-B provides excellent information regarding conflicting aircraft in the immediate airborne vicinity as long as the other aircraft's transponder is working. Should the transponder fail, the possibility exists of converging flightpath-related collision.

Parallel aircraft flying at a different airspeed than yourself, such as on approach to a parallel runway, may present orientation challenges as well. Stimulus in peripheral vision is a powerful cue for movement sensation, so unnatural object movement may convince our senses our own orientation is incorrect. Aircraft flying parallel flightpaths at a different airspeed may compel a pilot to sense a turning sensation which, if unverified with instruments, could cause a loss-of-directional control at inopportune times.

10.10 EFFECTIVE SCANNING

Several reasons exist why maintaining an effective visual scan inflight is necessary; however, the best reason is simply to avoid hitting objects. As a result of visual anomalies, an aviator simply cannot fly with their eyes focused straight ahead. To maximize one's visual effectiveness, pilots must utilize an effective scanning pattern, as the probability of spotting potential inflight collision threats increases with respect to the time spent scanning airspace as opposed to an instrument panel.

FAA studies indicate the time a pilot spends on visual tasks involving the instrument panel or flight deck should represent approximately one-fourth of the time versus visual tasks outside the aircraft. This equates to approximately 5 seconds scanning instruments for every 15 seconds scanning for obstacles outside the aircraft. The brain is trained to process visual information presented from left to right, so pilots may scan more effectively by starting the scan sweep over their left shoulder and proceeding across the windscreen to the right.

The eyes have the potential to observe approximately 200 degrees of arc at one glance; however, only the fovea centralis in the retina maintains the capacity to initiate and transmit clear, sharply focused images to the visual cortex of the brain. A broad horizontal and vertical forward scan should be maintained with the mission of identifying inflight collision threats at the earliest possible time with the best visual acuity possible, which is one's central vision. Any visual information not processed by central vision will be of low resolution, and not effective for object identification.

For example, aircraft at distances of 7 miles may appear in sharp detail using central vision, whereas the same aircraft would be at a distance of approximately 7/10 of a mile to be recognized by peripheral vision. As a result of central vision's effectiveness in threat identification, a series of short, regularly spaced eye movements merging areas of the sky should be used in one's scan.

To clear the immediate flight path, a 60-degree horizontal and 15-degree vertical sweep is recommended. The eyes should move across the scan plane in 10-degree increments, focusing at each increment for approximately three seconds. Focusing less than three seconds may not allow enough time to visually process and acquire a threat, and focusing more than three seconds on a small object against an infinite background may cause the object to "bleach out." One must also be aware of visual obstructions.

Visual obstructions may include window posts, instrument panels, eyeglass or sunglass rims, bug splatter on the windscreen, windscreen imperfections, sun visors, wings and front seat pilots or other occupants. Obstructions may not only mask some of the scan view completely, but may result in specific scan quadrants being visible to only one eye, making it less likely to be detected as a result of visual blind spots.

In addition to the forward scan-plane, attention must be given to the potential for converging flight paths of other aircraft. Clearing airspace in the difficult-to-see planes such as at 90-degree and greater angles to the cockpit in high, level and low planes must be included frequently, similar to looking back over one's shoulder when changing lanes in an automobile.

An important component of a pilot's scan is maintaining situational awareness with an integrated instrument scan. Human eyes tend to tire quicker when immediately adjusting from close-up focus to distances, such as one would experience focusing from the instrument panel to distant airspace. This eye strain and fatigue may be reduced by scanning from instruments to the left wing, past the wing tip, continuing to the first scan quadrant when transitioning the exterior scan. After scanning from left to right, focus the eyes along the right wing from the tip inward. Once focus is inside, commence the panel scan. This technique will allow eyes to accommodate less aggressively, thus reducing eye fatigue.

The importance of identifying threats at the earliest time cannot be stressed enough. Two aircraft flying directly towards each other with one nautical mile separation and a closure speed of 240 knots (120 knots each), would impact in a little over 14 seconds. Based on research performed by the FAA, a pilot would take an average of 12 seconds to see, comprehend, analyze, decide and react to that specific situation, leaving a mere two seconds for margin-of-error. It would be preferable to spot that aircraft at five miles, as opposed to one mile.

Glare may directly affect an aviator's ability to accurately detect other aircraft, particularly when the aircraft is in the same quadrant as the glare. Glare may originate directly from the light source, or may be veiling glare reflected from crazing or dirt on the windscreen. The book *Human Factors in Flight,* by Frank H. Hawkins and Harry W. Orlady, states when the source of the glare is only 5 deg. away from the line of sight, the loss of visual effectiveness is 84%. When glare is 40 deg. from the line of sight, the loss of visual effectiveness is 42%.

10.11 COMMON INFLIGHT VISUAL ILLUSIONS

A variety of illusions may be present in either day or night flight environments predisposing an aviator to erroneous orientation when the true horizon is obscured. In many cases, these orientation-related illusions manifest themselves when a pilot's composite scan breaks down as a result of fatigue, boredom, distraction, etc. In cases such as these, the brain takes over and tries to align the unsuspecting pilot with what *should* be the horizon under normal conditions.

Obviously, if the aircraft is being flown on autopilot orientation should not be an issue. However, if a pilot is not concentrating on the task-at-hand, these illusions make a pilot feel like "something just doesn't seem right," and may prompt the pilot to doubt the accuracy of their instruments. These illusions include:

- Misleading ground light patterns
- Mistaking ground lights for stars
- False atmospheric vertical cues
- False atmospheric horizontal cues
- Relative altitude of approaching objects

Misleading ground light patterns may compel a pilot to misinterpret the horizon in dark, moonless flight conditions. In many instances a line of artificial lights may be *close*-to-even with the true horizon. A pilot may be looking at the light-strewn edge of an urban area in the desert or close to water, an interstate highway, or some other relatively straight line of lights and convince themselves they are looking at the true horizon.

Mistaking ground lights for stars may compel a pilot to mistake distant ground lights for stars above-the-horizon. These illusions will typically occur in wide-open, relatively flat terrain away from urban congestion, where a lack-of-lighted visual references exist. For example, flying over desert terrain at night is an expanse known for this type of illusion. The error would be for the pilot to attempt to align the ground lights mistaken for stars above the alleged horizon, and ultimately fly into terrain.

False atmospheric vertical cues could include certain cloud formations, northern lights, spot-lights or laser lights from urban events.

False atmospheric horizontal cues generally are produced by clouds, haze, forest fire smoke, open water blending with an obscured horizon, and other atmospheric phenomena.

Relative altitude of approaching objects may be misinterpreted and improperly assessed, thus elevating the possibility for potential midair collisions. From a distance, an approaching aircraft may actually appear higher than your present altitude, only to eventually pass below your aircraft. Mountain peaks seen at a distance may also present the same illusion. To ensure an approaching object will safely clear your aircraft, look for movement of the object on the windscreen. If the object is moving up the windscreen, the object is at a higher altitude than yourself, and if the object is moving down the windscreen, the object is lower. If the object remains stable on the windscreen, a potential collision risk exists. Knowing those visual cues can enable a pilot to rapidly assess the conflict and apply appropriate control inputs.

The above-described illusions can be defeated with an effective and disciplined instrument scan. Frequent orientation checks should be made with aircraft instruments during level flight, and the pilot must understand these illusions exist so as not to drift off-course or off-altitude. Any heading changes and level-offs must be confirmed with aircraft instruments as opposed to visually leveling off.

10.12 AUTOKINESIS

Autokinesis is the apparent movement of a single point-of-light against a dark background, such a single, isolated star on a clear night. Single points-of-light in low-light conditions are difficult for the eye to perceive as the eyes naturally move to try to achieve a better perception of the light. With no other visual references, this involuntary, subtle eye-movement is not detected by the brain; thus, the brain perceives the light as moving. A light appearing to move in the path of an aircraft in flight may be misperceived as an airborne threat on a collision course.

The autokinesis effect may be produced by a singular star or distant ground light, prompting a pilot to make unnecessary collision-avoidance maneuvers which have the potential of creating a loss-of-control condition.

The autokinesis effect can be effectively mitigated with the following steps:

- **Do not stare at single-point lights.**
- **Use a diamond-shaped scan pattern around the light:**
  - **Start the scan 15 degrees above the light, then move to 15 degrees to the left, bottom and right of the object.**
  - **Maintain the diamond-shaped scan to stabilize the image until no longer necessary.**

Using the diamond-shaped scan will allow the aviator to differentiate between stabilized lights and lights that are truly moving. If the light is still moving while using the diamond-shaped scan, consider using object-avoidance techniques at that time.

10.13 VISION AND FAA STANDARDS

The following section is a reprint of the Aviation Medicine Advisory Service's synopsis of Vision and FAA Standards:

"Federal Aviation Regulations require a pilot's distant vision be 20/20 or better, with or without correction, in EACH eye separately to hold a first or second class medical certificate. The standard for near visual acuity (16") is 20/40 in each eye separately. Pilots aged 50 and older also have an intermediate visual standard measured at 32" of 20/40 or better in each eye separately. Third class medical certificates require 20/40 or better for near and distant vision. There is no intermediate vision standard for third class certification.

Nearsighted (myopic) individuals, those who have blurring when viewing distant objects, are required to wear corrective lenses (glasses or contact lenses) at all times during aviation duties. These lenses must correct distant vision to 20/20 in each eye.

Farsighted (hyperopic) individuals or *presbyopic* individuals (those who require reading glasses as they age), are required to have corrective lenses AVAILABLE during aviation duties. These lenses are usually bifocals, progressive lenses or the half cut reading lenses ("granny glasses").

Pilots and controllers with *cataracts* whose vision does not correct to 20/20 at distant may be recertified to fly and control after having a surgical implantation of an artificial intraocular lens. These individuals may also be required to wear glasses to provide optimum visual acuity.

With FAA Order 3930.3B, ATC vision standards were made similar to airman standards. With or without correction, air traffic controllers must demonstrate 20/20 distant vision in each eye separately, 20/40 in each eye at 16 inches near vision, and 20/40 in each eye at 32 inches intermediate vision if they are 50 years of age or older. Glasses or contact lenses are permitted.

Unilateral vision or visual field defects are waiverable for pilots, but typically not for controllers. However, controllers with visual field defects might possibly be considered for center operations on a case by case basis.

The ability to focus images on the retina of the eye is determined primarily by two components of the eye, the lens and the cornea. The cornea has a refractive power of approximately 45 diopters (ability to bend light rays). The lens has a variable refractive power (accommodation) of 1-18 diopters as a youth, but there is a progressive deterioration in accommodation so that the 50 year old pilot/controller may have less than 2 diopters of accommodation. The retina and macula may be affected by certain conditions that preclude good vision regardless of the status of the lens and cornea.

Distant vision requires less bending of light rays (lower diopters of refraction) to focus on the retina than near vision, such as reading, requires. The young farsighted individual, who has a flatter cornea and less corneal refractive power, can compensate for problems in near vision by using the accommodation of the lens to add refractive power. As one ages, the lens stiffens and loses the ability to accommodate (presbyopia) or add near focusing power. The first thing the pilot or controller will do when faced with this problem is hold objects they are attempting to read at greater distances from the eye. When those distances exceed the arm's length or cannot be moved (such as an instrument panel), the pilot usually reluctantly admits it is time for reading glasses or bifocals.

The nearsighted pilot or controller, who has been constantly wearing glasses to correct for the excessively curved cornea with too much refractive power, may not have to use bifocals for five to ten years after his farsighted counterpart has, because the loss of accommodation is compensated for by the larger refractive power of his cornea. Ultimately, they will require lenses with significant differences in the near and distant corrective powers.

Astigmatism is the irregular curvature of the cornea so that different portions have varying refractive powers. Glasses or toric contact lenses correct this condition.

For more information, see the AMAS article regarding Eyes and Physiology of Vision.

How will corrective eye surgery affect my FAA medical certificate?

The FAA will permit pilots and controllers who have undergone refractive surgery to fly and control, if they have had a successful outcome. If they meet the uncorrected visual acuity standards for the class of medical certificate applied for, the Airman Medical Certificate will not have any vision limitations. If the visual surgery does not result in meeting the FAA standards uncorrected, but does with corrective lenses, the certificate will bear the standard vision limitations (e.g.., "must wear corrective lenses"). If the outcome of the surgery does not allow vision correction to FAA standards or results in fluctuating vision, the airman or controller may be denied medical certification. The surgery must be reported to the FAA on Form 8500-7, Report of Eye Evaluation, at the next physical. Controllers must obtain specific clearance from the Regional Flight Surgeon before returning to duty.

Contact Lens Authorization by the FAA

Pilots and controllers wearing glasses or contact lenses must meet all of the FAA vision standards. Those requiring near and distant correction may do this with either bifocals worn all the time or wearing contact lenses that correct for distant and having reading glasses available for near vision.

Some contact lens manufacturers and eye specialists are touting the advantages of Mono Vision Contact Lenses (MVCL) to eliminate the need for glasses without surgery. The MVCL technique uses one contact lens to focus at near while the lens in the other eye focuses at distant. The pilot suppresses the blurred image from the eye not in use depending on the distance of the viewed object. The FAA continues to prohibit the use of MVCL's because each eye does not correct to 20/20 at distant and 20/40 at near separately. Because both eyes are not simultaneously focusing on an object at distant, the binocular component of depth perception may be reduced. Many other monocular cues to depth perception, such as shadows, relative size, motion parallax, contrast, and texture gradient still exist when using MVCL. These monocular cues are susceptible to illusions in a visually compromised environment, such as reduced lighting or weather. The FAA will only allow mono-vision correction if induced surgically (see our article on refractive surgery) though it does require at least a six months adjustment period before returning to flying. After that time, the FAA will most likely require a medical flight test and subsequent Statement of Demonstrated Ability (SODA) to remove restrictions. Currently, controllers are not authorized any method of mono-vision correction.

The FAA has approved the use of the newer multifocal contact lenses that correct at distant in the central portion while correcting for near vision at the periphery. This arrangement works fine when looking down at something to read, but blurs images in the periphery on lateral and upward gaze, particularly in low light conditions. Applicants must allow one month for adaptation before returning to aviation related duties, must be free from any vision defects, and must meet FAA vision standards.

Finally the FAA prohibits the use of X-chrome lenses. These are contact lenses of different colors to enhance color perception in those individuals who are "color blind."

Removal of Previous SODAs for Uncorrected Vision

The FAA removed the previous uncorrected visual acuity requirement. As a result, many individuals no longer required SODAs. You must specifically request that the SODA be removed from your records. This can be accomplished through your FAA medical examiner or through AMAS.

What is FAA current policy regarding glaucoma?

Pilots and controllers medically treated for increased intraocular pressure are usually not medically disqualified. Continued medical certification depends primarily on the status of the ophthalmologic condition. Individuals whose ocular pressure can be controlled while maintaining required visual acuity and normal fields of vision, are generally certified for all classes. Once treatment begins, the FAA must be provided with evaluation and treatment information. FAA form 8500-14 (Ophthalmologic Evaluation for Glaucoma) must be completed and forwarded to Oklahoma City. Controllers report through the regional flight surgeons. FAA will require periodic follow up which can be provided during the airman's routine FAA physical examination.

As noted previously, unilateral vision or visual field defects are waiverable for pilots, but typically not for controllers. However, controllers with visual field defects might possibly be considered for center operations on a case by case basis.

10.14 INTRODUCTION TO ENHANCED VISUAL SYSTEMS

Flight or flying approaches in visually-obscured terrain or low-visibility conditions is obviously not optimum for safe operations. Technology has been developed to enable aviators to operate in those conditions in a safer manner, and these technologies are known as *enhanced vision systems (EVS)* or *enhanced flight vision system (EFVS)* for aircraft. The main differentiation between the two is the location of the image. In EVS systems, the image is displayed on a screen on the aircraft instrument panel. With EFVS, the image is displayed on a *Head Up Display (HUD)* mounted above the glare-shield for the pilot to look through while in flight.

Enhanced vision systems are airborne visual systems designed to allow a pilot to more safely operate in visually-degraded environments through the use of *light intensification* or *infrared* vision systems. While the use of these particular systems does not allow for perfect visual clarity, they have the potential to allow pilots to see obstacles that may remain unseen with unaided vision. *Synthetic vision systems (SVS)* is not technically a "flight vision system," as its information is database-driven as opposed to real-time information and are not to be used for primary flight references.

Light intensification visual systems, commonly called *night vision goggles or NVGs,* take light energy (photons) into the device through the objective lens. As the photons pass through the photocathode screen, the photons are turned into electrons. The electrons pass through a microchannel plate (photo-multiplier) and multiplied. The multiplied electrons then pass through the phosphor screen where the electrons are changed back into photons, presenting the aviator with a visual image in the ocular lens.

Figure 10.6 Night Vision Goggles

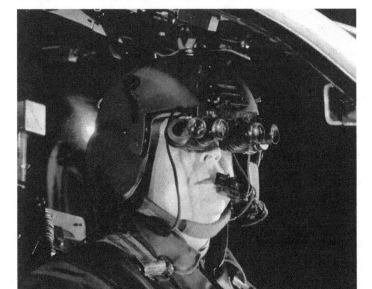

NASA 2021

The end result of this process is the NVG's capacity to increase the luminance of an object, making the object easier to see.

Infrared vision systems, commonly called *forward-looking infrared or FLIR,* create an image based on thermal contrast. Hotter objects emit more energy in the infrared spectrum than cold objects, thus allowing a FLIR user to differentiate between objects based their individual temperatures. As one can imagine, a temperature different exists between virtually everything in the natural world, revealing a scene for the user to interpret. FLIR systems are extremely sensitive to thermal contrast, so even slight temperature differences result in image transfer.

EVS provides the pilot with the ability to see certain objects such as terrain, runway, trees, nearby roads, etc. Unaided vision may allow a pilot to detect the lighted outline of the runway and cars on the road, but little else. EVS allows the pilot to build a better, more complete mental scene of the area as the approach is flown, thus allowing a safer transition from ILS to visual approach.

Issues with these devices remain regarding certain elements of vision, which will be discussed in the chapter "Human-Automation Engagement."

Conclusion

An aviator's knowledge of human orientation system strengths and weaknesses will give them an advantage in the flight environment. The pilot will know what to expect out of themselves, and when to rely on countermeasures to ensure flight safety is maintained should conditions exist where their own vision and/or orientation abilities are in doubt.

In the next two chapters, we will discuss specific spatial and visual illusions routinely occurring in flight conditions, and how to successfully defeat those illusions.

Chapter 10 Core Competency Questions

1. What are the three primary sources of orientation in aviation?
2. What percentage of inflight orientation does visual orientation provide?
3. Proprioceptive senses allow humans to sense what?
4. Vestibular sense allow humans to sense what?
5. What two components make up the vestibular apparatus?
6. What would be the speed of a turn for sub-threshold acceleration?
7. What are the two main components of human visual systems?
8. What are the three phases of vision?

9. Where is peak visual acuity located?
10. How large is human perceptible field of view?
11. Where is the night visual blind spot located on the visual field?
12. What are the two technologies used for enhanced vision systems?
13. What is the recommendation for visual scanning inflight for instruments versus outside the aircraft?

11. SPATIAL DISORIENTATION

Spatial disorientation (SDO) is a subject known by virtually all pilots as it is required knowledge to be covered in a pilot's training cycle. It would be safe to say, however, precious few pilots fully appreciate the magnitude of intellectual incapacitation SDO can produce under the right circumstances. While SDO looks fairly benign reading about it or talking about the subject in a classroom, SDO can create a psychologically terrifying life-or-death struggle for a pilot wrestling to maintain flight with no idea which way is up, and while attempting to keep their aircraft from hitting terrain at an extremely steep angle-of-descent.

The problem with SDO is not that it *will* occur, but rather *when* it occurs. Rarely is SDO a factor in IFR flight in IMC conditions, although it may produce disconcerting sensations during routine flights. Often times SDO becomes a major factor when the pilot is engaged in some other startling activity, such as trying to manage an icing, engine-out, loss-of-instruments, or loss-of-control event. In the course of trying to rectify the predominant issue the pilot loses intellectual command of their orientation, mistaken believes they are out-of-control, and in a panic actually <u>over-controls</u> the aircraft to the degree where a total loss of control and orientation is experienced. Often this results in the aircraft contacting terrain in a near-vertical descent resulting in total destruction of the aircraft and fatal injuries for the occupants.

In this chapter, we'll discuss:

1. History of spatial disorientation
2. Spatial disorientation definition, terminology and types
3. Flight conditions leading to spatial disorientation
4. Visual impairments to orientation
5. Effects of fatigue on spatial disorientation
6. Pilot response to spatial disorientation
7. Optokinetic cervical reflex
8. Spatial disorientation illusions
9. Spatial disorientation countermeasures

11.1 HISTORY OF SPATIAL DISORIENTATION

Before the development of high-speed, mechanized transportation, understanding human spatial orientation did not garner much interest in the scientific communities. Walking, running, riding horses, floating on a ship, or riding in horse-drawn carriages did not do much to cause a human to lose their orientation abilities.

In the late 1800's, Austrian Physicist Ernst Mach was riding on a train which was traveling at a high-rate of speed (for the time) around a long, sustained curve in the tracks. Mach noticed when the train track straightened out following the curve, he still had a sensation of turning. This event started Mach on the path to find out how human orientation systems worked. With the assistance of other scientists, a human's sense of balance and movement was traced back to fluid movement in the semi-circular canals of the inner ear.

In December of 1903, Orville and Wilbur Wright achieved the first flight of a heavier-than-air machine. For the first time in history, man was exposed to operation in three dimensions, as opposed the two-dimensional environment of having constant contact with the Earth in some way. In 1908, the first aviation-related fatality occurred to U.S. Army Lt. Thomas Selfridge while flying as a passenger on a demonstration flight of the 1908 Wright Military Flyer, piloted by none other than Orville Wright himself. The aircraft crashed and Lt. Selfridge died of head injuries.

Obviously, it did not take long before early aviators realized flight into clouds was eventually unavoidable, and questions concerning those possibilities arose. Scientists theorized a human would be able to maintain orientation with the Earth for some 15 to 20 minutes without visual contact with the ground or horizon. It would be safe to assume those theories lasted about as long as it took for the first pilots to fly into clouds, lose orientation, and crash. Aviators and scientists quickly realized as flights in lower visibility conditions occurred, flying became even more dangerous and new questions began to emerge. The term associated to a loss-of-orientation in flight was *vertigo*.

Vertigo was explored more seriously in the 1920's, and one of the first scientists to experiment with the types of vertigo experienced in flight was Dr. Robert Barany. Dr. Barany experimented with a special chair of his design capable of smoothly spinning on a very low friction bearing on the chair's vertical axis. This chair was appropriately named the "Barany Chair", and had been used in previous experiments regarding human orientation. In 1926, Dr. Barany definitively identified the first vertigo illusion experienced in flight, which he named the *somatogyric illusion*. In time, other common illusions were identified and vertigo eventually became known as <u>spatial</u> <u>disorientation.</u>

Scientists discovered a pilot could potentially artificially orient themselves in flying conditions with the advancement of aircraft instrumentation, and by 1929 developed the first experimental "fully" instrumented airplane cockpit. With these instruments, pilots could monitor the aircraft's flight altitude, attitude in relation to the ground, and airspeed, enabling flight in low- to no-visibility conditions.

Spatial disorientation research and subsequent training continued throughout the mid-1900s, although pilots continued to experience fatal accidents as a result of spatial disorientation (SDO). Around the late 1960's to early 1970's, the U.S. Air Force's School of Aerospace Medicine developed research teams to find definitive answers to the physiological issues continuing to plague the aviation community, including spatial disorientation. In 2010, USAF research revealed the SDO accident and fatality rate has not changed significantly since 1990. A study of SDO mishaps shows from 1990 to 1999, SDO accounted for 14% of all Air Force aviation-related mishaps and 30% of all fatalities. From 2000 to 2009, SDO accounted for 11% of all aviation-related mishaps, and 26% of all fatalities.

Spatial disorientation related-research continues to this day, as well as for many other physiological issues, and pilots are still experiencing fatal encounters with SDO in flight even with the current amazing technologies available. Even after more than 100 years of scientific effort, aviators are still dying from some of the same physiological issues causing the deaths of those aviators who flew first.

11.2 SPATIAL DISORIENTATION DEFINITION, TERMINOLOGY AND TYPES

Spatial disorientation may be defined as "an erroneous sense or mistaken perception of one's position and motion relative to Earth." Typically, SDO occurs when a lack of visual confirmation of the horizon is present; however, in some cases SDO can occur on clear days as well.

As spatial disorientation illusions have been identified, specific terminology have been assigned to them based on the following root terms:

- Vestibulo: refers to the vestibular system, both semi-circular canals and otolith organs.
- Oculo, ocular: refers to the eye
- Somato: refers to the body
- Gyric: refers to a turning motion
- Gravic: refers to gravity or a linear (straight-line) motion

Based on knowledge of these root-terms, a specific SDO illusion may be deciphered as to what the cause of the illusion is. For example, a *somatogravic* illusion refers to the body (somato) is affected by linear (gravic) acceleration. An *oculogyric* illusion refers to the eyes being affected by a turning sensation.

Spatial disorientation of any degree may be a dangerous situation in the making. The types of SDO can be separated into three categories:

- Type I: Unrecognized
- Type II: Recognized
- Type III: Incapacitating

Type I SDO is spatial disorientation occurring in such a way the pilot does not notice the incidence. This may be a slow roll or undetected turn.

Type II SDO is spatial disorientation occurring in such a way the pilot realizes orientation is not correct. This may be a physiological turning sensation while the aircraft is flying straight and level, or the involuntary eye movement following an extended bank.

Type III SDO is spatial disorientation so psychologically overwhelming the pilot has little chance of recovery. This could be an ever-tightening descending spiral the pilot cannot control as they have no conception of true attitude.

SDO can transition rapidly from Type I or II directly to Type III. Under the correct circumstances, any SDO illusion can startle and/or unnerve an aviator to the degree the brain simply cannot cope with the situation adequately, unless properly trained to respond effectively.

Military aviation experiences a large percentage of aircraft-related fatalities as a result of SDO mishaps. This is mainly due to the hazardous missions flown in combat aircraft, such as low-level night or all-weather missions, flying in adverse weather conditions, ordinance-avoidance maneuvering, etc.

11.3 FLIGHT CONDITIONS LEADING TO SPATIAL DISORIENTATION

Certain flight conditions exist increasing a pilot's chances of getting SDO. These conditions include:

- Co-existing visual illusions
- Decreased visibility (IFR) conditions
- Catastrophic electrical/instrument failure
- Sub-threshold acceleration

- Manual flight maneuvers or changes in angular acceleration

Co-existing visual illusions can cause a pilot to misinterpret approach parameters, thereby causing mental confusion to develop during a critical phase-of-flight. The brain may be attempting to reconcile visual information, creating a significant loss of situation awareness which can potentially cause the pilot to lose airspeed, altitude, and/or attitude perception.

Decreased visibility removes the eye's ability to confirm orientation to the true horizon, which provides 90% of our human orientation ability. Quite obviously a lack of visual references accounts for the majority of SDO incidents and accidents.

Catastrophic electrical/instrument failure obviously removes the pilot's ability to determine orientation via flight instrumentation, which is absolutely necessary during low visibility conditions.

Sub-threshold acceleration are those slight banks occurring below the human threshold to detect. Upon recognition, this condition may startle the pilot and initiate flight control over-correction actions.

Manual flight maneuvers will stimulate the vestibular apparatus and proprioceptive and visual systems creating false sensations of movement or orientation, particularly during any distractions as these immediately detract from pilot S/A. Examples of maneuvers which stimulate the vestibular system are holding patterns, prolonged turns, acceleration or deceleration with limited visual references, head movement during turns, and turbulence.

11.4 VISUAL IMPAIRMENTS TO ORIENTATION

Since vision equates to 90% of human orientation ability, any impairment to our visual ability may lead to disorienting conditions. The following are recognized visual impairments:

- Smoke
- Haze
- Night
- Artificial light at night
- Precipitations

The factors listed above may cause a pilot to visually misinterpret descent and intercept angles, altitude, distance, and depth perception. Any condition causing a loss of visual references can be powerful and overwhelming to the pilot-in-command, especially when combined with vestibular and proprioceptive stimulation. The orientation picture presented to the brain may be so confusing, the brain can not make sense of what is happening and panic ensues. Once a pilot lapses into panic, ability to rapidly reorient themselves drops dramatically.

11.5 EFFECTS OF FATIGUE ON SPATIAL DISORIENTATION

Fatigue is the enemy of operational effectiveness, and the same can be said for orientation effectiveness. Humans are not effective at paying attention for long periods of time, and fatigue makes this ineffectiveness worse. The main problem fatigue creates is *complacency*. In relation to orientation, complacency breeds a loss of situational awareness through the following conditions:

- Acceptance of normally unacceptable situations
- Routine tasks get skipped
- Recognition of the development of bad situations or attempt corrective actions in a timely fashion
- Reduction of swift and complex decision-making processes

Acceptance of normally unacceptable situations is a dangerous element of fatigue which may place the aviator into an inadvertent and undesirable flight condition. At the end of a long, boring flight the main focus may become simply landing at the destination, regardless of what may transpire on the way in. One of the most dangerous phrases in aviation is "Let's just…"; let's just push on, let's just see if we can push our fuel consumption a little, *let's just* see if we can beat the weather before it dips below minimums. "Let's just" means someone is usually compromising safety for time, which in aviation is never a good thing.

Routine tasks getting skipped may mean an aviator is no longer adhering to safe practices, such as maintaining a good visual scan of the flight path, or strict adherence to checklists. The thought is "nothing has happened so far and we're almost there, so we'll take a few short-cuts to make this easy."

Recognition of the development of bad situations or attempting corrective actions in time is a result of a fatigued mind. Aviators may be lost in thought about something not related to the flight, and subtle signs of equipment or control failure may be either missed or ignored.

Reduction of swift and complex decision-making processes occur when the brain is not integrated with the task-at-hand. The brain has to "catch up" to the current situation, and if the situation warrants rapid analysis and reaction time, the seconds it takes to catch up may be the difference between life and death.

It is critical to stay mentally engaged with the aircraft at all times, which will be discussed in depth later in this chapter.

11.6 PILOT RESPONSE TO SPATIAL DISORIENTATION

Spatial disorientation, in many cases, will occur when the aviator is distracted with other problems or issues. Few spatial disorientation incidents and accidents occur when the pilot is fully engaged and psychologically invested in the flight segment, as they are monitoring the aircraft with full efficiency.

However, if and when SDO does occur in flight, certain elements are common to the experience:

1. The pilot will pay attention to the most conspicuous source of information, whether it is correct or not.
2. Attention often narrows to one instrument or view. Human tendency is to visually lock on to the first piece of potentially helpful information available; a view out of the windscreen, artificial horizon, altimeter, turn indicator, etc. The pilot may realize the situation is rapidly spiraling out-of-control, and the early stages of panic are setting in.
3. Cognitive and motor skills degrade or disintegrate altogether. The brain is in the middle stages of panic, and rational thought is difficult or impossible to focus on.
4. Pilots experience an almost complete loss of situational awareness. Nothing makes sense, the pilot has no idea what their proper orientation is, and hope of survival is degrading quickly.

One would surmise less experienced pilots would be most susceptible to SDO incidents and accidents, but actually the reverse is true. According to FAA research, the average pilot experience level involved in SDO-related accidents is over 1,000 flight hours and 10 years of experience. If those statistics are accepted as fact, how could that be?

As in any skill or profession involving experience, more experienced pilots presumably may become a little too comfortable with the flight environment. If a pilot had been flying for a good number of years and had never experienced a radical SDO or visual illusions event, some tend to get the "superhuman syndrome,"; in other words, they begin to believe those events will never happen to them as a result of their individual "superior" abilities or physiology. Unfortunately, human physiology is the same for all and when those advanced pilots happen onto the "perfect storm" of ingredients (weather, visibility, aircraft movement), they find themselves unprepared and immersed in a terrifying SDO event that very well could take their life.

Let us examine an incident which could possibly attributed to this phenomenon:

Incident Review – Jan 2016: A Part 91 IFR pilot was flying in IMC at 14,000 feet over Utah as a single-pilot operation with no passengers.

While flying in the weather, the pilot reported failure of the FMS and advised ATC they would be exceeding their assigned altitude of 14,000. 25 seconds after that transmission, the pilot reported failure of the autopilot and requested a climb to clear air. 2.5 minutes following the previous transmission, the pilot declared "MAYDAY", again requesting an ascent to get out of the weather.

The aircraft reached a maximum altitude of FL210, went into a tightening right turn, broke up in flight, and the fuselage impacted terrain at a descent rate approaching 36,000 feet per minute.

Analysis: The NTSB investigation revealed the pilot most likely experienced SDO, and even though the pilot reported multiple instrument failures, no such failure could be proven by the investigators.

Conclusion: The pilot was flying in very low visibility conditions by themselves, and likely experiencing some degree of SDO. Between proprioceptive and vestibular input, the pilot convinced themselves the aircraft instrumentation was failing when, in fact, the pilot's physiological orientation systems were confused. The pilot chose to believe their body's input over the aircraft, at which point the aircraft went uncontrolled.

11.7 OPTOKINETIC CERVICAL REFLEX

The *Optokinetic Cervical Reflex* is a compensatory reflexive reaction to banking an aircraft. The optokinetic cervical reflex occurs when the body banks with the bank angle of a vehicle capable of banking into a turn; imagine riding a motorcycle or banking an airplane. The bank angle of the vehicle (and thus the bank angle of the body) causes the line of the eyes to rotate to try to stay oriented with the true horizon, so the head banks in the opposite direction of the body so long as the horizon is visible.

This reaction works naturally in visual conditions allowing the true horizon to be seen, but does not work when the horizon cannot be seen. This results in an exaggerated sense of movement, which in turn can startle the pilot. The pilot may question instrumentation accuracy, starting the chain-of-events leading to an invasive SDO incident or accident.

Let us now examine the individual illusions associated with spatial disorientation.

11.8 SPATIAL DISORIENTATION ILLUSIONS

Spatial disorientation illusions are described by the sensation the pilot may feel or the flight condition that develops as a result of stimulation of either visual, vestibular or proprioceptive input, or any combination thereof. The illusions are named as follows:

- Oculogyric
- Elevator
- Somatogyric
- Graveyard spiral
- Graveyard spin
- Coriolis
- Somatogravic
- Inversion
- G-excess
- Leans
- Stroboscopic effect

Oculogyric illusions occur typically at night upon roll-out following a sustained turn of over 20 seconds, whereas the pilot tries to focus on a single point of light.

The semicircular canal fluid equilibrates to the turn, and is subsequently re-stimulated upon roll-out. The re-stimulation of the semi-circular canal (SCC) fluid initiates nerve impulses to the eyes (vestibulo-ocular reflex), causing the eyes to move as if tracking the single point of light as a moving object.

The involuntary "tracking" movement of the eyes causes the brain to interpret the image as the <u>object</u> is moving as opposed to the *eyes*, possibly causing the pilot to believe they are observing a moving object in their flight path. This, in turn, may cause a pilot to initiate collision avoidance maneuvers with a ground-based light, creating an unsafe flight condition.

To overcome this illusion, the pilot needs to wait 20 to 30 seconds for the SCC fluid to re-equilibrate, while closely monitoring the light to ensure it does not truly belong to another aircraft.

Elevator illusions are another example of how the vestibulo-ocular reflex can be problematic in flight. These illusions occur as a result of unanticipated updrafts or downdrafts encountered in level flight.

In an updraft, the aircraft is suddenly lifted several feet, causing a vestibulo-ocular reflex of the eyes in the opposite (downward) direction. Without visual references, the sensation created is interpreted as the aircraft nose has pitched up, prompting an automatic and reflexive nose-down control input from the pilot. This may create a loss-of-control flight condition.

In a downdraft, the aircraft drops several feet, and the vestibulo-ocular reflex makes the eyes look up. The sensation created is as if the nose of the aircraft pitches down, prompting a reflexive nose-up control input, potentially causing the aircraft to stall.

Somatogyric illusions occur when engaged in a level-flight turn long enough to allow the SCC fluid to equilibrate (20 seconds), the pilot will feel as if they are flying straight and level. When rolling out of the turn to truly fly straight and level the pilot feels a physiological sensation of turning in the opposite direction as a result of re-stimulating the passive SCC fluid.

The error would be to re-enter the original turn to feel as if the aircraft was straight and level again. This could potentially cause a loss altitude or heading, ultimately creating a loss-of-separation condition with other aircraft.

The *graveyard spiral* is the condition in which a pilot is engaged in an undetected banking (subthreshold turn) descent without visual references, which would generally happen while distracted with another task and at night or in clouds. As the bank increases, the descent rate increases as well. Eventually, the pilot may notice the altimeter unwinding and pull back on the yoke to try to level off, which instead increases the bank angle and descent rate. The aircraft will start descending with increasing speed, which startles the pilot and, in a panic, pulls back on the yoke even harder, tightening the spiral into a corkscrew vertical descent.

The subthreshold turn initiates this illusion which can rapidly develop into an uncontrolled descent of terrifying proportions. The following are the proper recovery procedures to follow:

- **Reduce power to idle**
- **Level the wings**
- **Slowly pull back to a nose-level attitude**
- **Add power once recovered back to normal airspeed to avoid a stall**

Once straight and level, the somatogyric illusion may induce the pilot to feel as though they were spiraling in the opposite direction, so caution and strict adherence to the instruments must be maintained until the SCC fluid re-equilibrates.

Let us examine two incidents that appear to be Graveyard Spirals:

Incident – July 1999: A Piper Saratoga being flown by John F. Kennedy Jr., his wife, and his sister-in-law were flying from Essex County Airport, NJ to Martha's Vineyard, MA on the evening of July 16th. JFK Jr. was a low-time VFR pilot who purchased the aircraft three months prior with the flight occurring in VFR-legal conditions, although hazy atmospheric conditions prevailed and the horizon of the ocean was difficult to discern.

The flight departed later than anticipated at 2038, with the last 30 minutes of the flight over open water. Shortly before the accident, the aircraft was observed on radar to make increasingly steep turns, with radar contact lost at 2141 and 7 nm from the Martha's Vineyard shore. The aircraft impacted the water at a 4,700 feet-per-minute descent rate, where all occupants were deceased on impact. The ensuing NTSB investigation concluded JFK Jr.'s accident was a probable SDO event leading to a loss-of-control.

Incident – November 2011: A Cirrus SR-20 with the pilot and three passengers was on initial approach near Crystal Lake, IL when the VFR pilot inadvertently entered IFR conditions. ATC advised the pilot to divert to an alternate airport, which the pilot declined.

Radar returns indicated the aircraft entered weather in a gentle right turn, the turn continued to tighten, and the aircraft ultimately impacted the ground in a near-vertical descent.

Conclusion: Each one of these accidents could have been prevented with proper training and strict adherence to an effective instrument scan.

Graveyard spin illusions are similar in scope to the graveyard spiral, but in the case of the spin the lower wing is in a deeper stall condition than the upper wing and the airspeed is slower. The lower wing generates more drag, yawing the aircraft into a more aggressive spin.

The error would be for the pilot to stop the spin, feeling as though they were spinning in the opposite direction, and re-enter the original spin to feel as though they were now straight and level.

Spin recovery is straightforward, and should be accomplished as follows:

- **Power to idle**
- **Ailerons to neutral**

- **Rudder applied opposite to spin**
- **Elevator forward**
- **Once control is re-established, add power**

The main ingredient for successfully mitigating this condition is to not panic, and follow the instruments' guidance.

The *Coriolis illusion* occurs in flight conditions where the horizon is occluded and the aircraft is engaged in a prolonged turn over 20 seconds. When the turn is initiated the fluid of one semicircular canal will be stimulated, physiologically signaling the turn to the pilot. As the turn extends past 20 seconds, the fluid equilibrates with body movement and the turn is no longer sensed. When the head is moved side-to-side or (especially) up-and-down in a nodding motion, other SCC fluid will be stimulated, which in turn may cause the pilot to feel a violent tumbling sensation.

When the pilot feels the violent tumbling sensation, the initial response is to immediately start "correcting" the controls instinctively, placing the aircraft into a true loss-of-control condition. Once a genuine loss-of-control is occurring, the pilot panics and completely loses SA.

The Coriolis illusion often occurs due to distraction, such as dropping a pen on the floor and bending down to pick it up, or paying attention to a handheld electronic device instead of instruments.

Let us review an incident in which the Coriolis illusion likely played a factor:

Incident – November 2011: A Lancair 360 with one pilot and no passengers was flying in the vicinity of Milford, UT. The pilot was VFR-only qualified flying in VMC conditions.

The aircraft engine started running rough. Attempting to diagnose the problem, the pilot looked down into the cockpit at the control panel and started adjusting controls in an attempt to rectify the problem, and while doing so inadvertently flew into a cloud bank.

The aircraft departed the cloud bank in a near-vertical attitude and impacted terrain, destroying the aircraft and causing fatal injuries to the pilot.

Conclusion: This accident most likely occurred as a result of pilot distraction causing flight into IMC. When the pilot finally looked up to re-establish orientation, they likely panicked when they could not see the horizon, over-controlled the aircraft into a loss-of-control condition, and was unable to re-establish control prior to impact.

The *somatogravic illusion* is the exaggerated sensation of pitch when accelerating or decelerating with no visual references. Acceleration accentuates the pitch up sensation, while deceleration accentuates the pitch down sensation. This is particularly dangerous illusion, as it is one of the leading causes of CFIT accidents.

This sensation occurs as a result of acceleration or deceleration forces influencing the hair cells and possibly fluid movement in the otolith organs.

Common conditions in which the somatogravic illusion occurs are as follows:

- Acceleration on take-off or go-arounds
- Rapid transition from VMC to IMC, such as flying into a cloud layer or fog bank
- Deceleration in IMC
- Ascending or descending at varying rates of climb or descent
- Rapid changes in pitch in IMC
- Climbing flight path with power increases combined with gear and flap retraction

Somatogravic illusions have been attributed to many fatal accident sequences, a few of which we will examine below:

Incident – November 2013: A Boeing 737 was on approach at night and inclement weather into a runway in Kazakhstan. The pilots elected to perform a go-around for an unspecified reason. On go-around, the nose of the aircraft reached a 30-degree pitch, the autopilot disconnected and airspeed decreased, and the aircraft reached approximately 2,300 feet AGL. The pilots pushed the nose over to a 75-degree nose-low pitch, and impacted the tarmac. There were no survivors.

Analysis: Authorities initially assumed a mechanical failure occurred, and investigated the accident as such. Investigation findings indicate no mechanical malfunctions occurred. Cockpit voice recorder (CVR) data recorded sink-rate and ground-proximity warnings sounding in the cockpit; however, black-box data indicated the warnings caused the pilots to inexplicitly push forward even further on the controls as opposed to pulling back on the controls. The only explanation authorities could conclude was the pilots most likely experienced a somatogravic illusion on go-around.

Conclusion: This accident likely occurred as a result of the rapid change of pitch and forward acceleration experienced during the go-around procedure, resulting in a somatogravic illusion. With the lack of visual references and the pitch and acceleration properties, the pilots may have felt as though the aircraft was looping into an inverted state, erroneously forcing them to over-correct into the fatal dive.

Incident – December 2017: A King Air C90 was practicing ILS approaches in Florida with two commercial-rated pilots and one multi-engine instructor. Two minutes after vectoring to join the localizer with an approach clearance, ATC issued a low-altitude alert and instructed the pilot to climb to 1,600 feet. A pilot radioed "I am, sir, I am!" just before radio and radar contact was lost, at which point the aircraft dove nearly vertically into a lake.

Analysis: The aircraft was porpoising on approach. DVR data indicates after ATC issued the low-altitude alert, the aircraft made a rapid initial climb, followed by a near-vertical dive into the lake located under the approach path.

Conclusion: The pilot-in-command was likely experiencing some degree of difficulty maintaining the ILS approach, porpoising while on the approach path. After ATC issued the low-altitude alert, the initial rapid pull-back on the controls may have produced a somatogravic illusion, startling the pilot to instinctively initiate a steep, nose-low correction at low-altitude.

Incident – December 2017: A Boeing 767-375BCF cargo aircraft was on initial approach to Houston at 6,200 feet with three pilots on board. Precipitation and turbulence were present along the approach path, and the pilots were trying to vector around the weather to turn to base leg. The aircraft climbed to 6,300 feet, initiated a rapid dive and impacted a swamp 40 miles SE of the airport. All crewmembers suffered fatal injuries.

Analysis: The pilots were requesting vectors to go around the weather. While the aircraft was descending through the weather, it leveled briefly at 6,200 feet, climbing to 6,300 feet, during which time FDR data indicates vertical acceleration consistent with turbulence. Airspeed was steady at 230 KIA, and after the climb to 6,300 feet, engines went to max thrust as the PF inadvertently selected go-around power, the nose pitched up 4 degrees, then rapidly down to 49 degrees. Airspeed increased to 430 KIA, with the nose rising to 20 degrees nose-low prior to impact.

Conclusion: From the accumulated data the PIC may have experienced a somatogravic illusion from the combination of the initial nose pitch-up and turbulence, and instinctively pushed the nose down to counteract the effect.

Somatogravic Illusion Countermeasures

Somatogravic illusions can be intellectually difficult to negotiate, especially when occurring at low altitudes. The following are recognized steps pilots should initiate to mitigate the illusion:

- **Avoid flying into clouds or descending into fog in the first place, or at least anticipate the sensations likely to occur.**
- **Get your eyes on the instrument panel instead of outside the aircraft.**
- **Stop downward or lateral movement of the aircraft.**
- **Land the aircraft (if possible) or initiate a gentle climb. Aggressive climbs will exacerbate the illusion.**
- **Maintain gentle control inputs to avoid exacerbating the illusion as well.**
- **Realize it may take over 30 seconds to reorient with the instruments and establish full aircraft control.**
- **Communicate your problems with ATC. They may be able to provide life-saving advice or instructions.**

Inversion illusions occur following a climb-to-altitude, culminating with an abrupt level-off. This slight upward force may induce a pilot to believe the aircraft is either inverted or possibly tumbling backward.

This sensation occurs as a result of semi-circular canal (SCC) and otolith fluid and/or hair cell stimulation brought on through gravitational forces, combined with proprioceptive stimulation by the pilot's seat safety harness. The hyper-gravity experienced during the maneuver lifts the hair cells towards the top of the head, creating a tumbling sensation. The illusion is further confirmed by activating proprioceptive sensors produced by the pilot's body being pushed upward into the lap belt & shoulder harness.

The error would be to reflexively push the aircraft nose forward to avoid the perceived stall, or roll the aircraft truly inverted, erroneously believing the aircraft was now straight and level.

G-excess illusions occur when a pilot looks to the inside of an increasing G turn, producing an exaggerated pitch and tumbling sensation potentially causing the pilot to believe the aircraft is out-of-control. The typical scenario for this illusion would be a transition from the downwind-leg turning to base-leg, with the pilot looking over their shoulder to visually locate the runway threshold.

The G-excess illusion is produced when the increasing G-forces of the turn influence and deflect the hair cells of the SCC and otolith, producing the exaggerated pitch sensation (somatogravic illusion).) As the pilot turns their head to locate the threshold, SCC fluid is stimulated producing Coriolis. The resulting sensation convinces the pilot the aircraft has departed controlled flight at a low altitude, predictably causing reflexive control inputs, panic and true loss-of-control.

Let us examine an accident where the pilot likely experienced a G-excess illusion:

Incident – November 2014: A pilot flying a Cessna 182 in vicinity of Wendover, UT, was practicing touch and go's at the local airport. Upon one of take-off attempts, the pilot initiated a left climbing turn and oriented himself with the departure end of the runway by looking outside and behind the aircraft. The aircraft banked even harder left, descended, and impacted the ground, causing fatal injuries to the pilot.

Analysis: The NTSB concluded the pilot failed to maintain situational awareness during a turn, resulting in a loss of aircraft control.

Conclusion: While the pilot was looking outside the window and over their shoulder, it is possible the pilot experienced a false pitch sensation, and in a state of startle over-controlled the aircraft at a low altitude, resulting in ground contact and their death.

The *leans illusion* occurs as a result of the aircraft being engaged in an undetected turn, with the pilot perceiving straight-and-level flight as a result of SCC fluid stabilization. Once the undetected turn is quickly corrected, the pilot will lean to what they perceive as straight-and-level. This type of SDO illusion is very common, especially for less-experienced aviators.

The mechanism behind this illusion is as the aircraft flies its undetected turn, the SCC fluid gradually equilibrates to the turn. When the turn is quickly corrected, the SCC fluid is still equilibrated to the turn, causing the pilot to lean towards what felt like straight-and-level during the original turn. The leans may also be caused by peripheral visual orientation cues.

While not particularly dangerous, the leans can cause a loss of orientation which creates an over-bank in the opposite direction, or possible rolling of the aircraft in severe cases.

The *Stroboscopic Effect* is the phenomena which occurs as a result of a continuous rotational or other visual cyclic motion represented by a series of short or instantaneous samples at a sampling frequency close to the period of motion. For example, if one has observed a spoked wheel turning at a high rate of speed, the spokes may appear stationary or to turn backwards. This effect may occur as a pilot watches a spinning propeller or rapid strobe-light frequency, and may cause adverse physical symptoms such as annoyance, visual fatigue, headache, and reduced task performance.

A closely-related phenomena is *flicker-vertigo*, which can occur as a helicopter pilot looks through the blades of the main rotor as it turns into the sun causing the sunlight to strobe. Flicker vertigo is caused by a strobe light flashing at 1 Hz to 20 Hz, which is approximately the frequency of human brainwaves. This effect may cause aviators to experience disorientation, nausea, rapid eye movements behind closed eyelids, loss of fine motor control, and muscular rigidity. In rare cases this effect may even cause seizures. The best course of action is to limit visual exposure to rapidly strobing lights.

11.9 SPATIAL DISORIENTATION COUNTERMEASURES

Quite obviously, a pilot needs to have an established plan-of-action to counteract the effects of spatial disorientation in flight. The following are recognized methods of combating SDO:

- **Increased awareness**
- **Vigilance in high-risk situations**
- **Do not react to physiological inputs until confirmed with aircraft instrumentation**
- **Monitor and believe your instruments**
- **Fly straight-and-level until symptoms resolve**
- **Refer control to the other pilot or to autopilot**

Increased awareness includes maintaining systematic and frequent orientation checks with your aircraft instrumentation. Distractions need also be kept at a minimum. Flying an aircraft should be treated as serious business, not a place for casual discussions or taking pictures of clouds.

Vigilance in high-risk situations includes maintaining intellectual command over the aircraft and continuous awareness of the orientation and position of the aircraft, particularly in conditions known to cause disorienting sensory inputs. If one is mentally prepared for disorienting conditions, those conditions will be much easier to properly deal with.

Do not react to physiological inputs until confirmed with aircraft instrumentation. This step is absolutely essential to NOT instinctively reacting to sudden pitch, yaw, or roll sensations and potentially creating an unrecoverable loss-of-control event. Instinctive or reflexive control inputs to attitude sensations is the cause of many fatal accidents, especially at low altitudes, and true aircraft actions can be confirmed in a split-second's glance at the instruments for confirmation. Backing this discipline up with unusual attitude training would be preferable.

Monitor and believe your instruments. This statement may seem obvious; however, when the brain is completely and profoundly disoriented, the natural human response is to trust the body as opposed to mechanical or electronic instrumentation. Aviators must learn to <u>not</u> trust the physiological inputs of vestibular and proprioception in flight, but instead almost completely disregard them as useless information. The body's orientation senses will lie to you in flight, which one must never forget. Maintaining currency of IFR procedures would be preferred.

Fly straight-and-level until symptoms resolve. This step will allow the body and brain to reorient themselves with normality; however, the 30 seconds or so it takes for this to happen can seem like an eternity when a pilot is profoundly disoriented. The pilot has to trust in the process and keeps their eyes on the instruments.

Refer control to the other pilot or to autopilot. If this step is an option in your aircraft, this can relieve the affected aviator of decision-making processes which may compromise safety-of-flight. Allow the other pilot or the automated system to maintain control until normality returns.

Conclusion

As mentioned at the beginning of this chapter, precious few aviators respect the magnitude of orientation problems profound cases of spatial disorientation can induce on unsuspecting aviators, unless they have been exposed to those conditions and were lucky enough to survive. Aviators must never forget the three-dimensional environment they operate in is completely foreign to effective human orientation, and terrifying life-threatening events can develop in seconds. Respect for those facts and strict adherence to the SDO Countermeasures previously discussed will help ensure a pilot's journey in aviation, whether private or professional, is an enjoyable one.

Chapter 11 Core Competency Questions

1. True or false: SDO may rapidly transition from unnoticed to incapacitating.
2. SDO typically happens when an aviator cannot visually confirm orientation with what?
3. True or false: Fatigue may lead to SDO by causing routine tasks or scans to be skipped.
4. What is the average experience level for pilots involved in SDO-related accidents?

5. What compensatory reflexive action typically happens to a pilot's head in a banking turn?
6. Which SDO illusion affects a pilot's ability to focus their eyes after rolling out of an extended turn?
7. Which SDO illusion causes a pilot to feel as if the aircraft nose suddenly pitched up during acceleration in low-visibility conditions?
8. Which SDO illusion causes a turning sensation following roll-out from an extended turn?
9. Which SDO illusion typically starts with a subthreshold turn?
10. How long should one expect to fly straight and level for SDO symptoms to resolve?
11. How much should pilots rely on vestibular and proprioceptive inputs during flight?

12. VISUAL ILLUSIONS

Visual illusions in aviation occur as a result of unnatural visual perspectives and confusing visual orientation cues for pilots. It is one of the main causes of incidents and accidents in the approach and landing phases of flight, coincidently the most accident-prone phases of flight. This fact alone makes understanding visual illusions one of the most critical physiological issues to comprehend and master to truly reduce the sheer number of incidents and accidents in aviation.

Historically, approximately 50% of corporate and commercial aviation incidents are attributed to the initial approach, final approach, and landing phases of flight. Those same phases of flight are also implicated in the majority of general aviation incidents, accidents, and fatalities. This being the case, what is it about approaches and landings that make them so difficult for both less-experienced and professional pilots alike?

In this chapter, we will discuss:

1. Effects of Visual Illusions
2. Common Landing Illusion Components
3. Airport Environment Illusions
4. Runway Environment Illusions
5. Weather Conditions Illusions
6. Tools to Counter Visual Illusions
7. Causes of Unstable Approaches
8. The Go-Around
9. Physical Hazards to Vision

12.1 EFFECTS OF VISUAL ILLUSIONS

One facet of what makes an approach and landing visual illusion appear as such to a pilot is the fact the approach trajectory appears normal when, in fact, it is not. In these cases the brain may subconsciously attempt to correct the approach path so it appears normal to pilots, thus departing stable approach parameters. Another facet of landing illusions is the brain is unable to build a comprehensible scene fast enough to intellectually interpret it correctly.

We will investigate what factors cause these illusions and why they happen to us. If the brain can't reconcile the information quickly enough for the pilot to correct any approach imperfections, the brain may enter into a "holding pattern" while trying to make a complex decision, and the delay in making a decision results in glideslope deviation, ultimately resulting in an incident or accident.

The absence or alteration of visual references on the approach path modifies a pilot's perception of their:

- Relative position to the threshold (altitude, distance).
- Intercept angles (glideslope angles).
- Ability to acquire the runway during transition from IMC to VMC (rapid scene interpretation). Weather anomalies may distort the pilot's expectation of the scene, cause a loss of field flow, modify visual perception, or make identifying the runway difficult.

The end result of the above-listed factors is they may induce an unintended deviation from the pilot's intended vertical or lateral flight path as the brain attempts to reconcile the visual information or correct the approach to make it appear "normal."

The following factors interact with the absence or alteration of visual references creating confusing perceptions:

- *Unfamiliarity* with the approach environment is one issue. The more familiar a pilot is with subconscious visual cues along the approach path for a given airport, the easier it is for them to maintain orientation during that phase.
- *Visual perspective* is another problem when viewing the Earth from the air. Our visual perspective was designed to work well at the surface of the Earth, but when that perspective is changed to one from an elevated position, it may be more difficult for humans to build a comprehensive scene in our brain.
- *Depth perception* is also heavily affected in flight. As we learned in previous chapters, human vision can only perceive depth out to a distance of 200 meters, which is only effective for an extremely short period of time (mere seconds) in a vehicle moving at a speed anywhere from 80 to 180 knots on approach.

The faster the speed of the approach, the less margin for error the pilot has to work with if anything goes awry. These incidents or accidents may be landing short, landing long, or landing to the side of the runway; extreme touchdown angles; and extreme (slow or fast) touchdown speeds.

12.2 COMMON LANDING ILLUSION COMPONENTS

While considering the various issues affecting and creating visual interpretation anomalies with unfamiliarity, visual perspective, and depth perception, three major landing illusion components are present:

- Airport environment
- Runway environment
- Weather conditions

The features involved in these environmental components can create confusion in scene building for the pilot, causing erroneous judgements resulting in abnormal landing events. Addition or subtraction of these components will greatly influence a pilot's ability for subconscious orientation, which is an important part of approach situational awareness. We will investigate each component in depth.

12.3 AIRPORT ENVIRONMENT ILLUSIONS

When considering landing illusion components involving the airport environment, terrain, lighting patterns, and structures (or a combination thereof) creates the pilot's scene building interpretation confusion. The specific components of the airport environment include:

- Ground texture and terrain features
- Off-airport lighting patterns
- Black hole approach and departures
- Uphill or downhill sloping terrain on approach path
- Wires, towers and antennas in the approach environment
- Overlapping contours

Ground texture and features can highly influence a pilot's perception of altitude along the approach path. As we know, a major component of human orientation is peripheral vision. In order to use peripheral vision for orientation purposes (speed, altitude, glide angles, etc.), course patterns in that area of the visual field are required. If no patterns exist, orientation is negated.

Imagine flying over fields in the summer time, when hills, rows of corn and vegetation create an easily-interpreted sense of altitude along the approach path. Now imagine flying over a flat field of snow, where no such texture exists. It is almost impossible to determine altitude above terrain such as this, same as flying over calm water, which greatly influences a pilot's ability to orient using peripheral vision.

Ambient lighting conditions may also assist or hinder a pilot's ability to use texture as an orientation tool. Sunlight can create texture in a relatively flat field of snow by creating shadowing effects on an undulating surface, whereas flat light eliminates the shadowing effect. Skiers may find attempting to ski in flat light treacherous as moguls and bumps are difficult to see, where skiing in sunlight makes seeing those terrain features much easier.

When flight in cloudy, flat-light winter conditions is necessary, the horizon may be difficult to discern, creating conditions for inadvertent flight-into-terrain accidents. Flight in flat-light conditions may require the use of horizontal reference points to create vertical situational awareness.

The following are recommendations regarding flight in flat-light and reference points:

- **Don't fly until you only have one visual reference point left. Two or more reference points create more effective vertical awareness.**
- **Try not to lose sight of your reference points at any time.**
- **Plan your approach so your reference points are on your side when flying, as these create better vertical awareness as opposed to points to the front on the aircraft.**
- **Never turn away from your reference point; always try to turn towards them.**

Closely following a lack of texture are terrain features, such as mountain shadow and altered planes of reference.

Off-airport lighting patterns, especially in heavily populated urban areas, can create confusing visual images of the physical environment, leading pilots to believe their aircraft is lined up with a runway when, in fact, it is not. Runway misalignment is not uncommon phenomena, even for experienced commercial pilots.

Extenuating circumstances making identification of an airport runway at night difficult may be not only urban lighting patterns, but also atmospheric conditions, precipitation and fatigue. The following are some recommendations to make runway verification more precise:

- **Compare a nearby town or city on a chart to the airport's location.**
- **Be aware of any nearby highways or roads paralleling the runway which may appear to be the runway.**
- **Look for the airport's single white and green beacon.**
- **Back up visual approaches with ILS approach guidance.**

- Study the airport's diagram to familiarize yourself with runway layout and look for those patterns.
- If available, initially turn up the airport lights to their brightest intensity for positive location.
- Study airport approach plates for a generalized layout of runway approach lighting.

Employing common sense and study time for your destination airport, as well as maintaining focus, should alleviate the possibility of confusing the surrounding area for runways.

Black-hole approaches and departures are typically long, straight-in approaches or departures at night with no ambient cues along the approach or departure path. These can be intimidating as a typical approach is flown with various visual cues along the approach/departure paths, allowing pilots to subconsciously judge airspeed, altitude, and glideslope angle based on peripheral input. When those cues are absent and the pilot only has the visual image of a runway outlined in lights with which to gauge their approach or darkness on departure, confusion may rapidly develop.

On black-hole approaches, a pilot tends to feel high on the glide path, and consciously or subconsciously lowering the glide path appears to be provide the correct visual angle of the approach for the pilot. This increases the possibility of touching down prior to the threshold and thus experiencing an incident or accident.

Day or night over-water approaches may create the same effect as a black-hole approach, especially when the surface of the water is calm. No texture equals no visual ability to judge altitude. Water with waves does have texture, but the visual appearance of waves can be misleading, as size references are difficult to determine with waves even in the best of visual circumstances. The following accident represents some of the challenges associated with over-water approaches and the lack of subconscious peripheral orientation cues:

Incident – September 2018: A commercial aircraft flight was on short final to an island airport in Micronesia. Visibility at the time of the accident was limited due to rain and cumulonimbus clouds at 800 feet – 1,000 feet over the airport.

On short final approach to the airport, the aircraft landed in the ocean approximately 145 meters short of the threshold. Passengers reported they thought the aircraft had experienced a hard touch-down until they noticed waves outside of the windows and water seeping up the aisles.

46 People survived the accident. One passenger received fatal injuries, and six were injured.

Analysis: The Papua New Guinea Accident Investigation Commission concluded the aircrew did not comply with airline SOP's, nor approach or pre-landing checklists. The approach was not adequately briefed. The aircrew did not follow approach glideslope aids. The crew disregarded 13 enhanced ground proximity warning system (EGPWS) aural alerts, and the FO was ineffective and oblivious to the unfolding situation.

Conclusion: The aircrew did almost nothing right on this approach. It is possible the aircrew was over-confident and complacent in their ability to fly the approach regardless of atmospheric conditions, and found themselves "over their heads" very quickly. The FO should have been monitoring the instruments and glideslope aids, but was most likely looking outside the aircraft. The EGPWS should have alerted the crew to their low altitude condition, but they may have either ignored it as a result of hearing it too often (*sensory adaptation*), or did not comprehend it because of attempting to visually process the unfolding events. Proper monitoring most likely would have prevented this accident.

On black hole departures, a quick turn to a new heading and level off at a given altitude can easily by missed or misjudged by pilots looking outside the aircraft for absent orientation cues. This may quickly lead to a loss of situational awareness (S/A), once again leading to an incident or accident.

The following accident illustrates the danger of black-hole departures:

Incident – December 2016: A pilot and his five guests flew to Cleveland to attend a professional basketball game. Following the game, they departed from Burke Lakefront Airport in the aircraft close to 11 PM, at which point the pilot had been awake for some 17 hours. Atmospheric conditions at the time were clear skies, moonless and dark.

Departure instructions were to turn right to heading 330, and climb and maintain 2,000 feet. The pilot accelerated, rotated and climbed at 6,000 fpm to 2,925 feet, turned right at a bank angle of 62 degrees, and pitched down 15 degrees.

The aircraft impacted the waters of Lake Erie a little over 60 seconds from the take-off roll.

Analysis: The NTSB concluded the pilot had recently transitioned into this aircraft after having owned a similar, but slightly different, model Citation. The pilot may

212

have been unfamiliar with the autopilot and may have thought it was engaged, when in fact it was not. The NTSB also concluded the pilot probably experienced some degree of spatial disorientation.

Conclusion: The pilot's attention during climb-out was likely outside the aircraft looking "into" the turn, which may have caused him to momentarily lose S/A. When the pilot realized they had overshot the assigned altitude, they over-corrected, again searching for a horizon which was almost impossible to see, misjudging the decent to the assigned altitude. It is likely strict adherence to the instruments in this situation would have prevented this accident.

Uphill or downhill sloping terrain on the approach path provides erroneous peripheral subconscious orientation cues by appearing to show a high or low approach path to the pilot, even though the approach is on the proper glide path. These subconscious cues may not match memories of previous approaches, thus prompting an involuntary glide path correction by the brain to make the approach visually match previous approaches.

Uphill sloping terrain will provide the pilot with the subliminal impression the approach glide path is high; the error would be to lower the approach path and potentially contact terrain prior to the runway threshold.

Downhill sloping terrain provides the pilot with the subliminal impression of a low approach; the error being to raise the approach path, land long, and potentially suffer a runway excursion.

Wire, towers and antennas in the approach environment present problems as a result of visual clutter in the background of those objects, creating a low contrast image. When looking at wires, towers, and antennas from an aerial perspective those items may be almost completely invisible when the visual background has trees, buildings, rows of corn, etc., because the visual image of the obstacles may get lost in the background clutter. When flying into an unfamiliar airport, or at times even a familiar one, wires, towers and antennas can be easily missed if little attention is paid studying approach charts and scanning the approach environment thoroughly, using primarily central vision, to spot the threats. The following incident is representative of unintentional contact with towers close to the approach path:

Incident – November 2014: A Learjet 35A with two pilots and seven passengers was flying to Freeport, Bahamas. On its first landing attempt in Freeport, the crew executed a missed approach due to heavy rain and reduced visibility.

After going into a holding pattern for some time, ATC finally cleared the crew for an ILS approach. ATC advised the pilot weather had again deteriorated due to rain and haze. The crew continued the approach, deliberately descending below minimum descent altitude (MDA) and ignoring multiple ground proximity warnings, with the crew even turning off the terrain awareness warning system (TAWS).

The crew continued descending while visually searching for the runway, and the right wing of the aircraft struck a crane, sending the aircraft into uncontrolled flight and crashing into a shipyard. All nine people on board received fatal injuries.

Analysis: The aircraft and crew were flying an ILS approach into Freeport, Bahamas in marginal weather, with the precision approach path indicator (PAPI) unserviceable at the time of the accident. As the crew was on final approach, the crew knowingly descended below MDA and ignored terrain awareness alerts saying they were low on approach. The outboard portion of the right wing and fuel tank contacted a shipyard crane, sending the aircraft into an uncontrolled descent, after which the aircraft crashed inverted into the shipyard.

Conclusion: The pilot's attention during approach was likely outside the aircraft looking for the runway, without the aid of the PAPI. It is possible the pilots were unaware of descending below MDA due to the focused concentration of trying to find the runway, and may have turned off the TAWS because they had heard it before on multiple approach occasions (alarm fatigue). Had the pilot monitoring been focused on the instruments as opposed to visual, this accident may have been prevented.

Overlapping contours are approaches where terrain or obscuring weather conditions may impede low approach glide slopes. Overlapping contours due to terrain features may be difficult to discern from an aerial perspective, as terrain features may either appear to be a mound or a dip.

A properly flown approach will clear these obstructions, but flying a low approach at night may produce a condition in which the pilot sees the runway lights suddenly disappear for no apparent reason, creating a "black hole." If such a condition occurs, the pilot must gain altitude immediately as they are in imminent danger of flying into terrain.

12.4 RUNWAY ENVIRONMENT ILLUSIONS

When considering landing illusion components involving the runway environment, runway configuration, size, slope, features and condition (or a combination thereof) may contribute to a pilot's scene building interpretation confusion. The specific components of the runway environment include:

- Runway dimensions (size-distance illusion)
- Runway uphill or downhill slope
- Number of runways and taxiways
- Approach and runway lighting
- Runway condition (wet vs. dry)

Runway dimensions, also known as a *size-distance illusion,* may create a confusing visual image for the pilot to interpret with regards to distance from the threshold.

A pilot will generally be familiar with a small number of airports, such as the airport they trained at, or the airport they always fly into and out of. The end result of that familiarity is the subconscious image of a perfect approach into that airport becomes a well-worn neural pathway (memory) of what a good approach is supposed to look like. Images of surrounding terrain, buildings, roads, and runway dimensions become part of that memory so when a pilot is, say, a half-mile from touchdown, they intuitively know the approach is on glide path due to these cues.

When tasked with flying to a new destination, the approach features, including runway width and length dimensions, may very well differ from their "home" airport. Without the familiar landmarks, the approach from a half-mile out appears visually different and therefore possibly create a degree of cognitive confusion.

A *narrower-than-normal* runway will visually appear to be father away at the same glide path position as a pilot's home airport. The pilot may subconsciously lower the glide path to match memories of their home-airport memories, potentially landing short of the threshold.

A *wider-than-normal* runway will visually appear to be closer at the same glide path position than a pilot's home airport. The pilot may subconsciously raise the glide path, potentially landing long and experiencing a runway excursion.

Runway slope has the potential to create confusing visual images to the pilot as well. Typically, most runways are fairly level, with the surrounding terrain matching the slope of the runway. Again, this image becomes a subliminal cue the pilot judges the appropriate approach glide path against.

When the slope of runway is something other than level, or the slope of the terrain differs from the slope of the runway, the pilot has the potential to misjudge the glide slope.

A *down-sloping runway* provides visual cues to the pilot indicating their glide path is low, increasing the subconscious tendency to raise the glide path and land long.

An *up-sloping runway* provides visual cues to the pilot indicating their glide path is high, increasing the subconscious tendency to lower the glide path and contact terrain short of the threshold.

The number of runways and taxiways, especially at larger urban airports, may create confusing visual images due to the sheer volume of information to process. Lack of familiarity, unclear or confusing ground markings and lights, or poorly-marked closed portions of airports may contribute to the confusion.

The following incidents help illustrate how ambiguous airport layouts and create confusion on approach:

Incident – December 2015: A 737-900 was on approach to Sea-Tac Airport, WA. The aircraft was on an ILS approach and cleared to land on runway 16R, when tower ATC offered the crew a visual swing over to runway 16C. Runway 16C would put the aircraft closer to the terminal, shortening the taxi time, so the crew accepted the visual swing.

When the crew lined up on what they thought was the new runway, they inadvertently lined up on taxiway T, which bisected runways 16R and 16C. They crew continued to a safe landing on the taxiway as opposed to the correct runway.

Conclusion: Although potentially an extremely dangerous mistake, this incident did not result in any damage or injuries. Weather may have been a factor in why the pilots did not recognize the fact they were lined up with a taxiway, but the prevailing weather conditions at the time of incident are unclear. It is also possible the pilots were engaged in other activities during the descent which distracted them just enough to not completely verify they were lined up with the correct runway. Perhaps maintaining full intellectual command over the aircraft during the approach phase would have prevented this incident.

Incident – July 2017: An A320 was on visual approach to SFO, CA to runway 28R in clear night conditions, and this was the last segment for this crew for the day.

After reading back the landing clearance, the crew queried the tower to confirm they were cleared to land, advising they were seeing lights on the runway. Tower advised the crew the runway was clear, and the aircraft was indeed cleared to land, prompting the pilots to continue the short final approach.

Four aircraft were lined up on the taxiway adjacent to runway 28R, and the pilots of one of those aircraft called the tower to inform them the A320 was lined up on the taxiway as opposed to runway 28R. The tower immediately instructed the A320 to go around, which they did, and landed without further incident.

Analysis: The crew was on short final approach into SFO, and had mistakenly lined up on the taxiway as opposed the active runway. Runway 28L was closed, but the pilots may have felt the "runway closed" markings were ambiguous and difficult to discern from the air. The NTSB determined the A320 descended to 59 feet AGL before its go-around, missing colliding with at least one of the four aircraft on the taxiway by 14 feet. The NTSB determined possible causes of the incident were expectation bias, fatigue, and failure to use the ILS for the approach.

Conclusion: The pilots' intellectual command of the approach was obviously inadequate. The pilots allegedly did not recall seeing the four aircraft on the taxiway, but "something did not look right to them." They descended to within mere seconds and feet of potentially colliding with four other aircraft full of close to 1,000 passengers due to a failure to follow procedures. Being as approaches and landings are statistically the most dangerous phases of flight, those phases demand 100% attention-to-detail and adherence to standard operating procedures (SOPs). 2017 was touted as the safest year in aviation history; however, a few more seconds or feet could have produced the worst commercial aviation accident in history instead.

Approach and runway lighting, although standardized across airports, can cause confusion when combined with other factors such as brightness, weather or unfamiliar placement. Another issue which may occur is the absence of approach and runway lights when the pilot expects them to be available for the approach.

The following incident helps illustrate the ambiguity weather conditions and knowing runway lighting position can cause:

Incident – November 2014: A CRJ-200 was flying an approach into Dane County Regional Airport, WI. The aircraft was approach to the airport in snow and foggy conditions at 300 feet overcast. The pilots were familiar with the runway, and knew the runway was known for having a slightly offset localizer.

On short final, the FO calls "approach lights in sight...continue" and the captain transitions from instruments to visual. The captain aims for the left side of the PAPIs and crosses the threshold over grass with the runway nowhere in sight under the aircraft. The FO calls for go-around, which the suddenly shaken captain did. The aircraft landed without further incident.

Conclusion: The pilot flying's attention during approach was on the instruments with an offset localizer as their guide, with the pilot monitoring looking for the PAPIs in limited visibility. Once the PAPI was spotted and the captain transitioned to visual, the expectation was the aircraft would be landing to left of the PAPI when, in fact, they should have landed to the right of the PAPI. This incident may have been prevented with a more thorough approach and landing briefing, even though the pilots were landing at a known airport.

Runway condition (wet vs. dry) has the potential to create confusion for the same reasons flying over calm water does – ambiguity with altitude. Dry runway pavement provide adequate ambient visual orientation cues to judge altitude, whereas wet pavement may prevent the pilot from accurately judging flare altitude resulting in a less-than-perfect touchdown.

Most of these above-mentioned conditions could be prevented by using ILS and visual glide slope aids such as visual approach slope indicator (VASI) or PAPI. If VASI/PAPI systems are unavailable, flying a stabilized approach is advisable.

12.5 WEATHER CONDITIONS ILLUSIONS

As we have learned, certain weather conditions may influence human ability to correctly interpret vertical, horizontal and slant visibility. Weather, as an influence on safety of flight with respect to visual interpretation, can be unpredictable and ever-changing.

Examples of precipitation leading to reduced visibility include:

- Rain
- Fog or fog patches
- Haze
- Mist
- Smoke
- Snow
- Whiteout effects

Weather can play a major contributing role in controlled flight into terrain/uncontrolled flight into terrain (CFIT/UFIT) accidents where the crew may be distracted, subjected to extra workloads, and experience reduced situational awareness. Typical human response, albeit the wrong response, to flying in weather is to focus attention outside the aircraft in an attempt to see the airport or runway while on approach. This, in turn, causes pilot scan discipline to break down. Every second spent searching outside the aircraft equates to a loss of situational awareness (S/A) with regards to airspeed, attitude and altitude, as well as proper glideslope. As we know, the flight envelope on approach can rapidly turn dangerous in seconds, and often does.

The following incidents encapsulate some of the dangerous misperceptions associated with flying approaches in precipitation:

Incident – July 2012: A King Air 200GT was on approach with two pilots and six passengers to Juiz da For a Airport, Brazil, in foggy conditions which were found to be below minimums.

The aircraft impacted terrain some 800 feet short and 50 feet below runway threshold elevation. All occupants onboard the aircraft sustained fatal injuries.

Analysis: Investigators found the captain and FO maintained a contentious relationship. The captain was difficult to work with, and was prone to aggressive outbursts when their authority was questioned. It is unclear if the FO attempted to correct the glide path during the approach or called for a go-around. The approach was flown in below-minimum conditions, which was against company SOP. Investigators concluded weather, the pilot's lack of professionalism and co-pilot's lack of assertiveness contributed to the accident.

Conclusion: It is likely both pilots had their attention tuned to visually confirming the presence of the runway as opposed to assuming the traditional roles of pilot flying/pilot monitoring. The FO may have resigned himself to the fact the captain was unlikely to follow their input. Strict adherence to reduced-visibility approach SOPs may have prevented this accident.

12.6 TOOLS TO COUNTER VISUAL ILLUSIONS

Having discussed the various issues affecting and creating visual interpretation anomalies with landing illusion components, it is now necessary to look at established methods of counteracting these anomalies. It is critical for pilots to have the tools available to them to fly a stabilized approach, each and every time, as approach and landing incidents and accidents are the most pervasive in the aviation industry.

In this section we'll examine not only how to avoid visual illusions, but also the causes and implications of unstable approaches.

The following are recognized methodologies in avoiding the Visual Illusions conundrum:

- **Maintain instrument scan discipline until touchdown**
- **Cross-check instruments against outside visual cues**
- **Monitor VASI or PAPI**
- **Use ILS approaches when available**
- **If no ILS, fly a stabilized approach**

Maintaining instrument scan discipline until touchdown even at a familiar airport. Knowing and briefing the threshold elevation and approach speed ensures the pilot flying and pilot monitoring experience no ambiguity and are using the same parameters flying the approach.

Cross-checking instruments against outside visual cues ensures the pilot's visual processing of the scene matches expectations and are providing them with the correct glideslope information. If the scene does not seem to match glideslope information and confusion develops, consider a go-around.

Even though one may be flying a visual approach, purely visual cues do not provide the most appropriate airspeed/lateral/vertical guidance to maintain the glideslope. The pilot must use the best guidance for all parameters, such as airspeed indicator for airspeed guidance, PAPI, ILS, and/or altimeter for vertical guidance, and visual runway cues or ILS for lateral guidance.

Monitor VASI or PAPI on approach, but do not fixate on it. Ensuring knowledge of which side of the runway the VASI or PAPI is located in relation to the runway is critical, particularly in limited visibility conditions, to prevent runway excursions. It is important to visually transition from the VASI or PAPI to runway references such as the 1,000 foot marker, runway end, or runway edge as the pilot approaches the flare phase.

Use ILS approaches when available. ILS vertical and lateral guidance will place the aircraft in the optimum glideslope position to transition to visual approach and provide safe clearance of approach path obstructions. The pilot should maintain ILS glideslope track to at least the runway threshold, if not flare, cross-checking with visual confirmation. If the transition to visual does not provide the pilot with the proper scene expectation and confusion develops, go-around and try the approach a second time.

If no ILS, fly a stabilized approach. Know and understand stabilized approach expectations, and follow them. If the approach becomes unstable for any reason, the opportunity for an incident or accident increases exponentially and serious consideration must be given to performing a go-around immediately.

Another common misstep pilots may employ on approaches is the desire to *duck-under*. Ducking under on glideslope may be accomplished by pilots wishing to touch down early on the runway to avoid having to land down the runway to the ILS or visual aiming point, or possibly even to present themselves with a better view of the runway once they feel they are close enough to touchdown. Duck-under may be attributed to over-confidence in one's abilities, attempting to make an early exit off the runway, or simply a bad habit. Ducking-under can place the aircraft in such a position that any slight miscalculation or minor downdraft may cause the landing gear to contact either mechanical or terrain obstructions.

Ducking-under is considered unprofessional by most professional pilots and could potentially cause the approach to become unstable at a critical time.

Unstable approaches may be caused by a variety of reasons, which we will examine next.

12.7 CAUSES OF UNSTABLE APPROACHES

Unstable approaches, albeit undesirable, may present themselves on approach from a variety of reasons:

- ATC issuing a late descent combined with an altitude or airspeed constraint
- ATC issuing or offering a late runway change
- Inadequate of improper use of automation
- Lack of awareness of wind conditions, such as a tailwind
- Incorrect anticipation of aircraft deceleration characteristics
- Distractions

Obviously, ATC-caused unstable approaches may be somewhat unavoidable at certain times. If this is the case, hyper-situational awareness of flying the approach must be maintained by the pilot flying as well as the pilot monitoring.

The following accident reveals the dangers of continuing an approach once unstable:

Accident – July 2015: An Embraer Phenom 300 was entering base leg traffic for Blackbushe Airport, Farnborough, UK, for runway 25. The pilot noticed they were overtaking a smaller, slower aircraft in the pattern. The pilot decided to attempt to climb above the other aircraft, and once clear descended again in front of the smaller airplane.

The pilot attempted to reacquire the approach by diving for the runway at 3,000 fpm. The Phenom crossed the threshold at 50 feet and 42 knots faster than Vref, and touched down 2,300 feet down the 3,500 feet runway.

The Phenom suffered an overrun of the runway, and crashed into a parking lot past the end of the runway. All of the Phenom occupants suffered fatal injuries.

Conclusion: The Phenom pilot obviously exhibited extremely poor judgement in attempting to continue an approach that was grossly unstable. Once the slower aircraft was spotted, the Phenom pilot should have exited the pattern and reattempted the approach once clear.

12.8 THE GO-AROUND

Go-arounds occur as a result of the pilot or pilots deciding to discontinue the approach and/or landing, and may be executed at any point from the final approach fix to wheels-on-the-runway prior to any deceleration device being activated. It is a decision not to be taken lightly, and can only be made by the pilot or ATC. Organizational Standard Operating Procedures (SOPs) normally outline the specific situations demanding a go-around, including unstable approaches. That being said, multiple studies indicate more than nine in ten unstable approaches continue to a landing.

According to Flight Safety Foundation data, 97% of airline pilots admit to flying unstable approaches, and 83% of approach and landing accidents could have been prevented by a timely go-around decision. In fact, the Flight Safety Foundation goes on to say performing timely go-arounds is the "single most important decision to reduce accidents in the aviation industry," which is a powerful statement as to the importance of go-arounds. How, then, do pilots prepare themselves to be fully engaged when flying an approach?

According to airline training providers, the recommended best practices for preparing for approaches include the following:

- **Obtain pertinent landing data (such as ATIS, etc.) as soon as possible in cruise.**
- **Complete the approach briefing ten minutes prior to top-of-descent.**
- **Ensure no pilot is distracted by electronic media such as cell phones, tablets, or laptops.**
- **Ensure if any electronic media is used, it is in direct support of the approach.**

Strict adherence to standard operating procedures is a must while in critical phases-of-flight, and in particular the approach and landing phase as most aircraft incidents and accidents occur during this phase.

12.9 PHYSICAL HAZARDS TO VISION

A variety of vision-limiting or vision-damaging anomalies may occur in flight due to environmental conditions, mechanical failure or human interference. These anomalies include:

- Snow and rain
- Snow and sunlight blindness
- Flash blindness
- Hypoxia
- Smoke in the cockpit
- Laser blindness

Snow and rain impairs vision due to physical obstruction. Staring at snow or raindrops flying past the windscreen may be mesmerizing to the point of hypnosis, can major distraction and loss of situational awareness. More visual time should be spent inside the cockpit with the eyes on the instrument panel assuring proper airspeed, attitude and altitude.

Snow blindness has the potential to reflect more than 80% of the UV rays striking its surface. If stared at the intense glare long enough, this may cause a condition called *photokeratitis,* which is a temporary loss of vision. The underlying damage is essentially a sunburned cornea, which may take 24 to 48 hours to resolve itself. Quite obviously, this issue can be prevented by the aviator wearing a good pair of sunglasses which block at least 99% of UV rays below 400 nanometers.

Sunlight blindness impairs vision by overwhelming the eyes with light, potentially causing photokeratitis and temporary blindness. The sun may be aligned with the runway just above the horizon on approach or departure, or sunlight may reflect off water causing issues for pilots. If sunglasses are not available or providing enough protection, avoid looking directly at the sun and attempt to use alternate visual cues for orientation such as looking out of the side window 45 degrees off-center for orientation cues.

Flash blindness most commonly happens in low-light conditions to a dark-adapted individual as result of inadvertent exposure to intense light, which may happen while taxiing and getting flashed by another aircraft's landing lights, or a similar event. As we know, full visual dark-adaption takes from 30 to 45 minutes and flash-blindness will cause the dark adaption to be lost in seconds. The goal, then, is to protect the eyes (or at least one eye) as quickly as possible. Closing or covering both eyes to protect them may not be prudent, depending on the situation, so protection of one eye will ensure at least 50% of your night vision will be retained.

Hypoxia will cause a loss of visual acuity at relatively benign altitudes as low as 5,000 feet, particularly at night. Aviators must be cognizant of their lack of visual acuity at altitude, and remember to compensate for the loss by employing a strong scan pattern, spotting threats with central vision, and using supplemental oxygen to maximize visual acuity if necessary.

Smoke in the cockpit causes physical obstruction of vision, which in the case of a continuous smoke event, can develop to a density level so as to completely eliminate visual interpretation of instrumentation or windscreen views. Aviators should carry smoke goggles or smoke hoods with them in the event of a smoke contingency, and have emergency smoke evacuation procedures established to prevent catastrophic build-up of dense smoke. The most effective smoke mitigation system currently available is the Emergency Vision Assurance System (EVAS), which creates a clear visual connection with critical flight instruments and windscreen view via a vented and filtered inflatable plastic tunnel.

Laser blindness is caused by inadvertent visual contact with laser beams produced by laser light shows, Christmas decorations, or unlawful use of lasers by individuals. The resulting laser contact with the aircraft windscreen or eye can produce difficulty seeing out of the windscreen due to light refraction, or potential damage to the eye itself.

Laser strikes may be accidental or nefarious, but strikes can happen anywhere at any time. According to the FAA, the most common laser strike times in the United States are from 7 to 10 PM, between altitudes of 2,000 feet to 10,000 feet, although laser strikes have been reported in excess of 40,000 feet. The chart below depicts laser strike frequency through 2017:

Cumulative laser illuminations reported to FAA
January 1 through December 31, for years 2007 to 2017

FAA 2021

Even relatively weak 5mW lasers have the capability of being major distractions beyond two miles, with the strongest military-grade lasers capable of major distraction beyond 20 miles.

According to the FAA, the following steps should be taken to mitigate inadvertent laser strikes:

- **Fly the plane first**
- **Do not look directly at the laser**
- **Block the laser light with your hand, clipboard, electronic device, or by turning the aircraft away from the laser light**
- **Turn up cockpit lights, as a laser strike on the windscreen can minimize night vision adaption**
- **Do not rub the eyes vigorously, as you may tear the cornea**
- **Inform ATC, as they can notify local law enforcement agencies**
- **Consider reengaging Autopilot, Auto-land, or transfer control to the Pilot Monitoring**

- Consider a missed-approach procedure

Laser strikes are potentially life-threatening events, and should be taken extremely seriously as a few aviation laser-strike cases resulted in permanent eye-damage to the aviator.

Conclusion

Visual illusions and/or visual impairment can rapidly develop into extremely critical events for those who fly recreationally or professionally. As we know, approaches and landings produce the majority of aviation incidents and accidents, making the knowledge to avoid these issues of primary importance for any aviator. Developing the disciplines to survive low-visibility approaches and using instrumentation and visual aids to their fullest advantage is gained in every day, perfectly fine VFR conditions. When the time comes when those skills becomes absolutely necessary, it is automatic.

Remember, the Flight Safety Foundation labeled the go-around procedure as the "single most important decision to reduce accidents in the aviation industry." Always follow proper approach procedures, cross-check instruments with visual cues, and trust & follow glideslope aids.

Adhering to these guidelines and making them part of one's mental tool-kit will go a long way towards ensuring a long and prosperous career or journey in aviation.

Chapter 12 Core Competency Questions

1. Historically, what percentage of commercial incidents and accidents happen in the approach and landing phases of flight?
2. Visual illusions cause incidents and accidents for what reason?
3. What two physiological factors may help create approach and landing visual illusions?
4. What are the three major landing illusion components?
5. When a pilot looks at the ground, lack of what terrain feature may create difficulties for a pilot to estimate altitude?
6. What about Black Hole Approaches makes them create a visual illusion?
7. What illusion does an up-sloping runway create?
8. What illusion does a narrower-than-normal runway create?
9. What makes wire, towers, or antennas difficult to see on approach?

10. Why could precipitation cause an incident or accident on approach?

11. What mechanical approach aids may assist a pilot on approach?

12. What percentage of landing incidents and accidents may have been prevented by initiating a go-around?

13. If a pilot suffers a laser strike, what is the first thing to remember?

13. HUMAN-AUTOMATION ENGAGEMENT AND ENHANCED VISION SYSTEMS

One of the most important advances in aviation in modern years has been the development and advancement of automated aircraft systems. Modern aircraft are increasingly reliant on automated computer-controlled systems to safely and efficiently operate various flight parameters and functions. While these advances have brought definitive benefits, they have also created a new set of problems. Mismanaged or mishandled aircraft automation may cause undesirable situations to develop at unanticipated intervals, creating difficult-to-impossible conditions from which the pilot is expected to recover from. In recent history, the aviation industry has embraced increasingly complex automation for cost-savings and efficiency objectives, but with little consideration for the contingencies and consequences of what happens if the system fails as well as the cumulative effects on pilot flying skills.

While automated systems have brought many benefits, the hidden danger is the simple fact that these systems are electrical or mechanical in nature. Anyone who has had any experience with electrical or mechanical systems know these systems may fail, and there is virtually no way to predict when this may happen. Many of these systems are fed data via air probes, tubes and ports on the exterior of the aircraft, which can be rendered useless by damage, freezing conditions at altitude or even bug ingestion. Computer chips may have manufacturing and programming defects or suffer from erroneous function from water or heat damage. Electrical signals are carried via cables and wiring, which may be compromised by chaffing, loosened or corroded connections, or water or heat intrusion. Mechanical components may fail due to freezing conditions, material failure, manufacturing defects, or simply age.

As a result of automation malfunction possibilities, human pilots are currently a very important part of the automation loop, if nothing more than to monitor the system to ensure it works as expected; a redundant system, so to speak. Therein lies the next problem, as humans are extremely poor monitoring devices due to lapses in attention, boredom, overreliance on automation, and many others.

In this chapter we will discuss:

1. Human flight monitoring
2. Monitoring and perceptual modalities
3. Strategies for effective monitoring
4. Cognitive lockup

13.1 HUMAN FLIGHT MONITORING

In today's society, human ability to focus or concentrate on a singular task is challenged. A large part of this challenge is the advent of personal electronic devices, which are near-constant companions of literally everyone, with them every waking minute of one's day. Electronic devices such as computers, tablets, or cell phones allow individuals to constantly search for information, communicate with friends and family, check the weather or news, play games, perform personal finance functions, listen to music, and the list goes on. As a direct result, focus on singular tasks suffers, as individuals cannot perform almost any task without the "electronic companion" being present and active.

The lack of focus and concentration while engaged with electronic devices takes a dangerous turn when individuals attempt to check devices while operating a machine, such as bicycles, motor vehicles, scooters, or aircraft. Any time a machine is being operated by a human, distractions caused by electronic devices can cause fatalities in the blink of an eye.

As a professional commercial pilot, your job is to provide <u>safe passage for paying occupants</u> of the aircraft you are operating. Passengers are literally paying you, as well as trusting their lives with you, to fly them through the air to get to their destination safely. The possibility for safe passage goes down exponentially when the pilot is distracted, because they are no longer intellectually engaged with the aircraft. Knowing this, let us now discuss what is involved with properly monitoring how the aircraft is performing in flight.

The first item to understand is the definition of *monitoring*, which is the condition of <u>observing and checking the progress or quality of something over a period of time</u>, or to <u>keep something under systematic review</u>. An aircraft in flight needs to be monitored to ensure flight parameters are adhered to, and to prevent dangerous deviations or situations from developing unnoticed. An excellent definition of monitoring as it applies to aviation comes the Civil Aviation Authority's paper

"Monitoring Matters," published in 2013: "*The observation and interpretation of the flight path data, configuration status, automation modes and on-board systems appropriate to the phase of flight. It involves a cognitive comparison against the expected values, modes and procedures. It also includes observation of the other crew member and timely intervention in the event of deviation.*"

The mechanics of monitoring are complex and involve selective application of mental resources to encode sensory inputs in the midst of performing a goal-oriented task. While monitoring is generally considered a visual activity, auditory and tactile inputs from controls can influence the monitoring task in the event of a stall or control anomaly. Similarly, smell and taste senses may alert aviators in the event of fumes in the cockpit and therefore also perform a monitoring tasking.

In two-pilot operations, the aircraft commander or captain will normally designate who will take direct responsibility for flight control for that flight sector, or which portions of the flight sector, who will be known as the *Pilot Flying (PF)*. The pilot not directly controlling the aircraft is then designated the *Pilot Monitoring (PM)*, whose responsibilities include systemically checking the flight management and aircraft control of the pilot flying, and this role represents one of the most important reasons a two-person crew is required in modern aviation operations. The PM, in theory, should have ultimate responsibility to ensure aircraft flight path and waypoint adherence is maintained. The PM will also carry out support duties such as communications and the reading of checklists.

In a professional flight cockpit, ambiguity is the enemy of effective operations. Standard operating procedures must also be established as to which pilot has ultimate decision-making authority. At first glance, the easy answer would be the "captain," but let us examine a hypothetical cockpit scenario:

- While flying an approach the first officer (FO), designated as PM, calls for a "go-around" because approach parameters are not being met and by SOP is required to make the call. The captain is the PF and, having flown this approach many times, knows the landing will occur just fine and continues on with the landing and roll-out despite the "go-around" call.

Who was right and who was wrong? If the PM calls for go-around, the call MUST be adhered to despite what the PF thinks. The PM may have seen something occurring the PF did not see, with no time to explain the situation thoroughly. While the designated aircraft commander is ultimately responsible for all aspects of flight safety, part of this responsibility must lie with the fact the PM's callouts may potentially have life-of-death implications.

While some crews maintain their designated PF/PM roles for an entire flight sector, some crews (and organizations) prefer using the *monitored approach* concept. In this practice, the pilot designated PM during descent and approach phases transitions to PF for the landing phase, theoretically improving the operational safety aspects of transition from instruments to visual reference, which is required for touch down after most approaches.

If a pilot is engaged in a single pilot operation, they will be responsible for not only active control of the aircraft, but systems monitoring and communications as well. Quite obviously, this can create some rather intense moments if anything out-of-the-ordinary is occurring.

Single-pilot monitoring abilities comes down to one word: discipline. Discipline is needed to ensure self-initiated safety briefings are conducted for each phase of flight, to ensure instruments are scanned routinely and very frequently, avoiding short-cuts, avoiding performing checklists by memory, and ensuring emergency checklists are readily available.

Monitoring Disruptors

Human *monitoring disruptors* may prevent pilots to properly and effectively monitor instrumentation in flight. These may occur for a wide variety of reasons, but regardless of the reason, the end result is the same; loss of situational awareness. A loss of situational awareness (S/A) in any phase of flight may cause a departure from controlled flight, leading to the startle effect and related shortcomings, but a departure from controlled flight in the approach and landing phase can be especially deadly because momentum is already propelling the aircraft towards the ground.

The list below provides the most commonly noted disruptors:

- Fatigue
- Boredom
- Visual Illusions
- Spatial disorientation
- Distraction
- Workload
- Weather concerns
- Complacency
- Confusion

Fatigue causes a slow-down in mental processing and, among other issues, can cause a pilot to miss crucial cues (loss of S/A) signaling a dangerous event is developing.

Boredom, like fatigue, slows mental processing but can also cause a pilot to become easily distracted with something perceived as more interesting than monitoring instruments, creating a loss of S/A.

Visual illusions and *spatial disorientation* create a loss of S/A as a result of an overwhelming human tendency to lock on to one conspicuous cockpit instrument or one view out of the windscreen. This "competing task" phenomena cause additional orientation information to be ignored.

Distraction causes a loss of S/A as result of alteration of attention. Distraction could occur from something as simple as dropping an item on the cockpit floor, non-flight-related conversation, reading a cell phone or tablet, or gazing at scenery. Distraction may also occur as result of an alarm or abnormal condition developing, drawing the pilot's attention away from flight path monitoring.

Workload and/or task saturation may cause a loss of S/A if the PM is overwhelmed with activities in the cockpit, such as an unexpectedly high volume of ATC communication during a typically high tasking period such as approach and landing.

Weather concerns can cause a loss of S/A because human nature demands we attempt to see where we are going in low visibility conditions, leaving no one monitoring airspeed, attitude and altitude.

Complacency creates a loss of S/A because a pilot may become so familiar with particular flight segment routine that they go on "autopilot" themselves and are not truly thinking each step through intellectually, but rather simply going through the motions of following checklists and monitoring. Scanning the instruments may become so habituated, the pilot "looks but doesn't see", therefore not properly processing the data the instrumentation provides.

Confusion may be caused by unfamiliarity with automated systems, emergency or normal procedures, or ambiguity of critical V-speeds.

Ineffective Monitoring

An argument could be made that ineffective monitoring is related to every human factors-caused aircraft accident not related to medical or physiological incapacitation. After all, if the aircraft is mechanically airworthy and flyable, why else would the aircraft crash?

According to a 2002 study conducted by the NTSB, on "flight crew-involved" U.S. airline accident sequences, monitoring errors were present in 84% of those accidents, making monitoring (or lack thereof) an incredibly important human factor in accident prevention.

The International Air Transport Association (IATA) 2020 Safety Report found for flightcrew-induced errors, manual handling/flight controls topped the list with a 39% contribution, and SOP adherence/SOP cross verification at 29%. In other words, either pilots were not manually flying the aircraft correctly, or were not following company-initiated standard operation procedures.

The IATA 2020 Safety Report also mentioned for the past five years, the top contributors to fatal airline accidents were flightcrew errors/SOP adherence/SOP cross verification at 56%, and manual handling/flight controls at 50%.

The main takeaways from the IATA 2020 Safety Report is pilots were not intellectually engaged or "ahead" of the aircraft, did not perform satisfactorily when flying manually, and failed to follow company procedures at critical phases-of-flight.

13.2 MONITORING AND PERCEPTUAL MODALITIES

As previously mentioned, good flight monitoring accumulates and analyzes data received from sensory inputs involving all of the human senses. These senses are:

- Optical (visual)
- Olfactory (smell)
- Gustatory (taste)
- Somatic (feel)
- Auditory (hearing)

Theses senses are known as *perceptual modalities,* or the way humans experience stimuli. When modalities overlap, stimulus interpretation may be hindered, as interference between certain modalities can create confusion.

Let us examine an incident involving modality inference:

Incident – December 2013: A Cessna CJ2 was on departure and ascent out of Coventry, UK, with one pilot and one passenger on board. As the aircraft neared its level-off altitude of FL430, which is close to the aircraft's maximum certified ceiling of FL450, the autopilot disengaged and the aircraft stalled. The aircraft completed five 360-degree rolls, partially recovered at FL270, stalled again, and finally fully recovered at 16,000 feet.

Analysis: The ensuing investigation revealed the aircraft pulled between 3.6 and 5.4 G's during the deviation from altitude. It was determined the pilot-in-command (PIC) was heads-down during the climb getting weather data from their tablet, and the PIC was not monitoring the instruments. The PIC missed the autopilot disengagement, but "may have felt" the stick shaker as the aircraft pitched down.

Investigators also determined the PIC may have problems interpreting the flight display attitude indicator.

Conclusion: The pilot's attention was solely focused on getting weather data from their tablet as opposed to dividing attention between instruments and the tablet, and consequently missed the tactile input of the stick shaker due to attempted visual processing of their electronic device.

Perhaps the PIC could have waited until the aircraft altitude stabilized prior to attempting to get the weather data.

Think about the last time you were watching TV and listening to your significant other's conversation at the same time. You either listen to your significant other's conversation or what you are watching on TV, but not both. Or, remember trying to study for an exam while watching a movie? You are either watching the movie or understanding what you are reading, but rarely both at the same time. One more example would be driving a vehicle in an unfamiliar area and become somewhat lost, so you turn down the music so you can better concentrate visually.

Conversely, the combination of certain modalities may enhance stimulus interpretation. If you look at the TV while listening to it, it is easier to understand what you are hearing. Another example is if you hear a sound that does not make sense to you, you will turn and look at it so you can process the stimulus both audibly and visually.

Psychological research indicates humans are very poor at visual processing two separate situations at once, as well as auditory processing of sound from two different sources at once. National Department of Transportation research on texting and driving suggests attempting to text and drive increases one's chances of being engaged in potentially fatal automobile accident by 2,300%. It is easy to imagine how having two visual alarms and/or two audible alarms going off on the flight deck simultaneously may potentially create confusion and intellectual "lock-up" in an emergency.

Pilots must learn and discipline themselves to use perceptual modalities to their benefit, which will be discussed later in this chapter.

13.3 STRATEGIES FOR EFFECTIVE MONITORING

Now that we understand the critical nature of proper monitoring skills, let's examine a variety of strategies the Civil Aviation Authority (CAA) recommends the PM use to ensure effective monitoring performance:

- Stay in the loop by intellectually flying the aircraft - even if autopilot or the PF is actively controlling the aircraft. Be certain to assign the appropriate level of attention to the task. On a scale of 1 to 10, with 10 being the highest level of attention, the pilot should maintain a level of 5 or 6 as opposed to sinking to a 1 or 2.
- If distraction occurs, ensure that you always check the flight mode annunciators (FMAs) and your flight instruments to reengage mentally as soon as possible.
- Monitor the flight instruments same as if you are manually flying the aircraft.
- Maintain vigilance in monitoring all flight path changes:
  o Plan the flightpath change – stay well "ahead of the airplane"
  o Confirm the flightpath change
  o Monitor to ensure the flightpath change occurs as predicted
  o Correct the flightpath trajectory if not automation-enabled
- When flight path changes are initiated, make monitoring of the actions of the PF a priority task.
- Always cross check the FMA after a change has been selected on the autopilot mode control panel.
- During briefings promote inclusive comments to encourage intervention, such as "remind me if I do not ask for the After Take-off Checks."
- Provide occasional monitoring reminders, such as "make sure that the tail wind does not exceed 10 kt."
- During the flight the aircraft commander should ensure the shared mental model remains intact, achieved through expression of intent (I will be flying the descent at 200kt) and providing a situation update to the PM when they have been engaged in a non-monitoring task.
- Manage the workload efficiently and effectively:
  o Avoid multi-tasking as much as possible
  o In emergencies, monitoring is critical
  o Program flight management systems (FMS) during slow phases of flight – NOT critical phases
- Write down aural communications – avoid relying on memory.
- Mentally rehearse next phase of flight.
- Make cross checking the autopilot a habit.

- Verbally complete checklists or observations, particularly for single pilot operations.
- De-brief the flight on monitoring effectiveness and shared objectives.
- Ensure MEL-acceptable aircraft defects are considered in monitoring tasks.

Piloting an aircraft is a serious task, and monitoring aircraft actions is an essential part of this task. At no time, unless a planned activity, should vigilance in monitoring be subjugated to distraction and mind-wandering.

13.4 COGNITIVE LOCKUP

While overlapping perceptual modalities may cause sensory input processing interference, another psychological phenomenon exists which causes human cognition to hyper-focus on a singular task. This phenomenon is known as *cognitive lockup*.

Cognitive lockup is defined as "holding on to a task or sticking to a problem, or reluctance to switch to an alternative task or problem." In aviation, this refers to a pilot's reluctance to switch tasks after time is invested into the original task of flying to a destination. What exactly does this mean?

Pilots face the ever-present pressure of "completing the flight." From the very first flying lesson, a pilot's main mission is to depart from one airport and arrive at another. This mission becomes psychologically ingrained in the pilot, and their primary mission of completing the flight at the destination becomes the foremost task to accomplish. This pressure of task-completion increases the possibility and effect of cognitive lockup. Some psychologists believe the probability of cognitive lockup increase when a task is 90 – 95% complete, as it becomes too intellectually difficult to abandon a task so close to completion.

Humans tend to deal with disturbances sequentially. When pilots switch tasks, mental reconfiguration to address the other task takes time, which some call the *switching cost*. Therefore, the most efficient method of working is to complete one task before moving on to the next. Cognitive lockup is reduced when it becomes obvious the benefits of task switching exceeds the switching cost.

Along the same theoretical lines as cognitive lockup is *sensory adaption*. This condition may occur when a pilot or crew become immune to a particular alarm which continuously presents itself during a specific phase of flight, such as ground proximity warning system (GPWS) alarm sounding every time a certain approach is flown. There may come a time when the GPWS alarm sounds as the aircraft nears inadvertent terrain contact, with the crew ignoring it because the GPWS "always" goes off.

Ambiguity may also occur if too many alarms sound at once. The human brain has a finite ability to process information, and too much stimuli at the same instant could potentially cause confusion, leading to inaction.

Let us investigate a few incidents where perceptual modalities and/or cognitive lockup may have been causal factors:

Incident – December 2013: The flight crew of a Gulfstream G550 were on approach to London-Stansted Airport, landing runway 04 in fog and broken clouds at 100 feet AGL. The autopilot and autothrust were engaged.

The aircraft captured the localizer and glideslope successfully; however, autopilot disconnected due to a flap overspeed condition. Subsequent to autopilot disconnection, the aircraft went high on the glideslope. The pilot attempted to reacquire the glideslope manually, but was porpoising through the glideslope, could not recapture and went unstable on the approach.

The aircraft landed 109 feet short of the runway threshold, simultaneously damaging an ILS antenna and the undercarriage of the aircraft. The aircraft rolled out and taxied to a hanger with no further incident.

Analysis: The approach and landing occurred at 3:30 AM local time, so it would be fair to assume fatigue precipitated the pilot's decision to continue the approach.

Conclusion: Fatigue, combined with the pilot's desire to land regardless of the unstable approach, appears to be a demonstrable case of cognitive lockup. The crew was attempting a landing during an abnormal time of the day, had almost completed the mission, and ended up damaging airport equipment and the aircraft. A go-around decision the moment the aircraft went unstable most likely would have prevented this incident.

Incident – February 2014: A Citation 525 was on approach to Elk City, OK with one pilot and six passengers on board. The pilot was flying an ILS approach in night IMC. Visibility was 2.5 miles in mist and overcast at 500 feet AGL. MDA at the final approach fix was 2,480 feet.

The aircraft impacted an object two miles north of the airport, and the pilot flew a missed approach, after which the aircraft completed a safe landing with no occupant injuries.

Post-flight examination of the aircraft revealed substantial damage to the aircraft nose, lower and upper fuselage surface, and the left horizontal stabilizer.

Analysis: Radar data indicated the pilot descended below the MDA shortly after crossing the final approach fix. Immediately prior to impact, the aircraft's transponder reported 2,100 feet MSL Investigators believed the aircraft struck a 29 foot-tall electric utility pole at 10 feet, 7 inches AGL. The pilot told investigators they thought they had leveled off 2,500 feet MSL, and never heard the radar altimeter sound the alert indicating they were below 400 foot radar altitude. The pilot stated they "never saw the terrain, any obstructions, the runway lights or airport environment during the approach to ELK."

Conclusion: This appears to be a text-book case of overlapping perceptual modalities, as it is possible the pilot was so focused on trying to visually find the runway in IMC at night that they missed the descent below MDA and were unable to audibly process the low-altitude alert. Based on the damage pattern on the aircraft, it seems unlikely the aircraft hit a pole, but rather flew under and contacted wires at less than 11 feet AGL, and *the pilot never saw anything!* A disciplined instrument scan may have prevented this incident.

Incident – August 2013: An Airbus A300 Cargo Jet was on a night visual approach into Birmingham, AL on its last segment of the day. The captain was an experienced 8,600 hour pilot, and the FO had a substantial 3,200 hours of experience. The flight crew was flying into the alternate 7,000 foot runway, as the main 12,000 foot runway was closed. The alternate runway lacked electronics for an ILS system.

On short final, the aircraft impacted terrain less than a mile from the runway threshold, on rising terrain below threshold elevation. Both pilots sustained fatal injuries.

Analysis: NTSB investigators determined the captain never received the crew rest they were supposed to get, according to findings supported by cell phone usage. This was the crew's last flight segment of the day, leading investigators to conclude fatigue was a factor. Also determined to be contributing factors were flying an unstable approach, and failure to monitor altitude on approach.

Conclusion: This appears to another case where overlapping perceptual modalities and/or cognitive lockup were brought on with fatigue being the underlying cause. This led both pilots to visually search for the runway, leaving no one monitoring glideslope (or not cognitively processing the information provided by the instruments) and proceeding with an unstable approach. Strict adherence to the

PF/PM concept followed by a timely go-around likely would have prevented this accident.

Incident – September 2018: A Boeing 737 was on approach into Chuuk/Weno IAP, Micronesia. Visibility was limited due to rain and cumulonimbus clouds at 800 – 1,000 feet over the airport.

In the short final phase of the approach, the aircraft landed in the water 145 meters short of the threshold. Passengers commented they believed the aircraft simply experienced a hard touch-down until they saw water seeping into the aircraft and realized they had just landed in the sea. One passenger was deceased, and 46 survived the accident.

Analysis: Investigative authorities found the crew had ignored 13 separate aural alerts from the enhanced ground proximity warning system (EGPWS) system. Ultimately, investigators found the aircrew negligent in complying with pre-approach briefings and following checklists as described in company standard operating procedures, as well as using glideslope aids adequately.

Conclusion: This appears to be a case of cognitive lockup (the need to complete the mission regardless of circumstances), and overlapping perceptual modalities, likely from the crew trying to visually search for the runway and missing the EGPWS aural alerts. Proper use of the PF/PM concept may have prevented this accident.

Cognitive Lockup Prevention

Effective cognitive lockup prevention training should be the goal of any flight department, and the following are steps to be adhered to towards this goal:

- **Increase practicing task switching**
- **Departmental framing of go-arounds**

Increase practicing task switching of approach and flare followed by switching to the task of go-around and reattempting the approach a second time. Often the ratio of practice approaches versus go-arounds is heavily in favor of landing the approach as opposed to go-arounds. The ratio should be closer to 50-50 to ensure pilots are familiar and comfortable with the go-around decision, and are more willing to choose that option if necessary.

Departmental framing of go-arounds to depict go-arounds and diversions in a more positive light may have a profound effect on a pilot's decision to perform a go-around. Too often go-arounds and diversions are "officially" sanctioned by a flight department, but privately frowned upon, or possibly even ridiculed. The reasons for this are many and varied, but normally are directly influenced by a company's reputation of being "on time" or something similar.

Obviously, the vast majority of pilots will make the correct decision concerning a potential safety-of-flight event, but it only takes one wrong decision to create a catastrophe. The ability to influence a department's <u>unofficial</u> view of go-arounds and diversions starts at the top of the chain-of-command.

13.5 AIRCRAFT AUTOMATION THEORY

Now we have a workable understanding of monitoring aircraft automated systems, so let us take a basic look at what aircraft automation systems do. Enjoying the benefits of a machine such as a sophisticated aircraft that is largely able to control itself is an amazing experience, and the abilities of aircraft automation almost reach the level of magic...right up to the point where they fail to operate as predicted. That is the main event pilots have to prepare themselves for, and the reality is many pilots fail in that endeavor.

Automation is the technique of controlling an apparatus, process or system by means of electronic and/or mechanical devices which supplement or replace the human to provide assisted or autonomous control in the sensing, decision-making and deliberate output. *Aircraft automated systems* are a blanket term for those devices designed into an aircraft providing the above-mentioned services.

Aircraft automated systems normally fall into these categories:

- Information acquisition
- Information analysis
- Decision and action selection
- Action implementation

Information acquisition may include systems and displays such as moving maps, various electronic or mechanical systems monitoring, wind and weather conditions.

Information analysis may include systems to enhance the flight crew's situational awareness regarding traffic (ADS-B, TCAS) and terrain awareness, system failures and alarms.

Decision and action selection such as the flight management system (FMS) and flight data computers, designed to maximize efficiency in flight plan following, continually assessing and adjusting speed, pitch, yaw and roll, and implementing stall prevention measures.

Action implementation includes automated flight path (heading and altitude) control and power and fuel-flow management, such as autopilot and auto-throttle.

First Automated Systems

When humans started to fly aircraft, the act of flying was novel and exciting; however, it didn't take long for humans to realize that flying at one altitude, heading and speed for long distances could become somewhat tiresome.

Around nine years after the first flight of the Wright brothers, a gentleman by the name of Lawrence Sperry understood the potential of developing a system to automatically control an airplane to some degree, decided to invent a system to do just that. The innovative technology Sperry designed could automatically balance the aircraft in flight so the pilot did not have to do so themselves, relieving the pilot of the boredom of straight-and-level flight for long distances. Sperry called this system the "gyroscopic automatic pilot", which the pilots lucky enough to use it nicknamed it "George."

Fast-forward to today and most modern commercial aircraft rely on *fly-by-wire* flight control technologies, in which a pilot's control inputs are sent to computers rather than through direct mechanical linkages to flight control systems. These fly-by-wire software packages contain flight control laws and logic that are tasked with protecting the aircraft from commanded control inputs that could place the aircraft into an unsafe flying configuration, and for optimizing performance efficiency.

13.6 HUMAN-AUTOMATION ENGAGEMENT BASICS

One may believe with the magic of automated flights systems, flying in the present day has never been safer, and they would be correct. According to most experts, automated flight control systems have largely been viewed as, as well as responsible for, having a positive effect on safety, with incident and accident rates improving considerably in recent history. Although aircraft automation may make flying safer, flying is not necessarily easier, as more skill and intuition is required to use automation effectively.

Modern automated systems and displays are designed to enhance the safety-of-flight by improving operator situation awareness, reducing and relieving pilot workload, and monitoring aircraft and aircraft system states to prevent unsafe flight conditions and operations.

While these systems are designed to <u>enhance</u> safety-of-flight, they should never be completely <u>responsible</u> for safety-of-flight for a variety of reasons, the main reason being they cannot be designed or built to be 100% reliable. Other reasons to consider is the fact machines, at least at the current time, do not enjoy the benefit of intuition based on experience, nor include the moral or ethical compass necessary to make difficult decisions in the critical moments leading to potentially fatal event.

The ability for an automated system to maintain a 100% reliability rate with regards to adherence to programmed law and logic, not to mention mechanical or electrical reliability, has been proven time and again to be at fault. When this does occur, in far too many cases pilots have been either unprepared or unable to recover the aircraft in a critical phase-of-flight, or programmed the system incorrectly for the desired aircraft action. This fact brings up some important questions:

1. Are pilots relying too heavily on automated control of the aircraft?
2. Does automation truly reduce errors, or just change the nature of the errors that are made?
3. Is automation beginning to supplant, instead of augment, basic flying skills?

With this in mind, let us examine what makes automated systems advantageous, as well as some issues regarding interaction with the automated systems.

Advantages and Disadvantages of Automation

The following are recognized advantages, followed be recognized interaction issues, of aircraft automation.

Advantages:

-   Technical reliability
-   Lateral and vertical navigation accuracy and flight path control
-   Systems diagnoses, map displays and traffic and terrain awareness
-   Relief from repetitive and non-rewarding tasks

Interaction issues:

-   Skill and feel for the aircraft deteriorate
-   Situational awareness suffers
-   Unexpected automation behavior (engagement or disengagement)
-   Interaction distracts from flying basics
-   Data entry errors and system failures, and mode awareness knowledge may be lacking

- Passivity

Technical reliability increases as a result of predictable system input.

Lateral and vertical navigation accuracy and *flight path control* increases as a result of constant, minute control inputs which monitor the slightest flight path deviations and correcting them.

Systems diagnoses, map displays and traffic and terrain awareness improve as the aircraft is constantly monitoring its own systems and providing continuous feedback; providing moving-map displays alleviating wasted space for large charts and wasted time locating one's spatial position; and providing transponder-enabled traffic and radar-enabled terrain proximity warnings and alerts.

Relief from repetitive and non-rewarding tasks alleviates the pilot's constant vigilance in maintaining a given flight path, as well as airspeed/attitude/altitude control and manipulation.

Skill and feel for the aircraft deteriorate as a direct result of allowing the aircraft to fly itself, as opposed to manual operations. The vibrations and control feel indicating impending controllability issues may be missed.

Situational awareness suffers as a result of experiencing no intuitive physical feedback from aircraft controls, and visual scans break down as trust in automated traffic-awareness monitoring grows.

Unexpected automation behavior (engagement or disengagement) may occur as a result of "glitches" in the system, or flight conditions being met triggering an exit from automated control. Another consideration regarding automated systems is while individual computers may be of the latest generation, the networking system for these computers may not be resulting in slower-than-expected automation behavior.

Interaction distracts from flying basics occurs when pilots are more engaged with programming systems, such as FMS, as opposed to flight path monitoring and instrument scanning, causing missed cues the aircraft is about to stall or other conditions causing deviations.

Data entry errors and system failures, and *mode awareness knowledge* may be lacking as result of inattention to preflight or inflight system programming; system failure may occur simply because these are electrical or mechanical systems, which can and will fail occasionally; and inadequate training, preparation or knowledge of the system leading to a lack of pilot knowledge of what the aircraft is programmed to do.

Passivity occurs as result of constant reliance on the automated systems. Over-reliance on automation can have serious consequences when the aircraft system disengages during a critical phase of flight, and the pilot sits and waits for the aircraft to save itself instead of taking manual control to alleviate the condition.

Automation Engagement

As automated systems have advanced, predictably pilots' manual control of modern aircraft has decreased, which has raised many questions in the aviation human factors community. On a global scale, the most common causes of commercial jet accidents are *loss of control in flight (LOC-I)* and *controlled flight into terrain (CFIT)*. These two categories often involve incomplete pilot S/A, poor judgment, and human errors when interacting with complex aircraft systems. In addition to basic flight training, pilots require advanced training to understand and manipulate the various features, modes, capabilities, and limitations of advanced flight control systems under a wide variety of flight conditions.

The first question to examine is *are pilots relying too heavily on automated control of the aircraft?*

Human nature typically dictates if there is an easier way to do something, humans will take it. The same concept applies to automated control of aircraft; if it is available, why not use it to its fullest advantage? If automated systems were 100% reliable, this may be less of an issue; the problem lies in the fact electromechanical systems are <u>not</u> 100% reliable and could potentially fail. When system failure occurs, the pilot's ability to respond appropriately could be compromised as a result of a lack of recent manual flight experience, a lack of situational awareness (S/A), or lack of readiness due to complacency.

The second question to examine is *does automation reduce errors, or simply change the nature of the errors which are made?*

Technology has most definitely reduced incidents and accidents in the aviation industry over time. One issue which may arise from technological solutions, however, is the tendency for that solution to create another distinct problem. For example, let us assume the aircraft you routinely fly employs a flight management system (FMS), which allows the pilot to pre-program the aircraft's flight path waypoints, including changes to headings and/or altitudes. When the aircraft fails to automatically turn to a new pre-programmed heading or capture a new altitude, the pilot may instantly attempt to reprogram the FMS to initiate the heading/altitude change as opposed to simply manually controlling the aircraft to change the heading/altitude, and then worry about reprogramming. In current aviation operations, many pilots tend to attempt to fix an automation problem with an automation solution. This ingrained desire to turn to the automated system first may cause an unacceptable delay in establishing the new heading/altitude.

Ever-increasing complexity of automated flight systems has been implicated in causing confusion and uncertainty in pilots, contributing to improper control actions during critical phases of flight and high-workload situations. In more profound cases, this could lead pilots to unintentionally position an aircraft in an unsafe flight condition.

Another question to examine *is automation beginning to supplant, instead of augment, basic flying skills?*

As a result of modern aircraft being capable of controlling themselves to a large degree, pilots may be increasingly reliant on the aircraft systems performing all the basic flight actions such as ascent, cruise, and descent as opposed to themselves. The unintended consequence causes pilots to lose confidence in their own ability to fly, simply because they don't perform those skills on a normal and recurring basis. Loss of control-inflight (LOC-I) has been the number one cause of air transport fatalities for many years, which may ultimately point to a lack of a pilot's fundamental skill of flying on instruments or unusual attitude recovery procedures.

The Downside of Automation

Automation has created a flight environment in which professional pilots are increasingly more unlikely to face a raw crisis in flight, but also those same pilots are more unlikely to be able to cope with such a crisis if one arises. As mentioned previously, automated systems are wonderful additions to aviation, right up to the point where they do not work correctly. Pilots must always be cognizant of the fact electromechanical systems can, and will, fail.

The U.S. Department of Transportation Inspector General published a report in 2016 on aviation accidents stating "accident pilots who typically fly with automation made errors when confronted with unexpected events or when transitioning to manual flying." That is powerful statement indicating pilots are basically unprepared to take over control of the aircraft when a system failure occurs. In an effort to retain basic flight skills for pilots, the FAA currently recommends pilots spend more time hand-flying the aircraft as opposed to automated flight.

Improper design of automated systems may also create problems. If a pilot is required to navigate multiple layers of software to reach the desired input screen, the systems are poorly designed, or there are many different systems to manipulate, this contributes to distraction from basic flying duties as well as S/A. Human brains inherently have trouble multitasking and the end up making errors, as the human brain can only process a finite amount of information at any given time.

An important concept for pilots to understand is automation does not relieve the pilot of safety-of-flight responsibility. The pilot must always be ready to engage with the aircraft if necessary, regardless of the phase-of-flight.

Many automated systems are fed flight data via devices external to the aircraft, such as pitot tubes, static ports, and angle-of-attack sensors. If the data from these sensors is inaccurate or compromised, the bad data may potentially cause erratic flight actions of the aircraft. Improper manufacturing, wear, bad electrical connections, bird-strikes, insect ingestion and freezing precipitation all have the potential to fail these sensors. In addition, frozen or damaged control unit input arms or rods may render the actual control surfaces ineffective or inoperative.

The following incidents illustrate how automation may be defeated in flight:

Incident – May 2011: A Dassault Falcon 7X was on approach to Kuala Lumpur, Malaysia, descending through 13,000 feet.

The nose of the aircraft suddenly pitched up, bleeding off airspeed rapidly. The pilot flying (PF) was the first officer (FO), who also an experienced ex-fighter pilot. When the aircraft pitched up, the FO immediately commanded the aircraft into a steep bank to lower the nose and avoid a stall, a trick the FO had learned from military aviation.

The aircraft was acting erratically for approximately two minutes before finally normalizing flight, and the crew continued on for a safe landing.

Analysis: The aircraft was thoroughly examined following the incident, and an improper solder joint in one of aircraft's control units was found to cause the errant behavior of the aircraft.

Conclusion: The pilot experienced an unexpected departure from controlled flight during a critical phase of flight. Fortunately, the pilot had prior upset recovery experience from their time spent flying military fighter aircraft, and was able to respond immediately through muscle-memory.

Incident – December 2012: A 737-800 deiced prior to flight in Helsinki, Finland. Ambient temperatures at the time were -17C. After deicing, the aircraft departed for Kittila, Finland.

On approach to Kittila with the aircraft being controlled by autothrust and autopilot, the aircraft began a normal nose pitch-up in line with trim actuation, with a predictable loss of airspeed. The autothrust responded to the loss of airspeed by increasing power to counter the effect.

At that point, the nose pitched up to 38 degrees, and airspeed bled off to 118 KIAS, and the aircraft stall warning activated. The pilot pushed forward on the controls with a measured 207 pounds of force, thereby forcing the nose down, and landed the aircraft safely.

Analysis: Investigators found frozen power control unit input arms rendered the elevator system inoperative during this critical phase-of-flight. With the aircraft flying in automated mode, the pilots were unaware of any control anomalies until trim actuation.

Conclusion: Automated control of an approach and landing in potentially freezing conditions can create potentially hazardous operating conditions which may manifest themselves at the least opportune moment. Had the pilots maintained manual control of the aircraft during the approach, they may have felt the lack of elevator control and therefore been able to plan for the anomaly appropriately.

Incident – July 2013: A Boeing 777-200 was on a VFR approach to SFO as the ILS glideslope guidance was inoperative at the time.

Aircraft approach was high at five nautical miles out, which the PF tried correcting with autopilot and autothrottle. At 500 feet above threshold elevation, the approach was now low and slow, and being unstable dictated a go-around according to company directives. At 200 feet, the flight crew became aware of the low airspeed and low glideslope, but did not initiate a go-around until the aircraft was at 20 feet AGL. With a normal approach speed of 137 knots indicated airspeed (KIAS), airspeed by this point in the approach had bled off to 106 KIAS.

The aircraft tail struck the seawall located before the threshold, broke off, and sent the aircraft spinning and tumbling down the runway. Four flight attendants were ejected onto the runway still in their seats when the tail broke off. Of the 307 people on board, three people ultimately died in the accident, and 187 were injured (49 seriously).

Analysis: The accident predictably underwent an extensive investigation, with a long list of official findings. In the end, NTSB findings include: "The probable cause of this accident was the flight crew's mismanagement of the airplane's descent during the visual approach, the PF's unintended deactivation of automatic airspeed control, the flight crew's inadequate monitoring of airspeed, and the flight crew's delayed execution of a go-around after they became aware that the airplane was below acceptable glideslope and airspeed tolerances. Contributing to the accident were (1) the complexities of the autothrottle and autopilot flight director systems that were inadequately described in Boeing's documentation and Asiana's pilot training, which increased the likelihood of mode error; (2) the flight crew's nonstandard communication and coordination regarding the use of the autothrottle and autopilot flight director systems; (3) the PF's inadequate training on the planning and executing of visual approaches; (4) the PM/instructor pilot's inadequate supervision of the PF; and (5) flight crew fatigue, which likely degraded their performance."

Conclusion: The main reason this accident occurred was a result of inadequate monitoring and management of a VFR approach. Had the PM been more proactive in alerting the PF about the degrading flight conditions, this accident may not have occurred.

Incident – November 2014: An A321 was performing a departure and climb-out in Bilbao, Spain, with the crew reaching their assigned cruise altitude of FL310.

The crew placed the aircraft in autopilot, at which time the autopilot was acting erratically. The crew turned autopilot off, at which point the aircraft entered a descent at 4,000 fpm. The pilots tried backpressure on the control sticks to level the aircraft, with no response or effect. The pilots ran their respective checklists, eventually deactivating the alpha protection system, at which point they regained control of the aircraft. The pilots arrested the descent at FL270, and continued the flight in manual flight mode.

Analysis: Investigators concluded the aircraft went into an un-commanded descent resulting from angle-of-attack (AOA) sensors which were frozen in place, sending erroneous flight parameter data to the alpha protection system. The system interpreted the erroneous data to signify the aircraft was stalling, and forced the nose down to counteract the alleged stall. Turning off the system allowed the aircrew to resume manual controlled flight.

Conclusion: The pilots were placed in a temporary uncontrolled flight condition as a result from a frozen sensor. The pilots reacted appropriately by running the checklists, finding the issue, and turning the system off.

Incident – March 2019: A Boeing 737-800 MAX was departing Ethiopia with 157 passengers and crew on board. On departure, the pilots advised ATC they were experiencing control problems and requested a return to the departure runway.

The aircraft leveled off at approximately 9,000 feet MSL, and radar contact was lost shortly after level off. The aircraft entered a steep dive, and impacted the ground six minutes after departure in a high rate-of-descent. All occupants of the aircraft were deceased.

Analysis: Investigators found the maneuvering characteristics augmentation system (MCAS) was providing erroneous control inputs to the aircraft's control systems, presumed to be a result of faulty system software combined with incorrect input from the AOA sensors. The MCAS was attempting to force the nose of the aircraft down, mistakenly believing the aircraft was in a stall, when no such stall was occurring. A similar incident involving this airframe and MCAS occurred five months earlier resulting in 189 occupants deceased in another country.

Conclusion: Aviation investigators and human factors experts believe while the MCAS was ultimately found to be at fault, the fact one of the pilots was relatively inexperienced may have contributed to the accident. Some experts felt had the pilots been trained to simply turn the MCAS off, this accident may have been prevented.

13.7 DECREASING ERROR RATES

The goal of every pilot should be to be as accurate as possible when making control inputs in the cockpit, whether it involves heading or altitude changes, communication frequencies, programming the flight management system (FMS), speed settings, etc. Knowing the fact perceptual modalities may be used to one's benefit for the processing of information, techniques have been developed for pilots to use in the cockpit to help ensure error rates remain low- to non-existent. One such technique is known as *point and shoot.*

As discussed previously, visual senses may be enhanced using audible and tactile reinforcement, so the goal of using the so-called *"point and shoot"* system of automation and control system input is to use all three senses to confirm control actions. This system is based on research performed by Japanese train operators, which concluded this technique has the potential to decrease error rates to *zero.*

For example, the PM receives an ATC call requiring a turn to heading 330. The PF would verbally confirm the new heading, turn the aircraft to the new heading, and the PM would confirm the new heading has been achieved by pointing at the compass (tactile), looking at the new compass heading (visual), and confirm the change by saying the new compass heading (audible). Therefore, the correct new compass heading has been achieved and confirmed with virtually no room for error.

This same technique should even be applied to flight in automated conditions. If adhered to, this would ensure the pilots remained intellectually engaged with the aircraft thus ensuring all automated control inputs were as programmed and/or expected.

13.8 AUTOMATED SYSTEMS MANAGEMENT

We now have a good understanding of the human cognitive issues surrounding the use of aircraft automation. We will outline the most important aspects of ensuring the pilot will maintain situational awareness during the use of these systems:

- **Display only pertinent flight data**
- **Change the way you think about "automated systems" to "semi-automated systems"**
- **Stay intellectually engaged with the aircraft**
- **Flightpath management responsibility remains with the pilot**
- **If in doubt, disengage the system and fly manually**

Display only pertinent flight data means activating and displaying the flightpath data that will assist the pilot in maintaining situational awareness for a particular phase-of-flight. Some modern automated systems employ many different display options, depending on pilot preference, and superfluous information will simply add to pilot confusion.

Change the way you think about "automated systems" to "semi-automated systems" refers to an individual's basic intellectual view of a system. If the operator of an automated system views the system as *autonomous,* the operator may believe the system does not need any monitoring or operator input. Mentioned previously was the fact electromechanical systems can and will fail, which would require operator input. Intellectually viewing an automated system as *semi-automated* means the operator is fully aware of the fact operator input may be necessary, and will therefore be more thoroughly mentally prepared for that possibility.

Stay intellectually engaged with the aircraft is a basic flight necessity. Professional pilots are compensated to maintain safe flight conditions, not to be a professional cloud photographer, internet searcher, or online purchaser. The pilot should maintain S/A with the aircraft at all times; at a minimum mentally monitoring the aircraft flightpath if not physically performing those duties. If this is successfully accomplished, the vast majority of monitoring errors contributing to incidents and accidents would obviously drop considerably.

Flightpath management responsibility remains with the pilot. This means if the automated system fails to perform a heading or altitude change, trim actuation, course correction, or power management function, the pilot intervenes in a timely fashion to correct the error manually. Once manually corrected, the pilot may then diagnose the system to see what programming or performance errors occurred.

If in doubt, disengage the system and fly manually. If an automated system is acting erratically, the pilot must eliminate the system as a threat by disengaging it and assuming manual control. In previous incidents and accidents, pilots were so engaged trying to fix or reprogram the system (problem-solving) as opposed to simply flying the aircraft (decision-making) a loss of S/A occurred.

A pilot can discipline themselves to follow these rules (depending on aircraft and organizational variances) to literally insulate themselves and passengers from the possibility of errors due to automation failure.

13.9 THE FUTURE OF AUTOMATION

Predicting the future of technology is almost impossible, as technology changes literally on a week-to-week basis. One element that should be considered, but most likely will not be, is maintaining some manner of mechanical control, completely independent of any electronic or programmable control. At this time, no electronically-controlled system can be relied upon with a 100% certainty of non-failure, whereas a mechanically-operated system can be manipulated and controlled with nothing more than a human being at the controls. Additionally, human intervention should always be possible with any system, as opposed to allowing an errant or maliciously hacked program to over-control the aircraft into a dangerous condition without the opportunity for recovery by the pilots. As a result of this, humans currently are and should remain the ultimate redundant system. Regardless of what the future holds, we will briefly examine current expert predictions on where aircraft automated systems are predicted to go as of the writing of this book.

Aircraft in development are being designed to wholly integrated, with more electronic fly-by-wire systems, *full authority digital electronics control (FADEC)*, and more extensive electrification. This will enable almost limitless fine control adjustments to be analyzed and initiated in terms of microseconds.

Aircraft *integrated cockpit layouts* should progress to a state of being more intuitive and straightforward to operate, as well as simpler to manipulate. Currently many separate and distinct systems exist in the cockpit, which may contribute to control system ambiguity, particularly in periods of hyper-stress.

Adaptive automation may be integrated into future technology design, which holds the promise of allowing pilots to maintain basic flying skills while enjoying the protection of an electronically-controlled backup system. Adaptive automation would only assume control of the aircraft if pilot inputs became illogical to the system's law and logic programming, signaling the pilot was either about to make a grave mistake or was incapable of manual control for some reason.

Glass cockpits, touchscreen controls, voice-control, and innovative approaches to design would allow information be presented as a holistic picture of the aircraft and its operation. Attempting to monitor a variety of systems may lead to alerts or potentially dangerous developing conditions to be missed, as opposed to monitoring one or two screens allowing the pilot to monitor many systems at a glance. Voice-controlled prompts may enable a pilot to verbally prompt the aircraft systems to load a particular flight segment into the FMS and fly most of the segment "hands-off."

Cyber threats are an ever-increasing and omnipresent danger to internet-connected communications systems, including aircraft. As aircraft become increasingly connected, the opportunity for malicious hacking of those systems increases exponentially. Beyond simply hacking aircraft systems, ATC and peripheral communication systems are exposed as well.

Although no aircraft has been forced down as a result of malicious hacking as of this writing, contemplating the consequences from such an action is both terrifying and unimaginable in scope, thus making the case for pilot-initiated mechanical control of aircraft even more urgent.

Human error can and has caused accidents in the past and will again in the future, and the following questions must to be answered before commercial aircraft should be allowed to fly with only one pilot, or possibly completely autonomous without a human pilot onboard:

- One-pilot flight operations with a remote, on-ground back-up pilot may be feasible for many operations, but "many" is not good enough. Pilot incapacitation resulting from illness is a relatively common event in most major aviation markets. Additionally, having a second pair of trained eyes may be essential. Inflight emergencies can happen and need to be resolved expediently. If and when something goes wrong in flight, the crew must act quickly and communicate effectively in conditions of profound uncertainty.
- Will electronic data transfer and/or programming ever be fool-proof and 100% reliable? At the current time, it is not. A secondary question to ask is "how many aircraft have been saved by a pilot when the automation failed?" The current

scientific view is automation saves lives because human errors are responsible for some 75 – 98% (depending on who one asks) of all aviation accidents, which is true. However, how many of those events was the pilot attempting to save the aircraft after failure of a system, and the pilot failed?

- Will electronic data transfer ever be faster, more complete, and more intuitive than the human brain? The human brain remains the greatest computer available at the time of this writing, although artificial intelligence computers probably aren't far behind. However, intuition is hard to program into a machine and many times a pilot's intuition that "something isn't right" has saved lives. A pilot's senses are capable of picking up on subtle clues indicating something is amiss, whether the clue be an odd smell, an observable change in weather, a weird vibration, subtle changes in the way something sounds, or even just gut feel.

- Will electrical or mechanical failures ever be rendered obsolete? Although theoretically possible in someone's future visions, it is difficult to imagine a machine that never suffers from mechanical wear, signal interruption or distortion, corrosion, errant programming, improper assembly, impact damage or the myriad other issues that plague machines of the current era. Until that time arrives, the human mind continues to be the best back-up system to potential failures.

13.10 ENHANCED VISION SYSTEMS

In the chapter on Visual Vestibular and Proprioceptive Systems, the concept of enhanced vision systems (EVS), and the various types of EVS, was introduced. EVS exist for the sole purpose of enabling a pilot to visually perceive objects during flights in limited-visibility conditions in which, ordinarily, the pilot would not be able to perceive with natural vision. In a sense, EVS give a pilot "super-human" sight.

Since the dawn of the aviation era, lack of visual acuity in certain atmospheric, weather, or night conditions has been a major factor in the causation of incidents and accidents. If a pilot cannot see, they cannot fly, and the same holds true even for birds, whose primary mode of transportation is to fly.

Types of Enhanced Vision Systems in Aviation

As a review of previously discussed material, we will briefly examine the main types of EVS currently employed in aviation, which are:

- Infrared systems
- Light intensification systems
- Combined vision systems (CVS)

Infrared Systems use thermal variation, or contrast, to create an image human visual perception can identify. These systems are typically found in fixed-wing aircraft. Basic infrared EVS is projected to the pilot via an instrument-panel mounted screen. More advanced enhanced flight vision systems (EFVS) are projected onto a head-up display (HUD) mounted either from the ceiling or glare-shield in front of the pilot's visual field.

Light Intensification Systems turn photons (light energy) into electrons, amplify the electrons, and turn the electrons back into photons to create a visually perceivable image. Essentially, this process amplifies the luminance of an object, allowing human users to see obstacles in the dark; the only time these systems are useful. These systems are normally used in helicopter operations, and are typically helmet-mounted goggles (Night Vision Goggles, or NVG's) which the pilot may either use or flip up out of the way for certain phases of flight.

Combined Vision Systems use a combination of infrared imagery superimposed on synthetic database imagery, giving the pilot a fusion of the two systems for more complete situational awareness (S/A). As mentioned previously, synthetic vision systems use a database to create imagery, and will not include real-time obstacles or aircraft. These systems are normally found in fixed wing aircraft, and are normally displayed on a HUD.

Although these systems allow for almost super-human visual ability, they do have limitations:

- FAA rules stipulate a pilot still has to visually acquire the runway by 100 feet with their natural vision.
- Heavy precipitation, clouds and fog can impair EVS effectiveness.
- Peripheral visibility is poor in the best of circumstances, limited to an approximate 40 x 40 degrees field of vision, making side traffic extremely difficult to identify.
- LED runway lights are invisible to IR since they generate no heat, and painted markings on pavement or asphalt may be difficult to impossible to see with long wavelength infrared (LWIR). Medium wavelength infrared (MWIR) and Short wavelength infrared (SWIR) provide better contrast for reading markings and signs.
- Since these systems can only generate monocular, monochromatic images, depth perception is non-existent and color and contrast sensitivity is a challenge.

13.11 EVS/EFVS/SVS UTILIZATION

Although EVS, EFVS and SVS have their limitations, we know these systems increase S/A in specific aviation situations. The following are the main purposes these systems are employed in aircraft:

- **Runway alignment on approach**
- **Obstacle avoidance in flight**
- **Runway guidance during taxi**

Runway alignment on approach is optimized for the pilots as the thermal variation between the asphalt and surrounding terrain allows for visual alignment confirmation. Using a combination of ILS, EVS/EFVS, and natural vision allows the pilot to maintain proper approach glideslope S/A throughout the entire process, regardless of prevailing visual conditions. The pilot must keep in mind LED marker lights and/or VASI/PAPI lights may be unusable due to inability to see them, or from a lack of color contrast. The newest EVS designs are multispectral, enabling the systems to capture both visual light from LED lights as well as the thermal image generated by previous EVS generations. The runway must still be acquired with natural vision by 100 feet AGL.

Obstacle avoidance in flight visual performance is greatly enhanced with EVS/EFVS, as previously low contrast obstacles such as other aircraft, flocks of birds, unmanned aerial vehicles (UAVs), terrain, trees and towers may now be included in a visible scene, allowing the pilots the ability to see and avoid.

Runway guidance during taxi with EVS/EFVS allows pilots to see the runway edge lights or asphalt edges in foggy conditions, avoiding runway excursions, and any obstructions during low visibility conditions.

The pilot must always be cognizant of the lack of side visibility due to the restricted field-of-view. Taxiing too fast will not allow the pilot adequate time to avoid colliding with another aircraft or ground vehicle if not visually acquired in time, so the pilots should always adhere to their individual company directives regarding taxi speeds versus. runway visual range (RVR).

Head-Up Displays

Head-Up Displays (HUD's) will project flight data directly into a pilot's field-of-view, allowing an unprecedented level of S/A as opposed to dividing attention between the instrument panel and windscreen visuals. All critical flight data, such as airspeed, altitude, attitude, direction, and ILS vertical and lateral guidance may be programmed to be projected onto the screen, as depicted below:

Head-Up Displays with Enhanced Vision Systems (EVS)

HUD screens with EFVS provide even greater S/A, with the benefits of enhanced vision combined with the aforementioned flight data. With a HUD-generated EFVS, the pilot gains the visual S/A of infrared imaging along with natural peripheral vision, allowing for better natural orientation processing skills to be employed.

Head-Worn Display Systems

Head-worn display systems provide head-up flight data and EFVS displays directly in a pilot's line-of-sight, so regardless of where the pilot is looking flight parameter information is readily available. These systems are suitable for day and night operations, all weather conditions, and minimize dependency on airport instrumentation. Although currently available, this technology has yet to catch on with the general pilot population. The display features high-resolution symbology on a transparent visor.

Future Flight Vision Systems

Looking into the future of flight vision systems is just as cloudy as predicting any other future technology, but the following trends are developing as of the writing of this book:

Augmented Reality holds great promise for increased S/A, as this technology blends real-time visual information in a pilot's sightline with technical information relating to what the pilot is looking at. For instance, imagine visually acquiring an airport and included in the view are runway dimensions, threshold elevation, ambient temperature, distance from threshold, desired glideslope, an infrared image of the runway and other pertinent data.

Another emerging technology is *fly-by-sight,* which will enable pilots to reduce head-down time in high workload environments by allowing a pilot to conduct certain tasks simply by looking at a control or function using line-of-sight activation.

The display methodology for these emerging technologies promises to be equally exciting as the data content. Pilots should expect to see small, lightweight *retinal displays* generated on normal-looking eyeglasses *or contact lens* displays generating images directly into the fovea of the retina. The ultimate display system would be direct *retinal implants,* whereas chemical, electrical or mechanical stimulation could allow a pilot's retina to interact with computer-generated or visual-field enhancing technologies within their own body.

Whatever the future holds for aviation vision and S/A-enhancing equipment, it is sure to be amazing!

13.12 EVS MANAGEMENT

No matter what type of EVS a pilot uses, times exist when a pilot simply has too much information relayed to them to decipher and process at one time. Pilots must remember a human brain can only process a finite amount of information at a given point-in-time, so if too much information is displayed it may become more of an annoyance or distraction than benefit. Care must be taken to ensure only information or data relevant to the current task is displayed, or performance may suffer as a result. Some pilots have been known to stow the HUD on approach so they can simply concentrate on flying the aircraft. The following are tips to remember when using enhanced vision systems:

- **EVS is effective for object or terrain recognition and avoidance, and runway alignment during approach and taxi.**
- **Eliminate superfluous information on the display.**
- **Dim HUD symbology to lesson distraction.**
- **If displays are too annoying, simply stow or turn off.**

Conclusion

Technological enhancements to aircraft systems will continue to evolve, forcing the technology of the current time into obsolescence. No doubt tomorrow's automated systems will be amazing in their thoroughness and complexity; however, no matter how amazing aircraft automation becomes, the simple fact remains these electrical and mechanical systems are not immune to failure or unexpected behavior.

Above and beyond the failure or behavior possibilities are the moral and ethical dilemmas which exist concerning life-or-death decision-making processes, which will inevitably occur in any transportation setting. The professional pilot should seriously ponder whether a life-or-death decision be left to a machine or computer program. To many aviation experts, this is the one decision remaining the exclusive domain of human operators.

Pilots of advanced computerized aircraft need to understand and be able to decipher complicated software logic rules and procedures under stress, because if not it could mean imminent disaster.

Ultimately pilots need to respect automation limitations and when it is appropriate to trust it. Pilots also need to maintain awareness of when to be skeptical, when to disable the system, and initiate manual control. While safety features such as auto-descent or stall mitigation are a fantastic addition for safety, one should never want to fly an aircraft capable of taking control away from human operators with no means of overriding the system in some way.

Aircraft automated systems have been an effective addition in the battle to increase flight safety in the aviation industry and have been responsible for saving many lives. However, experts predict no machine, program, or computer will supplant a well-trained pilot's effectiveness and necessity in the cockpit for a long time to come.

Chapter 13 Core Competency Questions

1. What are the two designated responsibilities for a two-pilot crew?
2. In two-pilot operations, who has ultimate responsibility to ensure the aircraft flight path is maintained?
3. What is the end result of monitoring disruptors?
4. According to IATA 2020 Safety Report, what was the main contributor for flightcrew-induced errors?
5. Pilot pressures of completing the flight at the destination is called what?
6. What two methods may prevent cognitive lock-up?
7. Automated aircraft systems are designed to _____safety-of-flight.
8. True or false: aircraft automated systems can be counted on to 100% reliable.
9. If an automated system were acting erratically, the best course of action is to_____.
10. What are the three types of Enhanced Vision Systems in aircraft?
11. What three purposes do EVS systems have in aviation operations?

14. IMPACT ACCELERATION AND AIRCRAFT CRASHWORTHINESS

An aviator's understanding of impact acceleration is important as aircraft crashes may occur, and knowing and predicting vehicle impact angles and forces, along with potential injury patterns resulting from impact forces and how to mitigate those forces may be the difference between survivability or not. Fatality by impact makes no discriminations, and few other threats to the health of aviators can compare to the effects of impact trauma.

Impact acceleration, by its very nature, typically happens extremely quickly. Therefore, there is less time to observe the phenomena and understand the event. An objective understanding of the physical processes involved will result in improved protection of aircraft occupants in the event of one of the most potentially severe threats to human health as a result of flight. The outcome of the impact experience will depend greatly on the utilization and effectiveness of designed aircraft and occupant protection technologies. An aviator's use of the protection and the characteristics of the protection available will depend upon the education provided to aviators.

Aircraft crashworthiness refers to the structural deformation and induced impact forces occupants are exposed to in a crash event, and how the design characteristics of the aircraft reduce or contribute to those forces. The chances of being in an aircraft crash are incredibly small, and the chances of dying from aircraft crash even smaller, mainly as a result of engineering survivability factors into the seat supports, fuselage, and restraint systems. However, pilot manipulation of all these systems must be correct in order for the systems to provide maximum benefit to the occupants.

In this chapter, we will discuss:

1. Definition of acceleration
2. Brief history of aviation safety
3. Environmental challenges of inflight escape
4. Impact G-forces
5. Crashworthiness
6. Crash survivability considerations
7. Common injury patterns due to impact forces
8. Increasing crash survivability

14.1 DEFINITION OF ACCELERATION

Acceleration is simply the rate of change of velocity with respect to time. In effect, acceleration is a rate of change of position with respect to time, and a net result of all forces acting on a body. Typically, the shorter the time for a change of position, the more hostile the force.

Acceleration, velocity, and position are vector quantities inclusive of both direction and magnitude. Magnitude of an acceleration is expressed in terms of a given velocity unit per unit of time; for example: *feet per second per second* or *feet per second squared*. Acceleration in aviation is commonly expressed in terms of gravity, expressed as *G* or *g*. Gravity is the force of attraction between two objects. G refers to a gravitational constant, while *g* refers to changing gravitational forces.

One g is the magnitude of gravitational acceleration experienced by an unsupported object at the Earth's surface, the force of which acts on every molecule of the object. The value of one g is approximately 32.2 feet per second squared, in which we must negate the effect of air resistance. The unit of g is not a unit of force, but rather a unit of acceleration. Acceleration can and will be produced by a gravitational force.

Newton's Second Law states: "Force on an unsupported mass will produce an acceleration in the direction of the force that is directly proportional to the magnitude of the force and inversely proportional to the mass of the object." This relationship is expressed by equation $F = ma$. Force and acceleration can be directly measured but mass is deduced from the equation. The units of force are *pounds-force* or *newton*, which are typically expressed in *mass-units* times *acceleration-units*. Force is not expressed in g.

Newton's Third Law states: *for every action there is an equal and opposite reaction.* The inertial reaction forces applied by an accelerated body accelerated in the positive direction will be oppositely directed. For example, a head accelerated in the rearward direction by an impact will apply an inertial reaction force back against a headrest opposite the direction of acceleration.

Impact acceleration is short-term acceleration; not sustained long enough to result in meaningful steady state or sustained component regarding the mechanical response of the body. Impact acceleration forces must be of sufficient magnitude to produce a transitory, or short-term, mechanical response. Some aviation experts define impact acceleration as being an acceleration event of less than one or two seconds; however, the transitory response definition is generally more useful.

Sustained acceleration in aircraft produce specific physiologic stresses, taking place over time, and will be discussed at length in the next chapter. Impact acceleration tends to produce mechanical stresses that are of very short duration, generating potentially traumatic results.

14.2 BRIEF HISTORY OF AVIATION SAFETY

As defined by the Convention on International Civil Aviation, Annex 13, an *aviation accident* is "an occurrence associated with the operation of an aircraft, which takes place from the time any person boards the aircraft with the *intention of flight* until all such persons have disembarked, and in which a) a person is fatally or seriously injured, b) the aircraft sustains significant damage or structural failure, or c) the aircraft goes missing or becomes completely inaccessible." Annex 13 defines an *aviation incident* as "an occurrence, other than an accident, associated with the operation of an aircraft that affects or could affect the safety of operation." Aircraft impacts may pertain to either of these categories, although in most cases an aircraft impact would be considered an accident.

The first aviation accident involving a fatality was the crash of a balloon near Wimereux, France on June 15th, 1785, killing the balloon's inventor and another occupant. The first aviation accident involving powered aircraft was the crash of a Wright Model A airplane at Fort Myer, Virginia, USA, on September 17th, 1908, injuring the aircraft's pilot and co-owner Orville Wright and killing the passenger, Signal Corps Lieutenant Thomas Selfridge. Lt. Selfridge died from head injuries sustained when the aircraft crashed, thus providing the very first human factors lesson in the history of aviation: high-velocity head impacts may kill aviators.

One must realize that early aircraft were meant to fly, not crash. When something went wrong in the air, there was not a lot of technology to protect the pilots or passengers from almost certain doom. Admittedly, aircraft safety close to the dawn of modern aviation was horrendous, as (unfortunately) people had to die in aircraft-related accidents in order for aviation "experts" to realize more robust safety precautions were necessary.

Among the first safety mechanisms to be developed in 1910 were seat belts to prevent the occupants from being ejected out of their seats when the aircraft came to a sudden stop. Aircraft escape systems, in the form of personal parachutes, made their debut in 1912.

In 1917, a young pilot by the name of Hugh DeHaven was involved in an airplane inflight collision that killed the other pilot, but not himself. This started the young pilot thinking about developing ideas concerning aircraft "crashworthiness"; designs focused on minimizing or preventing aircraft accident injuries and death.

The Federal Government became involved in aviation safety with the enactment of the Air Commerce Act of 1926, although in 1926 and 1927 saw a total of 24 fatal commercial aircraft crashes, with an additional 51 in 1928.

Full flight instrumentation assisting in avoiding crashes was introduced in 1929. To avoid inflight mistakes, pilot checklists were developed in 1937. Shoulder restraint systems were introduced in 1939, and aircraft ejection systems in the early 1940's, with the first successful ejection occurring in 1942. In 1947, a military flight surgeon by the name of Dr. John Stapp began human deceleration and restraint system testing, and aircraft evacuation slides were patented in 1956.

The single deadliest aviation accident occurred on the Canary Island of Tenerife, Spain, when two Boeing 747s collided, killing a total 583 occupants. The deadliest single-aircraft accident occurred to a Japan Airlines 747 when the aircraft suffered an explosive decompression as a result of a faulty repair, killing 520 occupants.

At the time of this writing, over 30 aviation-related accidents have occurred in which at least 200 aircraft occupants were fatally injured, and countless more accidents involving fatalities of lesser amounts. In the vast majority of aircraft accidents involving fatalities, those fatalities occurred as result of terrain or water contact by the aircraft.

As we can see, aircraft safety research and development has evolved extensively throughout the 1900's, into the current century, and continues to this day. Accident rates across every aviation sector have decreased immensely as a result of these measures, but has not, and most likely will not, disappear until mechanical, electronic, or human failures can be completely eliminated.

14.3 ENVIRONMENTAL CHALLENGES OF INFLIGHT ESCAPE

One method of egressing out of an aircraft inflight to enhance pilot safety which brings about its own impact acceleration considerations is *ejecting*. Mainly a military-specific escape system, ejection seats provide a "last-resort" method of separating the pilot from the aircraft. Although mainly propelled by rocket motors in the current era, ejection seats have been activated by compressed air, springs, bungees, gunpowder, and other explosive charges. Once clear of the aircraft, the seat generally automatically deploys a personal parachute to allow the pilot to maintain a survivable descent to the ground. The very process of ejecting, however, can be extremely violent and carries certain risk considerations.

Some of the challenges involved regarding inflight escape are:

- Extremes in speed
- Ejection forces
- Low altitudes
- Vehicle (fuselage) clearance
- Environmental extremes of altitude

Extremes in speed can provide challenges with regards to windblast effects. If ejecting at high speeds, sudden exposure to air pressure can produce human extremity flail injuries causing trauma to the head, neck, arms, legs, hands, and feet. Air pressure may also cause the pilot to have clothing and equipment ripped off their bodies such as helmets, boots, gloves, survival vests, jackets, etc. Some current generation ejection seats use speed-sensing, combined with altitude-sensing, technology to best determine the optimum speed and/or altitude in which to deploy the personal parachute. Current generation seats (depending on the manufacturer) are rated for ejections anywhere from 0 mph to 870 mph.

Ejection forces impose differential effects on the human body, and generally range from 10g to 20g. The pilot must maintain optimum body position during the ejection process to ensure minimal physical damage to the neck, spine, and extremities. Optimum body position includes keeping the butt as far back into the seat as possible, forcing the head against the headrest, tucking the chin to straighten the cervical spine, forcing the back against the seatback, tucking the elbows into the arm guards on the seat with fingers on the ejection handles, and keeping the legs tightly together with the toes pointed inward. Failure to maintain proper body position may result in damaged cervical, thoracic, or lumbar spine vertebrae damage, hyperextension of the knees and ankles, flailing injuries to the legs, and flailing and/or dismemberment of the arms.

Low altitudes may produce hazards simply from a lack of time and altitude for the seat to clear the pilot and fully deploy the parachute. Newer generations of ejection seats have gyroscopic sensors to propel the ejection seat skyward in the event of low-altitude, inverted ejections.

Vehicle clearance is a major consideration when designing an inflight or ground escape system. The typical aircraft ejection system operates in two distinct stages.

First, the canopy (or hatch) immediately above the aviator is opened, shattered, or jettisoned, and the seat and occupant are launched through the opening using whatever propulsion system is designed into the seat. In early aircraft designs, this may have required two separate actions by the aviator, while later egress system designs, such as the Advanced Concept Ejection Seat - Model 2 (ACES II), perform both functions as a single action when the ejection sequence is initiated.

Non-standard egress systems in aircraft where upward ejections are not an option include downward track, which are used for some crew positions in bomber aircraft including the famous B-52 Stratofortress, canopy destruct (CD) and through-canopy penetration (TCP), drag extraction, encapsulated seat, and even a unique crew capsule.

Early models of the F-104 Starfighter were equipped with a downward track ejection seat due to the environmental hazard of the T-tail vertical stabilizer. In order for this system to avoid injuring the pilot, they were equipped with "spurs" attached to automatic cables designed to pull the legs inward so the pilot could eject safely. With the development of this innovation, other egress systems began using leg retractors to prevent injuries to flailing legs, and to provide a more stable center of gravity. Some models of the F-104 were equipped with more traditional upward-ejecting seats.

Aircraft designed for low-level use sometimes have ejection seats which fire through the canopy, as waiting for the canopy to be ejected is too slow. Some aircraft types use canopy destruct systems, utilizing an explosive cord (MDC – miniature detonation cord or FLSC – flexible linear shaped charge) embedded within the acrylic plastic of the canopy. The MDC is initiated when the ejection handle is activated, shattering the canopy over the seat milliseconds before the seat is launched.

Through-canopy penetration is similar to canopy destruct, but a sharp spike on the top of the seat, known as the "canopy penetrator" or "shell-tooth", strikes the canopy and shatters it if the canopy fails to jettison. In ground emergencies, a pilot can use a breaker knife attached to the inside of the canopy rail to shatter the canopy manually.

Environmental extremes of altitude potentially expose the pilot to those high-altitude physiological considerations discussed in previous chapters, such as hypoxia and hypothermia, to name a couple of examples.

Another consideration is inadvertent parachute deployment at high altitudes, the opening forces of which can reach extreme parameters. Due to the lack of atmospheric pressure, and therefore backpressure on the parachute canopy, the canopy can snap open at speeds producing opening shock forces strong enough to severely injure a human suspended by a parachute harness.

Current ejection seats typically incorporate altitude sensors into the seat-human separation process to ensure the human's separation from the seat and subsequent parachute opening shock are performed at low enough altitudes so as to not be unsurvivable.

Ejection Sequence and Force References

Healthy human beings can withstand certain levels of impact G's without sustaining significant physical damage. Extensive research has shown humans can tolerate, with little debilitation or traumatic effects, ejection and parachute opening forces between 10 to 20 G's.

Ejection seat forces will peak fractions of a second after seat activation, while parachute opening shock forces are distributed over periods of one to two seconds.

For the common and widely-used advanced concept ejection seat (ACES II), the typical ejection sequence would operate as follows:

0.0 Seconds: The pilot pulls the handles or overhead curtain; aircraft canopy is jettisoned or

shattered; the seat catapult is initiated launching the seat up the seat rails.

0.15 Seconds: Ejection seat clears the seat rails and surrounding cockpit travelling at 50 fps with the pilot experiencing approximately 14 G's, which quickly dissipate after cockpit clearance.

0.19 Seconds: The main rocket motor ignites, at which time the pilot experiences 10-11 G's; Vernier motor fires to counteract pitch changes; yaw motor fires, inducing slight yaw to ensure man-seat separation.

0.50 Seconds: Ejection seat has ascended 100 feet to 200 feet above ejection initiation altitude, at which point the G forces quickly drop off prior to pilot-seat separation.

0.52 Seconds: Pilot-seat separator fires, propelling the pilot and their survival equipment away from the seat; the parachute drogue gun fires, pulling the main parachute canopy from its pack for deployment.

1.8 to 2.8 Seconds: The main parachute canopy fully deploys.

5.5 to 6.3 Seconds: The survival kit deploys to hang below the pilot on an extended lanyard.

Although most healthy pilots can survive the ejection sequence without consequence, proper body position must be maintained for the best chances of sustaining no injuries. Even then, due to the variety of factors involved, it would be simply impossible to guarantee no physical harm will occur as ejecting out of an aircraft is an extremely dynamic, violent event.

14.4 IMPACT G-FORCES

When examining impact G forces, we have to understand the *energy* involved. Energy is defined as "the ability to do work;" therefore, during an impact an object's energy is converted into work. Work occurs when a force is applied to move an object a certain distance; therefore, work is equal to force multiplied by distance. As a result of force being a component of work and impact is the conversion of energy into work, we may use the equations for energy and work to solve for the force of impact.

The energy of a moving object is called *kinetic energy*. This kinetic energy is equal to one half of the object's mass, multiplied by the square of its velocity. Unless you are a crash investigator, you most likely won't be calculating your impact forces if your aircraft is about to crash. What this information does mean to you, however, is management of kinetic energy is crucial.

Because kinetic energy varies with the square of velocity, increasing the speed of the impact exponentially affects the impact force. A good rule to remember is when the speed of an impact is doubled, the impact force is quadrupled. If we converted this into the impact speed of a light aircraft, for example, an impact at 85 knots yields twice the kinetic energy as an impact at 60 knots.

Obviously, when an aircraft impacts terrain or another object, the aircraft will deform due to the deceleration forces involved. This deceleration deformation will absorb some, most, or all of the force of the impact. The deformation of the vehicle is an important component regarding impact survivability. If impact forces are of high velocity and applied over a short time, deformation occurs quickly and deceleration forces are greater, whereas if impact forces are of lower velocity and applied over a longer time, deformation occurs slower and deceleration forces are less.

Knowing this, we can formulate aircraft impact rules and parameters to minimize kinetic energy, which would increase our chances of survival.

Three Rules of Crashing an Airplane

Following are the three critical components, or rules, to remember if an aircraft crash is imminent:

- **Arrive at the ground at the lowest possible ground speed.**
- **Arrive at the ground under control.**
- **Allow the aircraft and environment absorb your kinetic energy.**

Arriving at the ground at the lowest possible ground speed allows the pilot to minimize the kinetic energy necessary to mitigate. A 12.5 knot wind can make the difference between an 85-knot impact versus a 60-knot impact, which mentioned previously can reduce the kinetic energy to half the impact force. Assuming the pilot has the time, every attempt should be made to turn the aircraft into the wind, as this maneuver has the potential to reduce impact forces significantly. Ground speed should weigh *heavily* on the pilot's mind as they attempt an emergency landing, as even a few knots' reduction in airspeed yields positive results in terms of survivability.

Arriving at the ground under control allows the pilot to expose those parts of the aircraft most effectively designed to absorb impact forces; those parts being comprised of the front and belly of the aircraft. Additionally, the aircraft restraint systems are designed to mitigate forward acceleration, as opposed to vertical or lateral accelerative forces.

The astute pilot should avoid the concept of stalling into the treetops as well. Should the aircraft assume an inverted position while contacting branches during descent, little protection is provided for aircraft occupants to prevent branch penetration into the cabin from the roof of the aircraft. A more effective approach to treetop contact is to fly into the treetops to gain maximum structural protection from the front and bottom of the airframe. Generally, trees with needles (i.e. pine trees) tend to be softer wood and potentially more forgiving than trees with leaves, which tend to be harder and less forgiving wood.

Pilots need also to fly into the crash as far as possible. In many circumstances, pilots will relinquish control of the aircraft following the first impact to assume some manner of an impact brace position, leaving aircraft control to fate. Instead, the pilot should attempt to influence directional control of the aircraft after the first impact, if possible. The crash is not over until the aircraft comes to a complete stop.

If the pilot allows the aircraft to arrive at the ground completely out-of-control, any crash force protection mitigation from the aircraft could be potentially negated.

Allow the aircraft and environment to absorb your kinetic energy to prevent occupant's bodies from absorbing any impact forces, if possible. Based on impact tests conducted by the FAA, an aircraft fuselage stopping from 50 mph in the space of two feet generates approximately 43 G's of impact force, and the same fuselage stopping from

50 mph in five feet generates approximately 17 G's of impact force. It is doubtful that 43 G's of impact force would be survival to the human body; however, it is certainly possible 17 G's of impact force *would* be survivable. Theoretically, an additional three feet of stopping distance may be the difference between survivability or fatality, so even sliding your seat back as far as possible prior to impact could make a difference.

Every attempt should be made by the pilot to break off the landing gear, wings, or tail of the aircraft during impact to allow those airframe parts absorb kinetic energy. Based on testing data, a stall and/or spin into terrain at 50 mph may induce fatal injuries, whereas a 50-mph impact with the front of the aircraft into the side of a building may not.

In the event of an upright touchdown on unimproved terrain, landing gear become a breakable, energy absorbing structure. With the landing gear absorbing kinetic energy after initial touchdown, the pilot may consider raising the landing gear to allow the aircraft to settle onto the lower structure of the aircraft, thereby absorbing more kinetic energy as the aircraft slows.

Water Ditching

Pilots may assume ditching as aircraft in water would provide for a softer, more predictable impact experience, and experience has proven those pilots would be mistaken. Factors exist contradicting those assumptions, listed as follows:

- Hypothermia
- Water is hard at speed
- Unpredictable aircraft disintegration characteristics
- Most airplanes are not made to float on water

Hypothermia will be an immediate physiological concern following immersion in water, providing the aircraft occupants survive the initial impact and the aircraft did not crash into a heated swimming pool.

Cold shock response is the bodies initial response to cold water exposure, with water temperatures in the range of 15 to 20 degrees C (59 to 60 degrees F) and usually last for one to two minutes. Rapid cooling of human skin results in a gasp reflex, hyperventilation, and a lack of human ability to hold their breath, causing people to drown.

Survivors of cold shock response face cold incapacitation and loss of neuromuscular skills needed to keep their heads above water or assist in their own rescue, which typically occurs in the first 10 to 15 minutes.

Those that last beyond cold incapacitation face hypothermia, normally starting between 30 and 60 minutes of continuous immersion. Hypothermia further decreases body core temperatures, resulting in loss-of-consciousness and drowning. Those individuals kept afloat from flotation devices may survive another hour or so before their heart stops beating.

Water is hard at speed is a factor to be highly cognizant of. An object or body, whether mechanical or human, impacting water at speeds typical of a flying aircraft will generate a tremendous amount of kinetic energy once the object contacts the surface tension of the water. As with contacting any other surface, the object will come to a stop in a very short distance.

Even if an aircraft occupant is properly restrained, the physics of inertia still apply. When the human body comes to a sudden stop, internal organs want to keep moving forward, causing them to tear loose from the force of impact, resulting in massive internal bleeding.

Unpredictable aircraft disintegration characteristics occur when an aircraft impacts water as once the first piece of the aircraft contacts the water, the aircraft is subjected to whip-like acceleration characteristics. This will result in the aircraft fuselage tumbling, rolling, or cartwheeling resulting in an unpredictable disintegration of the aircraft, with unconscious crew and passengers at best, and fatal injuries at worst.

Most airplanes are not made to float on water as airplanes are not made to be air or water-tight, making the unconscious survivability of aircraft occupants of less certainty. If an aircraft impact results in occupant unconsciousness on land, the survivability of occupants is much greater provided no post-crash fire occurs. Research has proven drowning is the leading cause of death with regards to unintended aircraft water impacts.

Deceleration

Research conducted by the FAA's Civil Aerospace Medical Institute (CAMI) has shown if aircraft cabin deceleration can be maintained at 9 G's or less, occupant survivability is exponentially better than with greater deceleration forces.

At an impact speed of 50 mph, the minimum stopping distance to maintain 9 G's or less would be 12.3 feet. At an impact speed of 60 mph, minimum stopping distance would be 17.8 feet. These speeds take into consideration contact speed is groundspeed into the wind, and deceleration is constant. Theoretically, if an aircraft impacts the ground at 50 mph and comes to a stop in the aircraft's wingspan, all occupants should survive. Injuries can not be ruled out, but survival is probable.

271

G Force Realities

Effective weight increases with G force, which may be demonstrated when a pilot turns into a 60-degree bank in an aircraft. The turn rate would generate approximately 2 G's, effectively doubling the weight of the pilot.

The basic determinants of forces projected onto an object in a collision are its mass and its velocity. An impact event changes the velocity of the object's mass, which it does by applying force. Force applied over time changes an object's momentum. The severity of impact damage on an object is determined by the object's velocity change and the time and/or distance over which velocity change takes place. If the object's velocity change is large and the time/distance is short, the force must be high.

The rate at which a body decelerates directly translates to G forces applied to the body. For example, if one considers the positive effects of airbags on decelerations and momentum, the airbag slows the occupant down at a rate considered more survivable than without an airbag. An aircraft or automobile has *crush zones* designed into the structure of the vehicle to serve the same purpose as airbags; as deformation of the crush zone occurs, it systematically slows the vehicle at a rate more survivable for the occupants.

The rate at which force is applied in impact events will vary throughout the aircraft. Airbags and crush zones work to decrease the G-forces and momentum, therefore the effective weight and damage, experienced by occupants. Head injuries to aircraft occupants remains the most common cause of death in impact events, as head protection is one of the most difficult to achieve.

Human Tolerances to Impact G Forces

When we consider the effects of stress and strain on humans, the total force applied does not adequately or completely characterize its injury potential. Human injury patterns result from distortion of body structures beyond their recoverable limits. This distortion, or strain, is produced as a result of stress, which is not total force but force per unit area. The more force per unit area equals greater damage potential to the object. Similar force applied by a person's thumb to a thumbtack will be appreciated differently depending upon which end of the thumbtack you choose to push on.

There are six different potential components of stress which may be applied to body parts:

- Compression
- Tension

- Bending stress (positive or negative – front-to-back)
- Bending stress (positive or negative - left-to-right)
- Shear stress (oppositely directed force pairs as applied by a pair of shears) may be applied positively or negatively in combinations of two directions
- Torsion or twist

Human tissue deforms as a natural response to stress. One component of this tissue deformation is analogous to a spring in which increasing stress results in increasing strain in a linear relationship. Another component involves the speed of stress application. The combined response is similar to suspension components in an automobile, which include both springs and shock absorbers. The shock absorbers do not resist displacement, but rather the velocity of a displacement. Human tissue acts similarly, and acts stiffer if attempts to deform it occur more rapidly. The physical behavior is called *viscoelasticity*.

Human occupants of aircraft vary in size and shape; therefore, restraint systems remain an effective equalizer for the purpose of controlling the energy of an impact event and can improve impact tolerance.

For unrestrained individuals, impact forces may create survivability issues at G loads as low as 10 G; however, extensive military research regarding impact G's and restraint systems has proven properly restrained occupants could withstand impacts as high as 45.5 G.

With these concepts in mind, let us now examine how pilots and aircraft may assist in lessening damaging effects of impact forces.

14.5 CRASHWORTHINESS

Crashworthiness may be defined as "the ability of a structure to provide protection to occupants during impact conditions." Crashworthiness can be assessed either *prospectively* using computer models, or *retrospectively* through analyzation of actual crash outcomes.

Prospective analysis may include criteria such as deformation patterns of vehicle structures, vehicle accelerations experienced during impact, or the probability of injury predicted by human body modeling. Injury probability may be defined by criteria such as mechanical parameters (force, deformation, or acceleration) correlating with injury risk, including head impact criterion (HIC).

Retrospective analysis assesses injury risk in real-world crashes. As a result of the massive number of cofounders present in crashes, controls such as regression or other statistical techniques are necessary to make sense of the information.

All things considered, it is the attenuation of vertical and horizontal velocity at the point of impact which determines human occupant survivability.

With regards to human tolerance limitations in aviation impact deceleration and restraint research, U.S. Air Force Col John Stapp was a pioneer in the field and began his studies at Holloman AFB, NM in the 1940's and 1950's. Dr. Stapp used a high-speed rocket sled for use in linear acceleration & deceleration, restraint and windblast effects on humans, frequently volunteering to perform the research on himself as opposed to asking others to be involved.

During Dr. Stapp's testing, he personally experienced -38 Gx forces, +46.2 Gx forces, and reached speeds of 632 mph on the rocket sled and 570 mph in a fighter aircraft with the canopy removed.

Now let us examine crashworthiness, also known as crash survivability, parameter considerations for aircraft.

14.6 CRASH SURVIVABILITY CONSIDERATIONS

In determining how an aircraft is designed to best attenuate crash forces, no isolated or singular solution leads to significant improvements in impact performance. All the small enhancements aimed at the ultimate goal of increased human survivability are the ones making the difference.

In the earliest days of aviation, crash survivability was atrocious, since very little experience or credible research was available on how to make aircraft impacts safer. After many decades of aviation experience, a relatively clear picture has emerged outlining best practices and designs.

These practices and designs have led to drastically reduced chances of aircraft occupants perishing during a crash event.

Based on aircraft accident data, over 95% of people involved in U.S. aircraft crashes between the years of 1983 and 2000 survived, and the statistics are only improving year after year. According to the National Safety Council, the odds of a person dying in an air transport crash as of 2018 are 1 in 9,821. By comparison, the odds of dying in a motor vehicle crash are 1 in 114. 2017 recorded the lowest number of commercial aviation fatalities since 1940, which includes an exponential increase in passenger miles flown since then.

As mentioned, certain considerations come into play to maximize human survivability in aircraft crashes, which are outlined in the following section.

Crash Survivability Characteristics

When determining *crash survivability characteristics,* CREEP is an acronym detailing those considerations determined to afford the most information. Generally, injuries in aircraft crashes arise from three separate and distinct sources:

- Excessive acceleration and/or deceleration forces
- Trauma from solid surface contact
- Environmental factors (chemicals, fire, smoke, water) resulting in exposure injuries such as burns, drowning, or asphyxiation.

Each component of CREEP identifies focal points to be aware of for occupants in survivable impacts, and CREEP may also be used as a checklist which investigators may use when researching individual crashes.

The CREEP acronym considers the following variables:

- Container (strength of the cockpit and cabin)
- Restraints (seat and safety belt adequacy)
- Environment (injurious objects in immediate locale)
- Energy (crash force impulse attenuation system adequacy)
- Post-crash hazards (fire protection and escape system adequacy)

We will now examine each of these components in depth.

Container

The *container* may be considered to be the occupiable portion of the aircraft. Container strength should strive to maintain sufficient intrusion protection to occupants in the event of a survivable crash. Intrusion may result from structural collapse or penetration of external objects into the occupied space. High-mass item retention is another consideration, meaning the container should strive to achieve adequate tie-down strength to ensure gear and engines for fixed-wing, and rotor systems, engines, and transmissions for rotor-wing aircraft do not break away and enter occupant areas during a survivable crash.

Obviously, each airframe and fuselage type present their own distinct container challenges, and we will examine some of the common issues.

Light aircraft have a tendency to suffer longitudinal structural collapse with nose-low impacts, creating a low-survivability condition for occupants. The frame and structure of light aircraft curl from tail-forward, which does not afford acceptable conditions for those inside the fuselage.

As the tail wraps forward, the collapsing container may compress seats and cause the wings to fold forward, possibly blocking exits. If dynamic deformation exceeds design crash pulse limits, light aircraft may also suffer from gear and engine penetration of the container, thereby reducing the likelihood of occupant survival.

Fuel is typically poorly contained as well, making post-crash fires a persistent threat. Another fuel-related consideration is the realization of where the fuel is located; over the cockpit in high-wing aircraft, or under the fuselage in low-wing aircraft, both of which may bring unique survivability challenges to the post-crash environment.

Medium transport-class aircraft container considerations include exit door size restrictions, which typically are smaller than their larger counterparts. Obviously, this may create evacuation difficulties when trying to exit a large volume of passengers, as well as larger passengers.

Same as light aircraft, considerations regarding fuel location include high-wing aircraft dousing the fuselage in fuel in the event of a high-G impact gear-up landing, or fuel located under passengers for low-wing aircraft, spraying fuel close to exit routes. Another concerning characteristic of high-wing aircraft with nose-low impacts is the possibility of the wings collapsing around the fuselage, potentially blocking exits.

For high-wing aircraft, fuselage separation under seats is a possibility, potentially severing seat mounting mechanisms and projecting occupants into hard interior bulkheads or rigid structures.

For multi-engine turboprop aircraft, the prop plane-of-rotation may cause occupant survival challenges if the aircraft performs a gear-up landing, as the props may shear off and penetrate the fuselage adjacent to the passengers, potentially causing severe object impact injuries.

Large transport-class aircraft retains the same container issues for low-wing aircraft in other categories, with fuel poorly contained if the approach airspeed exceeds 150 knots indicated airspeed (KIAS).

Helicopters are unique by the fact the mast, rotor, and transmission are located on top of the fuselage, creating penetration hazards during high-G impacts. As a result of their light airframe, helicopters suffer from insufficient structural strength to maintain a survivable, occupiable space.

Gear collapse, exterior object penetration and rotor contact with the fuselage are common occurrences as well.

Floatplanes have unique impact characteristics as well. In a typical water impact scenario, the floatplane does not execute a perfect landing; rather, the front tips of the pontoon gear dig into the water or the aircraft arrives at the surface of the water out-of-control, causing a multi-directional impact. The crash-pulse of multi-directional impacts may create a loss of high-mass retention of the landing gear, wings, engine, etc., causing the aircraft to break up and therefore ejecting occupants into the water. If high-mass retention is retained, the aircraft will typically come to a rest inverted, again exposing the occupants to water submersion. Thus, the most common human fatality cause in floatplane impacts is drowning.

Restraints

Restraints are a safety feature designed to keep the occupant in their seat. Contact injuries occur at a rate of five-to-one more frequently than acceleration injuries, as a result of the frequent occurrence of restraint system or seat attachment failure. Unfortunately, these events result in the ejection of occupants who, in turn, either strike hard surfaces inside the container or exit the container completely. Even as an adequately-strengthened container comes to a stop, improperly restrained occupants experience a drastically reduced opportunity for surviving the impact event.

Restraint systems, including seats, should strive to maintain adequate effectiveness to retain occupants during maximum crash pulse events. In the event of significant floor warpage during an impact, seat attachment points should strive to maintain adequate failure limits to avoid seats being torn loose and allowing occupant ejection. Properly restrained occupants will be controlled and maintained at the deceleration speed of the container, making crash pulse G-forces more tolerable, as well as survivable. Well-restrained occupants will be provided protection from potential impact on controls and hard surfaces.

Lap belts and upper torso harnesses are necessary for survivability of impact forces. Properly-designed belt or harness restraints should diffuse the crash pulse force over a large area, providing for effective distribution of acceleration loading across the body. Narrow belts or harness can cause serious injuries as a result of the more focused acceleration loading, even potentially severing the body as opposed to restraining it. Some harness restraints may be equipped with "pre-tensioner" systems, designed to retract the harness in high-G impact events, thus preventing forward strike injuries.

Incorporating a crotch-strap, or tie-down strap, into the restraint system assists in the preventing "*submarining*", which occurs when the lap belt rides up the pelvis structure and severely compresses the abdomen. The belt compressing the soft organs of the abdomen may result in serious internal organ injury or spinal fractures.

"Head-swing" may also cause cervical spinal fractures, and limiting the head-swing envelope prevents those injuries along with focal skull fractures from hard-surface contact. Airbag systems may assist in the prevention or minimization of head-swing, thus preventing head and neck flailing and strike injuries.

Unrestrained occupant's inertia typically carries them forward as well as downward, causing them to strike structures at greater speeds, and thus greater G-forces. Impacts tend to be on focal areas, resulting in penetrating injuries.

Environment

When designing aircraft interior *environments*, a variety of important considerations include:

- Occupiable space
- Stiffness of aircraft structure
- Seating positions
- Safety and accessibility of exits
- Objects posing strike hazards

Occupiable space refers to the space the body may occupy during dynamic crash conditions. The occupiable space should include adequate crush protection should deformation of the container occur resulting from crash pulse force. An example of low occupiable space occurs when light aircraft nose-low impacts produce longitudinal structural collapse.

Stiffness of the aircraft structure obviously assists in creating survivable occupiable space, and larger aircraft provide more effective crush characteristics due to robustness of their structure.

Seating positions of most aircraft will be oriented in the forward position, so consideration must be given to seat-mounting strength, flying object damage and deceleration characteristics. Seat mounts should be robust enough to not sheer under survivable crash forces. Seat backs should have sufficient strength to protect from flying foreign objects, and not collapse forward causing spinal or object impact injuries. Aft-facing seats allow for higher impact G-force tolerance, but expose the occupant to flying foreign object damage.

Safety and accessibility of exits refers to the ease of occupant use of the aircraft exits. The location of the exits should be clearly marked, even under low-visibility conditions, and should be readily accessible for any occupant of the aircraft. The exit size should allow passage for all occupants, and not exit into an anticipated dangerous exterior environment.

Objects posing strike hazards refers to the lethality of injurious object contact for the immediate occupant vicinity. In a perfect design, these objects should be padded, frangible, or placed outside the strike zone.

Adherence to these design elements will make the occupant environment more hospitable should the aircraft experienced an impact event.

Energy

The concepts of *energy absorption* or *energy transfer* for fixed-wing transport-category aircraft may be designed into the airframe to create safer impact characteristics, while light fixed-wing aircraft or helicopters do not enjoy the same design latitude. This design disparity is more prevalent with vertical as opposed to transverse impacts, as vertical impact velocity may reach extreme levels.

When designing for energy attenuation in aircraft, the most common areas of concern include:

- Landing gear
- Floor structure
- Forward crush zones
- Seat structures

Landing gear may be either fixed or retractable, but all are designed to absorb impact shock for normal landings. Landing gear play an important role in crash kinetic energy absorption as well. Extended landing gear enjoys better overall crash energy attenuation, as more distance exists between the ground and fuselage in which to absorb the energy. Landing gear may also absorb crash kinetic energy, as well as slow the structure to a more survivable speed, in the process of separating from the aircraft in shallow, transverse ground contacts. In more severe-angle impacts, landing gear penetration into the container may be an issue.

Floor structure rigidity is critical for the survivability of occupants. If the floor structure bends or buckles, occupiable space is compromised and the impact integrity of seats may be negated. Typically, high-wing aircraft suffer from less floor structure protection and higher incidence of landing gear penetration due to the lack of infrastructure, whereas low-wing aircraft enjoy a more complex, robust, and therefore more protective infrastructure which provides for improved occupant protection.

Forward crush zones provide crucial energy attenuation characteristics through the predictable collapse of nose structures. The goal of this design element is for the nose to systematically crush in longitudinal impacts as opposed to "digging" into the ground, which decreases structure speed, kinetic energy, and therefore impact G-forces. In turn, this action minimizes rollover or plowing events, creates increased survivability and decreased injury opportunities for occupants.

Seat structures have been under an almost continuous state of design improvement almost from the beginning of flight, as every crash investigation yields more seat-design feedback. The two primary factors determining aircraft seat effectiveness is the seat's ability to protect occupants from being thrown about the cabin (tie-down strength) and vertical acceleration (stroke distance).

Adequate tie-down strength, along with floor structure, is essential to ensure crash forces do not dislodge the seats, causing focal impact injuries to occupants as they are traveling unrestrained about the cabin.

Adequate seat stroke distance is critical to prevent the seat from collapsing on its supports and "bottoming out", therefore producing extreme vertical acceleration spikes causing lumbar and cervical spinal injuries, among others. Considerations in this realm include the thickness of seat cushions. Thicker and softer "comfortable" seat cushions actually produce higher lumbar loads (more injurious) in cases of high vertical acceleration pulse resulting from the occupant's body traveling further vertically when the seat supports bottom out. Thinner and denser "uncomfortable" seat cushions allow the occupant's body to travel closer to the speed of the structure and have less distance to travel as the seat supports bottom out, therefore causing fewer injuries.

Properly designed seats should protect occupants in excess of 30G vertical accelerations; however, poorly designed seats may produce spinal injuries as low as 8 to 10G.

Post-Crash Hazards

Post-crash hazards present life-threatening challenges to those fortunate enough to survive the initial crash forces. The main hazards survivors encounter includes:

- Fire
- Fumes

- Fuel
- Oil
- Water

Fire will always remain a hazard to any vehicle crash event, due to the flammable nature of damaged propulsion system fuel. The threat of fire from fuel or batteries combined with oxygen and compression is an ever-present possibility, although efforts have been made to mitigate this threat through crash-resistant fuel systems, flame retardant systems, and physical separation for occupants from ignition sources. As materials on the aircraft heat up subsequent to a crash, the fumes from those heated materials rise to the top of the cabin, and may heat to the point where those fumes spontaneously combust, creating a "flashover" event. Flashovers following a crash are quite obviously a major threat to human life.

Fumes inhalation or ingestion produce more human casualties following survivable crashes than any other threat. An incredible amount of potentially toxic material is used in construction processes as complex a machine as an airliner, and most of those materials can burn. The vast majority of fumes produced from toxic materials are lighter-than-air, and congregate towards the upper half-to-third of a cabin, creating an extremely dangerous environment for occupants trying to evacuate from the aircraft. The use of low toxicity materials helps mitigate this threat, as well as expedient evacuation of the aircraft, as fumes tend to become a mortal menace within approximately 90 seconds following aircraft impacts, based on research conducted by the FAA.

Fuel and oil contamination present chemical perils for occupants, not only for the threat of combustion, but also from absorption of contaminants through human skin and respiratory systems. Wearing long-sleeve shirts, long pants, solid-material shoes, and covering the face and mouth of occupants assists in the mitigation of this threat, although many passengers prefer more casual dress while traveling.

Water, or more specifically drowning or hypothermia, presents the most important post-crash hazard for over-water operations. Some aircraft are equipped with floatation devices for passenger usage during a water-ditching event, and some fixed wing aircraft themselves, mainly low-wing aircraft, will float for a period of time subsequent to water entry. Other aircraft, such as high-wing aircraft and helicopters, are less prone to maintaining buoyancy properties conducive to long-term occupant survival. Helicopters, as a result of their high-center-of-mass, have a natural tendency to rapidly invert, posing a serious egress issue for occupants and making drowning an increasingly certain proposition for those untrained in underwater egress procedures.

From the above discussion concerning CREEP, integrated crashworthy design features are an important consideration into aircraft design. In many cases, major design improvements are not the ones that produce more effective survivability for occupants, but rather the modest, more innocuous improvements. Improving impact survivability may simply include padding or moving a particular object in the cockpit or cabin, or changing occupant restraints.

14.7 COMMON INJURY PATTERNS DUE TO IMPACT FORCES

The knowledge of the mechanism of injuries and injury patterns in survivors of aircraft crashes are critical for investigators to evaluate and reconstruct the crash event, and therefore recommend improvements to aircraft design and safety systems and equipment.

The December 2009 issue of the magazine "Aviation, Space, and Environmental Medicine" published an article on aviation-related injury morbidity and mortality. What the article found was for approximately 6,000 U.S. patients hospitalized for aviation-related injuries during a six-year period, occupants of noncommercial aircraft accounted for 32% of patients, parachutists 29%, and occupants of commercial and unpowered aircraft (gliders) constituted 11% of patients.

For specific injuries, lower-limb fractures were the most common injury type at 27%, head injuries 11%, open wound 10%, and upper extremity fracture and internal injuries made up 9% of the total. Among fatal injuries, head injury was the most prominent and accounted for 38% of the fatalities.

Let us now examine some common aviation-related impact injuries.

Spinal Compression Fractures

Spinal fractures may be caused by vertical or transverse accelerative forces. The spinal segment where the lower ribcage attaches to the spine, at the juncture of the thoracic and lumbar vertebral regions, is typically most vulnerable. The increased weight of the skeletal structure above that point creates a "pivot" point in the spine, making it susceptible to compression fractures during aircraft impacts. Spinal injuries include fracture or dislocation of vertebrae and torn or ruptured discs.

Common causes of spinal fractures include poor body position during ejections from fighter aircraft, high-G vertical or transverse impacts, poor crash body position, and the wearing of lap-belts without shoulder harnesses during aircraft crashes.

The chart below depicts spinal cord vertebrae and potential injury impacts:

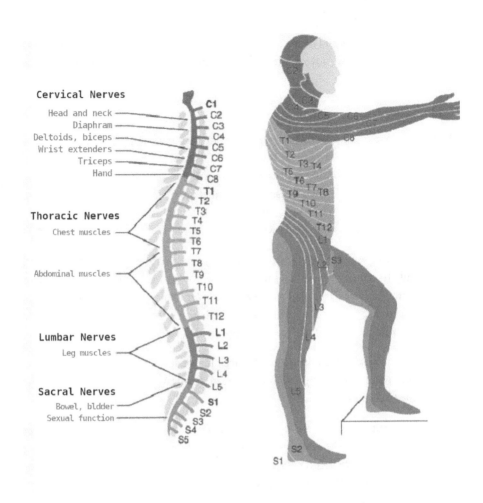

Cervical Nerves

Head and neck ——— C1
 ——— C2
Diaphram ——— C3
 ——— C4
Deltoids, biceps ——— C5
Wrist extenders ——— C6
Triceps ——— C7
Hand ——— C8

T1
T2
T3

Thoracic Nerves

Chest muscles ——— T4
 T5
 T6
 T7
Abdominal muscles ——— T8
 T9
 T10
 T11
 T12

Lumbar Nerves

 L1
Leg muscles ——— L2
 L3
 L4
 L5

Sacral Nerves

 S1
Bowel, bldder ——— S2
Sexual function ——— S3
 S4
 S5

Wpclipart 2021

Neck Compression Fractures

The neck, or cervical spine vertebrae and discs, are especially susceptible in impact events. When the vehicle comes to a sudden and profound stop, a whipping action occurs as a result of the occupant's head being unrestrained and neck muscles possessing insufficient strength to keep the head from moving. This sudden whipping effect can cause damage to the cervical spine vertebrae and discs, including fracture or dislocation of spinal vertebrae and torn or ruptured discs. The following picture depicts a dislocation between the fifth and sixth cervical vertebrae.

In addition to fractures and dislocations, the head is exposed to focal impact injury as a result of unrestrained movement. In extreme impact pulse events, decapitation is possible.

Head Injuries

The most common cause of fatal injuries from impact in all aircraft accidents is head injury. Some of the major reasons head injury fatalities are prevalent in crashes are resultant from lack of shoulder restraints, airborne foreign objects, lack of airbags, and a lack of crush zones. All of these issues contribute to an unrestrained *head-swing envelope* for occupants, allowing their head to strike injurious objects in the cabin. Once the skull strikes a solid object with sufficient force, focal injuries result.

The types of head injury which may occur include linear, depressed, comminuted and basilar skull fractures. *Linear* fractures traverse the full thickness of the skull in relatively straight lines. *Depressed* and *comminuted* fractures displace bone inward as a result of blunt force trauma, presenting a high risk of increased pressure on the brain. *Basilar* fractures are linear fractures occurring in the floor of the skull base.

Skull fractures caused by compressing the neck may lead to ring fractures at the base of the skull, mainly caused by striking the head during vertical G impacts of crush injuries due to container failure.

The key to limiting head injuries in aircraft impacts lies in limiting head-swing envelope. Normally, the head will not benefit from active restraint systems, so limiting head-swing envelope relies on controlling the energy, and therefore impact pulse, of the crash. The slower the speed of impact or the longer time impact forces to develop, the less chance head injury will occur.

Extremity Injuries

Extremity injuries generally occur due to the lack of arm or leg restraint, resulting in uncontrolled flailing of the extremities caused by impact pulse inertia. Uncontrolled flailing causes injuries to occupant hands, forearms, elbows, shoulders, upper and lower legs, knees and ankles. If one views slow-motion video footage of "crash dummy" testing, the arms and legs of the dummy flail regardless of how well restrained the dummy appears. Were occupants to consider the lethality of obstructions and, therefore, potential injurious surfaces immediately surrounding them in aircraft, more care may be taken with regards to the placement and stowage of themselves and their luggage.

The most common extremity injuries include the forearms and lower legs due to solid obstructions in the cabin and cockpit within short striking distance of those areas of the body. Buckling or collapsing seat supports may cause bone breakage in passengers whose lower legs are resting below the seat in front of their position. Dashes, seat supports, seat frames, seat frame and/or support failures, windows and windscreens, luggage, electronic equipment, bulkheads, buckling aircraft floors and/or containers, lavatory doors, drink carts, cockpit controls, and other occupants themselves may become injurious to crew and passengers given the correct impact acceleration and dynamics. Pilots have suffered numerous injuries to their knees as a result of contact with cockpit dashes. In many cases these injured extremities may not prove to be lethal in and of themselves, but may incapacitate an occupant's ability to egress the aircraft in a timely fashion.

Control Injuries

Pilots face special problems in the confined space of the cockpit. Typically, in the event of an aircraft crash event, the pilot's hands will be on the control yoke or stick, and their feet will be on the rudder pedals. Contact with the yoke or rudder pedals combined with the dynamics of impact pulse may result in contusions to the pilot's palm of the hands and/or soles of the feet, leading to significant bruising. Wrist and/or ankle fractures are a distinct possibility, as well as damage to the extensor (back) surfaces of the hands or feet.

We have covered an extensive amount of information regarding aircraft and human dynamics during impact events. Now we will investigate how to best protect ourselves, crew and passengers should this eventuality actually occur.

14.8 INCREASING CRASH SURVIVABILITY

The most obvious method of increasing aircraft crash survivability is to not crash in the first place, which is assumed to be the ultimate goal of every pilot. Increasing crash survivability opportunities involves not only optimizing aircraft crashworthiness, but also occupant awareness, preparedness, impact survival, timely evacuation and post-crash survival.

According to the European Union Aviation Safety Agency, approximately 90 percent of aircraft accidents are categorized as "survivable" or "technically survivable." That means, of course, 10 percent of aircraft accidents are considered "non-survivable." Those non-survivable accidents are not the focus of this discussion, even though this author has reviewed many so-called "non-survivable" aircraft accidents in which people somehow managed to survive anyway. The point is even though the pilot or occupant may believe whatever crash event they are about to be involved in is non-survivable, hope and the effort to survive should not stop. Instead of wasting time thinking about all the ways one could die, concentrate on all the ways one could live instead.

One of the most famous incidents of an aircraft occupant surviving "against all odds" occurred on Christmas Eve 1971, when lightning struck a commercial airliner over Peru, South America. As the aircraft exploded, one passenger named Juliane Koepcke was throw from the aircraft. She fell over 10,000 feet into the Peruvian rainforest, still strapped in her seat. Somehow Juliane survived the fall, and ten days later found civilization with serious injuries, but alive.

11 Most Dangerous Minutes

According to a variety of studies, approximately 80 percent of aircraft crashes predictably occur on the take-off or approach and landing phases of flight. Breaking that down further, these accidents occur within the first three minutes after take-off, or within eight minutes prior to landing. These critical minutes are aptly called "The Eleven Most Dangerous Minutes" for flight segments.

Sensibility would dictate occupants pay particularly close attention to potentially unfolding events during those eleven minutes. If one were to peer around the cabin of an airliner during those eleven minutes, however, the opposite usually occurs. Most passengers are already trying to take a nap, have taken their shoes off, are curling up with a book/magazine/electronic device, or already trying to order a drink. Precious few passengers pay attention to the flight attendant safety briefing, even though that information is critical for their own survival in the event of a catastrophe.

Regardless of how remote the chances are for a horrific tragedy to occur on your particular flight, the possibility always exists. For that reason, the Eleven Most Dangerous Minutes is the time for all occupants, crew and passengers alike, to be on guard for potential mishaps.

Planning Ahead

Crew members and passengers may drastically increase their odds of surviving aircraft crash scenarios by properly preparing and planning well in advance of the potential event. Again, no one can guarantee any given aircraft has a zero-degree chance of crashing once the aircraft is moving.

The below listed are recognized methods of minimizing the possibilities of fatal injury during an aircraft impact event:

- **Stay in good physical condition**
- **Use your seat correctly**
- **Be selfish**
- **Dress appropriately**
- **Sit close to an exit**
- **Formulate an action plan**

Staying in good physical condition is a basic survival rule. Individuals in good physical condition have a much greater chance of surviving injury-inducing trauma, experiencing less damage due to impact G-forces, having the strength to move debris off oneself, assisting others, egressing the wreckage, etc. Physically fit individuals also have a better chance of fighting off infections and fully recovering from sustained injuries. In essence, being physically fit makes a person "harder to kill."

Using your seat correctly means using the lap belt (and shoulder harness, if so equipped) correctly, such as ensuring the restraints are snug and not loose. Proper sitting posture should be maintained, with the individual's butt and lower back properly placed and supported by the seat structure. This will provide maximum effectiveness during crash pulse. Staying attached to your seat also provides more personal protection should one be thrown from the aircraft as well.

Being selfish may initially sound inappropriate, but one has to ensure their own survival first before they can be of assistance to anyone else. Quite obviously, every crash event has its own dynamics, but attempting to assist others before ensuring your own survival may only result in two fatalities.

Dressing appropriately requires forethought into possible scenarios. Natural fibers will provide more effective fire protection than synthetic fibers, which have a habit of sticking to human skin while those fibers burn. Long-sleeved shirts and long-legged trousers provide better fire protection than short clothing, and provide better protection against potential injuries sustained from contacting hot or jagged-edged metal and glass while trying to evacuate the aircraft wreckage. Solid-material shoes (leather) are preferable over soft-material shoes for the reasons mentioned above, and open-toed or high-heeled shoes should be avoided.

Sitting close to an exit, usually within five rows, provides occupants a greater opportunity to find and reach an emergency exit. According to research conducted at the University of Greenwich, sitting further than five rows from an exit drastically reduces survival chances.

Formulating an action plan gives occupants the opportunity to react from muscle-memory as opposed to intellectually. This includes listening to the flight attendant safety briefing, even though you may have heard it many times previously. Each airframe is different, and each has model-specific information you most likely will find valuable in the event of an emergency.

Formulating an action plan involves preparing for the crash, preparing for impact, and safely egressing the aircraft and vicinity, which is the information we will discuss next.

Preparing for a Crash

As mentioned previously, the more mental preparation one invests in emergency events, the more likely they respond appropriately and rapidly. Thinking through the steps necessary to reduce impact forces and increase personal and occupant protection will greatly influence injury outcomes. The pilots should take into consideration those items likely to affect passengers and crew, and the pilots or flight attendants should remind all occupants in simple, easy-to-understand terms what their immediate needs are. The steps to prepare for a crash include:

- **Prepare the aircraft and occupants for impact**
- **Prepare for egress**
- **Environmental considerations**
- **Prepare to vacate immediate area**

Preparing the aircraft and occupants for impact should include ensuring *the most shallow glide angle and slowest airspeed possible,* as these will have the highest ramifications on probability of occupant survival. An announcement must be made for all passengers and crew to prepare for impact; tightening restraints, assuming the brace position, ensuring children are properly restrained, and ensuring all loose items such as personal electronic devices, luggage, and beverage carts are stored as effectively as possible.

Preparing for egress includes informing the passengers and crew to locate the nearest exit, and to establish an alternate exit in the event the primary exit is inaccessible. Ensure all passengers know of any existing emergency lighting or signals directing them to the nearest exit. Remind occupants not to inflate water survival gear in the cabin.

Environmental considerations include informing all occupants what they may expect as they are actively exiting the aircraft, such as staying low to avoid smoke exposure in the cabin.

Additionally, address any necessary information regarding the environment occupants are exiting into, including engine fire locations, water evacuations, swampy terrain, mountainous terrain, etc.

Preparing occupants to vacate immediate area includes any information to assist occupants in avoiding smoke, fire and fume hazards or any other hazards particular to the event, such as "evacuate at least 500 feet to the North" and "it's nighttime, so watch for incoming emergency vehicles."

Personal Preparation for Impact

Pilots, cabin crew, and passengers can accomplish critical steps to minimize injury opportunities in the event of aircraft impact.

Pilots should try to position the aircraft for a shallow-angle, "hit and skid" impact to minimize impact energy. Lap belt and shoulder harnesses should be snug, all loose items stowed, and pilots should brace against aircraft controls as effectively as possible.

Passengers and cabin crew should remove sharp objects from pockets, ensure restraints are snugly secured, and assume the "brace" position. The brace position should compress the body as tightly as possible, consciously attempting to protect the head, neck, and torso from initial impact and blunt-force trauma and/or penetrating injuries.

The head and neck should be protected or braced by either the occupant's arms or the seatback in front of them so guard against secondary impacts as cabin deceleration or disintegration occurs.

Passengers and cabin crew should also keep their feet out of the aisles and not under the seat in front of them to avoid lower extremity injury should that seat collapse during impact. Once the aircraft comes to a complete stop, immediate occupant egress of the aircraft should begin.

Egress

Egress of the aircraft following an emergency or uncontrolled landing is extremely time-sensitive, and immediate implementation of aircraft evacuation procedures should be initiated by all crewmembers. For those occupants surviving the initial impact, fire, smoke and fumes present the most immediate threat to mortality statistically, according the FAA research. FAA research also finds occupants failing to egress the aircraft within 90 seconds of a survivable crash face an exponentially greater chance of being overcome by smoke and fumes.

The following steps should be taken to ensure a timely and efficient egress from the aircraft:

- **Leave personal belongings**
- **Stay low**
- **Do not push**
- **Do not inflate life preservers/life rafts in-aircraft**
- **No pictures**
- **Get out in 90 seconds**
- **Evacuate 500 feet upwind if possible**

Leave personal belongings behind, including luggage, purses, electronic devices, magazines, books, or anything else that does not fit in one's pocket. Any bulky item will slow you down getting through and out of the aircraft, which exponentially slows those behind you.

Stay low while moving through the aircraft; preferably in the bottom 1/3rd of the cabin. Most toxic fumes and/or heat will congregate towards the top of the cabin, making breathing that air potentially fatal. If possible, protect your airway with a mask or wet cloth.

Do not push occupants ahead of you. People will potentially panic, which in itself can render some to become irrational in their behavior. If those occupants ahead of you are in a state of panic and you push them, they may turn around and retaliate, slowing the process down for everyone. Instead, try to firmly assist those in front of you to egress as quickly as possible.

Do not inflate life preservers/life rafts in-aircraft which will, once inflated, render an efficient egress nearly impossible. Wait until you are through the exit portal to inflate water egress survival devices.

No pictures. As unbelievable as it sounds, many individuals are so vested in attempting to document every notable event in their lives they will actually stop in the middle of an extreme emergency to take a picture or video on their phone or other electronic device. Save useless actions for some other time, such as when people's lives are not in danger.

Get out in 90 seconds. Time is the enemy, as the buildup of heated materials can cause a flashover or produce deadly toxic fumes. Every second counts in the egress process.

Evacuate 500 feet upwind, if possible, to prevent potential exposure to heat, flames, or toxic fume plumes, and also to remain clear of any rescue forces responding to the event. Obviously, the environment the aircraft comes to rest in will determine the success of this step, as mountainous terrain, swamps, or open water may prevent this. Occupants must also be highly aware of incoming rescue vehicles, particularly at night or other limited-visibility situations, as rescuer attention will most likely be focused on the aircraft itself.

Conclusion

As mentioned in the beginning of this chapter, aircraft impact dynamics involve many different factors. Many passengers of commercial airliners have developed a fatalistic attitude towards the prospect of aircraft crash involvement, mistakenly believing "they're as good as dead" if the airplane goes down. In reality, the NTSB states airplane accidents, which are characterized by substantial airframe damage or occupants suffer serious injury or death, have a 95% survival rate.

We learned about the definition of impact acceleration; reviewed the history of impact research, discussed ejection considerations, impact forces and human tolerances, aircraft energy absorption, crash survivability concerns, crash injury patterns due to impact forces, and increasing crash survivability. This information makes you a more informed pilot as well as aircrew member or passenger. If one incorporates this information into operational practice, perhaps the aviation industry can raise aircraft crash survivability rates even higher.

Chapter 14 Core Competency Questions

1. The very first powered aircraft fatality in history taught aviators what?
2. Management of _____ is crucial when dealing with impact forces?
3. What are the three rules of crashing an airplane?
4. True or false: water ditching in an airplane is a good idea.
5. Research by CAMI indicates if a cabin decelerates less than _____ G's, survival is exponentially better.
6. What is designed into vehicles to systematically slow the vehicle during a crash to make the crash more survivable?
7. What term is used to describe the ability of a structure to provide protection to occupants during impact conditions?
8. What does "C" stand for in the acronym CREEP?
9. What does the "R" stand for in the acronym CREEP?

10. What do airbag systems attempt to prevent or minimize?
11. What is the most common cause of death in all aircraft accidents?
12. When are the 11 most dangerous minutes in flight segments?
13. How can aviators drastically increase their odds of surviving an aircraft crash?

15. SUSTAINED ACCELERATION

In the previous chapter we discussed the effects of impact forces. In this chapter, we will examine in depth what happens to aviators when they are exposed to the forces of gravity over a long period of time, or *sustained acceleration*. The main physiological anomaly regarding sustained acceleration is a lack of normal blood circulation due to gravitational forces, or stagnant hypoxia.

Reiterating previous information, human beings developed to effectively operate and function in essentially a one-G gravitational environment, which is an ever-present and constant force component in our daily lives. Our physiological ability to orient ourselves depends on gravity, to a degree. Our cardiovascular system relies on gravity, our muscular system works in concert with gravity, and we understand and are comfortable with gravity as presented in normal situations.

When we fly, however, everything we have learned, understand, and are comfortable with concerning gravitational forces suddenly and dynamically changes. Any time an aircraft accelerates in any linear or angular direction, our bodies are forced to deal with unnatural sensations and possibly disrupted physiological functions, some of which may escalate into serious problems in more extreme cases.

In this chapter, we will discuss:

1. The definition of sustained acceleration
2. Gravity and gravitational stresses
3. Increased G-force physiology
4. Cardiovascular and physiological anomalies
5. Gz accelerative forces
6. Zero-G physiology
7. G-Force research and training facilities
8. Improving +Gz tolerance
9. –Gz forces
10. Gx forces
11. Preparation for high-G flights

15.1 DEFINITION OF SUSTAINED ACCELERATION

To review from last chapter, *acceleration* is simply the rate of change of velocity with respect to time. In effect, acceleration is a rate of change of position with respect to time, and a net result of all forces acting on a body. Typically, the longer the time for a change of position, the more opportunity aviators have to compensate for the force's effects on physiological function, while the shorter the time for a change of position, the more hostile the force will be.

Whenever aviators are exposed to an unbalanced force for greater than a second, they undergo *sustained acceleration*. If they are moving in a constant direction, the acting force produces a continuous change in speed, known as linear acceleration. If they are moving at a constant speed, the acting force produces a continuous change of direction, known as angular acceleration. In many circumstances, aviators experience an acting force producing a change in both speed and direction. In aviation and space medicine, any human body experiencing a change in speed or direction (or both) experiences changes in perception of bodily weight, which is measured and characterized by g-forces.

To review, acceleration, velocity, and position are vector quantities inclusive of both vector and magnitude. Magnitude of an acceleration is expressed in terms of a given velocity unit per unit of time; for example: *feet per second per second* or *feet per second squared.*

History

As early as 1919, doctors and scientists realized pilots were mysteriously "fainting" in the air in the midst of aerial dogfights. All involved began to realize the human performance impacts increased maneuverability brought with it, and the desire to understand G-forces in flight was born. In order for scientists to research human limitations of G-force exposures, they had to consolidate their focus and efforts.

The first known U.S. Army Air Forces high-G research centrifuge was built in 1938 at Wright Field in Dayton, OH and in 1945 the Air Force Cambridge Research Laboratories were established. During the late 1950's, Brooks AFB in San Antonio, TX established the School of Aerospace Medicine where, following the end of the Viet Nam War in the mid-1970's, the mission of USAFSAM became focused on maximizing human pilot abilities in modern, high performance aircraft. USAFSAM started using their high-G centrifuge to not only research human G-limitations, but eventually to train pilots to maximize G-tolerance as well. In the late-1980's, a world-first fighter-pilot specific Physiological Training Unit was established to train fighter pilots in all physiological aspects associated with high performance aircraft, including high-G centrifuge, altitude chamber, physical training, spatial disorientation, and visual illusions for fighter operations. This author was intimately involved in the development of this training unit and its programs.

Sustained G Terminology

Acceleration in aviation is commonly expressed in terms of gravity, expressed as G or g. G refers to a gravitational constant, while g refers to changing gravitational forces. In aerospace, a change in *vector* refers to a change in an object's direction.

15.2 GRAVITY AND GRAVITATIONAL STRESSES

Gravity may be described as "the force of attraction between two objects." The standard gravitational force on the Earth's surface is 1G, and it is important to understand gravity acting alone does not produce g-forces. An object must experience either a change in speed or vector in order to experience acceleration and increased g's; therefore, g-force is a measurement of acceleration as opposed to the Earth's gravitational force. At 1G, the mass of an object equals the weight of the object. As the object experiences acceleration, the mass stays the same, but the perception of weight increases.

Gravity and accelerations act on every molecule of an object; one molecule in an object cannot be affected differently than another. For the human body, heart level is the fulcrum for gravitational activity. Human physiology developed and adapted to terrestrial life to function at the gravitational force of Earth, or 1G. Even at a nominal 1G, an upright person experiences higher blood pressures in the lower extremities and lower intracerebral blood pressure due to gravity; therefore, when a body undergoes significant accelerative forces, above heart level blood will drain, whereas blood will pool in the body below heart level. If a human is sitting upright and experiencing acceleration in an upward vector, blood will drain from the brain and upper body above heart level, and blood congests and pools in the lower extremities, creating stagnant hypoxia as result of impaired blood flow.

The cilia hair cells in the human vestibular apparatus may also be affected by accelerations, sending false sensations of orientation or movement to the brain.

Gravitational Stresses

With regards to the human body, gravity results in a *compressive* stress. At a normal 1G, this compression is not very noticeable; however, once aviators experience high g-levels the compressive effect may become very disconcerting. Remember, g-force acts on every molecule of the body. Even at 1G, short- and long-term effects become evident.

Short-term gravitational stresses may be noticed as lightheadedness or dizziness. Consider the feeling of standing up too fast after sitting on the floor for a period of time. The dizzying sensation results from a temporary blood-flow shift to the brain. The same may be felt if aviators fly through an updraft in flight.

Long-term gravitational stresses are quite evident in older adults. Most often, a lifetime of exposure to the Earth's gravity results in skin sagging, skeletal and joint degradation, and cardiovascular and skeletal muscular weakness.

Inertial Forces

As we know, g-forces indirectly produce a weight-like sensation. In an aircraft, g-forces are produced by the body of the pilot being pushed by the surface of another object (mainly the seat or restraint harness). The resulting reaction force to this contact between the pilot and the aircraft produces an equal and opposite weight for every unit of a pilot's mass.

In review, Newton's Second Law states: "force on an unsupported mass will produce an acceleration in the direction of the force that is directly proportional to the magnitude of the force and inversely proportional to the mass of the object." For example, a pilot's body in an aircraft directed in an upward or downward vector will want to continue in a straight line.

Newton's Third Law states: "for every action there is an equal and opposite reaction." The inertial reaction forces applied by an accelerated body accelerated in the positive direction will be oppositely directed. For example, a pilot's body in an accelerating aircraft will want to stay static, or a pilot's body in a moving aircraft will want to keep moving.

In straight and level flight, lift (L) equals weight (W). In a banked turn of 60 degrees, lift equals double the weight (L=W2), so the pilot is experiencing 2G as well as the sensation of doubling their weight. The steeper an aircraft's bank gets (generating more lift), the greater the g-forces the occupant is exposed to, with a corresponding increase in weight sensation.

15.3 INCREASED G-FORCE PHYSIOLOGY

Acceleration forces act on every molecule in the body; however, not all molecules are affected the same way. The body is formable and flexible; some molecules are supported and resist the force quite well, such as muscle and osseous (bone) tissue.

Other molecules are accelerated in the direction of the forces applied to the body, such as blood and fat. Next is the explanation of how the body is exposed to g-forces in various vectors.

Scientifically, acceleration is accepted as a vector quantity; however, g-forces are most commonly expressed as a scalar quantity, which is a physical quantity having no characteristics other than magnitude. Generally speaking, positive g-forces point downward or backward (indicating upward or forward acceleration), and negative g-forces point upward or forward (indicating downward or rearward acceleration). Therefore, g-force in aviation is a vector quantity of acceleration.

An aircraft in flight undergoes translational motion, which can be tracked in three dimensions with x, y and z coordinates, which is the basis of tracking human bodily g-force exposure.

G-Force Vector Terminology

Forces can be exerted on the body in a multitude of directions; however, we know translational motion can be tracked in the x, y, and z coordinates and from this, we can develop g-force exposure terms relative to the human body.

As a person is standing upright, g-force exposures are explained as follows:

- Forward - backward (transverse) g-forces: Gx axis
- Left - right (lateral) g- forces: Gy axis
- Headward - footward (vertical) g-forces: Gz axis

Types of Acceleration

Translational motion, or acceleration, for aircraft can be described as three types of acceleration:

- Linear
- Radial
- Angular

Linear acceleration refers to a change in velocity in a straight line, typically occurring during take-off, landing, or level-flight throttle adjustments.

Radial acceleration refers to a directional change, such as a pilot initiating a sharp turn.

Angular acceleration refers to a change in both speed and direction, typically occurring in climbing or diving turns.

Specific G-Force Vectors

Each g-force axis must be identified as either *positive* or *negative*. In order to experience the various positive or negative axes of g-force exposure, the aircraft must accelerate in a specific direction, which are outlined as follows:

- Forward vector (push forward on the throttle): +Gx
- Rearward vector (pull back on the throttle): -Gx
- Accelerate leftward (wings-level spin to the left): +Gy
- Accelerate rightward (wings-level spin to the right): -Gy
- Upward vector (pull back on the yoke): +Gz
- Downward vector (push forward on the yoke): -Gz

The Gy axis is difficult to achieve in most controlled aviation settings, so we will focus very little on this particular vector of acceleration. The chart below indicates the Gx- and Gz-axes on the human body:

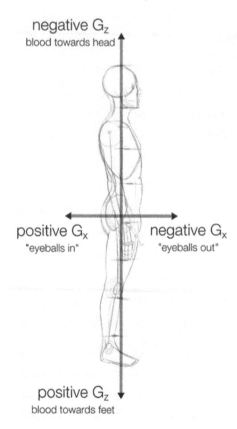

negative G_z
blood towards head

positive G_x
"eyeballs in"

negative G_x
"eyeballs out"

positive G_z
blood towards feet

Air Force 2021

15.4 CARDIOVASCULAR AND PHYSIOLOGICAL ANOMALIES

As we know, human physiological systems were designed to work at normal Earth's gravitational force, or 1G. Accelerative forces in excess of 1G will then adversely affect human physiology, dependent on the magnitude of the acceleration.

One of the main disruptive physiological anomalies is a lack of intracerebral blood delivery, resulting in stagnant hypoxia. Blood weight, and therefore blood flow, is directly influenced by g-forces, making circulatory efficiency and distance from the heart-to-brain critical depending on the g-vector.

The extent of circulatory disruption is dependent on the magnitude of acceleration, and the direction of acceleration relative to the human body. Acceleration vectors aligning with the human body's long axis (head-to-foot, or Gz) produce the largest hydrostatic pressure disruptions associated with redistributed blood flow. Those accelerations leading to hydrostatic increases (blood pooling) in the blood vessels of the head are tolerated most poorly, with accelerations leading to blood pooling in the legs most common. Accelerations aligning with the short axes of the body (side-to-side or Gy, and front-to-back, or Gx) produce less blood flow disruptions and are therefore tolerated more effectively.

Since the Gz axis is the most prolific g-axis pilots will be exposed to in aviation, Gz forces will be our primary focus of discussion.

15.5 GZ ACCELERATIVE FORCES

When a pilot is exposed to +Gz forces in flight, two main physiological problems present themselves:

- Restriction of movement
- Variance of systemic and pulmonary circulation

Restriction of movement occurs for the simple reason skeletal muscle is not prepared to move limbs weighing more than they normal weigh at 1G. If the pilot engages in a 5G bank, their forearms, head, and legs now weigh five times what they did at 1G. For example, if the pilot can move their arm at all, movement will be difficult and jerky at best, with fine motor skills non-existent. Musculoskeletal pain to the neck, lower back, and particularly the joints, is common.

Variance of systemic and pulmonary circulation is determinant on the g-axis being either -Gz or +Gz. The +Gz axis will cause an impairment of circulation above heart level, and a congestion of blood flow below heart level. In the case of +Gz exposure, maintaining adequate cerebral perfusion is critical, so heart-to-brain distance and blood pressure become of paramount importance. Increased +Gz forces also disrupts normal respiration processes by pooling blood to the base lung lobes, collapsing alveoli and creating a mismatch of ventilation versus blood diffusion as air remains in the upper lung, which is maintaining below-normal blood flow at that time.

The extreme blood perfusion in the lower extremities due to increased blood molecular weight may cause damage to the capillaries called *petechiae*. Petechiae presents itself as significant localized bruising where blood pooling occurs.

Conversely, the -Gz axis will perform exactly the opposite, with congestion above the heart and impairment below the heart.

Levels of +Gz Acceleration

Experiencing +Gz acceleration in aircraft can be categorized by three levels of magnitude: low G, medium G, and high G.

Low +Gz forces occur between 1G and 3G. At these exposure levels, the body will experience an adequate level of involuntarily cardiovascular compensation and the pilot should experience little-to-no visual light loss or intellectual impairment.

Medium +Gz forces occur between 3.1G to 5.9G. At these exposure levels, the pilot will experience marginal levels of involuntary cardiovascular compensation with the pilot experiencing visual light-loss, intellectual impairment, and possible loss-of-consciousness.

High +Gz forces occur above 6G, where mild-to-vigorous voluntary cardiovascular and muscular compensation must take place for the pilot to maintain consciousness.

+Gz Acceleration Physiology

The amount of sustained exposure time and magnitude of g-forces a pilot experiences in a given maneuver is important, as bodily functions must be either involuntarily or voluntarily modified to effectively compensate for the physiological ramifications of the +Gz exposure.

As mentioned previously, involuntary cardiovascular compensation occurs as a pilot undergoes +Gz exposure. This compensatory response results from a loss of blood pressure to the carotid arteries in the pilot's neck, which triggers a physiological *cardiovascular response*. Heart rate and blood flow volume automatically increase in an attempt to maintain adequate blood flow to the cranium, and thus the brain. The cardiovascular response resulting in increased heart rate will typically last for ten minutes.

Voluntary compensatory methods to maximize cardiac output, therefore increasing cerebral blood flow, include:

- Increased intrathoracic pressure
- Lung re-ventilation sequencing
- Isometric muscular contractions

Increased intrathoracic pressure essentially provides extra contractive pressure on the aorta, increasing blood pressure from the heart to the brain.

Lung re-ventilation sequencing is accomplished in short time-spans, such as three-to-four seconds, to allow for the removal of excess carbon dioxide from the cardiovascular system and lungs. This step also refills the heart with blood, providing fresh, oxygenated blood to reenter the cardiovascular system.

Isometric muscular contractions are performed by the pilot to assist preventing the pooling of blood in the lower extremities, thus overloading the capillaries and causing petechiae. The contractions squeeze the capillaries, preventing increased hydrostatic pressure in the capillaries.

Advantageous Positioning of Aircraft

We know exposure to +Gz forces results in more effective countermeasure utilization by the pilot. Intentional exposure to -Gz forces is not a wise decision to follow in flight, so proper positioning of the aircraft to ensure +Gz exposure in certain maneuvers is preferable. Rapid repositioning of the aircraft in terms of direction or altitude should always be performed in the +Gz axis, if possible.

Positioning the aircraft in the +Gz axis for a directional change is simple; bank into the desired turn, and gently pull back on the yoke or stick. The same rules apply for an ascent from level flight; simply pull back on the yoke to the desired pitch angle.

Positioning the aircraft in the +Gz axis for a descent from altitude, however, may be a little trickier. A common maneuver to perform to accomplish this is the *Split S*, a staple maneuver fighter pilots have used for decades to evade aggressor aircraft on their tails. The *Split S* allowed fighter pilots to trade altitude for speed, while accomplishing a rapid course reversal at the same time.

The aircraft turns inverted, pulls to a vertical descent, and then pulls out of the vertical descent to a level flight attitude. This maneuver can be performed very rapidly, ensuring a quick exit from the original altitude while positioning the pilot's body for +Gz forces, as opposed to more dangerous -Gz forces.

Long-Term High +Gz Exposure

Although not heavily researched, certain physiological anomalies have presented themselves as a result of spending a career flying in the high-G realm, such as fighter pilots or aerobatic pilots. Sufficient data has not been accumulated as of this writing to verify the long-term medical complications of the side-effects, although some of the effects may be somewhat self-evident.

The following are potential side-effects of profound, long-term high-G exposure:

- Cervical and lumbar spinal compression damage
- Hemorrhoids
- Cardiac hypertrophy (enlarged heart)
- Internal organ connective tissue damage
- Varicose veins

Cervical and lumbar spinal compression damage results from +Gz forces exerting extreme vertical compressive pressure on the vertebrae and discs of the spinal column.

Hemorrhoids presumably result from extreme Anti-G Straining Maneuvers (AGSM) pilots undergo in high-G aerial environments. A properly-performed AGSM closely resembles the actions one would go through to defecate, placing stress on hemorrhoidal tissue.

Cardiac hypertrophy (enlarged heart muscle) may occur as a result of the magnified exercise this muscle receives in the high-G environment. The long-term negative medical outlook on this issue remains unclear.

Internal organ connective tissue damage is presumably resultant from internal organ weight increases during high-G maneuvering, over-stressing connective tissue to the point of tearing and/or failure. Again, the long-term negative medical outlook on this issue remains unclear.

Varicose veins are presumably caused by repeated episodes of petechiae. The repeated damage to capillaries may develop permanent microscopic scar tissue in the blood vessels.

15.6 ZERO-G PHYSIOLOGY

As increased g-forces cause physiological modifications to be made, so does a complete lack of gravitational pull on one's body. Again, sufficient data on the effects of zero-G on humans has not been accumulated to any great degree as of this writing, as many human subjects have not been exposed to zero-G for long periods of time. However, some data has been accumulated and does point to specific anomalies:

- Increased disorientation
- Increased cranial fluid pressure
- Decreased cardiovascular system efficiency
- Heart muscle shrinkage
- Slight cognitive decline
- Atrophy of bone and muscle
- Excess flatulence

Increased disorientation results from a lack of normal orientation cues the body needs to maintain proper orientation. The cilia hair cells in the vestibular apparatus rely on gravity, as does the pressure-sensing proprioceptive system inputs of orientation. When gravity is lacking, visual, vestibular, and proprioceptive systems cannot reconcile erroneous sensory inputs and disorientation ensues, which may result in bouts of motion sickness.

Increased cranial fluid pressure is resultant from the bodily systems which rely on gravity for proper fluid distribution are no longer fighting gravity. Intracellular and extracellular fluids are no longer restricted or assisted by gravity. Additionally, the heart's left ventricle is now pumping blood through the ascending aorta without gravitational restriction and through the descending aorta without gravitational assistance.

The additional fluid-shift to the cranium, leading to abnormal fluid concentrations, results in astronaut "moon-face", or puffy facial features. In addition, increased cranial blood pressure results in over-pressurized optic nerves and retinas, slightly crushing them resulting in deformation-related visual disturbances known as "spaceflight-associated neuro-ocular syndrome."

Decreased cardiovascular system efficiency, or a decreasing of blood pressure, results from the over-pressurized carotid artery blood pressure sensors attempting to normalize blood flow to the cranium (cardiovascular response). Over time, this will also result in in reduced red blood cell counts, as the body realizes it does not require as much oxygen due to decreased physical effort. This may also lead to heart muscle atrophy.

Heart muscle shrinkage occurs from the reduced demand placed on the heart not having to provide adequate blood pressure force against the effects of gravity.

Slight cognitive decline may very well result from the above-mentioned decreased cranial blood-pressure, therefore less oxygen being delivered to neurons. Stress and fatigue may also contribute to this anomaly.

Atrophy of bone and muscle results from a lack of necessary effort, or physical challenge, to operate in the zero-G environment. Muscle and bone must be continually challenged, or worked, to maintain fitness and strength levels. The lack of stress on the bones and joints allow the human skeleton to fully stretch, which may result in increased heights of up to one inch after approximately one month.

Excess flatulence may be resultant from the reduced barometric pressures of spacesuits, as well as diets promoting fermentable substrate. For instance, the International Space Station (ISS) maintains an atmospheric pressure environment of 14.69 psi (SL pressure); however, an astronaut wearing an extravehicular activity (EVA) suit may only receive 4.7 psi in the suit, causing gas expansion in the gastrointestinal tract. One of the problems with life onboard spacecraft is the lack of expulsion of noxious gases, as these gases tend to linger in the habitable environment.

15.7 G-FORCE RESEARCH AND TRAINING FACILITIES

G-Research Facilities

One of the U.S. Air Force's (USAF) most advanced centrifuges for its time, also known as the Dynamic Environment Simulator, was developed in the 1960's for use at the Air Force Aerospace Research Laboratory at Wright-Patterson AFB, OH, and capable of producing up to 20 G's for animal and human occupants.

Another Air Force centrifuge was developed around the early 1960's at the USAF School of Aerospace Medicine, initially for research for the U.S space program, later for G-research for military fighter pilots, and eventually training those pilots during breaks in research.

G-Training Facilities

The USAF's first operational training centrifuge was installed at Holloman AFB, NM in 1988, with the mission of solely training US and allied fighter pilots. This centrifuge could accelerate from 1.2 G to 9 G's in 1.5 seconds.

The USAF's newest training/research centrifuge is operated by USAFSAM back at Wright-Patterson AFB, OH, where it all began. This centrifuge can accelerate from 1 G to 15 G in one second, with a maximum load of 20 G's (pictured below).

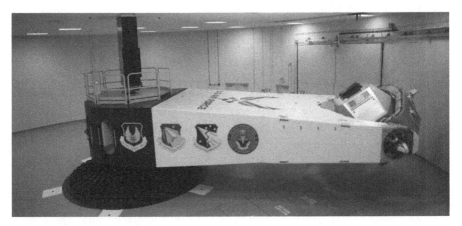

Air Froce 2021

15.8 +GZ ACCELERATION SYMPTOMOLOGY

As human pilots undergo positive g loads in aircraft, the main difficulties encountered center around maintaining adequate cerebral blood pressure for functional intellectual activity. In review, blood flow above heart level becomes inadequate, and blood flow below heart level increases, causing blood pooling in lower extremities. Difficulty breathing is also experienced as a direct result of G-forces acting on the muscles of the chest and ribcage.

Now, let us examine the common physiologic symptomology of experiencing G-forces. As a result of decreased blood flow to the cranium, symptoms include:

- Tunnel vision
- Greyout/blackout
- G-induced loss of consciousness

Tunnel vision will be the first profound symptom pilots experience as they increase G-loading. Intracerebral ischemia (lack of sufficient blood flow) prohibits sufficient blood flow to the sensitive photoreceptor cells of the retina, starting a cascading and progressive loss of peripheral vision.

Greyout/Blackout will be the second noticeable symptom the pilot experiences, for the same basic reasons mentioned above. Insufficient blood flow prohibits the retinal photoreceptor cells from full functionality, causing the loss of color vision. Ultimately, if G-forces continue to increase, vision will narrow to a pinpoint of light, followed by a complete loss of vision.

G-induced loss of consciousness is the last phase of intracerebral ischemia, with insufficient blood flow to the brain to continue normal intellectual function (Jedick R. , Pulling G's - The Effects of G-Forces on the Human Body, 2013).

+Gz Acceleration and Visual Loss

Mentioned above was the fact as G-forces increase, vision starts to fail. As pictured below, blood is fed to the retinal tissue through the retinal blood vessels. As the G-induced weight of the blood cells increase, blood flow through the retinal blood vessels lose hydrostatic pressure; therefore, the eye's globe pressure drops, capillaries furthest from the optic nerve completely lose blood flow, and begin to systematically collapse and will cause the pilot to lose peripheral vision. As blood flow continues to stagnate with greater G-forces, more peripheral vision is lost, eventually reaching the point where only a pinpoint of light can be seen in the center of the pilot's visual field. Beyond this point, total visual blindness occurs, to be followed shortly be a loss-of-consciousness.

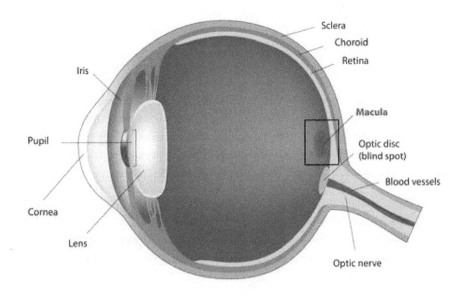

ghr.nlm.nih.gov 2021

With a gradual onset of G-forces, peripheral visual loss will occur more slowly, so pilot has a barometer as to when they are reaching the point where intracranial blood flow is being affected. At this point, the phenomena of visual loss may be used as a gauge for the pilot to know when to either strain against the G-forces with greater intensity or back off the G-loading.

At the opposite end of the spectrum, a rapid onset of G-forces may occur so quickly and profoundly the pilot may not recognize visual loss in time and lapse straight into unconsciousness.

G-Induced Loss of Consciousness

If humans are exposed to high enough G-forces for a long enough period of time, the final consequence is a total loss-of-consciousness, also known as G-induced loss of consciousness (*GLOC*). The phenomena will occur as a result of blood pooling in the lower extremities, and failing to return through the veins to the heart for re-oxygenation in a timely fashion, and therefore the brain. After perfusion cessation to the brain, a reserve time of approximately four-to-six seconds exists prior to a total loss of intellectual function (Jedick R. , Be a Better G-Monster: The Anti-G Straining Manuver, 2014). This condition will also produce an oxygen deficit at the cerebral level, resulting in complete incapacitation of the pilot.

Two phases of incapacitation exist with GLOC:

- Absolute incapacitation
- Relative incapacitation

Absolute incapacitation occurs while the aviator is physically unconscious, and lasts anywhere from an observed 2 to 38 seconds, with the average time of unconsciousness approximately 12 seconds. During this phase of incapacitation, the individual will experience two distinct sub-phases; *dreamlets* lasting approximately 8 – 10 seconds, and *myoclonic convulsive activity* lasting approximately 5 seconds.

During the dreamlet sub-phase, the individual will actually experience fully-formed dreams. This author personally experienced a GLOC on one particular centrifuge run and the dreams experienced were exactly as one would expect enjoying a full-night's sleep. It was a shock to wake up and realize my surroundings were not my home, but inside a centrifuge.

Myoclonic convulsive activity is involuntary muscular contraction occurring following a GLOC episode, similar to having a seizure. The physiology behind this sub-phase is when an individual lapses into unconsciousness from a lack of cranial blood perfusion, the person will let go of the stick controller in the aircraft or centrifuge, unloading the G-forces.

When the G-forces unload, blood flow will resume to the cranium region. As blood flow resumes, the first region of the brain to receive blood, and therefore oxygen, is the brainstem, which controls the primitive functions of the body such as breathing, heart rate, sleep and wake cycles, etc. The second part of the brain receiving a revived flow of oxygen is the cerebellum, which coordinates muscle movements.

These muscle movements occur randomly in the body with no intellectual motor control, and the aviator reawakening will inevitably jerk and thrash uncontrollably. It is also common for the aviator to snore loudly for a few seconds due to a loss of tension in one's tongue prior to bodily functions and muscular control resuming. The GLOC is affectionately nicknamed the "funky chicken" by high-G veterans, as the physical reactions an individual exhibits following a GLOC are somewhat humorous to watch in a controlled environment.

Relative incapacitation occurs as the aviator is waking up following the GLOC episode, which may last from an observed 2 to 97 seconds, with the average time approximately 15 seconds. During this phase of incapacitation, the individual will experience three distinct sub-phases: *neurological reintegration* lasting approximately

5 seconds, *reorientation* lasting approximately 7 seconds, and *memory impairment*, or full amnesia of the episode.

During the neurological reintegration phase, the brain is essentially re-booting as if one were re-booting their personal computer. Reorientation takes place as the individual begins to recognize their surroundings, and come to full understanding of the episode they are currently recovering from. Memory impairment may or may not occur, as the final seconds leading up to the GLOC may not be intellectually recoverable by the individual.

The rate of G-onset is as important as the G-load with regards to GLOC episodes. USAF research has suggested higher G-forces are required to GLOC for slower G-onset rates, as the cardiovascular response has more time to compensate for the increased G-forces (Jedick R. , Be a Better G-Monster: The Anti-G Straining Manuver, 2014).

Calculating +Gz Tolerance

Although everyone has distinct physiological characteristics affecting their tolerance to G-forces, a relatively accurate prediction of an individual's G-tolerance can be calculated from their blood pressure.

The average adult human heart-to-brain distance is approximately 32 cm, which absorbs 30 mmHg worth of blood pressure at Earth's normal 1G. If an aviator's blood pressure measured 120 mmHg at heart level standing on the ground, this would mean their cranial blood pressure was 90 mmHg.

When the above-mentioned aviator initiates a 3G turn, each G-force unit will decrease blood pressure by 22 mmHg at the brain level; therefore, a 3G turn reduces cranial BP by 66 mmHg. This equates to cranial BP being reduced to 24 mmHg at peak G during the turn. At 24 mmHg cranial BP, the aviator will most likely be experiencing at least some tunnel vision as blood flow is reduced to their brain.

To calculate an individual's resting g-tolerance, meaning the point at which the individual's vision is going into the blackout phase but is still conscious, can be figured out using the following equation:

G tolerance = 1 + (BP – 30 mmHg)/22 mmHg

Let us assume an aviator maintained a blood pressure of 118 mmHg. Using the above equation:

G tolerance   = 1 + (118 – 30)/22

$$= 1 + 88/22$$

$$= 1 + 4 = 5$$

Under the assumption most healthy aviators' BP falls into the general range of 100 mmHg to 120 mmHg, the average unprotected aviator doing nothing to counteract the forces of gravity, will have an unprotected +Gz tolerance in the 4G to 6G range.

15.9 IMPROVING +GZ TOLERANCE

Quite obviously, the goal of aviators anticipating flight in high-G environments want to maximize their performance in this environment. Many militaries have invested heavily in training programs intending to increase their respective fighter pilots' abilities in the aerial combat realm. Pilots flying aerobatics have also undoubtedly spent time developing their high-G skills, as well. With the appropriate countermeasures, +Gz tolerance can increase to 9G consistently for relatively short periods of time, and with more advanced equipment approach tolerance levels of 12G.

We will examine the most common examples of achieving improved G-tolerance, including:

- Anti-G suits
- Anti-G straining maneuver (AGSM)
- Positive pressure breathing
- Reclining cockpit seats
- Physical conditioning
- Nutrition and hydration

Anti-G suits are inflatable bladders designed to provide aviators with functional muscular compression to assist in the prevention of blood pooling in the lower extremities. These devices will be discussed in more detail later in this chapter.

Anti-G straining maneuvers (AGSM) provide aviators with controlled, maximal isometric muscular contractions to assist preventing blood drainage, as well as providing intrathoracic pressure to enhance blood flow from the heart-to-the-brain in +Gz force environments. Combined with muscular contractions is a timed respiratory sequence to enhance oxygen replenishment and carbon dioxide discharge. We will discuss this maneuver later in this chapter.

Positive pressure breathing is used primarily by military fighter pilots, using highly-specialized oxygen equipment combined with external pressure bladders for the aviator's torso designed to provide breathing assistance and lung counter-pressure to facilitate the AGSM during extreme high-G aerial maneuvering.

Reclining cockpit seats, such as the 30-degree in the F-16, shortens the heart-to-brain distance, making it easier for increased blood flow to the brain and which has proven to provide up to 1G additional protection for the pilot. Earlier aircraft (F-15, F-4) used 15-degree seats. Flying in the fully-reclined 30-degree position has proven unrealistic for most pilots; therefore, later-generation aircraft such as the F-22 and F-35 use a milder 20-to-22-degree seat.

Physical conditioning strengthens a fighter- or aerobatic-pilot's musculature, enabling them to function more efficiently in the highly-physical increased-G environment. While whole-body strength is necessary, focusing on the core and legs has proven to be most effective for high-G flying.

Nutrition and hydration provide the necessary cellular energy components for the body to operate at peak efficiency, and for quick recovery following high-G engagements. Maintaining adequate hydration and glucose levels is essential for high-G pilots to find success in these environments.

Anti-G Suit

Anti-G suits, normally simply referred to as *G-suits,* are pressurized leg and abdomen garments worn by aviators flying high-G aircraft to assist preventing vascular pooling in the lower extremities in high-acceleration conditions.

The first known use of G-suits was in the early 1940's by British Royal Air Force fighter pilots flying in Hurricane and Spitfire aircraft (g-suit, 2020). Initially, G-suits were filled with water; the prevailing theory being as G-forces increased, the water contained in the G-suit bladders would settle in the lowest parts of the suit to provide counter-pressure for muscles to strain against. Eventually, scientists realized this made the G-suits heavier and more cumbersome than the suits needed to be, and transitioned the suits to air-filled bladders fed by pressure regulators. The legacy air-bladder suits continued to be used relatively unchanged for over 70 years, providing bladder coverage over approximately 30 percent of the lower body.

Air-filled G-suits continue in use to this day in military fighter operations around the world, with the latest USAF iteration being the *advanced technology anti-gravity suit (ATAGS),* and the *full-coverage anti-gravity suit (FCAGS)* (Hatch, 2012). The newest generation of G-suits strive for greater lower-body coverage of up to 90 percent, thereby increasing anti-G strain efficiency and effectiveness, as shown below:

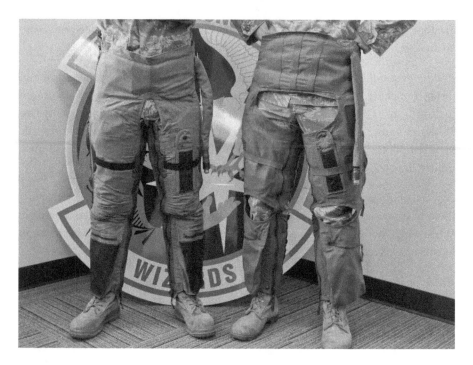

Air Force 2021

A properly-fitted, five-bladder legacy G-suit (above right) can increase a pilot's G-tolerance by an average 1 to 1.5G, with newer one continuous bladder FCGAS G-suits (above left) providing up to 3Gs' protection. Some anti-G systems have employed special positive-pressure breathing masks working in conjunction with full-torso and leg anti-G ensembles, capable enough to enable fighter pilots to sustain 12G's with a well-executed AGSM. All of the newer anti-G suit systems will allow pilots to sustain moderate-to-high G's with less effort than previous generations of G-suits.

Let us now examine how a properly-executed AGSM can provide outstanding G-force protection.

L-1/M-1 Anti-G Straining Maneuver

The AGSM was first introduced to aviation in World War II as a method for pilots to combat the effects of ever-evolving high-performance fighter aircraft. The premise of the AGSM is to increase intrathoracic pressure, thus squeezing the aortic arch (Jedick R. , Pulling G's - The Effects of G-Forces on the Human Body, 2013). This squeezing action increases aortic blood pressure, increasing cranial perfusion and therefore adequate vision and pilot consciousness. The two main components of the AGSM include isometric muscular contraction, and a measured, robust respiratory sequence. If executed effectively, this maneuver maximizes cardiac output, resulting in increased cerebral oxygen uptake while maintaining adequate levels of oxygen and carbon dioxide in the lungs and cardiovascular system. An effective and well-practiced AGSM has the capability to increase an aviator's G-tolerance by approximately three-to-four G's. We will now examine the muscular contraction and respiratory sequences in greater depth.

AGSM Muscular Contractions

To properly perform *muscular contractions* for the AGSM, maximum and continuous flexion of the skeletal muscles is maintained during the maneuver. The specific muscles involved in the strain are the calves, thighs, glutes, abdominals, arms and chest. The purpose of maximal flexion is three-fold; first to assist in increasing intrathoracic pressure for the purposes described in the previous paragraph, second to compress the capillaries to prevent pooling of the blood in the lower extremities, and third to avoid being physically overcome from the weight-like forces associated with +Gz forces. Anti-G suits provide necessary counter-pressure to allow the muscles to strain against a stiff surface, increasing strain effectiveness.

This extreme muscular contraction can prove very fatiguing in a short period of time, resulting in relatively short-term high-G engagements. Maintaining an effective strain for more than 15-to-20 seconds is monumentally difficult. In order for a fighter pilot to be at top performance in the high-G arena, they have to physically train with the intensity of a professional athlete.

AGSM Respiratory Cycle

The *respiratory cycle* is critical for AGSM effectiveness and (relative) longevity. This cycle is necessary to replenish the lungs, and therefore the bloodstream, with oxygen and to discharge excess carbon dioxide.

The first element of the respiratory cycle is to stock an adequate amount of air in the lungs by taking a deep breath immediately prior to initiating a high-G pull. To maintain those air levels in the lungs, the respiratory tract must be closed off to prevent leakage. The best place to accomplish this is at the *glottis,* which is a valve between the vocal folds in the throat controlling airflow in and out of respiratory passages. Closing the glottis results in an effective increase in chest pressure, assisting in the squeezing of the aorta. The glottis can be closed off by saying the word "hick". To put this sequence into practical application, the pilot would anticipate the high-G pull, take a deep breath, and say the word "hick" as they simultaneously pulled on the yoke or stick.

The next element of the respiratory cycle is to re-ventilate every 2.5 to 3 seconds. Holding one's breath for too long during a high-G turn would result in a rapid loss of blood pressure and oxygen to the brain, leading to a GLOC event. Conversely, not holding one's breath long enough will not generate adequate blood pressure to the brain as well as fatigue the pilot too quickly. To re-ventilate, the pilot would purse their lips as if trying to blow out a candle, and rapidly exhale 30% to 40% of the air in their lungs, and quickly inhale the same amount. The re-ventilation phase should take no more than .5 seconds. It is important to note this element is performed while continuously maintaining a maximal strain to prevent blood drainage to the lower extremities. Relaxing muscular contractions in a high-G turn even for one second may result in a dangerous drop in cerebral perfusion, with GLOC following close behind.

Complete AGSM

To perform a proper AGSM, the maneuver *must* be instinctive rather than intellectual; meaning the maneuver must be practiced judiciously. Most military pilots receive this crucial training in a controlled environment on a high-G centrifuge, while aerobatic pilots may practice in high-performance aircraft. For a pilot with access to neither, this maneuver may be practiced at 1G in a chair, but care must be taken not to perform maximal AGSM, as serious brain damage could potentially occur.

As the pilot anticipates a high-G maneuver, they begin contracting their skeletal and core muscles, take a deep breath, and immediately initiate the maneuver. Immediately upon reaching maximum G-force in the apex of the turn, a quick (.5 second) exhalation and inhalation (re-ventilation) of approximately 30-40% lung volume is performed, still "crunching" the muscular contractions. After three seconds of breath-holding, re-ventilation is performed again, and every subsequent three seconds during the high-G maneuver. At this point, if the maneuver is expected to last longer, the pilot may back off the AGSM intensity somewhat as long as vision is maintained. If peripheral vision starts to deteriorate, the AGSM intensity must increase or the pilot must unload the forces.

It is an important element of the AGSM to initiate the strain as entry to the high-G maneuver occurs. Starting to strain too early may inhibit the natural cardiovascular response of the body, and starting the strain too late is extremely difficult to overcome.

Changes in Anti-G Straining Maneuver

Occasionally, improvements to the AGSM are attempted with varying degrees of success. The latest (2015) iteration of the AGSM was to modulate the strain to the G-force level more effectively. Instead of performing a maximal AGSM for every mid to high-G maneuver the idea is to strain only as hard as needed, and only contract those muscles expected to experience blood congestion.

The modified AGSM calls for pilots to flex their hamstring and gluteus muscles, push out on the abdominals, only intake 60% lung volume at G-onset, exchange 20% of breath during the re-ventilation phase, and relax the shoulders and chest. This author had the opportunity to attempt this new AGSM in a centrifuge, and the reason the description sounds confusing to perform is because it is! The idea of the new AGSM is to prevent blood pooling in the lower body, and facilitate blood flow to the upper torso.

Physiologically, the concept of the new AGSM is sound, but in this author's opinion, it is simply too much to remember in the middle of a high-G engagement. A pilot's response to high-G maneuvering has to be instinctive as opposed to intellectual, mainly because during a high-G engagement the only thought going through a pilot's mind is "survive."

Anecdotally, the Air Force realized an increase in GLOC from an average of 7 per year to 12 in 2019, according to the USAF Safety Center (Verger, 2020).

Optimizing +Gz Tolerance

Recognized elements exist to optimize a pilot's tolerance to +Gz forces. Those methods are:

- **Good health**
- **Proper diet**
- **Proper hydration**
- **Physical conditioning**
- **Training**
- **Frequent G-force exposure**

Good health includes getting the correct amount of rest, not drinking excessive amounts of alcohol, and receiving the right amount of rest.

Proper diet includes balancing nutrition intake to produce optimum levels of glycogen (blood sugar for proper oxygen metabolization), and receiving adequate levels of vitamins, minerals, fats, carbohydrates and proteins. From a general perspective, avoiding "white" foods such as refined sugars, white rice, white bread, etc., and focusing on whole grains, fruits, vegetables, leans meats, moderate dairy intake and water is a great place to start. A good rule of thumb is to keep everything on your plate in portions small enough not to touch each other, and your various foods different colors.

Proper hydration includes drinking enough non-sugary fluids, such as water, in adequate levels to maintain the proper balance of water and electrolytes to allow for effective bodily function of nerves and muscles. This element is extremely vital for any pilot; not simply high-G pilots.

Physical conditioning is important for high-G pilots to enable them to physically perform at a high level during intense aerial aerobatics or combat engagements. Military fighter pilots should strive to maintain the physical conditioning of an elite athlete, as the physical demands of air combat maneuvers will rapidly overcome those unprepared for it. While all muscle groups are important to train, special focus should be given to those muscle groups most affected by increased +Gz blood pooling, such as the legs, Gluteus Maximus, forearms, and core.

Training is required to enable the pilot to react instinctively to counteracting high-G forces, as opposed to intellectually. When engaged in high-G maneuvering, and especially G-forces in excess of 7G's, "survival of the organism" is the main thought going through a pilot's brain.

High-level analyzation of the AGSM simply doesn't enter the thought-stream. The only thing a pilot should concentrate on regarding the AGSM is whether to strain with higher or lower intensity, depending on peripheral vision loss or not. This training may be experienced with an instructor pilot in an aircraft, or for those lucky few, in a high-G centrifuge.

Frequent G-force exposure plays a major role in pilot AGSM effectiveness. As with any other skill, the more recent the experience, the more effective the skill is applied. If the high-G environment is a frequent occurrence for the pilot, the less traumatic the environment is for the pilot, both physically and intellectually. Infrequent high-G exposure may result in pilots "relearning" the timing and required intensity levels for an effective AGSM.

Negative Effects on +Gz Tolerance

Certain elements exist which decrease a pilot's ability to engage high-G maneuvering, and those elements are:

- Physiologic/anatomic anomalies
- Thermal extremes
- Fatigue
- Alcohol
- Drugs

Physiologic/anatomic anomalies include personal characteristics precluding a rapid increase in blood pressure, physical strength and increased heart-to-brain distance such as low blood pressure, having a long neck and/or torso, tall and/or thin/slender physical build. The ideal high-G pilot would be shorter-than-average, stocky and muscular build, and slightly overweight with a short neck.

Thermal extremes may cause a pilot to react less effectively in the high-G environment, as the pilot's body is fighting to maintain normal body temperatures, detracting from their ability to respond to high-G maneuvering.

Fatigue will affect a pilot's physical response to extreme conditions, as the body is unable to operate at peak efficiency.

Alcohol and drugs will cause the pilot to experience varying levels of histotoxic hypoxia, once again preventing maximum physical effort in extreme conditions.

15.10 –GZ FORCES

When humans are exposed to -Gz axis forces (acceleration in the foot-ward direction), a head-ward bodily fluid shift will occur, creating extremely uncomfortable and potentially dangerous physiological changes. -Gz forces would be encountered in maneuvers such as an outside loop, uncontrolled roll, or flying in level, inverted flight.

As a result of gravity pushing blood to the head, vascular congestion of the cranium will occur creating potentially dangerous increases of blood pressure to the brain and retinal tissue.

Consequently, headache is a common symptom of -Gz forces, along with visual *red-out*. Red-out occurs as a result of the blood-overloaded lower eyelid being pulled into the pilot's field-of-vision, creating a noticeable red-haze occurring in a pilot's visual field. Based on reports of pilots being exposed to extreme -Gz forces of up to -4Gz, complaints of severe headache, a feeling of "eyeballs popping out of the head," red vision, facial swelling, petechiae, and bleeding in the eye (subconjunctival hemorrhages) (Moisseiev, 2013).

In extreme high -Gz circumstances, it is conceivable further organ damage or detachment may occur in the upper body. NASA research has indicated brain stem-spine separation may occur at 145 rpm in the -Gz axis.

Because of the unpleasant effects of -Gz forces, this G-force axis is considered the least tolerant G-vector for humans. The limit for human tolerance of -Gz forces is generally considered to be -2Gz to -3Gz.

Push-Pull Effect

We learned in Section 15.4 about the cardiovascular response temporarily increasing human heart rates in response to +Gz forces. The reverse occurs when exposed to -Gz forces. Blood flow increases to the carotid arteries as a result of the forces, thereby triggering a temporary reduction in heart rate, and thus cranial blood pressure, for up to ten minutes.

The *push-pull effect* occurs when a pilot experiences -Gz forces by entering an outside loop or inverted flight, followed immediately by a +Gz maneuver. This effect reverses the signal sent by the carotid artery blood pressure sensors, lowering blood pressure, which may exceed human response capabilities and cause pilots to experience GLOC at much lower +Gz levels then the pilot anticipates. Predictably, this means rapid transition from -Gz maneuvers to +Gz maneuvers is extremely dangerous in any aircraft, but high-performance aircraft in particular.

Let us examine an incident in which this effect resulted in tragic consequences:

Incident Review – April 2018: The USAF Thunderbirds Demonstration Team was practicing show maneuvers at Nellis AFB, NV, at an altitude of approximately 5,000 feet in their F-16 aircraft.

One Thunderbird pilot, call sign "Cajun," was an experienced F-35 pilot. Cajun was performing a maneuver requiring him to transition from -2Gz to +8.5Gz within a time period of five seconds. Cajun experienced GLOC on the +8.5Gz maneuver.

According to investigators, Cajun was "absolutely incapacitated for about five seconds. All indications point to Cajun regaining consciousness, only to impact terrain shortly after, resulting in fatal injuries.

Analysis: USAF Thunderbird Demonstration Pilot Cajun experienced G-induced loss of consciousness (GLOC) while performing a push-pull maneuver involving -2Gz forces, followed immediately by +8.5Gz forces, and failed to recover control of the aircraft, resulting in an uncontrolled flight into terrain (UFIT) accident.

Conclusion: Even though USAF Thunderbird Demonstration Pilots are highly-trained in G-force mitigation, one pilot succumbed to the push-pull effect. Even though Cajun regained consciousness prior to terrain contact, he was most likely experiencing a phase of relative incapacitation (reorientation) and unable to comprehend his dire situation at the moment of impact.

15.11 GX FORCES

G-forces affecting humans in the chest-to-back (or back-to-chest) axis or perpendicular to the spine, also known as *transverse G-forces or Gx forces,* are produced from forward acceleration or deceleration of the aircraft. Quite obviously, Gx forces are produced from engine thrust, air- or ground-braking actions, or nose-first impacts.

+Gx forces are produced by forward acceleration, also known as "eyeballs-in" forces because the sensation is the eyeballs are being pushed into the cranium. -Gx forces are produced by deceleration, also known as "eyeballs-out" forces because the sensation is the eyeballs are being pushed out of the cranium.

Outside of impacts, the main physical issues associated with Gx forces are aircraft occupants losing their footing if standing when the aircraft accelerates or decelerates, or if seats are not locked into position.

The main physiological issue associated with Gx forces are somatogravic illusions which, as we learned in section 11.8, cause pilots to feel a pitch-up sensation upon acceleration or a pitch-down sensation upon deceleration without visual references, and are responsible for a large number of CFIT/UFIT incidents and accidents.

Gx Force Physiology

Gx forces are considered the best-tolerated G-axis for human physiology, mainly due to the extremely short heart-to-brain distance. Consider a chest-to-back accelerative force for a pilot sitting in a seat and the lateral distance of the heart to the brain; at most, the distance may equate to a few inches. Normal heart ejection fraction (heart pumping force) is easily able to overcome large amounts of Gx-forces with relative ease, maintaining cerebral perfusion in adequate levels. Early experimentation suggested humans were able to tolerate +17Gx forces, and -12Gx forces; the main difference being the capillaries in the retina were more sensitive to -Gx forces. Based on more recent USAF research, the average human Gx-force tolerance level is considered + or – 15Gx.

Human limitations regarding Gx forces include:

- Increased effort with inspiration
- Fatigue
- Throat pain
- Swelling

Gx Research

One of the early pioneers in aviation acceleration, deceleration, windblast effect and restraint system research was USAF Col. John Stapp, whom was mentioned and introduced in Section 14.5.

Recall that U.S. Air Force Col John Stapp was an early pioneer in the research efforts of acceleration and restraint effectiveness, and initially conducted research at Muroc Dry Lake, CA (nor Edwards AFB, CA) and then Holloman AFB, NM in the 1940's and 1950's. In the course of conducting research, D. Stapp used a high-speed rocket sled for use in linear acceleration & deceleration, restraint and windblast effects on humans, frequently volunteering to perform the research on himself. Over the course of his research, Dr. Stapp suffered a fractured wrist, broken ribs, lost fillings in his teeth, and suffered permanent eye damage from retinal bleeding as a result of the forces he endured.

During Dr. Stapp's testing, he personally experienced -38 Gx forces, +46.2 Gx forces, and reached speeds of 632 mph on the rocket sled (a land-speed record) and 570 mph in a fighter aircraft with the canopy removed. As a result of his research, Dr. Stapp became known as "The Fastest Man on Earth." Dr. Stapp's ground-breaking research on restraint systems eventually was instrumental in the passage of the Highway Safety Act of 1966, requiring seat belt in all new automobiles as of 1968. Dr. Stapp was eventually inducted into the National Aviation Hall of Fame, among other awards (John P. Stapp, 2020).

15.12 PREPARATION FOR HIGH-G FLIGHTS

For a pilot to maintain maximum personal performance when flight in the high-G environment is imminent, the following recommendations should be adhered to:

- **Sleep well**
- **Maintain balanced diet**
- **Avoid alcohol**
- **Hydrate**
- **Eat a healthy snack**
- **Engage in G-warmup maneuvers**

- **Prepare to strain**

Sleeping well includes a restful seven-to-eight hours of sleep, which professional pilots know will enable their bodies to perform at their physical best in an intensely athletic environment, and keep intellectual activity as sharp as possible. A tired body and fatigued mind will not be able to maintain peak performance.

Maintaining a balanced diet will maintain proper glucose levels and oxygen metabolization processing necessary for the body and mind to perform and recover at near-peak capacity. Once again, proper diet means a good mixture of fruits, vegetables, grains, lean meats and fats as if one were preparing to run a long-distance race.

Avoiding alcohol should go without saying, as a body and brain recovering from alcohol consumption is dehydrated and unable to perform effectively. Alcohol can block the release of glucose, creating conditions of low and unbalanced blood sugars, which will not allow proper recovery following high-G maneuvers.

Hydrate by consumption of water or electrolyte-infused sports drinks. Avoid sugary drinks, which may lead to hypoglycemia and low energy levels during the flight.

Eat a healthy snack such as a piece of fruit immediately prior to the flight to give the body a healthy glucose boost. This helps the body recover faster following high-G maneuvers or engagements.

Engage in G-warmup maneuvers, if possible, to activate the cardiovascular response. This will prepare the cardiovascular system to respond quickly and effectively during the onset of G-forces.

Prepare to strain, or mentally prepare yourself to anticipate the onset of G-forces. If a pilot gets behind the power curve with the AGSM, it can be difficult at best to "catch-up" to the G-forces.

Conclusion

A pilot exposed to high-G flight is in an environment completely foreign to normal human physiological function. If the correct conditions exist, a pilot may be rendered incapacitated in a second, and must be highly aware of their own vulnerabilities in such flight conditions. Hence, pilots maneuvering in the high-G environment must possess the foundational knowledge of high-G physiology and be capable of performing an effective AGSM instinctively, which requires extensive training.

Chapter 15 Core Competency Questions

1. Acceleration is defined as a change in velocity with respect to _____.
2. A change in vector refers to a change in _____.
3. For humans, gravity results in a _____ stress.
4. What are the three accelerative forces on aircraft?
5. What are the three g-vectors humans are exposed to?
6. Which G-vector is least likely to occur in aviation settings?
7. Which G-vector is most likely to cause GLOC?
8. What two physiological problems exist when experiencing +Gz forces?
9. What are considered low G-forces?
10. What are considered high G-forces?
11. What is the first symptom of +Gz forces?
12. What is the unprotected Gz force tolerance most humans can endure?
13. The Push-Pull effect makes going from ____ Gz forces to _____Gz forces dangerous.
14. What is the average human + & - Gx tolerance level?

16. NOISE, VIBRATION AND RADIATION EFFECTS IN AVIATION

In the aviation environment, occupational exposure to *noise, vibration, and radiation* (ionizing and non-ionizing) will be an ongoing and continuous presence. Unlike other environmental factors such as smoke, fire, and fumes, pilots cannot detect these hazards by senses of sight, smell, or taste buds. Typically, the flight segment and altitude will dictate which of these factors will be more prevalent, such as take-off, climb-out, cruise, etc. The main physiological issues encountered with noise, vibration, and radiation are ear and/or eye tissue damage, and the potential cancerous effects on body tissues of radiation exposure. Most permanent physical damage occurs as a result of long-term exposure; however, instantaneous damage could potentially occur with some of these factors.

In this chapter, we will discuss:

1. Sound, noise and vibration concepts
2. Noise in aviation
3. Vibration in aviation
4. Flightcrew occupational radiation exposure

16.1 SOUND, NOISE AND VIBRATION CONCEPTS

Sound is produced by longitudinal, mechanical pressure waves, or impulses resulting from vibrating air particles. Sound and noise may be transmitted through not only air, but liquid or solid mediums as well. Very little impulse energy is transformed into tissue vibration energy, although the ear converts nearly 100% of sound energy into nerve impulses. Measurements of sound is accomplished in terms of frequency and amplitude.

Vibrations are periodic or random mechanical oscillations, or intermittent motion normally transmitted from one solid particle or body to another solid particle or body. When a human body is in contact with a vibrating surface, most vibration energy is transmitted directly into the body.

Vibrations may be either *free vibrations* or *forced vibrations*. Free vibrations may result from a brief solid object disruption and then the object is allowed to move freely at its natural frequency; forced vibrations occur upon repeated object disruption, which force specific frequency vibrations upon the object.

Vibrations may also be *damped* or *undamped*. Damped vibrations use external resistive forces to transfer energy to its surroundings, thus reducing the magnitude of oscillations; undamped vibrations do not transfer energy to resistive forces.

Noise and Vibration Sources

On the ground, aircraft noise and/or vibration sources may be produced by:

- Aircraft engines
- Takeoff preparations
- Ground-tire contact
- Aircraft braking
- Onboard equipment

In the airborne flight environment, noise and/or vibration may be produced by aerodynamically induced energy over the fuselage, such as:

- High speed operations at low altitudes
- Take-off near maximal weight limits
- Climbs, dives, and maneuvers

As a result of denser air molecule proximity sound is transmitted more efficiently at low altitudes. Regarding molecular density, the speed of sound in the air is approximately 343 meters per second, whereas sound travels much faster under water at a speed of approximately 1,480 meters per second (Baird, 2013).

Noise inflight may also be produced from sources such as:

- Jet efflux
- Hydraulic actuators
- Electrical actuators
- Propellers
- Rotors
- Environmental systems
- Pressurization systems
- Communications equipment

16.2 NOISE IN AVIATION

Noise is defined as unwanted sound, in which the brain deciphers acoustic sound and decides whether the sound is a wanted sound or unwanted noise. Australian Work Health and Safety legislation defines noise as "any sound that is potentially harmful to the health and safety of a person" (OHS Body of Knowledge, 2012). As most pilots are already aware, cockpit noise in aircraft has been around since the beginnings of aviation and is accepted as an inevitable byproduct of flying a mechanical device. What is not inevitable, however, is the potential tissue damage caused by noise, so long as the proper precautions are adhered to.

Sound Concepts

In order to understand noise, first we must understand the methodology behind how sound is transmitted and measured. The four characteristics of sound are:

- Frequency
- Intensity
- Speed
- Duration

Frequency, commonly referred to as *pitch,* is a measurement of the number of times per second a sound pressure wave repeats itself. Frequency is measured based on wave cycles or oscillations per second, with units of frequency called *hertz (Hz).* Lower frequencies produce fewer oscillations, while higher frequencies produce more oscillations. The normal range for human hearing is between 20 Hz to 20,000 Hz. *Ultrasound* encompasses frequencies above 20,000 Hz, while *infrasound* encompasses frequencies less than 20 Hz.

Intensity, also referred to as *amplitude,* is defined as the relative strength of sound waves, or transmitted vibrations. Human hearing perceives intensity as the volume or loudness of sound. Amplitude is measured in *decibels (dB),* referring to the sound pressure level. Lower thresholds of human hearing is 0dB at 1 kHz; moderate levels are under 60dB (normal voice levels), loud levels are approximately 70dB (vacuum cleaners), and the human pain threshold approximately 125dB (jet engine).

Decibels work on a logarithmic scale; the power ratio mathematically increases by a factor of ten for every increase of ten units (sound level), and a doubling of perceived loudness. (National Park Service, 2018). As a result, 20dB is perceived as twice as loud as 10dB, and 30dB would be perceived as four times as loud as 10dB.

The *speed* at which sound travels is dependent on the medium it travels through. With consideration to the pressure-wave characteristics of sound, it makes sense that stiffer chemical bonds between materials propagate sounds faster and more efficiently, whereas denser materials have slower sound propagation. Materials such as air do not have stiff chemical bonds, therefore propagate sounds more slowly (National Park Service, 2018).

Duration essentially is a measurement of the length of time a pitch or tone persists. Hearing damage occurs as a factor of duration and high-intensity sound. Damage may occur as a result of short, high-intensity sound or long, less-intense sound.

When air molecules vibrate due to pressure variation, the ear perceives the variations in pressure as sound. The vibrations are converted into mechanical energy by the middle ear, subsequently moving microscopic hairs in the inner ear, which in turn convert the sound waves into nerve impulses. If the vibrations are too intense, over time these microscopic hairs can be damaged, causing hearing loss (United States Department of Labor, 2013).

How Do We Hear?

Audible stimulus is processed through the ear, the organ making hearing possible. The ear's function is to gather, transmit, and perceive sounds from the environment.

The ear is divided into three distinct sections:

- Outer Ear
- Middle Ear
- Inner Ear

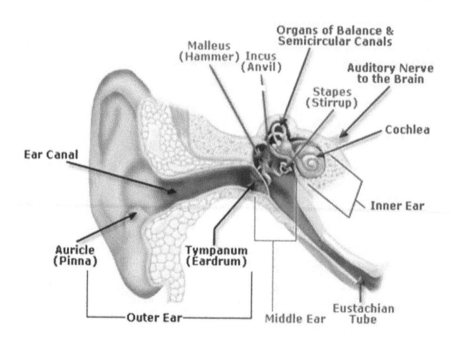

Osha 2021

326

The outer ear funnels ambient sound waves into the ear canal to the tympanic membrane (eardrum), at which point the variation of the sound waves vibrates the eardrum. This step is known as *modification.*

The middle ear transmits the vibrations from the tympanic membrane to the tiny bones of the Middle Ear, known as *ossicles.* The ossicles, called the Malleus, Incus, and Stapes, amplify the vibrations and transmits the stimulus to the inner ear. These steps are known as *conversion and amplification.*

The inner ear processes the sound vibrations in the cochlea, a snail-shaped structure filled with fluid. The vibrations cause waves in the fluid, and this wave energy influences the cilia of nerve cells in the inner ear, called hair cells. Depending on the hair cells' position in the decreasing radius of the cochlea, the hair cells' presentation of this stimulus activates the auditory nerve to transmit information to the brain, which will interpret the information as pitch and loudness. This step is known as *transformation.*

Impaired function in any stage will have a detrimental effect on hearing abilities (United States Department of Labor, 2013).

Types of Noise

Noise, as we know, is defined as "unwanted sound"; however, the definition is subjective and variable over time to each individual. The common characteristics for all humans is noise is considered loud, disagreeable, and/or distracting. One person may define a particular sound as "noise," while another may define the same sound as pleasant. A person with existing hearing damage may not be able to tolerate the same sound loudness levels as another, or vice versa.

Steady state noise is continuous, stable noise levels, which is very common in aviation settings. Examples of steady state noise would be the continuous drone of the engine or airflow over the nose.

Impulse noise is a sharp, sudden onset of noise, commonly with alarms suddenly sounding, gunshots or explosions. Typically, impulse noise consists of a single sound burst of less than one second, with peak levels at least 15dB higher than background noise.

Detrimental Effects of Noise Exposure

According to the FAA, the *detrimental effects of noise exposure* can include wide-ranging physiological and psychological impairment.

Some hearing loss should be expected throughout one's life, mainly through aging or work and environmental noise factors. For aviators, these issues may present themselves sooner, unless personal protection measures are implemented.

Many professional and general aviation pilots report unexpected fatigue on particular noisy flights, up to and including temporary hearing loss. Some pilots have experienced difficulty interpreting ATC communications. Noise exposure may produce harmful, cumulative physiological effects, which tend to increase with increases in sound intensity and duration. The Occupational Safety and Health Act was enacted to strictly limit the amount of noise U.S. workers are subjected to during eight hour work shifts in various jobs. Unfortunately for general aviation pilots, no restrictions exist, which makes this knowledge particularly beneficial for them.

Generally, prop-driven aircraft have the tendency to be noisy, with helicopters and open-cockpit aircraft obviously the noisiest. In any prop-driven airplane, the levels of sound are high enough for GA pilots to be concerned about continuous flight operations.

Cockpit noise related to engine and exhaust noises at maximum may be in a similar frequency range where speech has its maximum energy. Pilot reports reveal although volume or gain control on radios may be at maximum, tower transmissions can be unintelligible, masked by engine noise. FAA Civil Aerospace Medical Institute (CAMI) testing has shown full power take-offs may mask the intelligibility of ATC from 100% to zero.

We can divide noise effects into two distinct categories; physiologic and psychologic. The following are physiologic effects of high-intensity noise exposure:

- Ear discomfort, pain or rupture
- Temporary hearing impairment
- Permanent hearing impairment

Ear discomfort, pain, or rupture may occur at predictable dB levels. Ear discomfort may occur at exposures of 120dB, ear pain may occur at 130dB, and ear rupture may occur at 140dB.

Temporary hearing impairment may occur as a result of unprotected exposure to loud, continuous sound over 90dB for several hours. Typically, hearing returns to normal within several hours following cessation of the sound.

Permanent hearing impairment may occur as a result of unprotected exposure to loud sounds in excess of 90 dB for eight or more hours per day, spanning several years.

Permanent hearing impairment is thought to initially occur in the 4,000 Hz range, which is outside the range of normal conversation. This impairment may go unnoticed by the affected individual for a period of time, ranging from months-to-years.

The following are potential psychologic effects of high-intensity noise exposure:

- Subjective effects
- Speech interference
- Performance elements

Subjective effects may include distraction, acute fatigue, irritability, sleep and rest disruption, headache, disorientation, poor memory and concentration, sudden awakening or startle response.

Speech interference may make normal speech interpretation difficult or impossible. If noise is intense enough to mask verbal communication, it may have the potential to mask audible alarm systems as well.

Performance elements may create an increase in errors for tasks, particularly tasks requiring intellectual engagement such as calculations, concentration, monitoring, vigilance and complex diagnostics or judgements (FAA, Federal Aviation Administration, 2020)

Hearing Loss

According to CAMI, different individuals will respond differently to various noises. Within a particular individual, sensitivity may be different in each ear. Aside from individuality, average pilots may develop significant hearing loss flying in excess of eight hours per week, especially for aircraft such as helicopters and open cockpit fixed wing (crop-duster). For eight hours per week for ten years in a light twin-engine aircraft, pilots can expect severe-enough hearing loss to eventually have trouble understanding normal speech.

Hearing loss generally occurs gradually over a period of time. The loss may be imperceptible until speech intelligibility becomes difficult for aviators. By the time aviators recognize a problem, permanent hearing loss has most likely occurred. As a result of this issue, personal hearing protection must be introduced and utilized early in a pilot's flying career to prevent hearing loss in aviation.

CAMI and OSHA considers 90 dB of noise for eight hours to be the limit of what humans can endure unprotected (Permissible Noise Limit or PEL), with 85 dB of noise considered the "action" level. The action level is when individuals should seek hearing protection or remove themselves from the noisy environment.

OSHA PELs for Noise

Duration	PEL
8 hours	90 dB
4 hours	95 dB
2 hours	100 dB
1 hour	105 dB
1/2 hour	110 dB
15 minutes	115 dB

OSHA 2021

Hearing loss may be either temporary or permanent:

Temporary hearing impairment may also be identified as *threshold shift*. Unprotected exposure to loud, steady noise over 90dB for several hours may cause a shift in the auditory threshold, resulting in short-term hearing impairment. Typically the effect is temporary and normal hearing thresholds return a short time following cessation of the causal noise exposure.

Permanent hearing impairment may occur with unprotected exposure to loud noise (higher than 90dB) for eight or more hours per day for several years, causing permanent hearing loss. The same effect may occur with noise levels of 95dB for four hours per day.

Conductive hearing loss is the inability of sound wave transfer anywhere along the pathway through the outer ear, tympanic membrane, or middle ear. These issues may occur as result of ear wax, tumors, perforated ear drum, abnormal growths, barotrauma, and other factors. Depending on the nature and severity of the conductive loss, surgical or pharmaceutical treatments may be available to restore one's hearing.

Presbycusis is a common loss of hearing gradually occurring in individuals as they grow older. About 30-35 percent of adults age 65 and older experience hearing loss, and an estimated 40-50 percent of adults age 75 and older experience hearing loss. Hearing loss associated with presbycusis is typically greater for high-pitched sounds. For example, it may be difficult for the individual to hear the nearby chirping of a bird or the ringing of a telephone, but the same person may be able to clearly hear the low-pitched sound of a truck rumbling down a street. Prevention through adequate hearing protection is the best strategy; however, hearing aids may be employed to assist with this type of hearing loss.

Initially, permanent hearing impairment has proven to occur around 4,000 Hz (outside the conversational range) and may go unnoticed by the individual for some time. FAA research has shown hearing sensitivity normally decreases as a function of age at frequencies from 1,000 to 6,000 Hz, beginning around age 30 (FAA, Federal Aviation Administration, 2020).

In cases of hearing impairment, damage occurs to the *tensor tympani*, a muscle present in the middle ear which connects to the malleus ossicles. As the tensor tympani pulls the malleus, in turn tensing the tympanic membrane. This action creates a damping effect on the vibration of the tympanic membrane and transmission of vibrations to the Inner Ear, therefore reducing the perceived amplitude of sound and noise known as the *acoustic reflex*.

Damage occurs to the tensor tympani as a result of exposure to intolerable noise levels, which may over-contract the muscle leading to symptoms of ear pain, or a fluttering and/or fullness sensation in the ear. Repeated exposures to intolerable noise levels may result in *conductive hearing loss*, resulting from tympanic membrane perforation, increased stiffness or loss of continuity of the ossicular chain. Ultimate destruction of hair cells in the cochlea may also be a possibility (NAS, 2005).

Attenuating Noise Effects

According to the FAA, dealing with noise in flight is a relatively easy issue to mitigate. The first line-of-defense are earplugs or noise-cancelling headsets, which prevent most of the physiological problems identified to this point. Quite obviously, in order for hearing protection to be effective, it must be used properly and not forgotten in a pilot's flight bag.

Passive noise-reduction systems such as earplugs or standard communication headsets reduce or mask the effects of the low-frequency sound spectrum your ears would normally hear, but also reduce other sounds as well. Properly fitted earplugs allow the user to hear everything necessary to hear in the cockpit, with effective noise-reduction systems significantly enhancing an aviator's ability to distinguish audio communications. Unfortunately, poorly-fitted noise-protection devices are worse than none-at-all, as this condition gives users a false sense of security. Earplugs need not be uncomfortable, but must fit snugly to provide maximum benefit (FAA, Federal Aviation Administration, 2020).

Earplugs typically are inserted into or pressed against the external ear canal to reduce the effect of ambient sound on the auditory system. Individual ears are unique in shape and size, prompting a variety of approaches to solving the problem of designing adequate, universally-fitting earplugs.

Earplugs come in a variety of shapes, sizes, and materials, and generally will be effective for a noise reduction rating (NRR) of 10dB to 30dB, if employed correctly. Because earplugs and standard aviation headsets are passive, in many cases pilots must turn up the volume of communication devices to be able to hear clearly.

Active noise-reduction systems are typically headsets performing the same task as earplugs, in that they reduce the low-frequency sound spectrum. What differentiates active noise protection from passive protection, however, is active systems provide noise suppression and manipulation in the sound spectrum causing noise, but enables aviators to maintain clear communications without increasing radio volume, thus creating greater attentiveness. Active noise-reduction systems use electronic coupling of low-frequency noise waves with an exact mirror image of the noise, therefore canceling out the noise, but not other sounds. Average peak noise reduction for active noise-reduction systems is 15dB to over 30dB, depending on the effectiveness of the system.

Combining types of noise-reduction devices (earplugs plus headset) are recommended by the FAA for noise levels above 115dB. This provides the aviator maximum levels of hearing protection given the state of current noise-reduction technology.

Summary

Working and flying in an environment conducive to excessive ambient noise degrades an aviator's accuracy of comprehension, sharing attention, response times, and memory recall is impaired, along with the other physiologic and psychologic effects mentioned previously. The ability to control noise leads to better hearing, communication, concentration, and lessens distraction.

Detrimental noise-induced physiologic and psychologic effects are preventable. An aviator has to respect the potential for auditory system damage, maintain proper hearing protection for any environment producing potentially damaging noise, and remember if one's voice has to be raised to be heard, hearing protection is necessary.

16.3 VIBRATION IN AVIATION

Vibration in aviation operations can create and/or cause physiological issues resulting from the oscillatory motion of the aviator's body interacting with various vibrations transmitted from the airframe. A body with mass and elasticity is capable of motion, and the body holds a natural frequency in which motion repeats itself. The acute and chronic effects from airframe vibrations may range anywhere from negligible to serious impairment and pain.

Vibration Concepts

Vibration are generally categorized as either free vibrations or forced vibrations.

Free vibrations occur when an object or system is momentarily disturbed, then moves with no restraints on its movement.

Forced vibrations occur if an object or system is continuously driven by an external force.

Vibration in aviation operations may be more easily imagined as two types: *random (free) vibration* and *regular (forced) vibration*.

Random vibration may be described as not predictable, such as vibration produced by environmental effects such as aerodynamic effect on an airframe under differing atmospheric conditions, or the movement a tire makes on an uneven surface.

Regular vibration may be described as predictable vibration, such as vibration produced by an engine running at a constant speed, or the vibrations produced by a tuning fork.

In addition to the types of vibration, the following concepts play important roles in the severity of vibration injuries or impairments:

- Direction
- Frequency
- Amplitude
- Duration

Direction of vibration may be divided into three considerations: *linear, rotational, or combination*.

Frequency of vibration is measured in cycles per second, or Hertz. Aviation operations tend to deal with low-frequency vibrations, or those less than 100 Hz.

Amplitude of vibration, or the intensity of the vibration, correlates to the strength of the vibration, as well as the amount or distance of vibrational displacement.

Duration of vibration, or the time exposed to the vibration, will be a major factor in the severity and prolongation of symptoms in individuals affected by the effects of vibration.

Vibration-Induced Performance Problems

To generate an idea of how vibration may affect human performance, let us examine a few typical examples of how individuals driving a vehicle are exposed to vibration in everyday life.

Consider the factors of regularity, direction, frequency, and amplitude of these examples, and the human performance problems associated with them:

- Smooth road
- Rumble strips
- Washboard surface
- Railroad ties
- Potholes

On a smooth road, a driver would notice regular vibration in the steering wheel and seat in a combination of directions, at a high frequency and low amplitude with no ill effects.

Driving over rumble strips, vibration would be regular, linear, low frequency and higher amplitude; enough to cause numbness in hands after extended periods.

Washboard surfaces would cause random vibration, in a combination of directions, low frequency and high amplitude, causing whole body vibration (WBV) and fatigue after extended periods.

Driving over railroad ties and potholes would cause either regular or random vibration in the vertical linear direction, low frequency and very high amplitude, causing whole body vibration, fatigue, internal organ jarring, and likely spinal pain after extended periods.

Considering the same factors of factors of regularity, direction, frequency, and amplitude, let's examine how some handheld tools could affect human performance:

- Jigsaw
- Chainsaw

Using a handheld jigsaw would produce regular vibration with a linear direction, high frequency and low amplitude, causing hand, arm, shoulder, and possibly back pain after extended periods.

Using a chainsaw would produce regular vibration in a linear direction, high frequency and high amplitude, causing WBV, fatigue, internal organ jarring, and muscular pain after extended periods.

Human Response to Vibration

The human body has mechanical properties and our response to vibration may be classified under a range of descriptions. We can narrow down those descriptors to primarily *localized vibration* affecting the hands and arms, or *whole-body vibration* (*WBV*).

Localized vibration affecting the hands and arms may be experienced over a long enough time to cause issues such as creating a series of physiological issues with manual dexterity, fine motor control, circulation, premature fatigue, and pain.

According to a report conducted by the Naval Medical Center San Diego, CA, WBV affects up to six million workers and operators in vehicle transportation operations in the United States. As operators are continuously exposed to excessive levels of vibration, irreversible damage can occur to the body such as degenerative disc disease in the back, hand and foot numbness or tingling, as well as causing operator fatigue and impaired performance (SAFE, 2005).

Individual tolerance depends on a variety of factors, including body posture, muscle tension engaged for the activity, bodily dimensions, and body composition as vibration transmits through certain tissue better than others. The frequency of the vibration will also determine how energy is transmitted and/or attenuated throughout the body.

Human responses to vibration may be categorized as either *mechanical response* or *psychological response.*

Mechanical responses to vibration in the body are resultant from the tissues and organs attenuating the energy, which may lead to damage to internal organs in more extreme cases. A general feeling of discomfort begins at the 4-9 Hz frequency range, voluntary or involuntary muscular contractions begin at 4-9 Hz, increased urge to urinate starts at 10-18 Hz, a "lump in the throat" sensation begins in the 12-16 Hz frequency range, and increased muscle tone and influence on speech begins at 13-20 Hz. Psychological responses may include various stress reactions such as fatigue and irritability. Sleep is typically induced at the 2-4 Hz frequency range.

Vibration Syndromes

Vibration in general may be causal in direct vascular damage and neural dysfunction. Earlier was mentioned localized vibration causing physiological issues with the hands and the arms. Two such issues are:

- Hand-arm vibration syndrome (HAVS)
- Traumatic vasospastic disease

Hand-arm vibration syndrome (HAVS) has been described as a hand and forearm disorder including numbness, tingling, and loss of nerve sensation. This syndrome is typically linked to prolonged use of vibrating tools, although other activities such as extended riding of motorcycles (constant twisting pressure of the throttle) or gripping a yoke/stick in an aircraft may produce the same effects.

Traumatic vasospastic disease is commonly linked to repetitive trauma including vibration, mechanical percussive injury to the hand, electric shock injury, or significant cold exposure. Impairments may include reduced grip force, numbness, and difficulty with finger dexterity.

Both syndromes are similar, and known generically as *vibration white finger* or *dead-finger* to the general public. Onset rates for these conditions may take years or even decades of continual exposure to vibration or cold. Ultimately, these conditions will normally lead to unilateral digit dysfunction, brought on by a block in blood circulation in the hands and fingers. Fingers may by white, cold, and painful. Tactile sensitivity will be greatly reduced, preventing manual precision manipulation and fine motor control.

Resonance:

Resonance plays a major role in human impairment, and we will now examine the role resonance plays in the effects of vibration on humans.

Resonance in physics may be defined as "a phenomenon in which an external force or a vibrating system forces another system around it to vibrate with greater amplitude at a specified frequency of operation" (BYJUS, 2020). Applying this definition to humans, resonance is an excitation force equaling our natural frequency at which vibration amplitude is maximized, which may have significant effects results under certain circumstances. If one has ever driven down a rough road for a long period of time, it can feel as if one gets shaken apart by the resonance.

Specific resonance levels in the human structure can produce predictable results. At 5-10 Hz, a person's thoracic cavity and abdominal structures will be affected. At 20-30 Hz, shoulder and head structures will be impacted. At 60-90 Hz, a person's eyeball structures will be significantly impacted.

Human Performance – Vision

Human vision will be deteriorated when the image is blurred on the retina, which typically occurs in the range of 10-25 Hz, with most pilots noticing significant decreases in visual acuity around 20 Hz (Roderick, 1972). Since humans cannot control how blurry their vision gets from vibration, other mitigating factors need to be employed to minimize impacts. Perhaps the most important mitigation factors revolve around equipment designed to either attenuate vibration or minimize its effects. These mitigation factors may involve experimenting with issues such as aerodynamic effectiveness of the airframe, propeller design, engine operating characteristics, control placement, and so on. We will investigate a couple of the simpler concepts.

Once such mitigation strategy is seat design. Aircraft suspension seats can potentially decrease vibration by 4-8 Hz. Suspension seats attenuate vibration by elevating the occupant off the hard seat frame onto a liner "suspended" off the seat frame. This will attenuate vibration to an acceptable level for pilot vision to be more effective.

Another mitigation strategy is designing the instrument panel displays with increased visual efficiency in mind. Increasing the size of the display and the clarity of the information presented may enable the pilot to view the information more effectively. If gauges are employed on the instrument panel, the gauge should not have an information readout variability due to vibration (in other words, no shaking needles).

Human Performance – Control

Short-term, high-frequency WBV exposure has shown to increase pilot fatigue, decrease comfort, and interfere with piloting performance and overall operational safety.

Resonance will occur in the 4-8 Hz frequency range. Pilot control tracking errors appear to increase by significant amounts, possibly up to 40%, in the frequency range of 20-25 Hz (Roderick, 1972).

Vertical vibration produces more tracking issues then lateral vibration, and the residual effects may last up to 30 seconds after vibration has been terminated. The location and configuration of aircraft controls may have positive or negative impacts on control tracking errors, as better control has been realized with sidestick controls versus center stick controls.

Attenuating Vibration Effects

Knowing the effects of vibration in aviation may cause performance problems, we must then understand attenuation techniques to mitigate those problems. The U.S. Army has developed comprehensive anti-vibration strategies which can be employed in either fixed-wing or rotor-wing aircraft:

- **Maintain good posture/snug belts**
- **Maintain your equipment**
- **Isolate crew/patients**
- **Limit exposure time (if mission allows)**
- **Do not grip controls tightly**
- **Maintain excellent physical condition**
- **Maintain proper hydration and nutrition**

Maintain good posture/snug belts. By maintaining proper posture in the cockpit, the entire skeletal system, and in particular the spinal column, will be in the best possible mechanical position to absorb vertical and horizontal vibrations. Increasing restraint and decreasing mobility will keep an individual's body moving in the same relative motion as the aircraft. Decreasing reach, such as using a sidestick controller, will enable a pilot to maintain more precise control of the aircraft.

Maintain your equipment. Aircraft being mechanical devices, normal operation may cause fasteners and drive systems to wear or loosen, thereby producing increasing amounts of vibration. Proper maintenance will ensure the airframe and engine systems are as tight and balanced as possible, therefore minimizing vibration.

Isolate crew/patients. Crew and patients forced to sit or lie on the floor of the aircraft will receive more vibration then when placed in seats or patient racks. In addition, using firm seat pads will attenuate vibration more effectively, as soft seat pads may amplify the vibrational effect.

Limit exposure time (if mission allows). One of the main negative factors in the severity and prolongation of vibrational effects is the amount of time one is exposed to the vibration. If exposure time can be limited, it is an elemental way to attenuate vibration.

Do not grip controls tightly. The pilot should not maintain a "death grip" on aircraft controls, as this practice will transfer maximum levels of vibration to the hands and arms. Maintain firm contact with the controls, but let the aircraft do the work.

Maintain excellent physical condition. Vibration will transmit more effectively through fat tissue as opposed to muscle tissue. Maintaining excellent physical condition will ensure the body is as prepared as possible for vibrational attenuation.

Maintain proper hydration and nutrition. As with every other potentially physically fatiguing facet of aviation, one's body and mind will be at their peak if one maintains a proper hydration and diet schedule.

Summary

Vibration has the potential to cause significant negative effects on aviator performance due to resonance. The goal of aircraft designers is to provide protection to aviators through seat design, and improve performance through control and information display design.

The pilot can enhance their flight and mission effectiveness with their ability to understand and attenuate vibration in the aircraft using the personal techniques discussed.

16.4 FLIGHT CREW OCCUPATIONAL RADIATION EXPOSURE

According to the Centers for Disease Control and Prevention (CDC), as corporate and commercial aircraft fly through the air at typical enroute flight altitudes, increased radiation exposure may be an unwelcomed byproduct of the flight. Although not normally an expressed risk of air travel, radiation from flight has been attributed to a variety of issues in experienced aircrew members and frequent travelers. Research aimed at radiation exposure has been mainly focused on those individuals and groups exposed to relatively high levels of radiation, such as atomic bomb survivors, radiation therapy patients, nuclear power plant exposures, etc. However, long-term, low-level radiation exposure in aircraft poses many questions yet to be answered.

Sources of Radiation in Aviation

The recognized sources of radiation in aviation settings can be traced to several different factors:

- Ultraviolet radiation
- Galactic cosmic radiation (aka cosmic ionizing radiation)
- Solar storms

When flying outside the Earth's natural protective cocoon at the top or above the Troposphere, highly-charged radioactive particles are bombarding the Earth's atmosphere from all directions. These high-energy particles, which are the cores of atoms, can travel for millions of miles through space only to contact our atmosphere. Once these particles hit the atmosphere, they create showers of ionizing radiation, which are particles which dislodge electrons free of atoms and molecules. Fortunately for most humans, our ionizing radiation exposure at ground level has been largely mitigated by the atmosphere scattering the vast majority of Galactic Cosmic Radiation particles prior to reaching the ground (CDC, Aircrew Safety and Health, 2017).

Radiobiology

Ionizing radiation is common for humans to be exposed to from a variety of air- and ground-based sources, and *radiobiology* is the scientific discipline which studies the potential health effects due to radiation exposure. These radioactive particles have the potential to penetrate deep inside the human body, which may potentially cause damage to tissues and DNA, and have been linked to cancer, reproductive maladies and possible cognition problems in animals.

Research has shown several syndromes associated with radiation exposure are evident:

- Acute radiation sickness
- Radiation-induced cancer
- Fetal and genetic damage concerns

The CDC is not sure what levels of cosmic ionized radiation exposure are safe for every person.

Why does it Matter?

As mentioned earlier, commercial and corporate aircrew members are exposed to higher levels of ultraviolet A (UVA) and ionized radiation as a direct result of flight at common cruise altitudes. The National Council on Radiation Protection and Measurements reported professional aircrew have the largest average annual effective dose of all U.S. radiation-exposed workers. The International Commission on Radiological Protection considers aircrew to be exposed to galactic cosmic radiation on their jobs (CDC, Aircrew Safety and Health, 2017). The FAA formally recognized professional aircrew as occupationally exposed to radiation.

Although the risks of radiation-induced illnesses are relatively benign, awareness of the issues involved and making proper choices can assist aircrew in minimizing risks by decreasing levels of exposure.

Radiation Measurement

According to the CDC, many international scientists measure radiation using the System Internationale (SI), a unified system of weights and measures derived from the metric system. However, the United States still predominantly uses the conventional system of measurement.

Depending on the aspect of radiation being measured, different units of measurement will be used. Under the conventional system, emitted radiation is measured using the *curie (Ci),* radiation dosage absorbed by humans is measured in *rad,* and the biological risk of radiation is measured in *rem.* In aviation, biological risk is mainly measured in the SI format of *Sievert (Sv).*

Scientists have assigned a number to each type of ionizing radiation (alpha and beta particles, gamma rays, and x-rays) depending on that radiation type's ability to transfer energy to the cells of the body to determine a person's biological risk. This number is known as the Quality Factor (Q).

When an individual is exposed to radiation, scientists can multiply the dose in rad by the quality factor for the type of radiation present, therefore estimating a person's biological risk in rems. Thus, risk in rem = rad X Q. The rem has been replaced by the Sv. One Sv is equal to 100 rem. One Sv also equals 1,000 millisieverts (mSv) (CDC, Radiation Emergencies, 2018).

Comparison Doses

The following are examples of common radiation exposures for humans:

One dental x-ray: 0.15 mSv

One chest x-ray: 0.1 mSv

One chest CT scan: 7.0 mSv

One mammogram: 0.7 mSv

One year of exposure to natural radiation (from soil, cosmic rays, etc.): 3.00 mSv (CDC, Radiation Emergencies, 2018).

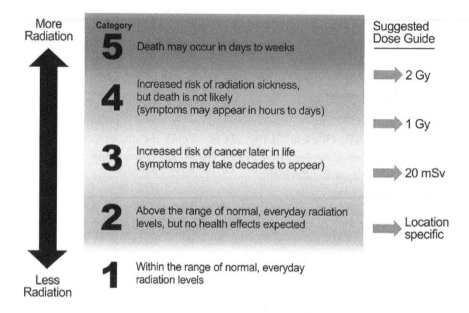

CDC 2021

FAA Advisory Circular 120-61B, *In-Flight Radiation Exposure,* breaks down the average annual doses of ionizing radiation a person in the U.S. typically receives from background sources:

Source	Effective Dose (mSv)	% of total
Galactic/Solar Radiation	0.33	11
Inhaled Radon/Thoron	2.28	73
Radioactive Ground Material	0.21	7
Radioactive Material in body tissues	0.29	9
Total:	**3.11**	**100**

As one can see, normal human existence on the surface of the Earth provides a certain amount of exposure to radiation.

Aviation Occupational Radiation Exposures

As we have discussed, flight in commercial aircraft at common cruise altitudes in excess of FL300 has been shown to produce relatively high doses of galactic cosmic radiation, which the FAA has deemed to be an *occupational exposure*. This effectively means commercial aircrew are considered *occupational radiation workers.*

Ultraviolet radiation, although missing in many scientific discussions on radiation exposure at altitude, is an increased risk in flight with its own set of potential physiological issues. According to a study published in the U.S. National Library of Medicine, UVB and UVC rays were effectively attenuated by the fuselage skin and windows of most aircraft, but UVA penetration may still present an issue. Meta-analysis indicates increased incidence rates of melanoma (skin cancer) in pilots and cabin crew, as well as cumulative eye damage.

Outside of the relative protection of the aircraft, UV radiation increases by some 3,500% at FL350. Flight above thick cloud payers and snow-covered fields may produce more UVA exposure, which could potentially reflect as much as 85% of UV radiation (Sanlorenzo, 2015).

Galactic cosmic radiation is a constant, low-grade, high-energy presence to professional aircrew. This type of radiation is primarily due to supernovae in space.

According to the FAA, ionizing radiation exposure will be less received on lower-latitude flights as a result of the shielding effects of the Earth's magnetic field. Predictably, this shielding effect is greatest close to the geomagnetic equator due to the thickness of the atmosphere, and will gradually decrease to near-zero close to the Earth's poles. In effect, radiation exposure over either pole would be roughly twice that over the equator (FAA, In-Flight Radiation Exposure, 2014).

On a roundtrip airplane flight segment from New York to Los Angeles, typical exposure to ionized radiation would equate to 0.03 mSv. One flight segment from New York to Tokyo over the North Pole would yield as much as 0.0754 mSv, or roughly the equivalent of one mammogram or close to one chest X-ray.

Solar storms tend to be episodic events in nature, therefore more rarely encountered. Peak dosage rates tend to occur in conjunction with solar flare activity. According to the FAA, solar peak energies occur much lower in the atmosphere than galactic peak energies, solar cosmic radiation dosage rates are negligible at latitudes close to the geomagnetic equator. Additionally, the Earth gains partial protection from the Van Allen Belts surrounding our atmosphere.

According to studies completed by NASA, one particular polar aircraft flight in 2003, which occurred during a large solar storm, produced 12% of the aircrew's annual radiation exposure limit on that one flight segment.

FAA Civil Aerospace Medical Institute (CAMI) developed the Solar Radiation Alert System to provide professional aviators with data concerning those times when solar disturbances are beginning on the Sun which may lead to high-dose rates of ionizing radiation in the Earth's atmosphere. If pilots take advantage of this information, they may opt to fly at lower altitudes in high-latitude areas of concern, therefore significantly reducing inflight radiation exposures (FAA, In-Flight Radiation Exposure, 2014).

Occupational Radiation Injuries

The major singular threat to aviators regarding exposure to increased radiation is the potential of various types of cancer. According to the FAA, estimates of harm or injury due to radiation exposure normally occur at higher doses and dose rates than predicted for air travel. However, any exposure to UV and ionizing radiation may result in damage to cells, DNA, and genetic damage to future generations. Flying while pregnant may induce fetal cancer risks, or potential genetic damage to offspring.

Let us now examine the relationship between atmospheric radiation exposure and carcinogenesis.

Exposure to radiation promotes *free-radical* formation, which means atoms or molecules have lost atomic orbital electrons, creating an electron imbalance or instability. This condition leads many free radicals to become unstable and highly reactive with other cellular structures. They may either donate or remove an electron from another molecule, effectively becoming either an oxidant or reductant.

An *antioxidant* is a donator of electrons, thus creating a balance in free radicals. A balance between free radicals and antioxidants is considered a necessity for proper physiological function. If this balance is not favorable, free radicals may overwhelm a body's ability to regulate them properly. The initiation of this condition leads to *oxidative stress* in the body, which has been linked to the promotion and progression of cancer (Lobo, 2010). Studies have indicated career aviators may experience an increase in fatal cancer risk by .5%.

According to Dr. Patrick Veillette, research conducted by Dr. Adrian Chorley, the original optometrist principal with Britain's Civil Aviation Authority, showed that between 2008 and 2015 long-wave ultraviolet A (UVA) proved to be the most harmful to pilots' eyes because a higher percentage of UVA penetrates the cockpit. Dr. Chorley noted "there is good evidence that long-term exposure to solar radiation, especially the ultraviolet and blue light components, is a risk factor for cataracts and, to a lesser extent, age-related degeneration of the retina."

Blue light is a short wavelength that progressively destroys light-detecting cells in the eyes, contributing to age-related macular degeneration, which is a leading cause of blindness. The hazard of bright sunlight and blue light increases with altitude (Veillette, 2020).

FAA Radiation Exposure Recommendations

The FAA's radiation exposure recommendations are the same as those limits recommended by the International Commission of Radiological Protection (ICRP).

The FAA's recommended occupational exposure limit for aviators regarding ionizing radiation is a five-year average effective dose of 20 mSv per year. No more than 50 mSv-worth of exposure should occur in a single year. This would equate to a total acceptable exposure amount of 100 mSv exposure every five years.

Radiation exposure due to a medical or dental procedure is not subject to recommended limits. It should be noted these limits are not thresholds beyond which the dose is intolerable; rather, these are upper limits of acceptability. These limits are based on accepted current risk coefficients and the health risks associated with exposure do not exceed those of what is normally considered a safe (FAA, In-Flight Radiation Exposure, 2014).

Fetal Radiation Exposure

The FAA contends pregnant woman, along with other medical and personal health concerns, should consider limiting the ionizing radiation exposure of their fetus. For pregnant crewmembers, the FAA recommends expectant mothers limit ionizing radiation exposure to no more than 1 mSv total, with no more than 0.5 mSv in any given month (Friedberg, 2016).

Examples of Exposure

The following chart depicts the actual measured ionizing radiation exposure rates for typical airline flights:

Route	Flight Level	Flight Time	mSv Exposure
SEA-POR	FL210	0.6	0.00017
STL-TUL	FL350	1.1	0.00171
JFK-ORD	FL390	2.3	0.00892
ORD-SFO	FL390	4.3	0.0194
JFK-TOK	FL430	12.5	0.0754

(Friedberg, 2016)

To determine the hourly rate of radiation exposure, divide the mSv exposure amount by flight segment hours. Using JFK-ORD, for example, the total flight segment exposure rate is 0.00892 divided by 2.3 hours = 0.0039 mSv per hour.

Remember, the FAA limit for radiation exposure is 100 mSv over five years. If a pilot were to fly the JFK-ORD route for 25 years, flying 700 hours per year, they would be exposed to 700 hours/year times 0.0039 mSv/hour = 68 mSv over 25 years, which certainly falls into the acceptable category according to the FAA.

For the pilot in the above mentioned scenario, on the surface the risk of increased ionizing radiation appears relatively small. However, according to the FAA this pilot now has a risk of one out of 360 to contract a fatal, radiation-induced cancer. For the general population base, normal risk equates to one out of 13,000, with approximately 23% of all deaths resulting from cancer.

As mentioned previously, less radiation will be received on flights close to the equator because of the greater amount of radiation shielding provided by the Earth's magnetic field. Predictably, flight segments spending less time in the air or lower-latitude routes will decrease the amount of potential ionizing radiation exposure levels.

Decreasing Radiation Risk in Aviation

Although flying does have an inherent risk of increased radiation exposure, several mitigation strategies recommended by the FAA may be employed to minimize the potential for damage:

- **Monitor solar radiation alerts**
- **Minimize time of exposure**
- **Decrease altitudes**
- **Fly at more central latitudes**

-   **Use of personal protection**

Monitoring solar radiation alerts, which are transmitted worldwide to subscribers of the NOAA's Weather Wire Service, allows aviators to be advised of periods of severe solar disturbances. Such periods account for excessive amounts of ionizing radiation to be present in the atmosphere. The NOAA sends messages advising aviators on estimations of radiation levels at altitudes from FL200 to FL800 for specified latitudes, and recommended maximum flight altitudes at these latitudes. Proper response to these alerts may significantly reduce exposure levels.

Minimizing time of exposure and *decreasing altitudes* equals reducing aviator radiation exposure levels, as well as flying at lower altitudes provides more atmospheric protection for the occupants.

Flying at more central latitudes provides the lowest possible radiation dosage rates due to the thickness, thus shielding effect, of the Troposphere near equatorial flight routes. This advantageous shielding effect gradually reduces to near-zero as aviators fly closer to the poles.

Use of personal protection includes wearing the proper protective eye-wear at altitude and anytime the eyes are exposed to UVA light. Sunglasses should block at least 99% of solar UV radiation below 400 nanometers, with wrap-around sunglasses being most effective at blocking UVA rays from the sides of the face. Sunglasses should not have dark tints providing less than 8% transmittance, and should not contain tints which distort color vision, as color perception is important for pilots.

Other personal protective measures include skin protection, such as wearing long-sleeved shirts or using high-SPF sunscreen when in the cockpit inflight.

Summary

Aviators may not definitively exclude illness or cellular damage from radiation exposure as an occupational hazard; however, science has yet to prove a particular disease or abnormality can be directly linked to these exposures. Uncertainty still exists in the dose-effect relationships established by the national and international organizations tasked with radiation dosage evaluations. Reasonable care should employed by aviation professionals to minimize their exposure to the potentially harmful effects of radiation exposures, with pregnant crewmembers of particular concern.

Conclusion

Noise, vibration, and radiation may greatly impact the ability of the pilot to maximize their performance on the flight deck. Learning to attenuate these effects early in an aviator's career will enable the aviator to more effectively focus on flight skills, rather than becoming prematurely fatigued. Protecting oneself from the environmental factors of noise, vibration, and radiation serves to protect not only the aviator's well-being and effectiveness as a crewmember, but also to prolong their career. Many of the harmful effects of these issues are cumulative, becoming only worse with time.

Chapter 16 Core Competency Questions

1. What are the four characteristics of sound?
2. Decibels increase by a factor of _____ for every increase in ten units.
3. What are the three distinct sections of the ear?
4. Steady state noise is defined as:
5. Impulse noise if defined as:
6. What are the recognized "action" and "damage" dB levels of noise according to the FAA?
7. What are the first lines of defense against hearing loss in aviation?
8. What are the directions of vibration?
9. What two types of vibration affect humans?
10. How would a pilot grip controls to reduce the effects of vibration?
11. According to the CDC, how much ionizing radiation does the average person in the U.S. receive each year?
12. Above what altitude has shown to produce increased amounts of ionized radiation exposure?
13. What is the FAA's recommended occupational radiation exposure limit per year for pilots over a five year period?

17. AIRCRAFT CABIN DEPRESSURIZATION

The vast majority of commercial passenger-carrying aircraft flown for civilian transportation purposes utilize an *aircraft pressurization system* to maintain a more comfortable atmospheric pressure in the cabin for occupants. The purpose of these systems varies depending on the focus of the benefits; aircraft engines enjoy increased efficiency at high altitudes, the aircraft can fly above slower traffic, weather and turbulence providing a smoother flight and less airframe fatigue. However, the main accepted purpose for cabin pressurization is heavily based on human physiological needs and demands.

Aircraft pressurization was first conceptualized as early as the 1920's, but the Boeing Stratoliner was the first commercial passenger-carrying aircraft to use a pressurized cabin in 1938. As the technology gained greater practicality and acceptance, pressurized cabins started to enjoy widespread use with the world's first jetliner in 1949, the de Havilland Comet.

While aircraft pressurization systems are generally reliable, the fact remains the system is mechanical in nature, and no mechanical system is fail-proof. Many sub-systems exist in an aircraft pressurization system, which means any number of factors may cause a loss of pressurization. When the pressurization system is functioning properly, aircraft occupants enjoy a relatively comfortable environment to travel in. The main problem comes when the system unexpectedly fails, exposing aircraft occupant to the potentially extreme hostility of high altitudes.

In this chapter, we will discuss:

1. Actual industry risk
2. Aircraft pressurization systems overview
3. Types of aircraft pressurization systems
4. Methods of pressurization – pressurization schedules
5. The positive aspects of pressurization
6. The negative aspects of pressurization
7. Loss of pressurization
8. Types of decompressions and emergency procedures
9. Explosive decompressions
10. Aircraft decompression incidents
11. Decompression prevention

17.1 ACTUAL INDUSTRY RISK

One of the fundamental misconceptions of professional pilots is the belief pressurization systems will not fail, or it will never happen to them. While aircraft decompression events are somewhat rare compared to the number of global flight hours accumulated, the fact is aircraft pressurization systems can and will fail without warning.

One factor contributing to a lack of awareness are systemic differences in how decompressions are tracked, which may lead to miscalculations in how many decompressions truly occur. One agency may only track rapid decompressions, a second agency may only track decompressions requiring a diversion, whereas a third agency may track any loss of pressurization, all leading to conflicting data. These decompression events may only be tracked in commercial aircraft as well, and not cargo, corporate, or personal aircraft as many of these decompression incidents are not properly reported or reported at all. This, in turn, may lead many professional pilots to a state of complacency.

In compiling all relevant data which can be retrieved from FAA, NASA, and independent university research, passenger-carrying aircraft decompressions occur approximately once every two-to-three days globally. Knowing this, it would be safe to assume most pilots will not experience a life-threatening decompression event in their career, but some pilots certainly will.

The question to answer is which pilots will experience such as event? Having personally trained 1,000s of professional military and civilian pilots, this author's experience is if a professional pilot flies for at least 20 years, the vast majority will either know a pilot who has experienced a decompression, or will experience one themselves.

17.2 AIRCRAFT PRESSURIZATION SYSTEMS OVERVIEW

Current commercial airliners have systems to manage the flow of ambient air entering the fuselage, and then venting excess air back out of the airtight fuselage. These systems are known as *environmental control systems (ECS)*. The purpose of the ECS is to allow the aircraft to fly at high altitudes, while maintaining an environment hospitable to humans in the aircraft interior. Typically, the main cabin and cargo holds are contained in the pressurized portion of the vessel.

Purpose of Pressurization Systems

The purpose of a pressurized aircraft cabin is to allow the occupants to fly at altitudes which would normally be physiologically hazardous, yet in relative safety and comfort. With commercial aircraft cabins pressurized to 8,000 feet or below, the occupants will minimize the stresses of trapped gas and fatigue due to extreme altitude exposure, but *primarily* to protect the occupants from the potentially detrimental effects of hypoxia and decompression sickness.

As we know, *minimizing* the physiological effects of trapped and evolved gas, hypoxia, and fatigue does not mean *eliminate* those issues. All of the aforementioned physiological problems may still manifest themselves in individuals, but not theoretically to the degree one would be exposed to flying at the ambient altitude of the aircraft.

17.3 TYPES OF AIRCRAFT PRESSURIZATION SYSTEMS

Two types of aircraft pressurization systems exist: those systems designed for flight outside the Earth's atmosphere, and those systems designed for aircraft flying well within the Earth's atmosphere.

Sealed Cabins

For aircraft, or more appropriately spacecraft, flying outside the Earth's atmosphere, the pressurization system used is called a *sealed cabin*. Sealed cabins maintain a given pressure differential and oxygen concentration in the near-vacuum of space by carrying their own supply of gases on the vessel, as a near-vacuum would not allow replenishment of the pressurization system. These gases must be regulated in proper proportions to provide the necessary atmospheric pressure and gaseous environment for the occupants to thrive.

According to NASA, the now-defunct space shuttle pressurization system was able to maintain a 14.7 (Sea Level) cabin pressure, plus or minus 0.02 psi, and maintained an average 80% nitrogen and 20% oxygen environment in the cabin.

The space shuttle pressurization system consisted of two oxygen systems and two gaseous nitrogen systems. The two oxygen systems were supplied by the *power reactant storage and distribution* (PRSD) oxygen system, which was the same source that supplied oxygen to the orbiter fuel cell power plants. The PRSD cryogenic supercritical oxygen storage system was controlled by electrical heaters within the tanks and supplied the oxygen to the *environmental control and life support system* (ECLSS) pressurization control system at a pressure of 835 to 852 psi in a gaseous state. The gaseous nitrogen supply system consisted of two systems with two gaseous nitrogen tanks for each system. The nitrogen storage tanks were serviced to a nominal pressure of 2,964 psi at 80° F. It would maintain the crew cabin at eight psi with oxygen partial pressure at two psi. For normal on-orbit operations one oxygen and nitrogen supply system were used. For launch and entry both oxygen and nitrogen supply systems were used (NASA, 2020). These systems also need to effectively eliminate CO_2 and trace contaminants.

Pressurized Cabins

Pressurized cabins use compressed ambient air to provide the higher atmospheric pressure requirements of standard air transport aircraft. In most aircraft, ambient air is ingested through the engines, with *bleed air* being extracted from the compressor stage of the gas-fed turbine engine. With the air being compressed prior to combustion, this will theoretically ensure no contamination of cabin air occurs. A portion of the compressed bleed air is cooled via a *heat exchanger* and *air cycle machine* known as a *pressurization and air conditioning (PAC) System*, then pumped into the cabin at a controlled rate. The ECS routes some the air through HEPA filters to filter contaminants, while the rest is directed to outflow valves, which are programmed and calibrated to maintain a desired atmospheric pressure (*cabin altitude*) in the aircraft cabin. The difference between the exterior altitude of the aircraft and the cabin altitude is known as the *pressure differential*. Typically, pressure differential values between pressurized aircraft range from 7.8 psi to 9.4 psi. The SyberJet SJ30 Light Business Jet can maintain a pressure differential of 12 psi, enabling a flight altitude of FL410 while maintaining a Sea Level cabin pressure.

For most commercial aircraft applications, at least two engines will provide compressed bleed air to maintain an acceptable level of mechanical redundancy. To supply the aircraft with compressed air on the ground prior to engine start, most commercial aircraft utilize an *auxiliary power unit (APU)*, which may also be used in emergencies. Further system redundancy is provided with duplicate electronic controllers, combined with a manual back-up control system.

The possibility of contamination by routing air through aircraft engines is an ever-present possibility. As a result of this, some aircraft utilize autonomous electric compressors to provide pressurization requirements, such as the Boeing 787. Whereas the autonomous compressors require significant re-engineering energy transfer as well electrical load on the engines, these systems do theoretically reduce the danger of engine-produced chemical contamination of the cabin via the ECS. As in many other cases, autonomous compressors may *reduce* the danger, but still allow certain contaminating chemicals into the cabin through a variety of means.

The factor determining the maximum pressure differential an aircraft can maintain is the structural limits of the aircraft, combined with the aircraft's maximum cruise altitude determined by the ability to maintain a cabin altitude at 8,000 feet or below for the occupants.

Aircraft *outflow valves* ensure air entering the cabin comes in quicker than it exits the cabin, thereby creating a higher-pressure environment in the cabin. Outflow valves ensure the fuselage does not become over-pressurized, and fresh air is continually being routed through the cabin at all times.

The rate at which the aircraft vents off excess air is controlled by the *cabin pressure regulator*. The cabin pressure regulator can increase or decrease pressure in the cabin, or be programmed to maintain either a constant cabin altitude or constant pressure differential as capable or necessary.

The outflow valves may also act as a relief valve to avoid over-pressurization; act as a vacuum relief valve to allow air into the cabin in the event exterior atmospheric pressure exceeds cabin pressure; or act as a dump valve allowing the pilots to manually release air from the cabin in the event of contamination (FAA, Introduction to Aviation Physiology, 2020).

As we can see, many components such as seals, clamps, ducting, metal, glass, and mechanized or electronic systems work in unison allow the pressurization system to function properly. Failure of any of those components may result in a loss of pressurization.

17.4 METHODS OF PRESSURIZATION – PRESSURIZATION SCHEDULES

Aircraft cabin altitudes may be controlled using two different methods of pressurizing aircraft cabins:

- Isobaric control
- Isobaric differential

Isobaric control is designed to maintain a stable cabin altitude despite the altitude of the aircraft. The crew will select the desired cabin altitude, which the cabin pressure regulator maintains by stabilizing the cabin at the specific atmospheric pressure necessary.

Isobaric differential is designed to control the cabin altitude using a constant pressure differential between the ambient atmospheric pressure of the aircraft versus the internal atmospheric pressure of the cabin. With this option, the cabin altitude will fluctuate with variations of aircraft altitude.

When an aircraft is set to the isobaric control mode under normal operating conditions, the pressurization system will maintain the specified cabin altitude until the maximum pressure differential (Delta P) is reached. If the aircraft were to continue to gain altitude, the pressurization mode would automatically switch to isobaric differential mode, maintaining the maximum differential capability of the airframe, causing an increase in cabin altitude.

The ascent and descent rates for the cabin can be controlled autonomously, either automatically or manually, from the actual ascent and descent rate of the aircraft. Typical cabin ascent and descent rates in commercial aircraft are controlled to 300 to 500 fpm. FAA research indicates cabin descent rates in excess of 600 fpm result in increased ear and sinus difficulties for passengers.

17.5 POSITIVE ASPECTS OF PRESSURIZATION

With an aircraft cabin pressurized to lower altitudes, the dangers of high-altitude flight are largely mitigated. Most commercial aircraft can fly at altitudes up to FL400, with corporate aircraft reaching up to FL510, with cabin altitudes maintained at a relatively comfortable 4,000 feet to 8,000 feet. With aircraft cabins maintained at these physiologically-friendly altitudes, a number of benefits may be realized:

- Oxygen mask use is minimized
- Hypoxia problems are minimized
- DCS risk is minimized
- Trapped gas problems are minimized
- Fatigue issues are minimized
- Less noise and vibration
- Temperature, ventilation and humidity is better controlled
- Freedom to move around the cabin

Oxygen mask use is minimized, but not completely eliminated. Regulatory wearing of the oxygen mask may still be required, depending on the altitude and number of crewmembers in the cockpit.

Hypoxia problems are minimized, but cannot be ruled out entirely. You may recall emergency procedures may still be difficult to recall even at relatively benign altitudes as low as 5,000 feet, and other forms of hypoxia exist than simply altitude-induced hypoxia.

DCS risk is minimized, but may still be an issue if SCUBA diving immediately prior to flight, where cabin altitudes as low as 6,000 feet may still present a risk.

Trapped gas problems are minimized, especially GI Tract gas expansion. With slower descent rates, ear and sinus clearing processes are easier to maintain. However, ear, sinus, and tooth gas expansion problems may present themselves in individuals with anatomic anomalies or occupants flying with colds.

Fatigue issues are minimized but not eliminated, as aircraft occupants are not physiologically exposed to higher altitudes. You may recall even mild hypoxic hypoxia may induce more prolific episodes of fatigue.

Less noise and vibration will be noticed due to better insulation and stronger airframe structural requirements necessary for pressurized aircraft.

Temperature, ventilation and humidity is better controlled using the aircraft ECS, as a constant flow of fresh air is continuously routed through the aircraft, as well as filtered up to once every two minutes.

Freedom to move around the cabin is realized as a result of not needing to wear oxygen equipment or robust thermal protective devices.

17.6 NEGATIVE ASPECTS OF PRESSURIZATION

While pressurization systems present a plethora of advantages, several disadvantages exist as well:

- Creates additional mechanical system
- Flight through contaminated ambient air
- Inadvertent loss of pressurization
- Improper use of oxygen equipment

An aircraft pressurization system *creates additional mechanical systems* for the aircraft. As a result of this, the additional mechanical equipment will increase the weight of the aircraft, thus affecting thrust-to-weight ratio, fuel consumption, and overall performance. The additional mechanical system will also increase the aircraft cost-of-operation, as well as maintenance required.

Flight through contaminated ambient air remains a threat, albeit a low-probability threat. Any flight through air contaminated with smoke from forest fires, volcanic ash, pollution, or other airborne contamination will be ingested into the engines, and therefore the pressurization system. Some of the contaminants will be filtered out;

however, some particulates and odors have been documented to permeate the cabin air, in some cases causing ill feelings among occupants.

Inadvertent loss of pressurization remains a low-probability, yet existential threat to any pressurized aircraft. As mentioned previously, a large number of components exist in a pressurization system, all needing to work together for the pressurization system to function properly. If and when a component fails, the entire system is at risk.

Improper use of oxygen equipment may be an issue in some professional aviation sectors. Because of the low-probability nature of loss-of-pressurization incidents and accidents, many pilots, if not the vast majority, truly feel a decompression accident will never happen to them.

While most pilots may be correct in this assumption, this assumption may lead many pilots to not adhere to FAA oxygen equipment-use rules. The few pilots facing a true rapid decompression emergency will most likely be taken completely off-guard and be woefully unprepared for the potential violence and physiological threats of the event.

17.7 LOSS OF PRESSURIZATION

Knowing decompressions may occur in transport-category pressurized aircraft, we will define an aircraft decompression as *a decrease in cabin atmospheric pressure as result of damage or mechanical failure.* A total loss-of-pressurization would result in the cabin altitude equaling the ambient flight altitude of the aircraft.

Decompressions may occur to certain aircraft more than others, and at varying times and severity levels, depending on a number of factors which we will examine next.

Susceptibility to Decompression

The following factors make an aircraft increasingly prone to experiencing a decompression:

- Improper inspections and maintenance
- Age of the aircraft
- Pressurization cycles on the airframe
- Higher differentials

Improper inspections and maintenance may be implicit in a number of decompression events, as mistakes by maintenance technicians can potentially contribute to mechanical failure of pressurization systems. Stress cracks or fractures in airframes or fuselage skin may be missed or misinterpreted, bolts may be not torqued to specification, loose ducting may have been missed, outflow valves could be misadjusted or left fully open, a faulty window or door seal may be overlooked; any number of mechanical mistakes may lend themselves to decompression events.

It would be safe to assume maintenance technicians do not intentionally cause these mistakes, but all humans are prone to distraction, inattention, lack of knowledge, or a myriad of other issues that may arise in the maintenance process.

Age of the aircraft can be a factor in mechanical failure, as with any machine. Anyone with any experience with mechanical objects, be it a dishwasher, automobile, or bicycle, knows the older a mechanical device gets, the more prone to failure it becomes. Aircraft are not immune from this rule. Door and window seals can wear out, windscreens may get brittle due to heating and cooling, or compressor bearings may fail, all or which can be causal in decompression events.

Pressurization cycles on the airframe may be a major factor in metal failure, due to metal flexion. A pressurization cycle is when a given aircraft pressurizes and depressurizes in the course of a normal flight segment. If one were to closely observe a fuselage undergoing a pressurization test on the ground, a fuselage may observably expand as pressurized air is pumped into the cabin, and once the air is released from the cabin, the cabin contracts. This expansion and contraction of the cabin contributes to metal fatigue over a period of time, so a commuter aircraft flying, for example, 15 flight segments per week will predictably experience more metal flexion than an aircraft flying two overseas flight segments per week.

Higher differentials will predictably place more stress on an airframe, therefore presenting a greater likelihood for potential failure as a result of any airframe anomaly.

Factors Controlling the Rate and Time of Decompression

According to the FAA, the faster aircraft pressurization is lost, the more detrimental the decompression becomes. FAA CAMI research has shown that effective performance time (EPT) can be cut by as much as 50% or more in a rapid decompression, especially above FL300. When an aircraft is cruising at FL400 the crew literally has only seconds to take proper and effective corrective action (FAA, Federal Aviation Administration, 2020). Dr. John Ernsting's research at the Royal Air Force Institute of Aviation Medicine also indicates that the maximum safe altitude an aircraft can decompress in five seconds and have the crew remain conscious at FL480, so long as the crew is receiving at least 40% oxygen prior to the decompression. If the crew is not wearing an oxygen mask above FL380 with a five-second decompression, a strong likelihood exists the crew will go unconscious.

The following are factors which will determine the rate and severity of a decompression in any given aircraft:

- Size of the cabin
- Size of the opening
- Pressure differential
- Pressure ratio
- Altitude at the time of decompression

Size of the cabin will determine how fast the pressurized air will depart the aircraft, with all other factors being equal. The large the cabin volume, the slower the decompression; the smaller the cabin volume, the faster the decompression will occur.

Size of the opening will determine the rate of the decompression, with all other factors being equal. A large opening in the aircraft will allow the pressurized air to depart very rapidly, whereas a small opening will allow the pressurized air to depart more slowly.

Pressure differential will determine the overall severity, as well as rate, of the decompression. The higher the differential, the more force will be generated during the decompression and the faster pressurized air will vacate the cabin.

Pressure ratio will determine how fast pressurized air will depart the aircraft. In most decompression events, aircraft compressors will continue to operate, and the greater the inflow of pressurized air from the compressors, the slower the decompression will occur.

Altitude at the time of decompression will determine the speed of the decompression. When higher atmospheric pressure air in the aircraft meets the lower atmospheric pressure air outside the aircraft, the internal air from the aircraft meets with less resistance as it leaves the aircraft, profoundly speeding up the loss of the pressurized air. The ambient altitude of the aircraft will also determine the physiological effects experienced by the occupants following the decompression.

One must remember an aircraft decompression does not have to be rapid to be dangerous. Slow decompressions may be extremely difficult to detect, and depending on the pressure differential and pressure ratio, even slow decompressions may generate tremendous force as air evacuates the cabin.

Historical Causes of Decompressions

Determining the most likely issue to cause an aircraft decompression event can be difficult at best. Different types of aircraft, as well as different flight missions, face different stresses. The list of potential failures is very long, indeed.

If one imagines the potential stresses and mechanical failures which may occur in commercial, corporate, cargo, general aviation, or military aircraft, each aircraft is exposed to a different flight environment with its own unique set of circumstances, risk factors, and stressors. Many of these decompression incidents may be quite benign; however, many decompression accidents have resulted in catastrophic loss-of-life.

When examining the historical causes of aircraft decompressions, several factors rise to the top:

- Metal fatigue
- Uncontained engine failure shrapnel
- Pressurization system incorrectly programmed
- Explosions
- Bird strikes
- Window or door seal failures
- Cracked or failed windscreens and windows

Metal fatigue normally occurs with older, high-cycle aircraft. All commercial transport aircraft undergo periodic Nondestructive Inspections; a non-invasive process for inspecting the aircraft structure for stress fractures & cracks, flaws, corrosion, delamination, impact damage, dis-bonding or excessive wear. Even then, some defects cannot be detected in a timely enough fashion to prevent failure at altitude.

Uncontained engine failure shrapnel may disperse engine parts when the engine fails mid-flight, causing cabin decompressions from those parts penetrating the fuselage and creating a hole. Typically, corporate aircraft certified for flight above FL400 have engines mounted adjacent an unpressurized portion of the fuselage to prevent shrapnel penetration-caused decompressions, whereas many commercial aircraft have engines mounted adjacent the pressurized portion of the cabin.

Pressurization systems incorrectly programmed have been implicated in several high-profile decompression events, some of which resulted in over one hundred fatalities. One of the most notable cases was Helios Airline Flight 522 in 2005, in which a series of mistakes resulted in the pressurization system being set to wrong setting, resulting in hypoxic incapacitation of 122 passengers and crew and eventual impact with the ground.

Explosions may cause decompression events. Explosions may be created by faulty fuel tanks and oxygen tanks, or intentionally detonated explosive devices by terrorist activity.

Window or door seal failures, while normally benign, may cause a decompression event. Seal leaks tend to be relatively slow, but may create a lot of noise, causing consternation among passengers.

Cracked or failed windscreens or windows may not only cause a decompression, but create an intense thermal event as well. Cracked windscreens are relatively common occurrences rarely resulting in decompression, but most emergency procedures dictate reducing pressure differential and altitude to reduce stress on the damaged windscreen. However, if a window or windscreen is lost completely, the event may turn dangerous due to the windblast, thermal stress, and potential for occupants being ejected from the aircraft during the initial stages of failure.

Bird strikes mainly present a lower-altitude decompression danger; however, the highest recorded altitude for a bird-strike was FL370 in 1973 in West Africa. Even at lower altitudes, windscreen destruction due to bird strike may present a significant thermal stress event for the flight deck crew.

17.8 TYPES OF DECOMPRESSIONS AND EMERGENCY PROCEDURES

We have examined factors making aircraft susceptible to decompressions, factors controlling the rate and time of decompressions, and historical causes of decompressions. We will now examine the resulting *types of decompressions* these issues may present.

The FAA recognizes three types of specific and well-defined pressurization events:

- Slow (or gradual)
- Rapid
- Explosive

Slow decompressions result in a loss of cabin pressure in a timeframe over 10 seconds.

Rapid decompressions result in a loss of cabin pressure in a timeframe from 1 to 10 seconds.

Explosive decompressions result in a loss cabin pressure in a timeframe of less than 1 second.

As we can see, the main factor separating the three types of decompression is time. Generally speaking, the faster the decompression occurs, the more detrimental the physiological effects become; however, each type of decompression carries its own set of threats.

Slow Decompressions

Slow decompressions, although not very dramatic, tend to be the most dangerous with regards to loss-of-life. The main reason for this fact is slow decompressions can be notoriously difficult to spot. Imagine losing your aircraft's cabin pressure over a time-period of 20, 30, or 40 minutes. The loss of pressure may so insidious many crew members or passengers fail to recognize any signs the event is actually occurring. As a result of the subtle nature of these events, more fatalities have been associated with slow decompressions in technologically-advanced aircraft than any other type of decompression.

Slow Decompression Indications

In the case of slow decompression detection, aviators may miss apparently obvious signs pressurization is slowly being lost. One of main reasons for this is individual failure to detect the subtle onset of hypoxia symptoms, which in many cases aviators may misinterpret as some other, more benign, anomaly. Once hypoxia has gained a foothold with the aviator, task fixation and loss of situational awareness contribute to the lack of recognition of the signs of decompression.

In addition to recognition of personal hypoxia symptoms, an observant aviator can monitor a variety of indicators to guard against the threat of slow decompressions:

- Pressure changes on the ears
- Temperature change
- Detection of hypoxia symptoms in others
- Instrument scans
- Warning devices
- Oxygen mask activation

Pressure changes on the ears causes the characteristic "popping and clicking" sensation aviators experience upon ascent. This sensation may arguably be the most prolific alarm in alerting an aviator they are experiencing a slow decompression. The sensation begins immediately upon ascent, alerting the aviator to an unexpected change in cabin pressure before the more dangerous higher altitudes are reached. Any detection of pressure change on the ears should prompt the pilot to starting checking the aircraft ECS and cabin altimeter.

Temperature change as a result of ascent, causing an environmental cooling effect, should be another obvious prompt alerting aviators to an unexpected loss of cabin pressurization.

Detection of hypoxia symptoms in others can be an invaluable asset in the realization environmental oxygen content is being reduced, giving aviators greater advanced awareness of their own potential impairment. Observance and recognition of the subjective symptoms of hypoxia in fellow crewmembers is a skill best learned in a controlled environment such as altitude chamber training.

Instrument scans should be maintained on a regular and routine basis to afford pilots early detection capabilities of any potential pressurization anomalies. Maintaining an effective cross-check of the cabin altimeter requires frequent scans, typically at 10,000 feet during climb-out, level-off, and hourly cruise segment checks.

Warning devices such as audible and visual warnings should provide early pressurization loss detection for pilots, although cases exist where these warnings were ignored and/or not appreciated for the potential severity of the emergency. Hypoxic intellectual impairment may have contributed in those cases.

Oxygen mask activation should be another obvious sign to a pilot cabin pressure is increasing, but again this indication has been ignored, unseen, or unappreciated in particular cases.

A pilot's own body may be the most reliable alarm system on the aircraft, as physiological awareness can alert pilots to unanticipated pressurization loss and prevent catastrophic events from happening in a safe and timely fashion.

Slow Decompression Emergency Procedures

Although slow decompressions may seem benign on the surface, the fact remains slow decompressions have caused more fatalities than any other type. Should a slow decompression occur, regardless of the speed and severity level, the following *slow decompression emergency procedures* should be performed to ensure one's physiological integrity:

- **Don oxygen mask with 100% oxygen and emergency pressure**
- **Monitor rate and depth of breathing**

- **Check connections**
- **Descend to safe altitude**

Don oxygen mask with 100% oxygen and emergency pressure is always the first step in responding to a high-altitude physiological contingency, as the pilot's intellectual effectiveness is paramount. FAR regulation guidance stipulates quick-don oxygen masks should be able to be donned, sealed, and properly configured with one hand, within five seconds or less. Although the time requirement may seem like "overkill" in responding to a slow decompression, the rate of the decompression may change at any time so a timely aircrew response is still necessary.

Monitor rate and depth of breathing to avoid transitioning into hyperventilation.

Check connections to ensure continued oxygen delivery is guaranteed and electronic communications are possible.

Descend to safe altitude, which as has been discussed previously, may or may not be below 10,000' depending on current circumstances regarding weather, terrain, traffic, distance to acceptable airport, and political climate of the country the flight segment is over. The decision to continue descent should be assessed above FL180 by the flight deck crew.

Rapid Decompressions

Whereas slow decompressions may occur with few obvious indications, *rapid decompressions* create signs a traumatic event occurred which are impossible to miss. While the indications of rapid decompressions may be difficult to miss, it is entirely possible those indications may be misinterpreted or so shocking in their onset pilots lapse into startle effect and fail to respond appropriately. Any lapse in pilot response time may result in incapacitation or unconsciousness in an incredibly short period of time; therefore recognition and immediate emergency procedure execution is paramount in ensuring crew survival.

As mentioned earlier in this chapter, the faster a decompression occurs, the more detrimental physiological effects become. Hence, the importance of immediate recognition and response is paramount in successfully mitigating the physiological effects.

Based on research performed by Dr. John Ernsting of the Royal Air Force Institute of Aviation Medicine on high-altitude decompressions in 1963 (Ernsting, 1963), an extremely rapid ascent (decompression) to FL380 or above may potentially cause unconsciousness in a pilot, even while wearing an oxygen mask. As gases expand on ascent in an aviator's lungs, all residual air (thus oxygen) will be expelled on ascent, so when the aviator reaches peak altitude, they will be left with virtually no oxygen in their lungs. If the pilot had no oxygen mask on or fails to don their mask in less than five seconds, they can expect to be unconscious in five to nine seconds. The accepted effective performance times at various altitudes have no value during a rapid decompression.

Fortunately for the pilot, if an oxygen mask is on their face at the time of the decompression or within seconds following the decompression, they will recover from the unconscious episode within 10 seconds or so.

The key to effective mitigation of rapid decompressions is to not misinterpret the physical signs, understand the physiological threats, and react instinctively as opposed to intellectually. The best method for instinctual reaction is training in an altitude chamber and being exposed to an actual rapid decompression in controlled conditions. Based on USAF School of Aerospace Medicine research, many pilots not receiving this training may be momentarily incapacitated by the startle effect for up to 15-30 seconds, and not react fast enough following high altitude rapid decompressions to avoid losing consciousness.

Rapid Decompression Physical Indications

The indications of rapid decompressions are profoundly obvious for most pilots. Although rapid decompressions may occur from a variety of causal factors, phenomena commonality exists in virtually all RD events:

- Loud noise
- Flying debris
- Windblast
- Fogging
- Audible/visible alarms
- Mask deployment

Loud noise is typically described by rapid decompression-exposed aviators as the first noticeable sign. With higher differentials, the noise heard at the onset of the decompression may closely resemble an unidentified explosion. The aural shock may cause uninitiated aviators to lapse into the startle effect, and fail to react appropriately or in a timely manner.

Flying debris will be a factor in most rapid decompression events, from particles as small as dust to as large as human bodies. The faster the decompression and higher the differential, the heavier and larger the debris will be. Under the right conditions, it is entirely possible for humans sitting next to a blown-out window to get partially or totally sucked out of the opening.

Windblast may occur in the event a large orifice develops, such as losing a door, window, or large portion of the fuselage skin and pressure rapidly departs the cabin. Tests conducted by the FAA have indicated wind speeds in an aircraft cabin can approach hurricane velocities, given enough pressure differential.

After pressure equalizes in the cabin, air may enter the cabin through the same opening as the aircraft is still maintaining flight speed. This effect may cause cabin wind chills capable of causing frostbite in literally minutes at high altitudes.

Fogging, or condensation, may occur resulting from the warmer air in the cabin mixing with colder ambient air outside the aircraft. Thick fog may permeate the entire cabin, particularly in smaller airframes, whereas fog tends to develop near the floor in larger airframes.

Audible/visible alarms will activate as the cabin pressure reaches predetermined "trigger" altitudes.

Mask deployment normally occurs at cabin altitudes of approximately 14,000 feet, unless the flight crew releases the masks manually.

Physiological Effects of Rapid Decompression

Following a rapid decompression, aviators must be concerned with immediate mitigation of the event in response to the potential physiological impacts of high-altitude exposure as listed below:

- Hypoxia
- Gas expansion
- Thermal factors

Hypoxia mitigation is always an aviator's main survivability concern following high-altitude exposure, lest the aviator lapse into incapacitation in possibly seconds.

Gas expansion will be a physiological consideration dependent on the maximum cabin altitude reached. Remember, trapped gas expansion ratios range from 2:1 at FL180 to 9:1 at FL430. Now, imagine trapped GI tract gas expanding to that degree in a few seconds!

Another gas expansion factor to consider is evolved gas. In aerial transport operations, most decompression sickness (DCS) events will occur following rapid decompressions. It will be up to the Captain to identify and provide appropriate assistance to affected individuals, as described in previous chapters.

Thermal factors may be an intense stress for the flight crew. Few aviators are totally prepared for incredibly cold wind chills during normal flight operations.

Physical Hazards of Rapid Decompression

The physical indications of rapid decompressions may not only startle the flight crew and create a physiological emergency, but may also provide immediate harmful physical hazards as listed below:

- Dust/condensation
- Windblast
- Windblast noise
- Flying debris
- Gas expansion
- Disorientation

Dust/condensation may cause visual impairment. Any dust on the aircraft capable of becoming airborne may swirl around the cabin with force, potentially blinding pilots. Condensation may develop instantaneously with the loss of cabin pressure with a density making a pilot's ability to see in the cockpit difficult-to-impossible.

Windblast from a missing door or windscreen may create an environment in the aircraft conducive to extreme thermal stress or frostbite in minutes. Thermal stress may potentially be induced in low-altitude settings with an ill-timed bird-strike on the windscreen.

Windblast noise may make crew or ATC communication extremely difficult-to-impossible, even with headsets.

Flying debris caused by the windblast or air leaving the cabin at near-hurricane forces may cause impact trauma from larger or heavier objects.

Gas expansion resulting from altitudes in excess of FL300 may cause pain in various body cavities. Gas expansion in the GI tract may cause crippling pain, severe tooth pain may develop, or gas in the middle ear may expand so rapidly ear pain could develop, or in extreme cases, perforate an ear drum.

Disorientation may develop from the suddenness and intensity of the event. This may cause pilots to lapse into the startle effect, potentially delaying a proper and timely response.

Physical Hazard Mitigation

The above-listed hazards should be planned for and mitigation strategies developed for flight crews. Although the probability of such a severe event may be low, failure to respond properly will be life-threatening should a rapid decompression event ever occur. The following are measures which may be employed by flight crews to assist mitigating each hazard:

Dust/condensation hazards may be mitigated through a thorough knowledge of emergency procedures and possessing the ability to perform those procedures by feel as opposed to visually.

Windblast and *thermal stress* may be reduced to a survivable level through the use of available equipment, such as smoke goggles to protect vision and the use of gloves to protect and maintain physical dexterity in the hands. The wearing of an insulated vest, if available, may assist in maintaining thoracic body core temperatures, as could chemical heat packs placed in the armpits and crotch. The warmer the blood leaving the heart, the more dexterity is maintained.

Windblast noise negating verbal communication may be mitigated through the use of pre-planned non-verbal emergency communication procedures, such as hand signals. Even a few standardized, rudimentary hand-signals indicating ascent, descent, or altitude increments can be useful.

Flying debris, while difficult to predict, may be reduced by conscious efforts to minimize clutter or loose objects on the flight deck, such as cell phones, laptops, electronic tablets, lunch boxes, flight bags, coffee cups, or other objects. All potential projectiles should be securely stowed.

Gas expansion in the GI tract may be managed through careful selection of preflight meals by avoiding meals known to produce copious amounts of intestinal gas. Tooth pain can only be mitigated by a rapid descent. If a middle ear fails to clear on ascent, attempt to clear it by yawning or swallowing.

Disorientation from shock may be mitigated through training. By experiencing a rapid decompression in an altitude chamber, aviators will experience the physical and physiological effects of rapid decompressions to build the muscle memory necessary to react <u>instinctively</u>.

Rapid Decompression Emergency Procedures

Above and beyond the preemptive measures one should employ to prepare for the physical hazards of high-altitude rapid decompressions, the following *rapid decompression emergency procedures* must be immediately initiated to ensure aircrew survival:

- **Get on 100% oxygen with emergency pressure, or descend**
- **Return rate and depth of breathing to normal**
- **Check oxygen equipment connects (if applicable)**
- **Descend below 10,000 feet if possible**
    - **Assess event prior to FL180 to ensure descent to 10,000 feet is currently feasible**

Failure to initiate these procedures immediately may result in pilot incapacitation. Under the worst-case scenario, an effective performance time of five seconds must be anticipated and appropriate measures employed. Responding to rapid decompressions should be practiced so as to elicit an instinctive (muscle-memory) response as opposed to an intellectual response.

Emergency Procedure Timeline

We will break down the rapid decompression emergency procedures into an effective timeline guide to maximize procedural effectiveness, starting from the moment of decompression:

- **Don oxygen mask – five seconds**
- **Initiate emergency descent – 10 seconds**
- **Attempt to determine structural integrity – 15 seconds**
- **Don personal thermal protection – 30 seconds**
- **Descent to FL250 – three minutes**
- **Check passengers – as possible**

Don oxygen mask and related activities (100% oxygen, emergency pressure, monitor breathing rate, check connections) should take place in the first five seconds to maintain intellectual integrity.

Initiate emergency descent should be accomplished within the first 10 seconds (FAA regulation stipulates an emergency descent should occur five seconds after mask donning).

Certain corporate aircraft models have the automated ability to begin an emergency descent to 15,000 feet following a detected decompression. This does not absolve pilots of those aircraft from donning an oxygen mask on time, as lack of adequate oxygen intake may result in pilot unconsciousness. There is no guarantee an unconscious pilot will regain consciousness at 15,000 feet after passing out at higher altitudes, which still creates an unacceptable risk.

Attempt to determine structural integrity within the first 15 seconds, as metal failure may have caused the decompression event. In the case of metal failure, a rapid descent may not be in the best interest of aircraft occupants.

Don personal thermal protection within the first 30 seconds, if thermal protection is available. Maintaining body heat is much more effective in extreme cold environments, as opposed to attempting to regain body heat.

Descent to FL250 within three minutes is recommended by the FAA to prevent medical damage to passengers. Continuing descent to 10,000 feet requires assessments of the current situation, such as weather, terrain, etc.

Check passengers as soon as practical to determine any immediate medical needs.

17.9 EXPLOSIVE DECOMPRESSIONS

According to the FAA, *explosive decompressions* are decompression events in which a total loss cabin pressurization occurs in less than a second with a 10 psi or greater pressure differential. A 10 psi pressure differential is roughly the equivalent of flight at an ambient altitude of FL420, while sustaining a cabin altitude of approximately 4,000 feet.

Explosive decompressions are physiologically characterized by the fact air cannot escape the alveoli in the lungs fast enough, resulting in *pulmonary barotrauma*. Pulmonary barotrauma means as air expands in the lungs, particularly in the alveoli, gas does not exit the lungs through the bronchioles, bronchi, or trachea effectively, and alveolar and other lung tissue ruptures as gas escapes though it.

Although many aircraft decompressions over the years have been described as "explosive" by the media, the reality is not many aircraft decompressions, if any, have met the explosive decompression criteria. For an aircraft to sustain the amount of pressure loss necessary in less than a second, massive damage to the aircraft would almost certainly need to occur, at which point the very airworthiness of the aircraft would be in question. Most often, explosive decompression occur in spacecraft or deep sea exploration devices.

17.10 AIRCRAFT DECOMPRESSION INCIDENTS

We will now examine real-life decompression incidents to gain a more thorough understanding of the potential causes of decompressions, as well as how flight crew actions following the emergency.

Incident Review – September 2015: A Boeing 737-800 was enroute at FL350 west-bound over Senegal in Africa at 1812 hours local time. Unknown to the 737 crew, a HS-125 air ambulance jet flying a medical transport mission was east-bound at FL350 along the same airway, flying an opposing flight path with the 737. The 737 pilots felt a momentary disturbance as if they had encountered clear air turbulence, after which they felt nothing further.

The HS-125 was carrying a doctor, two nurses, a patient, and three crewmembers. While their aircraft was flying east, the winglet on the right side of the 737 contacted their fuselage, apparently ripping a hole in the HS-125 fuselage and causing a rapid depressurization. The HS-125 continued flight on autopilot, and overflew Dakar at 1908 local time and FL350. The aircraft disappeared over the Atlantic, with no crew contact and likely eventually running out of fuel and crashing into the ocean.

Analysis: The two aircraft apparently collided at 1813 local time, approximately 80 miles east of Tambecounda, Senegal at FL350 flying in opposite directions. The remote area had no ATC radar coverage. The collision sheared off the top three feet of the 737's right winglet, registering on the FDR as a brief oscillation with uncommanded yaw, immediately corrected by the autopilot. The HS-125 was assigned a flight altitude of FL340. Both aircraft were equipped with TCAS, although no resolution advisory was ever issued.

Investigators believe the air ambulance was struck on the fuselage, causing a rapid decompression, leading to crew incapacitation. The aircraft continued flight for an additional 55 minutes with no crew response, eventually crashing into the ocean. The aircraft had been recently written up for discrepancies for faulty altimeters and transponder, possibly due to a faulty pitot-static system.

Conclusion: The HS-125 obviously had a mechanical fault, preventing it from being "seen" by the 737's TCAS. The HS-125's instrument failure may have corrupted the information fed to the TCAS and transponder.

This, in itself, does not absolve either set of pilots from using an effective inflight visual scan. The HS-125 crew could have potentially saved themselves through a proper response to the rapid decompression as well.

Incident Review – May 2016: A Cessna Citation I was enroute near Texarkana, TX at FL430 with one pilot and three passengers onboard. The aircraft lost cabin pressurization, and the pilot lost consciousness.

The pilot regained consciousness around 7,000 feet mean sea level (MSL), subsequently realizing the aircraft was in an uncontrolled descent. The pilot regained control, over-stressing the airframe in the process, and was able to fly to a nearby airport and land safely.

Analysis: Investigators found the primary pressurization duct into the cabin was separated from its connection to the water separator, causing the aircraft to rapidly depressurize. In the process of recovering from the uncontrolled descent, the aircraft sustained substantial damage to both wings due to excessive wing loading during the descent and subsequent recovery.

After an investigation by the NTSB and FAA, investigators concluded the pilot failed to utilize their oxygen mask as required for Part 91 operations in pressurized aircraft above FL350 with only one pilot in the cockpit. The pilot was subjected to disciplinary action from the FAA.

Conclusion: Failure to wear the oxygen mask as required nearly cost the four aircraft occupants their lives. Beyond failure to wear the oxygen mask, the pilot failed to recognize the decompression or properly respond the decompression event. Properly wearing the mask or responding to the event would have prevented this event.

Incident Review – April 2017: A Boeing 767-300 was enroute from Edmonton, Alberta to Kahului, HI at FL380 with 218 passengers and crew onboard. While over the Pacific Ocean 710 nm out of Kahului, the right hand windscreen shattered and the crew received a "R FWD WINDOW" EICAS message. The aircraft pressurization system was still operational, but could be compromised with a complete windscreen blowout. The crew, concerned about the damage, consulted with their Operations Center to calculate fuel burn to their destination.

The crew ultimately requested a descent to 14,000 feet for the remainder of the flight, and the aircraft landed safely at Kahului about 2:15 hours later.

Analysis: The aircraft, having shattered the windscreen, was in compromised state which may have led to a precarious position had the aircraft experienced a decompression.

Conclusion: While the event ended successfully, had the aircraft suffered a decompression the crew may have been placed in the difficult position of choosing

371

between adequate fuel to reach land or adequate oxygen to keep passengers completely safe. Pilots should always ensure their oxygen supply is sufficiently stocked with enough oxygen to cover any contingencies such as this event.

Incident Review – February 2017: An Airbus A340-600 was enroute from London, England to New York, NY at FL400. Southwest of Halifax, NS the crew received an "EXCESS CABIN ALT" warning. The crew checked the ECS Pressurization Displays, which presented no anomalies, and the crew elected to stay at altitude.

A short time later, the pilots and other crew members started getting symptoms of hypoxia, and the pilots donned their oxygen masks and initiated a descent. When the aircraft reached FL260, the cabin pressure apparently stabilized. 30 minutes later, the warning activated again with the pressurization displays still showing normal cabin pressure, so the crew descended to 11,000 feet for the remainder of the flight.

Analysis: On subsequent inspection of the aircraft, investigators found the warning system was functioning normally; however, the ECS pressurization displays were displaying erroneous information.

Conclusion: The crew received ambiguous information from their aircraft as the warning system was informing the crew of a cabin altitude issue while the ECS pressurization displays were reading normally. Unfortunately, the crew believed the erroneous source of information and started getting hypoxic. Fortunately, the pilots recognized their hypoxia symptoms and were able to safely descend.

Incident Review – April 2018: A Boeing 737-700 was enroute at FL320 near Philadelphia, PA with 148 passengers and crew onboard. The number one engine seized and suffered an uncontained engine failure, sending debris into the aircraft fuselage. Shrapnel impacted a passenger window, shattering it and causing a complete window failure. Most passengers and cabin crew responded by donning oxygen masks. The flight deck crew donned their oxygen masks with the captain initiating an emergency descent.

As the window departed the aircraft, the passenger immediately adjacent to the window was partially sucked out of the window hole. Other passengers and flight attendants immediately tried pulling the passenger back into the aircraft cabin, and were eventually successful; however, the passenger had already sustained fatal injuries. The aircraft was able to land without further incident.

Analysis: Investigators found the uncontained engine failure threw shrapnel into the fuselage, destroying the passenger window and causing it to completely fail. While the other passengers and crew tried valiantly to try to save the passenger sucked out the window, they were unable to save the affected passenger's life.

Conclusion: The flight crew did everything they could to mitigate this situation, following all prescribed emergency procedures.

Incident Review – May 2018: An Airbus A319-100 was enroute from Chongqing to Lhasa, China at FL320 over mountainous terrain and stormy weather. The first officer's (FO) windscreen cracked, then separated, from the aircraft, causing an uncontrolled rapid decompression. As the windscreen was separating, glass shards hit and injured the FO, damaged the flight mode control unit panel containing the autopilot controls, and partially sucked the FO out of the opening created by the missing windscreen.

The captain struggled to maintain control of the aircraft, while a flight attendant assisted the FO and pulled him back inside the cockpit. The FO never lost consciousness, and was able to use the transponder to squawk 7700. The captain, unable to communicate with ATC because of the windblast noise in the cockpit, initiated a descent to FL235, turned the aircraft to avoid mountains, and completed a descent to 9,000 feet.

Analysis: Investigators determined the root cause of the accident to be damage to the right-side windscreen seal as a result of moisture, eventually leading the damage to the windscreen layers, culminating in the windscreen bursting inflight. The FO sustained facial abrasions, minor eye injuries and a sprained wrist, while the flight attendant suffered from a sprained waist. The captain reportedly had no injuries, and was not able to don an oxygen mask during the entire descent. According to Chinese authorities, no crew member suffered from hypoxia or frostbite during the event.

Conclusion: The flight crew performed amazingly well during an incredible accident. Given the severity of the circumstances, it is implausible to believe the captain did not get hypoxic with no oxygen mask on, and no one suffered thermal injuries given the fact a windscreen was missing at high altitude. Squawking 7700 was essential, as verbal communication was impossible.

Incident Review – May 2019: A Citation 560 Encore flown as a single pilot flight was enroute at FL390 from St. Louis, MO to Fort Lauderdale, FL. Approximately one hour before reaching its destination, ATC communication was lost, and the aircraft overflew the destination. USAF fighters were dispatched to intercept the aircraft, but did not reach the aircraft until shortly before it went down in the Atlantic Ocean 300 miles East of Fort Lauderdale.

Analysis: The aircraft has yet to be recovered. Investigators assume the aircraft experienced a decompression, the pilot got hypoxic and became incapacitated, and the aircraft ran out of fuel.

Conclusion: Once again, assuming the pilot suffered from hypoxic hypoxia, the insidious symptoms of hypoxia were not recognized in time. The aircraft was equipped with oxygen equipment capable of sustaining cognitive function at that altitude and was either not used properly or at all.

17.11 AIRCRAFT DECOMPRESSION PREVENTION

Aircrews can take preventative measures to ensure they are not caught unaware by decompression events. The following are recognized steps for prevention of problems associated with cabin depressurizations:

- Address pressurization issues immediately
- Preflight oxygen equipment
- Cross-check cabin pressure frequently
- Observe the other pilot
- When checking pressurization issues, don oxygen mask first

Address pressurization issues immediately, thoroughly, and by-the-book. Do not let pressurization issues linger, as they may present themselves at the worst-possible time during the flight segment.

Preflight oxygen equipment each and every time you sit in the flight deck seat to fly. There is no guarantee anyone previously checked the oxygen equipment (or checked it correctly), just as there will never be a guarantee you will never need to use it.

Cross-check cabin pressure frequently at regular intervals during the flight segment. It is suggested pilots check the cabin pressurization at 10,000 feet during climb-out, at level-off, and at least once an hour in cruise flight. A loss-of-pressurization event normally will not alert the flight crew prior to when it decides to fail.

Observe the other pilot, as well as other crewmembers or passengers, for signs of intellectual impairment. Chances are good if other occupants are showing signs of impairment, you will not be far behind.

When checking pressurization issues, don oxygen mask first to ensure you are protected in the event of an unanticipated pressurization failure. Many serious incidents have occurred when pilots start troubleshooting pressurization issues, unintentionally causing a rapid loss of pressurization in the process.

Conclusion

Although decompressions are relatively rare events, keep in mind they occur often enough to be wary of the possibility. Decompressions may provide little warning, and may occur at almost imperceptible speeds or with incredible violence. One must be continuously vigilant to the signs and symptoms of decompressions, and constantly be prepared to react instinctively.

A pilot's greatest threats are hypoxia, decompression sickness (DCS), and thermal stresses, and one's most immediate need is 100% oxygen and descending the aircraft without delay.

Chapter 17 Core Competency Questions

1. What is the primary purpose of pressurization?
2. What are the two types of pressurization systems?
3. What are the two pressurized cabin schedules?
4. True or false – a pilot never has to wear an oxygen mask if the cabin is pressurized?
5. What physiological issues are minimized when using pressurization?
6. What makes an aircraft susceptible to decompressions?
7. What are the three types of decompressions?
8. Which type of decompression has caused the most fatalities in recent history?
9. What is arguably the most reliable "alarm" for slow decompressions?
10. What is normally the most prolific sign of rapid decompressions?
11. What is a pilot's most immediate need following a decompression?
12. According to FAA regulations, a quick-don oxygen mask should be able to be donned, sealed and properly configured with one hand in how many seconds?

18. FATIGUE IN AVIATION OPERATIONS

Fatigue is a ubiquitous fixture of everyday life; experienced by virtually everyone at some point. Normally, being fatigued presents a minor inconvenience with little-to-no consequence for most people. However, fatigue in aviation operations is one of preeminent threats to the health and well-being of everyone onboard the aircraft. Fatigue is not only manifested when a pilot falls asleep in the cockpit, but more importantly during the critical decision-making processes of the takeoff and landing phases of flight. Additionally, fatigue in a pilot may exacerbate virtually every other physical or physiological issue the pilot may experience. Making matters worse, fatigue does not exhibit definitive biomarkers such as developing rashes, headaches, cramps or anything else physically identifiable to individuals.

Many airlines and other flight operations operate with a 24-hour per day, seven-day per week schedule, forcing humans in such operations to confront significant physiological and physical challenges with regards to sleep and alertness. The prospects of flying odd hours, encountering various types of weather, personality conflicts on the flight deck, layovers, living out a suitcase, sleeping in hotels, eating on the road, and the rest which goes with professional aviation may wear on some individuals. Reported fatigue-related events include procedural errors, unstable approaches, lining up with the wrong runway, landing or taking off without clearances, and generally poor decision-making (FAA, Fitness for Duty, 2012).

A gap in human knowledge exists which few people may acknowledge, and this is the gap between what we *know* versus what we *do*. Every licensed driver knows it is illegal to drive above the speed limit, yet most drivers do. Most people know drinking excessive amounts of alcohol are harmful to our health, but many people do. Most people know eating a healthy diet is good for you, yet fast-food restaurants have thrived for decades and the average American is overweight. In aviation, fatigue lives in the gap between <u>knowing</u> the right thing to do versus intentionally <u>doing</u> the wrong thing. Fatigue affects aviators' decision-making processes, swift ability to make complex decisions, and recognition of impending failures. Quite obviously, the effects and resulting consequences of fatigue for pilots can be disastrous. Although being sleepy may be a byproduct of fatigue, fatigue is not about falling asleep on the flight deck; fatigue is about the potentially bad decisions a pilot makes getting to that point.

In this chapter, we will discuss:

1. The definition of fatigue
2. The types of fatigue
3. Subjective symptoms of fatigue
4. Objective signs of fatigue
5. Problems of fatigue reporting
6. Fatigue recognition in pilots
7. Individual fatigue countermeasures
8. Operation fatigue countermeasures
9. Use of caffeine
10. Fatigue-proofing strategies

18.1 DEFINITION OF FATIGUE

According to the FAA, the ability to define fatigue in humans may be difficult due to wide ranges of variability in the causes of fatigue. Fatigue may be caused by boredom, circadian rhythm disruption, heavy physical activity, repetitive tasks, and many other factors. Lack of adequate sleep is common cause of fatigue, as sleep often slips to the bottom of the list in lieu of other pursuits. For most people, fatigue may be described as simply "weariness."

For aviation operational purposes, however, a more accurate and all-encompassing description may be as follows:

> *Fatigue is a condition characterized by increased discomfort with lessened capacity for work, reduced efficiency of accomplishment, loss of power or capacity to respond to stimulation, and is usually accompanied by a feeling of weariness and tiredness.* (Fatigue in Aviation, 2020)

As stated by the accepted definition, fatigue creates a state of reduced mental and physical performance. The primary effects are a reduction in alertness, attention, memory, motivation, and work capacity. These effects may result in altered operational strategies, misjudged risk assessment, or potentially non-adherence to standard operating procedures.

One of the main problems in fatigue self-identification is no true *biomarkers* exist to tell us fatigue is present. When we are fatigued, we do not get a skin rash, headache, lose visual acuity, suffer from physical weakness, or anything else definitively telling us we are, indeed, fatigued. Certain intellectual markers do exist, however, which will be covered later in the chapter.

Fatigue in individuals may be derived from a variety of sources. While the source of fatigue may be important, it is more important to understand what negative impacts fatigue has on an aviator's ability to perform at a high level, or even more startling, to simply perform normally.

Based on our discussions thus far, fatigue leads to decreases in one's ability to carry out tasks. FAA research has indicated fatigue is responsible for significant impairment in one's ability to perform tasks requiring manual dexterity, concentration, and complex intellectual processing.

18.2 TYPES OF FATIGUE

Individual fatigue may manifest itself three different ways:

- Transient (acute) fatigue
- Cumulative (chronic) fatigue
- Circadian fatigue

Transient fatigue may occur in relatively short periods of time, following significant mental or physical activity. Examples of factors causing acute fatigue could be a recent loss of sleep, irregular or unpredictable shift changes at work, travel through time zones, working long hours, or experiencing a stressful event. If acute fatigue is noticed, it normally may be easily mitigated with increased periods of rest.

Cumulative fatigue occurs over longer periods of time. Examples of factors causing chronic fatigue include cumulative sleep debt over weeks or months, altered lifestyle, continuous poor sleep quality, increased personal demands over a long period, or long-term stress. Chronic fatigue is not easily mitigated in the short-term, but can certainly be managed given recognition and motivation.

Circadian fatigue generally refers to reduced cognitive performance during nighttime hours, particularly during an individual's "window of circadian low" (WOCL), which typically occurs between the hours of 2:00 a.m. and 05:59 a.m. (FAA, Fitness for Duty, 2012).

18.3 HAZARDS OF FATIGUE

While fatigue is present in all levels of society and professions, the presence of fatigue in transportation and health care industries is particularly frightening as the recipients of those services depend on the provider knowing their jobs and trust those providers will perform correctly. Professionals in those industries need to perform at a high-level of effectiveness and accuracy to ensure consumer safety and well-being.

As an aviation industry professional with passengers depending on your ability, a thorough understanding and awareness of the *hazards of fatigue* must be realized, and are as follows:

- Work avoidance mode
- Loss of situational awareness
- Channelized attention

Work avoidance mode refers to an individual's lack of willingness to engage in their normal work activities with any enthusiasm or motivation, or at all. Aviators may experience short attention spans, difficulty concentrating, and difficulty starting or finishing tasks.

Loss of situation awareness may become dangerous in the flight environment as aviators experience degraded computational and abstraction skills. Restructuring and interpreting night visual scenes and instruments or displays may be slowed or compromised. A lack of awareness to the development of potentially hazardous conditions may be realized.

Channelized attention results in reduced attention spans and vigilance due to fixation on a singular task or display. An aviator's visual and composite instrument scan tends to break down, and normal tasks and checklist items tend to be shortcut or omitted completely.

Sleep and Human Performance

Next to air, water and food, sleep must be considered a major physiologic necessity for human homeostasis. Sleep and human performance are intricately linked, as most research and experimentation repeatedly demonstrate adequate sleep sustains acceptable performance.

Varying levels of sleep are evident, and reflected in an aviator's sleep quality. Stage Three and rapid eye movement (REM) sleep are considered by the scientific community as most refreshing, as these sleep stages allow the brain to reorganize. For most adults, eight hours of sleep each 24-hour period sustains performance indefinitely.

Sleep researchers have found impairment caused by sleep deprivation is similar to alcohol intoxication. Studies show if one is awake for 17 hours, their level of impairment may be as impaired as one with a blood-alcohol content (BAC) of .05%; 24 hours awake can equate to a BAC of .10%.

Fatigue Consequences for Health

Individuals suffering from acute or chronic fatigue may realize physical and psychological impacts beyond job performance.

According to FAA research, fatigue may be related to increases in personal health issues, doctor visits, use of sick leave, impaired driving, and difficulty dealing with home and social life.

Health issues include, but are not limited to:

1. Heart disease and high blood pressure
2. Depression, anxiety, and stress
3. Gastrointestinal disorders (peptic ulcers, indigestion, heartburn, flatulence, upset stomach, or constipation)
4. Overeating
5. Higher alcohol and drug use
6. A lower sense of overall well-being (FAA, Maintainer Fatigue Risk Management, 2016).

18.4 SUBJECTIVE SYMPTOMS OF FATIGUE

One the main intellectual markers of fatigue in yourself is identifying when your mind is not on your work as it should be; in other words, being *distracted*. You may find yourself replaying pleasant or unpleasant scenes from home, or anticipating upcoming events which excite you, or many other examples.

Subjectively, mental fatigue manifests increased feelings of tiredness, a lack of energy, decreased motivation, and mental alertness. From a physiological perspective, mental fatigue has been proven to negatively influence performance and cognitive function, and may actually alter brain activity (Slimani, 2018).

One of the most dangerous phrases in aviation is "let's just", as a pilot uttering those words is typically starting to compromise safety. Imagine the consequences of using those words on a flight. "Let's just" fly this segment even though our oxygen supply is not quite where it should be. "Let's just" try to make it to our primary destination even though we are experiencing erroneous engine readings. "Let's just" try to make it through that sketchy weather up ahead, because going around may add too much time to the segment. If you find yourself starting to say "let's just…" it may be time to reevaluate your current situation more carefully and objectively.

Spotting fatigue in oneself may be difficult, but self-identifying intellectual subjective symptoms may exist as follows:

- Fixation
- Reduced situational awareness
- Lapses of attention and vigilance
- Delayed reactions
- Apathy or decreased motivation
- Negative mood
- Micro-sleep episodes

Fixation on one instrument or visual picture may occur as one's mind begins to wander. The brain may not even comprehend what the eyes are seeing at this point.

Reduced situational awareness will occur as cognitive processing slows. Once an aviator's ability to synthesize environmental data into a comprehensible picture is compromised, the potential for incidents and accidents rises. Advances in aircraft automated systems may play a part in this as well, as pilots may feel the aircraft systems will monitor flight conditions, relieving the pilot of the responsibility.

Lapses of attention or vigilance may occur, negatively affecting a pilot's instrument scanning ability and potentially missing subtle mechanical cues of impending failures, improper visual interpretation for inflight obstacle avoidance, misjudging approach glideslopes or landing visual cues, etc. Again, aircraft automated systems may play a role in this issue as well, with pilots feeling as though the systems are redundant enough to not have to rely on human monitoring. According to FAA studies, a fatigued aviator's propensity to commit errors on the flight deck doubles.

Delayed reactions to rapidly developing emergency events certainly decreases an aviator's ability to successfully navigate the intricate and necessary steps to mitigate the events, where seconds may be the difference between life and death. Based FAA studies, a fatigued aviator's reaction times to respond to novel stimulus increases approximately 60%.

Apathy or decreased motivation may become an issue for some aviators, as apathetic behavior is the lack of enthusiasm, interest, or concern in a task, regardless of how important the task may actually be to normal thought processes.

Negative mood may affect an aviator's ability to cope with normal complex tasks. Negativity is a result of irrational thinking about events, people, directives, and processes. Aviators with a negative mood tend to visualize a given situation as a "problem" rather than a "challenge" to be overcome.

Micro-sleep episodes are brief, uncontrollable sleep episodes occurring during wakeful relaxation. Aviators experiencing these episodes may actually fall asleep for periods lasting from one second to as many as thirty seconds, and may occur with the subject's eyes wide-open. During micro-sleep, parts of an individual's brain goes "offline" for a few seconds, and it is not uncommon for individuals to actually experience describable dreams during the episode. An aviator may experience excessive blinking, heavy eyelids, or lack of visual focus prior to a micro-sleep episode.

18.5 OBJECTIVE SIGNS OF FATIGUE

Spotting potential fatigue in colleagues may not only beneficial to the fatigued aviator, but the entire crew and passenger population as well! A flight deck crew absolutely needs to monitor each other, as successful completion of a given flight segment needs to be a team effort. One weak link in the chain can and has led to disastrous consequences.

The following factors are recognized as *objective signs of fatigue*:

- Inconsistent performance
- Degraded psychomotor skills
- Degraded sensory interpretation
- Poorer risk awareness
- Less risk aversion
- Loss of resource prioritization
- Reduced social interaction

Inconsistent performance for a pilot may indicate individual motivation is starting to wane. If a pilot normally performs a given task at a satisfactory level or better, but has shown recent skills degradation with the task, their focus may be directed elsewhere.

Degraded psychomotor skills resulting from fatigue may include task inefficiencies on behaviors requiring hand-eye coordination such as manually maintaining a glideslope, coordinated turn, and effective management of contaminated flight surfaces. Degraded psychomotor skills may also create a critical safety hazard for pilots through a reduction in their reaction time to emergency situations.

Degraded sensory interpretation may profoundly affect a pilot's ability to interpret visual scenes (particularly at night), suffer from an ineffective inflight scan, or properly identify approach and landing visual illusions. Spatial disorientation effects may be magnified under periods of fatigue as well, disabling a pilot's ability to mitigate dangerous events where rapid and complex cognitive action is necessary.

Additionally, aviators will experience increased susceptibility to acute hypoxic episodes.

Poorer risk awareness may cause the pilot to fail to acknowledge potential risks, or fail to actively reduce or eliminate those risks. Vigilance, attention-to-detail, and situational awareness suffer.

Less risk aversion may alter or eliminate an aviator's understanding of potential risks, or misjudge their threshold, ability to mitigate, or perception of risks. The pilot may fail to adequately manage operational threats.

Loss of resource prioritization may cause an aviator to misjudge their upcoming workload, effective sequential timing of events or tasks, delaying essential tasks, or ineffective implementation of crew resource management.

Reduced social interaction may occur with fatigued aviators, as they are less motivated to engage in reciprocal socialization. Fatigue may cause increased irritability with those surrounding the individual, which may cause further withdrawal from social interactions.

Identification and empathetic intervention for crewmembers suspected of acute or chronic fatigue should be a hallmark of any flight organization's Safety Management System. Timely intervention of fatigued individuals on the flight deck greatly reduces the potential for incidents or accidents, quite possibly preventing catastrophic events. Aviators may experience increased bouts of agitation resulting from minor incidents.

18.6 PROBLEMS OF FATIGUE REPORTING

As with any preventative safety program, potential issues need to be identified in order to be fixed, and in cases of aircrew fatigue the most effective identification processes start with the individual aviator. It is up to each individual aviator to be responsible for their performance on the flight deck; however, checks and balances between the certificate holder and all pilots in the system must be maintained to ensure joint accountability for these processes.

Scope of Problem

Based on studies conducted by a variety of organizations, including the FAA, NASA, EASA, and others, indications are the scope of fatigue in aviation is significant and widespread.

For the professional pilots surveyed in these various studies, the results are as follows:

- Pilots who have had to cope with fatigue: 85-92%
- Fatigue has affected piloting skills and performance: 50%
- Fatigue has caused pilots to make mistakes: 71-79%
- Pilots who have involuntarily slept on a flight: 43-54%

One has to keep in mind these responses are based on those pilots who admitted fatigue was an issue for them in the performance of their duties. It must be assumed there were pilots who did not admit to fatigue-related issues, but were affected as well.

Reasons Not to Report

If flight safety is paramount in aviation operations, why, then, do some pilots *not* admit to fatigue related issues? According to some reports, only 20% of pilots experiencing fatigue-related problems filed fatigue reports. Pilots have admitted some of the reasons encouraging them not to file a report are as follows:

- No benefit to filing a report
- Too tired to file a report
- Did not want to make a fuss
- Did not want management to have a less positive opinion of them

If pilots feel no beneficial qualities exist for them to report a fatigue-related issue, reporting will make management think they're ineffective, or pilots think management will not act on the reports, no amount of "talk" will make the situation better; only management action on the accumulated information will improve reporting.

Fatigue Management

For an organization to implement an effective *fatigue management strategy,* the organization must take into account the following measures:

- **Prevention**
- **Countermeasures**
- **Safety Management Systems (SMS)**

Prevention should include individual-initiated components such as effective off-duty rest strategies and appropriate allowances for circadian adjustments, and carrier-initiated components such as realistic scheduling policies and practices and educational and awareness initiatives.

Educational and awareness initiatives should include aircrew member training on how personal behavior may unintentionally lead to fatigue, how aggressive flight duty period (FDP) scheduling may induce aircrew member fatigue, and methods of fatigue mitigation in an industry known for nontraditional work cycles.

Countermeasures should include realistic inflight vehicle and environmental accommodation of fatigue mitigation, and personal strategies to be used in performance of duties in minimize fatigue impacts.

Safety Management Systems (SMS) are a top-down organizational plan containing the most recent fatigue information, aircrew education program, organizational fatigue trend analysis, and effective scheduling policies and practices.

This system needs to be embraced and enforced starting with top management officials. If the system does not elicit action from top managers, mid-level managers will not take the system seriously, which ultimately filters down to the line pilots. Effective fatigue management has to exist in a just culture, where all levels know, understand, believe, and share joint responsibility in the system for the system to do what it is intended to do – make flying safe for all.

18.7 INDIVIDUAL FATIGUE COUNTERMEASURES

According to the FAA, for flightcrew members to report for a flight duty period (FDP) properly and thoroughly rested, the certificate holder must provide the flightcrew member adequate and meaningful rest opportunities which will realistically allow each flightcrew member to get the proper amount of sleep. By the same token, each flightcrew member must accept and bear the responsibility of actually sleeping during rest periods, as opposed to using the time for other, less restful, activities. Each flightcrew member must report for any FDP properly rested, prepared for and fit to perform their duties.

The agreement between the certificate holder and each crewmember must be a joint responsibility to ensure fitness for duty. No certificate holder may assign, and no flightcrew member may accept an assignment to an FDP if the flightcrew member reports to their FDP too fatigued to safely perform their assigned duties (FAA, Fitness for Duty, 2012).

Fatigue Prevention

In developing an effective fatigue prevention strategy, one must look at long-term, chronic issues with regards to personal health, home and work environment, and stress levels. One must also aspire to improve circadian adjustments when necessary, and understand sleep quality and quantity issues.

Let us examine FAA recommendations for aircrew member-initiated mitigation for effective off-duty rest strategies.

Pre-duty activities: Flightcrew members residing in their domicile engaging in activities prior to reporting for duty may inadvertently expose themselves to similar fatigue exposure to pilots commuting to FDPs. Activities to attempt to avoid include working around the house, car repairs, yard work, and off-duty employment activities.

Flightcrew in the domicile versus commuting flightcrew: The total time of wakefulness for a flightcrew member residing in their domicile engaging in activities prior to duty may be similar to one that commutes to their domicile. The potential exposure to fatigue risks for the scheduled duty day affects both flightcrew members similarly. Essentially, both flightcrew members are awake for similar time periods prior to starting their FDP. While this may not be an issue for a midmorning report time, a mid- or late-evening report time exposes a flightcrew member to greater potential to experience a fatigue event, unless the flightcrew member has taken a nap prior to reporting.

Minimizing pre-duty activities: The National Academy of Sciences (NAS) conducted a study on the effects of commuting on pilot fatigue episodes. One recommendation of the study concluded: "Pilots should avoid planning commutes or other pre-duty activities that result in being awake beyond approximately 16 hours before the scheduled end of duty, endeavor to sleep at least 6 hours prior to reporting for duty, and obtain more than 6 hours of sleep per day whenever possible to prevent cumulative fatigue from chronic sleep restriction. Pilots should also consider the amount of sleep and time awake in their decision making relative to when to inform their supervisors that they should not fly due to fatigue."

Reducing risk of fatigue: It is imperative flightcrew members realize extended periods of wakefulness prior to starting a duty period may contribute to pilot fatigue episodes. Therefore, flightcrew members must initiate the appropriate fatigue mitigations by obtaining the proper rest prior to starting any FDP to reduce potential exposure to a fatigue-related event (FAA, Fitness for Duty, 2012).

Physiology of Sleep

To fulfill the human need for rest, four stages of sleep are believed to exist as follows:

- **Stage 1** is the transition between consciousness and sleep. You can generally hear and respond to someone. In this stage, it is not uncommon to actually hear yourself snore.

- **Stage 2** is a light sleep. You are easily awakened, but not immediately aware of your surroundings. You spend about half your sleep time in stages 1 and 2.
- **Stage 3** is deep slumber – this is a very restorative phase. Awakening during these phases may be difficult to achieve.
- **Stage 4** is known as *Rapid Eye Movement* (REM) sleep, and is the stage of sleep where you typically dream. Researchers believe your eyes move at this stage of sleep because you are scanning the images in your dreams. It is believed to be important for learning and consolidation of memory.

A complete cycle can last between 60 and 90 minutes. A typical sleep will move through the cycle several times, but each cycle will vary in length. Whenever an individual is sleep deprived, their body will first try to catch up on deep sleep (Stage 3) and REM sleep.

According to the FAA, the drive for sleep increases over time since the last sleep period and with any cumulative deficit in sleep relative to the average eight-hour day requirement. As a consequence, the sleep drive is at its lowest point in the morning, upon awakening. As the day progresses, the drive to sleep increases and the ability to sustain attention and engage in cognitive activities decreases. Once sleep begins, this drive gradually decreases until awakening (FAA, Fitness for Duty, 2012).

The Anatomy of Sleep

The *hypothalamus*, a peanut-sized structure deep inside the brain, contains groups of nerve cells acting as control centers affecting sleep and arousal. Within the hypothalamus is the *suprachiasmatic nucleus* (SCN) – clusters of thousands of cells that receive information about light exposure directly from the eyes and control one's behavioral rhythm. Some people with damage to the SCN sleep erratically throughout the day because they are not able to match their circadian rhythms with the light-dark cycle. Many individuals suffering from blindness maintain some ability to sense light and are able to modify their sleep/wake cycle.

The *brain stem*, at the base of the brain, communicates with the hypothalamus to control the transitions between wake and sleep (the brain stem includes structures called the *pons, medulla, and midbrain*.) Sleep-promoting cells within the hypothalamus and the brain stem produce a brain chemical called *GABA*, which acts to reduce the activity of arousal centers in the hypothalamus and the brain stem, also suppressing plasma *cortisol* production. The brain stem (especially the pons and medulla) also provides a special role in REM sleep; it sends signals to relax muscles essential for body posture and limb movements, so we do not act out our dreams. Core body temperatures will drop as well.

The *thalamus* acts as a relay for information from the senses to the *cerebral cortex* (the covering of the brain that interprets and processes information from short- to long-term memory). During most stages of sleep, the thalamus becomes quiet, allowing one to tune out the external world. However, during REM sleep the thalamus is active, sending the cortex images, sounds, and other sensations that fill our dreams.

The *pineal gland*, located within the brain's two hemispheres, receives signals from the SCN and increases production in the plasma of the hormone *melatonin*, which assists one to sleep once the lights dim. Scientists believe peaks and valleys of melatonin over time are important for matching the body's circadian rhythm to the external cycle of light and darkness.

The *basal forebrain*, near the front and bottom of the brain, also promotes sleep and wakefulness, while part of the *midbrain* acts as an arousal system. Release of adenosine (a chemical by-product of cellular energy consumption) from cells in the basal forebrain and possibly other regions supports one's sleep drive. *Caffeine* counteracts sleepiness by blocking the actions of adenosine.

The *amygdala*, an almond-shaped structure involved in processing emotions, also becomes increasingly active during REM sleep (NIH, Brain Basics: Understanding Sleep, 2019).

Circadian Rhythms and Adjustments

The human body works on a 24-hour cycle known as *circadian rhythm,* also known as our *body clock* or *biological clock.* This cycle controls a variety of bodily functions, such as sleepiness, digestion, melatonin production, and body temperature. Individuals living on a regular 24-hour routine who sleep at night have two periods of maximum sleepiness, known as *windows of circadian lows* (WOCL).

The primary WOCL occurs at night, occurring from roughly 2 a.m. to 6 a.m. This is the time when physiological sleepiness is greatest, and performance efficiencies, capabilities, and body temperature are lowest. The secondary WOCL occurs in the afternoon, occurring from roughly 3 p.m. to 5 p.m. During these timeframes, flightcrew members may find their performance degraded as a result of the body and brain beginning to fatigue and requiring sleep.

For the average person, the daily upswing in alertness produced by the circadian system tends to offset the decrease in alertness produced by depletion of the sleep regulatory process. The result is normal alertness and performance during the first 16 hours of continuous wakefulness. After about 16 hours of continuous wakefulness, most adults begin to notice reductions in the speed of performance and in alertness levels. However, the changes in behavior and alertness can be magnified by a prior history of insufficient sleep quantity and quality (FAA, Fitness for Duty, 2012).

Sleep-wake homeostasis keeps track of the human necessity for sleep. Homeostatic sleep drive prompts the body to sleep after a certain time and regulates sleep intensity. This sleep drive grows stronger every hour individuals spend awake and causes one to sleep longer and more deeply after periods of sleep deprivation.

Factors influencing one's sleep-wake cycle include medical conditions, medications, stress, sleep environment, and the types of foods and drinks consumed. The greatest influence may be exposure to light. Specialized cells in the retinas of one's eyes process light, informing the brain whether it is day or night and can advance or delay one's sleep-wake cycle. Exposure to light may cause difficulties falling asleep or a return to sleep once awakened.

Night-shift workers often have trouble falling asleep when they go to bed, and also have trouble staying awake at work resultant from natural circadian rhythm and sleep-wake cycle disruption. Regarding jet lag, individual circadian rhythms become out of sync with the time of day when aviators fly to a different time zone, creating a mismatch between their internal clock and the actual clock (NIH, Brain Basics: Understanding Sleep, 2019).

Let us now examine how to manage appropriate allowances for *circadian adjustments*.

Any time aviators travel across time zones and layover for more than 24 hours, those flightcrew members may find themselves struggling to operate normally as a result of the local circadian rhythm being offset from their own. For example, if a pilot departs LAX at 0700 and the flight segment arrives at MSP at 1300 after four hours of flight time, the pilot has advanced two time zones forward. The following day, if the pilot departs MSP at 0700 and the flight segment arrives at LAX at 0900 after four hours of flight time, the pilot has retreated two time zones backward.

Generally speaking, to physiologically adjust to a new circadian rhythm schedule synchronizing with local time, the body requires one day per time zone. Scientists have found most travelers find it more effective to adjust across time zones traveling west as opposed to traveling east. The reason for easier western adjustments is most individuals find it more desirable to stay awake longer to adjust to the new time zone, as opposed to attempting to go to sleep early to adjust traveling to the east.

Free running rhythm refers to circadian cycles naturally adopted by individuals whose approximately 24-hour sleep cycle is not guided by discernable external cues such as light or sleep-wake activities. For example, visually-impaired individuals unable to detect natural or artificial light may adopt free-running rhythms. Regardless of the reason, an abnormal free running rhythm may cause chronic fatigue, insomnia, sleep deprivation, and depression.

Sleep Optimization

Knowing the importance of rest opportunities, now we will examine methodology of *sleep optimization* to provide crewmembers the most favorable conditions for restful sleep. Aviators must avoid fragmentation of sleep opportunities from controllable factors such as interruption, environment, noise, or turbulence to ensure maximum performance enhancement.

According to the FAA, rest opportunities and sleep opportunities are two separate events. A rest opportunity is a designated and assigned time period in which flightcrew members are free from all duty prior to a duty assignment; while a sleep opportunity period resides within the rest period. The sleep obtained within the sleep opportunity is the essential element for being fit for duty.

Effectively managing rest and sleep opportunities are essential for reducing the risk of being unfit for duty due to fatigue. Again, joint responsibility is placed on the air carrier and the flightcrew member, which prescribes that no flightcrew member may accept an assignment for any reserve or flight duty period (FDP) unless that flightcrew member is given a rest period of at least 10 consecutive hours immediately before beginning the reserve or FDP measured from the time the flightcrew member is released from duty. The 10-hour rest period must provide the flightcrew member with an opportunity of a minimum of eight hours of uninterrupted sleep. If the flightcrew member determines that the rest period will not provide an opportunity of eight uninterrupted hours of sleep, that flightcrew member must notify their chain of command. The flightcrew member cannot report for the assigned FDP until he or she receives a minimum of eight hours of uninterrupted sleep opportunity (FAA, Fitness for Duty, 2012).

The following measures will assist aviators in taking full advantage of their assigned sleep opportunities:

1. Mitigate sleep space comfort issues. Ensure a cool, dark, humid environment is available.
2. Ensure sleep space is uninterrupted and quiet. Although this may prove challenging in some home environments, significant others should understand the role this plays in fatigue management.
3. Ensure sleep opportunities are anchored in body clock time, not local time.

4. Set a schedule for sleep opportunities. Make every effort to go to bed and wake up at consistent times each day, ensuring compliance with one's natural circadian rhythms.

5. Adjust timing of meals and exercise 20 to 30 minutes a day. Ensure these activities occur no later than a few hours before going to bed.

6. Make every effort to avoid disrupters, namely caffeine and nicotine late in the day and alcoholic drinks before bed.

7. Manage stress and relax before bed. Most stresses can be effectively mitigated simply be dealing with them, as opposed to letting them fester. One should try a warm bath, reading, or another relaxing routine.

8. Create a specific room for sleep. Avoid bright lights and loud sounds, keep the room at a cool, comfortable temperature, and don't watch TV or have a computer in your bedroom.

9. Do not lie in bed awake. If you cannot get to sleep, get out of bed and do something else, like reading or listening to music, until you feel adequately sleepy to try again.

10. See a doctor if you have a problem sleeping or if you feel unusually tired during the day. Most sleep disorders can be treated effectively if addressed by the appropriate professional (NIH, Brain Basics: Understanding Sleep, 2019).

Sleep Debt and Recovery Sleep

Humans require adequate amounts of sleep for peak performance, but unfortunately various circumstances may prevent this from happening, leading to *sleep debt*. To adequately manage or reverse the effects of fatigue, some individuals require *recovery sleep*. The time period for recovery sleep may vary for each individual, as one person's need for required sleep may vary from that of another person. Some people may require eight hours of continuous sleep while others may require more than eight continuous hours. Others may simply require a quick nap of 15 – 20 minutes to take the "sleep edge" off.

For more extreme levels of sleep debt, making the debt up may be more difficult. For example, if one misses ten hours of sleep in a given week, they should calculate out and plan to make up the missed sleep, or "pay back the debt." This may include sleeping an extra four hours during the weekend, followed by one-to-two extra hours of sleep each night during the following week until the sleep debt is paid in full.

Sleep Apnea

According to Dr. Eric J. Olson of the Mayo Clinic, some individuals may get adequate amounts of rest and sleep opportunities, only to continuously feel fatigued. Those individuals may suffer from *sleep apnea,* which is a potentially serious sleep disorder. Sleep apnea occurs when one's breathing repeatedly stops and starts during sleep periods, which typically causes one to snore loudly during sleep periods, and ultimately feel tired even following a full night's sleep. Three types of sleep apnea exist:

- Obstructive sleep apnea
- Central sleep apnea
- Complex sleep apnea syndrome

Obstructive sleep apnea (OSA) occurs when muscles of the throat relax to greater degrees than the general public.

Central sleep apnea (CSA) is a neurologic condition occurring as a result of the brain failing to send the proper signals to the muscles controlling breathing.

Complex sleep apnea syndrome (CSAS), also known as *treatment-emergent central sleep apnea,* occurs when an individual suffers from both obstructive and central sleep apnea conditions.

Symptoms of sleep apnea include:

- Loud snoring
- Gasping for air during sleep
- Awakening with a dry mouth
- Morning headaches
- Difficulty staying asleep, or insomnia
- Excessive daytime sleepiness
- Difficulty paying attention while awake
- Excessive irritability

Sleep apnea conditions affect approximately 8-10% of the population, and sleep apnea conditions increase in individuals with body mass indexes (BMI) over 40, being male, habitual alcohol or tobacco use, chronic congestion, and people who are older. Sleep apnea is currently part of FAA medical certification screening (Olson, 2020).

Sleep Apnea and Flight

A significant scientific study in 1999 demonstrated a six-fold increase in automobile accident rates in people diagnosed with Obstructive Sleep Apnea (OSA) over those not suffering from this condition.

The FAA has similar concerns regarding pilots flying with sleep apnea. In single-pilot operations, micro-sleeps or repeated "dozing off" may result in mishaps, deviations from ATC instructions and intended flight paths, or violations of Federal Aviation Regulations. In commercial operations requiring crew coordination, a pilot with uncontrollable fatigue presents an unacceptable risk to flight safety. Memory loss and impaired concentration present safety compromises, regardless of the absence of in-flight sleep

The primary concern of the FAA regarding pilot sleep disorders relates to alertness when on duty on the flight deck. Secondary concerns involve the personal complications and associated symptoms of sleep apnea, such as memory and concentration impairment, heart arrhythmias and other conditions causing subtle or sudden incapacitation when flying. Under current policy as outlined in the FAA Guide for Aviation Medical Examiners, any degree of sleep apnea is disqualifying for all classes of medical certification. The FAA requires AMEs to routinely screen airmen for Obstructive Sleep Apnea (OSA) risk and if necessary, refer them to their treating providers to apply Academy of Sleep Medicine clinical practice guidelines to determine if further assessment such as a sleep study is clinically indicated. If an airman is diagnosed with sleep apnea, the AMEs can clear the airman to return to flying once they have documented effective treatment and compliance and their records are submitted to the FAA.

Pilots diagnosed with sleep apnea may be granted medical certification under the special issuance provisions of 14 CFR 67.401. The essential elements for evaluation are a diagnostic sleep study and follow-up sleep study to ensure effective treatment. In some cases, such as use of autoPAP, a follow-up sleep study may not be necessary if the autoPAP compliance data also reports effective resolution of OSA. At least one week of compliance data documentation for continuous positive airway pressure (CPAP) along with attestation that the pilot no longer experiences any daytime sleepiness is required. There must also be a clinical narrative clearly indicating no evidence of daytime sleepiness and compliance with treatment.

The FAA usually requests an annual physician-initiated current status report in individuals requiring treatment as a requirement to maintain Special Issuance medical certification. They also require the attestation form and 12 months of compliance data for CPAP. More details on the FAA's policy along with a Question-and-Answer guide can be found in the FAA's Guide to Aviation Medical Examiners, or by contacting an AMAS physician (AMSA Sleep Apnea, 2020).

18.8 OPERATIONAL FATIGUE COUNTERMEASURES

Operational countermeasures to fatigue should be employed by air carriers for the obvious purpose of decreasing sleepiness during flight operations, and by proxy, increasing flight safety. Various countermeasures may be prescribed, and should include a holistic approach to flight crewmember fatigue issues. We have learned personal fatigue countermeasures in the previous section, so we will now examine active operational countermeasures, which may include:

- **Inflight napping**
- **Inflight breaks**
- **Bunk sleep**
- **In-flight rostering**
- **Flight deck lighting options**

According to the Aerospace Medical Association Fatigue Countermeasures Subcommittee of the Aerospace Human Factors Committee, one must be aware not all countermeasures are either currently sanctioned by the FAA, or even frequently utilized by air carriers. However, this list is intended to be inclusive and address effective varieties of potential fatigue countermeasures for pilots operating in restrictive flight deck environments. The need for safety and operational effectiveness at all times is paramount, and must be stressed incessantly.

Inflight napping in operational conditions where some sleep is possible, but the amount of sleep is limited, napping is the most effective non-pharmacological technique for restoring mental alertness. There is ample scientific evidence stating naps taken during long periods of otherwise continuous wakefulness is extremely beneficial for mental agility; however, inflight napping is not currently sanctioned by the FAA.

Inflight breaks can serve to increase mental alertness by reducing the monotony of highly-automated flight deck environments through conscious disengagement with monitoring and flight tasks. By allowing mild physical activity, depending on the type of break and the behaviors allowed during the break, one may allow their brain to reorganize and refresh. Although possibly not as effective as other countermeasures, anecdotal evidence indicates many pilots may take brief, out-of-the-seat breaks as a fatigue countermeasure.

Bunk sleep has proven to be one of the most important inflight fatigue countermeasures implemented to address sleep loss and circadian rhythm disruption during extended aviation operations. Obtaining sleep addresses the underlying physiology of sleep loss, and is the only proven method to reverse cumulative sleep debt. Significantly, it is an operationally feasible approach to address sleep loss associated with extended hours of wakefulness, crossing multiple time zones, and flying duties during nighttime hours.

Inflight rostering, although not commonly discussed as a fatigue countermeasure, may be used to minimize fatigue. Inflight rostering refers to the scheduling of flightcrew to assigned positions on the flight deck, allowing other flightcrew to obtain inflight rest or bunk sleep. Inflight rostering is directly related to the crew complement, or number of pilots assigned to the flight and is determined during the scheduling process in advance of the flight segment. Research predicts human performance starts deteriorating after 18 to 20 hours of continuous wakefulness with all aspects of cognitive functioning, as well as mood being affected. Furthermore, working shifts longer than eight to nine hours is thought to increase the probability of having accidents or making errors. Specifically, research has shown in aviation settings when the "time-since-awakening" extends beyond the median for crew positions, there is an increase in overall errors. Therefore, a sufficient number of crewmembers is necessary to provide multiple and equitable opportunities for crewmember rest.

Much is now known about the use of *cockpit lighting,* which may be used to assist in the shifting of human circadian rhythms using properly-timed bright light. While investigated to a lesser extent, light also appears to have an acute, immediate, and alertness-amplifying effect on mood and performance independent of its circadian phase-shifting properties. Research on the acute alerting effects of bright light shows it to be a potentially useful countermeasure at night where conditions effectively allow its use. Light's alerting effects are often believed to be tied to its suppression of melatonin, which is ordinarily released in the mid- to late-evening. Therefore, bright light has potential to mitigate the usual alertness and performance decline seen during nighttime hours, including flight deck conditions. Regarding light intensity, measurable increases in subjective alertness and reductions in slow eye movements were realized with room light levels. Short-wavelength light appears to have the greatest alerting effect, with the spectrum of typical room light containing enough energy in the shorter wavelengths to be effective. There is also some evidence that the alerting effects of light are independent of the time of day, leading to the possibility of employing light during the daytime to improve alertness and performance in individuals impaired due to prior sleep deprivation.

All of these aforementioned inflight countermeasures clearly have a place in sustaining alertness and performance of aviation personnel. However, the manner in which these strategies are employed should be based on the currently available scientific knowledge and should be implemented only after thoughtful consideration by the air carrier and flightcrew members (ASMA, 2009).

18.9 USE OF CAFFEINE

The use of caffeine in managing workplace fatigue has been a staple in society for many years, and aviation is no exception. According to Dr. Alexandra Holmes, Fatigue Management Specialist, caffeine is the world's most popular and widely consumed stimulant, mainly in the liquid forms of coffee, tea, and energy drinks. The popularity of caffeine is due in large part to its stimulating effects on the central nervous system, temporarily suppressing tiredness and improving mental alertness and performance. Many people consume caffeine in the morning to overcome sleep inertia, which leaves some individuals feeling temporarily groggy following waking up. Some people will consume caffeine in the afternoon as well, negating the effects of the mid-afternoon circadian performance slump. For industries such as aviation working on a 24/7 operations schedule, caffeine may be an effective strategy to combat work-related tiredness or low performance during circadian low-points.

At the other end of the spectrum, caffeine may produce significant negative consequences if more-than-recommended doses are consumed. Physiological signs of elevated levels of caffeine consumption may include jitteriness, anxiety, heart palpitations and arrhythmias, stomach discomfort, and ultimately sleep disruption.

Caffeine Realities

We will now examine some *caffeine realities* in the usage of this common stimulant so as to strategically harness and maximize its benefits, while minimizing negative effects and consequences.

Aviators must understand caffeine does not replace sleep. One should never purposefully skip adequate rest opportunities and depend on caffeine to take up the slack. While this strategy may be effective for short-term periods, in the long-term the lack of adequate rest will become dangerous for one's effective flightcrew performance.

Some may find their caffeine usage is limited to only morning hours for a good night's sleep, while others may drink coffee right up to bedtime and sleep fine.

Usually, the most effective single-use dosage for most people are moderate doses of 100 mg or less. Caffeine will realize its peak values in the bloodstream within approximately 30 minutes to an hour, and the benefits typically last three-to-four hours. Total daily dosages of less than 500 mg are generally considered harmless, although daily doses at the higher end of this range may still result in disrupted sleep patterns for some people. Excessive amounts of caffeine consumption (in excess of 500 mg per day) may point to one's attempt to mitigate high-levels of underlying fatigue, and efforts should be made to reduce caffeine intake and fatigue with more focus on adequate and effective sleep. According to research referenced by Flight Safety Foundation, consumption of caffeine amounts in excess of 300 mg per day may cause deterioration of psychomotor performance and mood changes which may potentially impair pilot efficiency and effectiveness for aircraft operation. According to Dr. Holmes, the following are four steps to follow when considering caffeine usage to combat fatigue:

1. Combine caffeine with a nap. Caffeine typically takes 20 minutes to affect the nervous system, and this window may be used to engage in a quick nap. Based on research findings, when one wakes up and the caffeine has taken effect, one will be more alert than simply using caffeine or a nap alone.
2. Avoid caffeinated beverages with high levels of sugar. Large amounts of sugar may cause an energy slump once the sugar wears off.
3. Consume caffeine only when it is needed. Individuals will rapidly develop higher tolerances to caffeine, so the more caffeine consumed on a daily basis, the more one will need to promote alertness.
4. Realize people differ widely in caffeine sensitivity. Some may find one cup of coffee effectively improves their alertness, while others may require several cups (Holmes, 2020).

Coffee and Tea Caffeine Content

As we now have a baseline of how much caffeine to consume for optimum performance, we must be aware of expected caffeine dosages from available sources. It must be noted caffeine amounts between different coffee and tea types may vary greatly; however, the following list will provide aviators with a general idea of the amount of caffeine to expect from standard sources:

- 8 oz. Brewed coffee: 95-200 mg
- 8 oz. Brewed decaffeinated coffee: 2-12 mg

- 8 oz. Brewed, single-serve varieties: 75-150 mg
- 8 oz. Brewed, single-serve varieties, decaffeinated: 2-4 mg
- 16 oz. Starbucks coffee, Blonde Roast: 360 mg
- 16 oz. Starbucks coffee, Pike Place Roast: 310 mg
- 14 oz. Dunkin' Donuts coffee: 210 mg
- 20 oz. Dunkin' Donuts Cappuccino: 252 mg
- 20 oz. Dunkin' Donuts coffee w/ Espresso Shot: 398 mg
- Keurig K-Cup, most varieties: 75-150 mg
- 16 oz. Starbucks Chai Latte Tea: 95 mg
- 16 oz. Starbucks Green Tea Latte: 80 mg
- 16 oz. Honest Tea Organic Lemon Tea: 63 mg
- 16 oz. Snapple Lemon Tea: 37 mg
- 18.5 oz. Gold Peak Unsweetened Tea: 47 mg
- 16.9 oz. Lipton Lemon Iced Tea: 21 mg
- 8 oz. Arizona Iced Tea, Black: 15 mg
- 8 oz. Brewed green tea: 28-38 mg
- 8 oz. Brewed herbal tea: 0 mg

Soft Drink Caffeine Content

- 20 oz. Pepsi Zero Sugar: 115 mg
- 20 oz. Pepsi: 63 mg
- 20 oz. Sunkist Orange (diet or regular): 31 mg
- 20 oz. Mountain Dew (diet of regular): 91 mg
- 20 oz. Diet Coke: 76 mg
- 16 oz. Coca-Cola or Coke Zero: 45 mg

Energy Drink Caffeine Content

- 2 oz. 5-Hour Energy: 200 mg
- 16 oz. Monster Energy: 160 mg
- 16 oz. Rockstar Energy: 160 mg
- 16 oz. Full Throttle: 160 mg
- 16 oz. NOS Energy: 160 mg
- 8.4 oz. Red Bull: 80 mg

One must be aware of the sugar content of energy drinks as this may cause a "sugar-crash", and drinks labeled "high-performance" or "extra-strength", as these may potentially provide elevated amounts of caffeine, which may lead to impairing side effects.

Over-the Counter Caffeine Pills

- 2 capsules Zantrex Blue: 300 mg
- 1 tablet NoDoz or Vivarin: 200 mg
- 2 tablets Exedrin Migraine: 130 mg
- 2 caplets Midol Complete: 120 mg
- 2 tablets Anacin: 64 mg

18.10 FATIGUE-PROOFING STRATEGIES

Times exist when flightcrew members faithfully follow anti-fatigue guidelines and still cannot sleep for one reason or another, or some unanticipated emergency presents itself, preventing adequate rest or sleep opportunities. Perhaps one loses sleep because they have a newborn infant in the house, and anyone having experienced this will agree sleep is difficult to come by. Perhaps a pilot is facing a known mentally and physically fatiguing series of flight segments or assignments.

Whatever the reason, one must be prepared to deal with situational anomalies when they are fatigued in the cockpit through no fault of their own. The best course of action would be to not fly in these situations, but at times acute fatigue or sleepiness presents itself after the aircraft has already departed.

During these times of unanticipated fatigue, comprehensive strategies should be employed to *fatigue-proof* flightcrew member intellectual and physical performance. Listed below are a synthesis of strategies employed by individuals in high-stress and high-fatigue environments, such as U.S. Military Special Operations Forces and fighter pilots, police SWAT teams, firefighters, and others:

1. Know and admit your mental processes are slowed. Understand more focus and vigilance is necessary at those times.
2. Strictly follow the checklist. Checklists are developed to assist operators not to skip critical steps, so use it for this purpose. You may need to go over the checklist multiple times, if necessary, to ensure all steps are completed.
3. Desynchronize activities so one pilot rests while the other is vigilant. Everyone gets fatigued from time-to-time, so be proactive to ensure one of the pilots is alert
4. Keep your brain engaged. Allowing one's brain to wander may become rapidly dangerous, especially during periods of fatigue.
5. Do not allow distractions to occur. When one's attention is drawn away from a task, particularly when fatigued, critical items may easily get missed.

6. Get sleep "in the tank" prior to engagement. If one is expecting to engage in a fatiguing event or flight segment, attempt to "preload" the body with more sleep than usual.

7. Use 100 to 150 mg of caffeine every two – three hours, as previously discussed.

8. Eat light (proteins/fats) and avoid carbohydrates. Eating light meals prior to fatigue-inducing shifts or events make it harder for one to feel sleepy.

9. Get moving or get some anaerobic exercise. Mildly strenuous bodily activity which produces endorphins, which makes it more difficult to be sleepy. Anaerobic exercise may be performed in confined spaces such as flight decks by engaging in isometric exercises (straining muscles against immovable objects).

10. Make yourself uncomfortable. It is difficult for one to be fatigued when plagued by discomfort, such as keeping the flight deck temperature colder than normal.

11. Talk to your crew members, preferably about inflammatory issues, but remember to keep the conversation civil. A heated discussion on politics, sports, religion or other inflammatory subjects will keep one wide awake, as it is extremely difficult to be sleepy when agitated.

The main element to remember when fatigued is not to allow oneself to slip into complacency, as the risk of incidents and accidents elevates exponentially in a complacent environment.

Conclusion

Fatigue is arguably the single greatest physiologic risk an aviator may face in the flight environment, as fatigue exacerbates many physiological issues such as hypoxia, hyperventilation, stress, emergency response times, vision and visual illusions, spatial disorientation, and others.

Intellectual and physical performance is more affected by fatigue than most individuals think. Similar in scope to drinking alcohol and driving a vehicle, most believe they can adequately cope with the effects of fatigue with little-to-no degradation of skill and abilities.

One generally needs less caffeine than one thinks. As described, 100 mg of caffeine per hour should be adequate to increase alertness without detrimental side-effects, although many will consume two-to-three times that dosage.

With careful and diligent adherence to recommended fatigue-mitigation policies, aviators may be assured of maximizing their effectiveness on the flight deck.

Chapter 18 Core Competency Questions

1. What is one of the main problems in self-identifying fatigue in oneself?
2. What are the three types of fatigue?
3. What is the problem with instrument scanning when affected by channelized attention?
4. What stages of sleep are most refreshing for humans?
5. What is one of the main intellectual markers of fatigue in yourself?
6. Based on studies, what is the percentage of professional pilots who have had to cope with fatigue?
7. What percentage of pilots who experienced fatigue-related problems in flight actually filed reports?
8. With regards to circadian rhythms, what are the two periods of maximum sleepiness called?
9. How many milligrams of caffeine per day is considered relatively harmless?
10. How much caffeine should be consumed every two-three hours for maximum effectiveness?

19. STRESS

Much like fatigue, *stress* can be a ubiquitous threat to aviation operations with few identifiable biomarkers. Aviators continuously work in complex and dynamic environments, synthesizing diverse data, while their brains attempt to make sense of all of this cognitive input. According to NASA, situational stress may create negative impacts on cognition and the skilled performance of aviators, and as mentioned, flying involves high-level cognitive ability.

Inflight emergencies and other unanticipated events require aviators to diagnose spur-of-the moment anomalies and execute nonstandard and infrequently practiced procedures accurately and in a timely fashion. Aviators must use their flying skills and accumulated knowledge to select appropriate courses of action; likely while experiencing high workloads, time pressures, and abstruse indications, all of which can be stressful in and of themselves. In addition to the unanticipated event, the aviator may be suffering from some level of physical, physiological, or psychological stressors distracting the aviator's intellect from full concentration on the task, which may redirect a survivable situation into a dire, nonsurvivable event.

It is imperative flightcrew understand how stress and anxiety may affect cognitive performance, particularly during the intellectual performance demands commercial pilots may encounter amidst inflight emergencies or under severely challenging standard operations. In these situations, even highly trained and skilled pilots may experience substantial acute stress in the process of performing complex, demanding cognitive tasks under conditions where minor errors may create major consequences.

Research performed by NASA indicates stress negatively affects core cognitive mechanisms of attention and memory. Regarding attention, stress may decrease cognitive ability to manage and distribute attention as a function of task requirements, prioritize and direct attention among competing task demands, manage multiple tasks concurrently, and perform normal perceptual scanning of environmental cues. Stress affects memory by decreasing working memory storage and processing capacity, and inhibiting retrieval of declarative information. However, long-term procedural memory (e.g., motor schemas) may be less affected by stress.

Research on stress effects on higher-order cognitive processes, such as decision making, also shows general decrements in performance both at the individual level and team or crew level. Stress causes decision makers to be more disorganized in their scanning and evaluating of alternatives and to consider fewer alternatives when attempting to decide.

Acute stress disrupts processes underlying team performance, primarily through undercutting communication and coordination, and so reduces overall task performance. Under stress, team members search for and share less information, tend to neglect social and interpersonal cues, and fail to recognize situations that require interpersonal interaction (Dismukes, 2015).

In this chapter, we will discuss:

1. The definition of stress
2. Physical, physiological, and emotional stress
3. Stress in the workplace
4. Self-imposed stressors
5. The effects of stress on individual and team performance
6. Stress management practices

19.1 DEFINITION OF STRESS

In a biological context, *stress* may be defined as "the sum of biological reactions to adverse stimulus, from internal or external physical, mental, or emotional causes, creating disturbances to an organism's homeostasis." Perhaps a simpler explanation would be "stress causes feelings of emotional or physical tension." Should an individual's compensatory mechanisms be inadequate or inappropriate, stress may lead to disorders or intellectual and physical failures.

Stress is the body's automatic response to any physical or mental demand placed on it. Although stress has a plethora of negative connotations, mainly thanks to modern media, some level of stress is good for people. Low levels of stress do not elicit high levels of performance from most individuals. Moderate levels of stress are necessary for humans to maintain high function and efficient performance. High levels of stress may cause drops in human performance, as human cognitive and physical capacities are exceeded.

When a body is exposed to extreme stress, the body will typically elicit a fight, flight (run), or surrender response. This response includes the body producing a hormone called *adrenaline*, which is a chemical naturally produced by the adrenal glands and a small number of neurons in the medulla oblongata of the brain, where the influx of adrenaline acts as a neurotransmitter responsible for regulating visceral functions, such as heart and lung activities. The introduction of adrenaline into visceral function regulation will increase heart and breathing rates, rapidly bringing more energy (in the form of oxygen) to the brain and muscles, which may dramatically improve their efficiency. Basically, the body is preparing to perform superhuman tasks, if necessary, to save itself from harm.

19.2 TYPES OF STRESS

The types of stress humans may be exposed to can be divided into groups based on how symptoms come on, how the stress is presented, or by how long the symptoms last. When aviators suffer from stressors, the ability to focus and pay attention is disrupted at a basic, fundamental level.

Aviators must gain a thorough understanding of the different types and periods of stress in order to understand how to battle it. The three recognized types of stress are:

- Physical Stress
- Physiological Stress
- Psychological Stress

Physical stressors originate from an individual's environment which place strain on the body. In the aviation environment, one of the main causal factors of physical stress is travel. Examples may include fatigue caused by unusual work hours and long days or nights, exposure to extreme temperature variations, acute or chronic illnesses, noise, vibration, medications, discomfort, and injury and unusual pains.

Physiological stressors originate from stressors which disturb the homeostasis of humans, which we know affects rest, nutrition, hydration, and oxygen. Examples may include frequent travel to different time zones creating circadian disruption creating sleep/wake cycle difficulties, variations in food intake, not being able to hydrate adequately, or mild hypoxic conditions.

Psychological Stressors are considered the most common forms of human stress, and originates from social factors. Examples may include work environments, decision-making anomalies, pressure from family or supervisors, negative criticism, information overload or task saturation, anxiety or worry, etc. Aviators in a negative psychological state may have problems with attention and detail-orientated tasks.

One may deduce psychological stress causes *emotions,* which definitively affects human performance. The effects of emotion on performance may be difficult for individuals to recognize; therefore, recognition of emotional stress is a main step in learning to control it. Once an individual has gained control over emotions, their performance will improve significantly, particularly in emergency situations. The most effective pilots learn to "check" their emotions at the flight deck door.

Boredom may be considered to be a form pf psychological stress as well. In today's society, people are bombarded with entertainment through constant accessibility to the wide variety of electronic devices available. Once access is to these devices is denied, such as on the flight deck, boredom may manifest itself rapidly. The very basic definition of boredom is "an inability to focus," which we know is the enemy of effective monitoring and therefore inherently dangerous.

19.3 STRESS IN THE WORKPLACE

Based on research conducted by the National Institute for Occupational Safety and Health (NIOSH), approximately half of U.S. workers report elevated levels of stress are common in their workplace. Stress is thought to contribute to about half of all lost working days, along with other psychosocial risks. Around 4 in 10 workers believe stress is not handled well in their workplace.

The World Health Organization (WHO) reports work-related stress is the response people may have when presented with work demands and pressures that are not matched to their knowledge and abilities and which challenge their ability to cope. Stress occurs in a wide range of work circumstances but is often made worse when employees feel they have little support from supervisors and colleagues, as well as little control over work processes. Pressure perceived as acceptable by an individual may even keep workers alert, motivated, able to work and learn, depending on the available resources and personal characteristics. However, when pressure becomes excessive or otherwise unmanageable it leads to potentially disruptive stress. Stress can damage an employee's health and work performance (WHO, 2020).

Scale of the Problem of Workplace Stress

According to the NIOSH, 26-40% of Americans find their work to be very or extremely stressful. Northwestern National Life Insurance Company states 26% of workers believe their job is the most stressful part of their lives. Yale University found 29% of workers are "quite a bit or extremely stressed at work." (CDC, Stress...at Work, 2014)

For aviation-related work positions, the resultant takeaway from this empirical data is pilots will certainly experience stress on the job which may impact their aviating performance. Based on a report published in Aviation Psychology and Applied Human Factors, 74% of pilots reported feelings of stress on the job (Bloudin, 2014). Workers in ground-based jobs may, in most cases, have the opportunity to step away from their job long enough to catch their breath and calm down. For pilots this will not likely be the case. Based on the fact the majority of pilots admit stress influences their performance, an understanding of how stress affects performance is warranted.

Stress, Arousal and Performance

As humans experience stress, focal attention may be narrowed in both good and bad ways. Stress may be so low the lack of stimulation causes a lack of attention. Stress may also assist aviators with focusing on major issues by intellectually eliminating nonessential information, thereby simplifying the task, up to a certain stress level.

If stressors exceed an aviator's cognitive capacity, focal attention may potentially narrow to the degree the aviator becomes "attention deaf," or completely loses situational awareness. Perceptual modalities become overloaded, and recognition of additional useful information is ignored, or not cognitively processed.

The following graph depicts how stress and performance are interlinked:

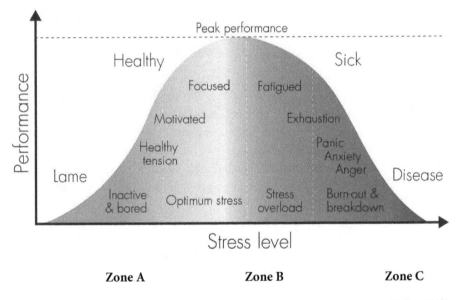

Air Force 2021

Zone A: Aviators experience decreased stimulation levels; and may become sleepy, fatigued, and bored. Attention is low as a result of inadequate mental challenges, and individuals may not maintain intellectual engagement with the aircraft. The result is lowered performance due to the inadequate stimulation. Chronic exposure to Zone A levels of stress may result in job dissatisfaction and lack of motivation and improvement.

Zone B: As aviators approach the top of the stress curve, they experience optimal performance levels as stimulation matches desired levels. Peak performance can be maintained for extended time periods, and the aviator is intellectually engaged with the aircraft. Aviators respond to challenges presented to them in a timely, motivated, and accurate manner. Rapid task completion is realized with well-learned tasks, and diagnostic and novel response aptitude is at its peak level for critical tasks. Work maintained at these levels is considered physically and mentally healthiest for employees.

As aviators extend beyond the top of the curve, optimal performance may be maintained for short bursts; however, extended performance at these levels of stimulation lead to acute fatigue and physical and mental exhaustion.

Zone C: Aviators exposed to extreme high stress levels find the influx of stimulation overwhelming, as arousal levels are too high for effective cognitive processing. Aviators reach maximum task saturation, leading to channelized attention and disregard for SOP's, and get "behind the aircraft." Anxiety levels build, which may lead to anger, panic, and irrational behavior or decisions. Chronic exposure levels to Zone C work stress may have negative impacts on one's health.

Synergistic and Individual Effects of Stress

Stressors can be synergistic, meaning two or more stressors may have greater effects. A singular stressor may be easily mitigated, yet when combined with one or more additional stressors, the cumulative effect may be enough stimulus to cause work disruption. Each and every individual maintains a personal stress limit, and when this limit is overloaded the ability to handle even moderate levels of workload or stimulation may be compromised.

As one contemplates the effects of stress on their own well-being, imagine mechanical stress to an airframe. As the airframe exceeds its designed load factor limits, the affected component may weaken or fail outright. Same as the airframe, if excessive demands are placed on an individual, their capacity to cope may deteriorate or fail.

Response to synergistic stress, as well as stress in generalized terms, varies with individuals based on their unique psychological profile. Acute stress may be handled effectively by individuals, but chronic exposure to the same stress may begin to affect their behaviors. What is stressful to one individual may not affect another. What is stressful today may not have an effect on you tomorrow. Experience is also important, as what is stressful to the inexperienced may be perfectly acceptable to the experienced.

19.4 SELF-IMPOSED STRESS

Measuring the full effects of stressors on an individual may be difficult; however, contributing factors may increase the amount of stress one experiences in a given situation. Although many of the stressors aviators will face are environmental or situational in nature, stress factors may result from individual behaviors. According to the FAA, these self-initiated contributing factors are appropriately termed *self-imposed stressors*.

These factors originate with the individual, such as the use of alcohol, drugs, and tobacco. Other life-style considerations include physical fitness levels, adequate diet, and disruption of circadian rhythm cycles and resultant fatigue from inappropriate life-style choices. We will investigate the effects of these stressors and potential effects on flight duty performance.

Alcohol

The dangerous side effects *alcohol* has on one's driving ability are widely known, so it's not difficult to imagine alcohol in any quantity may produce adverse effects on one's flying abilities.

First, we will examine how alcohol generally affects human systems.

Alcoholic beverages contain an active ingredient called *ethyl alcohol*. Alcohol is an anesthetic drug which, when ingested in any quantity, acts as a depressant. As alcohol is consumed, cellular metabolism is depressed, which is manifested most noticeably in the intellectual functions of the brain.

As cellular metabolism is depressed, the utilization of oxygen being delivered to the cells is depressed as well, which we have learned is called *histotoxic hypoxia*. According to the FAA, listed below is a list of potential physiological, physical and psychological performance losses caused by alcohol:

- Judgement lapses
- Efficiency of ocular movement and audible functions
- Muscular reflex speed and strength
- Sense of responsibility
- Reduced inhibitions and worries
- Relevance of response
- Skill reactions and coordination
- Low illumination visual ability
- Memory reduction and reasoning abilities

- Suppression of judgement, comprehension, and fine attention
- Altered situational perceptions
- Dehydration

Every individual is physiologically unique, causing the symptoms experienced by alcohol ingestion to vary in severity and intensity. Factors determining the rate of alcohol absorption is based on variables such as the type and quantity of food in the stomach, degree of dehydration, concentration of alcohol in the beverage, alcohol consumption rate, and body weight. Another determining factor is the human liver's rate of absorption of alcohol. On average, the human liver is capable of filtering approximately a third of an ounce of pure alcohol per hour.

Based on FAA data, if the average person ingests two shots of vodka in a one-hour period, complete alcohol metabolization by the body may take up to three hours (keeping in mind the other mitigating factors, such as food in the stomach and/or dehydration.)

Alcohol consumption symptoms are similar to hypoxic hypoxia, as the more stressors involved, the more intense the effects. With the effects of alcohol compounded by other stressors, each 10,000 feet of altitude doubles the effects of alcohol in the body.

Part 91.17 of the Federal Aviation Regulations, General Operating and Flight Rules, provides that no person may act as a crew member (or pilot-in-command) of a civil aircraft while under the influence of intoxicating liquor or until at least eight hours have elapsed since the last act of alcohol ingestion. One needs to realize although eight hours should be sufficient following light indulgence (four ounces of alcohol), eight hours is the *minimum* time allowed following alcohol consumption. Eight hours may not be enough time between "bottle to throttle" for some individuals, particularly those suffering the chronic effects of alcohol consumption.

Several chronic effects of alcohol exist, namely vitamin, mineral, and protein deficiencies, liver impairment, excess carbohydrate levels, alcohol psychosis, and others. In addition, one chronic effect which is most noticeable and poses enhanced levels of danger to aviators is the *hangover*. This condition may be more of a hazard than even mild intoxication, and it is more likely for pilots to be flying with a hangover as opposed to being mildly intoxicated.

Symptomology of hangovers may not be solely due to alcohol ingestion. Many symptoms may be attributed to activities accompanying drinking. Large amounts of alcohol, combined with increased amounts of gastric acid, may irritate the lining of the stomach. Blood vessels in the brain dilate, which is part of the reason for headaches being associated with hangovers. Other factors intensifying the symptoms of hangovers include excessive smoking, loss of sleep, and an inadequate diet.

Another major factor is dehydration, occurring from the loss of fluids in the cells of the central nervous system and cerebrospinal fluid surrounding the brain. Loss of these cellular fluids causes tension on the supporting structure of the brain, resulting in a headache. Dehydration may impair one's judgment and cause emotional changes seriously interfering with the pilot's ability to perform effectively. Dehydration may also compound the effects of disorientation due to its effects on the lower brain, or coordination center. Evidence shows human visual and vestibular systems may show the effects of alcohol for periods in excess of 24 hours (FAA, Introduction to Aviation Physiology, 2020).

Drugs

We as a society look for the "quick fix," particularly as the fix applies to illness. As aviators, if any type of *drug* is taken, one must know and understand its effects, especially with regards to drug side-effects combined with the hypobaric conditions of altitude. In aviation, this rule applies equally to over-the-counter (OTC) medications as it does to prescription medications.

Some pilots may be under the impression if a drug is safe enough to buy over-the-counter, it must also be safe enough to fly an aircraft while under its influence. Statistics show about 75-80% of all major aircraft accidents typically involve human factors. Since the effects of a particular drug can be intensified with altitude, it is up to individual aviators to be aware of the effects of any medication taken prior to operating an aircraft. An AME should be consulted as to possible side effects a particular medication may have. Similar in scope to alcohol effects, any medication side-effects will be amplified at altitude.

Aviators self-medicating with OTC medication present two potential dangers to themselves. One, OTC medications tend to simply mask unsafe conditions, which make the aviator unsafe. Two, the desired effect of a drug can may cause undesirable effects on the aviator's ability to adequately perform critical tasks. For example, if one takes an antihistamine for cold or allergy symptoms, one would not only experience relief of symptoms of the illness, but would also cause potentially undesirable side-effects such as drowsiness, impaired coordination, or even blurred vision.

As with any other maintenance medication, oral contraceptives should be cleared for use by an AME. The reason is many of side effects are unknown and the reaction to the medication varies with the individual. It has also been determined that pregnancy is not compatible with flying resulting from the possible effects of G-forces, mild hypoxia, and other stresses associated with the flight environment (FAA, Introduction to Aviation Physiology, 2020).

Tobacco

Extensive research shows smoking or chewing *tobacco* have long- and short-term effects. Long-term risks include conditions such as emphysema, heart conditions, and a multitude of cancers. The US Public Health Service reports cigarette smokers are 20 times more likely than non-smokers to die from cancer of the esophagus, bladder, and pancreas. Smoking causes a relative deprivation of oxygen to the heart muscle and contributes to circulatory problems by constricting the arterioles. Smoking also irritates the lining of the respiratory tract, causing edema and swelling, restricting proper respiration. These and other factors could lead to emphysema and other permanent lung damage. Of the many potentially harmful substances one receives from tobacco smoke, three are of particular importance to aviators. These include *carbon monoxide, tars,* and *nicotine.*

Carbon monoxide (CO) constitutes up to 2.5 % of the volume of cigarette smoke and even more in cigar smoke. If the smoke of three cigarettes is inhaled at sea level, a blood saturation of 4 % CO may result. One reason for this is CO combines with hemoglobin approximately 250 times more readily than oxygen. The hemoglobin is not available to carry oxygen to the tissues, producing slight degrees of hypemic hypoxia, therefore reducing individual altitude tolerance and increasing the effects of hypoxic hypoxia at any altitude.

Tar is the term given to the viscous residue left from tobacco smoke. One of the major cancer-causing agents, tar's primary effect is to cause destruction of the delicate mucous membranes of the respiratory tract. Tar also interferes with the natural cleansing action of the lungs and impairs proper oxygenation of the blood which reduces tolerance to hypoxia.

Nicotine is an extremely potent drug that acts primarily on nerve and muscle tissue. It is extremely poisonous. The amount found in two cigarettes, if injected directly into the blood stream, could be fatal. Some cigarettes contain 10 to 20 milligrams of nicotine, of which up to 2.3 mg is absorbed if the smoke is inhaled. Up to 1.5 mg is absorbed through the membranes of the mouth if the smoke is not inhaled. A 2.5 mg oral dose of nicotine can cause nausea, and 50 to 60 mg is considered a lethal oral dose. Individuals consuming two packs of cigarettes per day exceed these amounts, but rarely report any nicotine effects because of rapid detoxification and the development of individual tolerance.

In recent history, a certain stigma placed on smoking tends to make smoking in public socially unacceptable. As a result, many individuals are opting for smokeless tobaccos in the form of *snuff* or *chewing tobacco*. These forms provide the user with all the detrimental effects of tobacco, minus the carbon monoxide and toxic vapors. The absence of the CO and toxic vapors is more than made up for by the harmful effects of oral or nasal ingestion of various quantities of tobacco mixed with binding agents and synthetic flavors.

Circadian Rhythm and Stress

As discussed in the chapter on Fatigue, statistical studies in long-distance flight have shown most individuals are sensitive to travel-produced *circadian rhythm* shift, and may experience some rest discomfort for several days. Individuals experience hunger, sleepiness, or are awake at the wrong time with regard to the new local time. Their "body clock," "stomach clock," and elimination system are confused. After transcontinental flights in the US, these conditions typically last from 3-4 days; after transatlantic flights, 5-6 days. Crossing 12 time zones, which leads to a complete reversal of the day-night cycle, may take 10-12 days to re-synchronize. As a general rule, most travelers adjust to a new circadian cycle at a rate of nearly one hour per day, or one day per time zone. Some individuals adjust more easily after eastbound flights, while others after westbound flights, and some when returning to their home time zone with its familiar climate and social order. There are, of course, a few people who are not particularly time sensitive at all.

The problem of circadian de-synchrony is especially important for those whose occupations involve time zone changes. Flight crews of long-distance air routes fit in this category. They cross and re-cross time zones several times a month, or even fly around the world once every month. A too-frequent shift of the circadian cycles causes fatigue, which is well recognized by the pilot associations and medical directors of airlines (FAA, Introduction to Aviation Physiology, 2020).

19.5 EFFECTS OF STRESS

FAA research shows complex tasks requiring higher level thinking are more affected by stress. Another common effect is fixation, or focusing on one aspect or problem to the exclusion of other problems, which quite obviously may create potentially dangerous situations to develop as a result.

As flightcrew typically operate in teams, the *effects of stress* on how teams operate need to be addressed, such as startle effect, memory, skilled performance, decision making, and the effects stress has on team communication, performance, and decision making. We will also examine ways of decreasing stress effects of team performance.

Startle Effect

In many circumstances, abnormal events in aviation start with a sudden adrenaline-inducing indicator such as a master caution warning light, a sudden directional change of the aircraft, or a loud, unidentified noise. This unexpected stimulus triggers physiological and psychological responses in aviators, who automatically orient their senses to the stimulus, undergo physiological arousal, and experience an emotional state related to fear. These responses are collectively termed the *startle effect*.

Typically, the startle effect momentarily interrupts the aviator's functional task. If the aviator recognizes the indicators of the event, they may be able to quickly diagnose the indicators and summon the appropriate learned response from memory. If the indicators are unfamiliar and appear potentially threatening, stress may quickly follow. Some abnormal events make themselves obvious without an abrupt indicator, such as gradually rising engine oil temperature or slow ice accumulation on control surfaces. Unanticipated events may startle aviators because indications in the environment do not correlate with the individual's mental model of the situation and what is supposed to be occurring.

If the situation appears threatening, and the aviator cannot rapidly diagnose and respond appropriately, profound stress may occur resultant from the uncertainty of the outcome. Re-orienting attention to the abnormal event, combined with rapidly increasing stress, may cause the aviator to stop managing ongoing functional tasks or lose situational awareness (Dismukes, 2015).

Memory

Numerous aspects of *memory* have been identified by the scientific community. Three aspects concerning aviators are: Acquisition of new information to be used in ongoing tasks (such as a flight clearance), processing of this new information, and retrieval of well-established information from long-term memory (such as the procedure for programming flight parameters into the FMS). Working memory is involved in all three of these identified aspects, which we will examine next.

Working memory is central to human cognition and it is difficult to identify intellectual activities where it is not involved. Working memory is perceived as the active processing system in memory, serving as a kind of mental workspace. It temporarily makes a small set of information readily available from the operating environment or from long-term memory so the information can be continuously manipulated and used in the performance of diverse tasks.

Working memory allows one to focus on a central task and execute the required operations while excluding information not relevant to the task. Working memory consists of two distinct components: a storage component, consisting of temporarily activated and readily available information, and a central executive system that supports goal-directed behavior by manipulating information, shifting attention within or between tasks, and selecting among competing responses. Therefore, the functions of working memory and attention overlap considerably.

Individuals undergoing stress worry about the stressful event, in turn reducing the availability of working memory storage and processing capacity for dealing with ongoing tasks by competing for these limited cognitive resources. When stress consumes an aviator experiencing an unexpected and potentially dangerous event, a response system based on muscle memory as opposed to intellectual performance may be more useful (Dismukes, 2015).

Skilled Performance

Most of what pilots do in flight consists of performing highly-practiced tasks, also known as *skilled performance*. Abnormal situations impose unusual conditions and potentially unusual combinations of tasks; however, even when dealing with emergencies pilots are typically performing highly-practiced tasks, although under unusual conditions and circumstances. In essence, skilled performance equates to *automated cognitive processing* abilities, where situational response is automatic. This is opposed to *controlled cognitive processing*, which requires conscious cognitive effort for situational response.

Early studies on the effects of high environmental temperatures on skilled performance of navigation and piloting performance indicated more skilled operators showed less performance decrement than less skilled operators. These findings conclude greater expertise allows tasks to be performed through automated cognitive processing, creating fewer demands on limited cognitive resources required for controlled processing. This conclusion is consistent with what is known about automated cognitive processing, which found automatic processing is more resistant to stressors, such as fatigue and high workload situations, than controlled processing. Generally, highly-practiced skills are more robust than skills drawing heavily on limited cognitive resources, presumably because over-learning causes more elaborate representation in brain circuits, therefore easier retrieval of information. Similar in scope to automated processing, studies found pilot judgments requiring direct retrieval of facts from long-term memory to be relatively unimpaired by stress. However, retrieval of information that is not well-learned is apparently much more vulnerable to stress effects than deeply learned information.

Although the probability exists that highly-practiced, highly-automated skills are somewhat less vulnerable to disruption of stress than tasks relying on controlled processing, skilled performance may be more negatively affected than one may expect from the automated/controlled processing perspective. In real-world aviation settings, performance of practiced tasks does not take place in isolation; the human operator must decide how and when to initiate a skilled task, evaluate how well it is working, possibly modify how the task employed, and integrate it into performance of other tasks. All this involves controlled processing, so in stressful abnormal situations, exactly how automated skills are deployed may possibly be impaired.

The more familiar (automated) an aviator becomes with emergency tasks, the less controlled processing exposes the aviator to mistakes in high-stress situations (Dismukes, 2015).

Human Decision Making under Stress

Formal investigations into aviation accident causal factors frequently conclude pilot error, poor judgment, or inappropriate decision making were contributing factors. The typical good decision making of pilots failed for some reason, perhaps due to the stress of an unusually demanding maneuver or abnormal situation. For this reason, we must understand the effects of stress on judgment and decision making, particularly how and when aviation flightcrew decision making processes and performance fail under stress (Dismukes, 2015).

Decision Making, Team Performance, and the Effects of Stress

Commercial flight operations are a team effort, as flight decks contain multiple crew members and others outside the flight deck such as flight attendants, ATC, dispatch, and maintenance who may contribute to crew decision making and problem solving, particularly during abnormal events. The FAA has long recognized and recommended the critical importance of training and evaluating flight crewmembers above and beyond the performance of individual pilots. In fact, negligence in crew resource management (CRM) has been noted by the NTSB as probable causal factors of multiple accidents, specifically failures of decision making, communication, and coordination.

We must first consider how team decision making differs from decisions made by individual flightcrew members. The fact is there is little, if any, difference to the actual decisions made. On the flight deck, the same decisions regarding aircraft operation need to be made whether an individual pilot or flightcrew is in control; the same goals, parameters, environmental inputs, and available alternatives exist. However, the significant difference is the added interaction among flightcrew members. Team decision making fundamentally differs from individual decision-making stemming from the need to communicate and coordinate activities. To anticipate the effects of stress on team decision making, the primary hindrances to effective decisions appear to occur through disruptions to communication and coordination among team members.

The abnormal tasks involving flightcrew team performance are most often complex, cognitive tasks where deciding, planning, and problem solving all occur in an integrated manner, hopefully in a timely manner. A decider (usually the Captain) receives inputs, carries out mental operations of encoding, storing, and retrieving information, and finally transforms the information into an appropriate output, typically a selected flight control action (Dismukes, 2015).

The effects of stress on team decision making and performance research repeatedly predicts negative effects due to acute stress (Cannon-Bowers and Salas, 1998; Driskell and Salas, 1991). Studies occurring within personality and social psychology revealed team members under acute stress search for and share less information, tend to neglect social and interpersonal cues, and fail to recognize situations that require interpersonal interaction (Cohen, 1980; Janis, 1982). Furthermore, individuals find it more difficult to differentiate among people with differing areas of expertise (Rotten, Olszewski, Charleston, and Soler, 1978) and often confuse their roles and responsibilities (Torrence, 1954).

Stress hinders team performance, including decision making, primarily by disrupting communication and coordination. Coordinated action lies at the heart of effective team performance, and acute stress significantly reduces both the number of communication channels used and the likelihood that they will provide needed information to their teammates, thereby compromising their ability to retrieve and update information and coordinate its allocation to others crewmembers (Dismukes, 2015).

19.6 DECREASING THE EFFECTS OF STRESS ON TEAM PERFORMANCE

The negative effects of stress on team performance and decision making may be mitigated using scientifically-researched methodology. This is accomplished through training designed to help flightcrew understand and cope with the effects of stress. One such training method developed for military flight operations is four-phased approach, which has been shown to reduce stress impairment of complex tasks and team performance:

- Academic phase
- Procedure refinement phase
- Cross-training phase
- Practical training phase

The *academic training phase* is where trainees are provided information about physiological and psychological responses likely to occur during stressful environments and how their performance may be affected. Subjects include the physiological affects experienced under stress (elevated heart rate, rapid breathing,), psychological and cognitive effects (anxiety, narrowed attention, confusion), and team effects (ambiguous or impaired communication). This information would help prepare aircrew members for these effects, reduce distraction from these effects, and to be alert for alterations in team performance.

The *procedure refinement phase* provides trainees information on how to maintain performance under stress. This includes specific techniques such as making communications more explicit and periodic review of what the flightcrew members understand about an emergency situation.

The narrowing of attention is an adaptive response to the stress environment. This is an attempt to simplify an increasing complex and demanding task environment, and another approach to maintaining effective team performance is to *simplify the task environment*. For those settings in which effective teamwork is critical, it may be necessary to structure the task to make it less demanding (delegating subtasks), so attention can be maintained on essential task and teamwork cues. If stress restricts attentional resources, task completion or checklists may need to be restructured so flightcrew members are not forced to sacrifice attention to teamwork matters to maintain performance.

Unfortunately with real-world tasks, reducing the complexity of the task environment is a difficult undertaking; however, this may be accomplished through stream-lined checklists and communications necessary to accomplish the required task. Flightcrew attention must be maintained on high-priority items to the exclusion of information perceived to be of lower importance. The importance of teamwork coordination and communication must not be perceived as secondary to other basic, individual task demands (Driskell, 1999).

The cross-training phase eliminates reliance on one specific crewmember to accomplish a specific task. Cross-training essentially teaches flightcrew members the duties and responsibilities of their teammates. Cross-training assumes knowing the various roles & responsibilities, and understanding how one's own tasks and responsibilities relate to others, may improve communication and coordination. Improved communication and coordination effectiveness appears to maximize team performance under periods of high stress (Dismukes, 2015).

The *practical training phase* occurs so trainees have the opportunity to experience stressful situations in controlled environments, such as challenging abnormal situations presented in realistic flight simulations. Practical training should be accomplished in sufficient volume so as to develop flightcrew member instinctive and automated emergency response reflexes. This training assists in eliminating excessive or ambiguous communications.

19.7 INDIVIDUAL STRESS MANAGEMENT

Although stress affects virtually everyone to some degree, we will focus our discussions on individual stress management in aviation professionals specifically. Many options and expert opinions on reducing stress exists. While we will discuss some of those options later in this section, perhaps the most important component of individual stress management is an individual's *resilience*.

Resilience

Resilience may be defined as the ability to keep going in the face of adversity, or the process of adapting well in the face of adversity, trauma, tragedy, threats, or significant sources of stress. It is inevitable you, as well as your colleagues, will commit errors. Your ability to recover from those errors and move forward is crucial, as this ability is a critical component in dealing with individual stressors, as well as managing inflight emergencies.

Life itself is a constantly changing event, and everyone experiences twists and turns. These range from everyday challenges and irritations to traumatic events with lasting impacts, such as the death of a loved one, a life-altering accident or illness. Change affects individuals differently, bringing unique thoughts, emotions, and uncertainty. Through it all, people generally adapt well over time to life-changing situations and stressful situations, due in part to resilience.

Being resilient does not mean individuals will not experience major difficulty, adversity, or distress. Those individuals commonly experience emotional pain and stress, and the journey to achieving resilience is likely to involve considerable emotional distress.

While certain factors may make some individuals more resilient than others, resilience is not necessarily a personality trait that only some people possess. On the contrary, resilience involves behaviors, thoughts, and actions virtually anyone can learn and develop. An individual's ability to learn resilience is one reason research has shown that resilience is ordinary, not extraordinary.

Similar to increasing muscular strength, increasing resilience takes time, focus, and intentionality. To increase one's capacity for resilience to overcome and grow from difficulties, we will examine the challenges to building resilience as well as individual resilience building characteristics.

Challenges to Building Resilience

Times will emerge where individuals may experience difficulty, or even get stuck, on their way to building resilience. Managing difficult personal work relationships, differences in political or religious beliefs, and feelings of personal failure or constant criticism. A person may be challenged by the volume of work expected to perform, or the pace at which work completion is expected. Perhaps the nature of work itself may be outside of one's comfort zone, or beyond one's capabilities.

It is important for one to realize this journey does not have to be accomplished alone. Some individuals will encounter events which impact their ability to function in society, or possibly even daily activities. One cannot control all of life's circumstances, and in those situations asking for help is advised. Help or assistance may come from family, friends, support groups, or professional counseling. To ensure the best and most help is achieved, one must feel at ease with whatever help or assistance is chosen, and then follow through with whatever treatment plan or advice is rendered. One will experience personal growth through focusing on the manageable aspects of life's challenges with the proper support.

Individual Resilience Building Characteristics

According to the American Psychological Association (APA), individual ability to adapt may be developed through components which may empower one to overcome and learn from difficult and traumatic experiences. These four core components include:

- **Connection**
- **Wellness**

- **Healthy thinking**
- **Meaning**

Connection emphasizes connecting with empathetic and understanding people to allow one to understand they are in the situation alone. Trustworthy, compassionate people sharing one's viewpoint may assist one in validating feelings, empowering them to build resilience in adverse conditions. Find people who truly care about you, and accept their assistance and support.

Some may find connection with their religion an effective coping mechanism as well. One with deep religious convictions may find relief and reduced anxiety by practicing their faith.

Wellness may be thought of as "self-care." Self-care encompasses promoting healthy and positive life-style factors such as proper nutrition, sleep, hydration, and exercise. Focusing on such factors legitimately assists building resilience, and mental and physical health, all of which go a long way in stress management. Regular exercise, proper sleep, and healthy nutrition are effective in maintaining good attitudes and perspectives, as well as easing tension and anxiety. Relaxation techniques such as stretching, meditation sessions, breathing exercises, etc. may be useful, and could even be employed on the flight deck, if used within reason.

Although typically seen as a cliché, the fact is the better one feels about themselves, the harder is becomes to feel bad. Negative outlets should be avoided, including alcohol or drug abuse, rest avoidance, contact with negative people, or avoidable conflicts with coworkers.

Healthy thinking encompasses being able to "face down reality;" in other words, understand one cannot control everything, and at times needs to accept those things one cannot change. One's ability to improvise, overcome, or adapt to situations instead of opposing them will be more effective for long-term peace-of-mind. One should use what is available to them to accomplish their goals within the scope of their environment, and realize they are responsible for their own "luck." Optimism may be a useful tool for some; however, optimism cannot distort one's assessment of reality.

One needs to seek to identify and understand the stresses in their life, and act on the things they can change. Issues such as personal misunderstandings, toxic relationships, mounting debt, child problems, job dissatisfaction and many others will be a part of life. One needs to develop a plan to resolve those stressors, and act on those plans. One needs to cope with things they cannot change, as well as understanding not everything will go their way.

There will be times when issues may remain unresolved, yet one still has to perform their duties effectively and safely without psychological distraction. One effective technique used by military aviators is to "compartmentalize." Compartmentalization is a subconscious psychological defense mechanism allowing one to set concerns aside when preparing and operating aircraft. Although not effective in all situations, it may be useful in the majority of situations when conflicting emotions threaten operational flight safety. The basic concept is to mentally understand existing personal issues cannot be solved while performing one's duties, so those negative thoughts are pushed aside until such time uninterrupted intellectual thought may be assigned to those issues.

Meaning assists in minimization of stress through identification of one's core values and purpose to provide emotional guidance in one's life. For many, pursuing their identified "meaning" provides the thrust for their main reason to exist, possibly over and above their career. A deep sense of purpose and self-worth may be fostered through volunteer work with animals, the homeless, disadvantaged or medically-challenged children or older adults, church, and many others. Once one pursues a true meaning and experiences tangible results, resilience may grow exponentially.

According to the APA, additional individual stress-management techniques include being proactive, goal orientation, and self-discovery.

Being proactive includes acknowledgement and acceptance of one's emotions during difficult periods. This may be fostered through questioning what one can do about problems in one's life. Times exist when problems may seem too big to tackle; however, breaking those problems down into manageable pieces may lessen the intimidation of tackling the issue. As opposed to looking at the "mountain" in front of you, focus on each step necessary to climb the mountain. Taking personal initiative may also remind one to muster motivation and purpose during stressful periods of your life, increasing the likelihood one can and will rise to the task during difficult times ahead.

Goal orientation requires one to develop realistic goals and do something on a habitual basis, even if it seems like an insignificant accomplishment, enabling one to move forward on things one wants to accomplish. As opposed to focusing on tasks seemingly unachievable, focus on one thing one can accomplish *today* helping one move in the direction one wants to go.

Self-discovery refers to one having grown in some respect as a result of one's struggles. For example, after tragedies or hardships, some individuals report improved relationships and greater sense of strength, even while feeling vulnerable. This may increase one's sense of self-worth and heighten their appreciation for life (APA, 2012).

Conclusion

Much scientific evidence exists indicating stress may degrade human performance in many ways, specifically disrupting cognitive structures and processes. During inflight emergencies and other highly challenging events, aviators may be cognitively impaired to degrees whereas information, processing information, and assessment skills are impaired. Management of concurrent tasks, memory recall of facts, and communication and coordination with fellow flightcrew members is compromised. Not all experienced aviators will psychologically fall apart amidst life-threatening emergencies; fortunately, many aviators display remarkable abilities to manage such events, albeit not always with successful conclusions.

Highly-practiced skills of experienced aviators have proven to provide protection in such events; however, given the potential extreme demands of certain emergencies and the inherent vulnerability of aspects of cognition to stress, it remains crucial to devise countermeasures to stress effects. Success has been demonstrated utilizing phased training to develop performance of individuals and teams. Further countermeasures may be implemented in the design of flight deck interfaces, training, and operating procedures, based on current knowledge concerning the specific ways stress affects cognitive processes.

As cognitive capabilities of stressed aviators are likely impaired, performance should be supported by workload reduction measures and prompts to perform required tasks assisting keeping track of where aviators are regarding checklists or procedures. The abilities to shift attention among tasks without becoming locked into one task, maintaining situational awareness, identifying and analyzing decision options, and to psychologically step back from moment-to-moment demands of the event to establish a high-level mental model guiding actions as the event unfolds are of critical importance.

Chapter 19 Core Competency Questions

1. NASA research indicates stress negatively affects core cognitive mechanisms of _____ and _____.
2. What are the three recognized types of stress?
3. True or false: Hypoxia may be a physiological stressor.
4. True or false: Boredom may be a psychological stressor.

5. True or false: Stress can be good for maximum performance.
6. What are examples of self-imposed stressors?
7. What are the four phases of decreasing the effects of stress on team performance?
8. What is considered the most important component of individual stress management?
9. What are the four core components of individual resilience-building characteristics?

20. THERMAL STRESS

In aviation's beginnings, pilots flying open-cockpit aircraft were required to fly their aircraft with little protection from the environment to mitigate environmental stressors. With the advancement of modern aircraft, protective systems and clothing, and survival equipment, one would think thermal stress, be it from heat or cold, would no longer cause significant concern for aviators. The fact is, even in current technologically-advanced aircraft, thermal stress may be only seconds away.

On the commercial, corporate, or large military aircraft flight deck, one must consider the "greenhouse" effect of solar radiation penetrating windscreens and windows, which may quickly heat up the flight deck environment. Failure of environmental control systems (ECS) may result in immediate exposure to heat/cold conditions in short time-frames. In military fighter aircraft, the amount of flight and protective gear, and survival equipment pilots wear combined with a "bubble-top" canopy may generate copious degrees of heat stress. Aircrew members conducting flight operations in high-airflow environments such as open-door helicopters need be concerned with cold stress. Additionally, any environmental protection afforded by the aircraft may be potentially lost if the aircraft loses pressurization via a blown window or door.

Ground operations may cause thermal stress during periods of hot or cold temperature extremes, humidity, physical exertion, or solar radiation reflected off the asphalt or concrete of a ramp. Taxiing the aircraft in hot or cold environments may induce thermal stress as the doors are closed, and the aircraft may not receive adequate ram air for effective aircraft environmental control.

Aircraft can obviously cover great distances in relatively short periods of time, which may position the aircraft over hostile terrain or vast expanses of water. If an aircraft ditching is forced by circumstances, the aircrew may be exposed to extreme thermal variations based on the ditching environment, and may be aggravated by factors such as wind or rain, exacerbating human heat loss. Once on the ground or water, aircrews may be fully exposed to the environment, at which point their very survival depends on their ability to mitigate undesirable and/or challenging environmental conditions.

Understanding factors which contribute to human heat gain, heat loss, proper hydration & dehydration, and thermal injury are essential for aviators in the recognition of signs and symptoms of thermal stress and mitigation techniques. In this chapter, we will discuss:

1. The definition of human thermal comfort and stress
2. Physiological effects of thermal stress
3. Human thermoregulation
4. Heat stress and mitigation techniques
5. Cold stress and mitigation techniques

20.1 DEFINITIONS OF HUMAN THERMAL COMFORT AND THERMAL STRESS

Human thermal comfort may be defined as "a condition of mind, which expresses satisfaction with the surrounding environment." High or low environmental temperatures and humidity provide discomfort sensations, and potential heat or cold stress. These stressors reduce the body's ability to adequately cool itself, or maintain adequate heating capabilities.

Taking the above information into account, *human thermal stress* may be defined as "the effect of temperature extremes on motivation, dexterity, endurance, and the ability to maintain high cognitive functions."

20.2 EFFECTS OF THERMAL STRESS

The *effects of thermal stress* will be quite obviously be highly influenced be affected by a variety of factors, such the amount and value of protective clothing, ambient temperatures, physical activity, hydration, and fatigue. Many challenging tasks in aviation may be performed in environmentally stressful situations involving high or low ambient temperatures. Simply performing a preflight walk-around inspection of one's aircraft can be a challenge in the wrong atmospheric conditions.

Unlike ectothermic reptiles and various 'cold-blooded' animals, humans are endothermic, meaning we have the need and ability to regulate core body temperature within a relatively narrow range, despite the temperature of our environment. Heat is gained internally as a result of metabolic energy production, which increases during work or exercise. Heat may also be gained externally when the environmental ambient temperature is greater than the body's temperature. As overall heat gains exceed losses, core temperature increases, and as overall heat loss exceeds gains, core temperature decreases (Jedick, 2014).

The human body typically responds to heat gain in variety of predictable ways, all ultimately decreasing physical or psychological performance, which is a critical consideration for professional aviators. As previously mentioned, as sweating increases and blood vessels near the skin open up, the result is blood shift from internal organs, including the brain, to the skin's surface. Although muscular strength is apparently not impaired by excessive heat, one's muscular endurance, fine dexterity, and time-to-fatigue decreases. A crucial consequence of heat exposure to aviators is evidence in which heat alone, when controlled for fatigue and dehydration, causes deteriorations in motivation, attention, vigilance, memory, recall, and decision-making capacity (Jedick, 2014).

According to research, and noted in, for the Journal of Applied Physiology, Nutrition, and Metabolism, many factors, or modifiers, are involved when calculating the effects of thermal stress, including *environmental factors* such as temperature, wind, and water (precipitation or immersion); *activity factors* such as work intensity and work/rest cycles; *clothing factors* such as insulation, weight, and permeability; and *individual factors* such as age, physical condition, and hydration.

Acute effects of thermal stress include:

- Perceptual
- Physical
- Environmental

Perceptual effects of thermal stress include increases in physical discomfort and pain, and cognitive functions decrease.

Physical effects of thermal stress include decreases in manual dexterity and muscular strength, cardiovascular strain increases, and individual metabolic cost increases, meaning a body requires greater energy production to perform work,

Environmental effects of thermal stress include increases in slips, falls, and accidents, mainly due to decreases in manual dexterity and muscular strength.

Chronic effects of thermal stress include:

- Cardiovascular
- Respiratory
- Peripheral circulation
- Musculoskeletal
- Dermatological

Cardiovascular effects of thermal stress include increased morbidity risks. Increased cardiovascular stress amplifies frailties in an individual's system, rising the opportunity for failure.

Respiratory effects of thermal stress include increased opportunities for development of asthma and chronic obstructive pulmonary disease (COPD) as a result of breathing air whose temperatures are beyond homeostatic limits.

Peripheral circulation effects of thermal stress include episodes of frost-nip, frostbite, or white-finger vibration syndrome, potentially causing irreparable damage to peripheral capillaries.

Musculoskeletal effects of thermal stress include overuse and muscular strain issues, such as carpel tunnel syndrome, or strains due to muscular activity in environments beyond homeostatic limits.

Dermatological effects of thermal stress include skin issues such as psoriasis or atopic dermatitis as a result of cutaneous exposure to extreme temperatures, potentially causing permanent damage to the outer layers of the skin (Cheung, 2016).

20.3 HUMAN THERMOREGULATION

The human body processes a variety of strategies to regulate body core temperature. The primary method the body uses to cool itself is through sweating. For sweat to translate into heat loss, sweat must evaporate from the skin's surface; therefore, one's ability to decrease body temperature is highly influenced by clothing, the presence and speed of wind, and the relative humidity of one's environment. To a lesser degree, the body may also lose heat through shifting blood to the dermis layer of the skin, causing loss through convection and radiation to the environment, and through behavioral mechanisms such as seeking out shade, removing clothing, or hydrating.

Biophysics of Human Heat Transfer

Body core temperature changes are resultant form either positive or negative changes in heat storage. As the body core gains more heat than it dissipates, core temperatures increase; conversely, if heat loss exceeds heat gain, core temperature decreases.

Approximately 25% of energy expended during physical work goes toward performing the actual work and approximately 75% of energy expended is released in the form of heat. This heat is released from active skeletal muscles and transferred from the body core to skin, which then dissipates the heat to the ambient environment. Physical exercise may increase whole body metabolism by as much as 15 to 20 times above the resting metabolic rate in healthy young individuals. If heat production is not balanced by loss, body temperature will increase early in the work experience. In cold climatic conditions, the opposite occurs, where resting individuals must increase overall resting metabolic heat production through mechanisms such as shivering or other physical movement, which may increase metabolic heat production by 3 to 5 times, in order to maintain normal body core temperature (37°C) (Jedick, 2014).

Heat loss and heat gain mechanisms are highly dependent on the ambient temperature. When ambient temperatures are equal to or greater than one's skin temperature, evaporative heat loss predominates and accounts for virtually all body cooling activities. Dermis layer sweat glands secrete fluid onto the epidermal layer of the skin permitting evaporative cooling when liquid converts to water vapor. Sweat evaporation rates depend on air movement and the water vapor pressure gradient between the skin and the environment. If water vapor pressure is high, less sweat is able to evaporate from the skin to the environment, compared to a dry environment. In still or moist air, the sweat does not readily evaporate and collects on the skin. Sweat dripping from the body or clothing, as opposed to evaporating, provides no cooling benefit. When ambient temperatures are lower than one's skin temperature, dry heat loss (heat loss from radiation and convection) is greater than heat loss through evaporation.

In review, heat transfer between human skin and the ambient environment is influenced by air temperature and humidity, wind speed, solar/sky/ground radiation, and clothing.

Heat Transfer Mechanisms

Heat transfer is the physical act of thermal energy exchange through heat dissipation between two systems. Generally speaking, the greater the thermal differential, the higher the transfer rate. Three methods of human heat transfer exist, including:

- Conduction
- Convection
- Radiation (Heat emitted from a source)

Conduction is the transfer of heat between physically touching solid objects caused by thermal differential. For aviators, this may occur resulting from standing on hot or cold flight line tarmac, or contact with aircraft metal.

Convection is the transfer of heat through air or fluid movement over a body caused by thermal differential. This is the primary method of bodily heat movement from the core to the skin. For aviators, this may occur from exposure to ambient environmental temperatures through a window or door failure in an aircraft, or evacuating a downed aircraft into extreme temperatures on land or in water.

Radiation is the transfer of heat through the thermal motion of particles in matter, or heat emanation from a source. This transfer mechanism may originate from solar, sky, or ground sources. Radiation heat transfer is irrespective and independent from the motion of air.

Human Requirements for Heat

Human core body temperature is generally considered high compared to average ambient environments. Core body temperature must be maintained in a relatively narrow range for normal metabolic functioning, as this is highly dependent on core temperatures. Physiological temperature regulation is predominantly independent of intellectual behavior, but may be modified by it.

Average core body temperature generally ranges from 95-103.9 degrees F, with normal considered 98.6°F, and average skin temperatures at or about 93.2 degrees F. Altered core body temperatures are dangerous to human function, as even relatively slight core temperature fluctuations may cause serious consequences. Brain tissue is exceptionally sensitive to altered body temperatures, as brain thermal homeostasis may be affected from changes as little as 5.4 degrees F above normal causing structural changes. At 104 degrees F, loss of neural function and organ damage may occur.

As human physiology requires body core temperatures need to be regulated within a narrow range, the body core is the main controlled variable. The controller in this function is the *hypothalamus*. One of the main functions of the hypothalamus is maintenance of homeostasis, accomplished by responding to various signals from the body's internal and external environment.

Skin temperature signals are integrated with signals regarding body core temperature at the hypothalamus, and if body core temperatures deviate from homeostatic limits, an appropriate physiological response is activated. If the body is warm, *vasodilation* occurs, and if the body is cold, *vasoconstriction* occurs.

Vasodilation and Vasoconstriction

As mentioned earlier, humans are endothermic, needing to regulate body temperature independent of the environmental temperature and within a narrow temperature band. In response to environmental temperature variation, the body's two main mechanisms of human thermoregulation are *vasodilation* and *vasoconstriction*.

Vasodilation is basically the body responding to thermal variation by widening blood vessels to facilitate excess body heat loss, whereas *vasoconstriction* narrows blood vessels to facilitate maintaining body heat. Both conditions occur under the direction of nervous system, and *smooth muscles* are responsible for regulating blood vessel widening or narrowing.

Vasodilation widens (dilates) blood capillaries near the skin, while at the same time narrowing deeper blood vessels, to assist in excess body heat loss. Parasympathetic nerve impulses direct smooth muscles of the blood capillaries near the skin to relax, causing vasodilation. This condition reduces vascular resistance to blood flow inside blood vessels, allowing blood flow through the capillaries near the skin to increase, therefore decreasing blood pressure in these capillaries. As vasodilation increases blood flow to the cutaneous layer of the skin, it transfers metabolic heat to the epidermal layer of the skin, resulting in increased heat loss across the epidermis.

Vasoconstriction narrows (constricts) blood capillaries near the skin, while at the same time widening deeper blood vessels, to assist in body heat retention. Sympathetic nerve impulses direct smooth muscles of the blood capillaries near the skin to contract, causing vasoconstriction. This condition increases vascular resistance to blood flow inside blood vessels, allowing blood flow through the capillaries near the skin to decrease, therefore increasing blood pressure in these capillaries. As vasoconstriction decreases blood flow to the cutaneous layer of the skin, metabolic heat is prevented from leaving the body, and redirected to the body core.

Mild Fevers

An elevation in one's body temperature is a normal human reaction to infections. This increase in temperature is known as a *fever*, which is the body's perfect response mechanism in an attempt to destroy viral species.

A fever signals our immune response system is doing its job, and creates an environment within the body in which bacteria and viruses cannot easily survive. Every increase of 2 degrees F equates a 2% decrease in viral species invading the body, up to 103.9 degrees F. Fevers have been shown to increase the amount of anti-viral and anti-cancer substances in the bloodstream, and speed disease-fighting cells to an infection. *Slight fevers* are characterized by increases in body temperature up to 100.4

degrees F, while *high fevers* are characterized by body temperatures up to 103.1 degrees F.

The main infection-fighting cells are *T-cells*, which is a type of white blood cell. T-cells flow quietly through the blood by the millions, monitoring for harmful bacteria and viruses. Once potential danger is detected, T-cells aggressively react by converging on the nearest lymph node, which are glands scattered throughout the body. The T-cells mission is to trap disease-causing microbes near the infection site. This maneuver assists the T-cells to attack the invading microbes and clear them out. When one suffers from a cold or other infection, lymph nodes typically swell in the neck, typically behind the ears or under the jaw. When this swelling occurs, it is a sign one's immune system is performing its mission and fighting the infection one is experiencing.

Scientific studies reveal reducing fevers with medication increases the severity and duration of given illnesses. A normal, healthy adult should wait at least a few hours prior to taking fever-reducing medications to let the body do its job, as this will assist in building one's immune system. Copious amounts of water and rest may be the preferred option, so long as the fever does reach beyond 103.1 degrees F.

20.4 HEAT STRESS AND MITIGATION TECHNIQUES

Human adaptation to *heat stress* has evolved over time to be relatively efficient. One theory maintains humans are essentially tropical in nature, and therefore better equipped to adjust physiologically to heat than cold. Differing levels of heat exposure affect the body in increasing increments of severity.

Causes of Heat Stress in Aviation

Typical causes of heat stress in aviation may be produced by the environmental effects of hot environments such as temperature, humidity, clothing, physical activity, and radiant temperature of the ambient environment. These factors are influential during aircraft preflight walk-around inspections, environmental control system (ECS) cooling failure inflight, lack of adequate hydration, or potential survival situations.

Normal Heat Generation

Although thermal environmental factors may be the most obvious body core temperature influencer, other non-thermal factors exist such as dehydration, alcohol use, overdressing, physical activity, and acclimatization.

Dehydration increases body core temperature thresholds for sweating, therefore delaying sweating onset. Alcohol use affects the physiological ability to regulate body core temperature as a result of altered cerebral function. Overdressing for the climate disallows the body to effectively dissipate heat through the skin. Physical activity increases body metabolism, particularly in heat, increasing body core temperature and initiating physiological responses to attenuate the temperature rise.

Heat Regulation Processes

Increases in metabolic heat causes a dilation of blood vessels (vasodilation), with blood pooling towards the cutaneous layer of the skin, leading to a drop in blood pressure. Fluid loss also occurs from sweating, and the combination of these effects cause a decrease in blood volume available to the heart.

The increase in circulation to the skin bring metabolic heat to the body's surface, causing an increase in sweat production, and therefore evaporative cooling effects. Skin temperature alters the sensitivity of the relationship between sweating and homeostatic body core temperature; thus, at any given body core temperature, sweat rates increase when skin is warmer and decrease when skin is cooler.

Acclimatization represents an example of how a change in thermoregulatory control may impact physiological and physical performance. If an individual acclimatized to higher temperature environments, sweating may occur at lower body core temperature thresholds. This response mechanism allows for earlier metabolic heat dissipation and cooler skin temperatures, resulting from more effective cutaneous vasodilation and higher skin blood flows rates, improving dry heat loss. As the body secretes sweat onto the skin, evaporation takes heat energy from the skin, resulting in more effective cooling effects than convection alone. The end result from acclimatization is lower body core temperatures due to better evaporative, radiative, and convective heat loss.

Human physiology is adaptable and resilient. A human body has the capacity to acclimate to thermal stress after approximately 10-14 days of exposure to hot environments. To maximize this adaptive response, individuals need to be exposed to ambient heat a minimum of two hours per day. This adaptation may be accelerated by exercising during heat exposure. Heat adaptation may be reduced or lost approximately one week after reintroduction to cooler environments (Jedick, 2014).

Dehydration

The more fluid a body loses to the environment through sweat evaporation, the more fluid replacement is necessary. Humans can sweat faster than one can absorb water from the gut. As humans enter a deficit of bodily fluids, or hydration, the human then suffers from *dehydration*.

When one becomes dehydrated, physiological thermoregulatory control mechanisms for heat loss are impaired. Dehydration is often quantified as a percentage of body mass. Most studies isolating the effects of dehydration on human performance found cognitive performance is measurably decreased and mistakes are more frequent starting at 2% dehydration (Jedick, 2014).

The majority of Americans are considered "chronically dehydrated," mainly due to inadequate hydration sources. Proper human physiological and psychological function, as well as their very survival, depends on a homeostatic balance of fluids in the body. Unfortunately, thirst is not an adequate indicator of an individual's level of dehydration. If an individual becomes thirsty, it is typically an indication the individual is already dehydrated. The same holds true for the color of one's urine; if urine is clear, the individual is adequately hydrated, and if urine is yellow, dehydrated. Even during periods of physical inactivity, normal respiration and skin may account for up to 1,000 ml of insensible water loss per day in normal environmental conditions, and more so in dry environmental conditions.

Dehydration may cause symptomology including fatigue, poor memory, dizziness, constipation, headaches, decreasing motivation, or even mood shifts.

Proper Hydration

Every portion of one's body, including our cells, tissues, and organs, require adequate supplies of water to maintain optimum function. Water assists our bodies in disposing of waste through urination, bowel movements, and perspiration. Water also lubricates and cushions joints, provides protection for sensitive tissues, assists in respiration, and (of course) maintains homeostatic thermal control. Humans constantly lose water through perspiration, breath, urine, and bowel movements, and this water must be consistently replaced through consuming foods and beverages containing water.

In maintaining proper hydration, popular myths exist as to how water one should drink. One particularly persistent supposed truth maintains one should consume eight 8 oz glasses of water (64 oz) per day. In reality, according to the Mayo Clinic, no single formula is appropriate for every person in every conceivable situation.

The US National Academies of Sciences, Engineering, and Medicine (USNASEM) recommends approximately 15.5 cups (124 oz) of water per day for men, and approximately 11.5 cups (92 oz) of water per day for women. When considering these amounts, one must realize 20% of water consumption comes from foods, and the rest from beverages (water, coffee, tea, milk, juice, soda).

Individual water intakes may need to be modified from the above formula based on factors such type and volume of exercise, temperature and humidity of one's ambient environment, and overall current health concerns. USNASEM recommends drinking water (or appropriate substitute) before, during, and after meals and exercise, or if one feels thirsty.

Individuals may consider their fluid intake adequate if one rarely feels thirsty, or one's urine is colorless or pale yellow. Adequate hydration increases cell's metabolic and functional efficiency, provides better energy, clearer thinking, less muscular cramping, easier bowel movements, clearer skin, better stamina, and less bloated skin. Adequate hydration also reduces the chances of chronic health issues such as hypertension, urinary tract infections, coronary heart disease, gallstones, and glaucoma.

According to Dr. Donald Hensrud at the Mayo Clinic, in the rare event one consumes too much water, a condition known as *hyponatremia* may develop. Hyponatremia occurs when the concentration of sodium in your blood is abnormally low. Sodium is an electrolyte, and helps regulate the amount of water in and around one's cells. One or more factors ranging from an underlying medical condition to drinking too much water may cause the sodium in your body to become diluted. When hyponatremia occurs, one's body water levels rise and cells begin to swell. This swelling may cause many health problems, from mild to life-threatening (Hensrud, 2020).

When considering which fluids are best for hydrating purposes, water will suffice for most individuals, dependent on one's environment, level of exercise, and fitness level. For excessive work in hot environments, one may consider the use of sports drinks containing low-sugar electrolyte replacement formulas. Drinks with too much sugar draw too much water into the gut to process the sugar, causing insulin spikes and ultimately dehydrating properties.

Heat Emergencies

According to Dr. Edward Laskowski of the Mayo Clinic, heat emergencies include one of three heat-related syndromes; heat cramps, heat exhaustion, and heatstroke.

Heat cramps are the mildest of the three conditions; however, may include painful, involuntary muscle spasms. Heat cramps typically occur during periods of heavy exercise in hot environments. Spasms may be more intense and more prolonged than are typical nighttime leg cramps. Fluid and electrolyte loss typically contribute to heat cramps. Muscles most often affected include one's calves, arms, abdominal wall, and back, although heat cramps may involve any muscle group involved in exercise.

Should heat cramps be suspected, one must rest briefly and cool down, drink clear juice or an electrolyte-containing sports drink, and conduct gentle, range-of-motion stretching and gentle massage of the affected muscle group. Do not resume strenuous activity for several hours or longer following cessation of heat cramps. Seek medical attention if heat cramps fail to resolve within approximately one hour (Laskowski, Heat Cramps: First Aid, 2020).

Severe *heat exhaustion* is a condition whose symptoms may include heavy sweating and rapid pulse, resultant from one's body overheating. Causes of heat exhaustion include exposure to high temperatures, typically when combined with high humidity, combined with strenuous physical activity. Without prompt treatment, heat exhaustion can lead to heatstroke, a life-threatening condition. Fortunately, heat exhaustion is preventable.

If one believes they are experiencing heat exhaustion, stop all activity and rest, Move to a cooler place, and drink cool water or sports drinks. Seek medical attention if signs or symptoms worsen, or if symptoms do not improve within one hour. Seek immediate medical attention if individuals become confused or agitated, loses consciousness, or are unable to drink (Laskowski, Heat Exhaustion, 2020).

Heatstroke is a condition caused by one's body overheating, usually as a result of prolonged exposure and/or physical exertion in high temperatures. The most serious heat-related injury, heatstroke may occur if your body temperature rises to 104 F (40 C) or higher. The condition is most common in the summer months. Heatstroke requires emergency treatment. Untreated heatstroke can quickly damage your brain, heart, kidneys, and muscles. The damage worsens the longer treatment is delayed, increasing one's risk of serious complications or death (Laskowski, Heat Stroke, 2020).

Significant dehydration may occur in less than 30 minutes under the right environmental conditions. As one's body temperature rises, more sweat develops for evaporation. If evaporative mechanisms are impaired by wearing heavy clothing, the heat inside the clothing increases, causing more sweat and thus, more heat (wet heat). Body temperature increases reaching 103 degrees may cause organ failure. Once one's body temperature reaches the critical point of 104 degrees, internal organs cease adequate blood flow, leading to thermal runaway of body temperature to 108 degrees, which typically causes fatal injuries.

Avoidance and Treatment of Heat Emergencies

Should exposure to excessively hot environments be unavoidable, following recognized guidelines to minimize heat stress and avoid heat injury is necessary. The following steps should be adhered to:

- **Minimize exposure time.**
- **Acclimate**
- **Maintain proper hydration – 1½ quarts per hour of a proper electrolyte solution**
- **Wear proper clothing**
- **Avoid additional heat stress.**
- **Use ice packs**
- **Cold water immersion**

Minimize exposure time is the obvious first step to ensure heat stress does not develop to dangerous levels. One must limit the amount of time exposed to hot temperatures. The CDC defines a "heat wave" as indicated by daily temperatures in excess of 95 degrees F, or when the daily temperature exceeds 90 degrees F and 9 degrees F or more above the maximum temperature reached on preceding days. The CDC recommends a physically-fit, well-hydrated individual wearing normal work clothing may perform moderate work for no more than 30 minutes and rest 30 minutes on a 90- degree F day in full sun and 30% humidity. An increase to 95 degrees F under the same conditions warrants "caution," meaning safe work exposure time may only be a few minutes, if at all.

Acclimate to the environment over a period of 7- to 14-days. This may be accomplished by gradually increasing work exposure for oneself to hot environments, starting at approximately 20% of the normal work period on day one, followed by increasing work exposure 20% per day.

Maintain proper hydration with regular fluid-replacement breaks. CDC recommendations include consuming from .5 quarts per hour for easy work in 80-degrees F temperatures, to 1.0 quarts per hour for moderate to hard work in ambient temperatures above 90 degrees F. Fluid replacements will vary depending on environmental conditions and personal fitness levels; however, at no time should fluid consumption exceed 1.5 quarts per hour. The CDC also recommends fluid consumption not exceeding 12 quarts per day, except for "highly-conditioned" people. Urine should be maintained in a clear state for properly hydrated individuals.

Wear proper clothing appropriate for the environmental conditions. Natural, breathable clothing fibers are considered best for hot environments, wicking away moisture from the body improving evaporative cooling and comfort. Synthetic, non-breathable fabrics being undesirable as they cause one to sweat, losing moisture at higher rates, and disallowing for effective evaporative cooling. Clothing should allow for air circulation, as opposed to being tight, tucked-in or sealed. In most cases, light-colored long sleeves shirts and pants provide better protection from solar radiation.

Avoid additional heat stress through pre-planning to accommodate the conditions as much as practical. Keeping the aircraft parked in shade, allowing the flight deck to pre-cool prior to flight, minimizing preflight walk-around inspections during the hottest part of the day, and avoiding exercise for four hours prior to flight to avoid increasing body core temperature are possible methods to mitigate additional heat stress.

Use ice packs in the armpits and groin to cool body core temperature. This will also cool blood flow through the brachial and femoral arteries.

Ice water immersion may be used as an emergency treatment to individuals suffering from heat exhaustion or heatstroke. This method will cool body core temperatures by approximately ½ degree per minute. The individual being treated should remain in the water for approximately 10 minutes to cool body core temperatures to acceptable levels.

20.5 COLD STRESS AND MITIGATION TECHNIQUES

Human adaptation to *cold stress* has not evolved to be an efficient physiological process. As mentioned in the previous section, humans are able to relatively effectively physiologically adjust to heat; however, human physiological response to cold is limited and must be supplemented through behavioral activities. Behavioral thermoregulation requires conscious action including increased physical activity, wearing appropriately warm clothing, manipulating environments such as adjusting indoor thermostats, or creating a microhabitat increasing heat retention and providing shelter from the elements.

Causes of Cold Stress in Aviation

Cold stress in aviation may be produced by the environmental effects of cold environments during preflight walk-around inspections, environmental control system (ECS) heating failure inflight, loss of flight deck window or windscreen at altitude, or exposure to cold land or water environments in survival situations.

Cold ambient environments force the body to work harder to maintain body core temperature. As ambient temperatures drop below normal and wind speed increases, metabolic heat may leave the body more rapidly.

Wind chill is the temperature one's body feels when air temperature and wind speed are combined, and is of concern for those exposed to cold temperatures. For instance, if ambient air temperature is 40°F combined with a wind speed of 35 mph, the effect on exposed skin is as if the air temperature was 28°F. A given environmental air temperature may appear comfortable at first glance; however, wind, dampness, and clouds may make the temperature seem miserable. In fact, a given static temperature of -15 degrees F, for example, is much more tolerable to most humans than the same temperature derived from wind, which may make a wind chill factor of -15 degrees F feel 10 or 20 degrees colder.

Other individual factors contributing to cold stress are inadequate clothing, exhaustion, and poor physical conditioning, as well as predisposing health conditions such as hypertension, hypothyroidism, and diabetes.

Physiological Effects of Cold Stress

Cold stress occurs in humans by reducing skin temperature, eventually leading to a reduction in body core temperature. Most of the body's energy is utilized to shift blood flow to the body core, providing protection for critical internal organs. This shift in blood flow allows exposed skin and extremities to rapidly cool, increasing the risk of health issues such as hypothermia and frostbite.

Cold stress may be *generalized* through total body core temperature reduction, leading to serious health conditions, or *localized* through tissue damage of specific body parts, such as ears, skin, hands, or feet.

Cognitive and physical performance is affected by cold stress. Cognitively, decreased peripheral circulation also causes stagnant hypoxia to the cranium, leading to reduced blood flow to the brain and related cerebral hypoxia issues. Physically, manual dexterity and muscular motor control will be affected by decreased peripheral circulation and cooling of muscle tissue.

Cold Stress Protective Mechanisms

The body's primary initial response to cold environmental exposure is peripheral vasoconstriction, or slowing blood flow to the skin. Altered blood flow to skin, subcutaneous fat, and skeletal muscle effectively increases insulation, and reduces convective heat transfer between the body's core and skin, leading to decreases in skin temperature. Vasoconstriction occurs as skin temperature declines below 95°F. Extended exposure to cold environments causes blood vessels in subcutaneous tissues to constrict, effectively increasing the insulating layer. Cooling of subcutaneous inactive muscle tissue may cause these tissues to stiffen. Therefore, vasoconstriction to cold assists in reducing heat loss and protecting body core temperature, but in turn causes a decline in peripheral tissue temperatures. Even with maximal vasoconstriction of the skin, heat loss still occurs and only heat generation can counteract heat loss effects.

Human Heat Generation

In response to the physiological adaptions humans experience as a result of cold, increasing heat generation in the body is necessary. Humans generate heat by three methods:

- Metabolic
- Involuntary Shivering
- Physical Activity

Metabolic heat is generated on a cellular level through blood perfusion and energy production. Metabolic fuels such as carbohydrates and fatty acids are oxidized in cellular mitochondria to produce adenosine triphosphate (ATP). The hydrolysis of ATP causes energy to be released to support muscular contraction. Normal metabolic heat production is the amount of work produced by the body in a sitting, relaxed position.

Involuntary shivering increases metabolic heat production and voluntary behaviors such as increased physical activity, fidgeting, exercise, etc. Shivering produces rhythmic, repeated, involuntary muscular contractions. The intensity of shivering correlates directly to the severity of cold stress, and may produce metabolism rates three to four times more than normal. Cold water immersion may produce shivering intensities raising metabolic rates six times more than normal.

Physical activity is a voluntary compensatory mechanism one may use to increase metabolic activity. As one increases the intensity and duration of physical activity, greater oxygen consumption is required of cells. The more oxygen required, the more ATP must be produced, thus high levels of metabolic heat generation. If sitting relaxed produces normal levels of metabolic heat, doing medium levels of work while standing produces twice the metabolic activity. Walking at 2 mph produces 2.4 times normal levels, and walking at 3 mph produces 3.4 times normal levels (Olesen, 2001).

The inability of the body to generate sufficient levels of heat production may lead one to experiences effects of cold stress such as *hypothermia* and *frost bite.*

Hypothermia

Hypothermia is a progressive loss of body heat occurring as body heat drop quicker than it can be regenerated, and normal body temperature drops below 95 degrees F. As body temperature drops below 95 degrees F, cognitive and physical symptoms begin to develop. If these symptoms remain untreated in a timely fashion, severe hypothermia may ultimately lead to death.

Hypothermia is caused by cold stress, but may occur at ambient temperature levels as high as 55 degrees F, given wet and windy conditions. Protection and maintenance of body core temperature remains the single best option for individuals, as the effects of hypothermia are typically difficult and timely to reverse.

According to Dr. Edward Laskowski at the Mayo Clinic, mild symptoms of hypothermia include slowed mental processing skills, depressed muscular reflexes, and shivering, although the individual may remain alert. Moderate symptoms will be presented as a worsening of existing symptomology, including loss of coordination, confusion, and disorientation. Severe symptoms include a cessation of shivering, inability to walk or stand, dilated pupils, slowed breathing and pulse, and eventually loss of consciousness. At the point of unconsciousness, it is imperative the individual receive immediate and appropriate medical attention, as death is likely near (Laskowski, Hypothermia, 2020).

Individuals suffering from hypothermia need to be treated by medical professionals, but if medical assistance is not immediately available, the following steps may be taken:

- **Move the individual to a warm, dry space.**
- **Replace wet clothing with dry clothing.**
- **Cover the individual's head, neck, and body with layers of blankets, followed by a vapor barrier such as a large garbage bag or tarp (do not cover the face).**

- If the individual is alert, provide warm, sweetened beverages to them. Avoid alcohol or giving beverages to an unconscious individual.
- Place warm bottles or chemical heat packs in the individual's armpits, sides of the chest, and groin.

The more quickly an individual can be treated, the more complete their recovery will be.

Frostbite

Frostbite is a progression of cold stress injury to the body caused by freezing human skin and underlying tissues. Quite obviously, the lower the ambient environmental temperature, the more rapidly frostbite will occur. Frostbite typically will affect extremities such as the hands or feet; however, any exposed skin tissue to extremely cold temperatures for long enough time periods is subject to frostbite. In the most severe circumstances, amputation of the damaged body part may be required (Laskowski, Hypothermia, 2020).

The chart below illustrates windchill temperatures and time-to-frostbite:

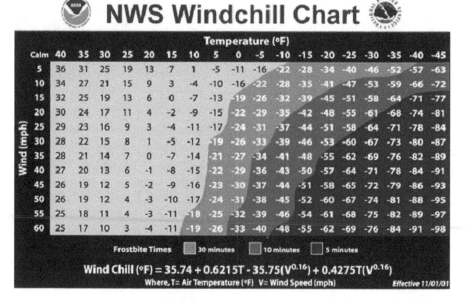

National Weather Service 2021

442

As we see on the chart, high wind speeds and below 0 degree F temperatures may lead to frostbite in a matter of minutes, meaning human protection measures need to be implemented immediately.

Symptoms of frostbite include numbness progressing to pain in the affected tissue; reddened skin progressing to gray or white patches of damaged skin; damaged tissue feeling firm or hard to the touch; and blisters potentially forming on the damaged tissue in severe cases.

Individuals suffering from frostbite need to follow the same recommendations listed in the treatment for hypothermia. In addition to those instructions:

- **Do not rub affected and damaged tissue as this action may cause additional damage.**
- **Do not attempt to treat by applying water or snow on damaged tissue, and do not break blisters.**
- **Loosely cover damaged tissue to protect the area from contact.**
- **Do not attempt to rewarm the affected area prior to receiving medical assistance.**
- **If the individual is alert, provide warm, sweetened beverages to them. Avoid alcohol or giving beverages to an unconscious individual.**
- **Protective Countermeasures for Cold Stress**

Insulating one's body by dressing properly for existing conditions is the most critical factor for cold stress mitigation. Selection of proper protective fabrics is crucial. Cotton may provide the worst protection, as cotton's insulation value is lost when wet. Wool, silk, and many synthetic fabrics provide more reliable protection, and retain their insulation values even when wet. The following are considerations for effective protection in cold environments:

- **Dynamic layering**
- **Semi-Permeability**
- **Extremity protection**

Dynamic laying provides thermal flexibility. Weather is dynamic, and one's ability to adapt to continuously changing environmental conditions is crucial. While one does not want to experience cold stress, one does not want to become too hot in clothing, as sweating in frigid condition may become rapidly dangerous. Once metabolic heat dissipates, wet clothing may draw heat out of the body faster than dry clothing. Cold weather clothing should prevent convective and radiant body heat loss.

When layering clothing, three loose-fitting layers provide the most productive insulation, as loose-fitting clothing traps warm air produced by the body, therefore maintaining the body's heat envelope. One may remove or replace layers as conditions dictate to maintain adequate heating properties, without the risk of becoming too hot or too cold.

Semi-permeability repels rain and wind, but breathable membrane allows air to move in and water vapor (sweat) to move out. An inner layer of wool, silk, or synthetic fabric provides vital wicking actions to move moisture away from the body. A middle layer of wool or synthetic fabric will provide insulation even when wet. An outer layer providing wind and rain resistance provides further environmental protection, but must provide ventilation as well.

Extremity protection is critical. One may maintain adequate protection for the body core, but if the extremities are exposed, much of the body heat one is attempting to maintain may be lost.

The use of an insulated hood or robust, full coverage hat assists in keeping the whole body warmer, as up to 40% of one's body heat can and will escape through the cranium. The face and mouth may be covered with a knit mask or covering to protect the lungs from extreme cold. Insulated and waterproof gloves should be utilized for hand protection, along with insulated and waterproof boots. Hats, gloves, and boots should provide not only insulation, but a snug fit as well. With gloves, one must consider how much dexterity one maintains while wearing the accessory, as having to remove the gloves to perform manual duties will impact heat loss.

Conclusion

Management of thermal stresses needs to be included in an aviator's intellectual checklist. In extreme cases, minutes matter to ensure homeostatic body core temperatures are maintained.

One must be aware of anticipated environmental conditions at their present location, along the route of flight, and final destination regarding temperatures, winds, and windchills. If temperatures are above or below normal, thought must be given to exposure times, and try to stay out of the wind as much as possible. Attempt to keep physical activities below levels which make one sweat.

One must be mindful of layering clothing, enabling dynamic adjustment to changing environmental conditions. Keep the body and clothing dry, replacing or drying them if they get wet. Be aware of fellow crewmembers' condition, and be watchful for signs of hypo- or hyperthermia.

Lastly, let others know of your travel plans and file a flight plan. If travelling alone or with a small crew, consider using ATC Flight Following in the event the aircraft goes down. This will give rescue forces a place to start searching for you and your crew, making the chances of rescue much more likely.

Chapter 20 Core Competency Questions

1. What are environmental factors to consider when calculating the effects of thermal stress?
2. What do the acute effects of thermal stress include?
3. What percentage of expended energy actually goes towards performing the actual work?
4. What are the three heat transfer mechanisms?
5. What is our average body core temperature range?
6. At what core body temperature may organ damage and loss of neural function occur?
7. An elevation in one's core body temperature in an effort to destroy a viral species is known as a _____.
8. What do humans suffer from when they enter a deficit of bodily fluids?
9. Under the right environmental conditions, humans may become dehydrated in as fast as _____ minutes.
10. What is the body's primary initial response to cold environmental exposure?
11. What are the three methods humans generate heat?
12. Hypothermia occurs when core body temperature drops below _____ degrees F.
13. How fast could a human become frostbitten at a temperature of -25 degrees F with 20 mph winds?

21. AIRCREW SURVIVAL

The subject of *survival* can be a complicated endeavor. Individuals have spent thousands of dollars, years of time, and volumes of reading pursuing survival subject matter, and still crave more information. At issue is even though one may be highly trained, situations may be encountered where chances of survival are slim at best; however, this does not mean knowing the basics of survival is invalid. The term "survival" must not be confused with "camping" or "enjoying the outdoors" as some modern media programs appear to suggest; survival can be an intensive, excruciating experience where difficult decisions are made and one mistake may cost one their lives.

Aircraft cover vast distances and wide varieties of terrain, weather, climates, and potential food and water sources. Some areas are hot, some cold, some humid, some dry. Some terrain lends itself to survival, and some terrain is so inhospitable seemly no living thing could possibly survive.

While this chapter will provide you effective, experience-based information, there is no way the information could possibly be considered "all-inclusive," and should not be treated as such. You will be provided basic information and knowledge to allow one to make informed decisions, and give one a good chance of making it through an unintentional downing in hostile, remote areas. The focus will be on relatively short-term survival episodes under one week in length, as technology exists enabling rescuers to find downed aircraft fairly effectively. However, even though "short-term survival" may seem benign, the reality is even several hours in the wrong environment may be life-threatening. It is highly encouraged if one desires more intensive survival information, they should certainly pursue it, as survival training can be a fascinating, confidence-boosting experience for those with enough courage to try it.

In this chapter, we will discuss:

1. The definition of survival
2. The survivor's attitude
3. Survival stressors
4. Survival factors
5. Critical survival needs
6. Survival health threats
7. Survival planning

21.1 DEFINITION OF SURVIVAL

A reasonable working definition of *survival* is "the continuation of life or existence, typically in spite of an accident, ordeal, or difficult circumstances." Another way of describing survival is simply staying alive despite potentially life-threatening circumstances. Although survival as it applies to aviation may be applicable to a wide variety of events, we will focus on problems aviators may face following an unintentional ditching or emergency landing in remote areas.

Those well-versed in the mechanics of survival maintain successful mitigation of survival situations are 5% skill, and 95% mental attitude. Most, if not all, of perceived mental stress in these situations may be diminished with a positive mental attitude. One's positive attitude may be translated as a positive outlook on any given situation. Many individual stories have surfaced depicting someone surviving seemingly insurmountable odds against them with little-to-no-skill, but a resolute refusal to give up despite the odds. This equates to the most essential aid to survival to anyone in a survival situation is simply their *will to live*. One's driving force to want to survive any and all obstacles must exceed the sum of one's fears.

Although it is understood positive mental attitudes assist greatly in survival situations, many obstacles to positive mental outlooks exist in the midst of trying to survive. Perhaps the largest obstacle to survival takes place before the emergency event even exists, which may be best summed-up as: "It can't happen to me." Individuals believing nothing will ever happen to them rarely take the time to prepare for a survival episode, as they're not willing to admit to themselves this may be a possibility. Much of this individual denial may stem from fear, as the unknown may be difficult thing for some individuals to face. Knowledge of what to expect during a survival episode may help one gain more understanding and confidence of their capabilities in such an episode, potentially dispelling some of this fear.

21.2 THE SURVIVOR'S ATTITUDE

As one's mental state is the most important component in successful mitigation of survival situations, one's mindset should be trained to reflect the proper attitude towards these events. The first step towards this epiphany is to realize survival events can and will occur. Like many other emergency events, the probability is you will never need to survive in remote wilderness; however, the possibility is always present.

A survival episode may present itself while flying over remote terrain, but also if your boat loses power on a fishing trip, you get caught in a blizzard on a hike in the mountains, your vehicle breaks an axel in the desert, or your vehicle slides into the ditch on the way home for Christmas. One never knows what will happen in the next minute, and the only way for one to be prepared is to <u>prepare today</u>. In addition to being prepared with survival equipment, one needs to ensure the equipment stays in and is available in whichever vehicle you intend on traveling in, whether a motorcycle, boat, car, truck, or aircraft.

As mentioned, the greatest obstacle to survival is a negative mental attitude. One needs to realize success is possible in extremely adverse conditions, and one needs to develop the ability to overcome adversity. As opposed to being irritated by small issues, one needs to overcome those obstacles, and those obstacles one is unable to overcome need to be adapted to and a new plan developed. The best way to deal with a problem is to handle it as soon as practical, as unresolved issues simply tend to fester and grow larger with time.

The most effective survivors are those who have eliminated the concept of "good luck" or "bad luck," but instead who specialize in "making their own luck." Consider the following scenarios:

- It is not bad luck your aircraft ran out of fuel, but rather from improper preflight planning.
- It is not bad luck your flight segment ended up in adverse weather, but rather a lack of good weather reports (or any weather report).
- It is not bad luck your aircraft went down in remote terrain and no one knows your estimated position, but rather lack of proper notification and following a flight plan.

Although these scenarios could on indefinitely, the concept is many life-threatening survival episodes may have prevented or minimized with more effective planning, forethought, and preparation.

Panic in a survival episode equals defeat. One cannot panic and expect to make rational decisions. Fear is to be expected, as survival episodes are not experienced by most people on a regular basis, but whereas fear can be managed, panic is exponentially more difficult to control.

The following incident review represents an example of how a positive mental attitude prevails despite debilitating circumstances:

Incident Review – May 2019: A Cessna 402C was being repositioned from Reno, NV to Columbia, CA, with portions of the flight occurring over mountainous terrain. Approximately 30 minutes into the flight, the aircraft impacted terrain at 10,000 feet in two- to –four feet of snow.

During the impact sequence, both wings, right engine, and left horizontal stabilizer were ripped off. As the flight deck was being torn apart, the captain was ejected from the fuselage and died on impact. The first officer (FO) was alive, but hanging upside-down from their seat and suffering from a compound fracture (bone penetrating skin) of the right femur and two broken ankles.

The FO released themselves from the seat and crawled out of the fuselage to reach their flight bag containing a hand-held survival radio, as the FO realized the emergency locator transmitter (ELT) was not working. Quickly beginning to suffer from hypothermia, the FO realized they needed to get back into the fuselage to stay warm; however, the only way in was through a window in the main cabin. The FO proceeded to kick out the cabin window and crawled back into the fuselage.

The FO proceeded to attempt to make contact with potential search aircraft with the survival radio, finally achieving success after 4.5 hours. The FO transmitted their position to the search aircraft immediately prior to the radio battery dying, leading to a successful rescue for the FO.

Analysis: The aircraft impacted mountainous terrain, with a severely-injured FO eventually making radio contact with search forces and being rescued.

Conclusion: Following a horrific aircraft accident and suffering from debilitating injuries, the FO maintained intellectual command of the situation by realizing the importance of retrieving the radio, protecting themselves from the elements, and trying to make radio contact with search forces. The fact the FO managed to kick out a cabin window with a compound fracture of the femur and two broken ankles is testament to the FO's will to survive. The FO managed to rapidly adapt to the situation and overcome seemingly insurmountable obstacles to ensure their own survival, regardless of the pain and discomfort involved in the process.

21.3 SURVIVAL STRESSORS

Certain stressors will present themselves in many survival sequences. The survival stressors presented in this section are not the only stressors one may face, as others certainly exist; however, what may provide stress to one may not be as stressful to another. One's experiences, training, physical and mental conditioning, and self-confidence level all contribute to mitigation of stress in survival environments. One will be unable to avoid stress, but what is important is to manage the stressors, adapt behaviors, and mitigate the stressors to prevent them from working against you.

Psychological stressors include:

- Fear and anxiety
- Loss of convenience and entitlement
- Boredom and frustration
- Loneliness and isolation

Physical Stressors include:

- Fatigue
- Stress
- Thirst and hunger
- Pain, injury, and illness
- Exposure
- Poisoning

Fear and anxiety are experienced by most individuals when placed in an unusual situation, typically brought on by fear of the unknown.

Loss of convenience and entitlement may be a problem for some, as some individuals may experience an inability to cope without a heater or air conditioner, without their phone, computer, or ability to simply drop by a supermarket or restaurant to get something to eat.

Boredom and frustration may present themselves in survival episodes, as times may exist where doing nothing feels counterproductive, or attempts to complete a task prove difficult and do not proceed as one thought.

Loneliness and isolation may affect some individuals, as humans are intrinsically social beings and require companionship, particularly in adverse conditions.

Fatigue will normally be an issue, as adequate sleep or rest may be difficult to achieve, given the prevailing environmental conditions.

Stress may quite obviously affect survivors, as trepidation as to how the survival episode may end or an inability to improve conditions inhibits intellectual focus.

Thirst and hunger typically present themselves as stressors, as adequate hydration or nutrition may be extremely difficult to mitigate in one's given environment.

Pain, injury, and illness may cause significant levels of individual stress, dependent on the level of malady.

Exposure may rapidly become a serious stressor, depending on ambient environmental temperatures, wind, precipitation, and ability to achieve adequate shelter to maintain homeostatic body core temperatures.

Poisoning may be a significant stressor if one ingests indigestible or contaminated food or water.

While the physical stressors may range in severity from mild to life-threatening, mitigating these stressors ultimately depends on the survivor's mental capacity to cope, making psychological stressor mitigation most important. Of psychological stressors, the most challenging stressor one must conquer to gain control of the event is *fear*.

Fear Factor

While most individuals possess a basic understanding of the concept of emotional *fear*, let us examine what fear truly is.

Fear may be defined as "to be afraid of something perceived to be dangerous, painful, or threatening; or to be afraid of the unknown." Fear may be perceived as a weakness by some; however, in reality fear may be a sign of good sense. Some unforeseen events or issues deserve to be feared, as this may provoke the appropriate level of response required to survive the event.

The real issue is whether one has control over their fear or not. As President Franklin D. Roosevelt said during a famous speech: "The only thing we have to fear is fear itself--nameless, unreasoning, unjustified terror which paralyzes needed efforts to convert retreat into advance." In other words, if one allows fear to control the outcome of a given situation, failure is imminent

As one is exposed to certain elements unfamiliar to an individual, the emotion of fear is perfectly normal. Not only is fear normal, but fear may actually enhance human performance (also known as the *fight or flight* response) during times of hyper-stress.

Physiological Symptoms of Fear

As an individual is surprised or startled by perceived dangerous events, fear of the unknown causes a biological response. The amygdala area of the brain plays a part of human emotional processing, and if danger is perceived by the amygdala, it generates a signal to the hypothalamus of the brain. The hypothalamus functions as the command center of the brain, and communicates with the remainder of the body via the sympathetic nervous system. The hypothalamus transmits signals through autonomic nerves to the adrenal medulla, which responds through the release of the hormone *adrenaline* (also knowns as epinephrine) into the bloodstream.

This introduction of adrenaline increases blood circulation, carbohydrate consumption, and breathing rates to prepare the body for maximum performance or exertion. Complex motor skills, visual reaction times, and cognitive reaction times are at their peak when heart rate is between 115 – 145 beats-per-minute (bpm), which in turn causes the presentation of physical symptoms.

These physical symptoms include:

- Neurological impulse speed amplifies 4x
- Dilation of pupils
- Rapid heart rate and breathing
- Increased strength and performance
- Decreased ability to feel pain
- Feeling jittery or nervous
- Sweating

The onset of these symptoms prepares one to perform at superhuman levels, with increased reflex speeds, better eyesight, more oxygen flow, more strength and endurance, and the ability to withstand injuries allowing a continuance of performance. So long as fear is controlled, fear assists one's abilities to cope with otherwise precarious situations.

Control of Fear

As mentioned, one needs to control fear as opposed to fear controlling oneself. The following remedies are recommended and accepted methods one may use in controlling fear:

1. **Admit being afraid.** The worst one can do is try to convince themselves they cannot or will not be afraid. One must not let fear turn to panic, as panic causes individuals to act irrationally.
2. **Think and plan logically.** As one enters a survival situation, the first thing to accomplish is to sit down and relax, if no immediate danger exists and conditions permit. Allow the mind to adapt to conditions, and develop a plan on what to do initially.
3. **Develop confidence in your abilities.** This includes practicing skills needed in survival episodes, such as building fires, shelters, or purifying water ahead of time.

4. **Be prepared** for survival situations every time one may be potentially exposed to survival episodes. Always have a stocked survival kit on hand and ready for deployment.
5. **Keep busy** to keep the mind off negative thoughts. Although keeping busy is helpful for mental health, be mindful of calorie consumption, as calories may be difficult to replace.
6. **Cultivate good survival attitudes.** Learn to tolerate personal discomforts. When one is exposed to adverse conditions, one may not be able to visualize the end-point of the condition. One must realize no situation lasts forever, and this must be one's focal point for the future.
7. **Practice your religion**, if this gives one comfort. It may provide the intellectual fortitude and calmness necessary for rational decision-making.

Psychological Symptoms of Panic

As mentioned, allowing one's fear to evolve to *panic* may lead to catastrophic and irrational intellectual decisions. Symptoms of panic include:

- Irritability, increased hostility
- Nausea
- Confusion, forgetfulness, and inability to concentrate
- Talkativeness in early stages leading to speechlessness
- Feeling of unreality, flight (unrestrained running through the area)
- Racing heart rate and shortness of breath
- Intellectual stupor

Once individuals succumb to panic, any hope of immediate rational response is lost. One's brain fails to select a reasonable course of action, typically leading to inaction or irrational behavior. Individuals in the midst of panic have been known to act wildly, running around a campsite without reason, removing their protective clothing in cold, or hiding from rescuers.

Individuals need to understand methods for managing panic prior to its onset.

Panic Management

As *panic* may lead to undesirable results, one can teach themselves efficient situational management through practicing visualization of emergency scenarios. Research has shown repeated visualization of specific events assists the brain in reacting effectively in those emergency situations may be effectively mitigated through visualizing the scenario, and mentally practicing the immediate response. An example of this is the immediate pilot actions following a rapid decompression; as the pilot hears the initial explosive noise, feels the wind blast, and sees condensation, their first instinctive action is to grab for their oxygen mask. The same *conditioned response* may be achieved with many scenarios one may encounter.

Individuals experiencing the early symptoms of panic may manage high stress environments by following the following steps:

1. **Maintain tactical breathing rates** of four second intervals. This controlled breathing rate assists in maintaining homeostatic O2 and CO2 levels in the body and allows one to maintain intellectual command of the situation.
2. **Talk yourself through the emergency.** Many times, one verbalizing the steps of emergency mitigation steps assists in keeping one intellectually focused.
3. **Stay outwardly focused on the task-at-hand.** Do not let yourself become side-tracked by nonessential issues. Focus on what is working or what you can do, not what is not working or what you cannot do.

Secret to Survival

If a *secret to survival* exists, it would equate to not allowing self-pity enter into the equation. An old saying states: "Pain is inevitable...suffering is optional." There is no doubt one will experience discomfort; however, maintaining a sense of humor may make the situation more tolerable.

Before one makes a decision on the next issue to tackle, one must think first, and act second. Many times, individuals waste valuable time and energy starting one project, realize something else must be done first, and then be forced to change directions. One must make objective decisions, not emotional ones.

21.4 SURVIVAL FACTORS

Certain *survival factors* exist in virtually all survival episodes. These factors change in hierarchal consideration and mitigation, depending on prevailing conditions. The survival factors include:

- Weather/climate
- Terrain
- Isolation
- Thirst
- Hunger
- Injury

An area's prevailing *weather and climate* conditions are important components in one's comfort level during a survival episode. Rarely is the temperature at a perfect level for sustained exposure. Temperature extremes in either hot or cold directions serve not only to make one miserable, but may turn deadly as well. Human bodies are prepared to withstand temperature variations externally, but as internal body temperatures change, many intellectual and physiological changes will result. Consequently, weather and climate needs must be mitigated as soon as possible, as not much deteriorates a positive mental attitude quicker than adverse weather.

Terrain may provide formidable challenges to the survivor. One may be subjected to desert, mountainous, swampy, prairie, forested, or open water environments, all of which may be a source of extreme discomfort and require remarkable coping skills. One's survival surroundings may provide a source of protection, food, and water, or create obstacles even the most adept survivors find difficult. The more adaptable one becomes, the better they will cope.

U.S. Air Force 2021

Isolation may provide challenges for some as distinct advantages exist facing adversity with others. Typically, aviators train to function as an integral part of a team; however, when facing obstacles individually the loss of information and guidance of others creates a sense of insecurity. One must build confidence in themselves, and understand they can contribute significantly to overcoming obstacles.

The presence of *thirst* will provide significant impacts on a survivor's mental attitude, as well as overall physical health. Absence of water for significant periods of time will cause one to weaken and eventually die. Thus, acquiring and preserving water increases exponentially in importance as the length of time in a survival situation increases.

Hunger may be feared by some as a severe stress in survival, but food is one of the last items on a survivor's list of issues to be concerned with. Humans are creatures of habit and most tend to eat at certain times of the day, and when one misses a meal the feeling is they are starving. The reality is one may survive for extended periods without food. If one were exposed to survival conditions for weeks, food may present itself as a problem, but generally simply ignoring hunger is effective so long as one does not burn extreme numbers of calories.

Injury and illness are, unfortunately, realities of survival episodes which must be planned for. Being alone and injured in a hostile environment can add significant levels of stress to an already uncomfortable situation. Injuries must be treated as soon and as thoroughly as possible, as typical methods of sterilization will be absent in nature. Wounds must be sanitized to the best of one's ability, and kept as clean and isolated as possible to avoid infections from developing. Prevention of injury and illness take on a major role of the experience, and one must exercise extreme caution when performing work or traveling so as not to injure oneself further. Even a sprained ankle or minor cut may turn a manageable situation into a disaster.

Preparing for the Elements

One's knowledge of thermal preparation for the various temperatures one may be exposed to in a given environment is paramount to their ability to *prepare for the elements*. The most obvious system for one to prepare for nature's elements is one's clothing. Clothing may be considered as one's first line of defense for dynamic thermal variation, and as such, one's clothing choices need to be binary and dynamic for not only hot and cold temperatures, but wet and windy environments as well. One needs to remember a static temperature may be much more tolerable than the same temperature derived from wind chill factor.

Hypothermia can occur at ambient temperatures of 50 - 55 degrees in wet and windy conditions, and water temperatures of 50 degrees F may cause death in one hour. One needs to determine their individual needs for what kind of clothing and gear is necessary when ambient temperatures range from -40 degrees F to 60 degrees F. Although one may believe they understand the clothing necessary for a given ambient temperature, the only true way one gains this knowledge is to actually <u>experience</u> those temperatures with their anticipated levels of protective clothing. If the clothing is adequate, one should be able to remain relatively comfortable for 60 minutes in the desired temperature range. One may quickly discover the clothing they thought was adequate is actually quite inadequate for anything other than a very short-term exposure.

A main focus in survival episodes should be one's attempt to work <u>with</u> nature, as opposed to against it. Examples of working with nature include resting when it is hot, moving when it is cold, collecting water when it rains, collect wood and build a fire when it is dry, or go around steep terrain instead of up or down it. Using nature to its fullest advantage will make the survival experience more successful.

Survival Travel

A major consideration for survivors is the question of whether or not to attempt to travel in search of assistance. Generally, the best option is to stay close to your aircraft (or any vehicle), as the vehicle will be easier for search and rescue (SAR) teams to visually identify as opposed to trying to spot a person walking in forested, mountainous, snowy, or flat terrain. The first place search teams will attempt to locate a downed aircraft is near the last known position (LKP) or along the flight plan route. The further one travels from the downed aircraft, the more area search teams have to cover, thus the longer time it takes to locate survivors. The chart below depicts how distance survivors travel affect the anticipated search radius and how long it would take to locate survivors once the wreckage was located, on the average:

Distance Traveled	Search Radius	Days to Find
— 1 mi	3.0 mi	0.9
— 2 mi	12.5 mi	3.5
— 3 mi	28.25 mi	8.25
— 4 mi	50.25	14.66
— 5 mi	78.5	23

According to the FAA, the average time from LKP to rescue is 27.3 hours. Filing a flight plan is great insurance to invest in, especially IFR flight plans, as it gives SAR teams a place to start searching. Not every survival episode is the same, so if your aircraft went down one mile from a town, you were certain where the town was, and conditions were favorable for travel, then attempting to make it to town may be the correct choice.

Survival Navigation

Travel may be necessary if one finds themselves in terrain which would prove difficult for SAR teams to find them, if one needs to get to higher terrain for a phone or radio signal, to find water or firewood, or many other reasons.

Should one discover a need to travel, *survival navigation* techniques enable the survivor to find their way back to camp or maintain a specific direction.. Although this revelation may sound logical, navigating through unfamiliar terrain isn't as easy as it sounds, as most experienced hikers will reveal. If one hikes in a one direction for an extended period of time, once they turn 180 degrees to walk back in the direction they came from, nothing looks the same. Landmarks one uses for directional guidance in one direction look entirely different from another direction.

One effective method for determining direction is called the *shadow-tip method*. To use the shadow-tip method, locate a straight stick approximately three feet long, as well as a level piece of ground open enough for the stick to cast a definite shadow. This accurate and simple method consists of four steps:

1. Place the stick into the ground at a level spot where it will cast a distinctive shadow. Mark the shadow's tip with a stone or twig. This first shadow mark is always west, true anywhere on earth.

2. Wait 10 to 15 minutes until the shadow tip moves a few inches. Mark the shadow tip's new position the same way as the first mark.

3. Draw a straight line through the two marks to obtain an approximate east-west line.

4. Stand with the first mark (west) to your left and the second mark to your right, at which time you are now facing north. Again, this is true anywhere on earth.

The most effective method of ensuring a return to the original starting point is to use a compass heading and time, assuming one has a compass and watch. For example, if one needs to travel to a distant peak, note the time started and compass heading in a line to the peak. Do not deviate from the heading until the peak is reached, then note the time. To reach camp, turn-around 180 degrees, walk the same amount of time it took to reach the peak, and one should be close to camp after the specified amount of time.

If a compass and watch are unavailable, attempt to use prominent terrain features such as a mountain top or large body of water. Small features such as a specific tree or a particular hill may be easily missed or misinterpreted once on the return trip. One should also make every attempt to anticipate declining weather conditions, as getting caught away from camp in rain or snow may make a successful return to camp impossible.

21.5 CRITICAL SURVIVAL NEEDS

Critical survival needs are elemental factors integral to maintaining life during any survival episode. The more effectively these needs are provided for, the better chance one stands of making it back to civilization alive. These needs include:

- Health
- Shelter (thermal protection)
- Signaling
- Water
- Fire
- Food

One of the most critical components in surviving is prioritization of these needs. How one determines which need is most important at any particular time can be accomplished using the Rule of Three, discussed next.

Rule of Three

When one considers the possibility of facing a survival episode, the chances are good one will find themselves in a particular place they didn't expect or anticipate, and at the worst time possible. The *Rule of Three* is a quick reminder for survivors on prioritizing their critical survival needs:

- 3 seconds - if you panic
- 3 minutes - without medical or oxygen
- 3 hours - without shelter
- 3 days - without water
- 3 weeks - without food

Although the Rule of Three exists in a variety of iterations, the first thing one must accomplished is avoiding panic and obviously ensuring they can breathe (if underwater or pinned under debris). Once the mind is calmed and immediate health threats neutralized, one must ensure body core temperature is attended to, followed by hydration. Food is a distant last place, as one may survive for relatively long periods of time without nutrition.

Personal Survival Kits

In attending to critical survival needs, individuals can make the effort far more effective with the proper tools to accomplish these tasks. These tools are contained in a *personal survival kit.*

Personal survival kits are individualized collections of gear to prepare survivors with the proper supplies they may require to meet the necessary needs to ensure their survival. Personal survival kits vary widely in size, shape, complexity, and contents, hence the reason for individualization.

What may work for one with extensive experience may not work for one with little-to-no experience.

When survival kits are packed in aircraft or any other vehicle, one must ensure the kit is accessible and protected from fire, separation, or destruction. Not much could be more devastating to a survivor to truly end up in a survival situation, only to find their kit was destroyed on impact or they could not reach it. The kit should provide expedient and easy access to signaling devises and other gear. Although not practical in all applications, the most useful and accessible survival kits are worn on the body, such as a vest.

When assembling a personal survival kit, including items addressing each critical survival need is essential. As survival kit space is limited, one also needs to consider the packing size and multiplicity of uses for each item; the more uses one items has, the more capabilities individuals possess for less space. One should also strive to maintain redundant capabilities for important functions, such as fire-starting, as items may become lost or broken.

Below is a sample of items to pack in personal survival kits:

1. First aid kit: may include bandages, gauze, disinfectant, insect repellant, aspirin, prescription medications, sun block, medical tape
2. Shelter materials: may include large orange (for visibility) plastic bags, tarps, material panels, duct tape
3. Tools/cordage: may include multi-use blades/knives, multi-tools, Swiss Army Knife, parachute cord, twine
4. Fire starting equipment: may include water-proof matches, flint and steel, disposable lighters, magnifying glass, steel wool, petroleum jelly-soaked cotton swabs
5. Food/water procurement and preparation: may include tinfoil, small plastic bags, cloth for straining water, water purification tablets, fish hooks and fishing line, snare wire
6. Signaling devices: may include large orange plastic panels, whistle, signal mirror, survival radio, Emergency Locator Transmitter, cell phone
7. Navigation aids: may include paper maps, compass, GPS
8. Portable cell phone charger, extra batteries (if necessary)

Some of the most important items in a survival kit may seem, at first glance, to be insignificant:

1. Tinfoil and plastic bags are extremely important items, because of the multitude of uses for both. Survival uses of tinfoil include boiling water, cooking food/solar oven, signaling, fishing lure, body heat retention blanket, sharpen blades, keep matches dry, or food/water container.
2. Survival uses for large and small plastic bags include water procurement and transport, personal rain protection, collecting and carrying small items (nuts, berries, tools), protecting maps/electronic gear/matches, signaling (orange bags), shelters, head or foot protection, or extra insulation.
3. Cordage may be used for slings (broken arm), ties for shelters, as handles to carry large objects, hold clothes together, snare lines, and a variety of other uses.

Knives are incredibly versatile tools, and should be included in any survival kit. One must consider, however, failure to use the right blade for the right job can result in severe injuries as one may severely injure themselves. Folding blades may be dangerous if the blade unexpectedly folds in on one's fingers, making locking blades a more obvious choice. Speed-assist lock blades can be opened with one hand, which may be useful if one sustains injuries to a hand or arm. Lock blades may be useful for not only cutting, but also drilling, sawing, digging, or as the head of a make-shift spear.

Signaling Considerations

Signaling provides one's best option of neutralizing the survival episode, as the ability to attract the attention of rescue forces expediently will lessen one's exposure to the elements. Since the necessity to signal rescuers arise at unanticipated times, signaling devices need to be ready to deploy at a moment's notice. In order for one to be prepared to effectively deploy signaling devices, it is best to practice first. One must also be mindful of what devices are available, and which devices provide the best deployment options for the environment. One must be mindful of the best contrast options for effective signal deployment, such as using bright light in dark settings, or using orange panels against a foliage background.

Reflective signaling is an efficient, simple signaling system effective for great distances in the correct ambient lighting conditions. Reflective signaling uses a highly reflective surface, such as a small mirror, to reflect light (normally the sun's rays) towards rescuers in an effort to attract attention. Signal mirrors may attract attention out to 15 miles. Reflecting light between two extended fingers as a "sight", one can direct the reflected light in the direction of rescue forces. If the survivor had a specific target to signal, the survivor would sweep the reflected light back and forth across the target, hopefully attracting attention. If no specific target exists, the survivor can sweep the light across the horizon, again hopefully attracting attention. If the survivor had no critical tasks to accomplish, the survivor should practice using the reflective signaling device so as to be effective at the task in the event of the necessity for immediate deployment.

If one does not possess a signaling mirror, one may look around the aircraft wreckage for other metal or glass pieces for use as a reflective signaling device. If necessity dictates, one may also use tinfoil from their kit as a reflective signal, as well as a watch lens, glass lens, cell phone face, or any other reflective object.

Although one may wonder what good a cellphone with no cell signal may possess in survival episodes, the correct answer is "a lot." The cell phone may be downloaded with survival manual applications, as well as navigation, flashlight, picture flash, or compass applications, along with the aforementioned reflective signaling option. Even the cellphone battery may be used as a fire-starter by using twisted steel wool bent in a "U" shape touching both battery posts, getting the steel wool hot enough to start tinder smoldering. If all else fails, the battery can be crushed, sending the battery into thermal runaway, and using this to start a fire.

Shelter Considerations

The primary purpose for a survival *shelter* is preservation of life through maintenance of homeostatic body core temperature. One's shelter must be thought of as a micro-habitat within a hostile environment for the survivor, creating as close-to-optimum thermal conditions as possible.

One's clothing should be considered one's first layer of shelter protection, with the goal of not only maintaining body core temperature, but protection from wind and rain as well. Remember, dynamic weather requires dynamic clothing, and layering clothing provides the most versatility. See the chapter on Thermal Stress for more information on effective clothing.

Maintaining body core temperature needs to be the main consideration for construction of a survival shelter. In adherence to this consideration, the shelter should be small enough to easily retain body heat with minimal waste of energy. If one thinks of the mechanics of a sleeping bag, its cocoon-like structure exercises maximum efficiency in body heat retention. The same should be attempted with a survival shelter; more extra room equals less efficiency, whereas less extra room equals more efficiency.

Along with the size of the shelter, one must consider the conductive effects of sleeping on the ground. Cold ground transfers cold temperatures to the body, whereas hot ground transfers heat to the body. With this is mind, keeping the body insulated from the ground is critically important to body heat maintenance. This may be accomplished by lining the shelter with a thick layer of vegetation, or constructing a platform to rest on six-to-eight inches off the ground.

One's survival shelter may also double as a signal. Constructing a shelter out of camouflage material will not attract attention from rescue forces, whereas constructing a shelter with bright material stands out from the background visual clutter, potentially attracting rescuers.

Once a survival shelter is established, sanitation needs must be considered. Human waste must be kept away from one's camp, as well as food and water sources. Human waste close to one's camp invites predatory animals to the site, as well as insects and pests such as mice and rats.

Illustrated below are simple shelter concepts from the U.S. Army:

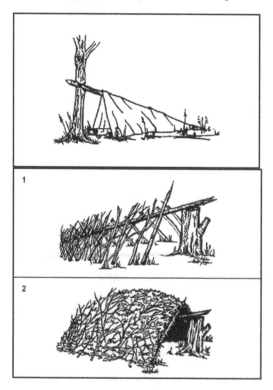

U.S. Army 2021

An aviator's obvious choice for a shelter may be the aircraft itself, provided the fuselage is still intact following the crash. Although the fuselage may provide effective protection from wind and rain, one must be carefully observant of ambient temperatures when attempting to use the fuselage as a shelter. If the prevailing ambient temperatures are too cold or too hot, those temperatures may be amplified inside the fuselage. In extremely cold conditions, the survivor may actually be warmer using the snow trench shelter as outlined below. According to the U.S. Army Survival Field Manual, a simple shelter may be constructed out of a few materials in open snow fields, as snow is an effective insulator and wind block:

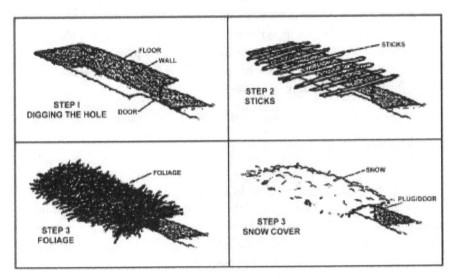

U.S. Army 2021

Water Procurement

Water is a vital resource for continuation of life efforts, and a primary concern for survivors. One should strive to secure a continuous source of water, as survival conditions necessitate the need for water more than normal environments. To prevent long-term dehydration, the normal adult would need to consume approximately 32 ounces (one liter or .25 gallons) of water per day while resting in a temperate environment, with the demand going higher in increasingly hostile environments. As one may calculate, this equates to a lot of water over a period of days or weeks.

In a perfect scenario, a survival "best practice" is to bring adequate water with you when considering flight over hostile terrain. This provides the best option to ensure one has sufficient, clean water immediately available, eliminating the difficulties of fulfilling this critical need in an already-negative situation. Unfortunately, many individuals will not adequately prepare for this crucial resource as a result of the "it will never happen to me" syndrome.

Finding potable water in survival environments is difficult at best, and near-impossible at worst. If one is fortunate enough to crash-land close to a natural water source, the water may still present a serious health threat due to parasitic, bacterial, or chemical pathogen contamination. Consuming contaminated water may cause vomiting and/or diarrhea, intensifying dehydration considerations.

As a general rule, running water as found in rivers or streams may be safer than stagnant water such as a swamp, as running water sources will naturally filter some of the contaminants out. Melting snow may be a viable option as a water source; however, melting ten gallons of snow equates to one gallon of drinkable fluid, making this a difficult and time- and resource-consuming option.

Methods exist survivalists may use to create water out of "thin air," such as desert solar stills and transpiration bags. Solar stills have proven to be extremely difficult to construct and yield minimal benefit, and as such, will not be discussed. Transpiration bags involve encasing green vegetation still attached to a tree in a large, clear plastic bag, tying off the neck of the bag to be air-tight, and allowing sunlight to create condensation in the bag. Depending on the water vapor content of the vegetation and the strength of the solar energy, condensed water will run to the bottom of the bag which one could use as a water source. The amount of water produced is highly variable and may not be worth the effort; however, it is an option for one to consider.

According to the EPA, water sourced from natural settings should be sterilized prior to human consumption, as many microbiological, chemical, or physical contaminants may be present. Microbiological contaminants include E. coli, streptococci, protozoa (Giardia), and cyanobacteria. Chemical contaminants may include nitrogen, bleach, salts, pesticides, metals produced from bacteria, and human or animal drugs. Physical contaminants may include sediment or organic material from soil erosion or animal waste (Contaminant Candidate List and Regulatory Determination, 2016).

Methods of sterilizing water include boiling for ten minutes, iodine tablets, straining with fine mesh cloth, or using a commercially available filtering device such as a *survival filter straw*. A survival filter straw allegedly removes bacteria (E. coli) & protozoa (Giardia), potentially allowing one to drink directly from a water source to one's mouth.

Fire Craft

Survival *fire craft* is an essential skill for life continuance, providing warmth, the ability to boil water or cook food, light at night, and even companionship. As an essential skill, fire craft should be practiced extensively prior to attempting to start a fire in a survival episode.

First, the survivor must determine if combustible natural materials are immediately available which provide adequate fire-making potential. If the natural material contains sap, such as pine branches, or is dry and not rotted or green, fire-making potential exists.

Second, the survivor must find suitable material to construct a *tinder-nest*. These are small pieces of combustible material allowing for easier starting for a larger fire. Materials for tinder-nests may be petroleum jelly cotton swabs from one's survival kit, lint, birch- or pine-bark shavings, pine needles, shredded paper, dry leaves, etc. It is best to create the potential fire-pit in a protected area which will heat the survivor and their shelter, but also be protected from wind and rain if possible.

Third, the survivor needs to select a fire-starting method. Fire-starters should be packed in the survival kit, as more primitive methods of starting fires is difficult at best and require expert-level ability. Considerations for fire-starters are how reliable are they for effectiveness, how easy are they to use, and is a back-up fire-starting system available if the first one fails? Items such as a fire striker/flint and steel, matches, and butane lighters are generally considered most reliable and easiest to use.

Fourth, the survivor needs to ignite the tinder-nest. The general idea is to produce an ember in the tinder-nest to start a small, smoldering fire, and gently build into a larger blaze. One must not get impatient at this stage, as the infant flames may just as easily be extinguished by trying to feed the fire too quickly. One must have larger material, such as small branches, immediately available to continuously feed the growing fire until such a point where the fire is self-sustainable for longer periods of time. Once the fire reaches self-sustainability, the survivor may carefully feed larger branches or logs into the growing blaze. The U.S. Army Survival Field Manual images below depict various fire-pit configurations:

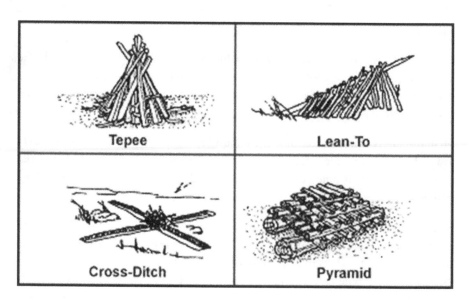

Tepee | Lean-To

Cross-Ditch | Pyramid

U.S. Army 2021

The survivor must always remember the need to monitor the fire in survival situations, as not only could the fire extinguish itself once out of fuel, but also not to allow the fire to grow out of control, potentially causing catastrophic environmental damage to vast areas of wilderness.

Food Procurement

As our discussions revolve around short-term survival events, food may not be considered a major factor for episodes of this duration. Although food may not be an initial consideration, one may want to begin the thought process of food procurement should the survival episode extend beyond a short time period, so long as the more important survival needs are met. In many cases, food procurement efforts can extend into days, or even weeks, before a sufficient food source is discovered.

The best option for survival food, like water, is to bring it with you from the onset. If one has the space in their personal survival kit, many effective options exist for freeze-dried, canned, or sturdily-packed survival food stuffs, available in most camping or outdoor outfitter stores. It is best to ensure expiration dates on these items is checked on a regular basis to ensure the food is not tainted should one need them.

In preparing to procure food in a survival situation, one needs to explore the most likely successful options for food gathering. For protein food sources, humans can eat virtually anything that crawls, swims, walks, or flies, so long as the food is prepared correctly.

Unfortunately, finding, trapping, and ultimately killing animal or bird food sources may be difficult for most to accomplish. Insect, plant, reptile, and fish food options are often the most abundant and easiest food sources for one to procure, so long as one knows what to look for and one can overcome their food aversions to eat them.

Many insect options provide 65 – 80% protein, compared to 20% protein for beef. Insects to avoid include adults which bite or sting, are brightly colored or hairy; specifically, caterpillars, spiders, ticks, flies, and mosquitoes. Good insect options include black ants, grasshoppers, beetles, termites, grubs, worms, and crickets. If possible, it is best to remove the head, and cook or boil the insect, which may make them more palatable to most individuals. Below is an incident involving a hunter lost in Australia's Outback where insects saved the individual's life:

Incident Review – Oct 2015: A 62-year-old male recreational hunter, a former miner, and his brother were hunting in the Great Victoria Desert in Western Australia State, driving the area in their vehicle. The two hunters spotted a camel, at which point the 62-year-old male left the vehicle to pursue the camel on foot. Daytime temperatures at this time of the year were in the vicinity of 100 degrees F.

Within a short period of time, the hunter became disorientated and lost. The brother looked for the individual, but could not locate him, and in turn, notified authorities. After six days of searching, police trackers finally located the former miner sitting under a tree approximately nine miles from where he had become lost. The man had survived an extremely hostile environment for nearly a week without water, simply by eating black ants.

Analysis: Although being an experienced hunter, the individual wandered away from their vehicle in unfamiliar terrain, and quickly became lost.

Conclusion: The hunter survived this desert survival episode by not panicking, and working with whatever food source he could find, which happened to be black ants. The black ants provided enough nutrition and fluid to sustain him until help could arrive, while the man conserved energy by not attempting to walk himself out of a perilous situation. The man used the tree for whatever shade the tree could provide, minimizing dehydration.

Plant food options are valuable resources as they require minimal effort to procure, but extreme care must be exercised to ensure one does not ingest poisonous plants. Although an entire book or two could be written on edible wild plants, the following rules apply for foods to avoid: mushrooms, milky/discolored sap, beans/bulbs/seeds inside pods, bitter/soapy taste, spines/hairs/thorns, almond scent in woody parts or leaves, colored red (unless known fruit), and three-leaf growth patterns. If one finds a plant appearing edible, it may be best to rub some on clean skin first to determine if a rash develops, or taste a small piece to determine palatability. Barks, roots, and berries may be food options, and may be cooked or boiled. A common plant containing many nutrients and is virtually 100% edible is the common dandelion.

Reptile food options include turtles, snakes, and lizards. If one were fortunate enough to catch a reptile, the entrails, head, and skin should be removed, and then cooked thoroughly to avoid salmonella poisoning.

Fish food options obviously only exist in areas with bodies of water, such as rivers or lakes. Once harvested, the fish should be filleted so one only cooks the side meat of the fish, excluding entrails, fins, and heads. The fish should be cooked thoroughly to avoid parasitic infection. Fish may be extremely difficult to catch with a hook and line, as many experienced fishermen may attest to, so survivors should direct their efforts to trap fish, which provides better odds of harvesting fish with less effort.

Some simple fish traps are shown below:

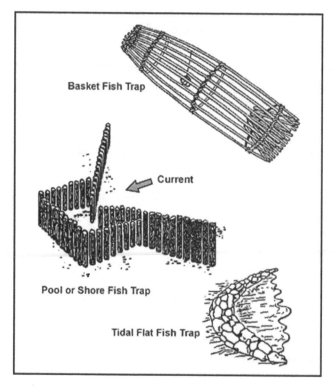

U.S. Army 2021

21.6 SURVIVAL HEALTH THREAT MITIGATION

Successfully navigating a survival episode necessitates maintaining one's health. Injuries or illness may turn a survivable event into a catastrophe in an instant, and as such, one must be on constant guard in order to not compromise their personal health and safety. In addition to your health, protecting the health of others who may be involved in your survival episode helps all involved, as a team effort is more effective than an individual effort.

We will briefly discuss mitigation techniques of the following health threats to survivors:

- Injury
- Weather/terrain
- Insects
- Animals
- Reptiles

Survival Injury Threats

Should survivors injury themselves, one may experience feelings of helplessness and apathy if incapable of protecting or treating themselves. One's ability to treat injuries in survival environments increases morale and a belief in themselves survival is possible. If multiple people are in the survival party, one with rudimentary medical treatment knowledge may positively change the outcome for all. Please note the following steps are extremely basic, and should be supplemented with additional training.

The following are steps one may follow to maintain an injury-free experience:

1. **Be careful during movement.** One may twist an ankle, cut themselves on jagged rock/metal/glass, injure an eye walking into a branch, fall down steep embankments, or falling through ice. Always be thoughtful and deliberate when moving.
2. **Maintain hydration and hygiene.** Hydration will assist one in maintaining peak cognitive skills, and therefore less prone to mental mistakes. Maintaining proper hygiene minimizes bacteria, fleas, lice, and germs by keeping hands, hair, teeth, and clothing as clean as possible, reducing the possibilities of becoming ill or infected. One may brush their teeth by chewing the end of a twig to separate the fibers and brushing with this, or wrapping a clean cloth around a finger to clean teeth with.

3. **Take care of your feet.** Your feet are one's one form of transportation, and as such must be in condition. Wash and massage feet daily, if possible, and keep socks as clean and dry as possible. If blisters form, attempt to pad the blisters to prevent breaking them.

4. **Get sufficient rest.** One must give the mind and body a break to avoid overstressing either, and to maintain peak endurance if needed.

5. **Control any bleeding and keep cuts or burns clean.** One may stop bleeding through direct pressure, elevation, or tourniquets. Dress the wound with clean cloth. Treat burns as open wounds and keep protected with clean cloth, and treat with honey if available to promote new skin growth.

6. **Stabilize fractures and sprains.** Splint broken bones with sticks or other stiff material and wrap with cloth to keep area from unnecessary movement. Sprains should be rest, ice (if available) the area for 24 hours, compression wrap the area to stabilize, and elevate the affected area.

7. **Maintain homeostatic body temperatures.** If one gets cold, get out of the wind, and perform work or some movement to heat up the body. If one gets hot, rest in shade to cool down.

Survival Weather/Terrain Threats

Weather and terrain characteristics may create health, comfort, and morale obstacles to survivors if not proper accounted for and controlled. In some environments, one's need for weather protection may take precedence over every other survival factor. One must anticipate potential issues which may arise resulting from weather and terrain, and position and construct the shelter appropriately to account for those issues. Weather considerations include heat, cold, rain, snow, flooding, high winds, and lightning.

The following are general rules regarding weather and terrain to consider when selecting a survival shelter site:

1. Stay out of low areas (depressions), as flash-flooding may occur and cause water to build up in the lowest terrain in the general area. Snow or terrain trenches are acceptable as a wind-block, so long as they maintain adequate drainage.

2. Create a natural wind and rain block with terrain features, if possible, such the down-wind side of a hill or tree/brush line.

3. Ensure the shelter is not constructed under dead trees or branches, in poisonous plants, under loose rocks or boulders, areas prone to mud slides or avalanches, or in areas of high insect or reptile activity.

4. Stay away from tall, singular items in open areas, such as the only tree or a radio tower in a field. Items such as these may attract lightning.

5. Stay away from metal in stormy, cold, or hot environments. Metal objects may attract lightning, or amplify hot or cold temperatures.

6. Use snow as an insulator against the side of a shelter, or as a shelter-building material itself, as snow is easy to work with and provides thermal insulation characteristics.

Survival Insect Threats

The survivor should wear long-sleeved clothing to minimize insect bites. One should use insect repellant and insect netting for their shelter, if available. Clean and dress bug bites and stings. Be prepared to treat for shock if necessary, and keep airway open. Cold compresses, mud and ash paste, or dandelion sap may reduce itching on the bite site.

Survival Animal Threats

Although animals may present a threat to survivors, most animals prefer to keep their distance from humans as much as humans from them. It is important for survivors to maintain situational awareness of any animal activity in their immediate area, and respect their habitat as effectively as possible. If animals have offspring in their area, the mother animal may become very aggressive if one approaches the offspring. Even docile-appearing and small animals may present an attack threat if approached or teased.

If one experiences a chance encounter with an animal, typically the best option is to remain as still as possible to avoid attracting attention. If possible, try to back away from the animal slowly, and one should avoid taking their eyes off the animal to prevent an attack from the rear. If one is actually attacked and has no effective escape route, attempt to appear as big as possible with outstretched arms, make as much noise as possible, and fight-to-kill with whatever weapon you can find. In some cases with larger animals such as bear, playing dead may cause the animal to lose interest and eventually wander off.

The following incident illustrates the necessity to fight as if your life depends on it should one be attacked by a large predator:

Incident Review – Oct 2015: A man was running on a mountain trail by himself near Fort Collins, CO. As he ran along the along the trail, he heard a noise behind him. As he turned around to see what had made the noise, an 80-pound mountain lion attacked him. The struggle caused the man to suffer facial cuts, wrist scratches and injuries, and puncture wounds to his arm, legs, and back from the lion's fangs and claws.

As the lion had a hold of the man's wrist with its mouth, the man picked up a rock with his free hand and smashed it repeatedly into the lion's skull. The man then wrapped his free arm around the lion's neck, immobilizing it with a headlock, and choked the lion to death. The man was able to walk back to civilization and get medical treatment for his wounds.

Analysis: Attacks by wild animals on humans are extremely rare occurrences. Although being an experienced outdoors enthusiast, the individual was running by himself in an area stocked with potentially dangerous wildlife. Against all odds and for reasons unknown, the individual was attacked by an adult mountain lion, and managed to survive the attack and kill the lion.

Conclusion: The runner survived this incident by not panicking and using whatever resources he could find to fight for his life. Although the chances of surviving an attack may seem small, the man did not give up and fought for his life. This incident provides proof to the concept if one fails to yield to fear, almost anything is possible given enough effort.

Survival Reptilian Threats

The most likely reptilian threats a survivor will encounter are snakes. While not all snakes are dangerous, no infallible rules exist for expedient and accurate identification of venomous snakes in the wild, as identification guidelines require dangerously close observation of the snake's body. According to the CDC, venomous snakes may be found in virtually every area of the United States. Rattlesnakes are found throughout the US, Cottonmouths/Water Moccasins are found the southeastern states, Copperheads are found in eastern states as far west as Texas, and Coral snakes may be found in the Southern US.

The best strategy one may employ when exposed to likely snake habitats is to leave all snakes alone. In areas which snakes inhabit and venomous species are present, the risk of being bit may negate their value as a potential food source. If one is willing to forego safety and attempt to catch a snake for food, it is essential the task be carried out with the utmost care. The head of the snake must be pinned securely to the ground with a forked stick placed on its neck, and the head must be severed completely. The head should then be buried in a deep hole, as even a severed head may pose a snake bite threat if one were to accidently step on it.

When traveling in venomous snakes habitats, apply the following safety rules:

1. Walk carefully and be observant where you step, as snakes may be well-disguised.
2. Step onto logs or rocks rather than over them in a survival situation.

3. Look closely when picking fruit or moving around water.
4. Do not tease, molest, or harass snakes. Some snakes, such as mambas, cobras, and bushmasters, will attack aggressively when cornered or guarding a nest.
5. Use sticks to turn logs and rocks.
6. Wear proper footgear, particularly at night.
7. Carefully check bedding, shelter, and clothing.
8. Be calm when you encounter serpents. Snakes cannot hear and you can occasionally surprise them when they are sleeping or sunning. Normally, they will flee if given the opportunity.
9. Use extreme care if you must kill snakes for food or safety. Although it is not common, warm, sleeping human bodies occasionally attract snakes.

If one does receive a venomous snake bite, one must restrict blood flow from the site of the snake bite. Keep as still as possible to reduce circulation, remove any rings or watches which may be constricting during swelling, place constricting bands between the wound and heart, maintain an open airway, and clean and cover the wound as best as possible.

21.7 SURVIVAL PLANNING

Survival planning is an essential task one must accomplish to ensure preparedness for not only continuation of life in remote environments, but also providing potential rescue crews the best opportunity to find you if you go missing. Many stories exist in which individuals get lost while completely unprepared, forgot their survival kit, or strayed from their intended route, making the possibility of finding them remote at best. If one disciplines themselves to ensure preparedness each and every time they fly (or travel), one stands the best chance of surviving any possible event. One popular survival saying states "failure to plan is a plan to fail."

The following are recognized steps one may take to avoid survival episode pitfalls:

1. **File a flight plan.** Once a flight plan is filed, stick with it. The quickest and most accurate opportunity for downed pilots to be found by rescue crews is along the intended route of flight, combined with the last known radar contact.
2. **Know the terrain and weather for your route of flight, and prepare accordingly.** One may research potential weather conditions, hostility of terrain, edible foods, water sources, and possible shelter materials prior to the flight.
3. **Pack adequate clothing for any anticipated weather conditions.** Remember to pack clothing with versatility and thermal variability in mind, as weather and temperature conditions may change rapidly.

4. **Ensure you have an operable emergency locator transmitter (ELT)**, as many lives have been saved by individuals successfully deploying and ELT. If one is renting an aircraft, remember some FBO's do not necessarily replace batteries in ELTs as recommended, so bringing one's own ELT may be a better option.

5. **Carry adequate survival equipment and know your survival kit.** One's survival kit should include core components necessary for any environment; however, one may supplement those components for increasingly harsh conditions. Ensure the survival kit is in the aircraft or vehicle, and understand how to effectively use or deploy the equipment in one's kit.

6. **Make your own luck with proper planning and execution.** With discovery research into weather and terrain for a given trip, one may realize the trip may be better off canceled. If one is nervous about attempting a trip, consider rescheduling the trip. Ensure "go" or "no-go" decisions are made objectively, as opposed to emotionally, as emotional decisions have cost many individuals their lives. The best "survival experts" are those who plan meticulously enough not to put themselves into a compromising situation in the first place.

Conclusion

As one prepares for survival events, one must remember these preparations must be accomplished on a physical (equipment & fitness) and psychological/intellectual level.

Physical preparation for survival episodes is relatively simple, as one may develop a survival kit to mitigate almost any contingency. One may maintain physical fitness, and pack sufficient water and food. However, nothing one packs in their survival kit may assist one's attitude and intellectual capacity for adversity. These attributes only develop from knowledge one attains through continuous assessment, practice, and planning. Once one becomes comfortable with the idea they possess the correct tools, equipment, and knowledge to survive, almost any contingency will seem surmountable.

One must also be comfortable with the idea in which unforeseen circumstances will happen, and not everything will develop as one hopes or plans for. One must not waste valuable mental energy wondering <u>why</u> something happened, but rather what one may do to modify the future of the situation. One must maintain a robust <u>will-to-live</u>, and control fear the likes of which they may have never encountered before. Be comforted by good preparation and accumulated skills. Work with what you have and can accomplish; do not concern yourself with what you do not have or cannot accomplish.

Chapter 21 Core Competency Questions

1. What is the most important component in successful mitigation of survival situations?
2. Can one's fear help in survival situations?
3. Why is panic worse than fear?
4. What is paramount in preparing for the elements?
5. With regards to survival travel, what is the best option?
6. How long may one last without water?
7. How long may one last without food?
8. What is considered one's best option for neutralizing a survival situation?
9. What is one first layer of shelter protection?
10. What can a pilot do to provide the quickest and most accurate opportunity for rescue crews to find a downed pilot?

22. PILOT MEDICAL CERTIFICATE MAINTENANCE

As one traverses the mountain of training necessary to accomplishing their goal of becoming a professional pilot, little else enters one's mind other than completing the next step. Eventually, however, one will finally complete all the training, classes, ratings, flight instructing and building flight hours, interviews, and sleepless nights to finally earn the coveted wings of their first professional pilot position. Unfortunately, the work does not end at this point, as this is where the work begins to maintain one's pilot status.

Aside from maintaining one's flying skills, currencies, and ratings, arguably the most important aspect of one's professional flying future is maintaining their *Pilot Medical Certificate*. Loss of one's medical certificate will equate to an instantaneous loss of flight privileges, as well as a loss of all the money paid and training time endured to become a professional pilot.

Additionally, consumer expectation of professional pilot performance is very high because consumer's lives depend on pilots...perhaps the highest of any industry outside of medical professions. For one to deliver consistent perfection in performance of their flight duties, one must maintain themselves at the highest physical and mental standards possible. If one maintains themselves in such a condition virtually guaranteeing consistent peak performance, one will enjoy the additional benefit of maximizing their potential to maintain their pilot medical certificate for as many years as one may desire.

As we discussed in early chapters of this text, for one to maintain homeostasis with their environment four essential components must be in equilibrium: oxygen, rest, nutrition, and hydration. Albert Einstein estimated humans may live to an average maximum life span of 115 years; however, the average life span averages merely 79 years due to poor nutrition, stress, and inactivity.

As a professional aviator, one must to possess a thorough understanding of optimizing bodily processes through a sustainable and effective personal diet, exercise, and medical certificate maintenance program. However, in the search for diet and exercise information, the volume and complexity of information available may be overwhelming to the degree one may simply disregard any desire to pursue beneficial programs. For this reason, we will concentrate on research-based, generalized information designed for practical implementation into one's professional life.

Professional aviators also need to understand they, alone, are responsible for maintaining their health. No one is more vested or interested in one's well-being than yourself; friends, spouses, employers, children, and circumstances all conspire against one's desire to maintain a healthy lifestyle. A concerted effort has to be maintained to ensure proper eating and exercise takes place on a consistent basis.

In this chapter, we will discuss:

1. Diet optimization
2. Physical fitness optimization
3. Medical maintenance

22.1 DIET OPTIMIZATION

The food one puts into their bodies is of critical importance to one's overall physiological and intellectual function. One's attention to *diet optimization* will provide the body with essential nutrients necessary for the building and maintenance of cellular metabolic activity and new cell growth, regulation of physiological functions, and providing biochemical energy.

Extensive research has shown optimized diet and exercise programs provide one with major medicinal benefits. These programs contribute to the control of many chronic illnesses and diseases related to lifestyle, such as heart disease, diabetes, stroke, obesity, chronic obstructive pulmonary disease (COPD), and certain types of cancer.

According to the United Nations (UN), prolonged exposure to the three modifiable lifestyle behaviors of smoking, unhealthy diet, and physical inactivity are responsible for the majority of chronic and non-communicable diseases in the world today. The UN maintains the combination of four healthy lifestyle factors including maintaining a healthy weight, maintaining a healthy diet, not smoking, and exercising regularly may be associated with an 80% decrease in the risk of developing the most common and deadly diseases (Al-Maskari, 2021).

When one focuses directly on the aviation profession, pilots are often at greater nutritional risk as pilots tend to suffer from unstructured eating patterns, resultant from varying work hours and destinations. This may contribute to insufficient nutrient intake and resulting deficiencies. While empirical research evidence between food and behavior anomalies are conflicted and complex, relationships between diet and cognitive performance have been confirmed by the National Institutes of Health

(NIH). NIH findings indicate individuals adhering to the so-called Mediterranean Diet may experience increased cognitive function, as well as playing a role in enhanced eye health and slowing cognitive decline as human's age (NIH, Diet May Help Preserve Cognitive Function, 2020).

According to the NIH, the *Mediterranean Diet* emphasizes consumption of whole grains, nuts, legumes, whole fruits, vegetables, fish, and olive oil, including reduced consumption of red meat and alcohol. The Mayo Clinic defines the Mediterranean Diet as follows:

- **Eat more fruits and vegetables.** Aim for 7 to 10 servings a day of fruit and vegetables.
- **Opt for whole-grains.** Switch to whole-grain bread, cereal and pasta. Experiment with other whole grains, such as bulgur and farro.
- **Use healthy fats.** Try olive oil as a replacement for butter when cooking. Instead of putting butter or margarine on bread, try dipping it in flavored olive oil.
- **Eat more seafood.** Eat fish twice a week. Fresh or water-packed tuna, salmon, trout, mackerel and herring are healthy choices. Grilled fish tastes good and requires little cleanup. Avoid deep-fried fish.
- **Reduce red meat.** Substitute fish, poultry or beans for meat. If you eat meat, make sure it is lean and keep portions small.
- **Enjoy some dairy.** Eat low-fat Greek or plain yogurt and small amounts of a variety of cheeses.
- **Spice it up.** Herbs and spices boost flavor and lessen the need for salt (Hensrud N. Z., 2019).

According to a study conducted at the University of North Dakota's John D. Odegard School of Aerospace Sciences, pilots consuming macronutrient high-fat and high-carbohydrate diets may experience increased cognitive performance in flight conditions compared to pilots consuming high-protein diets. The studies indicate pilot performance scores were significantly poorer for participants consuming high-protein diets compared to high-fat and high-carbohydrate diets. The results of this study may have broad implications for future pilot performance as peak performance of pilots is critical in today's complex flight deck environment (Lindseth, 2011).

Nutrition Terminology

While information on nutrition may fill volumes, it is important for aviators to possess a basic understanding of *nutrition terminology* to understand discussions involving nutrition, and assist in making informed dietary decisions. The following glossary is by no means all-inclusive, but does provide one with knowledge regarding commonly-used terms in nutritional descriptions and discussions:

Amino acids form the building blocks of all proteins. 20 different amino acids exist which combine in various sequences to construct all proteins necessary for metabolism and growth. Human bodies manufacture 12 of the amino acids from recycled proteins; however, the additional eight amino acids are derived from the food one consumes.

Antioxidants assist protecting one's body from damage caused by free radical destruction by neutralizing them. While the body manufactures antioxidants, extensive use of dietary antioxidants boosts the body's effectiveness and efficiency. Dietary antioxidants may be found in vitamins such as vitamin C, vitamin E, beta-carotene (converted to vitamin A in one's body); minerals such as selenium, zinc, and copper;phytochemicals (natural plant compounds) such as carotenoids (e.g. beta-carotene, lycopene and lutein); and flavonoids, which are phytochemicals found extensively in vividly-colored fruits and vegetables.

Bran is the separated outer layer of a grain, or grain husk. It is considered a good source of fiber, as well as vitamins and minerals. Bran is typically present in wholegrain cereals and breads, but is lost during refining processes used to make various products including white bread.

Calories are basically the nutritional energy value of a given food, and essential for human health. Foods providing high energy but little nutritional value are known as "empty" calories, such as refined sugar or solid fats such as butter. Adult males require 2,000 – 3,000 calories per day, while adult females require 1,600 – 2,400 calories per day, according to the U.S. Department of Health. Calorie consumption is dependent on physical activity.

Carbohydrates provide the body its most readily converted source of energy. Carbohydrate sources include rice, breads, cereals, legumes, fruits, and vegetables, all of which add additional nutrients. Alternate carbohydrate sources include refined sugars, which provide instant energy, but don't offer the nutritional value more complex carbohydrate sources do.

Cholesterol is a waxy, fat-like substance, considered a sterol, and made by one's body, as well as found in all cells of one's body. Cholesterol is necessary to make hormones, vitamin D, and digestive substances. Cholesterol is also found naturally in various animal products including meat, eggs, poultry, and dairy products.

Electrolytes are necessary minerals which keep the body's fluid balance at healthy levels. Electrolytes also assist in maintaining normal functions such as heart rhythm, muscular contraction, and nerve impulse transmission. Electrolytes include potassium, sodium, calcium, and magnesium.

Essential fatty acids are fatty acids the body cannot synthesize naturally in sufficient quantities for physiological functions, and therefore must be acquired through food consumption. Two essential fatty acids exist; linoleic acid, which is an omega-6, and alpha-linolenic acid, which is an omega-3 fat.

Polyunsaturated and monounsaturated fats are considered "good" fats assisting in cholesterol reduction. These fats exist in sunflower, olive, and canola oils and margarines, as well as various nuts, seeds, and soy foods. An important polyunsaturated fat is Omega -3, typically found in fatty fish such as salmon, herring, sardines, and oysters.

Saturated and trans-fats are considered "bad" fats which may raise cholesterol levels. This may cause development of fatty deposits in blood vessels, ultimately causing restriction in arteries, therefore increasing one's risk of heart disease. Saturated fats generally exist at elevated levels in animal-based foods, as well as commercially baked products. Trans-fats may exist in margarine and baked goods like biscuits and pastries. As a general rule, one should eat less food high in saturated and trans-fats, or select lean or low-fat alternatives.

Fiber plays an important role in preventing cancer, heart disease, and constipation. Good sources of fiber include whole grain breads, cereals, fruit, legumes, rice, pasta, and vegetables.

Free radicals are defined as atoms containing unpaired electrons in their outer layers. Free radicals are typically caused by pollutants, cigarette smoke, and the by-product of metabolism. Free radicals are believed to contribute to tissue damage, aging, and potentially cancer. Antioxidants are believed to contribute electrons to free radicals, neutralizing the possibly harmful effects.

Fructose is a type of sugar found naturally in fruit and honey. Honey is an excellent substitute for refined sugar in foods needing extra sweeteners.

Glucose is a simple sugar provided by the food one eats, and derived from the breakdown of carbohydrates. Glucose is an important energy source in living organisms, particular for providing energy to the brain.

Gluten is a family of proteins most commonly found in wheat, rye, barley, and triticale. Gluten provides dough its elastic texture and sticky cohesiveness, important in manufacturing food products such as bread, and assisting those foods maintain their shape. Gluten causes illness for individuals with celiac disease.

Glycogen is the condensed substance unused glucose assumes when stored in the liver and around muscles, making it available as energy requirements dictate.

Insulin is a hormone produced in one's pancreas in response to increased blood glucose levels in the bloodstream. Insulin's central mission is transporting glucose from the bloodstream into the cells for energy production.

Lactose is sugar found in milk. Known as a disaccharide (meaning it consists of two sugars), the body breaks lactose down to glucose and galactose, which can be absorbed in the bloodstream and used for energy production.

Macronutrients are key nutrients in one's diet providing humans with energy. Macronutrients consist of carbohydrates, proteins and fats.

Micronutrients is a general name given to compounds required in minute quantities to sustain healthy bodily function, such as vitamins and minerals. These are necessary for energy production, blood clotting, immune function, and other functions.

Minerals support the formation of teeth, bones, blood, and connective tissues. Minerals are important for making hormones and enzymes, as well as assist in regulating water balance, muscular contractions, and nerve transmissions. Trace minerals are required by the body in small amounts, whereas macrominerals are required in larger amounts. Minerals of all types are obtained from food; however, certain medical conditions may require mineral supplementation.

Potassium and *sodium* work in conjunction regulating the balance between acidity and water in the blood. Potassium is an electrolyte, assisting nerves function to cause muscles (such as the heart) to contract and helping heart rhythm to be regular. It also assists nutrient movement into cells, and waste product out of cells. Potassium can be found in fruits, vegetables, grain foods, meats and milk. Sodium is an electrolyte assisting maintenance of the blood acid-base balance, and helps regulate muscle contraction and nerve impulse transmission. Sodium also helps regulate blood pressure and water balance in cells. Highly-processed foods such as processed meats or table salt may contain copious amounts of sodium, and high levels may lead to high blood pressure and stroke.

Proteins are large, complex molecules important for body cell growth, completing most of their work in cells. Proteins are necessary for structure, function, and regulation of body tissue and organs. Protein may be provided by lean meat, fish, baked beans, peanut butter, nuts, eggs, cheese, dried peas, soy and wholegrains.

Vitamins are molecules required in small amounts for bodily health and growth. Vitamins will be obtained by the foods one consumes, with the exception being vitamin D (produced in the skin when exposed to sunlight) and vitamin K, which may be synthesized in small amounts by gut bacteria. Vitamins are essential to assist in releasing energy from food, plus hastening many chemical reactions occurring in one's body. Vitamins also assist in the formation of blood and bone, and may perform as antioxidants.

Whole foods are minimally processed or unprocessed foods naturally retaining high levels of nutrients. Whole food examples include raw fruits and vegetables, wholegrains, brown rice, nuts, and seeds. Whole foods should make up a large part of one's dietary consumption.

Whole-grain refers to grains where all parts of the grain including the germ, endosperm, and bran layer are intact and retained. Whole-grains are the healthiest type of grains, and their consumption is associated with depressed risks for several diseases. Examples of whole-grain include whole-grain wheat and brown rice.

Food Hygiene

Practicing adequate *food hygiene* assists one in ensuring the foods they eat will be safe, in particular when travel abroad is necessary.

Food poisoning is any illness or disease resulting from ingestion of contaminated food. Food poisoning may be caused by bacteria, viruses, parasites, molds, toxins, allergens, and other contaminants. Food poisoning may cause upset stomach, nausea, diarrhea, vomiting, dehydration, kidney failure, brain and nerve damage, and even death.

According to the World Health Organization (WHO), food safety can be maintained by keeping yourself and the food clean, separate raw and cooked foods, cook food thoroughly, keep food at safe temperatures, and use safe water and raw food materials.

When traveling abroad, one must realize food sanitation standards are not the same in every corner of the world. According to WHO, the most severe food poisoning potential exists in impoverished or low-income countries, and is most commonly

485

encountered in Africa and Southeast Asia. The following are tips from experts regarding food safety in foreign countries:

1. Plan ahead by researching your destination's food practices and water safety.
2. See your health care provider prior to departure to receive any vaccines, prescription medications, and other similar items.
3. Pack smartly with hand sanitizer, disinfectant wipes, and a travel health kit with insurance cards and authorized medications.
4. Keep your guard up by rethinking usual food choices, being adventurous with food, and do not be fooled by appearances.
5. Always err on the side of caution by avoiding raw foods and produce, and beware foods stored at room temperatures.
6. Watch out for all water sources. If one needs to ask if the water is safe, do not drink it and opt for beverages in sealed manufacturer's containers.
7. Wash your hands often using soap or hand sanitizer.
8. Take care of yourself if suffering from an illness. Stay hydrated and seek medical assistance for any serious medical anomalies.

Sample Diets

As previously mentioned, professional aviators may experience difficulty maintaining the "perfect" diet as a result of abnormal work schedules and other factors. Although difficult, it is possible to make heathy diet choices if one makes the effort to so, no matter where or what time one is able to partake in a meal. One critical component of maintaining healthy eating habits is to focus on consuming how much food one needs, as opposed to how much food one wants.

The following sample diet is designed to provide the professional aviator with general guidelines on how a healthy diet should look to assist them in making healthy choices.

This diet is based on research performed by a variety of government, university and private sources. It is designed to be nutrient-rich, promoting mental and physical well-being, cognitive alertness, enhanced memory and vision, boost one's immune system, provide for mitochondrial health, red blood cell production, and provide a steady supply of proteins, fiber, healthy fats, probiotics, and antioxidants. This diet will provide for stable blood glucose levels to avoid feeling rundown, shaky, and confused, as well as provide vital nutrients to maintain muscular growth and repair from regular exercise routines. These specific food items may be swapped for similar food items. One may also enhance a premade or homemade meal's nutritional value by adding healthy options, such as adding spinach leaves to a burger, taco, sandwich, or mac and cheese, adding green peppers to a pre-made salad, soup, or sandwich, adding frozen blueberries of other fruit to yogurt, etc. Adding additional spices assists in customizing one's food to personal taste preferences, as well.

Breakfast Options:

- Bowl of plain Oatmeal w/butter, two tablespoons wheat germ and honey; piece of fruit
- Greek yogurt with one tablespoon wheat germ, blueberries and/or red or black grapes and honey; piece of fruit
- Omelet (fried in olive oil) with vegetables, tomatoes, and onion; piece of fruit
- six to eight ounce fruit/vegetable drink

Lunch Options:

- One natural peanut butter/spinach/cheese sandwich on 12-grain bread with10 low sodium/fat chips or whole-grain crackers (may substitute peanut butter sandwich with salmon/tuna/chicken/roast beef/turkey/ham salad/egg and hummus sandwich); piece of fruit
- Chef's spinach salad with cheese, egg, bacon, black beans, plus any other fresh ingredients, olive oil-based dressing
- Tuna salad; piece of fruit
- Whole-grain sandwich with cheese and vegetables; nuts; piece of fruit
- Eight ounces of water or milk
- A few baby carrots w/hummus dip
- One-half dark chocolate bar

Dinner Options:

- Grilled chicken breast; one cup cooked vegetables
- Grilled lamb; brown rice
- Grilled tuna; small spinach salad w/fixings and olive oil-based dressing
- Broiled salmon; one cup cooked vegetables; baked potato
- Spinach Salad with flaked salmon/chicken, cheese, egg, bacon, black beans, plus any other fresh ingredients and dressing
- Eight ounces of water or milk

Snack Options:

- Banana
- Handful red grapes
- Baby carrots with hummus dip
- Apple slices with cinnamon and cheese slices

- Six ounces fruit/vegetable juice
- One to two hard-boiled eggs
- Handful of red grapes
- 10 – 15 almonds or cashews/mixed nuts
- One-half dark chocolate bar

Throughout Day: Drink water as needed. Drinking two to four cups of coffee throughout the morning and one to two cups of green tea throughout the afternoon is recommended.

22.2 PHYSICAL FITNESS OPTIMIZATION

One's pursuit of *physical fitness* should not be considered something extra in one's life to look good physically or to get extra healthy. Physical fitness is absolutely necessary for normal human function and longevity. Aviators need to be aware of the professional and personal benefits exercise provides the body; benefits which go far beyond building muscle tissue and burning fat.

Human development and function requires significant exercise every day to survive. In recent societal history, much of human daily exercise has been disappearing with technological advancements. Almost every opportunity to experience exercise in an average day has been replaced with remote controls, phone apps, switches, electronics, and a myriad of other devices designed make one's life "easier."

Empirical research has shown inactivity is foundational to the development of certain diseases. As humans have had physical exercise opportunities reduced by technology, the result has actually caused physiological dysfunction, physical weakness, and obesity, and as a result more disease.

According to Michael D Brown, PhD, professor of kinesiology and nutrition at the University of Illinois, Chicago, when the body is inactive, cells in the endothelium (a thin membrane lining the interior of heart and blood vessels) get sluggish and don't sit in the vessel wall properly. Exercise causes blood to flow more swiftly and under greater pressure, realigning the cells. Approximately 12 hours following a single exercise session, the cells have repositioned themselves to be in line with the flow of blood. In turn, this helps blood vessels work more efficiently by keeping them open and elastic, as opposed to stiff, narrow, and clogged.

Recent studies also indicate physical activity makes the brain more connected by bulking up the white matter, which functions as the wiring transmitting signals between nerve cells. Older adults who exercise have more gray matter in areas of the brain responsible for self-control, memory, and decision making. Exercise also beats medication for some ailments. In head-to-head tests, it works as well or better than pills for depression. In other conditions, like Alzheimer's and arthritis, it's been shown to delay disability. Individuals sleep better when they exercise routinely, resulting in one's body becoming more efficient (Goodman, 2015).

Regular exercise also assists in preventing debilitating *back pain.*

Back pain may be caused by a variety of sources such as a slipped disc or strained muscles. Typically, maintaining good sitting and standing posture combined with exercise specifically designed to stretch and strengthen back muscles will alleviate most back issues not requiring physical therapy or surgery.

Starting an Exercise Program

The first step in starting an *exercise program* is to receive a complete physical examination from an AME. As pilots need to maintain a current FAA Medical Certificate, one may believe that in itself is sufficient to begin an exercise program. However, if one maintains a Class II or Class III Medical Certificate, one may consider receiving a more comprehensive physical examination. One's medical physician needs to understand one's intention of beginning an exercise program and solicit advice on what the physician believes would be the most appropriate approach.

Once cleared physically to begin a fitness program, begin slowly and free from intimidation. One of the biggest obstacles to maintaining exercise programs are injuries resulting from individuals attempting too much exercise too soon. In the initial stages, muscular stiffness and soreness can be expected; however, as one develops muscular strength and endurance over the first month or so, those issues will resolve. Be aware muscles will develop faster than *tendons.* Tendons connect the muscle to bone and transfer the forces necessary for limb movement. Nothing halts the progress of an exercise program faster than tendon damage, and as such, must be an important consideration in the formulation of an exercise program. Simply because muscles can handle 50 push-ups or a certain weight does not mean the tendons can handle the strain as effectively, so it is important to listen to one's body. Muscles and tendons should be stressed, but one should not experience outright pain.

The most important key to starting the fitness program is to start. One does not need to perform at professional athlete levels in the beginning, or ever. Starting a program with stretching, 10 push-ups, and 10 stomach crunches every other day is fine, as long as one is simply doing something. As one develops physically, one may decide to add 20 minutes of brisk walking on alternate days, one more push-up and stomach crunch per workout, or perhaps another set of push-ups and crunches. Once fitness has developed to the point where one feels normal following exercise sessions, intensity levels may start incrementally increasing.

Exercise classifications:

Aerobic exercise targets the cardiovascular system. The main objective raising heart and breathing rates over extended periods of time to enhance endurance. A basic calculation one may use to calculate maximum heartrate for effective aerobic training is "220 minus age"; for example, if one is 25 years of age, 220 – 25 = 195. Therefore, a heartrate of 195 would be this individual's maximum heartrate during sustained aerobic exercise.

Anaerobic exercise targets the musculoskeletal system. The main objective is increasing muscular strength through resistance-type training, either with body weight combined with gravity or through mechanized exercise devices. Each singular muscle group should be allowed proper time to recover after anaerobic exercise, with many experts recommending 48 hours.

Exercise Safety

As exercise can and will produce injuries to those pushing their strength or endurance limits, one should be careful not to exceed their limitations. One should not push themselves to the point of total exhaustion or acute pain. If equipment is utilized in one's exercise program, ensure the equipment is used properly, and with a spotter for free weights. One's exercise program may benefit by having a partner present in case one experiences trouble, injury, or one requires external motivation.

The following safety tips should be adhered to for assisting with injury avoidance:

1. Stretch each joint and muscle group about to be exercised.
2. Exercise regularly and in different motions or planes of rotation to strengthen muscles around joints.
3. Allow 48 hours for recovery between exercising the same muscle group.
4. Begin new exercises and new routines slowly, incrementally increasing intensity.
5. Ensure frequent breaks from repetitive motions or specific exercises.
6. Change activities, routines, or exercises frequently to avoid boredom or plateauing.
7. Cease activities or exercises causing acute or chronic pain.
8. Rest no more than 60 to 90 seconds between sets to keep muscles engaged.

Exercise Time

As a professional aviator, finding adequate time to exercise can be the biggest challenge. If exercising early in the morning, ensure your program does not interfere with sleep requirements. If time is limited, one can find an exercise program providing maximum output in short periods of time, with consideration to one's limitations. As we will discuss in the following sections, an effective exercise program may be accomplished in as short as four minutes.

Injury-Proofing Exercises

Injuries are one of the biggest obstacles to ongoing fitness progress; therefore one should invest time into performing *injury-proofing exercises.* This may be important not only for maintaining a fitness program, but professional flying as well. If one imagines which parts of the body are stressed when climbing into one's seat on the flight deck, sitting for long periods of time, scanning, managing the rudder pedals and yoke, and having to twist and reach certain areas of the flight deck, a few body parts emerge: one's neck, shoulders (rotator cuff), elbows, wrists, lower back, core, and ankles. If one of these areas were injured one may have a difficult time exercising or performing flight duties, and as such these areas of the body should be given special attention to maintain flexibility and strength. While one may research exercises focusing on these vulnerable areas, listed below are a few exercises focusing on these body parts:

1. Chest-to-floor pushups (chest/shoulders/core)
2. Forearm plank for 60 seconds (core/spine/lower back)
3. Balancing on one leg for 30 seconds (ankles/knees)
4. Calf stretch (ankles)
5. Pull ups/chin ups (back/shoulders/elbows/wrists)

Injury-proofing exercises may be incorporated into one's normal workout, or performed at least once per week in stand-alone sessions.

Sample Exercise Schedules:

To save time in the gym and provide for adequate recovery time, one may break up the exercise schedule and work the following muscle groups together on the same day as listed: chest and arms, shoulders and back, and core and legs.

A typical six-day exercise schedule may look like this:

- Mon and Thurs – chest and arms
- Tues and Fri – shoulders and back
- Wed and Sat – lower body, core, aerobic exercise

A four-day schedule may look like this:

- Mon & Thurs – Chest, Arms, Core
- Tues and Fri – shoulders, back, lower body, aerobic exercise

Or

- Mon and Thurs – upper body
- Tues and Fri – core, lower body, aerobic exercise

Sample Exercise Routines

Exercise programs are highly individualized, as most people have preferences regarding what goals to achieve and which exercises they enjoy performing. Regardless of personal preference, one should attempt to set up one's routine so each different exercise warms up the next muscle group in line to exercise to minimize injury potential. The following exercise routine examples should provide one with time-sensitive ideas on how to configure their routine using weights and machine exercises or body-weight exercises only.

Full-Body Exercise Routine – Weights

These five exercises will work every major muscle group of the body, and may be performed every 48 – 72 hours, or broken up into body part specific workouts:

- Bench press – 3 x 12
- Dips – 3 x 12
- Chin up/pull ups with knee raises – 3 x max
- Dead lift – 3 x 12
- Squat – 3 x 12

10 Minute Quick Workout

Performing 10 minutes of intense circuit training may provide the same all-day metabolism enhancing results as a 30-minute-long circuit of the same intensity. Perform these exercises:

- 20 jumping jacks
- 12 squats
- 15 pushups
- 12 forward lunges with each leg

- 10 superman exercises: Lie on stomach with feet straight back and arms to the sides. Arch the back as you reach back with your hands towards your feet as far as possible, and hold this position for 15 seconds. Repeat for 5 – 8 sets.

Rest one minute between sets, and repeat as many times as you can before 10 minutes is up.

4 Minute Quick Workout

Although a four-minute workout routine may not sound impressive, this program is an interval routine developed for maximum efficiency and effect. Completing this routine will most definitely physically stress the individual.

To complete the routine, perform 15 seconds of maximal effort for one muscle group such as pushups, and rest for 15 seconds. Repeat with a non-competitive exercise such as squats, and rest for 15 seconds. Repeat for a total of four minutes.

According to studies performed by Japanese researchers, this four-minute workout may boost one's aerobic fitness by 14 percent. The routine may also boost one's anaerobic capacity, which is a measure of how long one can exercise at their highest intensity, by 28 percent. One may minimize cross-fatigue by alternating between non-competitive muscle groups like upper and lower body. As you develop appropriately, you may add cycles as necessary or perform a cycle using only one exercise.

With individual research you can find a comfortable workout which fits into your daily life, and achieves the desired fitness goals.

22.3 MEDICAL CERTIFICATE MAINTENANCE

Once an FAA Medical Certificate is issued to a pilot, it is up to said pilot to ensure the physical standards of the medical certificate are maintained. The FAA mandates all pilots, with the exception of those flying gliders and free air balloons, must possess and maintain valid medical certificates to exercise the piloting privileges of their aviator certificates. The recurring medical examinations required for aviator medical certification are performed by FAA-designated Aviation Medical Examiners; physicians with specializing training in aviation medicine and an interest in aviation safety.

Medical certification standards are stated in Federal Aviation Regulation (14 CFR Part 67). An updated (03/31/2021) synopsis of the medical standards are as follows:

Medical Certificate Pilot Types: First-Class Airline Transport Pilot, Second-Class Commercial Pilot, Third-Class Private Pilot

DISTANT VISION: 20/20 or better in each eye separately, with or without correction. 20/40 or better in each eye separately, with or without correction.

NEAR VISION: 20/40 or better in each eye separately (Snellen equivalent), with or without correction, as measured at 16 inches.

INTERMEDIATE VISION: 20/40 or better in each eye separately (Snellen equivalent), with or without correction at age 50 and over, as measured at 32 inches.

COLOR VISION: Ability to perceive those colors necessary for safe performance of airman duties.

HEARING: Demonstrate hearing of an average conversational voice in a quiet room, using both ears at 6 feet, with the back turned to the examiner OR pass one of the audiometric tests below.

AUDIOLOGY: Audiometric speech discrimination test: Score at least 70% reception in one ear at an intensity of no greater than 65 dB. Pure tone audiometric test. Unaided, with thresholds no worse than:

	500 Hz	1,000 Hz	2,000 Hz	3,000 Hz
Better Ear	35 Db	30 dB	30 dB	40 dB
Worst Ear	35 dB	50 dB	50 dB	60 dB

ENT: No ear disease or condition manifested by, or that may reasonably be expected to be maintained by, vertigo or a disturbance of speech or equilibrium.

PULSE: Not disqualifying per se. Used to determine cardiac system status and responsiveness.

BLOOD PRESSURE: No specified values stated in the standards. The current guideline maximum value is 155/95.

ELECTROCARDIOGRAM (ECG): At age 35 and annually after age 40.

MENTAL: No diagnosis of psychosis, or bipolar disorder, or severe personality disorders.

SUBSTANCE DEPENDENCE AND SUBSTANCE ABUSE: A diagnosis or medical history of "substance dependence" is disqualifying unless there is established clinical evidence, satisfactory to the Federal Air Surgeon, of recovery, including sustained total abstinence from the substance(s) for not less than the preceding two years. A history of "substance abuse" within the preceding two years is disqualifying. "Substance" includes alcohol and other drugs (i.e., PCP, sedatives and hypnotics, anxiolytics, marijuana, cocaine, opioids, amphetamines, hallucinogens, and other psychoactive drugs or chemicals).

Pilots with a history of specific medical conditions described in 14 CFR Part 67 are mandatorily disqualified from exercising flying privileges. These medical conditions include:

- Personality disorder manifested by overt acts
- Psychosis
- Alcoholism
- Drug dependence
- Epilepsy
- Unexplained disturbance of consciousness
- Myocardial infarction
- Angina pectoris
- Diabetes requiring medication for its control.

Other medical conditions may require temporary disqualification such as acute infections, anemia, and peptic ulcer.

Pilots not meeting medical standards may still attain medical qualification under special issuance provisions or the exemption process. This process may require either additional medical information be provided to the AME or practical flight tests be conducted for an FAA flight examiner.

Some of these issues or conditions include:

- Bone and joint issues
- Cancer
- Ear, nose, throat, and equilibrium
- Endocrine system
- Gastrointestinal
- Heart and circulatory system
- Immune system
- Mental health

- Neurological (nervous system)
- Pulmonary
- Sleep disorders
- Substance abuse
- Urology
- Vision

Student pilots should attempt to attain their medical certificate through an AME as soon as possible in their flight training to avoid unnecessary training time and expense should they not meet medical standards. Student pilots intending to enter commercial aviation should apply for the highest class of medical certificate anticipated for the pilot's career.

Taking the Medical Examination

An AME is not authorized new medical certificate issuance if a pilot fails to meet standards listed in FAR Part 67 and the Guide to Aviation Medical Examiners. Pilots requiring glasses or contact lenses need to bring them to the examination to optimize their opportunity of passing the vision tests. Similarly, pilots using hearing aids (authorized for flight duties with a limitation on their medical certificate, if necessary, to pass the exam) should also bring those devices to the exam.

Pilots attending their medical examination should arrive well-rested and should avoid high-sugar foods, tobacco products, caffeine, and stimulant-type medications before the examination. Foods high in sugar may create an erroneous result in the urinalysis, making it appear the pilot may suffer from diabetes. A meal of complex carbohydrates and proteins prior to the examination helps stabilize blood glucose levels and decreases the risk of an abnormal urine sample. Fasting prior to the exam is not necessary.

For pilots requiring electrocardiograms (first examination after age 35 and annually after age 40 for First Class certification), arriving well rested and avoiding caffeine, tobacco products, and stimulant medications such as decongestants decreases the possibility of abnormalities on the ECG. ECG abnormalities are shown to be not clinically significant in most cases; however, the time, expense, and anxiety associated with obtaining the required evaluation may be avoided by proper preparation.

FAA medical applications require pilots to report all medicines, prescription and non-prescription, the pilot is using on the FAA medical application. For first time reporting of the use of a medication, pilots should ensure to include a statement about the absence of any side effects, if applicable. "Nutritional supplements" purchased over-the-counter do not require reporting.

Applications will be returned to pilots if they fail to check any answer on questions 18.v. (convictions or administrative actions related to driving under the influence of alcohol or drugs) and 18.w. (history of other convictions) if these questions apply to the individual pilot. This question not only includes events since one's last FAA medical exam, but also requires a "Yes" response if one <u>ever</u> had a conviction or administrative action. The newest version of the FAA medical application, Form 8500-8, now asks if the applicant has ever been <u>arrested</u> for an offense involving drugs or alcohol while driving (18v). On previous applications only <u>convictions</u> required a YES response. For pilots required to respond affirmatively, an explanation of the circumstances plus one's police/driving records may be required.

Attempting to conceal moving violations involving the use of alcohol or illegal drugs is not recommended. One's signature at the bottom of the application authorizes the FAA to search the National Driver's Registry for any violations. Not only will concealment of an offense trigger a medical evaluation, but the Securities Division of the FAA may pursue enforcement action against one's Pilot Certificate. Falsification of a medical application is subject to up to 5 years in prison, a $250,000 fine, and revocation of pilot certificates and ratings.

Maintaining Fitness for Flight

Although a pilot may optimize their lifestyle to the best of their ability, other factors may present themselves to create less-than-optimum flight duty conditions. Thus, we will discuss factors to consider when *maintaining fitness for flight*.

Obesity: *Obesity* is defined as the condition of being grossly fat or overweight, and is a major health crisis from which aviators are not immune. According to the FAA, some 300,000 deaths per year occur from complication related to obesity, second only to smoking. Medical issues related to obesity include heart attack, stroke, gout, diabetes, gallbladder disease, arthritis of weight-bearing joints, depression, fatigue, breast and uterine cancer, hypertension, and increased risk of falls and accidents. In addition, obesity may negatively affect one's ability to withstand elevated G-forces and hypoxic conditions, and may make decompression (DCS) issues more likely in the event of high-altitude exposure.

Obesity may lead to decreased self-esteem and less professional success, and public scorn and ridicule is possible for gross obesity. As one may have noticed the tight spaces for some flight decks, pilots may have difficulty fitting into their seat. As of yet, no FAA regulations exist concerning obesity, although this should not detract one from attempting to avoid the issue.

One popular method of determining obesity is to use the *body mass index* (BMI), and the only accurate way to measure true BMI is by total body immersion in a tank of water, and then performing mathematical calculations to determine body fat percentage. A BMI of 25 is considered normal, with a BMI of 18 being abnormal and 27 being overweight. Much quicker and less complicated methods of determining one's weight is to simply look in the mirror, see how one's clothes fit, or see how much fat one can pinch between their fingers. Most people know when they are overweight, and the methods for losing weight may be determined by reading the diet and exercise sections of this chapter.

Illness: Although seemingly benign, a *minor illness* may seriously degrade performance of various flying tasks vital to safety. Illnesses may produce fever and distracting symptoms impairing judgment, memory, alertness, and cognitive functions. Although symptoms of an illness may be adequately controlled with medications, the medication itself may decrease pilot performance or potentially wear off in flight. The safest rule for one to follow is not to fly in the midst of suffering from any debilitating illness. If one feels they may be capable of flying with any given illness, individuals should contact their Aeromedical Examiner for practical advice.

Medication: Pilot physical and cognitive performance may be seriously degraded by not only *prescribed medications*, but over-the-counter medications as well, rivaling the medical illness conditions for which they are taken. Medications such as tranquilizers, sedatives, strong pain relievers, and cough-suppressants have primary effects which may impair judgment, memory, alertness, coordination, vision, and cognitive functions. Antihistamines, blood pressure medications, muscle relaxants, and agents controlling diarrhea and motion sickness may have side effects impairing the same critical functions. Any medication depressing the nervous system such as sedatives, tranquilizers, or antihistamines may make a pilot susceptible to hypoxia at lower altitudes and inhibit novel procedure recall.

Alcohol: Extensive FAA research provides various facts concerning the *hazards of alcohol* consumption combined with flying. Research has shown one ounce of liquor, one bottle of beer, or four ounces of wine may impair flying skills, even without combining the effects of alcohol with altitude. The alcohol consumed in these amounts is detectable in one's breath and blood for at least three hours. Even after one's body completely metabolizes moderate amounts of alcohol, one may still suffer impairment for hours more by the effects of hangover. Although many myths exist to the contrary, no ways of increasing the destruction of alcohol or alleviating hangover effects truly exist. As discussed previously, alcohol consumption exposes pilots to more disruptive events concerning disorientation and hypoxia.

Aircraft accident fatality rates have consistently proven to remain high when alcohol-related, serving to emphasize the potentially lethal combination regarding alcohol and flying. FARs prohibit pilots from performing flying crewmember duties within an eight-hour period following drinking any alcoholic beverage or while under the active influence of alcohol. Thus, the recommended rule is to allow at least 12 to 24 hours between "bottle and throttle" determinant on the quantity of alcoholic beverages consumed. Males should realistically consume no more than two alcoholic beverages per day, and females should consume no more than one alcoholic beverage per day on days when alcohol is consumed. The best and most effective plan is to drink no alcoholic beverages if flying the next day.

Travel Safety

As a professional aviator, part of one's job is to travel, which may bring its own set of health risks. Being safe during travels requires conscious thought and preparation, particularly when traveling abroad.

The following are tips on traveling safely:

1. **Keep your vaccinations current.**
2. **Research destination insect risks and prepare preventative measures if necessary.**
3. **Research and maintain destination water and food hygiene.**
4. **Reduce ground transport and recreational risks. Be alert to the possibility of muggings and only use reputable ride-share or taxi services.**
5. **Do not let your luggage out of your sight, and do not carry anything for anyone you do not know well.**
6. **Know your blood type.**
7. **Avoid unnecessary overexposure to sunlight which may lead to sunburn.**
8. **Only use local medications from reputable sources.**
9. **Remain clear of unfamiliar animals, birds, or reptiles.**
10. **Avoid casual sex and avoid going to someone's private room or residence unless you know them well.**
11. **Avoid verbal arguments which may lead to physical altercations.**
12. **Obey local laws and rules and respect local inhabitants.**

Conclusion

Pilots must take proactive steps to protect their medical fitness to fly. Fortunately, many of these protective steps can be implemented into one's normal life such as exercise and diet. One should exercise responsibility for monitoring one's health and ground oneself if medically unfit to fly, as your condition may endanger not only yourself, but other crewmembers and passengers as well.

To be considered a professional aviator, one must think and act as a professional. Be professional in the way you take care of your personal life and in your interactions with others.

Chapter 22 Core Competency Questions

1. Extensive research has shown optimized diet and exercise programs provide major _____ benefits.
2. What are the three behaviors responsible for the majority of chronic and non-communicable diseases in the world today?
3. Practicing adequate _____ ensures the food one eats will be safe.
4. Aerobic exercise targets the _____ system of the body.
5. Anaerobic exercise targets the _____ system of the body.
6. A pilot falsifying their medical application may be fined up to $_____.

INDEX

BIBLIOGRAPHY

Accident Statistics. (2020, August 12). Retrieved from ICAO Safety: icao.int

Al-Maskari, F. (2021, February 22). Lifestyle Diseases: An Economic Burden on the Health Services. *UN Chronicle.* un.org.

AMSA Sleep Apnea. (2020, November 19). *Aviation Medicine Advisory Service .* Centennial, CO, USA: Aviaiton Medicine Advisory Service.

APA. (2012). Building Your Resilience. *American Psychological Association.* apa.org.

ASMA. (2009, January 31st). Fatigue Countermeasures in Aviation. *Aviation, Space & Environmental Medicine.* Aerospace Medical Association Fatigue Countermeasures Subcommittee - Aviation Human Factors Committee.

Baird, D. C. (2013, November 12). *How Does Sound Going Slower in Water Make it Hard to Talk to Someone Underwater?* Retrieved from Science Questions with Surprising Answers: wtamu.edu

Bloudin, D. R. (2014, January 1st). Effects of Stress on Perceived Performance of Collegiate Aviators. *Aviation Psychology and Apllied Human Factors.* Hogrefe Publishing.

BYJUS. (2020, September 9). *Resonance.* Retrieved from byjus: byjus.com

CDC. (2014, June 6th). Stress...at Work. *The National Institute for Occupational Safety and Health.* Centers for Disease Control and Prevention.

CDC. (2017, May 9th). *Aircrew Safety and Health.* Retrieved from The National Institute for Occupational Safety and Health: cdc.gov

CDC. (2018, April 4th). *Radiation Emergencies.* Retrieved from Centers for Disease Control and Prevention: cdc.gov

Cheung, L. O. (2016, June 9th). Thermal Stress, Human Performance, and Physical Employment Standards. *Applied Physiology, Nutrition, and Metabolism.* Canadian Science Publishing.

Contaminant Candidate List and Regulatory Determination. (2016, September 16th). *Environment Topics*. epa.gov.

DeHart, D. R. (1996). Respiratory Physiology pg 98-99. *Fundementals of Aerospace Medicine 2nd Edition*. Baltimore, MD, USA: Williams & Wilkins.

Dismukes, R. K. (2015, August). Effects of Acute Stress on Aircrew Performance. *NASA/TM - 2015 - 218930*. Ames Research Center, Moffett Field, California, USA: NASA.

Driskell, S. J. (1999). Does Stress Lead to a Loss of Team Perspective? *Group Dynamics, Theory, Research and Practice*. Educational Publishing Foundation.

Ernsting. (1963). Aerospace Medicine. *A Textbook of Aviation Physiology*. Farnborough, Hampshire, England: RAF Institute of Aviation Medicine.

FAA. (2012, October 12). Fitness for Duty. *Advisory Circular 117-3*. Okalahoma City, OK, USA: Federal Aviation Administration.

FAA. (2014). *In-Flight Radiation Exposure*. Oklahoma City, OK: Federal Aviation Administration.

FAA. (2016, 12 2). Maintainer Fatigue Risk Management. *FAA Advisory Circular 120-115*. Oklahoma City, OK: Federal Aviation Administration.

FAA. (2020, August 28). *Federal Aviation Administration*. Retrieved from Hearing and Noise in Aviation: faa.gov

FAA. (2020). *Introduction to Aviation Physiology*. Oklahoma City, OK: Federal Aviation Administration.

Farlik, I. (2015, February 26). *U.S. Military Aerospace Physiology*. Retrieved from Go Flight Med: goflightmedicine.com

Fatigue in Aviation. (2020, April 4). *Aerospace Medical Education*. Oklahoma City, Okalahoma, USA: Federal Aviation Administration.

Federal Aviation Administration Medical Facts for Pilots. (2021, May 10). *Sunglasses for Pilots*. Oklahoma City, OK, USA: Federal Aviation Administration.

Friedberg, C. (2016). *What Aircrews Should Know About Their Occupational Exposure to Ionizing Radiation*. Oklahoma City: Civil Aerospace Medical Institute.

Goodman. (2015, June 22nd). The Benefits of Exercise Go Way Beyond the Muscles. *Webmd Fitness & Exercise*. webmd.com.

g-suit. (2020, August 11). Retrieved from Wikipedia: en.wikipedia.com

Hatch, S. C. (2012, December 7). *New G-Suit Comes to Luke*. Retrieved from Luke Air Force Base: luke.af.mil

Hensrud. (2020, December 30th). Hyponatremia. *Mayo Clinic*. Rochester, MN, USA: mayoclinic.org.

Hensrud, N. Z. (2019, June 21). Mediterranean Diet: A Heart-Healthy Eating Plan. *Mayo Clinic Healthy Lifestyle; Nutrition and Healthy Eating*. mayoclinic.org.

Holmes, D. A. (2020, November 15th). Using Caffeine Strategically to Combat Fatigue. *From the Briefing Room*.

How the Heart Works. (2017, November 17th). *Congenital Heart Defects*. cdc.gov.

Jacobson, S. (2013, August 24). *Aircraft Loss of Control Causal Factors and Mitigation Challenges*. Retrieved from NTRS - NASA : ntrs.nasa.gov

Jedick. (2014, May 14). Thermal Stress in the Cockpit. *Go Flight Medicine*. goflightmedicine.com.

Jedick, R. (2013, April 5). *Pulling G's - The Effects of G-Forces on the Human Body*. Retrieved from Go Flight Med: goflightmedicine.com

Jedick, R. (2014, January 30). *Be a Better G-Monster: The Anti-G Straining Manuver*. Retrieved from goflightmedicine.com: http://www.goflightmedicine.com

John P. Stapp. (2020, August 23). Retrieved from New Mexico Museum of Space History: nmspacemuseum.org

Laskowski. (2020, June 26th). Heat Cramps: First Aid. *Mayo Clinic*. Rochester, MN, USA: mayoclinic.org.

Laskowski. (2020, November 10th). Heat Exhaustion. *Patient Care and Health Information*. Rochester, MN, USA: mayoclinic.org.

Laskowski. (2020, November 10th). Heat Stroke. *Patient Care and Health Information*. Rochester, MN, USA: mayoclinic.org.

Laskowski. (2020, April 2020). Hypothermia. *Mayo Clinic Diseases - Conditions.* mayoclinic.org.

Lindseth, L. J. (2011, July 5th). Dietary Effects on Cognition and Pilots' Flight Performance. *US National Library of Medicine, National Institutes of Health.* Grand Forks, North Dakota, USA: ncbi.nlm.nih.gov.

Lobo, V. (2010). Free Radicals, Antioxidants and Functional Food: Impact on Human Health. *Pharmacognosy Review,* 118 - 126.

Moisseiev, E. (2013, October 12). *Negative g-Force Ocular Trauma Caused by a Rapidly Spinning Carousel.* Retrieved from US National Library Of Medicine National Institutes of Health: ncbi.nlm.nih.gov

NAS. (2005, January 31). *Hearing Loss: Determining Eligibility for Social Security Benefits.* Retrieved from National Academy of Sciences: ncbi.nlm.nih.gov

NASA. (2020, October 01). *Crew Compartment Cabin Pressurization.* Retrieved from National Aeronautics and Space Administration: spaceflight.nasa.gov

National Park Service. (2018, July 30). *Natural Sounds.* Retrieved from National Park Service: nps.gov

NIH. (2019, August 13). Brain Basics: Understanding Sleep. National Institute of Neurological Disorders and Stroke.

NIH. (2020, April 14th). Diet May Help Preserve Cognitive Function. *NIH News Releases.* nih.gov.

OHS Body of Knowledge. (2012). *Physical Hazards: Noise and Vibration.* Tullamarine: Safety Institute of Australia.

Olesen, H. (2001). Target Levels of Metabolic Heat Production. *Metabolic Heat Production.* sciencedirect.com.

Olson. (2020, July 20th). Sleep Apnea. *mayoclinic.org.* Rochester, MN: Mayo Clinic.

Roderick, P. T. (1972, March 30). *Vibration Effects on Pilot Tracking Performance Using Rigid Control Stick.* Retrieved from Fulltext: apps.dtic.mil

Role of Human Factors in the FAA. (2014, December). *HF Action Items.* Oklahoma City, OK, USA: faa.gov.

SAFE. (2005). *Whole Body Vibration Exposure for MH-60S Pilots.* Creswell, OR: SAFE Association.

Sanlorenzo, D. M. (2015, June 22nd). *US National Library of Medicine.* Retrieved from The Risk of Melanoma in Pilots and Cabin Crew: UV Measurements in Flying Airplanes : ncbi.nlm.nih.gov

Slimani, M. (2018). The Effect of Mental Fatigue on Cognitive and Aerobic Performance in Adolescent Active Endurance Athletes. *Journel of Clinical Medicine,* 4.

United States Department of Labor. (2013, August 15). Retrieved from Occupational Safety and Health Administration Technical Manual: osha.gov

Veillette. (2020, August 28th). Quality Eyewear More Than A Fashion Accessory For Pilots. *Aviation Week Network.* aviationweek.com.

Verger, R. (2020, January 3). *Technology.* Retrieved from Popular Science: popsci.com

Vision and FAA Standards. (2021, April 07). *Aviation Medicine Advisory Service.* Centennial, CO, USA: aviationmedicine.com.

WHO. (2020, October 19th). Occupational Stress; Stress at the Workplace. *WHO Newsroom.* World Health Organization.

CHAPTER CORE COMPETENCY ANSWER KEY

Chapter 1

1. 60-80% 2. 90 3. Royal Aeronautical Society in 1866 4. 46%

Chapter 2

1. 3.5 degrees F 2. The top of the Troposphere 3. Below 10,000 feet 4. 18.4 days per mile of altitude 5. 10,000 6. O2 21%/N2 78% 7. SL – 10,000 feet 8. 10,000 feet – 50,000 feet 9. 50,000' 10. 159 mmHg 11. Trapped Gas 12. Evolved Gas 13. Pressure gauge fluctuation 14. Respiration 15. Hypoxia

Chapter 3

1. An exchange of gases between a living organism and its environment. 2. Brain cells/neurons 3. Carbon dioxide 4. Oxygen 5. True 6. Alveoli 7. Ventilation, respiration, transportation, utilization 8. Red blood cell 9. Hemoglobin 10. Oxygen, nutrition, rest, hydration

Chapter 4

1. Cognition 2. Hypoxic, hypemic, histotoxic, stagnant 3. Hypoxic 4. Hypemic 5. True 6. Below 60% 7. Histotoxic 8. True 9. Isolate, extinguish, cool 10. Stagnant 11. Insidious onset 12. True 13. 100% oxygen 14. No 15. False

Chapter 5

1. 12-20 2. Carbon dioxide 3. Oxygen 4. False – it is the loss of carbon dioxide 5. Stagnant 6. Emotional 7. Oxygen 8. True 9. True 10. Conditioned or muscle-memory

Chapter 6

1. Boyle's Law 2. Ears, sinuses, GI tract, teeth, lungs 3. Teeth, GI tract 4. Ears, sinuses 5. The eustachian tube 6. False 7. Valsalva 8. No – emergency use only 9. Pass flatus or belch on ascent 10. Three times that of sea level 11. Do not fly with a cold

Chapter 7

1. Henry's Law 2. Nitrogen 3. 1.5 4. FL180 5. Type I 6. Type II 7. The bends 8. The chokes 9. SCUBA diving 10. 100% oxygen 11. Pressurization 12. AME 13. Bends, skin, chokes, CNS

Chapter 8

1. False 2. 10,000 feet 3. Gaseous and chemical 4. Gaseous 5. No 6. Continuous-flow, diluter-demand, pressure-demand 7. To raise oxygen partial pressure at the lung level 8. False 9. 14,000 feet 10. Preflight and inflight check of the aircraft oxygen system

Chapter 9

1. True 2. Catalytic ozone converter 3. External, internal, aircraft systems 4. 90 seconds 5. Carbon monoxide 6. 250 times 7. Cyanide 8. Respect the emergency and protecting your lungs

Chapter 10

1. Proprioception, vestibular, visual 2. 90% 3. Movement and body position 4. Angular acceleration 5. Semi-circular canals & otolith organs 6. Less than 3 degrees per second 7. Central and peripheral 8. Photopic, scotopic, mesopic 9. Central vision, central 2 degree cone 10. 120 x 120 degrees 11. Central 2 degrees/central vision 12. Light intensification and infrared 13. ¼ time inside, ¾ time outside

Chapter 11

1. True 2. The horizon 3. True 4. 10 years/1,000 hours 5. Optokinetic cervical reflex 6. Oculogyric illusion 7. Somatogravic illusion 8. Somatogyric illusion 9. Graveyard spiral 10. 20-30 seconds 11. Not at all

Chapter 12

1. 50% 2. Deviation from glideslope 3. Visual perspective and depth perception 4. Airport & runway environment, weather conditions 5. Lack of texture 6. Lack of ambient visual cues along approach path 7. Steep approach path 8. Higher and father away from threshold 9. Background clutter 10. The pilot spends too much time visually searching for the runway, not enough time on instruments 11. VASI, PAPI, ILS 12. 83% 13. Fly the aircraft first

Chapter 13

1. Pilot Flying (PF) and Pilot Monitoring (PM) 2. PM 3. Loss of S/A 4. Manual Handling/Flight Controls 5. Cognitive lock-up 6. Increase practicing task-switching,

departmental framing of go-arounds 7. Enhance 8. False 9. Turn it off 10. Infrared, light intensification, combined vision system 11. Obstacle avoidance, runway alignment during approach, runway guidance during taxi

Chapter 14

1. High-velocity head impacts kill 2. Kinetic energy 3. Arrive at the ground at lowest possible speed, under control, and allow aircraft/environment absorb kinetic energy 4. False 5. 9 G's 6. Crush zones 7. Crashworthiness 8. Container 9. Restraints 10. Head-swing 11. Head injuries 12. Three minutes after take-off, eight minutes prior to landing 13. Planning ahead

Chapter 15

1. Time 2. Direction 3. Compressive 4. Linear, angular, radial 5. Gx, Gy, Gz 6. Gy 7. +Gz 8. Variance of circulation, restriction of movement 9. 1 – 3 G's 10. Above 6 G's 11. Tunnel vision 12. 4-6 13. Negative to positive 14. 15 G

Chapter 16

1. Frequency, intensity, speed, duration 2. 10 3. Outer, middle, inner 4. Continuous, stable noise levels 5. Sharp, sudden onset of noise 6. 85, 90 7. Earplugs or noise-cancelling headsets 8. Linear, rotational, combination 9. Localized or Whole-body 10. Loosely 11. 3.11 mSv 12. FL300 13. 20 mSv per year

Chapter 17

1. To protect occupants from hypoxia and DCS 2. Sealed cabins and pressurized cabins 3. Isobaric control and isobaric differential 4. False 5. Hypoxia, trapped gas, evolved gas, fatigue, thermal stress, noise and vibration 6. Improper inspections and maintenance, age and cycles of aircraft, higher differentials 7. Slow, rapid, and explosive 8. Slow 9. The popping and clicking of the ears on ascent 10. Explosive noise 11. 100% Oxygen 12. Five

Chapter 18

1. No biomarkers 2. Transient, cumulative, circadian 3. Scan discipline breaks down 4. Stage I and REM 5. Distraction 6. 85-92% 7. 20% 8. Windows of circadian lows (WOCL) 9. Less than 500 mg 10. 100 – 150 mg

Chapter 19

1. Attention and memory 2. Physical, physiological, psychological 3. True 4. True 5.True 6. Alcohol, drugs, tobacco, circadian rhythm 7. Academic, procedure refinement, cross-training, practical training 8. Resilience 9. Connection, wellness, healthy thinking, meaning

Chapter 20

1. Temperature, wind, water (precipitation) 2. Perceptual, physical, environmental 3. 25% 4. Conduction, convection, radiation 5. 95-103.9 degrees F 6. 104 degrees F 7. Fever 8. Dehydration 9. 30 10. Vasoconstriction 11. Metabolic, Shivering, physical activity 12. 95 13. 10 minutes or less

Chapter 21

1. Mental state/attitude 2. Yes 3. Panic leads to irrational decisions 4. Knowledge of thermal preparation 5. Stay with the vehicle 6. 3 days 7. 3 weeks 8. Signaling 9. Clothing 10. File a flight plan

Chapter 22

1. Medicinal 2. Smoking, unhealthy diet, and physical inactivity 3. Food hygiene 4. Cardiovascular 5. Musculoskeletal 6. $250K

ABOUT THE AUTHOR

As a subject matter expert in aerospace physiology, Mr. Martin's direct involvement in the specialty of aerospace physiology has spanned over 30 years, having been personally involved in training well over 13,000 pilots and aircrew members, both military and civilian. This author's operational experience has included training military pilots in not only flight physiology subject matter, but also aircraft ejection and ground egress procedures, parachuting and parachute landing falls, survival techniques, high-G centrifuge training, extreme high-altitude training, spatial disorientation training, night vision and enhanced vision systems training, and fighter pilot physical conditioning programs. Civilian aerospace physiology teaching experience has included aerospace physiology academics, high-altitude chamber, spatial disorientation, visual limitations and optimization, enhanced vision training, and cockpit smoke training.

This author's education has included academic studies at the US Air Force School of Aerospace Medicine, University of North Dakota, Community College of the Air Force, and National Air Security Operations Center, but most importantly _practical_ experience.

Mr. Martin's goal has revolved around providing the most current, accurate, relevant, and innovative training possible involving this scientific specialty. Consequently, Mr. Martin has strived to experience what he teaches. As a result of this pursuit, Mr. Martin's personal training included various military and civilian survival schools, military parachutist training, research and observation flights in virtually every airframe including fighters/helicopters/corporate aircraft/light fixed wing/simulators, live-fire ejection seat training, over 70 six to nine-G human centrifuge profiles, unmanned aerial system training (MQ-9 Predator), thousands of high-altitude and rapid decompression hypobaric chamber flights, and episodes of hypoxia, hyperventilation, fatigue, acute extreme stress, thermal stress, life-threatening situations, as well as many others.

CPSIA information can be obtained
at www.ICGtesting.com
Printed in the USA
LVHW022341300422
717629LV00017B/1796

9 781662 917653